EDINBURGH UNIVERSITY PUBLICATIONS

History, Philosophy and Economics

18

Lord Salisbury, 1888

A STUDY IN THE PARTITION OF AFRICA

ENGLAND, EUROPE &
THE UPPER NILE

1882–1899

G. N. SANDERSON
formerly Professor of History, University of
KHARTOUM

EDINBURGH
University Press

© G. N. Sanderson 1965
EDINBURGH UNIVERSITY PRESS
George Square, Edinburgh 8
North America
Aldine Publishing Company
320 West Adams Street, Chicago 5
Australia and New Zealand
Hodder & Stoughton Ltd.
Africa, Oxford University Press
India, P. C. Manaktala & Sons
Far East, M. Graham Brash & Son

Printed in Great Britain
by T. & A. Constable Ltd., Edinburgh

PREFACE

THIS is a long book; but its length is perhaps excused by the importance and wide ramifications of its subject. In Africa, these ramifications extended far beyond the Sudan and Egypt. At one time or another the Upper Nile basin was the focus of European activities in a vast arc of territory extending from Eritrea and Somalia to Lake Chad, by way of Ethiopia, 'Kenya', Uganda, the Congo and Ubangi basins, and the Shari basin. Two great Powers, Britain and France, were potential or actual competitors almost from first to last. So too was another major Power in Africa, King Leopold's Independent Congo State. Between 1889 and 1894 Italy was from time to time a competitor in the eastern Sudan. Germany renounced direct competition, if indeed she had ever seriously contemplated it, in 1890; but she did not thereby cease to interest herself in the politics of the Nile basin. Even Russia ultimately became involved in Ethiopia, though not directly in the Upper Nile itself.

The European competitors did not however operate in 'an Africa without any Africans'. Speculations about the strength or weakness of the Mahdist State, and about its attitude to European Powers, were important and sometimes decisive factors in both British and French policy. Ethiopia under the Negus Menelik played an active and very important part in the international politics of the Upper Nile, especially in the closing phases of the struggle. In 1886 the policy of Mwanga, Kabaka of Buganda, unwittingly helped King Leopold to gain control of the Emin Pasha Relief Expedition; two years later the politico-religious loyalties of Emin's Sudanese soldiers completely frustrated the policies which had been planned in London and in Brussels.

The waters of the Nile, and the *de jure* status of the Sudan as Egyptian and ultimately Ottoman territory, linked the remote wildernesses of Equatoria and the Bahr al-Ghazal with Egypt and with the Mediterranean. As the rivalry between Britain and France became more open and acute, the Upper Nile dispute gained in importance, not only as a factor in British imperial strategy and in the Mediterranean balance, but also as an issue in which national prestige was at stake. On both counts, the Upper Nile had by the summer of 1894 become part of the mainstream of Great-Power diplomacy. Moreover, in Britain from 1892 to 1895 and in France almost continuously from 1893 onwards, policy towards the Upper Nile generated important internal conflicts at the very centre of political power.

I have tried to do justice to all these facets of the subject without deviating too far from a plain factual narrative. If I have not succeeded,

v

I must plead in mitigation Professor William L. Langer's judgment on the problem of the Upper Nile: 'Its complexity is simply baffling and the many contradictions on all sides only serve to enhance the confusion'. Some of these contradictions I have tried to resolve in the light of the very copious material which has become available since Langer wrote. But one or two key episodes still remain more or less obscure; my reconstructions of these are at best tentative, and sometimes admittedly speculative. In discussing the origins of the Marchand Mission, in particular, I have sometimes been forced, in order to tell an intelligible story, to neglect the very sound rule that a historian should assert only what his evidence compels him to assert. Here the crucial evidence has been removed from the archives and probably no longer exists. But the few fragments which have escaped suppression all point in the same direction and do seem to suggest very strongly, if not to compel, the interpretation which has been put forward.

I have not attempted, except at a very elementary level in the final chapter, any analysis of the 'deeper' or 'underlying' motives for the competition of European Powers on the Upper Nile, still less of the motives for imperial expansion in general. It can, I think, be quite clearly shown that, whatever the importance of defensive strategy in British policy, strategy was no longer predominant during the final crisis of 1898-99. It is also easy to illustrate the thesis that French policy, especially between 1894 and 1898, was dominated by an 'imperialism of prestige'. But the very use of so vague a word as 'prestige' is in itself a warning that a much more precise analysis is required. The body of the book is devoted to a detailed account of the strategy and tactics of the 'policy-makers'; not because I believe this to be the whole of the story, but because such an account seems an indispensable preliminary to any fruitful investigation of other and more elusive, but perhaps no less important, factors in imperial policy.

*   *   *

I have many debts to acknowledge: to the late Dame Lillian Penson, who taught me whatever I may know of the art of historical research; to my colleagues past and present in the Department of History at the University of Khartoum, and especially to Professor Mekki Shibeika. In more ways than they perhaps realise they have helped the prosecution of a long-term research project in the stimulating but strenuous environment of a University and a Department growing at times with almost explosive rapidity. I am indebted to the Marquis of Salisbury for his kindness in allowing me to use the Salisbury Papers; to Professor Pierre Renouvin for permitting me to work from certain French diplomatic documents in advance of their official publication; and to Dr F. H. Hinsley for permitting me to use certain paragraphs from a paper published in *The Historical Journal*.

My debt to the officials of the archives and libraries in which I have worked will be obvious; but it is none the less great for that, and I thank them for their unfailing patience and courtesy. I am however especially grateful to the Librarian of the University of Khartoum for his generosity and efficiency in obtaining microfilmed material. I also owe a special debt to Sayed Muhammad Ibrāhīm Ahmad, Archivist to the Sudan Republic, who has not only drawn my attention to relevant Mahdist sources but has most generously furnished me with translations of some of these.

Others to whom I am indebted are Professor P. M. Holt, who has placed at my disposal his unique knowledge of Mahdist history; Dr Ihsān Rashīd ʿAbbās, Dr J. A. S. Grenville, Mr M. Jolliffe, Dr J. F. A. Mason, Sayed Mūsa al-Mubārak, Dr Sālih Muhammad Nūr, *Hofrat* Dr Oskar Regele, the late Professor Charles Schmidt, and Dr A. B. Theobald.

I owe a very real debt to the Honours students of the University of Khartoum to whom I have taught 'The Upper Nile' as a special subject. They have done more than merely keep the subject alive in my mind; their questions and comments have often prompted me to reconsider my views.

But my greatest debt is to my wife, who has helped me in ways too numerous to specify and without whose constant interest and encouragement this book would probably not have been written.

G. N. SANDERSON, Khartoum, 1965

TO MY PARENTS

CONTENTS

ix

LIST OF ILLUSTRATIONS AND MAPS

ACKNOWLEDGEMENTS

Plates I, II, III, IV, V, VIII, IX, XI, XII, XIII and XIV are reproduced by permission of Radio Times Hulton Picture Library and plate X by permission of Sir Ronald Wingate.

ABBREVIATIONS

I. References to unpublished sources

FO	Foreign Office papers deposited at the Public Record Office, London.
SP	Papers of the third Marquis of Salisbury, deposited at Christ Church, Oxford.
MAE	Archives of the Ministère des Affaires Etrangères, Paris.
MC	Archives of the Ministère des Colonies, Paris.
— C.F.S.	Correspondence, Côte française des Somalis
— G.C.	Correspondence, Gabon-Congo
Mahdia Cairint Intel	Archives of the Republic of the Sudan, Khartoum, in the classes: Archives of the Mahdist State; Papers of the Egyptian Army Intelligence Division; Other Intelligence Archives.
I.R.E.	Intelligence Reports, Egypt (confidential print).
S.I.R.	Sudan Intelligence Reports (confidential print).

II. Other References

Ann. Sci. Pol.	*Annales des Sciences Politiques* (Paris)
A.R.	*The Annual Register*
B.C.B.	*Biographie Coloniale Belge*
B.D.	*British Documents on the Origins of the War*
Bull. C.A.F.	*Bulletin du Comité de l'Afrique Française*
Bull. I.H.R.	*Bulletin of the Institute of Historical Research*
Bull. I.R.C.B.	*Bulletin de l'Institut Royal Colonial Belge*
Bull. Soc. Roy. Belge Géog.	*Bulletin de la Société Royale Belge de Géographie*
C.H.B.E.	*The Cambridge History of the British Empire*
C.H.J.	*The Cambridge Historical Journal*
D.D.F.	*Documents Diplomatiques Français* (First Series)
D.D.I.	*I Documenti Diplomatici Italiani*
D.K.	*Deutsches Kolonialblatt*
E.H.R.	*The English Historical Review*
G.P.	*Die Grosse Politik der Europäischen Kabinette*
Hertslet	E. Hertslet, *The Map of Africa by Treaty* (Third Edition, London 1909)

H.J.	*The Historical Journal*
J.A.H.	*The Journal of African History*
J. Mod. Hist.	*The Journal of Modern History*
J.O.	*Journal Officiel*
L.Q.V. 2	*The Letters of Queen Victoria,*
L.Q.V. 3	Second and Third Series
M. Géog.	*Le Mouvement Géographique* (Brussels)
New C.M.H.	*The New Cambridge Modern History*
Proc. Sud.	
Hist. Assoc.	*Proceedings of the Sudan Historical Association*
Q.D.C.	*Questions Diplomatiques et Coloniales* (Paris)
Rev. Belge	
Phil. Hist.	*Revue Belge de Philologie et d'Histoire*
Rev. Hist.	*Revue Historique*
Rev. Hist. Cols.	*Revue d'Histoire des Colonies*
Rev. Hist. Dip.	*Revue d'Histoire Diplomatique*
S.N.R.	*Sudan Notes and Records*

Note on Spelling

For the spelling of Arabic personal names, the system used in R. L. Hill's *Biographical Dictionary of the Anglo-Egyptian Sudan* has been followed, but with the omission of subscript diacritical marks.

For Sudanese place-names, I have followed the conventions of the Sudan Survey Department (except for the use of the form Bahr *al*-Ghazal). Elsewhere, African place-names have been written with the usual English-style spelling wherever such a spelling exists (e.g. 'Jibuti', not 'Djibouti'; 'Chad', not 'Tchad'). When in doubt, I have used the form most likely to be recognised by other workers in this field of study. Where place-names and personal names occur in quotations, the spelling of the original has always been retained.

The names of the Ethiopian months have been spelled in a form approved by the International African Institute.

Note on Dates

Documents originally dated by the Islamic or the Ethiopian calendar have been cited with both their original date and its Gregorian equivalent. Documents from Russian sources have been cited with a New Style (Gregorian) date only.

'We go to gain a little patch of ground
That hath in it no profit but the name.
To pay five ducats, five, I would not farm it'
Hamlet, iv, iv

Introduction

THE UPPER NILE BASIN AND THE
NILE WATERS

ON 30 October 1898, when war with France seemed to be the almost inevitable outcome of the Fashoda dispute, Queen Victoria wrote that she could hardly bring herself to consent to 'a war for so miserable and small an object'.[1] The Queen doubtless had in mind the squalid and pestilential site of Fashoda itself; but Fashoda was, if anything, a rather superior sample of much of the country within the upper basin of the Nile. This region, which may be roughly defined as the Nile basin north of Lake Albert and south of the tenth parallel, had moreover no intrinsic attraction whatever for the 'official mind' of British imperialism. In Lord Cromer's view, it consisted of 'large tracts of useless territory which it would be difficult and costly to administer properly'.[2] In 1898 Lord Salisbury disposed in two words of a memorandum which expatiated on the supposed wealth of the Bahr al-Ghazal region: 'wretched stuff'.[3] Yet this unpropitious country, which has been either a financial liability or a security risk—and usually both—to every government which has so far attempted to administer it, appears to have provoked a conflict which, alone among 'Partition of Africa' questions, brought two Great Powers to the very brink of war. This paradox, which distressed the Queen in 1898, still persists in spite of two generations of study by publicists and historians.

The geography of the Upper Nile region, considered in isolation, offers no solution to this paradox; nor does the political and social condition of its inhabitants during the period of European competition. North of the 'Albert Nile' reach between Lake Albert and the present Sudan frontier at Nimule, the Upper Nile basin resembles a vast shallow saucer. This saucer collects and transmits the rainfall of the entire region lying between the Nile-Congo divide in the south-west and south, and the Ethiopian highlands in the east. It also receives the waters of two streams that rise outside it: the Albert Nile, which continues northwards as the Bahr el-Jebel; and the Baro, which escapes

[1] L.Q.V. 3, iii, p. 305, the Queen to Salisbury 30 Oct. 1898.
[2] SP Cabinet Memoranda, Cromer to Salisbury 5 Nov. 1897.
[3] FO 78/5051, minute on a report by Gleichen of 20 Oct. 1898.

A

westwards into the basin from the tangled Ethiopian massif. The waters thus collected are drained by the White Nile, which flows northwards through a third gap in the rim of the saucer, and its only outlet—the broad, usually featureless plain lying between the hills of southern Kordofan and the western ramparts of Ethiopia.

This work of collection and transmission is however performed very inefficiently. The western half of the basin is occupied by an elaborate system of tributaries rising on the Nile-Congo divide and all flowing towards the White Nile, mostly by way of the Bahr al-Ghazal; but of the estimated sixteen milliard cubic metres run-off of the Bahr al-Ghazal basin less than a milliard is actually delivered to the Nile. The south-eastern sector of the Nile basin is drained by the Pibor, which flows northwards to join the Baro; downstream of the confluence the river, here known as the Sobat, meanders westward across the plain to join the White Nile a few miles upstream of Malakal. But the contribution made by the Pibor is again an almost negligible fraction of the run-off for the large area which it drains. As for the Bahr el-Jebel, it gains no water, even in the rainy season, from its passage through the Upper Nile basin. On the contrary, almost half the water which the Albert Nile transmits to the basin has been lost when the Bahr el-Jebel flows out of it at Lake No.[1]

This strange state of affairs is brought about by the peculiar relief and surface geology of the Upper Nile basin. Except in the south-west, where the country adjacent to the Nile-Congo divide consists of a low, gently sloping, ironstone plateau, the floor of the basin is formed by an almost level plain of impermeable clay. On this clay plain the river channels are mere shallow ditches, quite inadequate to transmit even the local rainfall. During the wet season, this rainfall, augmented by the run-off from the peripheral regions with a more definite relief, spills over to inundate many thousands of square miles of plain, and is ultimately lost by evaporation and by transpiration from the tall grasses which cover the whole clay region. Even where no considerable rivers transmit water to it, the clay plain is completely waterlogged and often actually under water during the rainy season. After the rains most of it dries out into a waterless 'sour veldt'—a desert of tall grass devoid of crops, pasture and human habitation. Its pastoral inhabitants contrive to live by practising transhumance between the small 'islands' of higher land which are not totally flooded during the rains, and the almost equally limited tracts of riverain swamp-pasture which persist through the dry season.

In the centre of this seasonally flooded plain—at the bottom of the saucer—lies a large area of permanent swamp. It is here that the Bahr el-Jebel loses, by spillage and consequent evaporation and transpira-

---

[1] For the general geography of the southern Sudan, see: K. M. Barbour, *The Republic of the Sudan* (London 1961), esp. pp. 234-64. For the hydrology of the Upper Nile basin: H. E. Hurst, *The Nile* (London 1952); P. P. Howell *et al.*, 'The Equatorial Nile Project', *S.N.R.*, XXXIII, I (1952), pp. 3-41.

tion, so much of its water. In this region too, the river-channels, unless kept open artificially, become completely choked by masses of swamp-vegetation known as 'sudd'.[1] Partly because of the diminution in river traffic during the Mahdia, but also from natural causes which are still very ill understood, the sudd in the eighteen-nineties became particularly formidable; more impenetrable indeed than it had been when the Upper Nile was first explored half a century earlier. Immediately to the north of this sudd region, however, there has always been an open reach of the White Nile, running eastwards to the Sobat mouth from the confluence of the Bahr el-Jebel and the Bahr al-Ghazal at Lake No. Here, in this unobstructed reach, lay the natural cross-roads of the north-south and east-west routes across the Upper Nile Basin. A little further downstream, where the White Nile swings northwards to Khartoum from its confluence with the Sobat, isolated tongues of firm ground[2] begin to penetrate the fringing swamp and to reach the open waters of the river. Ever since the Egyptian government post of Fashoda was founded in 1855, one or other of these 'landing-places'— Fashoda, Tawfiqia, Malakal—has always been the site of the military and administrative headquarters for the river and swamp country to the south. This strategically critical reach of the White Nile from Lake No to Fashoda was therefore the ultimate goal of almost all the European expeditions which entered the Upper Nile basin between 1890 and 1900.

The severity of the natural obstacles which barred the way to this region was not however usually recognised by the planners of these expeditions. Only from the north was access naturally easy. The White Nile from Khartoum to Lake No, navigable at all seasons and un-encumbered either by cataracts or by swamp vegetation, forms a natural canal with a current so gentle that it can be ascended under sail alone when the winter northerlies blow. Ever since 1839, when Turco-Egyptian military explorers had first begun to penetrate the southern Sudan, the White Nile had been the standard approach route; but in 1884-5 this route was completely closed by the successes of the Mahdi and the Egyptian withdrawal from the Sudan. Approaches from other directions by river, which look so promising on the map, are in fact frustrated by the physical geography of the Upper Nile basin. Almost all these rivers are in their upper courses mere seasonal torrents, rarely if ever navigable. Many of them never reach the main stream at all, even in the rainy season; their lower courses lose themselves in the waterlogged plain. Those that finally reach the Nile almost always do so only after flowing through the zone of permanent swamp, and permanent sudd, on either the Bahr al-Ghazal or the Bahr el-Jebel. In the period of active European competition the sudd was a natural barrier comparable in severity with a desert or a range

---

[1] Arabic *sadd*, an obstruction or barrage.
[2] Arabic *mashra'*, a landing-place.

of very high mountains, and a complete obstacle to all ordinary navigation.[1] Any approach by the Bahr el-Jebel was indeed not merely very difficult but, after about 1895, frankly impossible. In 1894 the Bahr el-Jebel sudd had closed; its clearance rapidly became a major engineering operation which could not then have been organised from the southern end.[2] Of all the rivers flowing towards the White Nile only one, the Sobat, afforded reasonably easy navigation; but the Sobat begins its navigable course in a region which was itself very difficult of access to European expeditions at that time. Nor did it profit the military explorer to abandon the rivers in favour of an over-land march, except of course on the ironstone plateau of the south-west. The clay plain was an insuperable obstacle: during the rains a vast swamp or shallow lake; in the dry season a parched wilderness which posed insoluble problems of provisioning and water-supply. Marchand, who seems to have studied the geography of the Upper Nile much more carefully than most of his colleagues or rivals, was so impressed by all the difficulties that he originally planned to by-pass almost the whole of the basin, and to work his way around its 'rim', first along the ironstone to Deim Zubeir and thence northwards and eastwards to Fashoda through the savannah country of southern Darfur and Kordofan.[3]

The distribution within the Upper Nile basin of the White Nile and its tributaries endows this region with a certain physiographical unity. But this unity is in no way reflected by its human geography. Its physical boundaries, for the most part identical with the present frontier of the Sudan Republic south of the tenth parallel, are scarce-ly anywhere ethnic boundaries. In the south-west the Azande strad-dle the Nile-Congo divide, and are now partitioned between three different states; in the south-east the Acholi, the Latuko and the Turkana dwell on both sides of the frontier. Within the basin, on the other hand, the ethnic, linguistic and socio-economic diversities are manifold and profound. There are about a dozen 'major' tribes; but the total number of separate tribal entities is very much larger. Tribes range in size from the Dinka, in 1956 more than a million strong, down to tiny groups of a few dozen individuals. These peoples are broad-ly classified into three ethnic groups: Nilotics, Nilo-Hamites, and a rather embarrassingly miscellaneous group called 'Sudanic' or 'speakers of Sudanic languages'. The Nilotics (Dinka, Nuer, Shilluk, Anuak) dwell in the northern, central and north-eastern districts of the basin; roughly, in the region occupied by permanent or seasonal swamp. In the south and south-east are the Nilo-Hamites, of whom

[1] Marchand did indeed penetrate the Bahr al-Ghazal sudd in 1898; but his was no ordinary navigation. Cf. *infra*, Ch. xii, p. 286.
[2] S.I.R., Nos. 66-70 (Dec. 1899-June 1900), describe the clearing operations. M. F. Gage, 'Sudd-Cutting', *S.N.R.* xxxi, 1 (1950), pp. 7-20, describes an unsuccessful and nearly disastrous attempt to pierce the sudd from the Uganda end in 1899-1900.
[3] *Infra*, Ch. xii, p. 285.

the Bari and the Latuko are typical representatives. The 'Sudanic' peoples, a group comprising a large number of often very small tribes, are found in the west and south-west. The largest tribe of this group, the very distinctive and cohesive Azande of the extreme south-west, played an important part in the internal politics of the Upper Nile during the period of European competition.[1] Ethnic diversity is reflected in linguistic diversity. Among the many languages spoken in the southern Sudan, no less than twelve could in 1956 be classified as 'major languages', spoken by thirty thousand people or more. But none of these—not even Dinka, which may have been spoken in its various dialects by as many as 40 per cent of the population—had ever developed into anything approaching a *lingua franca*.[2]

The manifold ethnic and linguistic diversity is reinforced by differences, not so numerous but certainly no less profound, in mode of living. These differences are clearly linked to regional variations in the physical environment, which is however almost everywhere difficult enough to impose upon the inhabitants very specialised techniques of subsistence. The conditions of the clay plain for the most part preclude effective agriculture; and the Dinka and the Nuer depend for survival upon their cattle. Cattle provide not only the milk and blood which are staple Nilotic diet; their dung is normally the only fuel available to feed the smudge fires without whose protection neither men nor cattle could survive the attacks of nocturnal insects. But the raising of stock in these hard conditions is in itself a *tour de force* which demands a highly specialised and therefore inflexible mode of life. The Azande, in sharp contrast, live in tse-tse country where the raising of stock is impossible. They live by shifting bush cultivation, eked out by hunting and collecting; their chronic protein deficiency is occasionally alleviated by feasting upon termites.[3] Elsewhere in Equatoria, bush cultivation, more or less shifting and often combined with some stock-raising, is the normal means of subsistence; though some groups in the extreme south-east practise true cattle-nomadism, as opposed to the short-distance transhumance of the Nilotics.

Religious and political institutions were just as varied as ways of life; among the peoples of the Upper Nile there was nothing resembling the broad similarity of beliefs and practices to be found, for instance, among the southern African Bantu. The Shilluk, with their 'divine kingship', had perhaps gone furthest on the road towards centralisation of political and religious authority; but there was nowhere a political structure comparable in its elaboration with that of the Baganda or even the Banyoro. Moreover, the most strongly integrated groups, like the Shilluk and the Azande under their ruling clan of the Avongara, were by no means the largest numerically. The really big

[1] Cf. *infra*, Ch. v, pp. 95-6; Ch. xii, p. 277.
[2] The figures in this paragraph are derived from the *Last (9th) Interim Report* of the First Population Census of the Sudan, 1956.
[3] And, in earlier times, by occasional cannibalism.

tribes, notably the Dinka and the Nuer, had no formal political organisation at all above the clan level; and even in the clans, authority was widely distributed, especially among the Nuer. No tribe ever seems to have been strong enough to establish a widespread preponderance outside its homeland, or even to act as a focus for the inter-tribal relationships of any large area.

Until the advent of the Turco-Egyptians in the fifth decade of the nineteenth century, all these local forces making for disunity and tribal isolation had never been counteracted by any external unifying influence. Unlike the northern Sudan, which has throughout historic times been a province, albeit often a rather backward province, of some major civilisation—Ancient Egyptian, Eastern Christian, Arab-Islamic—the Upper Nile does not seem ever to have been influenced, to any significant extent, by cultures more developed than its own.[1] From the seventeenth century onwards the Arab north had indeed slowly encroached upon the Negroid south; but the southerners had simply given ground and had remained remarkably impervious to the Arabic language, to northern political institutions and to Islam. The southerners who bore the brunt of this contact were in fact the Nilotic Dinka and Shilluk, whose highly specialised and self-sufficient mode of life seems always to have made them unresponsive and even hostile to all external influences. The Turco-Egyptian advance pierced at last this 'Nilotic shield' of the south, though the invaders did not in the end attempt any wholesale subjugation of the Nilotics themselves.[2] The far south and the south-west, where the tribes were more accessible and less formidable and where above all there was ivory to be hunted, were the regions in which the newcomers were most active.

New and very powerful forces now began to work upon, and to disrupt, many of the archaic societies of the Upper Nile. Of these new forces the most important were the much more active penetration of Islam and, above all, the rapid development of large-scale commerce. The ivory trade, which the Khartoum Government at first attempted to monopolise, soon fell into the hands of European and later of northern Sudanese merchant adventurers (the 'Khartoumers'). From the outset the ivory traders had been all too ready to use violence as a short cut to profits; but violence became endemic when the Negroid peoples, their very modest demand for trade-goods satisfied, refused to deliver ivory except in return for cattle. Cattle could be obtained only by raiding; private armies were therefore created whose members were paid by being allowed to acquire and export as slaves the prisoners captured in these raids. Meanwhile, the establishment of an effective administration in the South was

[1] The only obvious exception seems to be the working of iron, acquired, presumably, directly or indirectly from the Meroitic civilisation of the northern Sudan.
[2] Except for the more accessible Shilluk, who occupied the strategically important left bank of the White Nile between Lake No and about Lat. 13°N.

delayed for almost a generation.[1] After about 1865, the southern trade, by now mainly a trade in slaves, was entirely in Khartoumer hands, but the situation in the South was much more complex than that implied in the traditional stereotype of 'Arab' exploiters and Negroid victims. Some groups were indeed slaved almost to the point of tribal disintegration; but even among these some fortunate individuals found in enslavement not a life of misery but an attractive career. Half a century later, tribesmen of the heavily slaved Banda were to recall the old days with something like nostalgia. Being raided and enslaved 'happened once, and all was soon over. Then you were given a home, food, clothes, etc., and above all a *gun*; you were a man.'[2] Other tribes, for instance the Njangulgule of the Raga district, co-operated actively in the trade, and seem to have reached a satisfactory *modus vivendi* with their Khartoumer overlords. In some regions, friction between southerners and outsiders was eased by the assimilation of Arab customs and even by conversion to Islam. But this process was much too patchy to make for any wide unity. It had gone furthest in the north-western Bahr al-Ghazal, where a number of small tribes had been more or less thoroughly Arabised and at least one, the Feroge, had been fully converted to Islam. In some parts of Equatoria the chiefs had adopted Arab dress and certain Arab social customs, and a pidgin colloquial Arabic ('Mongallese') was beginning to develop as a *lingua franca*. But the Nilotics, by far the largest southern group, remained almost untouched by these influences. Even among the comparatively accessible Shilluk, Arab customs had made little headway and Islam none at all.[3]

By the eighteen-sixties the organisers or protectors of the slave trade, Zubair Rahma al-Mansūr in the Bahr al-Ghazal and the al-'Aqqād family in Equatoria, had in practice supplanted the Egyptian Government as rulers of these areas. But from about 1869 onwards the Khedive Ismā'īl strove to administer the southern Sudan more effectively, and above all to suppress the slave trade, by the employment of European senior officials. These efforts aroused strong opposition, not least among some of those whom they were intended to benefit. Sir Samuel Baker, in his dealings with the Bari of Equatoria, soon found himself involved in the now traditional pattern of violence. Violence for violence, the Bari preferred that of the slavers to that of the Government, for the slavers were in a position to offer immediate and tangible advantages to certain individuals and groups. Govern-

[1] J. R. Gray, *A History of the Southern Sudan, 1839-1889* (London 1961), pp. 27-69. Cf. M. F. Shukry, *The Khedive Ismail and Slavery in the Sudan* (Cairo 1937), pp. 91-107.

[2] S. Santandrea, 'Sanusi, Ruler of Dar Banda and Dar Kuti, in the History of the Bahr-el-Ghazal', *S.N.R.* xxxviii (1957), pp. 151-5, citing (at p. 155) the remarks of Banda tribesmen.

[3] S. Santandrea, 'A Preliminary Account of the Indri, Togoyo, Feroge, Mangaya and Woro', *S.N.R.* xxxiv, 2 (1953), pp. 230-64. Gray, *op. cit.*, pp. 142-4. G. N. Sanderson, 'Islamic "Spheres of Influence" in East-Central Africa on the Eve of European Partition' (Paper presented to the International African Institute's Seminar on 'Islam in Africa', Dec. 1963).

ment taxation, levied in kind, appeared as legalised and recurrent plunder. Forcible recruiting by the Government was indistinguishable in its operation from ordinary enslavement; but soldiering for the Khedive was a much less attractive career than membership of the private armies of the Khartoumers.[1] In the Bahr al-Ghazal, Gordon's attempted repression of the trade was intensely resented far outside the ranks of the Khartoumer merchants and their 'Arab' following. Here the Mahdist cause was embraced, not as an Islamic 'New Order' but simply as an anti-government revolt, by the partially Arabised Njangulgule and even by certain sections of the frankly pagan Dinka.[2] The Equatoria tribes, though they did not rally to Mahdism, seized the opportunity to rise on their own account as the conflict developed between the Mahdists and the Egyptian garrison. By 1880 the tribes of the Upper Nile, divided one from another in so many profound and far-reaching ways, were united only in their detestation of 'the Government'. Some resented its attempted destruction of a business in which they were active partners; many others found its yoke heavier and less rewarding than that of the Khartoumers. Many of the Nilotics had indeed never been under either Khedivial or Khartoumer administration, and did not distinguish between government agents and other light-skinned foreigners. But they had learned enough of the predatory ways of all these 'Turks' to welcome their ejection with no less enthusiasm than other groups whose experience had been more direct.

The effect of the Mahdia in the southern Sudan was to destroy all trace of Westernised administration and indeed all authority above the level of the tribe. Paradoxically, it also arrested the development and consolidation of Islamic influence on the Upper Nile.[3] In Equatoria, the Mahdists were never able effectively to fill the vacuum of power left by the withdrawal of Emin Pasha and the Egyptian garrison between 1889 and 1891.[4] Indeed, even as early as 1886, before the total collapse of Egyptian authority, the missionary Mackay could write that while Egyptian rule in Equatoria had been almost 'as bad as any government could be', it had at least been much better than the chaotic violence which had followed it.[5] In the Bahr al-Ghazal, except perhaps in the extreme north, Mahdist control declined to vanishing point after 1885, when the force under Karamallāh Kurqusāwi was called away to deal with an emergency in Darfur. This withdrawal, even more than the campaign by Karamallāh which had preceded it, left the Bahr al-Ghazal in turmoil and

---

[1] Gray, op. cit., pp. 85, 92-8, 112-4. Santandrea, 'Sanusi . . .', loc. cit. G. N. Sanderson, article 'Fāshōda' in Encyclopaedia of Islam (New Edn.), II, p. 828.

[2] Gray, op. cit., pp. 155-61. Shukry, op. cit., pp. 302-13. Santandrea, 'A Preliminary Account of the Indri . . .', S.N.R. 1953, at pp. 244-9. F. R. Wingate, Mahdiism and the Egyptian Sudan (London 1891), pp. 24-9.

[3] Sanderson, 'Islamic "Spheres of Influence" . . .', ubi supra.

[4] Ibid. Cf. infra, Ch. II, p. 40.

[5] FO 84/1775, Mackay to Kirk 24 Aug. 1886, enclosed in Holmwood to Iddesleigh No. 191, 18 Oct. 1886.

a prey to chronic inter-tribal war; local traditions represent this period as one of devastating violence and as a catastrophic breach with a comparatively peaceful and uneventful past.[1]

By 1890, when King Leopold of the Belgians initiated active European competition by launching the Van Kerckhoven expedition towards Equatoria, the Upper Nile was indeed 'Darkest Africa'. It had not always been so. The map of Africa prepared for the Egyptian General Staff in 1877 shows a wealth of detail in the Upper Nile basin which contrasts sharply with the surrounding blank spaces. Indeed, at that time the Upper Nile was, outside southern Africa, by far the best-explored and best-known region of the African interior. Less than fifteen years later it had become well-nigh inaccessible to the European Powers who were beginning to compete so hotly for it, and of its internal condition scarcely anything was known apart from a vague general impression of confusion and conflict. In October 1897 Salisbury remarked that it was 'as difficult to judge what is going on in the Upper Nile valley as to judge what is going on on the other side of the moon'.[2] These words were prompted by the difficulty experienced in obtaining reliable information about European expeditions, but they applied with even more force to the internal politics of the Upper Nile. The sudden and total collapse of external control had come at a moment when this control had in many regions already shaken tribal institutions and utterly destroyed the previous pattern of inter-tribal relations, but before any stable new adjustments had begun to emerge. The murderous confusion which followed made the always unpromising wildernesses of the Upper Nile a most unattractive field for imperial expansion to the British 'official mind', if not always to other imperialist circles in England and elsewhere.

But however inaccessible the Upper Nile basin might be, however unpromising its lack of natural resources other than slave manpower and however desperate the confusion and violence of its internal politics, through it and from it the waters of the White Nile still flowed northwards to fertilise Egypt. It had of course always been obvious, even from the remotest antiquity, that Egypt was 'the gift of the Nile'. Less obvious, but beginning to be appreciated by hydrologists, was the increasingly critical importance of the contribution made by the White Nile during the low season when the Blue Nile is not in flood. Until the nineteenth century the low-season flow of the White Nile had indeed been of only marginal importance to the Egyptian economy. During the low season, primitive mechanical devices—the *shādūf*, the *sāqīa*, the Archimedean screw—lifted small volumes of water to irrigate slender ribbons of land immediately adjacent to the Nile; but as in the days of the Pharaohs, dearth or plenty in Egypt still de-

[1] Santandrea, 'A Preliminary Account of the Indri . . .', at pp. 243-9, 255-6, 259-60. Sanderson, 'Islamic "Spheres of Influence" . . .'.
[2] S P Egypt, Salisbury to Cromer 29 Oct. 1897.

pended on variations in the height of the flood and therefore in the area of land which could be effectively inundated by it.[1] To the Nile flood the White Nile normally makes a negligible contribution, compared with the immense spate of water sweeping down the Blue Nile and the Atbara from Ethiopia.[2] But in the eighteen-nineties the Blue Nile and Atbara floods, in spite of medieval legends and more recent fears, were pretty adequately protected against malicious interference by their own quite unmanageable volume.[3] In any but the most abnormal of years the effect of human interference would have been insignificant compared with that of the natural variations in the height of the flood. In the occasional catastrophically high or low year, occurring perhaps once a century, such interference could hardly have much increased the gravity of what was already a major disaster for Egypt.

In the low season the roles of the Blue and White Niles are reversed, and the White Nile now contributes more than four-fifths of the Nile waters.[4] Early in the reign of Muhammad 'Ali, techniques had been introduced for the distribution of the low-season water by gravity; and the area of Egyptian soil irrigated all the year round, and not merely in the flood season, began steadily to increase. By 1886 the area under permanent irrigation was already nearly 50 per cent greater than that under seasonal flood irrigation. In 1890 repairs were completed to the Delta Barrage, originally built in 1861 but until 1890 little more than an architectural ornament owing to faults in its construction. With the Barrage repaired, it was possible to raise the low-season level of the Nile sufficiently to command a system of canals providing permanent gravity irrigation for the Delta; and before long the new Delta cotton fields and sugar plantations were taking up the whole low-season discharge.[5] Already by 1895 the demand for water towards the end of the low season was beginning to outstrip the supply, and plans were being made for the building of a dam at Asswan to store part of the flood surplus for use during the season of shortage. Any interference with the White Nile would now have impoverished Egypt; interference serious enough to prevent the low-season Nile from commanding the new gravity irrigation systems would have completely dislocated the

[1] Hurst, op. cit., pp. 38-46. The shādūf consists of a bucket attached to a pivoted and counterpoised beam; the sāqia is the bullock-powered wheel-lift sometimes called a 'Persian wheel'.

[2] Average maximum discharge (as at Asswan): White Nile, 70 million cubic metres per day (10 per cent); Blue Nile, 485 million (68 per cent). The Atbara contributes the remaining 22 per cent (157 million cubic metres). Even today, in spite of the construction of storage dams at Asswan, Sennar and Roseires, in any normal year much of the flood runs to waste (Hurst, op. cit., pp. 12-13, 241-2).

[3] Cf. W. L. Langer, The Diplomacy of Imperialism, Second Edn. (New York 1951), pp. 103-6. The capacity of the Sennar dam (780 million cubic metres) is less than two days' discharge of the Blue Nile at its peak.

[4] White Nile, 37·5 million cubic metres per day (83 per cent); Blue Nile, 7·5 million (17 per cent). (Hurst, op. cit., p. 242.) The Atbara contributes nothing during the low season.

[5] Hurst, op. cit., pp. 12-13, 46-54. The figures in 1886 were: Basin irrigation, 2 million feddans; permanent irrigation, 2·9 million feddans (ibid., p. 284).

Egyptian economy. The volume of the White Nile discharge, unlike that of the Blue Nile in flood, is at all seasons modest enough to be easily controllable. To hold back the discharge of several weeks, and then perhaps to release it in an untimely flood, would not in principle have been a difficult operation.[1] The skill of the Western hydraulic engineer had greatly enriched Egypt; but it had also made Egypt vulnerable as never before to interference with the White Nile waters at the very moment when she lost control of the remote African wilderness from which those waters flow.

[1] The capacity of the Jebel Aulia dam on the White Nile above Khartoum is 3500 million cubic metres (Howell *et al.*, *S.N.R.* 1952 *ubi supra*, at p. 34). The daily discharge of the White Nile varies between 37·5 and 70 million cubic metres (Hurst, *op. cit.*, pp. 241-2).

I

PRELUDE TO EUROPEAN COMPETITION

1882–86

So long as Egypt herself controlled the Sudan, no European Power was seriously interested in the fate of the Upper Nile basin. From about 1870 British official attention was directed to this region with increasing frequency because British subjects were often the agents of Egyptian expansion towards territories where some of their fellow-subjects—missionaries and merchants—had interests or aspirations. But this interest took, far more often than not, a resolutely negative form. In April 1869 Stanton, the Consul-General at Cairo, was warned by the Foreign Secretary Clarendon that H.M.G. would 'undertake no responsibility whatever for [Baker's expedition] or as regards any matter connected with it'.[1] In 1875, however, the Khedive Ismāʿīl's expansion towards Uganda began to clash with the interests of the Sultan of Zanzibar in this region. This was awkward, for both these African Powers were to a greater or a lesser extent British clients. In order to forestall the establishment of European rivals on or near the Suez route to India, London was encouraging Egypt to extend her possessions on the African shores of the Red Sea and the Gulf of Aden, and at the same time supporting the hegemony of Zanzibar over the African coast of the Indian Ocean. But this again did not imply a positive official interest in the basin of the Upper Nile. To the Foreign Office the Upper Nile was no more than a minor complication in the management of two small Powers who could be encouraged to play a defensive part in British ocean strategy.[2] Unofficial British interest was indeed more active and sustained than that of the Foreign Office; humanitarians and missionaries campaigned against the slave trade in the southern Sudan. Even when Ismāʿīl attempted to suppress the trade, Egypt still remained suspect to these groups, often designated by the nickname 'Exeter Hall';[3] and Exeter Hall continued to oppose the expansion of Egypt, as a Muslim Power, even when that

[1] Gray, *History of the Southern Sudan*, p. 170, citing FO 78/2091, Clarendon to Stanton 15 Apr. 1869.

[2] *Ibid.*, pp. 175-85. R. E. Robinson and J. Gallagher, 'The Partition of Africa', *New C.M.H.*, xi (Cambridge 1962), pp. 593-640, at pp. 611-2.

[3] So called from the usual place of their meetings and rallies (a site now occupied by the Strand Palace Hotel). Cf. R. L. Hill, 'The Period of Egyptian Occupation' [*sc.*, of the Sudan], *S.N.R.* xl (1959), pp. 100-106.

expansion took place under the enthusiastically Christian Gordon. The humanitarians were often supported by certain commercial interests, who believed that the suppression of the slave trade, and the restriction of Egyptian influence, would open up greater opportunities for 'legitimate commerce' in Uganda and the Upper Nile basin.[1] But unofficial agitation had very little effect upon official policy. True, in 1866 Clarendon had asked Stanton how 'we might best put a stop to the horrible state of things which undoubtedly exists on the White Nile'.[2] But no action followed, apart from almost routine diplomatic remonstrances addressed to Ismā'īl. Indeed, after the retirement of Petherick in 1865, London ceased even to maintain a consul at Khartoum. In 1881, under very strong humanitarian pressure, Gladstone agreed to revive the Khartoum consulate; but so languid was the interest of the Foreign Office that minor administrative difficulties were allowed to prevent the filling of the vacancy, and the outbreak of the Mahdia found Britain still without any official representative in the interior of the Sudan.[3]

By 1887, however, the basin of the Upper Nile was rapidly becoming an object of serious political concern to Britain; and within the next three years British concern was greatly increased by the growing interest of other European Powers. This rapid and surprising transformation had its roots in the British occupation of Egypt in September 1882 and in the Mahdist insurrection which, combined with heavy British pressure, forced Egypt into withdrawal from the whole of the Sudan. Since the Mahdist State neither sought nor obtained the recognition of other Powers, the Sudan could be plausibly—and temptingly—regarded as *res nullius*; and in the southern Sudan, where Mahdist control was so limited and uncertain, this juridical concept was a pretty accurate label for the actual state of affairs. Then in 1884-5 the political partition of East Africa was suddenly and unexpectedly inaugurated by the way in which Bismarck exploited certain diplomatic consequences of the British occupation of Egypt. The establishment of a British monopoly of influence in Egypt had been followed almost immediately by developments which placed the waters of the Upper Nile, at least potentially, within the reach of a rival European Power.

For some time after the occupation of Egypt the British had continued to look upon the Upper Nile, and indeed upon the Sudan as a whole, merely as an incidental complication—though this time a very

[1] Gray, *op. cit.*, pp. 167-8, 174-7, 181-4. R. Oliver, *The Missionary Factor in East Africa* (London 1952), pp. 87-9.

[2] Gray, *op. cit.*, p. 169, citing F O 84/1260, Clarendon to Stanton 9 May 1866.

[3] The Khartoum consulate had in fact been suppressed in 1864, largely as a means of quietly dropping Petherick, whose conduct had given rise to embarrassing controversy. In Dec. 1883, after the Shaikān disaster, Frank Power, the correspondent of *The Times* at Khartoum, was hurriedly appointed consul. Cf. Gray, *op. cit.*, pp. 186-7; R. L. Hill, *Egypt in the Sudan, 1820-1881* (London 1959), p. 125; R. L. Hill, *A Biographical Dictionary of the Anglo-Egyptian Sudan* (Oxford 1951), pp. 308-9.

important one—in an operation which had been prompted almost entirely by the needs of imperial strategy in the Near East. Britain had intervened in Egypt by force of arms only when the 'anarchy' and 'fanaticism' of Ahmad 'Urābi Pasha's revolt had begun to threaten the Suez Canal. The Canal was the indispensable link between the Mediterranean Fleet and the Indian Army, those two great factors of power which backed the paper of English diplomacy both east and west of Suez. Its security could apparently be guaranteed simply by suppressing a military mutiny and restoring the Khedive Tawfīq to his rightful authority; once this had been achieved, the British troops could be speedily withdrawn. In fact, 'Urābi's insurrection was no mere putsch by a group of discontented officers. To some extent at least it was a widely based movement of popular protest against the subservience of the Egyptian 'Establishment', and of the Khedive in particular, to the foreigner and the infidel.[1] It was begotten by Western nationalist ideas upon Muslim faith and tradition, and especially upon the undoubted religious duty of *jihād* against infidel political control. The force and vitality of nationalist movements which thus combine the 'modern' and the traditional are now obvious enough; but in 1882 such movements were less familiar than they are today. It does not seem to have occurred to Gladstone and his colleagues that to restore the Khedive at the point of alien and infidel bayonets would exacerbate the feeling of outrage and destroy what little remained of Tawfīq's credit as a worthy ruler for Muslim Egyptians.[2] When Sir Evelyn Baring, later Lord Cromer, arrived in Egypt in September 1883, it did not indeed take him long to discover that 'recent events have completely shattered the system of government which prevailed under Ismail Pasha and his predecessors'. But Baring still thought it possible to create 'new systems of administration and judicial procedure' to replace the old régime. These institutions, when they had 'gained stability', would be handed over to 'a strong native government' consisting of Egyptians patriotic enough to be respected by their fellow-countrymen and moderate enough to be acceptable, not only to London but to the other Powers with interests in Egypt. The British evacuation would then follow immediately. Premature evacuation was however, in Baring's eyes, the road to almost certain disaster, for it would jeopardise the 'exotic superstructure' of European inhabitants, interests and institutions which had grown up in Egypt since the time of Muhammad 'Ali.[3] Any serious threat to this 'superstructure' would

---

[1] It is probably just to call 'Urābi's insurrection 'a recognisably modern nationalist revolution' (Robinson and Gallagher, *ubi supra*, at p. 597). But a serious study of this movement, based on Egyptian sources and publications, has yet to be undertaken.

[2] Cf. R. E. Robinson and J. Gallagher, *Africa and the Victorians* (London 1961), pp. 76-159; Robinson and Gallagher, *New C.M.H.* XI, *loc. cit. et seq.*; R. E. Robinson, 'Imperial Problems in British Politics, 1880-1895', *C.H.B.E.* III (Cambridge 1959), pp. 127-80, at pp. 150-6.

[3] Cromer [E. Baring, Earl of Cromer], *Modern Egypt* (London 1908), II, pp. 354-65, printing Baring to Granville 9 and 28 Oct. 1883. FO 633/6 (Cromer Papers), No. 6, Baring to Granville 14 Oct. 1883; cf. No. 68, Baring to Iddesleigh 31 Oct. 1886.

invite the intervention of other Powers, who might well threaten British security at the Suez Canal no less dangerously than Ahmad 'Urābi himself.

Six years later, Baring was curtly to state that this policy was 'impossible of execution'.[1] This was not his view in October 1883, when he wrote:

> Give me 2000 men and power to settle matters between the
> English and Egyptian governments and I will guarantee that in
> twelve months there shall not be a British soldier in Egypt, and
> that the country is put in such a position as to render it very
> improbable that any Egyptian question will be raised again for
> many years to come at all events.[2]

Baring's optimism was not entirely unjustified. Egyptians qualified to play the governmental part for which British policy had cast them were scarce, but they were not non-existent. The most prominent of them, Sharif Pasha, was a statesman of considerable ability who was widely respected in both Egyptian and European circles. But whether or not the policy of 'restore, reconstruct and retire' was originally incapable of execution, it was very soon to become so. The reaction of Baring, and of the British Cabinet, to the Mahdist insurrection in the Sudan made it impossible for patriotic and moderate Egyptians to collaborate with the occupying Power even for the purpose of bringing the occupation to an end.

The note of *jihād* and Islamic resistance, somewhat muffled in the protest of Ahmad 'Urābi, rang out loud and clear in that of Muhammad Ahmad al-Mahdi. Oppressive taxation and a fairly high level of administrative corruption were certainly grievances in the Egyptian Sudan of the eighteen-eighties; but they were not new grievances. What was new, and what was bitterly resented by the Muslim fundamentalists of the Sudan, was the Westernising, reforming tendencies of the Egyptian administration under Ismā'īl and his successor, and the increasing employment of Christian officials in positions of ever higher authority.[3] Was the government of the Khedive a Muslim government at all? The Mahdi was convinced that it was not: 'Religion fell into the hands of the Turks, who changed it and replaced it by *kufr*. They annulled the laws of the Merciful and revived the ways of Satan after their own inclinations.'[4] One of 'their own inclinations' was of course opposition to the slave trade; and all those in the Sudan— and they were not a few—who depended directly or indirectly on the trade for their livelihood and their ability to pay taxes, were natural recruits for the Mahdia. Among the Mahdi's first adherents, and for a

[1] FO 633/6, No. 147, Baring to Salisbury 15 June 1889.
[2] Cromer, *op. cit.* II, p. 359, citing Baring to Granville 28 Oct. 1883.
[3] P. M. Holt, *The Mahdist State in the Sudan, 1881–1898* (Oxford 1958), pp. 25-36; *idem*, 'The Place in History of the Sudanese Mahdia', *S.N.R.* XL (1959), pp. 107-12.
[4] Mahdia 1/34/11, the Mahdi to the Negus Yohannes 1302/1884-5 (no day or month). *Kufr*=atheism, godlessness.

time the backbone of his military strength, were the tough and turbulent northern Sudanese frontiersmen who dominated the slave and
ivory country of the Bahr al-Ghazal.[1]

For some two years, from 1881 to 1883, the Egyptian Government
had under-rated the Mahdi, in much the same way and for much the
same reasons as England and France had under-rated 'Urābi. Cairo
scarcely seems to have recognised that a serious military problem
existed until the fall of El Obeid in January 1883; even then, the true
dimensions of that problem were not understood until on 5 November
1883 the Mahdi annihilated at Shaikān the expedition under Hicks.
Shaikān clearly demonstrated that the Egyptian army, dissolved by
Khedivial decree after the battle of Tel-el-Kebir and then hurriedly
reconstituted, was quite incapable of suppressing the insurrection in
the Sudan. It was not clear then, and it is not clear now, whether this
fact necessarily implied the abandonment of the riverain Sudan from
Khartoum northwards, a region where there had so far been no
Mahdist activity. As early as 19 November 1883, however, Baring contemplated abandoning the whole of the Sudan south of Wadi Halfa;
and throughout December he pressed this policy consistently on a
wavering and divided London Cabinet as the only possible one—
unless of course the Sultan would provide Turkish troops at his own
expense.[2] At the beginning of 1884 the British Government finally
decided to insist on the total evacuation of the Sudan. Sharif Pasha
resigned rather than be responsible for so great a humiliation of
Egypt. Baring had expected this, and was prepared if necessary to
force a ministry of British officials upon the Khedive; but he found a
more pliant Prime Minister in Nubar Pasha Boghos. Nubar was an
Armenian Christian who spoke neither Turkish nor Arabic, a Le-
vantine who personified many of the influences and tendencies most
detested by Egyptian nationalism. He had no illusions about his own
position, and more than once told Baring that if the British troops withdrew, he would take good care to 'leave Egypt with the last battalion'.[3]
Baring, too, recognised that the abandonment of the Sudan and the
political consequences of this decision would force Britain to exercise
in Egypt 'a far more direct interference . . . than has hitherto been contemplated'.[4] Alike to protect the southern frontier against the Sudanese
Mahdists and to protect the Khedive and Nubar against the Egyptian
nationalists, the British garrison would have to be increased and
evacuation postponed. What Baring did not yet realise was that with
the resignation of Sharif there had disappeared his last chance of find-

[1] Holt, *The Mahdist State*, pp. 34-5, 68-72. In 1877-9 there had been a series of pre-
monitory outbreaks, backed by the slavers, in the northern Bahr al-Ghazal and in
southern Darfur. Cf. Shukry, *The Khedive Ismail and Slavery in the Sudan*, pp. 302-13.
[2] Cromer, *op. cit.* I, pp. 372-82. FO 633/6, No. 14, Baring to Granville 22 Nov. 1883.
M. T. Shibeika, *British Policy in the Sudan, 1882-1902* (London 1952), pp. 112-35.
[3] FO 633/6, No. 16, Baring to Granville 17 Dec. 1883. Cromer, *op. cit.* I, pp. 383-4;
II, p. 339.
[4] FO 78/3665, Baring to Granville No. 7, 1 Jan. 1884.

ing a 'strong' yet 'reliable' government to which a reformed Egypt could be handed over. On 7 January 1884, the day of Sharif's resignation, Baring could still promise Gladstone's government military withdrawal from Egypt 'eventually . . . if only you will keep the Tories out of office'.[1]

In November and December 1883 the weight of British military opinion in Egypt had swung steadily in favour of more or less total withdrawal from the Sudan.[2] This was a valid argument, and Baring made a perfectly proper use of it; but it was probably not his only motive for insisting on complete evacuation. In 1908 Baring remarked that: 'the work of reorganisation and reform in Egypt proper . . . could not have been undertaken . . . with any prospect of success so long as the Soudan hung like a dead-weight round the necks of Egyptian reformers'.[3] This consideration, in a rather different context, probably influenced his views in 1883. If Egypt were forced to give up the Sudan, Baring's prospect of being able to hand over a reformed Egypt to 'a strong native government' would recede; but it would not, he believed, disappear completely. But if Egypt attempted to hold even the riverain Sudan, administrative reform would for the foreseeable future be completely subordinated to the military emergency and might never even be effectively started. This would reflect no credit on Sir Evelyn Baring, to whom a Liberal government was looking to create the conditions in which Egypt could be safely evacuated. In London, too, motives were mixed. Northbrook, having read the works of Baker and the reports of Gordon, found himself 'greatly troubled' in conscience at the prospect of supporting continued Egyptian rule in the Sudan, which had in his view been 'a great evil to the people of that country'. He doubted in particular whether the Khedive Tawfiq really wished to discourage the slave trade.[4] For Granville, the Foreign Secretary, the crux of the question was financial: in his view the Sudan was simply an expensive luxury for Egypt. 'It takes away somewhat of the position of a man to sell his racers and hunters, but if he cannot afford to keep them, the sooner they go to Tattersall's the better.'[5]

Hustled by the military emergency, obsessed by the mountain of Egyptian debt, troubled by misgivings about the character of Egyptian rule, and prompted by Baring in moments of indecision, the British Cabinet enforced the evacuation of the Sudan with scarcely a thought for the security of the Nile waters. Engineering opinion in Egypt believed that interference was at least a possibility; but on the advice of a senior British official who had just visited Egypt, the Cabinet rejected this view, without investigation, as 'chimerical'.[6]

[1] FO 633/6, Nos. 16 and 20, Baring to Granville 17 Dec. 1883, 7 Jan. 1884.
[2] Shibeika, loc. cit. Cromer, op. cit. I, pp. 375-89. Cf. L.Q.V. 2, iii, pp. 455-7, Evelyn Wood to the Queen 27 Nov., 10/11 Dec. 1883.
[3] Cromer, op. cit. I, p. 392.
[4] Shibeika, op. cit., p. 129, citing Northbrook to Granville, private, 24 Dec. 1883.
[5] Cromer, loc. cit., citing Granville to Baring, private, 28 Dec. 1883.
[6] Shibeika, op. cit., p. 131.

B

Baring, to do him justice, was not so sure. He did not agree with Sharif Pasha that the whole valley of the Nile from the sources of the river was necessary for the safety and even existence of Egypt.[1] He did, however, recognise the grave danger to Egypt inherent in any European penetration towards the central Sudan and towards the Nile in the Berber-Khartoum reach; and he was always very sensitive to threats of encroachment on the Red Sea coast, the natural starting-point for such penetration. As early as December 1884 he warned Granville against the danger of permitting a French or German foothold here, 'in view of the foolish earth-hunger which appears to have taken possession of Gaul and Teuton alike'.[2] Baring seems to have believed that Egypt was safe so long as no European Power reached the Nile near Khartoum; it does not seem to have occurred to him that the Nile waters might be threatened in the far south. This attitude was reasonable enough in 1883 and 1884, when the danger of European penetration into Equatoria must indeed have seemed 'chimerical'. But as late as January 1889, when the German 'Emin Pasha Relief Expedition' was in active preparation, Baring totally rejected the eloquent plea of Riaz Pasha that 'le Nil est la vie d'Egypte et le Nil, c'est le Soudan', and still insisted that full security could be achieved by maintaining watch and ward on the Red Sea coast.[3] Even in 1890 Baring was preoccupied by the dangers—which he much exaggerated—of an Italian advance into the eastern Sudan, and was apparently blind to the possibility of German encroachment in the Uganda-Wadelai region.

This blindness was probably not fortuitous. As early as November 1883, discussing the possibility of total evacuation of the Sudan, Baring remarked that while Egypt must some day return to the northern Sudan, there could 'be no question of the Egyptian Government reconquering any of the provinces south of Khartoum'.[4] Fifteen years later his views were unchanged. In January 1898, when it still seemed possible that the reconquered Sudan would be Egyptian and not 'Anglo-Egyptian', he reluctantly admitted that 'sooner or later we shall have to put up an Egyptian flag at Fashoda' but continued to insist that 'no further military operations on a large scale . . . will be undertaken for the recovery of the [southern] provinces'.[5] Baring never seems to have explicitly stated his reasons for this settled hostility to the restoration of Egyptian rule in the southern Sudan; but these reasons are not far to seek. 'Exeter Hall' had never succeeded in provoking British official intervention in the southern Sudan; but it did succeed in converting British official opinion, thoroughly and perma-

---

[1] Cromer, *op. cit.* I, p. 380, citing Sharif to Baring 22 Dec. 1883.
[2] Shibeika, *op. cit.*, pp. 138-9. FO 633/6, No. 32, Baring to Granville 8 Dec. 1884.
[3] *Egypt No. 1 (1889)* [C.-5668], No. 35, Baring to Salisbury 15 Jan. 1889; and enclosure, Riaz to Baring 9 Dec. 1888.
[4] FO 633/6, No. 14, Baring to Granville 22 Nov. 1883.
[5] Zetland [L. J. L. Dundas, Marquess of Zetland], *Lord Cromer* (London 1932), pp. 260-1, citing Cromer to Salisbury 28 Jan. 1898. FO 141/336, Salisbury to Cromer tel. No. 8, 26 Jan. 1898—an instruction which faithfully reflected Cromer's own views.

nently, to its own rather one-sided view of the iniquities of Egyptian rule in the south. That Baring shared this view is clear from his own published remarks in *Modern Egypt*. He also believed, doubtless correctly, that the Sudan had 'for many years been a source of loss to the Egyptian Government'; and that the southern Sudan was the least profitable part of an unprofitable region.[1] To the ultimate fate of the southern provinces Baring seems to have been, and to have remained, utterly indifferent. In 1898 he had of course long been aware of the need to safeguard the waters of the upper Nile; but once the Nile waters had been secured he was prepared to give away the mere territory of the southern Sudan to anyone who would take it—to King Leopold, to the Negus Menelik, even to the French if they would stop their 'constant heckling' in Egypt.[2]

In 1884 and 1885, however, Gladstone's government had troubles in Egypt and the Sudan far more pressing than the ultimate fate of Equatoria. Gordon's mission, originally comparatively straightforward, was complicated by Baring's directive instructing him to 'establish some sort of rough government under the tribal chiefs', and authorising him for this purpose 'to retain the [Egyptian] troops for such reasonable period as you may think necessary'.[3] This was a programme as 'impossible of execution' in the Sudan as the policy of 'restore and retire' in Egypt itself. Its sequel was British military intervention in the Sudan, which boxed the compass of futility from relief which came too late, through a punitive expedition to 'smash up the Mahdi', to final and precipitate withdrawal—a withdrawal hastened by fears that Russia was preparing to destroy the Afghan buffer on the north-west frontier of India. The Pendjeh crisis of April 1885 found Britain isolated in the face of an indifferent or hostile Europe; but Gladstone had already for some months been attempting to work his passage back to the Concert of the Powers by instituting an international control of Egyptian finances, with its corollary of early, if not immediate, evacuation. While British policy in the Sudan fluctuated wildly, at the mercy of divided counsels and short-lived waves of intense public excitement, in the privacy of the Cabinet Gladstone pursued his Egyptian financial policy with tenacious consistency. By the end of 1884 he had worn down the opposition of the 'pay and stay' group who wished to remain in Egypt indefinitely at the price of using English money to pay Egypt's debts.[4] In March 1885 Gladstone's efforts bore fruit in the adoption by all six Great Powers of the London Convention on Egyptian finances.

The London Convention perpetuated international control through

[1] Cromer, *op. cit.*, I, pp. 349-51.
[2] SP Cabinet Memoranda, Cromer to Salisbury 15 Nov. 1898. FO 1/35, Cromer's draft instructions to Harrington, in Cromer to Salisbury No. 40, 5 Mar. 1898; cf. *infra*, Ch. XI, p. 260.
[3] FO 633/6, No. 23, Baring to Granville 21 Jan. 1884; Cromer, *op. cit.* I, p. 445.
[4] Robinson and Gallagher, *Africa and the Victorians*, pp. 141-50; cf. Cromer, *op. cit.* II, pp. 366-71.

the *Caisse de la Dette*. Egypt was permitted a 'current' debt of up to one million pounds; beyond that figure she could not borrow without the consent of the *Caisse*. Even more crippling was the stipulation that all surplus income, beyond what was needed to pay the 'coupon' and to provide an arbitrarily fixed 'administrative' revenue, was to be divided equally between the *Caisse* and the Egyptian Government. The 'administrative' revenue was sufficient to maintain, rather precariously, the existing machinery of government; it left nothing for schemes of reform and development. 'The result was', in Baring's words, 'that if the Government wished to spend £10 in excess of the administrative limit prescribed . . . , revenue to the extent of £20 had to be collected'.[1] France welcomed the London settlement as an important first step to further negotiation on 'the question of neutralising Egypt and consequently the British evacuation of the country'.[2] This view was fully accepted by Gladstone and his supporters: 'those who object to a proposal of this kind will be compelled to show their hand, and to say "we do not mean to go out of Egypt at all, either now, or hereafter" '.[3] But not many months later, in October 1886, Baring was forced to admit that he could find no Egyptians capable of forming the 'strong native government' to which he had hoped to hand over his reformed Egypt. He warned the Foreign Secretary, Lord Iddesleigh, that so far ahead as he could see, the withdrawal of British troops would be followed by a revival of 'anarchy' and 'fanaticism' which would invite renewed European intervention; and he recommended that the question of evacuation should not even be discussed for another ten years.[4] A financial settlement designed to pave the way for early evacuation had soon been followed by an authoritative warning that this policy was ruled out by the internal condition of Egypt itself.

Thanks to Baring's skilful management, the current finances of Egypt were soon sufficiently buoyant to prevent the London Convention being used as a means of enforcing evacuation. By 1889 the race against bankruptcy had been won, and thereafter Baring was able to build up a modest but growing surplus. But he had throughout to work within very narrow limits; and his remaining within these limits was for many years the first and strongest line of defence for the British position in Egypt. All Baring's financial skill could not however rescue British policy from the diplomatic consequences of the London Convention. The *Caisse de la Dette* had previously consisted of Commissioners representing Austria-Hungary, France, Great Britain and Italy. At London Bismarck demanded and obtained a seat for Germany; Russia followed suit. The new constitution of the *Caisse* ensured that in almost any conceivable pattern of European align-

---

[1] Cromer, *op. cit.* II, p. 307.
[2] Robinson and Gallagher, *op. cit.*, p. 151, citing Waddington to Ferry 22 Jan. 1885.
[3] *Ibid.*, *loc. cit.*, citing Derby to Granville 17 Jan. 1885.
[4] FO 633/6, No. 68, Baring to Iddesleigh 31 Oct. 1886.

ments Germany would hold the key position in Egyptian finance. When Rosebery became Foreign Secretary in the short-lived Liberal administration of February 1886, Baring at once warned him that 'Berlin, and not Cairo, is the real centre of gravity of Egyptian affairs'.[1] Bismarck's *bâton égyptien* was not of course created simply by Germany's position on the *Caisse*, but that position gave him a very useful handle by which to wield it. The handle became more useful still when in July 1888 an Egyptian reserve fund for extraordinary expenditure was created, and disbursements from this fund made subject to the previous assent of the *Caisse*. The reconquest of the Sudan would obviously entail 'extraordinary expenditure' of dimensions not easily predictable. When the time for reconquest came, the attitude of Germany on the *Caisse* would probably be crucial.

In 1881 and 1882 Gladstone's government had considered many plans for avoiding a military occupation of Egypt; when they stumbled into occupation after all, they had no plan whatever for meeting the diplomatic liabilities which their position in Egypt brought with it. For a time, however, the very existence of those liabilities was concealed. Bismarck professed a benevolent disinterest, and promised not to oppose whatever Egyptian settlement the British decided to make.[2] The President of the French Republic expressed his profound gratification at the result of Tel-el-Kebir.[3] Europe seemed to stand by and applaud while Britain brought about the first major change in the balance of power since 1871. But Wolseley had not fought a purely British battle at Tel-el-Kebir. It was not merely that he had defended the interests of French as well as British bondholders; more important, he had demonstrated the crushing superiority of Western armed force over Muslim resistance. Britain had acted as the gendarme of Europe in a region of *Dar al-Islām* which had long been subordinated to the 'European system', and this general subordination all the Great Powers were determined to maintain, however their particular interests might conflict. The Powers applauded; but they expected to be paid for their applause. France hoped, and seems to have expected, that after Tel-el-Kebir Britain would restore the Anglo-French Dual Control of Egyptian finance. When Britain refused to do so, France 'reserved her freedom of action', which meant in practice that she began to work to enforce an early evacuation. Gladstone and Granville were however quite prepared to accept an early evacuation; and in May 1884 Jules Ferry had agreed to co-operate in the restoration of Egyptian finances in return for a conditional promise of evacuation by the end of 1888. But the French bondholders objected to the detailed British proposals, which involved 'taxing the coupon';

[1] *Ibid.*, No. 48, Baring to Rosebery 9 Feb. 1886.
[2] G.P. iv, No. 729, memo. by Herbert Bismarck Sept. 1882; No. 730, H. Bismarck to Bismarck 13 Sept. 1882; No. 731, memo. by H. Bismarck 22 Oct. 1882; No. 735, H. Bismarck to Bismarck 14 Jan. 1883.
[3] A. J. P. Taylor, *The Struggle for Mastery in Europe, 1848-1918* (Oxford 1954), p. 290.

and the bondholders' lobby was strong enough to force Ferry to reject these.[1] The Anglo-French 'liberal alliance' had perhaps never a-mounted to much more than a unity of sentiment between Gambet-tists and Gladstonians, and a tacit agreement not to push differences to the point of open dispute; but it was at least some counterpoise to the *Dreikaiserbund*. It was an inevitable casualty of disputes over Egyptian finance and of the later British refusal to name a date for evacuation. In January 1884 Baring could still congratulate himself on the friendly and co-operative attitude of his French colleague in Cairo. But in October 1886 he complained that the French 'have left no stone un-turned to make our task impossible', and warned Iddesleigh that 'we are not likely to solve the Egyptian question without passing through a state of serious tension with France'.[2]

Bismarck too expected to be paid. By the middle of 1884, with the Triple Alliance in his pocket, Britain and France estranged, and the Balkans quiet enough to permit the cordial renewal of the *Dreikaiser-bund*, Bismarck could name his own price. He had, as he said, 'all the honours in his hand'.[3] Until May 1884 he seemed to favour the acquisition of Heligoland, then suddenly threw all his weight behind the German colonial demand at Angra Pequena in South-West Africa.[4] His motives for this decision have been variously estimated. Doubtless he hoped to use a colonial quarrel with England as a means of persuading the French 'to forgive Sedan, as . . . you came to forgive Waterloo'—as early as April he was suggesting to the French a League of Neutrals against England.[5] Quite possibly he was taking out a cheap insurance against the growing colonial enthusiasm of those classes who helped to support him against the *Reichsfeinde* at home.[6] What may well have tipped the balance was Bismarck's anger at the dilatory and off-hand way with which Granville dealt with Germany's colonial claim, and above all at the British pretension to exclude other Powers from regions where she neither had, nor intended to acquire, legal rights of her own.[7] In British eyes, this was a policy with respectable antecedents: as long ago as 1845 Lord Aberdeen had remarked, when refusing to establish a protectorate in the South Pacific, that 'H.M.G. will not view with indifference the assumption by another Power of a

---

[1] Robinson and Gallagher, *op. cit.*, p. 143.

[2] FO 633/6, No. 22, Baring to Granville 19 Jan. 1884; No. 66, Baring to Iddesleigh 24 Oct. 1886.

[3] He had indeed been confident of this as early as Oct. 1882 (G.P. iv, No. 731, minute by Bismarck).

[4] *Ibid.*, Nos. 738, 740, 741, Bismarck to Münster 5, 11 and 25 May 1884; No. 742, Hatzfeldt to Bismarck 24 May; No. 743, Bismarck to Münster 1 June 1884.

[5] Taylor, *op. cit.*, pp. 295-7. Cf. *eundem, Germany's First Bid for Colonies* (London 1938).

[6] The distribution of this enthusiasm is evident from the analysis in F. F. Müller, *Deutschland-Zanzibar-Ostafrika* (Berlin 1959), pp. 97-114, 134-76. For a different 'domestic' interpretation of Bismarck's colonial policy cf. E. Eyck, *Bismarck and the German Empire*, English edn. (London 1958), pp. 272-81.

[7] G.P. iv, No. 742, minute by Bismarck; No. 743; Nos. 744 and 746, Münster to Bismarck 7 June 1884, H. Bismarck to Bismarck 17 June, minutes by Bismarck. These various explanations are not of course mutually exclusive.

Protectorate which they . . . have refused'.[1] To Bismarck, who dominated Europe in 1884, it was an intolerable example of Britain's naïve egoism and a flagrant deviation from international law. In May 1884 Bismarck decided, not merely to acquire colonies, but to destroy this 'Monroe Doctrine for Africa'[2] and to demonstrate that Germany must be treated with deference not only in Europe but overseas. This meant a challenge to the British sea-power which had hitherto validated London's pretensions; and to make this challenge was beyond the power of Germany acting in isolation. But by collaboration with France Bismarck hoped to create an 'equilibrium on the seas', and so bring to an end the easy unofficial predominance which Britain had enjoyed in most maritime regions outside Europe, and on the coasts of Africa in particular.[3]

For Bismarck, serious collaboration with France against England in Egypt would have been self-defeating;[4] but an Anglo-French quarrel over the Congo basin provided him with the opening which he needed. In October 1882, as an insurance against the encroachments of King Leopold's International Congo Association, the French Chamber had ratified de Brazza's treaties in the Congo basin. Granville foresaw the disappearance of the Congo trade behind a high French tariff wall, and had no confidence whatever in Leopold's 'non-descript association'[5] as a safeguard against a French monopoly. His solution was to recognise and support the decayed claims of Portugal to the mouth of the Congo. The Anglo-Portuguese treaty was signed on 26 February 1884; for some weeks French attempts to drum up opposition to it met with little success at Berlin. But by May Bismarck had begun to link it with Germany's colonial demands; on 7 June he informed Granville that Germany would not recognise the treaty and would insist on a conference to settle the Congo question.[6] By August the Anglo-French deadlock over Egyptian finance had hardened sufficiently to favour a serious essay in collaboration between Paris and Berlin. Bismarck had already prepared the ground for this: in July he had sharpened and extended his own colonial quarrel with England by declaring protectorates over Togoland and the Cameroons. In the course of August and September he persuaded Jules Ferry to accept, not without some misgivings, a joint programme of action in a conference on West Africa and to co-operate in creating the indispensable 'equilibrium on the seas'.[7]

[1] Quoted in J. Gallagher and R. Robinson, 'The Imperialism of Free Trade', *Economic History Review*, 2nd Series, VI, 1 (1953), at pp. 3-4.
[2] G.P. IV, No. 743; No. 742, minute by Bismarck.
[3] D.D.F. V, No. 407, Courcel to Ferry 23 Sept. 1884. Cf. *ibid.*, No. 249, same to same 25 Apr. 1884; and S. E. Crowe, *The Berlin West African Conference, 1884-1885* (London 1942), pp. 68-9, 219.
[4] The 'Egyptian stick' was too valuable a weapon to be used where a lesser threat would serve; moreover, Bismarck did not intend to push London into irreconcilable enmity but rather to 'inquiéter la Grande-Bretagne pour l'amener à chercher un accord avec l'Allemagne' (P. Renouvin, *Histoire des Relations Internationales*, VI, ii [Paris 1955], p. 59).
[5] Thus described, in another connection, by Granville to Gladstone 14 Jan. 1884 (Shibeika, *op. cit.*, p. 149).   [6] G.P. IV, Nos. 738, 743. Crowe, *op. cit.*, pp. 1-33.
[7] Crowe, *op. cit.*, pp. 34-77; Renouvin, *op. cit.*, pp. 57-9.

Bismarck's successful demand that Germany be treated as a major Power in extra-European affairs had more important results than the mere acquisition by Paris and Berlin of regions where Britain had hitherto exercised a predominant influence. The Berlin West Africa Conference promulgated a code of rules governing the acquisition of coastal annexations and protectorates in Africa. The final draft was much less far-reaching than the original German proposals; but the British ambassador in Berlin was mistaken in his belief that it was therefore harmless to British interests.[1] The simple requirements concerning the formal proclamation and notification of protectorates nullified the standard British techniques of 'unofficial empire' in Africa. On the East African coast, Britain held in 1884 not a single square mile of territory; but from Somalia to Mozambique, and far into the interior, she enjoyed paramount influence through her client the Sultan of Zanzibar, whom she had protected against European encroachments and whose hegemony on the mainland she supported. In 1885 and 1886 Bismarck devoted himself to the destruction of this unofficial empire. On 27 February 1885, the day after the signature of the General Act of the Berlin Conference, Carl Peters obtained an imperial *Schutzbrief* for his acquisitions in the interior of East Africa. In August, under the muzzles of Commodore Paschen's guns, the Sultan of Zanzibar was forced to cede to Germany not only these territories, but also Dar-es-Salaam and the coastal region of Witu north of the river Tana.[2] Salisbury had not even a legal card to play, and could only advise the Sultan to submit. In June 1886 Berlin extorted British assent to the proposition that south of the river Tana the Sultan's dominions extended inland for no more than 'ten sea miles', and that north of the Tana the sovereignty of Zanzibar was confined to a few isolated coastal settlements.[3] The Zanzibari coastal strip, already pierced at Dar-es-Salaam, was the feeblest of barriers against further European encroachment; and north of the Tana even the coastal strip did not exist. East Africa, and more especially that part of it whose hinterland could be extended to Lake Victoria, Lake Albert and the Upper Nile, was wide open for annexation *à la mode de Berlin*.

In 1885, however, the coast of East Africa still seemed a very long way from the Upper Nile. The interests which Salisbury and Rosebery were defending here, in so far as they could or did defend them, were those of ocean strategy, not of Egypt's water supply. The interior seemed unimportant except as a possible field for commercial enterprise. But the merchants in fact showed very little enterprise; Mackinnon the Glasgow shipowner and Hutton the Manchester exporter

---

[1] Crowe, *op. cit.*, pp. 176-91, citing (p. 191) Malet to Granville 21 Feb. 1885.

[2] Technically, Dar-es-Salaam was not ceded; but it became, in Sir John Kirk's words, 'to all intents a German settlement'. Cf. R. Coupland, *The Exploitation of East Africa, 1856-1890* (London 1939), pp. 402-42.

[3] *Ibid.*, pp. 448-68. Cf. Lady G. Cecil, *Life of Robert, Marquis of Salisbury*, IV (London 1932), pp. 225-6, citing Salisbury's speech in the Lords 10 July 1890.

refused to hazard their capital unless the Government provided not only political but financial guarantees.[1] In the summer of 1885 Salisbury saw no point in 'keeping every other nation out on the bare chance that some day or other our traders will pluck up heart to go in'. He preferred to use concessions in East Africa to buy Bismarck's 'help in Russia and Turkey and Egypt', and considered that 'on the whole I have as yet got my money's worth'.[2] Indeed, although Bismarck was evidently still determined to damage beyond repair the structure of British unofficial empire in East Africa, he had by this time good reason to cultivate friendly relations with England elsewhere. In March 1885 Jules Ferry was driven from office amid angry demonstrations which owed something at least to the belief that he was too much in Bismarck's pocket. Thereafter the Franco-German rapprochement rapidly faded out; on 1 June Bismarck complained that 'the French will never become even dependable defensive allies for us'.[3] In September the *Anschluss* between Bulgaria and Eastern Rumelia inaugurated a new and ultimately very severe Balkan crisis. Easier relations with Germany enabled Salisbury to postpone any solution of the Egyptian question, in the hope that a more favourable situation would develop. Meanwhile, in the Sudan, he overrode Wolseley's reluctance to preside over a complete military fiasco, and in July 1885 ordered him to retire 'to a point which in your judgment provides for the security of Egypt'. This point, on Wolseley's own showing, was Wadi Halfa, protected to the south by the second cataract and the very difficult broken country of the Batn al-Hajar.[4]

In October 1886 the East African situation was to all appearances stabilised by an Anglo-German partition, which drew a line from Wanga on the Indian Ocean to the point where the first parallel of south latitude crosses the eastern shore of Lake Victoria.[5] But this appearance of stability was an illusion. For reasons which never seem to have been adequately investigated, European military explorers at the head of very small detachments were able, in the last two decades of the nineteenth century, to penetrate Africa and to impose their authority with unprecedented ease and rapidity. Egypt's greatly increased dependence on the White Nile (and Sobat) waters had brought with it 'new frontiers of insecurity' extending to the Abyssinian plateau, the Nile-Congo divide, and the Great Lakes. In 1886 the threat to these regions still seemed very remote. Three years later, European expansion from apparently harmless coastal establishments —that of Italy at Massawa or of Germany at Witu—was already reaching far out towards the Nile waters and threatening to jeopardise

---

[1] Robinson and Gallagher, *op. cit.*, pp. 190-8.

[2] Cecil, *op. cit.* III, p. 230, citing Salisbury to Iddesleigh 24 Aug. 1885; Coupland, *op. cit.*, pp. 433-4, citing Salisbury's minute (17 Sept. 1885) on Kirk's despatch of 21 Aug.

[3] J. Chastenet, *La République des Républicains* (Paris 1954), pp. 163-8. Taylor, *The Struggle for Mastery*, p. 301.

[4] L.Q.V. 2, iii, pp. 613-82, *passim*. Shibeika, *op. cit.*, pp. 303-8.

[5] Hertslet III, No. 263.

the British position in Egypt. Ironically, the British themselves stimulated the competition of other Powers by an act of intervention on the Upper Nile which was initiated long before the Nile waters were seriously threatened and which was, in origin at least, quite irrelevant to their protection. The Emin Pasha Relief Expedition, approved by Salisbury in December 1886, was made possible by Baring's determination to complete the administrative disengagement of Egypt from the southern Sudan. It was launched when Salisbury was already preparing the ground for a serious attempt to preserve British preponderance in Egypt without incurring the diplomatic penalties inherent in an indefinite occupation. True, this attempt might not succeed. Even if it did, evacuation with a right of re-entry did not necessarily relieve British policy of all concern for the security of the Nile waters. But never again was this concern to be so remote and hypothetical as it seemed to be at the end of 1886 and in the early months of 1887.

II

THE EMIN PASHA RELIEF EXPEDITION

1886–89

IN January 1884 Baring had seen no reason to arrange for the
evacuation of the Egyptian garrisons in the Bahr al-Ghazal and
Equatoria. He believed that they were in no danger and would in
any case be unwilling to return to Egypt.[1] A year later, the situation
of the Equatoria garrison, although unknown from any recent reports,
was correctly believed to be precarious; and in May 1885 Nubar wrote
at Baring's prompting to its commander Eduard Schnitzer, better
known by his Turkish name of Emin. Emin was warned that Cairo
could give him no assistance, and was advised to retire with his
garrison through Uganda to the East African coast.[2] In November
1886, however, Baring's willingness to spend £10,000 out of an un-
balanced Egyptian budget in order to secure Emin's retirement was
not prompted by any concern for the safety of the Governor or his
troops. Emin was by this time known to have surmounted his immediate local difficulties. Possibly this very fact strengthened Baring's
determination to remove him, lest his success frustrate Baring's decision that Egyptian rule in the southern Sudan should never be restored. This anxiety to remove Emin did not, however, imply any
desire to establish British control over Equatoria. Any such arrangement would in 1886 have doubtless involved at least the formal
recognition of Egypt as sovereign; and even a ghost of Egyptian
sovereignty in the southern Sudan seems to have been too much for
Baring. In November 1886 he objected to the proposals of the German
geographer Schweinfurth for reorganising and consolidating the
Equatorial province 'pour un avenir plus propice', not because these
might ultimately give Germany a foothold on the Upper Nile, but
because the operation would be carried out, theoretically at least, on
behalf of Egypt.[3]

Baring's indifference to the ultimate political fate of the southern
Sudan was not however shared by all his countrymen. Ever since

[1] FO 633/6, No. 21, Baring to Granville 14 Jan. 1884.
[2] G. Schweitzer, *Emin Pascha* (Berlin 1898), p. 315, printing Nubar to Emin 13 Sha'bān
1302 / 27 May 1885.
[3] FO 78/3932, Baring to Iddesleigh No. 482 (enclosing memo. by Schweinfurth) 23
Nov. 1886. FO 84/1770, same to same tel. unnumb., 25 Nov.

Baker had written up parts of the South as a potential El Dorado, British humanitarians and merchants with interests or aspirations in the southern Sudan had tended to unite 'on a platform of defeating the slave trade by the introduction of legitimate commerce'.[1] The missionaries in particular saw in 'English commerce, industry and civilisation' an influence which might counteract that of Muslim Egypt. In 1882 a committee with humanitarian and commercial backing had been formed to promote the construction of a Suakin-Berber railway, in the rather odd belief that this would facilitate the opening up of the South; the desire to by-pass Egypt is however obvious enough. Speaking in support of this project, the geographer R. W. Felkin had in February 1883 dilated upon the supposed peace and prosperity of Emin's province, 'the extent and significance of which do not seem to be fully realised, either by governments or businessmen'. Two years later, when the Liberal government ordered the construction of the Suakin-Berber railway during its short-lived resolve to 'smash up the Mahdi', the Sudan lobby took up a proposal by H. M. Stanley for the formation of a 'Gordon Association for the Nile', to operate in the southern Sudan on the model of the Congo International Association. In July 1885, after the railway project had been abandoned, a strong campaign was launched to promote an expedition which should unite the tribes of the South into 'a confederacy for their own self-preservation'. The precise political status of this 'confederacy' was not specified. The expedition was indeed to co-operate with 'the remnants of Egyptian administration'—that is, with Emin; but the project seems to have implied the 'sarawaking' of the southern Sudan, perhaps under Emin's more or less nominal headship. Among its supporters were such diverse figures as Cardinal Manning; the Rev. Horace Waller, a leader of the anti-slavery movement; and J. H. Hutton, as President of the Manchester Chamber of Commerce. But its leading promoter was Stanley, at that time in the paid service of Leopold of the Belgians, King-Sovereign of the newly-created Independent Congo State. Stanley urged very strongly that the proposed expedition should approach the Upper Nile by way of the Congo and Aruwimi rivers—a route which had originally been suggested to the King by Gordon in January 1884 and which Stanley, doubtless on Leopold's instructions, had studied in detail later in the same year.[2]

Towards the end of 1885 A. M. Mackay, the principal C.M.S. missionary in Uganda, had suggested that Britain, in order to forestall German encroachment towards the Upper Nile, should intervene to assist Emin in his struggle against the Mahdists.[3] This appeal naturally fell on deaf ears; but in September 1886 Consul Holmwood at Zan-

[1] Gray, *Southern Sudan*, pp. 173-4.
[2] *Ibid.*, pp. 174-6, 184-95. P. Ceulemans, *La Question Arabe et le Congo, 1883-1892* (Brussels 1959), pp. 88-9, 93.
[3] Oliver, *Missionary Factor*, p. 130.

zibar, who consistently favoured a forward policy in East Africa, be-gan to press for action. Mahdist pressure on Emin had now relaxed, and he no longer wished to evacuate his province; indeed, it was clear that his own troops were strongly opposed to any evacuation south-wards. Emin's main difficulties now were a shortage of supplies—particularly ammunition and cloth—and the absence of a reliable line of communication with the outside world. Both these difficulties had recently been aggravated by the action of Mwanga, the Kabaka of Buganda. In May 1886 Mwanga had launched a ruthless persecution of the Buganda Christians; and for a time the lives of European missionaries seemed to be in danger. He had also refused all facili-ties for the transmission of supplies to Emin.[1] The Russian explorer Junker, who reached Zanzibar with this news in September 1886, pressed strongly for an expedition to overawe Mwanga, open the road to Emin, and supply the Equatoria garrison with its needs. Holmwood enthusiastically concurred. He saw not only an opportunity of sup-pressing the 'bloodthirsty tyrant' Mwanga, but also of creating on Lake Albert 'a base from which any further operations . . . for the retention of the Upper Nile could be undertaken effectively and with-out anxiety'. Holmwood suggested, as an adequate force, 1200 porters escorted by 500 'seasoned Nubian or Egyptian troops'; ultimately the relief expedition would join forces with Emin's own troops in 'any measures for dealing with Uganda'.[2]

It seems unlikely that when Holmwood wrote of 'the retention of the Upper Nile' he was thinking of its permanent retention by Egypt; but Salisbury was the last man to be dazzled by these vistas of imperial expansion. Moreover, the War Office treated Holmwood's amateur military planning with complete contempt. Brackenbury, the head of the Intelligence Division, wrote rather testily that plans for an ex-pedition to central Africa were not kept in stock at his department: 'our interests there are not so great that we have ever made this a special subject of study'. But his immediate impression was that a force large enough to deal with Mwanga would be prevented by difficulties of supply from ever reaching Uganda. Further study confirmed this view, in which Wolseley concurred. Such an expedition would be difficult enough even if Mwanga were friendly; with Mwanga hostile, it would be 'the height of folly'.[3] Sir John Kirk, previously for many years Consul at Zanzibar, remarked, when asked to comment: 'From these papers I understand the only question is how to communicate with Emin Bey and enable him to retire. The question of holding the Equatorial province is not now under consideration.' Kirk suggested

---

[1] Coupland, *Exploitation*, pp. 425-6, quoting Holmwood to Hutton 10 Apr. 1885. Oliver, *op. cit.*, pp. 103-6, 129-30. Gray, *op. cit.*, pp. 195-6.

[2] FO 84/1775, Holmwood to Iddesleigh No. 173, 23 Sept. 1886 (enclosing letters from Emin and Mackay, brought by Junker); *ibid.*, same to same tel. No. 122, 23 Sept. FO 78/3930, Holmwood to Baring Nos. 354 and 355, 25 and 27 Sept. 1886.

[3] FO 84/1790, Brackenbury to Wolseley 29 Sept. 1886. FO 84/1775, minutes by I.D. and by Wolseley (2 Oct.) on Holmwood's tel. No. 122.

that an armed relief caravan might be despatched at a cost of £25,000. It would proceed under the auspices of the Sultan of Zanzibar; and it should not attempt to pass through Buganda.[1]

On 17 October, a few days after Kirk had written this minute, a telegram from Holmwood reported that Emin had offered, in a letter of 7 July, to hand over his province to Britain if she would take it.[2] This offer seems to have whetted the interest of Sir Percy Anderson, the head of the African Department, who now began to press strongly for the despatch of an 'armed' (but not 'military') caravan which should by-pass Uganda. He soothingly pointed out that 'failure would not involve awkward contingencies'; and he urged that 'if the expedition goes it should start *at once*'.[3] But Salisbury's minute a day or so later seemed completely to kill the whole project of intervention. 'An armed expedition is out of the question. It simply means war with Uganda, conducted out of British resources, in which we should be forced to enter into a close alliance with the Sultan of Zanzibar.' Such an alliance could hardly have been reconciled with Salisbury's current policy of using the Sultan's mainland interests as a means of paying Bismarck for support elsewhere. Salisbury was less opposed to a 'diplomatic' mission to Mwanga, which should in effect bribe the Kabaka to release the missionaries and open the road to Emin. But even here he saw difficulties. If a servant of the Crown were sent to Buganda, 'we might have to rescue or avenge him'. Salisbury concluded: 'I think the Germans should be put in possession of our information. It is really their business if Emin is a German.'[4]

In spite of this rebuff, Anderson continued 'to study Emin's position'. So did Portal, Baring's assistant at Cairo, to whom Holmwood had communicated his despatches concerning Emin. On 8 November the British and Foreign Anti-Slavery Society sent to the Foreign Office a resolution asserting that 'the position of Dr Emin Bey presents a very strong claim on H.M.G.' and demanding all aid short of 'any measure of a military character'. This was the signal for an agitation for relief on humanitarian grounds which attained respectable dimensions in the course of November.[5] Meanwhile Mackinnon and Hutton had secured the services of Stanley as leader of a relief expedition; on 15 November Mackinnon informed the Foreign Office that Stanley would serve without demanding any official recognition.[6] On the 16th, Baring telegraphed enquiring what answer he should give to Holmwood's latest proposals for the relief of Emin. Anderson

---

[1] FO 84/1775, minute by Kirk 13 Oct. 1886, on Holmwood's tel. No. 122 and attached papers; cf. *ibid.*, Kirk to Anderson 14 Oct.
[2] *Ibid.*, Holmwood to Iddesleigh tel. No. 60, 17 Oct. 1886.
[3] *Ibid.*, minute by Anderson 18 Oct. 1886.
[4] *Ibid.*, minute by Salisbury 19(?) Oct. 1886.
[5] FO 78/3930, Portal to Iddesleigh No. 419, 19 Oct. 1886. FO 84/1793, British and Foreign Anti-Slavery Society to F.O. 8 Nov. 1886; minute by Anderson 13 Nov.; Mackinnon to Fergusson 15 Nov. FO 84/1794, memorial from the Scottish Geographical Society 23 Nov. 1886. Gray, *op. cit.*, pp. 197-200.
[6] FO 84/1793, Mackinnon to Fergusson 15 Nov. 1886.

strongly recommended that the Mackinnon-Stanley offer be accepted; so did the Parliamentary Under-Secretary, Sir James Fergusson. Fergusson emphasised that Stanley and Mackinnon contemplated a private expedition operating 'by moral influence only'; to him the question was now simply one of finance—'whether H.M.G. can find such a sum as is required for a private expedition, though for an object political as well as philanthropic'.[1] But Salisbury, and more particularly his Foreign Secretary, Iddesleigh, still saw grave objections of principle, and were quite unimpressed by Holmwood's pleas for 'the development of Africa . . . on a scale more commensurate with the magnitude of the undertaking'.[2] On 23 November the Cabinet declined 'to entertain the [Mackinnon-Stanley] proposal as it would involve Government in responsibilities similar to those in Gen. Gordon's case' with their 'risks of future entanglements in case of disaster'.[3]

On 20 November Fergusson had suggested that the British Government might escape responsibility if Egypt were to finance the expedition.[4] Three days later Baring telegraphed offering £10,000 from Egyptian funds for the relief of Emin. The question which the Cabinet decision seemed to have closed was at once re-opened. Fergusson pointed out that this offer opened 'fresh possibilities': 'it is very possible that Messrs Mackinnon and Hutton may supplement the Egyptian undertaking if it is sanctioned'.[5] Mackinnon did in fact offer a further £10,000 on the 27th.[6] Meanwhile, Anderson strongly urged that Baring's offer be accepted; but he was less happy about Cairo's proposals for the leadership of the expedition. The geographer Schweinfurth, whose reports on the Equatoria situation seem to have prompted Baring's proposal, was pressing strongly in Cairo for the appointment of his friend Junker. Baring had transmitted this suggestion with no more than a query as to its acceptability; Holmwood thought that 'Junker would be a most suitable leader'. Anderson was suspicious of this interest by a German whose publications proved him to be no particular friend of Britain; in any case, Mackinnon was insisting on the employment of 'an Anglo-Saxon'—in fact, of Stanley. After consultation with Kirk and Mackinnon, Anderson was convinced that 'we can have nothing to do with Schweinfurth and Junker'; and on 25 November Baring and Holmwood were informed of this negative decision.[7]

[1] FO 84/1770, Baring to Iddesleigh tel. No. 138, 16 Nov. 1886; minute by Anderson. FO 84/1794, minute by Fergusson 20 Nov.; memo. for the Cabinet by Anderson 20 Nov.
[2] FO 84/1775, Holmwood to Iddesleigh No. 191, 18 Oct. 1886 (received 22 Nov.); same to same No. 176, 27 Sept. 1886; Holmwood to Anderson, private, 28 Sept.
[3] FO 84/1794, minutes by Pauncefote and Fergusson 23 Nov. 1886.
[4] Ibid., minute by Fergusson 20 Nov. 1886.
[5] FO 84/1770, Baring to Iddesleigh tel. No. 142, 23 Nov. 1886. FO 84/1794, minute by Fergusson, 23 Nov.   [6] FO 84/1794, Mackinnon to Iddesleigh 27 Nov. 1886.
[7] FO 84/1770, minute by Anderson on Baring's tel. No. 138. FO 84/1794, minutes by Anderson 24 Nov. 1886, on Fergusson's minute of the 23rd, and on R. W. Felkin to Iddesleigh 23 Nov. FO 84/1770, Baring to Iddesleigh tels. unnumb., 24 and 25 Nov.; minutes by Anderson and Iddesleigh. Ibid., Pauncefote to Baring Africa No. 12 (extender), 25 Nov. FO 84/1771, Pauncefote to Holmwood No. 155B (extender), 25 Nov. 1886.

Meanwhile, the opponents of the expedition fought what was rapidly becoming a rearguard action. On 24 November Pauncefote, the Permanent Under-Secretary, had suggested that the whole pro-. ject was otiose, since 'Emin Bey appears to be quite safe and happy judging from these [latest] letters'. Iddesleigh concurred; but Fergusson retorted that Baring, with his greater knowledge of Emin's situation, was urging 'steps for his relief'.[1] On the 25th the Cabinet were still 'of opinion that they could not take part in sending out an expedition, even of a peaceful character, to rescue Emin Bey, without exposing the country to the risk of having to rescue the rescuers'.[2] But would the Cabinet really be 'taking part' if no money were provided from British funds? By the 27th, when Mackinnon's detailed plan for a purely 'private' expedition had been received, the question of official responsibility seemed to turn on a mere procedural detail—whether the Egyptian £10,000 should be paid to Mackinnon directly or through London.[3] On the 28th Iddesleigh rather desperately reminded Salisbury of the Cabinet decision to avoid 'any action which might by any possibility lead to our being obliged to rescue the rescuing party'.[4] But the arrival on the 29th of the extender to Baring's telegram of the 23rd enabled Anderson to drive home the point that 'there is a distinct offer in this of £10,000'; and on the 30th he submitted a memorandum which evidently won over Salisbury and therefore the Cabinet.[5]

Anderson pointed out that Stanley would act as the private agent of a private company, at his and their own risk. His object would be to communicate with Emin on the Company's behalf; but he was willing to carry official letters from the Egyptian Government to Emin, and to assist him to withdraw if Egypt ordered him to withdraw. 'If he fails the Egyptian Government lose their money: otherwise they are no worse off than before. If he succeeds they rescue their last Soudan garrison—or at least so many of them who wish to retire—and thenceforth wash their hands of the Equatorial provinces'. To lay the ghost of Gordon, Anderson emphasised that the risks of such a mission 'could not be compared to that of a Soudan expedition'—indeed, to a man of Stanley's character and experience, they were almost negligible. But if unfortunately Stanley did lose his life 'there would be no more obligation on the British Government to avenge him than there is to avenge Bishop Hannington'. Three days later, on 3 December, Baring was informed that Mackinnon's 'purely pacific' expedition for the 'relief' of Emin Pasha had been approved.[6]

[1] FO 84/1794, Felkin to Iddesleigh 23 Nov. 1886, enclosing Emin to Felkin 7 July 1886; minutes by Pauncefote, Iddesleigh, Fergusson (27 Nov.).
[2] *Ibid.*, memo. by Iddlesleigh 25 Nov. 1886.
[3] *Ibid.*, Mackinnon to Iddesleigh 27 Nov., and minute by Pauncefote.
[4] Robinson and Gallagher, *Africa and the Victorians*, p. 199, quoting from SP Northcote, Iddesleigh to Salisbury 28 Nov. 1886.
[5] FO 78/3932, Baring to Iddesleigh Nos. 481, 482, 483, all of 23 Nov. 1886 and received on the 29th; minute by Anderson on No. 482. FO 84/1794, memo. by Anderson, 30 Nov. 1886.
[6] FO 84/1794, *ubi supra*. FO 84/1770, F.O. to Baring tel. unnumb., and Africa No. 15, 3 Dec. 1886.

1 Emin Pasha (Eduard Schnitzer)

II Leopold II, Sovereign of the Independent Congo State

It is not easy to say what exactly had been approved. The ambiguous word 'relief' covered two quite different concepts of the expedition's objective. Baring, as he plainly told London, was solely concerned to 'relieve' Emin of his command, to write *finis* to the story of Egyptian rule in the South by withdrawing Emin and any troops who would follow him.[1] Indeed, on 28 November, before London had authorised the expedition, Baring had instructed Emin through Nubar 'to retire . . . to the best position for ultimate withdrawal via Zanzibar when circumstances allow'.[2] But Mackinnon and his associates were concerned to 'carry relief to Emin Bey', and to employ Emin and his troops as the protective garrison for the interior posts of a 'large trading company' based on Mombasa.[3] This would indeed involve Emin's immediate retirement to the Kavirondo country north-east of Lake Victoria; but Mackinnon almost certainly hoped that sooner or later Emin would return to Equatoria as the Company's agent. It was of course this project, with its implications of the forestalling of German encroachment, and not any acute concern for an Egyptian withdrawal, which prompted Fergusson and Anderson to press for the expedition in the face of steady discouragement by Iddesleigh and the Cabinet. The same motive inspired Anderson's later zeal in furnishing this 'purely private' and 'purely pacific' expedition with free Admiralty coal, free War Office Maxim ammunition, and powers to call upon British official representatives for full countenance and support.[4]

Salisbury's initial opposition to the project has often been noticed and emphasised. His ultimate concurrence has attracted less attention; yet it is the more remarkable in that the façade of a 'purely private' expedition had become very flimsy indeed by December 1886. It became even flimsier in January 1887, thanks to Anderson's exertions at the Admiralty and the War Office, and thanks still more to Salisbury's orders enjoining Baring to override Egyptian objections to Stanley's proposed route.[5] Had Stanley himself—and not merely some of his obscure subordinates—come to grief in some spectacular fashion, the Government could hardly have avoided incurring 'responsibilities similar to those in Gen. Gordon's case', for all its careful Blue-Book publication of the correspondence disclaiming such responsibility;[6] and Salisbury cannot have been blind to this danger. Salisbury's approval may well represent his first step towards a policy which he was gradually to develop in the course of 1887 and 1888— that of encouraging private enterprise to peg out claims in regions of

[1] FO 84/1770, Baring to Iddesleigh tel. unnumb., 25 Nov. 1886.
[2] *Ibid.*, Baring to Iddesleigh Africa No. 21, 28 Nov. 1886, enclosing Nubar to Emin 28 Nov.
[3] FO 84/1794, Mackinnon to Iddesleigh 27 Nov. 1886; *ibid.*, minute by Fergusson 20 Nov.
[4] FO 84/1856, F.O. to Admiralty 8 Jan. 1887. FO 84/1857, same to same 13 Jan.; F.O. to War Office 17 Jan. FO 84/1796, F.O. to Holmwood 22 Dec. 1886. FO 84/1878, Salisbury to Baring Africa No. 2, 24 Jan. 1887.
[5] FO 84/1878, Salisbury to Baring tel. Africa No. 8, 24 Jan. 1887.
[6] *Africa No. 8 (1888)* [C.-5601].

C

East Africa where the Germans were sooner or later likely to be active. He may even have already been insuring, at what doubtless seemed a very low premium, against the still remote possibility of German penetration towards the Upper Nile. In March 1887 Salisbury was particularly anxious that no Red Sea port should fall into French or German hands. Even the Italians were now unwelcome here: 'Massowah was a mistake'.[1] No doubt Salisbury had the Suez route to India mainly in mind. But the Italians at least were hardly a serious threat to British ocean strategy; and Salisbury may also have been moved by Baring's fears that ports on the Red Sea might develop into bases for penetration, sooner or later, into the central Sudan. If Salisbury foresaw possible difficulties here, there is no need to assume that, with his much greater knowledge of the East African situation, he shared Baring's blindness to the potential dangers further south. Germany's first colonial thrust had shattered at a blow the British unofficial empire in East Africa and had already carried the German flag as far as Lake Nyasa and Mount Kilimanjaro. It was not absurd to fear that a second thrust, if it came, might reach Uganda and the Upper Nile either from Witu or through the still unpartitioned territory to the west of Lake Victoria.

By the end of November 1886 the Emin Pasha Relief Expedition was being promoted by three different interests—Baring, Mackinnon, the African Department of the Foreign Office—with three different objects in view. To these interests was now to be added a fourth: that of King Leopold. Leopold held Stanley under contract to himself and could therefore make his own terms for releasing him to lead the expedition; in this way he soon came to dominate its planning. During his early correspondence with Mackinnon, Stanley had been careful not to specify the route which he favoured for the expedition.[2] Having already drafted plans, on Leopold's instructions, for a Congolese advance to the Upper Nile by way of the Aruwimi, Stanley must have guessed that the King might well insist on this route; but it would have been impolitic to reveal this information until Mackinnon had definitely accepted Stanley's offer of leadership.[3] Indeed, there are indications that Stanley himself, as an explorer rather than as an agent of King Leopold, was not altogether happy about the Congo-Aruwimi approach and would have avoided it if he could. On 24 December he told Anderson that he might 'have to alter it', and he does not seem to have dissociated himself from Mackinnon's protest against it.[4] But the Foreign Office itself helped Leopold to override Mackinnon's op-

---

[1] FO 78/4066, memo. by Salisbury, 21 Mar. 1887.
[2] FO 84/1793, Stanley to Mackinnon 15 Nov. 1886; FO 84/1794, memo. by Mackinnon, 27 Nov. Cf. H. M. Stanley, In Darkest Africa (London 1890), I, pp. 32-3, where the recommendation of the Congo route looks rather like an interpolation from later correspondence.
[3] FO 84/1795, Mackinnon to Stanley 11 Dec. 1886. FO 84/1796, Anderson to Pauncefote 24 Dec.
[4] FO 84/1796, ubi supra. Stanley, op. cit. I, pp. 34-5, 43-7. Ceulemans op. cit., pp. 92-7.

position. There were fears in both London and Paris that Mwanga might react to the presence near his borders of a large armed expedition by murdering the English and French missionaries, and at the end of December the Quai d'Orsay formally enquired 'what precautions could be taken against such a calamity'.[1] The Congo route set these fears to rest and also avoided arousing the jealousy of the Germans. Anderson was therefore strongly in favour of this route; so was Iddesleigh, whose main anxiety now was that the expedition should strictly maintain its 'pacific character'.[2]

The Egyptian Government held other views; and so, at first, did Baring. On 19 January 1887 Salisbury telegraphed to Baring: 'Congo route decided on as safest and quickest and easiest for return of women and children'. Evidently puzzled by this development, Baring replied: 'Do I understand rightly that Stanley is going by Zanzibar and intends to return by the Congo?'[3] Three days later, when he was better informed, Baring transmitted the objections of the Khedive and Nubar to the Congo route; but he was careful not to associate himself with these objections, and clearly hinted that they could if necessary be overridden. The Egyptians very sensibly objected that it would take Stanley at least fifteen months to reach Equatoria by the Congo route, and that it was doubtful whether Emin could hold out for so long. Moreover, they suspected that 'the expedition is rather one of exploration than relief and somewhat demur to applying Egyptian money to [this] object'.[4] Well might they demur—'exploration' in this context was simply a euphemism for European penetration and acquisition. The Khedive and Nubar seem indeed to have made a serious attempt to withdraw the Egyptian ten thousand.[5] But on 24 January a personally drafted telegram from Salisbury ordered Baring in the most uncompromising terms to give Stanley his complete support; the Egyptian objections were not answered, they were simply ignored. Under Baring's pressure Egyptian resistance soon collapsed; by 2 February Tawfīq and Nubar had, in Baring's words, 'expressed themselves' as convinced by Stanley's arguments in favour of the Congo route.[6]

Leopold's motive for intervention in the affairs of the expedition was simple and clear-cut: he wished to annex to the Congo State the Bahr al-Ghazal and at any rate western Equatoria. At the beginning of 1884, when Gordon had momentarily taken service under King Leopold, he had impressed upon the King that in order to strike at the

[1] FO 84/1770, Baring to F.O. tel. No. 222, 26 Dec. 1886; tel. unnumb., 27 Dec. FO 84/1796, minute by Pauncefote 28 Dec. 1886.

[2] FO 84/1878, minute by Anderson 5 Jan. 1887. FO 84/1856, F.O. to Admiralty 8 Jan.

[3] FO 141/247, Salisbury to Baring tel. Africa No. 4, 19 Jan. 1887. FO 84/1878, Baring to Salisbury tel. unnumb., 20 Jan.

[4] FO 84/1878, Baring to Salisbury tel. Africa No. 8, 23 Jan. 1887. Cf. FO 84/1857, minute by Anderson on Admiralty to F.O. 25 Jan.

[5] Ceulemans, op. cit., p. 96, citing d'Aunay to Flourens 29 Jan. 1887.

[6] FO 84/1878, Salisbury to Baring tel. Africa No. 8, 24 Jan. 1887; Baring to Salisbury tel. Africa No. 9, 2 Feb. 1887.

root of the slave trade it was necessary to occupy the Bahr al-Ghazal. Thereafter the acquisition of the Bahr al-Ghazal remained permanently on the King's agenda.[1] Gordon himself seems to have been given authority by Leopold to retire to the south after his work at Khartoum was completed, and to administer the Bahr al-Ghazal as a Congolese province.[2] In 1887 the King cast Emin for the part which Gordon had been prevented from playing in 1884-5; and in May 1888 he offered to Emin, through Stanley, the post of Congolese Governor of Equatoria. It has never been clear whether, or how, the King's plans for Emin's future were to be reconciled with those of Mackinnon. Mackinnon appears to have acquiesced in Leopold's proposed annexation of at least a part of Equatoria; but he can hardly have acquiesced in Leopold's attempt to monopolise Emin and his troops, whom Mackinnon himself wished to employ in the Kavirondo region.[3] The proposals of Leopold and of Mackinnon were in fact presented by Stanley to Emin as mutually exclusive alternatives.[4] Evidently the King intended to over-reach Mackinnon; characteristically, in 1888 he began to fear that the East Africa Company would do likewise, and perhaps already 'nourrissait [des] projets ténébreux à l'égard de l'E.I.C. . . . de connivence avec le *Foreign Office*'.[5] But however much or little Mackinnon knew of Leopold's plans, he did not reveal his knowledge to Downing Street. Nor did Anderson show the slightest apprehension, or even curiosity, about the King's motives even when it became clear that Stanley would not be released unless the Congo route were adopted. Like most people in 1886, Anderson probably did not take King Leopold's African hobby very seriously. Even if the so-called Congo State should by some miracle survive, it could surely never embarrass the policy of a major Power. Indeed, it might perhaps play on the Upper Nile the part for which England had cast Portugal on the lower Congo four years earlier.

The planners in Cairo, London and Brussels had reckoned without Africa. They knew little, and cared less, about the complex internal situation in Equatoria, where the views of Emin's Sudanese troops and of Emin himself were—in that order of importance—the crucial factors. Nubar's original order to Emin of May 1885, recommending him to retire southwards and bluntly informing him that no help would be forthcoming from Egypt, had produced some unexpected results. It had profoundly distressed and even demoralised Emin him-

---

[1] B. M. Allen, *Gordon and the Sudan* (London 1931), pp. 190-2, 211-2, 260, 273, 446-9, citing Gordon to Charles Allen 5 Jan. 1884; Gordon to Leopold 1 Feb., 18 Feb. 1884. Gordon also wrote in similar vein to Stanley on 6 Jan. 1884: cf. H. M. Stanley, *The Congo and the Founding of its Free State* (London 1885), II, pp. 226-7. Cf. *infra*, Ch. v, pp. 89-90.

[2] Shibeika, *op. cit.*, p. 237, citing Gordon to Baring 9 Mar. 1884. Cf. Allen, *op. cit.*, pp. 307-8.

[3] Robinson and Gallagher, *op. cit.*, p. 199. Cf. Ceulemans, *op. cit.*, p. 121.

[4] Stanley, *In Darkest Africa*, I, pp. 386-93; Schweitzer, *op. cit.*, pp. 404-6.

[5] He was reassured by a report of the Emin Pasha Relief Committee, transmitted to him by the F.O. in May 1888 (Eetvelde to Leopold 12 May 1888, cited Ceulemans, *op. cit.*, pp. 113-4).

self. For three years, ever since March 1883, Emin had been awaiting some official word from Cairo. On 26 February 1886 it arrived at long last: the Egyptian Government washed its hands of Emin and of his province. More important, Emin's troops could not believe that the Khedive would thus have deserted them, after their long years of loyal service and tenacious defence against the Mahdists, and they refused to accept Nubar's letter as authentic. They had some excuse for this, for all that Emin had received was an unnumbered French translation of the Arabic original. When Emin attempted, as a first step towards evacuation, to concentrate his troops in the Wadelai region, his northernmost garrison of Lado came out in open mutiny. By June 1886 it was clear that any attempt to evacuate the troops southwards would cause a general mutiny throughout the province.[1] Under the influence of these events Emin had written to his English friends— Felkin, Kirk, Mackay—early in July, announcing his intention to remain indefinitely in Equatoria and offering, since Egypt had deserted him, to 'aid in the annexation of this country by England'.[2]

By April 1888, when Stanley at last met Emin, order and stability had been largely restored in Equatoria. Emin's authority, which had been severely shaken in the summer of 1886, was now fully recognised everywhere except in the extreme north. The external difficulties and internal dissensions which plagued the mutinous garrisons served to emphasise the good order and comparative prosperity enjoyed by the region under Emin's administration.[3] With the general revival of confidence in Emin's leadership, Emin himself became more determined than ever not to desert his 'people'. He had by 1887 made up his mind to stay whether Britain took over or not. He left it to the diplomatists to settle the final fate of his province; meanwhile, he would devote himself to repairing the damage done by the Mahdist wars. True, Emin's province now consisted of little more than the riverain region from Lake Albert northward to about the fourth parallel. But even in this shrunken remnant of the old Equatoria, he was still at least somebody. He had no desire whatever for the role of a superfluous ex-governor at Cairo—'to go and beg in Egypt' as he put it.[4] Least of all did he wish to go with Stanley, whose advance party had arrived at Lake Albert in the last stages of want and exhaustion and who was clearly in no shape to rescue anyone. What Emin needed in 1888 was still what he had asked for in 1886: ammunition and cloth (of which Stanley had been able to bring only miserably small quantities), and a reliable line

[1] Schweitzer, *op. cit.*, pp. 312-30.
[2] FO 84/1794, Emin to Felkin 7 July 1886, enclosed in Felkin to Iddesleigh 23 Nov. 1886. FO 84/1775, Emin to Kirk 7 July, to Mackay 6 July 1886, enclosed in Holmwood to Iddesleigh No. 191, 18 Oct. 1886. Cf. Emin to Mackay 1 Oct. 1886, quoted Oliver, *op. cit.*, pp. 131-2.
[3] Schweitzer, *op. cit.*, pp. 367-79, especially Emin's diary during his tour of inspection, Aug.-Dec. 1887. Cf. Stanley, *op. cit.* 1, pp. 371-408.
[4] Schweitzer, *op. cit.*, pp. 330-42, citing Emin's letters to Junker, esp. those of 20 Jan. and 15 Apr. 1887. R. W. Felkin, 'Introduction' to the English edn. of Schweitzer, *op. cit.* (London 1898), pp. xxvii-xxxvii, citing Emin to Felkin 5 May 1886; 17 Apr., 15 Aug. 1887.

of communication to the exterior. In May 1888 Stanley made his proposals on behalf of Leopold and of Mackinnon. Leopold's offer Emin rejected out of hand; he had no confidence either in the future of the Congo State or in its ability to maintain communications with him. He was more attracted by Mackinnon's proposal, but he must have known how very unlikely it was that his 'people' would follow him to Kavirondo. Partly to gain time, partly perhaps genuinely to test feeling, Emin agreed that he and one of Stanley's officers, Jephson, should visit the garrisons and explain the situation. Stanley composed an address to be read to the troops together with the letters from the Khedive and from Nubar which he had brought with him; and then retired to join his rear party.[1]

Stanley's appearance in Equatoria revived and strengthened the hostility of Emin's troops to all projects of evacuation southwards. Fear of the unknown—'we know only one road, and that leads down the Nile to Khartoum'—and a reluctance to leave the domestic amenities of Equatoria for barrack life in Egypt, doubtless contributed to this hostility. But the troops, not least the Sudanese, were also inspired by a genuine loyalty and devotion to the Khedive. They refused to believe that *Effendīna* could really have ordered his soldiers to desert their posts or face total abandonment.[2] The Khedive's rescript was indeed a strange and utterly ambiguous document. In one breath it ordered Emin and his troops to retire with Stanley; in the next it gave them complete freedom to remain, but without the slightest prospect of further assistance from Egypt.[3] Stanley's 'proclamation' to the troops attempted to remove this ambiguity by representing withdrawal as the Khedive's order, with abandonment and total loss of pay as the punishment for disobeying it; but many of Emin's soldiers were quite intelligent enough to notice this distortion. For the troops, the very ambiguity of the Khedive's order cast doubt on its authenticity; and if it were really genuine, why had it been brought by a foreigner and an infidel, a mere adventurer who held no position in the Khedive's service, and who was evidently concerned to falsify it?[4] Moreover, to retire with Stanley seemed a road to almost certain death; the horrors of the march through the Aruwimi rain-forest and of Stanley's ruthless indifference to casualties had lost nothing in the telling when his survivors reached Equatoria. On 13 August 1888 the garrison at Laboré broke out in mutiny when Emin read the Khedive's rescript. 'All you have been telling us is a lie, and the letter you have

---

[1] Stanley, *op. cit.* I, pp. 377-404. Schweitzer, *op. cit.*, pp. 404-13. A. J. M. Jephson, *Emin Pasha and the Rebellion at the Equator* (London 1890), pp. 30-3.

[2] Jephson, *op. cit.*, pp. 102-10, 116, 153-4.

[3] The Khedive's rescript of 8 Jumāda al-Awla 1304 / 1 Feb. 1887 is printed in English translation at Stanley, *op. cit.* I, pp. 56-7; in German translation at Schweitzer, *op. cit.*, pp. 407-8. Nubar wrote in similar vein—Nubar to Emin 9 Jumāda al-Awla 1304 / 2 Feb. 1887; cf. FO 84/1878, enclosure in Baring to Salisbury Africa No. 9, 2 Feb. 1887.

[4] Stanley's 'proclamation' is printed at Stanley, *op. cit.* I, pp. 403-4. For the reaction of the troops, see Jephson, *op. cit.*, pp. 102-214, *passim*. The indictment against Emin specifically called Stanley 'an adventurer'.

read out is a forgery', cried their spokesman. On the following day, without interference from the mutineers, Emin and Jephson turned back towards Wadelai, but on arrival at Dufilé they were at once arrested and imprisoned. On 24 September Emin was sentenced to deposition and imprisonment by a council of officers; he was held to have betrayed the Khedive by conspiring with Stanley to utter forged Khedivial documents and to hand over his troops as slaves to the English.[1] It was a charge false as to the letter, but not totally false as to the spirit; and there seems no reason to doubt the good faith of Emin's accusers.

European intervention in Equatoria had, in its own small way, destroyed confidence in Emin even more completely than European intervention in Egypt had undermined the authority of Tawfīq—and, ironically enough, precisely because Emin's troops, insulated by their remoteness from the politics of Egypt, were by 1888 perhaps the only important group of Tawfīq's subjects who still retained a deep loyalty to *Effendina*. The apparent stability of Equatoria in April 1888 was in fact based upon a very delicate equilibrium between the wishes of Emin's troops and Emin's authority as Governor. Although Eduard Schnitzer had taken a Turkish name, and had found it useful and convenient to conform to the social proprieties of Islam, he was after all no more than a non-Muslim expatriate official. Respected for his impartiality and administrative skill, and for his personal qualities of tact and patience, Emin would be trusted and obeyed so long, and only so long, as no suspicion arose that his policy was in conflict with the deeper loyalties of his 'people'. A man less fitted than H. M. Stanley to understand the subtleties of such a relationship would have been hard to find. Even after the damage had been done Stanley never seems for a moment to have suspected that his own actions might have contributed to it; it was all the fault of Emin, who was lacking in 'firmness'.[2] Stanley's behaviour in Equatoria was that of a bull in a china-shop—a china-shop of whose very existence he seems to have had no inkling.

In November 1888 Emin was released, and he later regained some influence over a part of his troops, but his authority as Governor had been irreparably damaged.[3] When Stanley returned to Lake Albert in January 1889, he reacted to the situation in Equatoria with bewildered fury; but he soon saw, through his bewilderment, that an Emin without either authority or troops was of no value to either Leopold or Mackinnon. To Stanley, however, he was still of value; a spectacular 'rescue' of Emin would help to cover the total failure of Stanley's political mission. Emin also recognised that he had now no

[1] Jephson, *op. cit.*, pp. 145-215. Cf. Jephson to Stanley 7 Feb. 1889, printed Stanley *op. cit.* II, pp. 121-7.   [2] Cf. Stanley's estimate of Emin, *op. cit.* II, pp. 208-29.
[3] The most coherent account of the situation is that of Jephson, at Stanley, *op. cit.* II, pp. 123-7. The immediate cause of Emin's release was the invasion of northern Equatoria by the Mahdists under 'Umar Sālih in Oct. 1888.

alternative but to leave Equatoria; but he procrastinated, hoping that enough of his 'people' would join him to enable him to march out as a Governor at the head of his troops, not as a mere refugee in Stanley's train. Stanley, for his part, wished to get away as quickly as possible and to take as few of Emin's troops as he decently could. To do him justice, his motives for haste went beyond the reflection that the more troops Emin brought, the less like Stanley's trophy he would look. Stanley had work to do for Mackinnon forestalling the Germans west of Lake Victoria. Large numbers of Egyptian troops, with their numerous camp-followers and endless impedimenta, would have been an intolerably cumbersome addition to his caravan. Worse, they might even be dangerous. Some of them had already mounted a *coup d'état* against Emin, a man whom they normally liked and trusted; why not against Stanley, whom they intensely disliked and saw no reason to trust? On 4 April 1889 Stanley detected an attempt by Egyptian officers to steal the rifles of his Zanzibaris. Ignoring Emin's pleas for further delay, Stanley marched out on 10 April; Emin had no alternative but to accompany him. Very few of Emin's troops had, when it came to the point, volunteered to join him; and most of these deserted once Stanley got under way.[1]

Even before Emin's departure the troops in Equatoria had split into two hostile factions. The majority followed Fadl al-Mūla Bey Muhammad, who had taken a leading part in the arrest and deposition of Emin and who was consistently opposed to evacuation. Salīm Bey, the leader of the rival faction, had been making a rather half-hearted attempt to concentrate such troops as would follow him for the march out of Equatoria. Stanley's precipitate departure left Salīm dangerously isolated against Fadl al-Mūla, and he soon withdrew to Kavalli's near the southern end of Lake Albert.[2] Fadl al-Mūla now made his headquarters at Wadelai; here he engaged in negotiations with the Mahdists under 'Umar Sālih, who had occupied northern Equatoria in October 1888. But when the Mahdists appeared before Wadelai in March 1891, Fadl al-Mūla's troops forced him to give battle. The Mahdists were beaten off; but almost immediately afterwards eight hundred of Fadl al-Mūla's force marched south to join Salīm Bey at Kavalli's. With his remnant of perhaps six or seven hundred men Fadl al-Mūla could not hope to control Equatoria. But, as it turned out, the Mahdists were equally incapable of holding the province. In October 1891 a general rising of the tribes in Equatoria and the Bahr al-Ghazal forced 'Umar Sālih to retire to Bor from his former headquarters at Rejaf.[3] As a result of European intervention, political control in Equatoria had slipped by easy stages into the hands of the local Negroid peoples, who were quite unable to make any constructive

[1] Stanley, *op. cit.* II, pp. 109-207.
[2] *Ibid., loc. cit.* Cf. R. O. Collins, *The Southern Sudan, 1883-1898* (New Haven 1962), pp. 67-70.
[3] Collins, *op. cit.*, pp. 55-85.

use of it. From a European point of view, the vacuum of power in the southern Sudan could not have been more complete.

*   *   *

Salisbury's approval of the Emin Pasha Relief expedition in December 1886 had been followed almost immediately by a sustained and serious attempt to shake off the burden of Egypt. By 1887 the Bulgarian crisis, coinciding with a bout of French chauvinism of which General Boulanger was the inadequate symbol, was compelling Bismarck to seek British support. But thanks to Britain's vulnerability in Egypt, he could still seek it on his own terms. 'Egypt', wrote Salisbury, 'is a disastrous inheritance, for it enables the Chancellor to demand rather unreasonable terms as the price, not of his assistance, but of his refusal to join a coalition against us'[1]. In February 1887 Salisbury bought, by an agreement to assist Italy in the Mediterranean, Bismarck's prospective approval for an Anglo-Turkish arrangement for the early evacuation of Egypt.[2] Bismarck seemed to be selling the *bâton égyptien* at a bargain price; but perhaps he calculated—if so, correctly—that other Powers would serve him by wrecking the Anglo-Turkish 'Drummond Wolff Convention'. Salisbury had indeed expected that France and Russia would oppose this arrangement. What he had not foreseen was that these two Powers would succeed in preventing the Sultan from even ratifying the Convention. Salisbury discovered with dismay that Turkey was even weaker than he had thought, and had become 'for all practical purposes . . . the "Janitor" of Russia'.[3] This discovery threw doubt on the major premise behind the policy of evacuation—that the route to India could be defended as effectively at the Straits as at Suez. But Salisbury made no sudden change in his policy. Indeed, the Second Mediterranean Agreement, concluded in December 1887, was in effect a Near Eastern Triplice of Austria-Hungary, England and Italy, with definite commitments to protect the Ottoman Empire against Russian aggression. Salisbury concluded this arrangement, reluctantly, as a lesser evil than breaking his link with Bismarck altogether. He resented being forced to carry Bismarck's Austrian burden at the Straits; he resented still more the consequent deflection of Russian hostility from Berlin to London. But he made a shrewd bargain by committing the allies to the defence of Asia Minor as well as of the Balkans; and as an interim defensive arrangement at the Straits the Agreement was at least as valuable to England as to Germany.[4]

[1] Cecil, *Salisbury* IV, pp. 40-1, citing Salisbury to Malet 23 Feb. 1887. Cf. *ibid.*, pp. 41-2, 45-6, citing Salisbury to Wolff 23 Feb.; to Baring 6 May 1887.
[2] G.P. IV, No. 883, Bismarck to Hatzfeldt 3 Feb. 1887; No. 884, Hatzfeldt to Bismarck 5 Feb., and Bismarck's minutes.
[3] Cecil, *op. cit.* IV, p. 48, Salisbury to A. Austin 3 July 1887; to Lyons 20 July.
[4] *Ibid.*, pp. 69-71, Salisbury to the Queen, 27 Oct. 1887; to White 2 Nov. Cf. F. H. Hinsley, 'Bismarck, Salisbury and the Mediterranean Agreements of 1887', *H.J.* I, 1 (1958), pp. 76-81; *eundem*, 'International Rivalry, 1885-1895', *C.H.B.E.* III, pp. 256-60.

By 1888, however, doubts had arisen whether the fleet was in fact strong enough to make defence at the Straits anything more than a bluff. The Navy was now doubtful of its ability to cope with the French Toulon squadron; a commitment to defend the Straits against a Russian *coup de main* was quite unacceptable, if France were also hostile.[1] France seemed very likely to be hostile; by 1888 she was no longer a mere disgruntled rival, but an active menace. Side by side with the Boulangist agitation for *revanche* against Germany, and stemming from the same root of humiliated frustration, there had arisen a violent Anglophobia with 'Egypt' as its main war-cry. A week after Boulanger's electoral success, Salisbury told the Queen that 'France is, and must always remain, England's greatest danger'.[2] The only safe solution was to remain in Egypt to guard the Suez route; and though in August 1888 Salisbury still referred to the occupation of Egypt as a 'burden', he also gave notice that there was no prospect of its early termination.[3] Baring for his part was beginning to wonder whether it could ever be terminated. He doubted the wisdom of a compromise by which (as in the proposed Drummond Wolff Convention) preponderance would be maintained by a right of re-entry after evacuation. Baring's attempts to improve the lot of the *fallāh* had been frustrated by a fall in the prices of Egyptian products and by his own role as bailiff for the bondholders. If the British troops left, peasant discontent and 'Mohammedan fanaticism' would soon bring about a very dangerous 'upset'. Baring was of course further than ever from finding reliable Egyptians to man the 'strong native government' which might contain this situation. In June 1889 he reported that 'the real reason why the evacuation policy is well-nigh impossible of execution' was not the Mahdist danger; this was merely 'an excellent working argument'. The core of the difficulty was 'the utter incapacity of the ruling classes', to whom it was impossible to hand over without inviting disaster.[4] When Salisbury next publicly mentioned Egypt, in November 1889, he no longer referred to it as a burden; and he announced Britain's intention to remain as long as she thought necessary, 'whether assisted or obstructed by other Powers'.[5]

By the end of 1889 the retention of Egypt implied the active defence of the Nile waters far more clearly than it had even two years earlier. In 1888 there had been the lowest flood on record. Defence of the *White* Nile waters had of course no relevance to the Nile flood; but the disaster of 1888 emphasised in the most spectacular possible way

---

[1] Robinson and Gallagher, *op. cit.*, pp. 268-70; cf. W. C. B. Tunstall, 'Imperial Defence, 1870-1897', *C.H.B.E.* III, pp. 241-4.
[2] Chastenet, *La République des Républicains*, p. 207. L.Q.V. 3, i, pp. 436-8, Salisbury to the Queen, 25 Aug. 1888. Cf. Cecil, *op. cit.* IV, p. 95, Salisbury to Baring 17 Feb. 1888.
[3] Speech of 6 Aug. 1888, cited Cecil, *op. cit.* IV, p. 135.
[4] Robinson and Gallagher, *op. cit.*, pp. 276-81. Cf. FO 633/6, Nos. 146, 147, Baring to Salisbury 5 and 15 June 1889.
[5] Speech of 9 Nov. 1889, cited Cecil, *op. cit.* IV, pp. 137-8.

the total dependence of Egypt on the waters of the Nile.[1] In 1888-9 the Mahdist State underwent a series of internal crises—famine, dissensions within the ruling circle, and the rising in Darfur under the pseudo-Khalifa abū Jummaiza—which were widely misinterpreted as heralding its early collapse. The total rout by the Egyptian Army of the Khalifa's invasion of Egypt, at Tushki in August 1889, led to equally unwarranted assumptions about the military decadence of the Mahdia.[2] There was, however, no comfort in this for Baring; after a surplus of £E100,000 in 1887, his 1888 accounts had shown a small deficit. It would be very embarrassing if the vacuum of power in the Sudan were to occur while Egypt was financially hamstrung; as Salisbury had pointed out, 'the House of Commons would certainly decline to bear the cost' of reconquering the Sudan on behalf of Egypt.[3] Still, in the northern Sudan an Egyptian reconquest would in principle provide a final and clear-cut solution; and for a few months early in 1890 this solution appeared to be almost within reach. But by 1889 the threat to the Nile waters was not confined to possible Italian penetration towards Khartoum; Salisbury, if not Baring, was now well aware that Equatoria lay open to German encroachments. Here Egyptian reconquest was not a possible solution. It was ruled out by Baring's decision never to restore Egyptian rule in the southern Sudan; and perhaps also by Salisbury's fears of the outcry which such an attempted restoration would have evoked from missionary and philanthropic interests in England. At all events, Salisbury never quarrelled with Baring's verdict. Official British occupation of the South, or as much of it as was necessary to protect the White Nile, seemed equally out of the question. No House of Commons, least of all one in which the Liberal Unionists held the balance of power, seemed at all likely to provide money for the administration of a region where, it was now becoming clear, the prospects were not of profits but of unceasing and expensive difficulties with the turbulent inhabitants.

In 1887 and 1888 Salisbury had hoped that private enterprise—Mackinnon and his associates—would do something to fill the gap which was left by the inability of either London or Cairo to act on the Upper Nile. Even if the southern Sudan itself were beyond Mackinnon's reach, he might at least stake British claims in the regions through which German penetration was possible. In May 1887 Salisbury approved the lease to Mackinnon by the Sultan of Zanzibar of the coastal strip immediately to the north of German East Africa; and the Treasury was told that Mackinnon's East Africa mail subsidy would have to be renewed in order to encourage him to undertake responsibilities in the interior.[4] In 1887, however, the fate of the coast,

---

[1] Langer, *The Diplomacy of Imperialism*, pp. 106-7, 574.
[2] Holt, *The Mahdist State*, pp. 125-40, 156-64, 173-4. Cf. *infra*, Ch. IV, pp. 70-1.
[3] Robinson and Gallagher, *op. cit.*, p. 276. L.Q.V. 3, i, pp. 459-60, Salisbury to the Queen 25 Dec. 1888.
[4] Robinson and Gallagher, *op. cit.*, pp. 199-201.

and of Mombasa in particular, still presented a much more urgent problem than that of the hinterland. In the following year perspectives began to change. In June 1888 plans were initiated for a German Emin Pasha Expedition. Its promoters, who included figures as influential as Admiral Livonius and Rudolf von Bennigsen, scarcely troubled to conceal their territorial objectives in Uganda and on the Upper Nile.[1] Almost simultaneously, Mackinnon's Imperial British East Africa Company, formed in April, wrote to Emin making a take-over bid for his province as a going concern.[2] In September the Company was granted the Charter for which Mackinnon had long been pleading; it was expected by the Foreign Office to justify this privilege by forestalling the Germans in Uganda and by barring their route to the Upper Nile.[3] In February 1889 the Company took its first practical steps towards these ends when an expedition under F. J. Jackson left the coast for Wadelai, where it was instructed to join forces with Stanley and Emin.[4] The encouragement of private enterprise seemed in 1888 a sound enough policy even for the Upper Nile itself. Emin was still believed to be in full control of his province; and the letters from him which R. W. Felkin received in the first half of 1888 left no doubt that Emin would be happy to run Equatoria as a 'Sarawak' either under direct British protection or under that of a British Chartered Company.[5] In June 1888 Felkin, who had played a leading part in prompting Mackinnon's offer to take over Equatoria, could write to Emin 'You at the present time hold the key to the whole Soudan problem'.[6]

Meanwhile, in spite of the exertions of the German Emin Pasha Committee, Berlin refrained from official competition on the Nile approaches. In July 1887 Britain and Germany had agreed to 'discourage' annexations in the hinterland of one another's spheres;[7] but as the lines could quite well be drawn to exclude Britain, rather than Germany, from the Upper Nile, this was not in itself much safeguard. In December 1888 Salisbury asked Bismarck to define his attitude to the German Emin Pasha Expedition. Salisbury had in effect for the

---

[1] C. Peters, *Die Deutsche Emin Pascha Expedition* (Munich-Leipzig 1891), pp. 1-17. Idem, *Die Gründung von Deutsch-Ostafrika* (Berlin 1906), pp. 236-8, 254-61. Müller, *Deutschland-Zanzibar-Ostafrika*, pp. 463-4.

[2] De Winton to Emin, 9 June 1888, printed at F. Stuhlmann, *Die Tagebücher von Emin Pascha*, IV (Brunswick-Berlin-Hamburg 1927), Appendix, pp. 445-8. Cf. *ibid.*, pp. 439-45, Felkin's letters to Emin, July 1887-Nov. 1889.

[3] M. Perham, *Lugard: I—The Years of Adventure* (London 1956), p. 181, citing FO 84/2069, minute by Anderson 31 Mar. 1890. Robinson and Gallagher (*op. cit.*, pp. 201-2) doubt whether Salisbury shared Anderson's motives. Their scepticism is not however backed by any very convincing evidence; and cf. Harry Johnston's article in *The Times* of 22 Aug. 1888 (written after a week-end at Hatfield) in which Johnston looks forward to 'our sphere of influence in the Egyptian Sudan [which] Emin Pasha will rule in England's name . . .' (cited R. Oliver in *Rev. Belge Phil. Hist.*, XXXV, 3/4 [1957], pp. 729-30).

[4] P. L. McDermott, *British East Africa or IBEA* (London 1893), p. 111. FO 84/2036, Mackinnon to Stanley, 5 April 1889.

[5] Felkin, *ubi supra*, pp. xxix-xxxvii.

[6] *Ibid.*, pp. xxxvi-xli. Stuhlmann, *op. cit.* IV, pp. 440-1, printing Felkin to Emin 4 June 1888.

[7] By exchange of despatches: Hertslet III, No. 267.

first time given notice to a foreign Power that Britain had a special interest in the basin of the Upper Nile. But Bismarck's reply had been quite reassuring—he would give the expedition no official support or countenance whatever.[1] He was better than his word: German naval officers co-operated with the British in attempting to prevent Carl Peters from landing in Africa.[2] When Peters nevertheless slipped ashore north of Witu on 17 June 1889, Bismarck gave an explicit assurance that 'Uganda, Wadelai and other places to the east and north of Lake Victoria' were outside the sphere of German colonisation.[3]

In the second half of 1889, however, Anglo-German relations began to run less smoothly in Africa. The Germans resented British encroach-ment in the region between Lakes Tanganyika and Nyasa, which they regarded as their own hinterland; and they were increasingly dis-satisfied with their situation in Zanzibar. Complaints began to be heard that German goodwill was not being reciprocated in London.[4] In October 1889 Berlin suddenly declared a Protectorate over the Benadir coast north of Witu, a region where the rather squalid bicker-ings of Mackinnon and the Denhardt brothers had hitherto completely failed to interest either Bismarck or Salisbury.[5] The only conceivable importance of this poverty-stricken region was that its hinterland could be held to extend to the Upper Nile; and it was rapidly becoming standard German doctrine that a coastal Protectorate, duly notified under the Berlin Act, established a right to a hinterland bounded only by the internationally recognised spheres of other Powers. In Dec-ember 1889 Stanley and Emin arrived at the coast in a blaze of publicity. The Germans gave Emin a hero's welcome: a salute of twenty-one guns from the warship *Sperber*, and a personal telegram of congratulations from the Kaiser.[6] Colonialist enthusiasm in Germany was intensely stimulated;[7] henceforward it would be more difficult for both Salisbury and Bismarck to keep the smouldering African disputes well damped down. Moreover, Emin and Stanley had left behind them an Equatoria dissolving into chaos. Such a vacuum of power would have been acceptable enough in 1886; at the end of 1889, with Carl Peters at large in the interior and Bismarck proclaiming new Pro-tectorates on the coast, it was anything but welcome. In any case, it completely ruled out the possibility of a take-over by private enterprise in the southern Sudan; and only if Bismarck continued to keep his word to Salisbury would it be even tolerable for very long. But the

[1] Müller, *op. cit.*, p. 466, citing Reichskolonialamt 249/4, précis of a despatch from Bismarck to Hatzfeldt 11 Dec. 1888. Cf. F.O. to B.E.A. Co. 11 May 1889, cited McDermott, *op. cit.*, p. 87.
[2] Peters, *Die Gründung von Deutsch-Ostafrika*, pp. 245-6; *Die Deutsche Emin Pascha Expedi-tion*, pp. 18-42.
[3] FO 84/1954, Salisbury to Malet Africa No. 266, 25 June 1889.
[4] D. R. Gillard, 'Salisbury's African Policy and the Heligoland Offer of 1890', *E.H.R.* LXXV, 297 (1960), pp. 633-6, 643.
[5] Hertslet II, No. 210. McDermott, *op. cit.*, pp. 45-54.
[6] Schweitzer, *op. cit.*, pp. 460-4.
[7] Müller, *op. cit.*, p. 462.

rising tide of colonialist enthusiasm in Germany, not least among Bismarck's strongest supporters,[1] might make it very difficult for him to do this, especially if Germany's grievances elsewhere in Africa remained unrequited. Official British or Egyptian action to forestall the Germans on the Upper Nile was utterly out of the question. The ultimate future of the southern Sudan was more obscure than ever; but while British policy was seeking a solution to this riddle, other Powers must be kept out in order to safeguard the Nile waters. If Bismarck were to change his mind, the strategic protection of the Upper Nile would at once cease to be a rather hypothetical affair and would become a major issue of Great Power diplomacy. By the end of 1889 the security of the Nile waters, both in the central Sudan and in Equatoria, had perforce become 'a separate and dominating factor' in Salisbury's foreign policy.[2]

[1] *Ibid.*, pp. 466-70. Müller even suggests that 'in der Emin-Pascha-Krise wetterleuchtet bereits der Sturz Bismarcks'. He also emphasises Bismarck's difficulties in weaning the Emperor from his 'Equatorial enthusiasm'.

[2] Cecil, *op. cit.* IV, pp. 139-40.

III

DEFENCE BY DIPLOMACY

I—SALISBURY, GERMANY AND

THE UPPER NILE, 1889-91

B Y 1889 Salisbury's rather precarious tactical situation in East Africa was counterbalanced by a diplomatic strength in Europe greater than at any time since 1885. The Second Mediterranean Agreement had acted as a satisfactory deterrent at the Straits without creating any serious danger of war with Russia, and had usefully linked Britain with the Bismarckian system without binding her to its total support. The crescendo of Boulangist agitation, and the increasingly visible rapprochement between France and Russia, had forced Bismarck to court England more warmly. True, in 1888 Salisbury had still feared that Germany might use her local superiority in East Africa to bring about forcible changes in the *status quo*; he took part in a joint blockade of the Zanzibari dominions lest the Germans, uncontrolled by British collaboration, should 'turn their arms against the Sultan in the Island of Zanzibar' itself.[1] But by the end of 1888 Bismarck was declaring that 'my map of Africa lies in Europe'; as an earnest of his words he had totally disavowed the German Emin Pasha Expedition without attempting to make even a minor profit on the transaction.

In January 1889 Bismarck made to Salisbury his famous proposal for a defensive alliance against France;[2] it was accompanied by protestations that Germany was tired of 'colonial quarrels and flag-hoistings', and that British friendship was worth more to Germany than the whole of East Africa.[3] The danger to England from France seemed real; and here was a tempting offer of a free hand in East Africa. Yet Salisbury politely declined the offer, for he was unwilling to commit himself irrevocably to Germany. He still hoped to improve his relations with France in order to decrease his dependence on

---

[1] L.Q.V. 3, i, pp. 443-4, Salisbury to the Queen 29 Oct. 1888. Cf. Cecil, *Salisbury* IV, pp. 234-6: Salisbury to Malet 18 Sept. 1888; to Goschen 14 Oct.

[2] G.P. IV, No. 943, Bismarck to Hatzfeldt 11 Jan. 1889.

[3] Bismarck in the *Reichstag* 26 Jan. 1889, when he declared himself 'von Hause aus kein Kolonialmensch'. Cf. Herbert Bismarck in the *Reichstag* 14 Dec. 1888; H. Bismarck: to Hatzfeldt 19 Dec., cited G.P. IV, p. 176.

Bismarck. Indeed, throughout the difficult years from 1886, he had attempted to limit this dependence by making minor concessions to France. In the course of 1887 he concluded with France an interim settlement of the New Hebrides dispute and a Convention guaranteeing free passage through the Suez Canal; in February 1888 an Anglo-French agreement on Harar was concluded, with a definite, if small, point against Italy.[1] So long as the Boulangist tide was flowing, French public opinion did not respond to these *douceurs*; indeed, Salisbury sometimes feared that hysterical anglophobia might stampede France into an unplanned war with England.[2] But between January and April 1889 the Boulanger bubble was burst by the General's own incompetence and irresolution; and although the French continued to press for the evacuation of Egypt,[3] a government with the old Gambettist Spuller at the Quai d'Orsay could not be regarded as systematically hostile to England.

By the middle of 1889 Salisbury's determination to avoid a downright quarrel with France—a quarrel which Bismarck would have welcomed[4]—had succeeded to a point which seemed very unlikely at the beginning of the year. But although Salisbury could insure in this way against being too much at Bismarck's beck and call, he could not afford to be too distant with Berlin. As he told the Queen in June 1890, the only alternative to 'terms of amity with Germany' was an entente with France which 'must necessarily involve the early evacuation of Egypt under very unfavourable conditions'.[5] By 1889 evacuation would already have been a very stiff fence to ride at. Even if Baring's prophecies of disaster were ignored, the 'acquisitional feeling' in Britain, whose strength Salisbury had lamented as early as 1887,[6] was stronger than ever by 1889—especially in Salisbury's own party. Moreover, the recent instability of French politics made France seem a highly unreliable partner—far too unreliable to justify an attempt to overcome such formidable Egyptian and British obstacles. There was in fact no safe alternative to the continued occupation of Egypt. This left the *bâton égyptien* in Bismarck's hands; and it was a formidable weapon, especially when the Egyptian budget was still fluctuating between deficit and surplus. Moreover, the collapse of Boulangisme, which had given Salisbury's policy more elbow-room, also made it no longer necessary for Bismarck to court England quite so warmly; by the second half of 1889 the Chancellor was no longer parading his total lack of interest in African questions.[7] England still

---

[1] G.P. IV, No. 945, H. Bismarck to Bismarck 22 Mar. 1889. Cecil, *op. cit.* IV, pp. 49-54, 71, 95. Hertslet II, No. 225.
[2] Cecil, *op. cit.* IV, pp. 41-2, 47-52, 95, citing: Salisbury to Baring 11 Feb. 1887; to Holland 3 June; to Lyons 20 July; to White 10 Aug. 1887; to Baring 17 Feb. 1888.
[3] Robinson and Gallagher, *Africa and the Victorians*, pp. 270-2.
[4] Cecil, *op. cit.* IV, pp. 40-2, Salisbury to Malet and to Wolff 23 Feb. 1887.
[5] L.Q.V. 3, i, pp. 613-4, Salisbury to the Queen 10 June 1890.
[6] Cecil, *loc. cit.*; and pp. 44-5, Salisbury to Wolff 4 May 1887.
[7] G.P. VIII, No. 1673, H. Bismarck to Hatzfeldt 18 Dec. 1889.

needed Germany more than Germany needed England; in the last resort Bismarck could dispense with British friendship by changing his policy towards either France or Russia in the Levant.[1]

All the same, the Anglo-German friendship was mutually advantageous, and neither Bismarck nor Salisbury wished to disrupt it by quarrelling seriously about Africa.[2] Neither Bismarck nor Salisbury, however, could completely ignore the pressure of their own colonialists. Germany was no doubt a 'managed autocracy'; but the enormous Bismarckian 'cartel' majority in the Reichstag of 1887 was a card which Bismarck might some day wish to play in his difficult relations with the young Emperor. It was precisely among the classes who supported the 'cartel' that colonialist enthusiasm ran highest. Bismarck might restrain the colonialists from new adventures, but he could hardly sit tamely by while other Powers encroached on German hinterlands. Already by the summer of 1889 a number of 'otherwise right-thinking' newspapers were complaining of the Chancellor's excessive pliancy in colonial questions.[3] Salisbury's domestic situation seemed, and perhaps was, far more precarious than that of Bismarck. In the Commons he was completely dependent on the Liberal Unionists, whose support on 'main lines of policy' did not necessarily extend to African questions. The Government's credit had been severely shaken by the report of the 'Parnell Commission' in February 1890; Irish obstruction had thrown its legislative programme into hopeless arrears; the Conservative back-benchers were frustrated and dissatisfied; by-election results were consistently unfavourable. On 17 June 1890 the Government majority on a critical division fell to four.[4] This was a situation which colonialist pressure-groups were not slow to exploit; and Salisbury's main difficulty in negotiating the Anglo-German Agreement of 1890 was not with Berlin, but with domestic opposition strongly represented even in his own Cabinet. On 24 May 1890 he confessed to the Queen that an African agreement with Germany, however desirable in the interests of European policy, simply could not be concluded unless it was 'acceptable to our Companies and missionaries who are first in possession of the disputed ground'.[5]

By the autumn of 1889 there was all too much disputed ground. There was the island of Zanzibar; the Anglo-German boundary west

[1] Cecil, *op. cit.* IV, pp. 50-1, Salisbury to White 10 Aug. 1887. There was also the danger, to which Salisbury had adverted in Feb. and Nov. 1887, that the Powers might treat the possessions of an isolated England 'as divisible booty, by which their differences might be adjusted'. (L.Q.V. 3, i. p. 272, Salisbury to the Queen 10 Feb. 1887; Cecil, *op. cit.* IV, p. 71, Salisbury to White 2 Nov. 1887.)

[2] In Aug. 1889 Bismarck attacked the supporters of the German Emin Pasha Expedition as 'playing the game of France and Russia' (Müller, *Deutschland-Zanzibar-Ostafrika*, p. 469).

[3] G.P. VIII, *loc. cit.* Cf. Müller, *op. cit.*, pp. 465-70, which demonstrates the strength of these attacks.

[4] Cecil, *op. cit.* IV, pp. 153-5, citing Salisbury to the Duchess of Rutland 15 June 1890. L.Q.V. 3, i, pp. 606-7, 612, Salisbury to the Queen 24 May and 8 June 1890. W. S. Churchill, *Lord Randolph Churchill* (London 1907), p. 775.

[5] L.Q.V. 3, i, p. 607, Salisbury to the Queen 24 May 1890.

D

of Lake Victoria; the hinterland, with its possible access to the Upper Nile, behind Witu and the new German protectorate to the north of it; and the territory west of Lake Nyasa claimed by Berlin as the hinterland of German East Africa. In none of these regions had Salisbury much to give away. Zanzibar still had its value for Indian Ocean strategy; and its cession would doubtless have been a serious blow to British prestige not only in East Africa but in the Arab world. On the Witu hinterland he could compromise, so long as British access to the Upper Nile were preserved and German access excluded; but the 'Mackinnon clan' would bitterly oppose any serious concessions either here or to the west of Lake Victoria. The most serious difficulty was however the Nyasa-Tanganyika problem. The German claim here was a good one, not only on Berlin's own hinterland doctrine, but on any fair reading of the understanding of July 1887 by which Britain and Germany had agreed to 'discourage' competitive hinterland annexations.[1] This region had however been opened up and occupied by Scottish missionaries; and to incur the wrath of the Kirk by abandoning it would, as Salisbury himself admitted, 'certainly help Mr Gladstone very much'.[2] To the influence of the Kirk was added the not less powerful influence of Cecil Rhodes; in August 1889 Salisbury had agreed that the South Africa Company's Charter should set no limit to the Company's northward expansion towards Lake Tanganyika.[3] Since the outbreak in September 1888 of Abushiri's Arab-Swahili revolt in the German coastal sphere, the Germans had been unable to extend their occupation to the disputed Nyasa-Tanganyika hinterland. They were therefore the more uneasy both at the plans of Rhodes and at Salisbury's refusal to recognise the 'archaeological' Portuguese claims in south-central Africa, which they had hoped to use as a buffer against British expansion.[4] When on 25 June 1889 Hatzfeldt had transmitted Bismarck's assurances about Uganda and Wadelai, he had added that Berlin 'count[ed] upon similarly fair conduct on the part of H.M.G.' in the Nyasa-Tanganyika region. The British reply had been evasive; but when in August Hatzfeldt pressed the point, Salisbury took a firm stand on the prior occupation of the Scottish missionaries: 'It is not possible . . . to abandon the rights that they have so acquired or to recognise over the territory in which they have so settled the sovereignty of any [other] Power'.[5]

If the Germans were becoming 'very fidgety'[6] about the Nyasa hinterland, Britain for her part was under heavy German pressure at

[1] On the general situation in East Africa, see: Gillard, 'Salisbury's African Policy', E.H.R. 1960; G. N. Sanderson, 'The Anglo-German Agreement of 1890 and the Upper Nile', ibid. LXXVIII, 306 (1963), pp. 49-72.
[2] Oliver, Missionary Factor, Chs. I-III. L.Q.V. 3, i, pp. 608-9, Salisbury to the Queen 1 June 1890.
[3] Robinson and Gallagher, op. cit., pp. 228-9, 242-6. Cecil, op. cit. IV, pp. 239-42.
[4] Cecil, op. cit. IV, pp. 258-63. Gillard, ubi supra, pp. 633-5.
[5] Gillard, ubi supra, pp. 635-6, citing FO 84/1954, Salisbury to Malet Africa No. 266, 25 June 1889; Salisbury to Beauclerk Africa No. 301, 6 Aug. 1889.
[6] Minute by Sir T. Sanderson Nov. 1889, cited ibid., p. 642.

Zanzibar. In December 1888 Sultan Khalīfa *bin* Saʿīd had launched a policy of anti-European reaction. The Sultan was too unstable a character for this to amount to very much; but it was accompanied by picturesque atrocities which furnished a classic pretext for European intervention.[1] Germany was by now actively working for some arrangement at Zanzibar which should formally embody her practical equality of status with Britain; and Bismarck at once suggested that 'the sultan ought to be, if not set aside, at least reduced to the impotence of the Bey of Tunis'. In July 1889 he was still complaining about 'the hampering, useless deadweight of the nominal authority of the Sultan'. In August Bismarck himself took steps to make that authority even more nominal. On the pretext of ending the blockade 'with a flourish', he extorted from the Sultan the right to search for slaves all Arab dhows in Zanzibari waters—yet another blow to the Sultan's credit with his subjects. By November 1889 the German Ambassador Hatzfeldt was suggesting a joint (or perhaps alternate) Anglo-German control of the Zanzibar customs, which would doubtless have meant the end of the sultanate even as a political expression.[2]

In 1889 Salisbury was playing for time, which was working on his side in the Nyasa hinterland,[3] and meeting as they arose the increasing difficulties on the coast. In November 1889 he recognised the German coastal protectorate north of Witu; a little later he forced the British East Africa Company to evacuate the offshore islands of Manda and Patta, which the Germans claimed, on flimsy enough grounds, as part of this protectorate. However, while recognising the *coastal* protectorate, Salisbury reserved the treaty rights of British subjects in the hinterland, and officially communicated to Berlin a schedule of relevant treaties.[4] Under further German pressure for a settlement, on 21 December Salisbury proposed arbitration on a number of minor questions and on one major issue: 'whether any of the treaties recently concluded by the British East Africa Company in the interior between the Tana and Juba rivers [i.e. behind the German coastal protectorate] infringe on the well-attested rights of the Sultan of Witu or any other native chief or chiefs under the protection of Germany'.[5] Salisbury's list of topics did not include either the Nyasa hinterland or the country

---

[1] L. W. Hollingsworth, *Zanzibar under the Foreign Office, 1890–1913* (London 1953), pp. 29–36. Gillard, *ubi supra*, p. 640.

[2] Gillard, *ubi supra*, pp. 640–1, 643, citing FO 244/443, Malet to Salisbury Africa No. 152, 29 Dec. 1888; FO 84/1979, Euan Smith to Salisbury 19 July 1889. Hollingsworth, *op. cit.*, pp. 34–5.

[3] Indeed, in this region Salisbury then feared, not German encroachment, but 'a British victory of adventure over the Germans too complete for the continuance of friendly relations'. Cecil, *op. cit.* IV, pp. 244–5.

[4] FO 84/1961, Salisbury to Hatzfeldt 12 Nov. 1889. For the Manda and Patta affair, see McDermott, *British East Africa*, pp. 43, 56–71, 303–4. Cf. Cecil, *op. cit.* IV, pp. 277–8; Hertslet, II, No. 210, III, No. 269.

[5] FO 84/1961, Salisbury to Hatzfeldt 21 Dec. 1889. Cf. G.P. VIII, No. 1674, Hatzfeldt to Bismarck 22 Dec. 1889; Cecil, *op. cit.* IV, pp. 248–9. One of the minor questions was the Manda-Patta dispute—a sop to the B.E.A. Co.; but Salisbury specifically refused to re-open the question of the coastal protectorate (Gillard, *ubi supra*, p. 644).

to the west of Lake Victoria; it was not, as the Permanent Under-Secretary Sir Philip Currie remarked, 'a bill of fare that will be tempting to the Germans'. Nevertheless, Bismarck accepted it, merely adding three more trivial disputes to the schedule.[1] By April 1890 it had been arranged that Sir Percy Anderson should meet Krauel of the *Kolonialabteilung* in Berlin in order to define the questions more closely and agree on the procedure for arbitration.

Given the importance of the Tana-Juba hinterland as a means of access to the Upper Nile, it is at first sight remarkable that Salisbury was willing to leave it to the hazards of arbitration. He seems to have still been confident that, whatever the upshot of arbitration on the interior treaties, Bismarck would continue to honour his undertakings and would not claim a hinterland extending to Uganda and Wadelai. Bismarck's very willingness to accept arbitration, thereby waiving in this case the much-cherished doctrine of hinterland, was in itself a reassuring sign; and it was a reasonable calculation that the Chancellor would not risk disrupting the intricate network of his European diplomacy by a deliberate defiance of the implicit English veto on German expansion to the Nile. So long as the Germans kept well clear of the Nile basin, they were welcome to their coastal protectorate and as much hinterland as they wanted. Moreover, the arbitration proposal kept the Nyasa hinterland completely out of the picture. It seemed not unlikely that the Germans had acquired their Tana-Juba protectorate in the hope of exchanging it for a favourable settlement west of Lake Nyasa.[2] This bargain Salisbury was unable to contemplate. The Nyasa country seemed the more valuable both intrinsically and in terms of the British interests involved; more important, Salisbury could not afford the dispute both with Cecil Rhodes and with the Scots Kirk which its abandonment would have implied. Mackinnon's East African interest seemed less formidable. Salisbury therefore ignored Mackinnon's complaints about the German coastal protectorate and as far as possible avoided becoming involved in the East Africa Company's Tana-Juba squabbles. Meanwhile he pushed as hard as he could for an arbitration which should exclude the Nyasa hinterland and at the same time avoid a head-on collision with Mackinnon. 'Any terms which we might get for him from the Germans by negotiation he would denounce as a base truckling to the Emperor', wrote Salisbury in April 1890. He was well aware that Mackinnon's hostility, though not so dangerous as that of Rhodes and the Scots, was still not to be taken lightly.[3]

On 10 April 1890 Salisbury was still 'pushing as hard as he could for arbitration'.[4] On 13 May he offered Hatzfeldt a comprehensive

[1] Gillard, *ubi supra*, p. 645, citing minute by Currie 18 Dec. 1889.
[2] *Ibid.*, pp. 642-3. Marschall hoped in fact to strike this bargain in May 1890; cf. FO 84/2031, Malet to Salisbury Africa No. 64, 17 May 1890.
[3] Salisbury to Goschen 10 Apr. 1890, cited Cecil, *op. cit.* iv, p. 281.
[4] *Ibid., loc. cit.*

settlement in Africa, throwing in Heligoland as a counterpoise to his very heavy African demands.[1] Salisbury's earlier tactics had been based on the assumption that the African disputes could be treated in a very dilatory manner without endangering the indispensable 'terms of amity' with Germany. By the second week in May this assumption had become obsolete. Thanks to the exploits, or prospective exploits, of Stanley, Peters, and Emin, colonialist excitement on both sides of the North Sea had risen to a point where the rather shaky governments in London and Berlin found difficulty in containing it. Unless the East African questions were settled quickly, both governments might be forced into a quarrel in Africa in order to escape grave embarrassment at home.[2] Salisbury had hitherto relied upon Bismarckian prudence as the ultimate guarantee against German encroachment in the Nile basin. But in March 1890 Bismarckian prudence had ceased to guide German policy. The new government under Caprivi, with Marschall at the Wilhelmstrasse, professed the greatest friendship for England, which Salisbury was of course prepared to reciprocate. But Salisbury feared the predominance of the young Emperor William, for whose 'unreasonable and blameable' impulses he had a profound distrust.[3] He seems almost from the first to have doubted the ability of the new team in Berlin to keep the colonialists in check as Bismarck had done; and the Emperor's enthusiasm for colonial expansion was of course no secret. A week before the fall of Bismarck Salisbury had mocked at his Zanzibar consul's excessive alarm 'as to German projects' in East Africa. But when on 1 April Consul Euan Smith reported that Emin had entered German service and was to lead a mission to Uganda, Salisbury instructed Malet at Berlin to make enquiries and to remind Marschall of the existing understandings.[4]

Salisbury also attempted to meet the changing situation by a last attempt to stimulate private enterprise. Early in April Portal, the Consul-designate at Zanzibar, was sent to attend a meeting of the East Africa Company's directors, and to urge the despatch of a second caravan to the interior in support of Jackson. The Company was in fact already urging its agent F. D. Lugard to advance to Uganda; but a few days later it became pretty clear that Peters had already reached Uganda, while Jackson had reached neither Uganda nor Wadelai.[5] By 10 April Salisbury seems to have abandoned all hope of serious assistance from Mackinnon: 'he has none of the qualities for pushing an enterprise which depends on decision and smartness'.[6] On 26 April Emin marched out from Bagamoyo at the head of a hastily organised German expedition whose rumoured objective was

[1] G.P. VIII, No. 1676, Hatzfeldt to Marschall 14 May 1890.
[2] *Infra*, pp. 55–8. Cf. Müller, *op. cit.*, pp. 492–3.
[3] L.Q.V. 3, i, pp. 398–9, Salisbury to the Queen 21 Apr. 1888; 441–2, the Queen to Salisbury 15 Oct. 1888; 573–4, Salisbury to the Queen 24 Feb. 1890.
[4] Gillard, *ubi supra*, pp. 645–7; Sanderson, *ubi supra*, p. 53.
[5] Perham, *Lugard I*, pp. 179–82.
[6] Salisbury to Goschen 10 Apr. 1890, cited Cecil, *loc. cit.*

Equatoria. Berlin assured Salisbury that the expedition would not encroach on the British hinterland; in fact, the instructions given to Emin by the Imperial Commissioner von Wissmann stated that *any* extension of the German sphere 'would be regarded by me as redounding to Your Excellency's special merit'.[1] By 3 May Marschall had begun to retreat from Bismarck's unconditional assurance that Uganda was outside the German sphere.[2] It remained to be seen what view he would take of Wadelai which, more plausibly than Uganda, could be represented as within the German hinterland north of the Tana. The new German Government was, to say the least, already riding the colonialists with a much lighter rein than that of Bismarck. Salisbury's behaviour from about the end of April suggests that he fully recognised this; and that he was less impressed by the German assurances about Emin[3] than by the fear that the northern hinterland question would soon become an acute embarrassment unless Germany could be brought to renounce all access to the Nile basin.

On 30 April Salisbury signed Anderson's instructions for his conversations with Krauel. These instructions still listed as one of the matters for arbitration 'the internal frontiers of the German Protectorate north of the Tana, having regard to the treaties made in the interior by the British East Africa Co.'.[4] A day previously, however, Anderson had told Hatzfeldt on Salisbury's instructions that 'above all [the German] possession of Witu was the stumbling-block and the reason for English lack of confidence', and had suggested that the only satisfactory delimitation would be one 'which should completely separate the two spheres so that the German sphere would lie to the south, and the British sphere to the north, of the frontier in question'. Salisbury was in fact inviting Germany to state her terms for the cession of Witu and the Tana-Juba protectorate; but Hatzfeldt refused to commit himself beyond hinting that if Germany did name a price it would be a high one.[5] Evidently Salisbury was by now beginning to doubt the wisdom of leaving the Tana-Juba hinterland to arbitration; but on the very eve of the Anderson-Krauel conversations he could hardly delete from the arbitration agenda its only item of any serious importance.

In his instruction of 30 April Salisbury had also included certain 'questions of another order', on which Anderson was to explore the possibility of a direct negotiation. By far the most important of these, bringing in as it did the disputed regions to the west both of Lake Victoria and of Lake Nyasa, was 'the practical application of the Hinterland Agreement of July 1887'.[6] On 9 May, after six days of

---

[1] Schweitzer, *Emin Pascha*, pp. 493-503; cf. Gillard, *ubi supra*, p. 647.
[2] Gillard, *ubi supra*, p. 648.
[3] *Ibid.*, p. 647.
[4] FO 84/2030, Salisbury to Malet Africa No. 129, 30 Apr. 1890.
[5] G.P. VIII, No. 1675, Hatzfeldt to Caprivi 30 Apr. 1890.
[6] FO 84/2030, *ubi supra*.

negotiation, the frontier to the west of Lake Victoria was provisionally settled. Anderson abandoned the British pretensions to territory on the south-western shore of the lake; Krauel abandoned the German claim that the frontier should run north-westwards to Lake Albert, and admitted that 'Uganda at least as far as one degree south was in the British sphere'.[1] But this concession did nothing to protect the Upper Nile from German access through the Tana-Juba hinterland. The name 'Uganda', as used in the late nineteenth century, referred exclusively to the restricted region now more correctly termed 'Buganda';[2] and in May 1890 the most generous delimitation of 'Uganda' could not have drawn its northern and eastern frontiers so as to close off the Tana-Juba hinterland from the Upper Nile. Indeed, Krauel still regarded these frontiers, which had not yet been discussed, as completely open; on 14 May he proposed to Anderson, as one item in a comprehensive settlement, that 'in return for the assignment to Germany' of the immediate Tana-Juba hinterland, 'the watershed of the Nile with a sufficiently wide radius should be secured to England'.[3]

Except as part of a settlement which should recognise all or most of the German claim west of Lake Nyasa, Krauel was quite uncompromising in the Tana-Juba region. He insisted that the treaties of the British East Africa Company were worthless, because all the chiefs with whom they had been made were in fact vassals of the German-protected Sultan of Witu. The most important of these treaties in British eyes seems to have been that with Chief Avatula of the Waboni; but Krauel 'seemed amused at the mention of this ruler who was, he asserted, a petty feudatory of the Sultan of Witu whose vast possessions existed only in his imagination or in that of those who treated with him'.[4] Anderson for his part was equally uncompromising in the Nyasa hinterland; and it was probably Krauel's failure to obtain even a hint of concession in this region which prompted Berlin, on about 10 May, to instruct Hatzfeldt to approach Salisbury directly.[5]

Meanwhile, during the first and second weeks of May, the policy of piecemeal arbitration-cum-negotiation was being overwhelmed by the rising tide of agitation in both England and Germany. By the middle of the month the Lakes hinterland dispute, especially its northern branch, had become so acute that its speedy settlement was

[1] FO 84/2031, Anderson's despatch No. 4, 9 May 1890, enclosed in Malet to Salisbury Africa No. 53, 9 May.

[2] Sanderson, *ubi supra*, pp. 54-5, for detailed evidence.

[3] FO 84/2031, Anderson's despatch No. 7, 14 May 1890, enclosed in Malet to Salisbury Africa No. 61, 15 May.

[4] FO 84/2031, Anderson's despatches Nos. 4 and 7; cf. FO 84/2035, Malet to Salisbury tel. Africa No. 17, 10 May 1890.

[5] FO 84/2035, *loc. cit.*; FO 84/2031, Anderson's despatch No. 10, 17 May 1890. The first sentence of Hatzfeldt's despatch of 14 May (G.P. VIII, No. 1676) makes it pretty clear that Hatzfeldt had been *instructed* to approach Salisbury. Moreover, his remarks to Salisbury on the dangers of a 'steeplechase' in the Nyasa hinterland follow very closely those of Marschall to Malet some ten days earlier (cf. FO 84/2031, Malet to Salisbury Africa No. 44, 3 May 1890).

essential if Salisbury were to avoid serious friction with Germany and political embarrassment at home. On 2 May, even before Anderson had begun his negotiations, the East Africa Company had demanded the proclamation of a protectorate 'with as little delay as possible' over certain territories to the west of Lake Victoria where Stanley claimed to have made treaties with six 'powerful and important tribes'.[1] The Germans were especially sensitive about these claims; they already knew, from correspondence which had fallen into their hands, that in the course of 1889 Mackinnon had ordered Stanley to stake a claim in the region between Lakes Victoria and Tanganyika in order to link the East African sphere with that of Cecil Rhodes.[2] Salisbury refused even to consider declaring a protectorate, did not communicate the treaties to Anderson, and warned the Company that 'in view of the negotiations now pending with the German Government . . . it is . . . desirable that these treaties should not be made public at present'.[3] But Stanley had already mentioned the treaties in a public speech; and on 8 May *The Pall Mall Gazette* commented: 'I am informed that they are now lodged with the officials of the Foreign Office, who will hardly venture to render futile the efforts of Mr Stanley and the British Company by raising any difficulties as to their ratification. British subserviency to Germany in East Africa, has, it is to be hoped, reached its limits'. On the following day the treaties were the subject of a Parliamentary Question.[4] The East Africa Company's agitation had begun.

On 6 May the Company again demanded an immediate protectorate over the territories covered by Stanley's treaties. They also now demanded a protectorate over Uganda itself. Once again Salisbury declined to communicate this information to Anderson, although it was clearly relevant to Anderson's terms of reference. Almost simultaneously, Salisbury similarly withheld information directly relevant to Anderson's work on the Tana-Juba hinterland. On 5 May the Company had notified the Foreign Office that two of the Company-protected chiefs in this region, including Avatula of the Waboni, had certified by affidavit that the Germans had used threats of death in order to extort from them an admission of their dependence on Witu.[5] Salisbury's refusal to communicate this letter is the more remarkable in that a day or two earlier he had transmitted to Anderson a letter in which the Company reminded the Foreign Office specifically of its treaty with Chief Avatula.[6]

---

[1] FO 84/2081, I.B.E.A. Co. to F.O. 2 May 1890. Cf. Perham, *op. cit.*, pp. 258-9.
[2] Gillard, *ubi supra*, p. 647.
[3] FO 84/2081, *ubi supra*, minute; *ibid.*, F.O. to I.B.E.A. Co. 8 and 13 May 1890.
[4] *Ibid.*, cutting from the *Pall Mall Gazette*, 8 May 1890; draft answer to P.Q. by Mr. Bryce 8 May.
[5] *Ibid.*, I.B.E.A. Co. to F.O. 6 May 1890; same to same 5 May; minutes on these two letters. In each case an instruction to communicate to Anderson has been deleted by Salisbury personally; cf. Sanderson, *ubi supra*, pp. 60-1.
[6] FO 84/2081, I.B.E.A. Co. to F.O. 2 May 1890, and minutes thereon.

These suppressions, especially the latter, were evidently signs of an intention to remove the hinterland questions, including the Tana-Juba hinterland, from the competence of Anderson; for this was in fact Salisbury's next step. On 9 May, after Anderson had reported that Berlin would concede no more than the one-degree line in Uganda and that no compromise seemed possible west of Lake Nyasa, he instructed Anderson 'to put aside the Hinterland negotiations for the present and to do what was the original object of your mission, namely to settle terms of arbitration as to East Coast and West Coast questions'.[1] This instruction was as it stood ambiguous, for the internal Tana-Juba treaties had of course been included in 'the original object' of Anderson's mission. But in no sense did they constitute a *coastal* question such as (to mention two other items from Anderson's arbitration agenda) Walfisch Bay or Wanga. On the contrary, Salisbury had always made a sharp distinction between the German coastal protectorate, which he was prepared to recognise; and their claims in the interior, which he was not. But it was obviously impossible for Salisbury to delete an item from Anderson's agreed agenda while the conversations with Krauel were actually in progress; and the ambiguity in Salisbury's instruction would no longer matter once he had personally taken over all the hinterland negotiations, as by now he had doubtless decided to do.

Salisbury's motives are not far to seek. By 9 May the East Africa Company's campaign for Stanley's treaties, with Stanley himself as its chief standard-bearer, was provoking a strong counter-agitation in Germany. Marschall was already loud in complaint at the failure or refusal of the Foreign Office to control the British companies; he indignantly pointed to his own undertaking to disavow any treaty which Carl Peters might have made in Uganda.[2] If the hinterland questions in Uganda and 'Nyasaland' were to remain unsettled, and the British Companies permitted to present Berlin with a *fait accompli* which should include Stanley's hated treaties, the new German Government might well retaliate—might well be forced to retaliate—by extending their Tana-Juba hinterland to the Nile basin. Indeed, before very long Marschall was to warn Salisbury that if no settlement were reached he would be unable to prevent Peters playing the part of a German Stanley[3]—and Peters had never troubled to conceal that his crowning ambition was to obtain for Germany a foothold on the Upper Nile. East Africa had quite suddenly become the question of the hour in both Britain and Germany. In London, Stanley was 'the lion of the season', and his roars were soon loud enough to provoke Salisbury to a public defence of his African policy.[4] In Berlin 'the

[1] FO 84/2034, Salisbury to Malet (for Anderson) tel. No. 27, 9 May 1890.
[2] FO 84/2031, Malet to Salisbury Africa No. 44, 3 May 1890; FO 84/2035, same to same tel. Africa No. 11, 3 May.
[3] G.P. viii, No. 1683, Marschall to Hatzfeldt 31 May 1890; FO 84/2031, Malet to Salisbury Africa No. 68, 31 May.
[4] *A.R.*, 1890, pp. [137], [144-5]. Cecil, *op. cit.* iv, pp. 285-6. Cf. Sanderson, *ubi supra*, p. 59.

German public were intensely interested in East Africa'.[1] On 12 May Caprivi, introducing an appropriation of 4½ million marks 'for the suppression of the Slave Trade and the protection of German interests in East Africa', announced to the Reichstag his conversion to the cause of colonial expansion.[2] On the following day Hatzfeldt warned Salisbury, in courteous but grave terms, that an early settlement of all the hinterland disputes was the only way to avoid dangerous friction and the development of 'an insoluble situation'.[3]

Salisbury's dealings with Anderson in the second week of May had been signs of 'a fundamental change . . . in his conception of the problem'.[4] The problem was three-fold: to maintain 'terms of amity with Germany'; to satisfy at least the more important aspirations of the British 'Companies and missionaries'; and to obtain those regions —Zanzibar and the Tana-Juba hinterland—where German 'black-mail' was possible. The 'fundamental change in . . . conception' was Salisbury's recognition that this three-fold problem had now to be solved very speedily and in one single operation. By 13 May Salisbury's change in conception was complete, and he had found a possible solution for the complex of African questions, which were evidently interlocked in such a way that no satisfactory settlement was possible within the framework of a purely African bargain. The clue to the tangle was Heligoland, which the young Emperor coveted, although since 1884 Bismarck had shown scarcely any interest in it. In return for Heligoland, and a promise to obtain for Germany full sovereignty over the coastal strip which she held on lease from Zanzibar, Salisbury demanded African concessions on a scale intended to satisfy companies, missionaries and strategic interests alike: a British protectorate over Zanzibar, total German cession north of the river Tana, access from Uganda to the northern end of Lake Tanganyika, and the lion's share of the Nyasa hinterland.[5]

The offer of Heligoland was an invitation to the Emperor to sacrifice colonial expansion to his naval ambitions; but the bait was not taken at once. On 17 May Marschall, cannily recognising that the Tana-Juba hinterland was a crucial British demand, offered 'Witu . . . and the Somali coast' in return for a favourable partition west of Lake Nyasa and a common German frontier with the Congo State, which would automatically interrupt British access to Lake Tanganyika from Uganda. As for Heligoland, Hatzfeldt was merely told 'not to adopt an *a priori* attitude of refusal'.[6] On 21 May Salisbury waived

---

[1] FO 84/2031, Anderson, despatch No. 7, 14 May 1890, citing Krauel. On 10 May a certain Delfmann had indeed written to Krauel: 'Der Nil und Ägypten müssten mit der Zeit an Deutschland fallen . . .; das wünscht das Deutschtum im Ausland . . . Afrika für Deutschland!' (Müller, *op. cit.*, pp. 492-3).
[2] Cf. his speech as reported in *A.R.*, 1890, pp. [316-7].   [3] G.P. VIII, No. 1676.
[4] Cecil, *op. cit.* IV, p. 281.   [5] G.P. VIII, *loc. cit.*
[6] *Ibid.*, No. 1677, Marschall to Hatzfeldt 17 May 1890. On the same day Marschall offered a similar 'compromise' to Anderson: FO 84/2031, Anderson's despatch No. 10, enclosed in Malet to Salisbury Africa No. 64, 17 May 1890.

his claims south-west of Lake Victoria and conceded the German-Congolese common frontier. But he could not afford to give up the Nyasa hinterland for Witu and the Somali coast. Pleading the conviction of British public opinion that 'the interior of Africa in the line of the Great Lakes . . . offered the attractions of the El Dorado of the 16th century', the most Salisbury would offer in the Nyasa-Tanganyika region was a very grudging partition which would give Germany far less than Hatzfeldt's instructions permitted him to accept. When this proposal was rejected, Salisbury suggested a postponement of the whole negotiation until public opinion should have recovered from Stanley's campaign of agitation.[1] On 23 May Salisbury and Hatzfeldt were still 'as far from agreement as ever'—not surprisingly, since the ambassador had in the meantime received no new instructions. By the 24th Salisbury evidently feared that his Heligoland offer had fallen completely flat, and that it might be wiser to abandon the negotiation rather than risk incurring the wrath of 'our Companies and missionaries' by yielding to the German demands.[2]

Salisbury's suggestion of a postponement had been at least partly a tactical move; he guessed that Berlin's anxiety to reach a settlement was not less than his own. On 23 May Marschall told Hatzfeldt that any postponement was 'most undesirable' lest further disputes should arise out of the activities of rival expeditions. In fact, having just jettisoned the Reinsurance Treaty with Russia, the new team at the Wilhelmstrasse was the more anxious to avoid all friction with England. Marschall now offered to cede 'Witu und die Somaliküste samt Hinterland' and to recognise a British protectorate over Zanzibar, in return for Heligoland and full German sovereignty over the East African coastal lease.[3] On the Nyasa hinterland he was for the moment silent; but on 25 May he telegraphed accepting Salisbury's proposed partition and emphasising the major importance of Heligoland.[4] Salisbury's bait had been swallowed, and by 28 May agreement was in sight. Germany was to have Heligoland and her coastal sovereignty; Britain, her protectorate at Zanzibar together with 'Witu, and any claims [Germany] might have on the hinterland of that territory'. West of Lake Victoria Salisbury confirmed his concession of the one-degree line; but west of Nyasa he had now increased his demands and had extorted from Hatzfeldt a straight line from the northern end of Nyasa to the southern end of Tanganyika. However, Hatzfeldt had accepted this last demand only *ad referendum*; and Salisbury's pro-

---

[1] FO 84/2030, Salisbury to Malet No. 186a, 21 May 1890; G.P. viii, No. 1678, Hatzfeldt to Auswärtiges Amt 22 May.
[2] L.Q.V. 3, i, pp. 606–7, Salisbury to the Queen 23 and 24 May 1890.
[3] G.P. viii, No. 1679, Marschall to Hatzfeldt 23 May 1890.
[4] *Ibid.*, No. 1680, Marschall to Hatzfeldt 25 May 1890. Salisbury's proposed partition followed the line: Lat 8°S. from Lake Tanganyika eastwards to the 32nd meridian; that meridian southwards to the 11th parallel; that parallel eastwards to Lake Nyasa.

posals were subject to consultation with the British interests concerned.[1]

On 29 May Marschall telegraphed the Emperor's well-known directive that Heligoland was to be regarded as the object of the negotiation and the African questions treated merely as bargaining factors.[2] On the 31st, Berlin conceded Salisbury's new demand west of Lake Nyasa and permitted Hatzfeldt, if he found it necessary, to make concessions west of Lake Victoria so long as the common frontier with the Congo was preserved.[3] Meanwhile, however, Salisbury had run into strong domestic opposition. In order to obtain the Tana-Juba hinterland, he had abandoned some of the more extreme British claims at either end of the Great Lakes. These concessions were trifling indeed compared with the German sacrifices for Heligoland; but the 'Companies and missionaries' did not regard them as trifling. The South Africa Company was 'reasonable'; but the Scottish churches objected to the straight line between Lakes Nyasa and Tanganyika—already a demand exorbitant enough in German eyes— because it would cut the missionary highway of the 'Stevenson Road' between the two lakes. Salisbury shrank from a collision with the Scots, and begged the Queen 'to point out to the Emperor that a great deal of sentiment gathered in Scotland round the Stevenson Road', adding that 'any attempt to sacrifice it to Germany might produce serious feeling and would certainly help Mr Gladstone very much'.[4] But the East Africa Company was even more unreasonable than the Scottish churches. On 2 June it officially put forward the quite baseless contention that the Anglo-German hinterland understanding of July 1887 implied access from Uganda to Lake Tanganyika. It asserted that the shareholders had subscribed on this assumption, and that 'the Directors would be acting *ultra vires* did they now accept conditions' which would interrupt this access.[5]

Salisbury was prepared to fight Mackinnon—'he has got all he really has a right to, which is Uganda'.[6] But Mackinnon's ultimatum of 2 June was no empty threat. On the following day the African proposals came before the Cabinet. Salisbury pointed out that the Germans would not give way on the Congo frontier, and that if Mackinnon's objections were upheld 'no arrangement at all will be arrived at'. He insisted that the collapse of the negotiation would be 'a step into the unknown' in the whole field of foreign policy, and demanded that 'Sir William Mackinnon and Mr Stanley . . . be over-

[1] FO 84/2030, Salisbury to Malet No. 208a, 28 May 1890. G.P. VIII, pp. 17-18 fn.; No. 1682, Hatzfeldt to A.A. 30 May. Cf. Sanderson, *ubi supra*, p. 65 fn.
[2] G.P. VIII, No. 1681, Marschall to Hatzfeldt, 29 May 1890.
[3] *Ibid.*, No. 1683, Marschall to Hatzfeldt 31 May 1890.
[4] L.Q.V. 3, i, pp. 608-9, Salisbury to the Queen 1 June 1890. Cf. FO 84/2081, memorials from the Church of Scotland and the Free Church of Scotland, 9 and 27 May 1890. For the 'Stevenson Road', see Oliver, *op. cit.*, pp. 43-4.
[5] FO 84/2083, Kemball (vice-president, I.B.E.A. Co.) to Anderson 2 June 1890. Cf. *infra*, Ch. v, pp. 90-2.
[6] L.Q.V. 3, i, *loc. cit.*

ruled'. But it was Salisbury who was overruled. The Cabinet insisted on retaining not only the Stevenson Road, but territory covered by Stanley's treaties south of the one degree line.[1] Salisbury's colleagues even tried their very unskilled hands at an arrangement of their own. They appear to have suggested, as an equivalent for these demands, that Witu should be left to Germany and the islands of Manda and Patta reserved for arbitration.[2] The proposed cession of Heligoland, which Salisbury had not yet revealed even to the Queen,[3] was not on the agenda of this Cabinet; but when Salisbury discussed it informally with some of his colleagues their reaction was not encouraging.[4]

At his interview with Hatzfeldt after the Cabinet of 3 June, Salisbury dwelt upon his colleagues' grave misgivings about the cession of Heligoland, and suggested a postponement of the Heligoland-Zanzibar section of the negotiation. He also transmitted the Cabinet's demands for the Stevenson Road and the region to the west of Lake Victoria, together with their proposals for Witu, Manda and Patta. Salisbury was not surprised when Hatzfeldt rejected out of hand any division of the negotiation. Apart from Heligoland, Germany was not obtaining much that was worth having; and Hatzfeldt's rejection was heartily approved by the Emperor—'Nein! Zusammen oder Nichts!'[5] But the Wilhelmstrasse, which had within the last few days finally decided not to conclude any form of agreement with Russia,[6] was now more anxious than ever 'to abolish for the foreseeable future all considerable points of conflict' with England in Africa, lest they should 'arouse ill-feeling which might react in an unpredictably disturbing manner upon the continuity of European policy'. The British proposals for Witu, Manda and Patta, which so far as the hinterland was concerned would have perpetuated rather than removed 'points of conflict', were rejected by Berlin as worthless—a rejection which again can hardly have come as a surprise to Salisbury. Marschall was however now prepared to concede the Stevenson Road, as part of a comprehensive settlement to be treated as 'a single indivisible whole', if London would definitely accept the first parallel as the frontier west of Lake Victoria.[7] The Stevenson Road was the one concession that Salisbury deemed

---

[1] Cecil, *op. cit.* IV, pp. 283-5; Robinson and Gallagher, *op. cit.*, p. 293 (both cite extracts from Salisbury's Cabinet Memorandum of 2 June 1890). Cf. L.Q.V. 3, i, pp. 610-1, Salisbury to the Queen 4 June 1890; and G.P. VIII, p. 21 fn., summarising Hatzfeldt's tel. No. 94 of 3 June.

[2] The only surviving trace of this proposal seems to be a sentence rejecting it in Marschall to Hatzfeldt, 4 June 1890 (G.P. VIII, No. 1685). It is hardly conceivable that Salisbury can have fathered such a suggestion; and it evidently emerged from the deliberations of the Cabinet on 3 June. Salisbury is silent about it in his letter to the Queen on 4 June (L.Q.V., *loc. cit.*), and this silence is probably significant.

[3] Salisbury had not mentioned it in his letter of 4 June; but on that day the Queen learned of it verbally from Lord Cross (L.Q.V. 3, i. p. 610, the Queen's journal).

[4] L.Q.V. 3, *loc. cit.* Cf. G.P. VIII, No. 1684, Marschall to the Emperor 4 June 1890.

[5] G.P. VIII, p. 21 fn.; No. 1684, and minute by the Emperor; No. 1685. Cf. Cecil, *op. cit.* IV, p. 296—'This reply was no doubt anticipated'.

[6] Cf. G.P. VII, Nos. 1373-80. The final decision had been transmitted to St Petersburg at the end of May.

[7] G.P. VIII, No. 1685; cf. No. 1681.

'indispensable'; having obtained it, and having satisfied himself that Berlin was still 'quite uncompromising' west of Lake Victoria, he closed with Hatzfeldt on 5 June, subject to the approval of the Cabinet.[1]

On 3 June Salisbury had seen Mackinnon, and had permitted him to ratify a private arrangement with King Leopold by which the Congo State ceded to the East Africa Company a corridor of territory behind the German sphere between Uganda and Lake Tanganyika. On 7 June Mackinnon completed this ratification and at once wrote to Salisbury withdrawing his objections to the one-degree line west of Lake Victoria.[2] On the same day the Cabinet accepted Salisbury's proposed African settlement as embodying Berlin's last word. To the cession of Heligoland, now officially mooted for the first time, there was however vigorous opposition.[3] But on this occasion Salisbury did not expatiate to Hatzfeldt on the misgivings of his colleagues; he reserved these observations until he had at last obtained their approval on 10 June.[4] Two more days, and several lengthy telegrams, were then required to overcome the objections of the Queen, who believed quite simply that 'Giving up what one has is always a bad thing'.[5] More insidious and dangerous were the guerilla tactics of the East African lobby, which continued to oppose the settlement in spite of Mackinnon's *agrément*. On 11 June *The Saint James's Gazette* published an accurate statement of the 'Bases' of the Agreement, which were by now in draft at the Foreign Office, but still unsigned and of course still secret. This disclosure produced a crop of embarrassing Parliamentary Questions, to which very uninformative replies had to be given.[6] Even at the beginning of July Sir Donald Currie, a Scottish shipowner M.P., was trying to organise opposition among Conservative backbenchers to what was now a *fait accompli*.[7] On 4 July, however, Salisbury silenced the malcontents by a statement which amounted to a *mot d'ordre* from the Leader of the Party. The Government could not 'support pretensions which are inordinate; and incompatible with the fair claims of other nations': the Companies and Missions had been fully consulted, and were believed to approve 'generally' of the Agreement.[8] The Parliamentary Debates on the Agreement were dull

---

[1] L.Q.V. 3, i, p. 610, Salisbury to the Queen 4 June 1890. FO 84/2082, minute by Salisbury, 4 June 1890, on Anderson's record of the meeting with Mackinnon (3 June). G.P. VIII, No. 1686, Hatzfeldt to A.A. 5 June 1890.

[2] FO 84/2082, Anderson, Minutes of meeting between Salisbury and Mackinnon 3 June. FO 84/2083, Mackinnon to Salisbury 7 June 1890 (two separate letters). Cf. *infra*, Ch. v, *loc. cit.*

[3] L.Q.V. 3, i, pp. 611-2, Salisbury to the Queen 8 June 1890. Cf. G.P. VIII, No. 1687, Marschall to Hatzfeldt 6 June; and Cecil, *op. cit.* IV, p. 297. The Cabinet still made some minor reservations in West Africa and southern Africa.

[4] L.Q.V. 3, *loc. cit.*; and pp. 613-4, Salisbury to the Queen 10 June 1890. Cecil, *loc. cit.* G.P. VIII, No. 1688, Hatzfeldt to Caprivi, 11 June.

[5] L.Q.V. 3, i, pp. 612-5.

[6] FO 84/2083, P.Q.s by Messrs. Pease, Beckett and Bannerman 11 and 12 June, and draft replies. FO 84/2084, P.Q. by Mr Hanbury and draft reply 16 June. Mr Conybeare was induced to withdraw two particularly awkward questions about East African frontiers.

[7] FO 84/2085, MacDonnell (private secretary) to Salisbury 3 July 1890.

[8] *Ibid.*, P.Q. by Mr Beckett, and reply drafted by Salisbury 4 July 1890.

and desultory;[1] Salisbury had fought and won his battle with the African pressure-groups almost entirely behind the scenes. But in the first week of June it had been touch-and-go. To save the Agreement, Salisbury had been forced to appease Mackinnon, a man whom he disliked and despised; and to provoke the Germans, by gratuitous information about misgivings over Heligoland, to say a 'last word' which he could use as a means of pressure on his colleagues.

In defending the Anglo-German Agreement, and justifying the cession of Heligoland, to the Queen and to the public, Salisbury emphasised the value of excluding all European competition between the first parallel of south latitude and 'the borders of Egypt';[2] and in his speech in the Lords on 10 July he had referred frankly to the previous danger of German encroachment from Witu towards 'the sources of the Nile'.[3] Indeed, except for a moment when his colleagues compelled him to transmit proposals which made nonsense of the whole negotiation, Salisbury had treated the acquisition of the Tana-Juba hinterland as essential, and had been prepared to pay for it by concessions which were domestically hazardous. In the negotiation with Hatzfeldt the real importance of this region was not however explicitly revealed—the word 'Nile' does not even appear in the published German documents. Nor did the project of bases, as initialled on 17 June, contain any specific reference to a British sphere in the Nile valley or even to the Nile valley at all. It had simply delimited the *German* sphere in East Africa (Art. I); and had then, after two articles relating to West and South-West Africa, baldly stated that: 'Germany will cede to England its protectorate over Vitu [*sic*] and over the Somali country to the north of the English sphere.' (Art. IV).[4] But when Anderson and Krauel set to work in Berlin to fill in the details, the question of the Upper Nile at last shed its modest disguise of 'Witu und die Somaliküste samt Hinterland' and came nakedly into the open.

On 18 June Anderson telegraphed from Berlin: 'Good progress is being made with Dr Krauel as to details. . . . I have trouble with him about our hinterland on the Nile, but I insist that we cannot risk an expedition of Dr Peters and Emin Pasha to Wadelai and I think he will not hold out. . . .' Salisbury replied forthwith: 'Nile hinterland. Count Hatzfeldt examined my despatch before it was sent and expressed his approval. We therefore consider the statement of the effect of the German concession to be accepted.'[5] The despatch in question was one

---

[1] Robinson and Gallagher, *op. cit.*, pp. 298-300.
[2] L.Q.V. 3, i, pp. 613-4, Salisbury to the Queen 10 June 1890. FO 84/2030, Salisbury to Malet No. 223, 14 June 1890.
[3] Cited Robinson and Gallagher, *op. cit.*, p. 299.
[4] FO 84/2037, draft of Bases, undated, by Anderson; cf. Cabinet Print, 24 June 1890.
[5] FO 84/2035, Anderson to Salisbury tel. Africa No. 27; FO 84/2034, Salisbury to Anderson tel. No. 48, both of 18 June 1890. The despatch, No. 223 of 14 June, was published as *Africa No. 5 (1890)* [C.-6043].

written to Malet on 14 June for Blue-Book publication, and actually published on 18 June. In it, Salisbury had mentioned the German cession north of the existing British sphere, and had then remarked that 'the effect of this arrangement will be that, except so far as the Congo State is concerned, there will be no European competitor to British influence between the first degree of south latitude and the borders of Egypt, along the whole of the country which lies to the south and west of the Italian Protectorate in Abyssinia and Gallaland'.[1] Krauel had presumably not been fully informed, or had been exceeding his instructions; but Salisbury was now on his guard. Not only did he insist on the explicit recognition of a British sphere; he rejected Anderson's suggestion that it should be defined as merely extending to 'the basin of the Nile'. It was to be 'conterminous with the territory reserved to Italy . . ., as far as the confines of Egypt' and bounded in the west 'by the Congo Free State, and by the western watershed of the basin of the Upper Nile'.[2] Everywhere except in the north, the sphere was defined with the greatest precision; in the north, where England had only her vassal Egypt to contend with, the boundary was left completely and conveniently nebulous.

When Salisbury began his negotiations with Hatzfeldt, he was perhaps not yet thinking in terms of anything so positive as a 'British sphere' in the southern Sudan. Especially since the Brussels Act, so definite a commitment implied responsibilities which England would obviously find it very difficult to fulfil. Moreover, the reconciliation of a British sphere with Egyptian and Ottoman rights in the Sudan might well lead, as in the event it did, to awkward diplomatic complications. But the Germans were sticklers for formality and precision in African diplomacy; they would recognise only definite spheres, and Salisbury was therefore forced to claim one. Having thus been saddled with a sphere, Salisbury was prepared to accept the practical consequences. He already recognised, far more clearly than many 'advanced' imperialists, that the sphere would remain a diplomatic fiction so long as transport from the coast to the lakes took three to four months and cost £300 a ton.[3] A railway into the interior was the indispensable key, not only to the effective administration of the lake regions, but to any token occupation in the southern Sudan. Direct Treasury expenditure on a railway was of course unthinkable; but private enterprise, which had failed to protect the Upper Nile from foreign encroachment, might yet succeed in this purely technical task if given some public assistance. In December 1890 Salisbury approached the Treasury for such assistance to the East Africa Company; and by March 1891 he seemed to have persuaded Goschen at the Exchequer to guarantee 5 per cent interest on a capital of 1¼ million which Mackinnon was to

[1] FO 84/2030, Salisbury to Malet No. 223, 14 June 1890.
[2] Robinson and Gallagher, *op. cit.*, p. 295. Cf. Hertslet III, No. 270 (Anglo-German Agreement, 1 July 1890), Art. 1 (3).
[3] Portal to Rosebery 1 Nov. 1893, in *Africa No. 2 (1894)* [C.-7303].

raise.[1] But once again private enterprise broke in Salisbury's hand. It was becoming increasingly apparent that the East Africa Company was plunging into insolvency. Goschen, originally not unsympathetic, yielded to the preaching of his 'Gladstonian' permanent officials on the sheer immorality of subsidising bankruptcy; and Goschen, as Salisbury's indispensable link with the Liberal Unionists, could not be overruled.[2] In May 1891 Salisbury attempted to arouse public interest in the railway project by emphasising its humanitarian motives—'I do not see that any slave-dealer who presented himself with a body of slaves to be carried on trucks to the coast would be very civilly received'.[3] In vain. By July the project had been whittled down to a £20,000 grant-in-aid for a preliminary survey.[4]

The refusal of the railway subsidy was a crushing blow to the East Africa Company. Without this mark of government confidence and support, it had little hope of raising new capital, especially in a market still shaken by the Barings' failure for over twenty-one million in November 1890. On 16 July 1891 the Company decided that Uganda at least must be relinquished, and ordered its agents to withdraw at the end of the year. However, humanitarian and missionary interests, aided by a press campaign led by *The Times*, succeeded in raising sufficient funds to enable the Company to remain in Uganda until December 1892.[5] In May 1892 Mackinnon sent to Lugard the final order to withdraw; communicating it to Salisbury, he made a last despairing appeal for government assistance. To this appeal Salisbury did not even reply.[6] The Company was obviously finished; a general election was approaching; a decision on the Mombasa railway had been postponed until the completion of the preliminary survey.[7] In August 1892, after its electoral defeat, Salisbury's government resigned with the fate of Uganda still unsettled and the future status of the southern Sudan not much nearer definition than it had been in 1886.

Salisbury's failure to follow up the brilliant *coup* of the Anglo-German Agreement by clinching the railway project has been attributed to his queasy attitude to public opinion and his reluctance to initiate the profane herd into 'the sacred mysteries of African strategy'.[8] True enough, *odi profanum vulgus et arceo* might well have

---

[1] McDermott, *op. cit.*, pp. 173-91. Cecil, *op. cit.* IV, pp. 309-10. Perham, *op. cit.* I, pp. 388-91. Robinson and Gallagher, *op. cit.*, pp. 308-9. Cf. *Africa No. 2 (1892)* [C.-6560], F.O. to Treasury 20 Dec. 1890 and 9 Feb. 1891; Treasury to F.O. 10 Feb. 1891.

[2] For Goschen's original attitude, see Cecil, *op. cit.* IV, p. 242.

[3] Speech at Glasgow (Perham, *op. cit.*, I, p. 391).

[4] McDermott, *loc. cit.* Perham, *op. cit.* I, pp. 391-2. Cecil, *op. cit.* IV, pp. 311-2. *Africa No. 2 (1892)*, Treasury to F.O. 20 July 1891. Even the grant-in-aid was held up by Harcourt's decision (17 July 1891) to treat it as 'in the highest degree contentious'. Salisbury's renewed pleas for a subsidy in September (Cecil, *op. cit.* IV, pp. 312-4) were therefore doomed from the outset.

[5] McDermott, *op. cit.*, pp. 192-5. Perham, *op. cit.* I, pp. 392-9. *Africa No. 1 (1893)* [C.-6847], pp. 1-2.

[6] *Africa No. 1 (1893)*, I.B.E.A. Co. to F.O. 17 May 1892; F.O. to I.B.E.A. Co. 26 May 1892.

[7] Cecil, *op. cit.* IV, p. 314.

[8] Robinson and Gallagher, *op. cit.*, pp. 310-1.

E

been the Cecil family motto in the time of the third Marquis. But any statesman, however popular his touch, would certainly have experienced difficulties with the House of Commons, and with some of the colleagues, that frustrated Salisbury in 1891. Moreover, he did attempt to arouse public opinion, if not to initiate it into African strategy, by his Glasgow speech on the Uganda railway in May 1891. Nor should his domestic failure be allowed to detract from his diplomatic success. In 1890, when private enterprise had proved a broken reed, and when it was impossible to 'ask Parliament for money and send a Major Wissmann out . . . to hold the country',[1] Salisbury had achieved a diplomatic squaring of the circle. The threatening African difficulties were converted into a means of actually strengthening the 'terms of amity' with Berlin. The Africa lobby he could not fully satisfy; but he satisfied enough of it to make the opposition to the Agreement just manageable. Salisbury was well aware of the domestic risks he was running, though he may not at the outset have realised how narrow his margin of success was to be. But his bitter experience of German 'blackmail' at Zanzibar in 1885-6 strengthened his determination to avoid any repetition of it on the Upper Nile.

[1] Minute by W. H. Smith 2 April 1890, cited *ibid.*, p. 294.

IV

DEFENCE BY DIPLOMACY

II—ITALY, THE IMPORTUNATE FRIEND,

1889–94

SALISBURY'S African settlement with Germany in 1890 had been simplified by the desire of the Wilhelmstrasse to remain on good terms with England. Close Anglo-German friendship was however in 1890 a 'New Course' for Berlin, confirmed for the time being by the rapid and successful solution of the African difficulties in the July Agreement. But Anglo-Italian friendship was an old theme in European diplomacy, whose survival was now threatened by Italian attempts, under the leadership of Francesco Crispi, to obtain a foothold within the Nile basin. Since the Mediterranean Agreements of 1887 the loose alliance with Italy had indeed become the keystone of Salisbury's foreign policy. It was not Italy's strength—least of all her naval strength—but rather her weakness, which made her valuable to England as an ally. Without British naval support Italy could scarcely have remained in the Triple Alliance in the face of French hostility; even had she done so, her long and vulnerable coastline would have more than neutralised her value as an ally. As Caprivi put it in April 1891, 'the military value of Italy as an ally is mainly dependent on whether Britain is a fourth member of the league'.[1] Berlin was therefore concerned to maintain the Anglo-Italian entente as an insurance against Italy's being forced out of the Triplice and into the arms of France; and this preoccupation was Salisbury's strongest guarantee that Germany would treat British interests with respect. Further, the carefully non-committal wording of the First Mediterranean Agreement enabled Salisbury to keep Crispi 'within bounds' in his not infrequent 'trumpery quarrels' with France.[2] In this way Salisbury was able to keep open a line to Paris, a line which functioned well enough so long as the anglophile Ribot was at the Quai d'Orsay. The entente with Italy allowed Salisbury to 'lean towards' the Triple

---

[1] G.P. VII, No. 1412, memo. by Caprivi 23 April 1891. British naval men had a very low opinion of the Italian fleet—cf. A. J. Marder, *The Anatomy of British Sea-Power* (New York 1940), pp. 141-2, 172.

[2] L.Q.V. 3, i, p. 272, Salisbury to the Queen 10 Feb. 1887. D.D.F. VIII, No. 390, Waddington to Ribot 25 June 1891 (citing Salisbury). Cecil, *op. cit.* IV, p. 105, Salisbury to Dufferin 28 Dec. 1888.

Alliance without committing himself to an alignment with Berlin which would have excluded all friendly contact with Paris, and so gave him considerable freedom of tactical manœuvre. In August 1892 Salisbury was to describe England's link, through Italy, with the Triplice as 'the key of the present situation in Europe'.[1]

Great as the value of Italy's friendship was, Salisbury was not prepared to pay for it by concessions in the Nile valley. For Italy, the entente with England was almost a necessary condition of her recognition as a Great Power. For Crispi, its existence was the strongest defence against accusations that his foreign policy had brought Italy nothing but the sacrifice of *Italia Irredenta* and the unrelenting hostility of France. Salisbury could be confident that not even the headstrong Crispi would risk the total loss of English goodwill by openly hostile action in Africa. At the same time he refused to accept Baring's urgent pleas that Italy should be warned off the Nile basin, immediately, in the strongest possible terms, and if necessary at the sacrifice of her friendship. Instead, Salisbury took refuge in procrastination and evasion; only as a last resort did he bluntly tell Crispi that the Italian demands were totally unacceptable. In 1891 his patience was rewarded. He found in di Rudinì a minister who was not merely indifferent, but positively hostile, to Italian expansion in *East* Africa, and who was for other reasons exceptionally anxious to conciliate England.

Crispi's technique of intervention was to offer, as a keen and loyal ally, military co-operation—'parallel action'—against the Mahdists, in the hope of obtaining a territorial reward and ultimately achieving a status equivalent to that of England as a self-appointed 'trustee' of Egyptian rights in the Sudan.[2] This policy had been initiated by Mancini and Depretis as early as 1885, but had been almost immediately frustrated by Salisbury's decision to withdraw to Wadi Halfa and remain strictly on the defensive.[3] Thereafter, until 1889, the Italians were far too occupied in maintaining their position on the Red Sea coast to be able to make offers of 'parallel action' in the Sudan. Casualties among the Italian garrison at Massawa, with its murderous climate, soared to such heights that the East African adventure was likely to die of unpopularity in Italy unless a foothold could be obtained on the healthier Eritrean *altipiano*. This operation was attempted in January 1887; the Italian expedition was ambushed and annihilated by the Ethiopians under Ras Alula at Dogali, almost within sight of the Massawa outposts.[4] By August 1887, when Crispi became foreign minister, the Italian position seemed not far from total

---

[1] Cecil, *op. cit.* IV, pp. 404-5, Salisbury to Currie, 18 Aug. 1892.
[2] The policy of 'co-trusteeship' was not however openly avowed until 1894. Cf. G. N. Sanderson, 'England, Italy, the Nile Valley and the European Balance, 1890-1891', *H.J.* VII, 1 (1964), pp. 94-119, at p. 105.
[3] M. P. Hornik, *Der Kampf der Grossmächte um den Oberlauf des Nil* (Vienna, n.d.). pp. 16-9, 21.
[4] *Ibid.*, pp. 32-4. G. Bourgin, 'Francesco Crispi', in *Les Politiques d'Expansion Impérialiste* (Paris 1949), pp. 123-56, at pp. 131-3.

collapse. Such a fiasco could only have strengthened the Radical, Irredentist and Francophile elements in Italy; and Salisbury thought it worth while to bolster up the Italians by sending Portal from Cairo to argue the Negus Yohannes into granting them a less constricting frontier. Portal's mission was a total failure. Yohannes rejected, in anger and scorn, all the demands presented on Italy's behalf; and British prestige in Ethiopia was seriously damaged by this inept attempt to exercise it in support of the hated and despised Italians.[1]

It was not the British but the Mahdists who were, quite unwittingly, to save the situation for Italy. In January 1888, when it seemed quite possible that the Tigre chiefs Alula and Mangasha would drive the Italians out of Massawa itself, the Mahdists under Hamdān abu 'Anja invaded Gondar. The menacing Ethiopian concentration above Massawa dispersed; Crispi was able to reduce the pestilentially over-crowded garrison at Massawa and at the same time feel his way on to the *altipiano*. By February 1889 an Italian advance party had reached Keren. But this position could not be permanently held; and the Italian detachments in the highlands were already faced with the alternatives of withdrawal or annihilation at the hands of Alula when on 9 March the Negus Yohannes was killed in battle against the Mahdists. The generally recognised heir of Yohannes was Menelik, King of Shoa; but Menelik's claim was contested by Ras Mangasha of Tigre, the illegitimate son of Yohannes. A struggle for the succession was inevitable; and Menelik, who had been in treaty relationship with Rome since May 1883, was regarded by the Italians as their client. Antonelli, the able Italian agent at the court of Shoa, enjoyed con-siderable influence with Menelik; and in 1889 his credit was partic-ularly high thanks to a recent shipment of 8000 rifles and 'millions' of cartridges.[2] On 2 May 1889, by the Treaty of Uccialli, Italy recognised Menelik as Negus and in effect agreed to support him against Mangasha.[3] While Tigre and Shoa were locked in combat, the Italians, on the pretext of supporting their ally Menelik, were able to make a military promenade into the Eritrean highlands. On 2 June Keren was occupied; on 3 August, Asmara.[4] From Keren, perched on the westernmost bastion of the *altipiano*, the Italians looked down over the foothills to Kassala and the valley of the Nile beyond. 'Parallel action' in the Sudan at once returned to Crispi's agenda.

---

[1] G. H. Portal, *My Mission to Abyssinia* (London 1892). *Abyssinia No. 1 (1888)* [C.-5431]. There is some interesting correspondence on the Portal Mission in FO 78/4051 and FO 95/746.
[2] Holt, *The Mahdist State*, pp. 153-5. Hornik, *op. cit.*, pp. 32-4, 38-9. Bourgin, *op. cit.*, pp. 134-8. MAE, Mémoires et Documents Afrique 138 (Abyssinie 5), Lagarde to Spuller, 14 June 1889.
[3] Hertslet II, No. 120. By a notorious mistranslation of Art. xvii, Antonelli attempted to create an Italian protectorate over Ethiopia. C. Zaghi, *Crispi e Menelich* (Turin 1956) prints a facsimile of the Amharic text between pp. 152-3; the Amharic version of Art. xvii is discussed at pp. 168-9.
[4] Hornik, *op. cit.*, p. 41. Bourgin, *op. cit.*, pp. 138-9. Cf. FO 141/274, report of military attaché, Rome, 20 Dec. 1889, enclosed in Salisbury to Baring No. 4, 3 Jan. 1890.

Baring, sensitive as always to encroachments into the central Sudan from the east, had already taken alarm. By August 1889 he was complaining to Salisbury that the Italian advance, if not checked, would soon begin to threaten the security of the Nile waters. Salisbury 'concurred fully as to the inviolability of the Nile valley, even in its affluents', and assured Baring that the 'misplaced and suicidal' Italian aspirations would not 'be gratified at the cost of any solid sacrifice on our part'.[1] These merely general assurances did not satisfy Baring. On 3 August, the very day on which Baldissera had entered Asmara, the Khalifa's invasion of Egypt had been shattered at Tushki.[2] This rout of the Mahdists by Egyptian troops, and exaggerated rumours of internal conflict in the Sudan, had by December 1889 inspired Baring with the fear that the Mahdist State might soon become too weak to resist an Italian offensive; and that the Italians, who were already hankering after Kassala, might strike before Egypt had completed her financial and military preparations for reconquest. At best, Egypt might then be hustled into action before 'the *dégringolade* of Mahdiism'[3] was complete; this would entail not only military hazards, but perhaps insolvency on Egypt's current account and international interference in Egyptian administration. At worst, Egypt might find herself forestalled by Italy not merely at Kassala, but at Berber and Khartoum. On 15 December Baring demanded, in his most forthright style, that the Italians be warned off; 'if they are allowed an inch, they will take an ell'. To permit the establishment of any 'civilised' Power—even a friendly Power—in the Sudan would be a gross dereliction of duty towards Egypt, for it would jeopardise 'the headwaters of the river on which the whole life of the country depends'. Nor did Baring shrink from the conclusion that 'it would be paying too high a price, even for Italian friendship, to make any serious sacrifice on a point of this importance'.[4]

Throughout December 1889 and January 1890 Baring continued to plead that the Italians be 'kept back for a few years'; if only this could be done 'the Soudan [would] probably come back to Egypt without much trouble'.[5] But Baring seems to have doubted Salisbury's ability to do this; and his anxieties were increased by the mistaken belief that the Mahdia was approaching its death-agony. In January 1890 he had been convinced, on military grounds even if on no other, that 'the time for advancing on Khartoum ... has certainly not come yet'.[6] But by 15 March 1890 he believed that 'the military power of

---

[1] Cecil, *op. cit.* IV, pp. 325-6, citing Salisbury to Baring 15 Nov. 1889. Cf. F O 78/4243, Baring to Salisbury No. 405, 15 Dec. 1889.

[2] Holt, *op. cit.*, pp. 158-63.

[3] S P Egypt, Baring to Barrington (private secretary) 19 Jan. 1890.

[4] FO 78/4243, *loc. cit.*; FO 633/6, No. 150, Baring to Salisbury 15 Dec. 1889. Cf. Holt, *op. cit.*, pp. 165-6.

[5] FO 78/4243, FO 633/6, SP Egypt, *loc. cit.* FO 78/4307, Baring to Salisbury No. 23, 18 Jan. 1890.

[6] FO 78/4307, *loc. cit.*

the Dervishes is broken' and that a total collapse of the Mahdist State
was imminent. He again reminded Salisbury that 'any civilised Power
holding the upper waters of the Nile at Khartoum will in reality
dominate Egypt'. Then, recalling an earlier remark by Salisbury himself on the difficulty of keeping 'other people out of savage territory
which we are unable to occupy ourselves', Baring concluded, though
without quite committing himself to a definite proposal for immediate
reconquest, that 'actual occupation would, without doubt, be a much
more effectual safeguard' than mere diplomatic remonstrances.[1]

Within the next few weeks events on the frontier forced Baring to
admit that the Mahdists still presented a formidable military problem.[2]
It also became clear that Salisbury's diplomatic defence was quite
strong enough to prevent Italian adventures in a Sudan which was not
after all on the verge of political and military dissolution. On 7 March
the Italian ambassador had submitted to Salisbury proposals for a
delimitation of the Italian and 'Anglo-Egyptian' spheres, with the
proviso that in case of operational necessity military commanders
should be permitted to cross the proposed frontier. Alert to the possible
implications of this proviso, Salisbury warned Tornielli not to suppose
that the retirement of Egypt 'a few years ago from Khartoum and
Kassala was . . . an abandonment on her part of a title to those regions'.
Britain, as the guardian of Egypt, 'could not in her name surrender any
portion' of Egyptian dominion over this territory.[3] Tornielli, who was
no enthusiast for African expansion, was soon convinced that Salisbury
would not yield more than a temporary and strictly 'operational'
occupation of Kassala. But Crispi insisted that he persevere, and
despatched to London the Africanist Luchino dal Verme, ostensibly as
technical adviser; his real mission was to confer unofficially with his
personal friend General Brackenbury, the D.M.I.[4] On 26 March
Tornielli showed to Salisbury a trace of the proposed frontier, which
dal Verme had doubtless brought with him. Salisbury remarked with
disapproval that the line 'if prolonged, would strike Khartoum and
leave Kassala in the Italian sphere', but noted 'as a point in its favour
that it merely affected country draining into the sea and not country
draining into the Nile'.[5] Tornielli was by now thoroughly alarmed at

[1] FO 78/4308, Baring to Salisbury No. 87, 15 Mar. 1890.
[2] In March 1890 it had been believed that an Egyptian reconnaissance to Firka might
alarm the Mahdists into evacuating Dongola. Instead, they reinforced Dongola; and on
19 April Baring confessed that the reconquest of the Sudan was 'quite beyond the existing
resources at the disposal of the Egyptian Government' (FO 78/4309, Baring to Salisbury
No. 137).
[3] FO 141/274, Salisbury to Baring No. 60, 14 Mar. 1890, enclosing Salisbury to
Dufferin No. 60, 7 Mar. Cf. C. Zaghi, 'La Conferenza di Napoli tra l'Italia e l'Inghilterra'
(hereafter cited as: Zaghi, 'Conferenza'), Rassegna di Politica Internazionale, III (1936),
pp. 663-4.
[4] Zaghi, 'Conferenza', pp. 664-5. Idem., 'Il Problema di Cassala e l'Italia' (hereafter
cited as: Zaghi, 'Problema'), Storia e Politica Internazionale, 1940, 2, pp. 413-4. FO 45/648,
Dufferin to Salisbury tel. No. 21, 21 Mar. 1890. Cf. FO 78/4318, Brackenbury to Francis
Bertie 27 Mar.
[5] FO 141/274, Salisbury to Baring No. 76, 26 Mar. 1890.

Crispi's persistence, and confided to Hatzfeldt his fears lest this obsession with the Nile should jeopardise British support for Italy in Europe. The Emperor William personally ordered his ambassador at Rome to remind Crispi of the overriding importance of Anglo-Italian co-operation in the Mediterranean; but the only reply was a harangue on the urgent need for co-ordinated Anglo-Italian military action both in Ethiopia and in the Sudan.[1]

For all dal Verme's reputation as a reliable Africanist, his conclusions were the same as those of Tornielli: that Salisbury would make no territorial concessions whatever within the Nile valley, but was prepared to consider adjustments in regions draining into the Red Sea.[2] Here Salisbury's responsibilities as guardian of Egypt sat lightly enough upon him. The legal and historical claims of Egypt on the Red Sea littoral were as good as anywhere else in the Sudan; but they had no relevance to the security of the Nile waters, and Salisbury was quite prepared to sacrifice them as a sop to Crispi. On 28 March he told Baring, in explanation of his refusal to authorise an advance on Tokar, that it was 'only by a forced process of reasoning' that the Red Sea coast could be 'represented as essential to the safety of Egypt'. Baring rather grudgingly concurred, but he warned Salisbury that the Suakin-Berber route might ultimately be compromised by 'Crispi's Bersaglieri running all over the Eastern Soudan'.[3] On 25 April Salisbury suggested that as the temperature of the dispute seemed to be 'at boiling point in the Soudan', but was 'at zero' in London, Baring himself might undertake a negotiation when he was next on leave. With his administrator's love of a clear-cut situation, Baring chafed at this delay. The Italian encroachments on the coast were a constant irritant to him and he was still far from easy about Kassala. On 2 May he suggested that Crispi be invited to send a representative to Cairo to discuss a delimitation 'in principle', the principle being that the Egyptian title to Kassala should be unconditionally recognised. Salisbury concurred, though he doubted whether Crispi would accept.[4] But Crispi was anxious to demonstrate, as an offset to the already deteriorating situation in Ethiopia, that 'perfect accord and understanding' existed between Britain and Italy in Africa.[5] A frontier agreement would have afforded some tangible proof of this, and dal

[1] G.P. viii, No. 1972, Hatzfeldt to A.A. 26 Mar. 1890, and minute by the Emperor; No. 1974, Solms to Caprivi 8 April.
[2] Zaghi, 'Problema', pp. 414-7, 430-2, 437-42, citing dal Verme's letters to Rome. L. dal Verme, 'L'Italia nel Libro di Lord Cromer', Nuova Antologia, Series v, cxxxvii (1908), pp. 373-4.
[3] FO 78/4313, Salisbury to Baring tel. No. 27, 28 Mar. 1890. Cecil, op. cit. iv, pp. 327-8, citing Salisbury to Baring 28 Mar., Baring to Salisbury 4 Apr. 1890.
[4] Cecil, op. cit. iv, pp. 328-30, citing Baring to Salisbury 4 Apr., Salisbury to Baring 25 Apr. 1890. FO 141/274, Salisbury to Baring No. 98, 25 Apr. 1890, enclosing Salisbury to Dufferin No. 98, 23 Apr. FO 78/4313, Baring to Salisbury tel. No. 49, 2 May 1890; Salisbury to Baring tel. No. 39, 3 May.
[5] Since the advance of Gen. Orero across the Mareb to Adowa in Jan. 1890, Menelik had become much more reserved towards his Italian 'ally'. For Crispi's domestic difficulties, cf. FO 45/646, Dufferin to Salisbury No. 47, 7 March 1890; No. 86, 14 May.

Verme was therefore sent to Cairo in the hope that he would redeem the setback he had suffered in London.[1]

Baring had by this time accepted Salisbury's thesis that a sop for Italy could be provided on the Red Sea littoral; but in his negotiation with dal Verme he attempted a squeeze by putting forward extravagant coastal claims, which he then offered to withdraw in return for the unequivocal renunciation of Kassala by Italy. Indeed, in this case he was prepared to throw in an extra thirty miles or so of coastline. Dal Verme's reaction was to advise the postponement of the negotiation (25 May); but Crispi, more anxious than ever for a settlement which could be represented as a diplomatic success, refused to authorise this. On 4 June Baring pressed very strongly for a settlement in principle on Kassala. Dal Verme evaded this demand by suggesting that it was premature to draw a line before detailed topographical studies had been made, and again pressed Crispi to suspend the discussions, lest Italy be faced with a blunt and final refusal of all concession on Kassala. Crispi concurred, very reluctantly, on 11 June; but by the 23rd he was already pleading for a resumption.[2] Meanwhile, Baring had passed the problem back to Salisbury for action: 'The hesitation of the Italian Government to agree in principle to a frontier which will keep them from the Nile shows, I think, how necessary it is to get this point arranged'.[3]

Salisbury was not to be hustled. He was still determined to evade the dilemma of either recognising an Italian title within the Nile valley or quarrelling downright with Rome. He had not indeed been opposed to what he called Baring's 'informal consultations' with dal Verme.[4] These occupied time and committed nobody. But when on 23 June Crispi requested a formal negotiation, Salisbury concurred in Currie's proposed reply that 'the arrangements with Germany must be concluded before we can enter into negotiations with Italy'. 'Yes—put in some civil phrases'; an ironical courtesy, for 'the arrangements with Germany' were already complete in all but mere form. On 20 July Crispi renewed his request, pointing out that the Anglo-German negotiations had been completed some time previously. Salisbury no longer had a presentable excuse for delay, but he moved as slowly as possible. Not until 31 July did he instruct Lord Dufferin, the Ambassador at Rome, to make enquiries as to the precise matters which Crispi wished to discuss.[5]

[1] FO 141/279, Salisbury to Baring tel. No. 41, 5 May 1890. Dal Verme, *ubi supra*, p. 374.
[2] FO 78/4313, Baring to Salisbury tels. No. 69, 24 May 1890; No. 76, 4 June; No. 80, 11 June. FO 78/4310, Baring to Salisbury No. 193, 12 June 1890, enclosing dal Verme to Baring 11 June. Zaghi, 'Problema', pp. 417-9, 443-7, 452-4, citing dal Verme's reports to Crispi. FO 84/2038, Dufferin to Salisbury No. 37, 23 June 1890.
[3] FO 78/4313, Baring to Salisbury tel. No. 80, 11 June.
[4] Cf. FO 45/648, Salisbury to Dufferin tel. No. 25, 24 Apr. 1890.
[5] FO 84/2038, Dufferin to Salisbury tel. No. 37, 23 June 1890, and minutes by Currie and Salisbury; Salisbury to Dufferin tel. Africa No. 1, 25 June; Dufferin to Salisbury Africa No. 9, 21 July; Salisbury to Dufferin Africa No. 32, 31 July 1890. Dufferin moved just as slowly; he did not transmit Salisbury's enquiry until 13 Aug. (FO 170/439).

Towards the end of August, however, Salisbury at last agreed to a formal negotiation to take place in Italy and to be conducted jointly by Baring and Dufferin. At the end of July Crispi had asked Salisbury for his countenance in a project to 'forestall' a French occupation of Tripoli, and had at the same time suggested to Paris an arrangement which should leave Italy and France a free hand in Tripoli and Tunis respectively. The Germans, particularly Holstein, feared that this move portended a Franco-Italian partition of Tripoli, which would be followed by 'an immediate flare-up in the Balkans and the secession of Italy from the Triple Alliance'. Hatzfeldt therefore 'entreated Lord Salisbury for some display of practical sympathy', in the form of 'a written guarantee that [Italy] shall some day be the heir of Tripoli'. This guarantee Salisbury refused to give; Crispi professed himself content with verbal assurances and the scare blew over.[1] But some gesture was needed to pacify Rome and to reassure Berlin. The proffered negotiation on East Africa was doubtless intended to serve this purpose, especially as Crispi was soliciting the help of Italy's allies in getting it started.[2] But if Salisbury now felt it necessary to make amends for the 'contemptuous indifference' of which Tornielli complained to his German and Austrian colleagues, this did not imply any weakening in his resolve to exclude Italy from the Nile basin. If Baring could not 'persuade the Italians . . . to keep their hands off the affluents of the Nile', he was to adjourn the conversations, 'putting in a note to make it quite clear what our claims are'. 'I do not think', wrote Salisbury, [that] 'England will lose by delay . . . I daresay things will go on as they do now so long as Crispi is at the head of affairs.—But he is 71! . . .'[3]

The negotiation opened at Naples on 24 September 1890. It was easy to agree that Italy should be permitted an operational occupation of Kassala subject to her restoring that place to Egypt 'under certain conditions'. The difficulty lay in defining these conditions. The Italians began by suggesting that the 'claims'—not the 'rights'—of Egypt should remain in abeyance until after an Anglo-Egyptian re-occupation of Khartoum. Baring of course rejected this out of hand. But in his anxiety for a definitive settlement he was inclined to accept an unofficial statement that Italy did not in fact intend to occupy Kassala, until Salisbury warned him that any such 'private assurances' would be quite worthless coming from Crispi. Though Crispi did not totally exclude the use of the word 'rights', he nevertheless contended that Egyptian rights in the Sudan had lapsed, and would recognise them only as a subject for future discussion. Thereupon

---

[1] The citations are from: G.P. VIII, No. 1890, Holstein to Hatzfeldt 3 Aug. 1890; Cecil, *op. cit.* IV, pp. 372-5, citing Salisbury to Dufferin 12 Aug. For a fuller account cf. Sanderson, *ubi supra*, p. 102.

[2] G.P. VIII, No. 1977, Hatzfeldt to Caprivi 29 Aug. 1890. Hornik, *op. cit.*, p. 63, citing Deym to Kálnoky 27 Aug.

[3] Cecil, *op. cit.* IV, pp. 330-1, citing Salisbury to Baring 31 Aug. 1890.

Baring, with Dufferin's concurrence, suggested on 7 October that Britain should with the tacit assent of Crispi unilaterally declare that any Italian occupation of Kassala should not derogate from Egyptian rights, which would remain in abeyance until Egypt was 'in a position to resume effective possession'. 'We think that this solution, although not nearly so satisfactory as a distinct pledge of evacuation, would be preferable to stopping the negotiations and leaving everything unsettled.'[1]

Salisbury did not agree. The Italian argument about the lapse of rights at Kassala was capable of indefinite extension within the Nile valley. On 10 October he replied:

> We cannot sanction any occupation of Kassala unless we receive
> a clear recognition of Egyptian right and an undertaking to give
> it back whenever the Egyptian Government are ready to take
> charge of it. . . . It is ridiculous to say that by four years' with-
> drawal the right has lapsed.

This blunt rejection was communicated by Baring to Crispi immediately after a conversation in which Crispi had evidently gained the impression from Dufferin that the project of a unilateral declaration was not entirely unacceptable to the British. Taken aback, Crispi attributed this rebuff to the machinations of Baring, moved by supposed 'personal enmity . . . towards the Italians'. He at once retorted that it was 'impossible to acquiesce' in Salisbury's demands, and the conference broke up. It had not however been a complete waste of time. It had furthered Baring's political education by convincing him that it was not possible simply to hustle Crispi into a satisfactory settlement. He also recognised that his Cairo viewpoint had tended to magnify the Italian danger.

> 'It is a pity', he wrote, [that Crispi] 'would not come to terms, as
> it may cause a certain amount of trouble, although not, I think,
> of a very important kind. In the long run the Italian policy in
> Africa will probably collapse—More especially if they are too
> ambitious. All I have seen and heard here impresses me greatly
> with the weakness of Italy as a Power.'[2]

Crispi could not accept 'the miscarriage at Naples' so philosophically. His parliamentary position was by now so precarious that he dared not admit a setback; and, as Dufferin told Salisbury, 'he was in a real fright lest it should be supposed that the suspicion of a cloud had arisen between Italy and England, as it would tell so greatly against him at the elections'.[3] Crispi was forced to swallow his resentment. He

---

[1] FO 170/442, tels. unnumb.: Baring to Salisbury 30 Sept. 1890; Salisbury to Baring 3 Oct.; Baring to Salisbury 7 Oct. Dal Verme, *ubi supra*, pp. 374–5; Zaghi, 'Conferenza', pp. 665-6.

[2] FO 170/442, Salisbury to Baring tel. unnumb., 10 Oct. 1890. SP Egypt, Baring to Salisbury 11 Oct. (source of final quotation). FO 170/426, memo. by Dufferin 10 Oct.; Dufferin to Salisbury No. 175, 17 Oct. Cf. dal Verme, *ubi supra*, pp. 375–6; Zaghi, 'Conferenza', p. 666; Cecil, *op. cit.* IV, pp. 331-2; Sanderson, *ubi supra*, pp. 103-4.

[3] SP Italy, Dufferin to Salisbury 13 Nov. 1890.

declared in the *Riforma* that there was no serious difference with England and that the negotiations had been 'suspended rather than broken off'. Indeed, within a week he was again pleading for a resumption. On 15 October Tornielli complained to Salisbury that it was damaging to Italy's international position that she should be unable to conclude an African agreement with England when Germany and even France had been able to obtain satisfactory terms from London. Salisbury retorted that neither Germany nor France had demanded that England should 'give up territory of which we [*sic*] had been in occupation as territorial owners within a period of four years', and emphasised that he was not prepared to discuss the absolute right of Egypt to Kassala. In fact, he was unwilling to resume the discussion at all so long as Crispi was in office; and in December, perhaps as an indirect way of letting Rome know this, he admitted it to Hatzfeldt.[1]

By October 1890 Crispi needed Kassala to offset the dismal prospect in Ethiopia, where it was becoming very clear that the attempt at indirect control through Menelik had broken down and that if Italy wished to retain her predominance she would have to fight hard for it.[2] But Crispi had always hoped that Kassala would be a base for further expansion in the Sudan, to be achieved by 'parallel action' with the British. At the outset of the Anglo-Italian discussions in March 1890, Crispi had proposed through Tornielli that the two countries should concert their military operations if the Mahdists appeared in force on the shores of the Red Sea. Salisbury had evaded discussion of this proposal, doubtless seeing the direction in which it tended; and Crispi, dissatisfied with Tornielli's report, had instructed dal Verme to sound British military opinion on the subject of 'parallel action'. But dal Verme found that the British were quite unmoved by Italian forecasts of a powerful Mahdist drive towards the coast, and that in any case they desired no partner in the Nile valley and were determined to preserve their full freedom of action—or inaction. He added that if the British public were ever to suspect the full scope of Crispi's aspirations 'a hornets' nest' would be aroused and Italy would have no hope of even the slightest concession.[3]

The more the Ethiopian situation deteriorated, the more attractive to Crispi became the prospect of a military success in the Sudan in collaboration with the British; and after the Naples fiasco he more than once attempted to stimulate Britain into action which would enable him to offer military collaboration. In October 1890 he was con-

[1] Zaghi, 'Conferenza', pp. 666-8. FO 45/647, Dufferin to Salisbury No. 161, 16 Oct. 1890. FO 170/432, Salisbury to Dufferin No. 219A, 15 Oct. G.P. VIII, No. 1981, Hatzfeldt to Caprivi 15 Dec. 1890.

[2] Menelik was already beginning to challenge the Italian interpretation of the Treaty of Uccialli; by Dec. 1890 Antonelli was lamenting that twelve years' work was in ruins and that 'tout était à recommencer' (MAE, *ubi supra*, Lagarde to *Colonies* 7 Dec. 1890; cf. *ibid.*, Menelik to Sadi Carnot 30 Oct. 1890).

[3] FO 141/274, Salisbury to Baring No. 60, 14 Mar. 1890, enclosing Salisbury to Dufferin No. 60, 7 Mar. Zaghi, 'Conferenza', pp. 663-4; 'Problema', pp. 413-7, 432-3, 437-42, citing dal Verme's reports.

templating an arrangement by which Italy would agree to retrocede
Kassala if within a prescribed period either England or Egypt had
re-occupied Khartoum, and if England would guarantee the western
boundary of the Italian sphere—wherever that boundary might then
be. But Crispi seems to have shrunk from actually communicating to
London this remarkable proposal.[1] On 12 November, however, he
attempted by shock tactics to push Salisbury either into military action
or into giving Italy a free hand at Kassala. 'An urgent message' from
Rome announced that 'the Italians are menaced by the Dervishes at
Kassala. Will the English associate themselves with Italy in resisting
this attack? If not, the Italians must defend themselves.' Salisbury
refused to be pushed; but he did not conceal his irritation. Abandoning
the 'civil phrases' with which he was wont to mollify Crispi, he spoke
with blunt severity.

> I did not conceal my regret at the course Signor Crispi was tak-
> ing: or my wonder that he should pursue such a policy, which
> could bring Italy no profit, and could scarcely fail to injure her.
> If a menace from Kassala was to justify him in seizing Kassala,
> a further menace would not be wanting to justify him in
> occupying Khartum.[2]

By December 1890 Crispi was complaining bitterly of England's
cold response to Italy's 'constant and unwavering friendliness'. Salisbury remained unmoved, and approved Dufferin's attitude of being
'at a loss to understand' these accusations.'[3] Dufferin, a *grand seigneur*
who always found it difficult to condescend to African questions, had
little inkling of Crispi's daemonic urge towards imperial expansion
and seems genuinely to have believed that the Kassala dispute was a
trifle.[4] However, in December Salisbury did authorise discussion on
the boundary between the Blue Nile and the Indian Ocean, the sector
which did not include Kassala. This negotiation was complicated by
the existence of a previous agreement, of 3 August 1889, between Italy
and the Imperial British East Africa Company, which Crispi now
wished to modify so as to include Kaffa in the Italian sphere. This
claim was sharply contested by the Company, and Salisbury did not
exert himself to hasten a solution. When Crispi fell from office on 31

---

[1] Zaghi, 'Conferenza', pp. 668-9. There is no trace of this proposal in the London
archives.
[2] FO 45/648, Salisbury to Dufferin tel. No. 56, 12 Nov. 1890. It was found on enquiry
that neither Baring nor the Italian War Ministry knew anything of an immediate threat
to Kassala. The incident did not enhance Crispi's reputation in Roman diplomatic
circles. Cf. Hornik, *op. cit.*, pp. 65-6; Sanderson, *ubi supra*, p. 106.
[3] FO 45/647, Dufferin to Salisbury No. 222, 22 Dec. 1890. FO 45/664, Salisbury to
Dufferin No. 4, 2 Jan. 1891. Cecil, *op. cit.* IV, pp. 377-8, citing Salisbury to Dufferin 7 Jan.
1891. SP Italy, Dufferin to Salisbury 8 Jan.
[4] Indeed, Dufferin believed that Crispi was 'by no means in favour of a forward policy'
and had no intention of advancing to Kassala. He attributed 'the miscarriage at Naples'
to the intransigence of dal Verme rather than of Crispi, and was 'very much startled'
by the incident of 12 Nov. 1890. 'That [Crispi] should now fly in the face of England . . .
seems very extraordinary.' (SP Italy, Dufferin to Salisbury 1 Oct. and 13 Nov. 1890.
FO 45/647, same to same No. 222, 22 Dec. 1890.)

January 1891 the negotiation had already lost itself in a maze of detailed argumentation about the obscure tribal geography of Kaffa.[1]

Although the fall of Crispi was 'a consummation . . . long desired by the Prime Minister', Dufferin was instructed to express to him 'our deep sympathy and regret . . . and our high sense of the friendship and consideration which he has always shown for England'. Civil phrases cost nothing, and some day Crispi might return to office. Meanwhile, Salisbury hastened to profit by the advent of di Rudinì. Dufferin was told to 'hint that if economies are wanted it might be worth while to consider what profit the African expenditure has brought or is likely to bring to Italy'.[2] But di Rudinì needed no prompting. On 14 February he announced a policy of financial and territorial retrenchment in Africa, which was generally understood to imply the restriction of direct Italian activity to the Massawa-Asmara-Keren triangle. On 20 February, in reply to Dufferin's invitation to resume the African negotiation, di Rudinì suggested that the whole frontier from the Red Sea to the Indian Ocean might be settled in one operation. He was, thought Dufferin, anxious 'to be able to say [that] he has settled the matter' and he would probably accept 'the ultimatum which Baring presented to Sr. Crispi' at Naples in October 1890. Three days later Dufferin was unofficially informed that di Rudinì was prepared to meet Salisbury's wishes 'in regard to Kassala and similar matters, as the goodwill of England was in his opinion of far greater importance than any Italian interests that might be connected with these outlying districts.'[3]

Salisbury preferred first to complete the pending negotiation on the southern sector of the frontier. The task did not take long. The East Africa Company still attempted to insist on its claim to Kaffa, which it had no prospect of ever occupying and which Salisbury for his part was perfectly willing to relinquish; but the Company's opposition was now quickly overcome, and on 24 March 1891 a Protocol was signed delimiting the frontier from the Blue Nile to the Indian Ocean.[4] The northern delimitation, from the Blue Nile to Ras Kasar on the Red Sea, was then undertaken and even more speedily settled. Although the Protocol was not actually signed until 15 April, as early as 30 March di Rudinì had agreed to terms 'identical with those proposed by Baring at Naples'. These terms conceded to Italy a temporary military

---

[1] FO 84/2038, Dufferin to Salisbury Africa No. 15, 22 Dec. 1890. FO 170/426, same to same No. 221, 22 Dec. SP Italy, same to same 25 Dec. 1890; 7 and 21 Jan. 1891. FO 84/2131, Currie to Anderson 31 Jan.

[2] Cecil, op. cit. IV, p. 334. FO 45/667, Salisbury to Dufferin tels. No. 2 and 3, 4 Feb., 8 Feb. 1891.

[3] FO 45/667, Dufferin to Salisbury tels. No. 9 and 10, 14 Feb. 1891; No. 15, 23 Feb. SP Italy, Dufferin to Salisbury 20 Feb. G.P. VIII, No. 1982, Solms to Caprivi 3 Mar. 1891; and footnote. C. Zaghi, 'La Conquista di Cassala' (hereafter cited as: Zaghi, 'Conquista'), Nuova Antologia, Oct. 1934, pp. 603-4.

[4] FO 84/2131, F.O. to Dufferin tels. Africa No. 13, 13 Mar. 1891; unnumb., 21 Mar. Ibid., Dufferin to F.O. tel. unnumb., 20 Mar.; tel. Africa No. 1, 24 Mar.; minute by Anderson 2 Mar. Text, Hertslet III, No. 288.

occupation of Kassala, subject to an explicit recognition of Egyptian rights and an obligation to retrocede as soon as 'the Egyptian Government shall be in a position to re-occupy the district in question ... and there to maintain order and tranquillity'. Italy further undertook, if she did occupy Kassala, 'not to construct on the Atbara ... any work which might sensibly modify its flow into the Nile'. But di Rudinì assured Dufferin that 'there was not the slightest chance of the Italians going to Kassala so long as he was in power'.[1] Di Rudinì meant what he said; indeed, his only motive in stipulating for any right to occupy Kassala seems to have been to avoid trouble with the Africanists in the Italian Chamber.[2] Far from wishing to advance to Kassala, he was in fact willing to contemplate the abandonment of all Italy's Eritrean possessions, except perhaps Massawa. The arrangements of 30 March included a secret Agreement—unpublished and apparently unsuspected until 1964—by which Italy undertook, in the event of her retirement from any part of her newly defined sphere outside the Ethiopian frontier, to 'offer no objection to such abandoned territory being permanently occupied by the Egyptian Government'. This arrangement, which ironically enough was never revealed to the Egyptian Government, was embodied in a 'Protocole Séparé' also signed on 15 April 1891.[3]

It has been stated that by the Protocols of 1891 'the most extravagant and ambitious demands of the Italians were met' in order to safeguard the Atbara waters.[4] Even allowing for necessary lack of knowledge of the Secret Protocol, this judgment seems very wide of the mark.[5] Of Crispi's programme for an 'Anglo-Italian Sudan', which may fairly be taken as representing Italy's 'most . . . ambitious demands',[6] nothing whatever had been achieved. In return for the right to occupy Kassala merely as a temporary military convenience, Italy had abandoned all claim to any political foothold within the Nile basin. Further, the territories recognised by Italy as within the 'British sphere' included not only the regions 'as far as the confines of Egypt' which were specified in the Anglo-German Agreement but also, by implication at least, certain Egyptian territories within the

---

[1] SP Italy, Dufferin to Salisbury 30 Mar. and 16 Apr. 1891. FO 45/667, Dufferin to Salisbury tel. No. 24, 15 Apr. Text, Hertslet III, No. 289.

[2] Di Rudinì had despatched the Borgnini-Martini commission to investigate the situation and prospects in East Africa. Its report (*Gazzetta Ufficiale*, 2 Oct. 1891) was remarkably sanguine, and laid particular emphasis on the retention of Agordat as a starting-point for 'parallel action' in the Sudan.

[3] SP Italy, Dufferin to Salisbury 30 Mar. 1891. FO 45/665, same to same No. 65, 15 Apr. 1891, and enclosure. Text printed, Sanderson, *ubi supra*, p. 119. FO 45/664, Salisbury to Dufferin No. 93, 7 May 1891.

[4] Langer, *The Diplomacy of Imperialism*, p. 112.

[5] C. Zaghi, Crispi's most scholarly modern apologist, regards the 1891 arrangements as a severe defeat for Italy. Zaghi, 'Conferenza', p. 669; 'Conquista', p. 607; 'Problema', p. 420. *Idem*, 'I Protocolli italo-britannici del 1891' (hereafter cited as: Zaghi, 'Protocolli'), *Rassegna di Politica Internazionale*, IV (1937), pp. 938–9.

[6] Hornik is not far out, so far as Crispi is concerned, when he states (*op. cit.*, p. 61): 'Um die italienische Afrikapolitik zu verstehen, muss man daran festhalten, dass ihr wichtigstes Objekt der Nil war.'

Sudan. The preamble to the April Protocol announces the intention to complete the delimitation 'of the respective spheres of influence of Great Britain and Italy'; but Article II of the Protocol reserves the rights of the *Egyptian* Government to Kassala and stipulates for its retrocession to Egypt. Nor did the Italians question the assumption by Britain, without even a courtesy mention of the Khedive, of authority to treat on behalf of Egypt.[1] Italy had in effect recognised that Britain had a free hand throughout the Nile valley, and had thrown in the reversion of Eritrea as a *pourboire*. It is not easy to see what more London could have asked or Rome have granted.

The diplomatic protection of the central Sudan was now so complete that the projects of early reconquest, widely canvassed in both London and Cairo during 1890, no longer seemed very relevant. Moreover, even before the conclusion of the Anglo-Italian Protocols, the action against the Mahdists at Tokar had conclusively shown that the fashionable belief in Dervish military decadence was quite unfounded. Baring, who was never very happy about Salisbury's willingness to permit moderate Italian encroachments east of the Red Sea Hills, had pressed very strongly for an advance to Tokar as early as March 1890.[2] On 28 March Salisbury firmly rejected this proposal. It would be unpopular in England: the electorate would 'shrink instinctively from any proposal to advance into the Egyptian desert'. Further, until Baring was ready for general reconquest, such limited and 'merely destructive attacks' would weaken the Mahdists to the profit of Italy, not of England or Egypt. 'Until you have money enough to justify you in advancing to Berber, you had better remain quiet.'[3]

On his return from leave in November 1890 after the 'miscarriage at Naples', Baring renewed his pressure for the Tokar advance. It would, he insisted, greatly alleviate the situation at Suakin; the operation would be safe and easy, and could be controlled so as to prevent the soldiers getting the bit in their teeth. Salisbury was utterly unconvinced, and repeated his previous argument: why harass the Mahdists when they 'are rendering us a service by keeping Italy out'? 'Surely, if you are *not* ready to go to Khartum, this people was created for the purpose of keeping the bed warm for you till you can occupy it.'[4] Baring persisted; Tokar would be a useful observation post from which to detect Italian designs upon Kassala. He was backed by an impressive

[1] The French ambassador at Rome was at pains to point this out to the Quai d'Orsay (D.D.F. VIII, No. 339, Billot to Ribot 17 Apr. 1891). But Ribot addressed no observations either to Rome or to London.
[2] FO 78/4308, Baring to Salisbury No. 87, 15 Mar. 1890. FO 78/4309, same to same Nos. 102, 23 Mar.; 109, 27 Mar.; 110, 28 Mar. FO 78/4313, same to same tel. No. 39, 27 Mar. SP Egypt, same to same, 27 Mar. 1890.
[3] Cecil, *op. cit.* IV, p. 327; Robinson and Gallagher, *Africa and the Victorians*, pp. 286-7 (both citing Salisbury to Baring, private, 28 Mar.). Cf. FO 78/4313, Salisbury to Baring tel. No. 27, 28 Mar. 1890.
[4] FO 78/4312, Baring to Salisbury No. 298, 7 Nov. 1890. Cecil, *op. cit.* IV, pp. 332-3; Robinson and Gallagher, *op. cit.*, pp. 304-5 (both citing Salisbury to Baring 21 Nov. 1890).

weight of military opinion both in England and in Egypt. The Adjutant-General, Sir Redvers Buller, thought that 'from a military point of view the time for the occupation not only of Tokar but of Berber and Khartoum has fully come, and an advance has I fancy been restrained by political, not by military considerations'. In this appreciation, which was typical of much British military thinking in 1890, the Commander-in-Chief concurred.[1] On 7 February 1891 Salisbury gave way, doubtless against his better judgment and mainly because of Baring's reports that the Mahdist garrison at Tokar had recently been very greatly reduced in strength.[2] On 20 February Grenfell, the Sirdar of the Egyptian Army, reported from Suakin that Tokar would be occupied 'with slight opposition if any'. On the following day battle was joined at Afafit. The Mahdist strength proved, in the words of the official account, to be 'curiously at variance with reports received'; and Tokar was taken only after a sharp engagement in which the Egyptian troops suffered severe casualties.[3]

Baring afterwards confessed to Salisbury, 'If I had known how strong the Dervishes were, I should certainly have hesitated to recommend the advance'.[4] In fact Baring's hopes of an early reconquest, always rather a tender plant, withered and died on the dusty plains of Tokar. Even in 1890, Salisbury had been willing to authorise reconquest as soon as Baring was 'financially ready';[5] but as the years went by Baring seemed to become less and less ready. In his Annual Report for 1890, drafted after Tokar, he insisted that 'for some long time to come, it is neither possible nor desirable that the territory under the rule of Egypt should be extended'. Baring was as good as his word. His reports for 1891 and 1892 dismiss all plans for reconquest as 'altogether premature'—'neither possible nor desirable'. In 1893 he insisted that Egypt remain strictly on the defensive; in 1894 and 1895 he did not mention the prospects for reconquest at all.[6] Baring agreed in principle that Egypt must some day reconquer the Sudan—though no further south than Khartoum;[7] but he shrank more and more from an operation which would interfere with the smooth running of his Egyptian administration and might compromise the solvency upon which the whole administrative structure depended. From 1891, down to and even beyond the inauguration of the Egyptian advance in March 1896, all Baring's increasingly powerful influence was exerted against launching a reconquest even of the northern Sudan.

[1] Cecil, op. cit. IV, p. 333, Baring to Salisbury 28 Nov. 1890. FO 78/4319, War Office to F.O. 29 Nov. (for the appreciations of Buller and others). Egypt No. 2 (1892) [C.-6561], No. 1, Grenfell to Baring undated. FO 141/279, Baring to Salisbury tel. No. 137, 21 Dec. 1890.
[2] Egypt No. 2 (1892), Nos. 3, 4, 5, 6, 8, 14 (correspondence, Baring-Salisbury, 23 Jan.–7 Feb. 1891).
[3] Ibid., Nos. 16, 17, 18, 28.   [4] Cecil, op. cit. IV, p. 334.
[5] Ibid., pp. 327, 333, citing Salisbury to Baring 28 Mar. and 21 Nov. 1890.
[6] Egypt No. 3 (1891) [C.-6321]; Egypt No. 3 (1892) [C.-6589]; Egypt No. 3 (1893) [C.-6957] Egypt No. 1 (1894) [C.-7308]; Egypt No. 1 (1895) [C.-7644]; Egypt No. 1 (1896) [C.-7978].
[7] Zetland, Cromer, p. 222, citing Cromer to Kimberley 29 Mar. 1895.

F

Cromer's intense distaste for re-opening 'this abominable Soudan question'[1] was clearly shown in the spring of 1894, when Rosebery appeared for a moment to be listening to renewed proposals by Crispi for 'parallel action'. Crispi had returned to office in December 1893 to find the Ethiopian situation more hopeless than ever. But on 21 December General Arimondi defeated the Mahdists at Agordat; and Crispi again began to dream of an Anglo-Italian Sudan created by military collaboration with the British. In February Tornielli suggested 'parallel action' against 'Uthmān Diqna, the Mahdist leader in the Red Sea Hills; meanwhile, Saminiatelli of the Italian General Staff was sent to Cairo to consult with Cromer. Cromer had no objection to the regular exchange of military information between Suakin and Massawa; but when Saminiatelli hinted that the time was ripe for an Italian occupation of Kassala under the 1891 arrangements, Cromer told him bluntly that this move would be unwelcome. Saminiatelli then proposed a joint Italian and Egyptian advance on Kassala, to operate under the Egyptian flag. This plan Cromer flatly rejected. Much as he disliked independent Italian action at Kassala, he evidently preferred even this to a premature Egyptian advance. Crispi then put forward proposals for purely defensive collaboration, which Rosebery seemed at first inclined to accept; but he ultimately deferred to Cromer's insistence that 'any action had better be independent'.[2]

In 1894 even Cromer was prepared to accept an Italian occupation of Kassala under the 1891 arrangements, without serious misgivings even if with considerable distaste.[3] There could be no more striking tribute to the strength of the diplomatic defences which Salisbury had built. In the Anglo-German Agreement of 1890, using a completely different diplomatic technique, he had achieved an equally satisfactory result. But the very skill and versatility with which Salisbury had reached these African settlements introduced complications into his European diplomacy. Salisbury's combination of freedom of manœuvre with a bias towards the Triple Alliance was possible only so long as he could retain a measure of French confidence by declining to conclude formal alliances with the Triplice Powers. To this end he developed a technique of evasion which made much of 'the misgivings of his colleagues' and 'the fluctuations of British opinion'.[4] But the protection of the Nile waters required specific delimitations; and these

---

[1] Zetland, *Cromer*, p. 221, citing same to same 8 Nov. 1894. (Baring had been created Baron Cromer in May 1892).

[2] G.P. VIII, Nos. 1987-1990, Bülow to Berlin, 30 Jan.-19 Feb. 1894. Shibeika, *British Policy in the Sudan*, pp. 328-30, citing correspond. F.O.-Cairo, F.O.-Rome, Feb.-Apr. 1894. Cf. Zaghi, 'Protocolli', pp. 942-4; Anon., *History of 'The Times'*, III (London 1947), p. 253.

[3] One of Crispi's motives in advancing to Kassala in July 1894 was to force the hand of the British, and he was very irritated when London made no move (G.P. VIII, No. 1996, Bülow to A.A. 21 July 1894). Cf. the Kaiser's comment—'Nun sollte England gegen Chartum losgehen.' (*ibid.*, minute on No. 1997).

[4] He used the first in parrying Italo-German pressure for a closer link with Italy in Apr.-May 1891; the second in refusing Bismarck's offer of a defensive alliance against France in Jan.-Mar. 1889.

had to be embodied in formal treaties with those very Powers whose too close embrace Salisbury was anxious to avoid. Salisbury's skill in combining territorial safeguards for the Nile waters with an actual improvement in relations with Germany and Italy strengthened the natural suspicion that these Agreements contained more than the publicly announced delimitation of spheres. The Anglo-German Agreement, doubtless because it included Heligoland, was particularly suspect to French and Russian diplomatists. Staal at London, Shuvalov and Herbette at Berlin, all thought for a time that it marked the definite adherence of England to the Triple Alliance. Indeed, Staal believed that it marked an Anglo-German entente so complete that it was pointless to speculate on the existence of secret clauses.[1]

However, in 1890 these suspicions had not affected existing alignments. The French reaction to the Anglo-German Agreement had indeed been at first very violent. Salisbury had concealed from the French his negotiation over Zanzibar, where Paris had an interest—admittedly a long-dormant interest—consecrated by a treaty dating as far back as March 1862.[2] The French press, already inflamed by recent British proceedings in Egypt and Newfoundland, for a time talked 'as if we were almost on the eve of war'.[3] But Salisbury, with the tacit co-operation of Ribot at the Quai d'Orsay, was able to demonstrate to the French public, and to Europe, that Germany was not the only Power capable of obtaining a satisfactory African settlement with England. The French obtained the recognition of their Protectorate over Madagascar and a delimitation in West Africa which at the time seemed not ungenerous[4]—and would have seemed more generous still had not Salisbury permitted himself that tactlessly ironical remark about the 'very light land' relinquished to France.[5] It was typical of Salisbury's moderation and balance that he did not ask for a recognition of the Anglo-German Agreement, which would have raised Egyptian issues and thereby frustrated rather than promoted the appeasement of France; while at the same time, to avoid shaking Italian confidence in England, he rejected the French request for a bilateral arrangement on the Tunisian customs duties.[6]

[1] A. Meyendorff (ed.), *Correspondence Diplomatique de M. de Staal*, II (hereafter cited as: Staal, *Correspondence*), (Paris 1929), pp. 88-9, Staal to Giers 1 July 1890. D.D.F. VIII, Nos. 83, 140, Herbette to Ribot 17 June and 5 Aug. 1890.
[2] Salisbury excused himself to the French ambassador by the plea that he had forgotten all about the French interest in Zanzibar; and Waddington was inclined to accept this excuse (D.D.F. VIII, Nos. 91, 132, Waddington to Ribot 21 June and 26 July 1890). But cf. Cecil, *op. cit.* IV, p. 318—the French reaction 'had not been unforeseen', and 'the propitiatory terms to be offered were brought forward with a smooth rapidity which suggested a plan prepared'.
[3] Cecil, *op. cit.* IV, p. 318, citing Lytton to Salisbury 29 June 1890. Apropos of the cession of Heligoland, Ribot remarked to Lytton: 'I suppose you will not mind handing Jersey over to us?'. Cf. D.D.F. VIII, No. 95, Ribot to Waddington 25 June 1890.
[4] The Anglo-French Agreement of 5 Aug. 1890 (Hertslet II, No. 229). As Salisbury said to Waddington, 'J'avais commencé par Tombouctou et j'ai fini à Say.' (D.D.F. VIII, No. 136, Waddington to Ribot 1 Aug. 1890).
[5] Salisbury in the Lords 11 Aug. 1890. Cf. Cecil, *op. cit.* IV, pp. 322-4.
[6] D.D.F. VIII, Nos. 121, 123, 127, Waddington to Ribot 18, 19 and 22 July 1890.

The Anglo-German Agreement had represented, if not a change in British alignments, at least a considered decision not to make such a change—not to seek 'the alliance of France instead of the alliance of Germany'.[1] The Anglo-Italian Protocols of 1891 did not have even this limited importance for Salisbury's general foreign policy. Yet this purely local African settlement initiated a diplomatic chain-reaction which Salisbury found himself quite unable to halt, and which ultimately produced a major and very unwelcome change in the European balance of power.

Di Rudinì's distaste for the hazardous and spendthrift Italian adventure in East Africa was of course common knowledge; but this was not the only motive for his sweeping concessions to England in March 1891. On 30 March, à propos of the Secret Protocol, Dufferin had 'happened to say to Rudinì that the best thing Italy could do would be to get out of [East] Africa altogether, to which he replied that he quite agreed and that he would like nothing better than to surrender the whole of Eritrea to us "for a consideration" '. The 'consideration' which di Rudinì had in mind was a formal and binding agreement for mutual defence in the western and central Mediterranean.[2] Di Rudinì was already engaged in discussions with Paris through which he hoped, by holding out quite illusory hopes that Italy would weaken her links with the Triplice, to bring the French to relax the severe and very effective pressure on the Italian economy by which they had retaliated against Italy's unfriendly diplomatic alignment.[3] His ultimate object, as the French shrewdly discerned, was to 'bénéficier à la fois de l'appui militaire de l'Allemagne et du concours financier de la France'.[4] In this quest he had already been forced to give some dangerously misleading impressions both at Paris and at Berlin. A fully fledged naval alliance with Britain would be a valuable insurance against his duplicity being unmasked; meanwhile, it would help to convince the already suspicious Germans that Italy did not contemplate any real change in her alignments.[5]

The manœuvres of di Rudinì at Paris did not extract any economic concessions from the French, but they did make the Germans so uneasy that they quickly took up his offer to renew the Triple Alliance in May 1891, a year ahead of its expiry. Di Rudinì, who was as greedy for empire in north Africa as he was indifferent to it on the Red Sea, insisted that the renewed alliance should bind Germany to support Italy in a possible occupation of Cyrenaica, Tripolitania and Tunisia.

[1] L.Q.V. 3, i, pp. 613-4, Salisbury to the Queen 10 June 1890.
[2] SP Italy, Dufferin to Salisbury 30 March 1891.
[3] The principal French weapons were prohibitive duties on Italian wines and silks; and an embargo on Stock Exchange dealings in Italian government stocks.
[4] D.D.F. VIII, No. 259, Billot to Ribot 14 Feb. 1891. This episode was represented by di Rudinì to the Germans as a French attempt to increase the financial pressure upon Italy. Langer, working from Die Grosse Politik, accepted this account (W. L. Langer, The Franco-Russian Alliance [Cambridge, Mass. 1929], pp. 151-8). But the published French documents tell a very different story.
[5] For details, Sanderson, ubi supra, pp. 109-12.

This commitment had no attractions for Berlin; but the Wilhelm-strasse recognised that 'the surest way of preventing Italy from falling into the arms of France is to foster Italian aspirations in North Africa', and finally compromised by making the German engagement conditional, in fact if not in form, on the acceptance of a similar engagement by England. Di Rudinì also asked for German support in pressing the British for a naval alliance; Berlin agreed at once, feeling that such an alliance would be the best possible insurance against any repetition of the recent disturbing vagaries of Italian policy. Meanwhile, to coincide with the publication of the Anglo-Italian Protocols, di Rudinì launched a campaign of rumour and innuendo designed to give the impression that England was already completely committed to Italy in the Mediterranean.[1]

Di Rudinì never got his naval agreement. Indeed, Salisbury was so disturbed by 'these extraordinary stories as to special engagements between Italy and England' that he refused the invitation to meet di Rudinì at Ventimiglia which both Rome and Berlin were pressing upon him.[2] But the 'extraordinary stories' evoked persistent enquiries in the House of Commons. The Foreign Office could and did deny that any binding military or naval agreements existed; but it was forced to confirm that an exchange of Notes had taken place in 1887 and to give a forthright pledge of support for Italy in the maintenance of the Mediterranean *status quo*. Berlin and Vienna agreed that the Italian request for a regular alliance had lost much of its point in view of this parliamentary demonstration of solidarity, and that it would be unwise to risk a refusal by pressing it. To console di Rudinì for his failure, Salisbury sent the Mediterranean fleet on a courtesy tour of Italian ports.[3]

Le flirt anglo-triplicien, the traditional nickname for these transactions, is evidently a misnomer. There was no flirtation; only a rather clumsy attempt at seduction. Nevertheless, di Rudinì, by his graceful concessions in East Africa, by his effusive gestures and above all by his calculated indiscretions to which it was impossible to reply by a complete *démenti*, had contrived to create the illusion that his advances were being reciprocated. On 16 June Salisbury lamented that 'we have been unable so to frame our answers as to avoid giving the impression that we are more "Tripliste" than people thought; and France is consequently out of humour'.[4] The French were more than out of humour; they were seriously alarmed. On 23 June Ribot instructed his ambassador at London to sound Salisbury about the content of the 1887 Agreements. Salisbury attempted reassurance by

[1] *Ibid.*, pp. 112-3. The quotation is from a memoir by Caprivi 15 May 1890 (G.P. VIII, No. 1862).
[2] Cecil, *op. cit.* IV, p. 379, Salisbury to the Queen 17 Apr. 1891. Cf. N. Rich and M. H. Fisher, *The Holstein Papers; III Correspondence* (Cambridge 1961), pp. 378-9, Hatzfeldt to Holstein 14 Apr. 1891.
[3] Sanderson, *ubi supra*, pp. 113-5.
[4] Cecil, *op. cit.* IV, p. 381, Salisbury to Lytton 16 June 1891.

denying the existence of any obligation linked to the presumptive *casus foederis* of the Triple Alliance. He tried to convince Waddington that the Agreements had so far worked to the positive advantage of France by 'keeping the Italians within bounds' and by shoring up the Ottoman Empire.[1] But the effect of Salisbury's soothing words was more than neutralised when in July the German Emperor's state visit to England coincided with the presence of the Mediterranean fleet at the launching of a new Italian battleship by King Humbert.[2]

The French were not alone in their disquiet. To the Russians, the Kaiser's brilliantly successful visit seemed a clear demonstration of England's new alignment. What St Petersburg feared was not so much the 'flirtation' with Italy as the full adherence of England to the Triple Alliance. England would hardly have joined without some firm understanding about Constantinople and the Straits; if Berlin was now prepared to back an Anglo-Austrian solution of this question, the outlook for Russia was bleak indeed.[3] By the first week of July the Russian Court had become convinced, in spite of the scepticism of its London ambassador, that British adherence was already an accomplished fact.[4] On 23 July, the day on which the visiting French naval squadron reached Cronstadt, Paris accepted the Russian proposals to 'faire un pas de plus dans la voie de l'entente'; and they mentioned as the principal cause of their disquiet the supposed increase of intimacy between England and Italy.[5]

Salisbury still attempted to demonstrate 'that England [had] no antipathy to France or any partisanship against her'.[6] The Queen was persuaded to postpone the normally immutable date of her departure for Balmoral, and a grant was even extorted from the Treasury, in order to welcome and entertain the French squadron on its way home from Cronstadt. All in vain.[7] In 1891 Salisbury's skill in negotiating settlements with friendly rivals in Africa incurred the penalty which he had foreseen and avoided in 1890. The Anglo-Italian arrangements must indeed have seemed a harmless enough affair. Even had Salisbury known more than he did about di Rudinì's manœuvres at Paris and Berlin, he might well have reckoned that Crispi's return to office with the Kassala question still unsettled would be a greater hazard than the possible European repercussions of so purely local an agree-

---

[1] D.D.F. VIII, No. 386, Ribot to Waddington 23 June 1891; No. 390, Waddington to Ribot 25 June.

[2] *Ibid.*, No. 421, report of d'Estournelles de Constant, enclosed in Waddington to Ribot 14 July 1891. Cf. Sanderson, *ubi supra*, pp. 115-6.

[3] Cf. Shuvalov's comment on the published Bases of the Anglo-German Agreement of 1890: 'On compte . . ., à Londres, barrer le chemin de notre politique traditionnelle en Orient' (D.D.F. VIII, No. 83, Herbette to Ribot 17 June 1890).

[4] Staal, *Correspondance*, pp. 137-8, 140-1: Giers to Staal 29 May 1891; Staal to Giers 16 June, 1 July and 14 July 1891. D.D.F. VIII, No. 415, Vauvineux to Ribot 9 July 1891.

[5] D.D.F. VIII, No. 430, Laboulaye to Ribot 20 July 1891; No. 434, *Projet de Note pour le Gouvernement russe*, 23 July.

[6] L.Q.V. 3, ii, pp. 64-5, Salisbury to the Queen 22 Aug. 1891.

[7] D.D.F. VIII, No. 431, Waddington to Ribot 21 July 1891. Sanderson, *ubi supra*, pp. 117-8.

ment. Yet had the Kassala dispute remained unsettled, di Rudinì could hardly have launched his campaign for a regular Anglo-Italian alliance. Without the atmosphere of 'flirtation' engendered by that campaign, St Petersburg would certainly not have read so sinister a significance into the Kaiser's visit to England and would not have been prompted to make so definite a proposal to the French. Like a single pebble which starts a landslide, Salisbury's African settlement with Italy set in motion forces which led to the formal Franco-Russian alliance which he was particularly anxious to avert and which was itself ultimately to play a part of some importance in the diplomatic history of the Upper Nile.

V

THE ASCENDANCY OF KING LEOPOLD

I—THE CHALLENGE TO THE BRITISH

1888–94

TO the problems presented by potential German and Italian encroachment on the Nile, Salisbury had found elegant and effective diplomatic solutions. But in 1892 he discovered, two years too late, that he had been outwitted by King Leopold; and although by this time the King was an actual and not merely a potential trespasser on the British sphere, Salisbury was forced to bequeath the Anglo-Congolese dispute as an unsolved problem to his successor Rosebery. Some of Leopold's diplomatic techniques must have been disconcerting to Salisbury, though they are familiar enough today. In local African disputes the King was not slow to resort to force or threats of force; but at the same time he exploited his own modest political status to pose as the victim of bullying Great Powers. He made extensive use of spies and secret agents, some of them hired mercenaries, others unwitting tools. He was not fastidious in choosing his means of pressure or persuasion; nor did he shrink from arousing the lasting resentment of those he blackmailed or duped, so long as he gained his immediate point. In short, he broke most of the rules of the diplomatic game as it was played, between European Powers at least, in the Bismarck-Salisbury era. He was able to do so with impunity because the conflict of greater Powers in Africa, which had indeed generated the Congo State itself, usually protected him from reprisals. Like some of the 'non-aligned' states today, and for fundamentally similar reasons, Leopold had little to lose and much to gain by pursuing a policy that was in appearance provocative to the point of utter recklessness. Salisbury and Rosebery were baffled by Leopold in much the same way as the Western diplomatists of today often find themselves baffled by a Sukarno or a Jamāl 'Abd al-Nāsir.

King Leopold's greatest strength, however, lay in the widespread failure to take the Congo State seriously as a political force. In 1887 the Foreign Office had been serenely incurious about Leopold's motives for intervention in the Emin Pasha Expedition. In 1890 Salisbury treated him as a mere makeweight in African diplomacy and indeed, indirectly, in British domestic politics.[1] Meanwhile, the King had not been idle in his drive for the Bahr al-Ghazal and the Upper Nile, and Stanley's expedition was only one of several irons in the fire. As early as 1886 he had commissioned Alphonse Vangele to explore the Upper Ubangi. By June 1890 the Congo State had a post at Yakoma, on the M'Bomu-Uele confluence; and a treaty with the important Nzakara chief Bangasso, whose territory extended north-wards from the M'Bomu towards the Nile watershed.[2] In the summer of 1888 Leopold hatched a project, which came to nothing, for pushing forward the Zanzibari Tippo Tip from the 'Arab Zone' of the Congo State to occupy the Bahr al-Ghazal on the State's behalf.[3] Later in the same year, prompted by Carl Peters' Emin Pasha agitation, he turned to Berlin with proposals for the neutralisation of the Upper Nile under Congolese trusteeship as a means of obviating Anglo-German friction. He even suggested that Berlin should do him a favour by ceding Witu to England 'à condition que les Anglais renoncent à étendre leur influence à la rive gauche du Nil'![4]

These projects were intended to insure against the total failure of Stanley's expedition, or against its possible subordination to purely British interests.[5] Leopold's proposals to Berlin were not of course accepted; but they were not quite so absurd as they may appear. In the autumn of 1888 the Germans had their hands full with Abushiri's revolt, and might well wish to guard against new complications with England in the interior. Nor was Leopold's approach to Germany entirely without result. The joint Anglo-German blockade of the Zanzibari mainland dominions was of course an operation of war against Abushiri; but its official pretext was the suppression of the slave trade. When Leopold was asked by Berlin to participate by suppressing the traffic in arms from the Arab Zone of the Congo State to the German hinterland, he at once consented; but at the same time he suggested that Germany might request him to operate against the internal slave trade by preventing 'la sortie des esclaves allant au Soudan par le Bahr el Gazal'.[6] When Gordon had momentarily taken service under Leopold at the beginning of 1884, he had pressed strongly for a Congolese occupation of the Bahr al-Ghazal as a measure against the slave trade; and the King himself now stated that he wished to act 'conformément aux conseils de Gordon'.[7] Berlin

[1] Supra, Ch. II, pp. 34-6; infra, pp. 93-4.
[2] B.C.B., 5 vols. (Brussels, 1948-); I, Bangasso, Milz, Roget; II, Vangele. L. Lotar, La Grande Chronique du Bomu (Brussels 1940), pp. 7-14, 28-30. A. Thuriaux-Hennebert, 'L'expédition du commissaire de district L. Roget au nord de l'Uele', Bulletin de l'Académie Royale des Sciences d'Outremer (Brussels), New Series, VIII, 4 (1962), pp. 559-79.
[3] Ceulemans, La Question Arabe, pp. 153-62.
[4] Ibid., pp. 137-41.
[5] Cf. ibid., pp. 112-7.
[6] Leopold to Greindl 8 Nov. 1888. Fuller accounts and detailed references at: G. N. Sanderson, 'Leopold II and the Nile Valley, 1880-1906', Proc. Sud. Hist. Assoc., I, VI (1955), pp. 12-17; Ceulemans, op. cit., pp. 142-6. Both these accounts are based on the Belgian documents published in D.K. XXVII (June 1916), pp. 135-61.
[7] Leopold to Eetvelde 4 Nov. 1888 (Sanderson, ubi supra).

raised no objection to the King's proposal. Bismarck accepted, and indeed published in a White Book, a Congolese Note of 30 November 1888 which stated that 'measures have been taken for the occupation of those points the possession of which appears to be essential for the achievement of the objective indicated by the Imperial Government'.[1] Leopold now had a humanitarian cover, officially approved by Berlin, for his projects of Nilotic expansion; and on 30 December 1888 he sent orders to Stanley to occupy 'a few suitable places' in the Bahr al-Ghazal.[2]

In the summer of 1888, with the British East Africa Company's charter in the offing, Leopold had begun to work for a delimitation between his own sphere and that of the Company on the Upper Nile.[3] Mackinnon himself was so completely under the King's influence that his personal activities caused little disquiet; but Leopold suspected some of the Company's directors of a design to take over, with Emin's assistance, the Mangbetu country on the upper Uele. Desultory discussions between Leopold and Mackinnon took place in 1888 and 1889; but in April 1890 a regular negotiation was launched in which Stanley, previously briefed by the King, acted as Congolese negotiator.[4] In the third week of May a draft treaty was concluded, and was submitted to Salisbury for approval on the 18th. The Congo State obtained access to Lake Albert, and the Company access to the Ruwenzori region; more important, the Company recognised the 'sovereign rights' of the State on the west bank of the Nile as far north as Lado, while Leopold recognised the Company's 'sovereign rights' over a corridor of territory from Uganda to Lake Tanganyika. On 19 May Salisbury minuted that the Agreement 'is complete and is only waiting for F.O. sanction', and directed that 'it should be examined in the office: copied: and returned with our approval to the King ... with as little delay as possible'.[5] On the 21st he told the King in writing that 'no objections will be raised on the part of the Foreign Office to the engagements which have been entered into by Your Majesty ... and Sir William Mackinnon's Company'. He repeated these assurances verbally to Leopold, who was then in London.[6] Meanwhile, the relevant documents were duly docketed and the transaction treated, so far as can be seen, as fully 'official'.

---

[1] German White Book No. 4 of 1888-9.

[2] Ceulemans, op. cit., p. 116.

[3] From about May 1888, the question of the Upper Nile seems to have taken on a new urgency in Leopold's eyes. Cf. Leopold's correspondence with Banning, Ledeganck, Stanley and Strauch, May-July 1888, cited Ceulemans, op. cit., pp. 113-6, 130-8.

[4] Ibid., pp. 113-5, 121, 131-3, 137, 278. D. Stanley (ed.), The Autobiography of Sir Henry Morton Stanley, G.C.B. (London 1909), pp. 412-4. M. Luwel, 'Catalogue des manuscrits exposés lors de la commémoration H. M. Stanley', Bull. I.R.C.B. xxv,5 (1954), plate facing p. 1421 (facsimile of drafts by Leopold and Stanley).

[5] FO 84/2082, two undated drafts; minute by Salisbury 19 May 1890.

[6] Ibid., Salisbury to Leopold 21 May 1890. Cf. FO 10/604, memo. by Salisbury 6 Feb. 1893; L. Guebels, 'Rapport sur le dossier J. Greindl', Bull. I.R.C.B. xxiv, 2 (1953), pp. 607-10, printing Leopold to Greindl 10 Oct. 1892.

The 'Mackinnon Treaty'[1] is a very clumsily drafted document; nor is it easy to see how a mere Company, however Imperial or Chartered, could either cede or acquire 'sovereign rights'. Salisbury's hasty approval of this strange transaction seems to have been prompted by the need to appease Mackinnon and the Cape-to-Cairo enthusiasts, lest they should wreck his delicate negotiations with Germany. It was only on 21 May, after he had approved the creation of a British corridor through Congolese territory, that he conceded the German-Congolese common frontier to Hatzfeldt.[2] By 27 May Anderson had become very uneasy about this apparent hoodwinking of the Germans.[3] Salisbury ignored this warning: he was before long to tell Berlin that the Mackinnon Treaty was not to be taken seriously, and to give a solemn assurance that the corridor would never be occupied.[4] He was more impressed by Anderson's warning that an outright cession of the corridor to the Company might enable the French to invoke their 'right of preference'—a right, recognised by the Congo State in April 1884, which gave France the first refusal when the King wished to cede Congolese territory.[5] The last thing Salisbury wanted, in May and June 1890, was to give France a pretext for disrupting the delicate web of his African negotiations.

Mackinnon was therefore warned on 31 May that 'it would be injudicious . . . to accept any formal cession of territory in view of the French treaty rights. But this objection would not apply to a concession as to a private Cy.'. The Agreement should therefore be re-drafted; but Mackinnon was assured that 'the principle of the agreement would meet with no objection on the part of H.M.G.'.[6] On 2 June Mackinnon replied that it was impossible to alter the treaty, as Leopold expected ratifications to be exchanged forthwith. On the same day the East Africa Company notified to Salisbury its refusal to accept any Anglo-German settlement which did not provide access to Lake Tanganyika from Uganda.[7] On 3 June the Cabinet threw out Salisbury's proposed settlement with Germany in favour of the Stanley-Mackinnon claims

[1] The 'treaty' in its final form, which does not differ significantly from the drafts submitted to Salisbury, is printed at *D.K.*, *ubi supra*, p. 142. Some of the subsequent correspondence between Leopold and Salisbury is printed *ibid.*, pp. 142-3.

[2] G.P. viii, No. 1678, Hatzfeldt to A.A. 22 May 1890. Hatzfeldt suspected that Salisbury had reached some arrangement with the Congo State (*D.K.*, *ubi supra*, p. 143, citing Hatzfeldt to Marschall 25 May 1890).

[3] FO 84/2086, memo. by Anderson 27 May 1890.

[4] Statements to this effect were made in June 1894 to Malet both by the Emperor and by Marschall; and they were never contradicted by London. FO 64/1333, Malet to Kimberley No. 70, 9 June 1894; G.P. viii, No. 2047, the Emperor to Caprivi 11 June 1894.

[5] FO 84/2086, *ubi supra*. For the 'right of preference', see Hertslet ii, No. 151. In Apr. 1887 the Congo State had asserted that this right 'could not be opposed to that of Belgium'; France had 'taken note of', without formally accepting, this declaration (Hertslet ii, No. 155; cf. *infra*, Ch. vi, pp. 134-6). In 1890 the Foreign Office seems still to have been unaware of what had passed in Apr. 1887.

[6] FO 84/2086, minute by Salisbury on Anderson's memo. of 27 May; minute by Anderson of conversation with Kemball 30 May. FO 84/2082, Sanderson to Mackinnon 31 May 1890.

[7] FO 84/2083, Mackinnon to Sanderson 2 June 1890; Kemball to Anderson 2 June.

to the west of Lake Victoria. In April Salisbury had refused Mackinnon an interview to discuss East African affairs; on 3 June he begged Mackinnon to call on him.[1] It was agreed that the Mackinnon Treaty should be ratified forthwith as it stood; but that there should be annexed to it an 'explanatory paper . . . making it clear that the Congo State was not making any cession of territory which might entail interference from France'. So great was Salisbury's anxiety to appease Mackinnon that he insisted to Anderson that this 'Additional Declaration' must not limit the Company's rights 'more than is indispensable to protect the Congo State from French reclamations'.[2] On 7 June Mackinnon announced that he had on the 3rd ratified his treaty, availing himself 'of the permission Your Lordship had just given me'. On 7 June, also, he notified the withdrawal of his Company's objections to the proposed settlement with Germany.[3]

In his minutes of the interview with Mackinnon on 3 June, Anderson had noted that after the signature of the Additional Declaration 'a letter would be written to the Co. giving the approval of the Government which is a condition of the validity of the Agreement'; and he prefaced his draft of the Declaration by a preamble which ran: '. . . in the event of the approval of the British Government being given to this agreement, that approval will be subject to the condition . . .', et cetera. But the Declaration had to be submitted to Leopold as well as to the Company; and Salisbury therefore deleted Anderson's preamble. Indeed, on 9 June he reiterated to Leopold that 'there is nothing [in the treaty] to which the British Foreign Office is entitled to object', and merely suggested that Anderson's draft Declaration be appended in order to protect the Congo State from 'embarrassing claims on the part of France'.[4] The King concurred, but submitted a counter-draft designed to escape any implied admission that the French right of preference applied to exchanges of territory.[5] By 18 July the wording of the Declaration had been agreed, King Leopold had formally notified his willingness to sign it, and the Company had been informed of these facts.[6] But on 24 July Mackinnon, who had just returned from Brussels, told Anderson that Leopold was 'much disturbed about the French claims'. Leopold was at that time under heavy French pressure to declare explicitly that the right of preference applied to all types of cession, including exchanges. Apparently because of Leopold's diffi-

---

[1] *Supra*, Ch. III, pp. 60-2. Robinson and Gallagher, *Africa and the Victorians*, p. 307, citing Mackinnon to Salisbury 8 Apr. 1890 and Salisbury's minute thereon. Cf. L.Q.V. 3, i, pp. 595-7, Mackinnon to Ponsonby 14 Apr. 1890.
[2] FO 84/2082, record by Anderson of the meeting with Mackinnon on 3 June 1890; minute thereon by Salisbury.
[3] FO 84/2083, Mackinnon to Salisbury 7 June 1890 (two separate letters).
[4] FO 84/2082, draft by Anderson 4 June 1890; FO 84/2083, Salisbury to Leopold 9 June 1890, and enclosure.
[5] FO 84/2084, Leopold to Salisbury 22 June 1890.
[6] FO 84/2085, Salisbury to Leopold 9 July 1890. FO 84/2086, Currie to Mackinnon 10 July; Leopold to Salisbury 12 July; Salisbury to Leopold 18 July; F.O. to Mackinnon 18 July 1890.

culties, Mackinnon was no longer enthusiastic about the Treaty, and his fellow-directors were 'now disposed to think that their best plan will be to cancel [it]'. Anderson, who must have been expressing Salisbury's views, 'encouraged this idea, saying that perhaps that might be the simplest way of solving the difficulty'.[1]

On this inconclusive note the transaction ends. The Additional Declaration remained unsigned, for Salisbury never formally called upon Leopold to sign it. The Company for its part never formally cancelled the Agreement but, according to Anderson, they 'always considered [it] as null and void', and never attempted to occupy the corridor ceded—or perhaps 'conceded'—to them.[2] The oddest feature of the Agreement, however, was one which provoked no discussion whatever in 1890—the proposal to hand over to Leopold a large and ill-defined sphere on the Upper Nile. It seems usually to be assumed that Salisbury was already seeking to insure against French encroachments, and that the Mackinnon Treaty was an—admittedly defective —preliminary sketch for the Anglo-Congolese Agreement of May 1894. But in May 1890 there was no shadow of a French threat to the Upper Nile; this problem did not even begin to preoccupy the African Department until the middle of 1892.[3] It was certainly not like Salisbury to guard against remote and hypothetical contingencies by immediate and far-reaching cessions of territory.[4] Moreover, the installation of Leopold in full sovereignty—a provision against which Salisbury raised not a word of objection in 1890—might in certain circumstances actually present the French, through their right of preference, with a valid claim to territory within the Nile basin.

This apparent *insouciance* is however quite explicable if Salisbury never intended the Mackinnon Treaty to have any permanent validity, and regarded it simply as a means of keeping Mackinnon quiet until the Anglo-German Agreement was safely in his pocket. The precise rights granted *by* the Congo State to the Company had to be carefully defined, lest their incautious formulation should provoke an *immediate* and very embarrassing protest from France. But the assertion of the French right of preference in the territory ceded *to* the Congo State was a remote contingency which could only arise if Leopold should at some future date wish to dispose of these regions. It could never arise at all if meanwhile the Mackinnon Treaty had been invalidated and Leopold deprived of his title. Salisbury seems to have intended from the outset to prevent any occupation of the corridor by the Company, and he undoubtedly gave the Germans assurances to this effect. This would in itself provide a pretext, if not a very strong

[1] FO 84/2087, Anderson, 25 July 1890, record of conversation with Mackinnon on the 24th. For Leopold's difficulties with the French, see *infra*, Ch. VI, *loc. cit.*
[2] FO 84/2200, minute by Anderson 8 Mar. 1892, on Vivian to Salisbury No. 9, 3 Mar. 1892 (FO 84/2201).
[3] *Infra*, p. 97.
[4] 'I will wait till I *am* a tiger', Salisbury once retorted when someone asked him what he would do in hypothetical circumstances (Cecil, *Salisbury* IV, pp. 87-8).

one, for considering the treaty as void, and forbidding a Congolese occupation on the Upper Nile. Better, so long as the Additional Declaration remained unsigned (and Salisbury carefully refrained from reminding Leopold to sign it), the arrangement could be invalidated on the ground that it was incomplete. The confused drafting of the Agreement and its undoubtedly illegal assertion of the Company's authority to deal in 'sovereign rights' were also weapons in Salisbury's hand. The more vices of form and substance the Mackinnon Treaty contained, the easier it would be to brush aside once it had served its purpose.

Once the Anglo-German Agreement had been concluded, Salisbury made short work of Mackinnon's Central African corridor. In his Lords speech of 10 July—the day after he had approved Leopold's counter-draft of the Additional Declaration!—he launched a withering attack upon the Cape-to-Cairo enthusiasts, with their 'very curious idea which had lately become prevalent', and upon corridors in particular:

> . . . I can imagine no more uncomfortable position than the
> possession of a narrow strip of territory in the very heart of
> Africa three months' distance from the coast, which should be
> separating the forces of a powerful empire like Germany and
> [of the Congo State]. Without any advantages of position we
> should have had all the dangers inseparable from its defence.[1]

Salisbury seems to have used Leopold throughout merely as a means of pacifying Mackinnon, and to have regarded him as a completely negligible quantity. Two years later he was to rue this error and to recognise—too late—that the King-Sovereign's claims could not be brushed aside so unceremoniously as those of Mackinnon. Leopold had been quite shrewd enough to see which way the wind was blowing in July 1890. Instead of repeating his offer to sign the Additional Declaration—a proposal which would doubtless by now have been received evasively in London—he launched a major expedition to the Upper Nile, with Wadelai and Lado as its objectives. While other Powers drew frontiers round the Upper Nile on paper, King Leopold was going to stake his claim on the spot.

Advanced elements of the Van Kerckhoven expedition, which had a strength of twenty European officers and 500 African rank-and-file, left Marseilles as early as 10 August 1890.[2] Exactly two years later the expedition had reached the Nile watershed. In October 1892 it took into Congolese service the remnant of Emin Pasha's troops which had

---

[1] Cited Robinson and Gallagher, *op. cit.*, p. 296. Cf. Cecil, *op. cit.* IV, pp. 300, 322-3.
[2] Leopold had begun his preparations even before the signature of the Mackinnon Treaty (Ceulemans, *op. cit.*, p. 283).

For a detailed account of this expedition, with full source-references, see: G. N. Sanderson, *Anglo-French Competition for the Control of the Upper Basin of the Nile, 1890-99* (London; unpubl. Ph.D. thesis, 1959), pp. 119-31. Cf. *eundem*, 'Contributions from African Sources to the History of European Competition in the Upper Valley of the Nile', *J.A.H.* III, 1 (1962), pp. 69-90; Collins, *The Southern Sudan*, pp. 94-121.

remained at Wadelai under the command of Fadl al-Mūla. But after this promising start the expedition met increasingly serious difficulties. Relations with Fadl al-Mūla did not prosper, especially when the Sudanese learned that they were to re-occupy the posts to the north of Wadelai and to hold them against any Mahdist attack, while the Congolese concentrated their forces in comparative security on the Nile-Congo divide. By January 1893 the outlook was so unpromising that the Congolese commander (now Delanghe) postponed in-definitely any advance on Lado; the Congolese regulars had already been pulled back from Ganda on the watershed to Niangara in the Uele valley. The local inhabitants, at first terrorised by the expedition's ruthless suppression of all resistance, were now exasperated into retaliation as the Congolese and their Zande irregulars ate the country bare. So far the Mahdists had not been encountered, but by the summer of 1893 there were rumours of their return to Equatoria. News that there were whites in the far south had indeed reached the Khalifa early in 1893. He at once ordered 'Umar Sālih to advance from Bor and to re-take Rejaf. By April 'Umar Sālih had occupied Rejaf; by June the Mahdists were fully informed of the strength and location of the Congolese and were preparing to drive these 'enemies of God' out of the Nile valley.

Delanghe, who had returned to Ganda in May, chose this un-propitious moment to advance to the Nile itself. He was about to be relieved, and he seems to have feared that his relief intended to rob him of the honour of being the first to hoist the Congolese flag on the river. Ignoring orders to withdraw all regulars from the Nile basin and concentrate them at Niangara, Delanghe founded posts in July and August on the Nile at Muggi and Laboré. But with the whole country now aroused against the Congolese and the Mahdist threat rapidly developing, these posts were utterly untenable and by the end of September Delanghe had been forced to evacuate both of them. The inevitable withdrawal to the Uele, which could have been carried out in good order had Delanghe obeyed his instructions in July, had by now become a desperately hazardous operation. The local tribes-men now attacked the Congolese whenever they emerged from their stockades; and the retreats from the Nile to Ganda in October, and from Ganda to Mundu on the Uele in December, were continuous running fights in which the Congolese suffered heavy casualties. Early in 1894 their principal Zande ally, Chief Renzi, turned against them. The irregulars mutinied, killed their officers, ambushed isolated parties and even attacked Congolese posts.

In March 1894 Renzi and the mutineers laid siege to Mundu, and enforced a further Congolese retreat. By this time the Congolese position on the upper Uele was almost as precarious as it had been on the Upper Nile six months earlier; and now the long-threatened Mahdist offensive took place. In January 1894 'Arabi Dafa'allāh, the newly appointed Governor of Equatoria, marched out against Fadl al-Mūla, and annihilated the 'rebel' who had dared to support 'the enemies of God, the Christians'. In the summer of 1894 'Arabi's lieutenant, al-Tāhir 'Adnān, invaded the Uele valley and for some months threatened Niangara itself. The Mahdists were not expelled from the Uele valley until December 1894; and Congolese casualties were so heavy that this seems to have been a Pyrrhic victory for them. It certainly did not restore Congolese military prestige among the Azande; on the day *after* the decisive battle, Renzi announced that he considered himself henceforth independent both of the Mahdists and of the Congolese. The days were gone when the mere presence of a modest Congolese detachment sufficed to secure the submission and co-operation of the Azande. Indeed, Zande resistance was not completely suppressed until April 1896. Meanwhile, Leopold's plans for a second and more permanent occupation of the Upper Nile were frustrated.

The British did not learn of the near-disaster which had befallen King Leopold's Nile expedition in 1893 and 1894 until it was too late for the information to be of any use to them. But early in 1892 they discovered its probable destination and launched the first of a series of quite fruitless protests against it. On 19 February 1892 Lord Vivian, the British minister at Brussels, was instructed to demand an assurance that the expedition would remain within the conventional frontiers of the Congo State (in this region the fourth parallel and the thirtieth meridian) and, in particular, that 'no attempt will be made to extend the dominion of the State over the western watershed of the Nile'.[1] Leopold professed bewilderment. He pointed out that he was acting within his rights under the Mackinnon Treaty; if Salisbury now wished him to sign the Additional Declaration which had been agreed in July 1890, he was perfectly willing to do so. He also drew attention to the assurances personally given to him by Salisbury on 21 May 1890. Vivian could not rebut these arguments, for his archives contained neither the Mackinnon Treaty itself nor the relevant correspondence.[2] Salisbury, for his part, seemed to have forgotten what had passed in May 1890. On 8 March 1892 he minuted: 'I don't think the cession of land near Lado was in the draft I saw', whereupon Anderson produced the draft which Salisbury had originally approved.[3] The Mackinnon Treaty had come home to roost.

With the Mombasa railway project at a standstill and the East Africa Company preparing to evacuate Uganda at the end of the year, there was no hope of competing with Leopold on the spot. Nothing remained but to repudiate the assurances of 1890 and to attempt this particularly ungracious task of trying to keep 'other people out of

[1] FO 84/2200, Salisbury to Vivian No. 24, 19 Feb. 1892.
[2] FO 84/2201, Vivian to Salisbury No. 9, 3 Mar. 1892.
[3] FO 84/2200, minutes by Anderson and Salisbury 8 and 10 Mar. 1892, on Vivian's No. 9 of 3 Mar.

savage territory which we are unable to occupy ourselves'. In a despatch of 19 March 1892 the Foreign Office denied that the Mac-kinnon Treaty had ever been anything more than an informal 'basis of an arrangement between the State and the Chartered Company', and asserted that even in this humble role it 'was inchoate only, and [had] never been completed' by the signature of the Additional Declaration. But Leopold could easily have met these objections by offering to sign the Additional Declaration and to accept something less than full sovereignty in the Nile valley. The Foreign Office there-fore attempted to empty the treaty of all meaning by asserting that even if it had been completed and were now in full force, it could have recognised Congolese authority on the Nile only 'if such authority were legitimately established there'. But all prospect of such legitimate establishment had disappeared as from 1 July 1890, when the disputed region had been recognised as in the British sphere. It was 'con-sequently . . . not open to the occupation of a Foreign State'.[1] The Congolese reply of 23 April did not attempt to rebut these disingenuous subtleties. It was content to recall Salisbury's repeated verbal and written expressions of approval: as for the Additional Declaration, 'Rien . . . ne l'amenait à conclure de cet incident que la convention elle-même eût perdu son caractère définitif'. However, if Salisbury was now dissatisfied with the original arrangement, Leopold would recognise the British sphere if he were permitted to retain the 'non-political' rights which his agents had acquired there—an offer which Anderson neatly described as a project 'to keep the carcase and leave us the skin'.[2] On 20 May the Foreign Office in a formal Note re-capitulated the British case and again demanded the immediate with-drawal of the expedition.[3]

This curt notice to quit was soon to be modified by fears of Franco-Congolese collaboration in the Nile basin; and Leopold did his best to exploit these fears. On 21 May Baron Lambermont, the permanent head of the Belgian Foreign Ministry, told Gosselin of the Brussels legation that while the Congo State would be satisfied with the Nile watershed as its frontier (a completely untrue statement, but possibly made in good faith), 'the French hoped eventually to push on to the river itself'.[4] Anderson was sceptical at first, but by the end of May he admitted that 'all the recent infmn. points to the united action of France and the Congo State in pressing towards the Nile'.[5] There had indeed recently been some discussion in Paris, prompted largely by

---

[1] *Ibid.*, Salisbury to Gosselin No. 35, 19 Mar. 1892.
[2] FO 84/2201, Note by de Grelle 23 Apr. 1892, enclosed in Gosselin to Salisbury No. 29, 25 Apr.; minute by Anderson 4 May.
[3] FO 84/2200, Salisbury to Gosselin No. 72, 17 May 1892; FO 84/2201, Gosselin to Salisbury No. 38, 24 May.
[4] FO 84/2201, Gosselin to Salisbury No. 37, 21 May 1892; cf. same to same Nos. 27 and 45, 20 Apr. and 28 May.
[5] *Ibid.*, Gosselin to Salisbury Nos. 37 and 46, 21 and 29 May 1892; minute by Anderson on No. 46.

G

Leopold himself, of a French advance to the Nile.[1] On 10 June Count de Grelle-Rogier, who was negotiating in Paris on behalf of the Congo State, warned Gosselin that if Ribot discovered that Leopold had received from London 'what practically amounted to an ultimatum', he 'would feel in honour bound' to administer 'un second coup de pied' so violent that Leopold might be forced to accept a frontier giving France access to the Nile. Impressed, the Foreign Office warned Phipps at Paris to be discreet about the Anglo-Congolese dispute, 'as . . . it wd. be more advantageous to us to have the Congo as a neighbour than the French'.[2]

On 17 June Gosselin suggested that Leopold might formally recognise the British sphere if he were permitted to extend his north-eastern frontier to the Nile-Congo divide. Anderson and Salisbury concurred; but before a project could be drafted Leopold had replied on 18 June to the British Note of 20 May.[3] The King repeated that Salisbury had, after all, given his written consent in 1890: 'Ce point, qui n'est du reste pas contesté, domine tout le débat'. If the Mackinnon Treaty were now repudiated, failing any new arrangement the Congo State must treat the Upper Nile as *res nullius* and appeal to her right of prior occupation. Anderson admitted defeat—'We have now come to negotiation'—and suggested that Gosselin's proposal be pursued. Salisbury languidly concurred: 'Yes—it is worth trying'.[4] But in the general election of July 1892 the Conservatives were defeated; and Salisbury, at the head of a caretaker government, suspended further action.

Indeed, even before Salisbury's resignation in August, it had become very clear that the Gosselin proposals were so unlikely to satisfy Leopold that there was no point in proceeding with them. At the end of June Vivian had been replaced at Brussels by Sir Edmund Monson; and Leopold at once attempted to hustle the new British Minister into supporting a settlement favourable to the Congo State. Monson was plied with reports that a Franco-Congolese arrangement was imminent; then, at a carefully staged interview on 6 July, he was warned by the King that the Anglo-Congolese dispute would end by the French securing a road to the Nile 'with a view to future designs on Egypt'. The French could reach the Nile in four months from their existing bases, and England could not stop them. But Leopold, given British support, could stop them by insisting on a frontier running as far north as the eighth parallel, beyond which France would have to contend with the Mahdists. All that Leopold asked in return was a

---

[1] *Infra*, Ch. VI, pp. 137-8. Cf. FO 84/2202, Gosselin to Salisbury No. 53, 17 June 1892.
[2] FO 84/2202, Gosselin to Salisbury No. 50, 10 June 1892; Gosselin to Anderson, private, 12 June; minutes by Anderson and Salisbury.
[3] *Ibid.*, Gosselin to Salisbury No. 53, 17 June, and minutes by Salisbury and Anderson; No. 56, 21 June 1892, enclosing Note by de Grelle 18 June.
[4] *Ibid.*, Note by de Grelle 18 June; minutes by Anderson and Salisbury 23 June; Gosselin to Salisbury No. 57, 21 June.

'perpetual delegation of sovereignty' in those regions lying between the conventional boundary of the Congo State and the Nile-Congo divide. However, Leopold stipulated that should the 'sultanates' in these parts include any territories situated within the Nile valley, 'ceux-ci aussi seraient réunis à l'Etat du Congo'.[1] Had this arrangement been concluded Leopold would undoubtedly have maintained that the Nzakara and Zande sultanates on the north bank of the M'Bomu extended indefinitely into the Nile basin. The Foreign Office of course saw the trap; and no official reply to this proposal was ever vouchsafed.[2] Instead, on 27 July Salisbury replied in quite uncompromising terms to the latest Congolese note, and left to his successor the responsibility of negotiating with Leopold.[3]

Rosebery had not been in office a week before Leopold was making new proposals for Anglo-Congolese collaboration against France. On 18 August he complained that he had 'been completely misunderstood at the Foreign Office'. His dearest wish was to co-operate with London; but unless the British made some response, and were in particular prepared to 'maintain and consolidate' their East African sphere, he would be forced to come to terms with Paris. Rosebery replied that he wished to do 'what is agreeable to the King', but was reluctant 'to add to the number of questions . . . pending with France'.[4] Leopold replied through the Queen, emphasising the French determination 'de s'emparer de suite du haut-Nil', and suggesting that an Anglo-Congolese entente would so discourage the French that they would abandon their Nilotic ambitions. In this way an Anglo-French dispute would not be provoked, but averted. The Foreign Office was not impressed by this argument; nor was it yet fully convinced of the French threat. Currie commented, very shrewdly, that 'we know nothing definite as to the advance of the French . . . except what the King of the Belgians has told us'.[5]

Still, Leopold's remark about the need for the British to 'maintain and consolidate' their sphere had made its impression. Without access through East Africa, the 'British sphere' on the Upper Nile would be a mere theoretical concept even by the very easy standards which guided paper partitions of Africa. Moreover, British control of the East African interior would be essential if, as Anderson suggested on 6 September, London had ultimately to seek 'a reasonable arrangement' with Leopold: 'as the King bluntly says, the question hinges on the decision as to the retention of Uganda'. However, Anderson thought

[1] *Ibid.*, Monson to Salisbury No. 61, 1 July 1892; Nos. 63, 64, 65, all of 7 July. Cf. *B.C.B.* 1, Eetvelde.

[2] Cf. Leopold to Greindl 10 Oct. 1892, printed Guebels, *ubi supra.*

[3] FO 84/2022, Monson to Salisbury No. 67, 29 July 1892, citing Salisbury to Monson No. 104, 27 July.

[4] *Ibid.*, memo, by Monson 30 Aug. 1892, on a conversation with Leopold 18 Aug.; minute by Rosebery 30 Aug.

[5] *Ibid.*, Rosebery to Currie 13 (?) Sept. 1892, enclosing extract (undated) from Leopold to the Queen; minute by Currie, 13 Sept. Cf. *L.Q.V.* 3, ii, p. 152, the Queen to Rosebery 23 Aug. 1892.

that such an 'arrangement' might still be avoided: 'if we retain Uganda we ought to be able to settle the question of the Nile basin by prior occupation'.[1] Leopold and Anderson were not the only ones to draw Rosebery's attention to Uganda as the key to British strategy on the Upper Nile. On 23 August F. R. Wingate, D.M.I. to the Egyptian Army, had warned the Foreign Office that the French might reach Equatoria through Uganda; Anderson took this opportunity of reminding Rosebery that Paris had never recognised the British sphere. Even the sceptical Currie noted that if the French got their way in their frontier dispute with Leopold they would be 'within measurable distance of Uganda'.[2] Meanwhile Egypt in its turn was becoming ever more clearly the key to Mediterranean strategy. Naval preponderance sufficient to guarantee the Straits against a Russian *coup* seemed as far off as ever, in spite of the Naval Defence Act of 1889. By June 1892 the development of the Franco-Russian entente, and the rapid naval construction of these two Powers, had forced Salisbury to write off 'the protection of Constantinople from Russian conquest' as 'a policy of false pretences'.[3] Rosebery did not, and probably could not, go so far; but the situation which confronted him forced him to regard security on the Nile—everywhere on the Nile— as a major priority of policy.

The salient facts of the Uganda situation in August 1892 were simple. The East Africa Company would evacuate by 31 December unless it received the subsidy which Salisbury had refused it in May. On the other hand Salisbury had been forced by the outcry against Lugard's controversial proceedings in the Uganda civil war of January 1892 to take a step, if not a very long one, towards engaging official responsibility. On 24 June 1892 he had instructed Capt. J. R. L. Macdonald, the director of the railway survey, 'to draw up a report . . . which should explain the causes of the outbreak and the actions of British officials'.[4] On 24 August Rosebery asked Anderson to prepare a précis of the Uganda question. Convinced that Uganda was the key to Nile strategy, Rosebery himself amended Anderson's memorandum into a strongly argued brief for immediate annexation, the revival of the railway project, and the rapid extension of British influence into the southern Sudan.[5] Circulated to the Cabinet on 13 September, the memorandum had a very hostile reception. Gladstone bitingly remarked: 'I thought it was a pleading from a Missionary society or from the Company, or should have thought so, but for the date from

---

[1] FO 84/2022, memo. by Monson 30 Aug. 1892; minute by Anderson 6 Sept.
[2] Robinson and Gallagher, *op. cit.*, pp. 314-5. Cf. Cairint 3/214/11, Kitchener, memo. on Uganda 16 Sept. 1892.
[3] L. M. Penson, 'The New Course in British Foreign Policy, 1892-1902', *Transactions of the Royal Historical Society*, Fourth Series, xxv (1943), pp. 121-38, at p. 134, citing minute by Salisbury 4 June 1892.
[4] *Africa No. 8 (1892)* [C.-6817], Salisbury to Portal 24 June 1892.
[5] A. G. Gardiner, *Life of Sir William Harcourt* (London 1923), ii, pp. 191-3, citing Harcourt to Gladstone 20 Sept. 1892. Perham, *Lugard I*, pp. 404-5.

the F.O.'. For Gladstone there was 'no Uganda question'; Salisbury had already settled it by acquiescing in the Company's decision to withdraw.[1] Sir William Harcourt denounced the proposals in even more violent language: 'Jingoism with a vengeance'; he would 'die a thousand deaths rather than have anything to do with it'.[2] Rosebery's humanitarian plea, that evacuation 'must inevitably result in a massacre of Christians' was rejected by both Harcourt and Gladstone as a cynical pretence. Nor were they impressed by the need to protect the Nile waters. Gladstone and his friends still hoped to solve the Egyptian question by evacuation, not (as they saw it) to embroil things further by African adventures which would provoke 'no end of trouble with the French and Germans'.[3]

On 23 September Gladstone made a constitutional issue of the Uganda dispute by invoking the ultimate responsibility of the Prime Minister for all policy. On the 28th Rosebery threatened to resign unless some positive action were taken. Gladstone affected to treat this threat with contempt, but he promptly begged Harcourt 'not to drive [Rosebery] to despair'. Rosebery's resignation might well have split the Liberal Party; it would certainly have brought on a major crisis with the Queen and, even more important to Gladstone, have jeopardised the cause of Irish Home Rule in the Commons.[4] To this master-passion of his declining years Gladstone sacrificed his convictions on Uganda. On 29 September Gladstone proposed, and Rosebery accepted, a compromise by which the Government was to subsidise the Company's occupation until 31 March 1893. On the 30th it was formally adopted by the Cabinet, after Gladstone had read a letter from King Leopold 'which appeared to glance at some plan for the administration of Uganda and Unyoro by the King'. But Rosebery had not won his battle yet. The official motives for the reprieve were to gain information and to enable the missionaries to retire; in principle, the policy of evacuation still stood.[5] On 28 October Salisbury strengthened Rosebery's hand by a public statement that the previous Government had intended to retain Uganda; a week later Rosebery raised another Cabinet storm by proposing that an Imperial Commissioner be sent out to take over the administration from the Company. On 7 November Rosebery was forced to settle for a mere investigating and reporting commissioner; and at the same time the Company was invited to undertake 'a short further prolongation of its occupancy'. But the Company now asked for at least three years'

[1] R. R. James, *Rosebery, A Biography* (London 1963), pp. 261-4, citing Gladstone to Rosebery 17 Sept. 1892. Gardiner, *op. cit.* II, pp. 193-5, citing Harcourt to Rosebery 23 Sept.
[2] Gardiner, *op. cit.* II, pp. 195, 193.
[3] Perham, *op. cit.*, pp. 405-7; James, *op. cit.*, p. 262; Gardiner, *op. cit.* II, p. 192.
[4] James, *op. cit.*, pp. 263-8, citing Gladstone to Rosebery 23 Sept. 1892. Perham, *op. cit.*, pp. 408-10. Gardiner, *op. cit.* II, p. 196. L.Q.V. 3, ii, p. 158, the Queen to Rosebery 28 Sept. 1892.
[5] James, *loc. cit.*; Perham, *loc. cit.*; Gardiner, *op. cit.* II, pp. 196-7. L.Q.V. 3, ii, p. 159, Rosebery to the Queen 29 Sept. 1892; p. 161, Gladstone to the Queen 30 Sept.

tenure at a subsidy of £50,000 a year. Even to Rosebery this seemed exorbitant, and he rejected it out of hand.[1]

Rosebery may not have entirely regretted the impending vacuum of administration in Uganda, for this would at least make it more difficult for the Government to evade a decision. In an attempt to influence this decision, Rosebery sponsored a campaign of agitation in which the speeches of Lugard played a major part. This campaign has been written off as a failure in that it had no perceptible effect upon Liberal opinion and did not compel the Cabinet to adopt a clear-cut policy of retention.[2] But it certainly made a decision for total abandonment more difficult than ever; even Gladstone and Harcourt from time to time toyed with anachronistic schemes for managing Uganda through the Sultan of Zanzibar.[3] It demonstrated, too, the extent to which imperialism had captured the imagination of the upper classes —the 'Establishment'. Lugard was lionised by fashionable society, by the City, by the Universities, by aristocratic magnates in both London and the provinces. When he spoke in London, 'Lords and Dukes and all sorts of swells were turned away at the door for want of standing room'.[4] Men like Gladstone, Harcourt and Wilfrid Blunt, as much members of the Establishment as any Lord or Duke but convinced opponents of imperial expansion, were already beginning to look like survivals from a bygone age. The new generation of Little Englanders were often men of lower middle-class origin, politically suspect as extreme Radicals and quite impossible people socially. No wonder Gladstone and Harcourt fought a losing battle against Rosebery.

All the same, they fought a hard battle. Throughout November 1892 Rosebery wrangled with them, and on occasion threatened resignation, over the choice of a commissioner and the instructions to be given to him. On 30 November the Cabinet accepted Rosebery's nomination of Portal, now consul at Zanzibar, although he was known to be a convinced retentionist. Possibly the fact that Salisbury had in March 1892 designated Portal as 'Commissioner in the British sphere . . . on the East Coast of Africa' enabled an exhausted Cabinet to avoid a further quarrel over his precise status.[5] Rosebery, who was privately warning Portal that he must not consider evacuation, bowed to Gladstone's insistence that his instructions must not contain any reference to 'administering the country'; instead, Portal was asked to advise on the best way of 'dealing with' Uganda. But it was clear that Portal could not complete his task before the expiry of the Company's tenure in March 1893; and he was given an establishment—five officers and

[1] James, *op. cit.*, pp. 273-5; Perham, *op. cit.*, pp. 417-8, 427-9; Robinson and Gallagher, *op. cit.*, pp. 318-9.
[2] Perham, *op. cit.*, pp. 411-27; Robinson and Gallagher, *op. cit.*, pp. 317-8. A. Low, 'British Public Opinion and the Uganda Question, October-December 1892', *The Uganda Journal*, XVIII, 2 (1954), pp. 81-100.
[3] Perham, *op. cit.*, pp. 417-8, 429; Gardiner, *op. cit.* II, p. 198.
[4] Perham, *op. cit.*, pp. 421-4, citing a letter by Edward Lugard, 4 Nov. 1892.
[5] James, *loc. cit.*; Perham, *op. cit.*, pp. 429-31, 434. *Africa No. 4 (1892)* [C.-6555], No. 1.

'an adequate force of armed natives'—which seemed very generous for a mere investigator. In fact, Rosebery's private instructions went far to transform Portal into the administrative commissioner which the Cabinet had refused to authorise.[1] Rosebery admitted as much when in February 1893 he bluntly told Gladstone that Portal was not 'a mere reporter—to take something down in writing and hurry away bag and baggage, leaving the population to its fate'.[2] Portal certainly lived up to this description. On 1 April 1893 he hauled down the Company's flag and replaced it by the Union Jack. On 29 May he induced the Kabaka Mwanga to place Uganda formally under British protection, covering himself by the stipulation that the treaty was not to be binding on England unless subsequently approved in London. Before he left for the coast he appointed Macdonald 'Acting Commissioner in Uganda and its dependencies', and put at his disposal a force of seven Europeans and about 1100 African soldiers—some of them Emin Pasha's former troops, whom Lugard had found at Kavalli's in September 1891 and had taken into the Company's service.[3] Portal had created an administration for Uganda 'and its dependencies' with an establishment more generous than that of many existing colonies and protectorates.

Meanwhile, Rosebery had scored a decisive victory over his colleagues on Egyptian policy. In January 1893 Cromer had seen in the attempt by 'Abbās Hilmi to choose his own ministers a revival of 'Urābist 'anarchy' under khedivial sponsorship, and had demanded the immediate reinforcement of the British garrison.[4] Gladstone declaimed that 'they might as well ask him to put a torch to Westminster Abbey as to send more troops to Egypt'. All the same, for the sake of Irish Home Rule, Gladstone once more gave way and persuaded his colleagues to give way, when Rosebery again brandished his resignation.[5] The evacuation of Egypt, which had in November 1892 been under preliminary discussion between Gladstone and the French ambassador Waddington, was now in effect permanently vetoed by Rosebery.[6] This situation logically implied the retention of Uganda if only for the security of the Nile waters. But Gladstone, Harcourt and their supporters could hardly be expected to think in these terms; and in fact they fought their rearguard action as obstinately as ever. Although Portal's activities had created a situation where the Uganda question could be settled by a mere stroke of the pen, Rosebery still found himself quite unable to enforce a positive decision.

[1] For Portal's official instructions, see: *Africa No. 1 (1893)* [C.-6847], No. 40, Rosebery to Portal 10 Dec. 1893. Cf. Perham, *loc. cit.*
[2] Perham, *op. cit.*, p. 434, citing Rosebery to Gladstone 4 Feb. 1893.
[3] For Portal's despatches from Uganda, see: *Africa No. 8 (1893)* [C.-7109]; *Africa No. 2 (1894)* [C.-7303].
[4] L.Q.V. 3, ii, pp. 203-15. Cromer, *Abbas II* (London 1915), pp. 7-41. Cf. T. B. Miller, 'The Egyptian Question and British Foreign Policy, 1892-1894', *J. Mod. Hist.* XXXII, 1 (1960), pp. 1-15, at pp. 2-5.   [5] James, *op. cit.*, pp. 279-80.
[6] D.D.F. x, No. 37, Waddington to Ribot 2 Nov. 1892; No. 153, Waddington to Develle 31 Jan. 1893. Cf. *infra*, Ch. VII, pp. 140-1.

This delay was all the more unwelcome in that by the summer of 1893 both the Congolese and the French appeared to be actively threatening the Upper Nile. Anderson's hopes of settling this question by prior occupation had of course proved utterly fallacious; and the Uganda impasse also prevented Rosebery from seeking any 'reasonable arrangement' with King Leopold. Rosebery had at first attempted to carry matters with a high hand. On 22 October 1892, following a Brussels report that the Van Kerckhoven expedition had reached Wadelai, he brusquely demanded its unconditional withdrawal from the British sphere. On 4 December Leopold replied by offering mediation under Article XII of the Berlin Act, whereupon Rosebery rejected all further negotiation until the expedition had been withdrawn and threatened 'to adopt a policy of retaliatory annexation'.[1] But it was the King who retaliated. On 28 January 1893 he sent for Monson and told him that in May 1890 Salisbury had approved a Congolese occupation as far as Lado; Leopold therefore refused to dishonour himself by an unconditional withdrawal. 'You may do what you like with me; you may cause me to lose the whole Congo if you choose, but I will never give way on this point . . .'. The King backed up this open defiance by a threat to publish the Mackinnon Treaty and his correspondence with Salisbury in 1890. 'If he is attacked and accused of dishonourable conduct either in Parliament or in the Press, he would not hesitate to invite the judgment of that tribunal upon the four important documents in his possession.'[2]

Anderson, who was only too familiar with the transactions of 1890, again recognised defeat. Adverting to rumours of a setback to Van Kerckhoven, he minuted: 'should he fail it would be a real godsend'. But Currie thought it 'obvious that Lord Salisbury cannot in 1890 have given the King . . . authority to take possession of Lado'; and Rosebery took the unusual course of submitting Monson's despatch to Salisbury for comment.[3] Salisbury's comments were lengthy and obviously embarrassed. Their main gist was that nothing more than 'a confidential exchange of ideas' had taken place in May 1890. 'If I had thought that [King Leopold] was proposing a formal convention to me I should respectfully have declined to receive it at his hands.'[4] This was useless to Rosebery; a glance at the archives showed that Leopold had in his possession letters clearly indicating that there had been much more than 'a confidential exchange of ideas'.[5] After January 1893

---

[1] FO 84/2203, Monson to Rosebery No. 98, 22 Oct. 1892; No. 109, 7 Dec., enclosing Congolese Note of 4 Dec.; No. 119, 19 Dec., enclosing copy of Note based on Rosebery to Monson No. 160, 16 Dec. 1892.

[2] FO 10/595, Monson to Rosebery Nos. 21 and 23, 28 Jan. 1893.

[3] *Ibid.*, minutes by Anderson and Currie. FO 10/604, minute by Rosebery 31 Jan. 1893.

[4] FO 10/604, memo. by Salisbury 6 Feb. 1893.

[5] *Ibid.* Moreover, Salisbury now admitted that in 1890 he had been prepared to consent to a real transfer of *some* rights to Leopold. So unsatisfactory did Rosebery find this that he watered down Salisbury's admission in an elaborate letter of explanation to Monson (FO 10/594, Anderson to Monson, private, 15 Feb. 1893). This letter was in fact drafted in the office and heavily amended by Rosebery himself.

Rosebery never dared to repeat his demand for unconditional with-drawal; he confined himself to requests for information, which were met with blandly ironical protestations of complete ignorance. Mean-while Leopold treated with complete unconcern Rosebery's periodical warnings that the British Government were 'très froissés' by the King's behaviour, which 'must one day lead to most unpleasant conse-quences'.[1] In March 1893 the Belgian Foreign Ministry unofficially informed Sir John Kirk that Van Kerckhoven was 'now firmly established at Lado' and had 'been from first to last in constant com-munication with the Congo State'. Anderson minuted, 'It is clear that we are being trifled with'; but no action followed—except by Leopold who, doubtless to emphasise the strength of his position, secured the removal of Monson by complaining to the Queen that he had been lacking in deference.[2] By the summer of 1893 Rosebery was nervous even of pressing too hard for information. On 6 August the Belgian press announced the occupation of Wadelai, and Sir Francis Plunkett, the new British Minister at Brussels, was instructed to make a written enquiry. This produced a written protestation of ignorance; and the African Department strongly urged Rosebery to 'press the point definitely as to Wadelai'. But Rosebery, evidently fearing to provoke Leopold, repeatedly evaded action on the pretext of awaiting further press reports.[3]

By August 1893 the French threat to the Upper Nile—perhaps in collaboration with Leopold, for Franco-Congolese discussions were known to be in progress at Paris—seemed almost as dangerous as the supposed Congolese occupation. In May 1893 Delcassé had com-missioned P.-L. Monteil to lead an expedition to the Upper Nile.[4] Leopold, who had secretly encouraged French action, partly no doubt as a further means of pressure on the British, at once warned London of these plans. But the King had already cried 'Wolf!' so often that at first even Anderson was not much impressed: 'The risk of a [Congolese] collision with France is increasing; and again the appeal is made to our suspicions of French rivalry in the Nile Basin.'[5] But the departure of Monteil's advanced elements made it clear that the warning had to be taken seriously; and on 8 August the French press carried a premature report of Monteil's own departure.[6] Rosebery was almost helpless. Hamstrung by his colleagues, especially by Gladstone and by Harcourt

[1] FO 10/597, Plunkett to Rosebery No. 169, 26 Nov. 1893; No. 177, 2 Dec. 1893.
[2] FO 64/1316 (sic), Kirk to Anderson, private, 3 Mar. 1893; minute by Anderson 4 Mar. L.Q.V. 3, ii, p. 244, Rosebery to the Queen 5 Apr. 1893. Cf. Crewe [R. O. A. Crewe-Milnes, Marquess of Crewe], Lord Rosebery (London 1931), ii, pp. 423-4. Monson was in fact promoted to the Vienna Embassy.
[3] FO 10/596, Adam to Anderson, private, 6 Aug. 1893. FO 10/594, Rosebery to Plunkett No. 92, 16 Aug. FO 10/596, Plunkett to Rosebery No. 125, 25 Aug.; minutes by Sir C. Hill and Rosebery. FO 10/597, Plunkett to Rosebery Nos. 130 and 131, 6 and 8 Sept. 1893, minutes by Currie, Hill and Rosebery.
[4] Infra, Ch. VII, pp. 140-3.
[5] FO 10/596, Monson to Rosebery No. 90, 13 May 1893; minute by Anderson 15 May.
[6] FO 2/60, Rosebery to Portal 10 Aug. 1893.

at the Exchequer, he could neither approach Leopold for a 'reasonable settlement', nor earmark men and money for a steeplechase with Monteil. All that he could do was to instruct Portal, 'should the means at [his] disposal . . . permit, to send emissaries into . . . the Nile basin, in order to ascertain the state of affairs in . . . the British sphere [and] to negotiate any treaties that may be necessary for its protection'; and even this inadequate substitute for a forward policy had to be carefully concealed from Gladstone and the Cabinet.[1] These orders were not received and carried out until January 1894, when Colvile, Macdonald's successor in Uganda, despatched E. R. Owen to Wadelai. Owen made a treaty with the Wadelai chief, hoisted a Union Jack on either side of the river, engaged with two months' advance of pay a 'garrison' from the survivors of Fadl al-Mūla's troops, and left Wadelai within twenty-four hours.[2] This was the merest parody of occupation. When a similar visit was made to Wadelai three months later there was no sign of either the flags or the garrison.

A few weeks after he had despatched his orders to Portal, Rosebery attempted an even longer shot in his growing anxiety about the Upper Nile. In September 1893 Kitchener, prompted by Wingate, revived a proposal which Baring and Salisbury had rejected in July 1891—that Rabīh Zubair should be induced to resist any attempted French penetration into the Nile valley by way of Darfur and Kordofan.[3] Rabīh, a former follower of Zubair Pasha Rāhma, had after the collapse of Egyptian rule in the Sudan migrated to Bagirmi, east of Lake Chad, and was by 1893 the ruler of a powerful military empire.[4] Although the Foreign Office was warned from Cairo that this proposal had previously been rejected, Anderson, who feared that a push through Darfur and Kordofan was included 'indirectly' in Monteil's programme, pressed hard for its adoption. Rosebery concurred; and again he did not inform the Cabinet of his action.[5]

Owen's 'dash for Wadelai' had no political results. He had indeed discovered that the Congolese were not after all at Wadelai; but this news did not reach London until May 1894, too late to be of any practical use.[6] But the attempt to enlist Rabīh Zubair's support had some unexpected and very important consequences. By October 1893 it had become clear that the forthcoming Anglo-German 'Nigeria-Cameroon' Agreement (signed on 15 November)[7] would place Rabīh's dominions mainly within the German sphere. Nevertheless

[1] FO 2/60, loc. cit. Gardiner, op. cit. II, pp. 315-6, citing Harcourt to Kimberley 14 May 1894.
[2] Africa No. 7 (1895) [C. 7708], No. 17, Cracknall to Kimberley 7 May 1894; cf. Nos. 18, 19, 22, 23, 29. H. E. Colvile, The Land of the Nile Springs (London 1895), pp. 169-70, 202-7.
[3] I.R.E., No. 13, May 1893. Cairint 3/15/302, Wingate, memo. on Maistre's expedition to Bagirmi, June 1893. FO 2/118, Hardinge to Rosebery No. 171, 18 Sept. 1893, enclosing memo. by Kitchener, 13 Sept.
[4] R. L. Hill, A Biographical Dictionary of the Anglo-Egyptian Sudan (Oxford 1951), s.v. Rabīh Fadl Allāh.
[5] FO 2/118, ubi supra; minutes by Anderson 3 Oct. and 31 Oct. 1893.
[6] Africa No. 7 (1895), ubi supra.   [7] Hertslet III, No. 275.

Anderson persisted in the project, apparently doubtful of the Germans' ability to defend themselves against the ubiquitous Monteil; and Rosebery concurred again. The letters to Rabīh were revised; and at last, on 18 December when all was ready, Rosebery very belatedly explained to Hatzfeldt 'what we are doing'. This communication was not a mere tentative request; it notified what was very nearly a *fait accompli*.[1] The whole procedure showed a complete lack of consideration for German susceptibilities; Rosebery could hardly have been more off-hand had he been dealing with the Sultan of Zanzibar. Rosebery's remarks to Hatzfeldt about his wishing to dissipate 'the atmosphere of suspicion which seems to pervade all African politics' seemed to the Wilhelmstrasse a bare-faced confidence trick, by which Rosebery hoped to insinuate British influence into territory which he had recognised as German a bare five weeks earlier. The Germans decided not to protest but to retaliate, just as they had silently retaliated on the Egyptian *Caisse de la Dette* when in December 1892 Rosebery had opposed certain German railway concessions in Asia Minor.[2]

An opportunity of retaliation lay ready to hand. Germany was engaged in negotiations with France on the Cameroon hinterland;[3] but by mid-December these were deadlocked, largely because of Monteil's arrogance and incompetence as a negotiator. By 16 December the French ambassador and Kayser of the *Kolonialabteilung* were tacitly agreed that further discussion should be postponed until the New Year, and that Monteil should meanwhile be dropped. However, on 18 December, the day on which Rosebery spoke to Hatzfeldt, Kayser suggested that the final session, originally planned for the 19th, should be postponed to the 21st.[4] On the 19th Hatzfeldt sent Metternich, his *Conseiller d'ambassade*, to the Foreign Office 'to get some details' about the Rabīh Zubair project. Anderson read to Metternich the text of the letter to Rabīh and, according to Anderson, he 'expressed himself as satisfied'.[5] But at Berlin, on the 21st, Kayser restored the moribund Franco-German negotiation to very active life by offering to France access to the navigable system of the Niger at Bifara, a village on an affluent of the Benue. This offer was unsolicited and utterly unexpected; the French had already abandoned all hope of such access.[6] To the British, engaged in a bitter dispute with Paris

---

[1] FO 2/118, minutes by Anderson and Rosebery 31 Oct. 1893; by Anderson 4 Dec.; by Rosebery 10 Dec. Rosebery to Malet No. 149a, 18 Dec. 1893.

[2] For this episode see G.P. VIII, Nos. 1814–1818; FO 64/1292, 1293, 1296.

[3] By November 1893 Marschall was dissatisfied with Rosebery's policy towards Germany both in Europe and in Africa (cf. *infra*, Ch. VIII, pp. 176–8). He had initiated the negotiation with Paris as a means of bringing pressure to bear upon England by a tactical Franco-German entente in 'the colonial sphere'. Cf. D.D.F. x, No. 434, Herbette to Develle 18 Nov. 1893; No. 471, Herbette to Casimir-Périer 15 Dec. 1893; also P.-L. Monteil, *Souvenirs Vécus* (Paris 1924), pp. 90–1.

[4] D.D.F. x, No. 474, Herbette to Casimir-Périer 17–19 Dec. 1893.

[5] FO 2/118, minute by Anderson on the conversation with Metternich 19 Dec. 1893.

[6] D.D.F. x, No. 478, Herbette to Casimir-Périer 21 Dec. 1893. Monteil, *loc. cit.* M. Blanchard, 'Administrateurs d'Afrique Noire', *Rev. Hist. Cols.*, XXXIX (1953), pp. 377–430, citing (at pp. 380–2), Haussmann to Maurice Lebon 10 Dec. 1893.

about the encroachments and aggressions of the Mizon mission on the Niger-Benue,[1] it was a gesture so pointedly hostile that Rosebery, when he learned of it, could not at first believe that Berlin really meant it—the French must have 'jockey[ed] the Germans by superior information'; while Anderson thought that his great bogey Monteil must somehow have hypnotised 'the less quick-witted Dr Kayser' into supporting 'his anti-English policy'.[2] Although by December 1893 Rosebery evidently had grave misgivings about how Berlin would receive the Rabīh Zubair business and himself remarked very justly that 'the Germans are so suspicious',[3] he never seems to have recognised its connection with the German cession of Bifara to the French. Yet, but for the Rabīh Zubair episode, it seems very unlikely that this cession, so deliberately offensive to London, would have been included in the Franco-German Protocol of 4 February 1894.

The Franco-German Protocol of 1894 is often held to have restored French access to the Upper Nile, which Rosebery is supposed to have hoped to close in the previous November by the diplomatic defence of the Anglo-German Agreement. This Agreement ceded to the Germans the territory to the east of Lake Chad and the Cameroons as far as the western boundaries of Darfur, Kordofan and the Bahr al-Ghazal. But when in February 1894 Germany ceded Bagirmi and Wadai to France this supposed barrier collapsed, and Rosebery was forced hastily to build another by coming to terms with King Leopold.[4] In fact, the Franco-German Protocol did not re-open the French road to the Nile. It could not do so because, as the Foreign Office was very well aware, the Anglo-German Agreement had never closed it. Nor did the February Protocol in any way determine the timing of the British approach to King Leopold in March 1894.

It was in the first place very nearly a geographical impossibility for the Germans to close completely the French route to the Nile. Short of throwing out a bridgehead from the Cameroon hinterland to the Ubangi, which would have been a gross trespass on French-occupied territory, their only means of doing so was to occupy the long slender salient between the Nile watershed and the fourth parallel, which was still the official frontier of the Congo State. This was in 1893 an indefinitely remote prospect; moreover, much of this salient was already occupied in some strength by King Leopold. However, the specific mention of the Bahr al-Ghazal in the Anglo-German Agreement

---

[1] For Mizon's proceedings and the British reaction to them, see: J. E. Flint, *Sir George Goldie and the Making of Nigeria* (London 1960), pp. 168-79; D.D.F. x, No. 410, Dufferin to Develle 30 Oct. 1893.

[2] FO 64/1333, Rosebery, minute of 21 Feb. 1894 on Malet's No. 19, 17 Feb.; Anderson, minute of 13 Mar. 1894 on Malet's Nos. 28, 29 and 30, 7 Mar.

[3] FO 2/118, minute by Rosebery 10 Dec. 1893.

[4] Taylor, *The Struggle for Mastery*, pp. 350-1. Cf. Langer, *The Diplomacy of Imperialism*, pp. 131-4. This view seems to derive ultimately from the lengthy but very misleading footnote to the single unimportant document that the editors of *Die Grosse Politik* saw fit to publish on the Franco-German negotiations (G.P. vii, No. 1598, Marschall to Herbette 15 July 1893; footnote, pp. 335-6).

seems to have fostered the belief that the Foreign Office did indeed expect Berlin to undertake these far-flung operations. But this is misplaced subtlety. In May 1893 Anderson had insisted on the specific mention of Darfur and Kordofan in the Agreement simply because 'otherwise it might be interpreted as shutting out England' from those provinces. Early in November, and for precisely the same reason, Wingate had insisted on the specific mention of the Bahr al-Ghazal, which was conceivably accessible from Wadai without passing through Darfur.[1]

The principal object of the Agreement, which grew out of unofficial discussions between Sir George Taubman Goldie of the Niger Company and a German 'Committee for the Cameroons', was indeed to use Germany as a buffer—but not on the Ubangi approach to the Nile. The area to be protected was Bornu, where Goldie could not get a local treaty. As Anderson put it: 'in future troubles with France about her push [from the south] to Lake Chad, which are certain to come, Germany will have to be counted with, and we shall be quit of the danger of collision'.[2] Anderson certainly hoped that Germany would retain Bagirmi and Wadai, and so relieve him of his recurrent nightmare that Monteil might, with the assistance of Rabīh Zubair, 'sweep to the Nile' through Darfur and Kordofan. But he explicitly recognised that there was still 'danger of Monteil getting at the Nile through the Bahr el-Ghazal country';[3] and this was, after all, the most direct route and the most obvious danger-point.

Jules Develle at the Quai d'Orsay, who supported a French mission to the Bahr al-Ghazal in principle at least,[4] never complained that the Anglo-German Agreement had destroyed French access to the Upper Nile. His silence is the more significant in that he protested strongly against the threatened denial of access to Lake Chad.[5] Nor did the Foreign Office ever complain, either in 1894 or in later retrospect, that the Franco-German Protocol had 're-opened' the road to the Nile for the French. Kimberley, who had succeeded Rosebery as Foreign Secretary in March 1894, never mentioned the Nile either in his conversations with Hatzfeldt or in his despatches to Berlin. A decade later, J. A. C. Tilley, in his well-known *Memorandum respecting the Relations between Great Britain and Germany 1892-1904*, still regarded the Franco-German Protocol as a major grievance; but even in this prosecutor's brief there is not a word about the Nile. What rankled in London and aroused the desire to retaliate even in the placable

[1] FO 64/1301, minutes by Anderson 17 May and 31 Oct. 1893; Anderson to Le Poer Trench, private, 21 May; Rosebery to Malet No. 133, 1 Nov. 1893. Cf Map 4.
[2] FO 64/1302, minute by Anderson on Malet to Rosebery No. 64, 4 Aug. 1893. For the part played by Goldie, who dominated the British side of the negotiation, cf. FO 64/1301, 1316, 1317, 1318, *passim*.   [3] FO 2/118, minutes by Anderson, 3 and 31 Oct. 1893.
[4] *Infra*, Ch. VII, pp. 140-2.
[5] D.D.F. x, No. 334, Herbette to Develle 12 Aug. 1893, and footnote; No. 448, Develle to Herbette and Decrais, 29 Nov. 1893. Langer, who implies (*op. cit.*, p. 131) that Develle's protest concerned access to the *Nile*, has evidently been misled by the footnote at G.P. VII, pp. 335-6.

Kimberley, was the 'treachery' (as Anderson called it) of combining with France to harass Britain on the Niger.[1] Except as an insurance against the imaginary danger of French penetration through Darfur, the Anglo-German Agreement had played no part in Rosebery's almost desperate attempts to protect the Upper Nile in the second half of 1893.

Towards the end of 1893 there were indeed welcome signs that the position on the Upper Nile was not after all so critical as it had seemed in the summer. The African Department hoped that Colvile's offensive against Kabarega of Bunyoro 'would secure the road to Wadelai'.[2] Monteil continued to postpone his departure; then, instead of going to Africa, he went to Berlin. Towards the end of November *L'Indépendance Belge*, a newspaper usually sympathetic to Leopold's African policy, began to carry rumours of a serious setback to the Congolese Nile expedition; and Lambermont admitted to Plunkett his fears that something was gravely amiss. These rumours doubtless reflected genuine information, received through the 'bush telegraph', of the serious difficulties which the expedition had begun to encounter in the summer of 1893. Plunkett thought that 'there must have been a serious disaster'; Anderson, that 'the expedition is not now in our sphere and has difficulty in advancing'[3]—a perfectly correct conclusion and one which was to remain correct, had Anderson but known it, throughout the following months. But then, just at the moment when official confirmation of the collapse on the Nile must have begun to reach Brussels, the Belgian press suddenly changed its tune. On 1 December *La Réforme*, a 'Progressiste' organ normally bitterly hostile to Leopold's African adventure, announced that the Congolese had re-occupied Wadelai. On the next day Lambermont volunteered the opinion that recent gloomy reports had been much exaggerated; and in January and February 1894 *La Réforme* vied with *L'Indépendance Belge* in celebrating a series of fictitious successes on the Upper Nile.[4] Leopold's African expeditions were indeed more successful in Europe than in Africa; for although they were all officially secret, he skilfully leaked news of successes and completely suppressed news of failure. His successful manipulation of the Belgian press in 1893-4 hoodwinked the Foreign Office so completely that when Leopold, after the signature of the Anglo-Congolese Agreement, began to admit the true position, Anderson found difficulty in believing it.[5] Wingate's intelligence

---

[1] Tilley, 5 Jan. 1904 (B.D. 1, at p. 323). FO 64/1333, minute by Anderson 13 Mar. 1894 on Malet to Rosebery Nos. 28 and 29, 7 Mar.; minute by Kimberley 22 Mar. on Malet's No. 34, 16 Mar. Cf. J. R. Rodd, *Social and Diplomatic Memories*, 1 (London 1922), pp. 346-7.

[2] FO 83/1310, Hill, memo. on work in the African Dept. 10 Mar. 1894.

[3] FO 10/597, Plunkett to Rosebery Nos. 167, 169 and 172, 26 and 29 Nov. 1893; minutes by Anderson.

[4] *Ibid.*, Plunkett to Rosebery Nos. 174 and 177, 1 and 2 Dec. 1893. FO 10/614, same to same Nos. 5 and 19, 13 Jan. and 21 Feb. 1894.

[5] Cf. Anderson in July 1894 on Congolese reports of clashes with the Mahdists on the Uele: 'It is scarcely credible that the fight can be rightly placed if the assailants were really Mahdists.' (FO 10/616, minute on Plunkett to Kimberley No. 159, 8 July 1894).

service, so admirably informed about the northern Sudan, was no help at all in the deep south; in March 1894 Wingate confessed that for all he knew the Congolese might be anywhere between Wadelai and Zemio, on the M'Bomu five hundred miles away.[1] But by February 1894 Anderson already suspected that, if there had been a setback, it had been overcome; and in March the official Foreign Office view was that the Congolese were on the Nile at Wadelai and had made a treaty.[2]

Once Monteil had completed his task in Berlin, Leopold was quick to play on British fears of revived French activity. On 10 February 1894 Lambermont warned Plunkett that if the British wasted much more time they would find themselves forestalled on the Upper Nile by France; and Anderson thought it 'certainly probable that when the negotiations with Germany are finished, Capt. Monteil will push towards the Nile'.[3] Meanwhile, there were also strong hints from Lambermont that King Leopold's negotiations with the French, at a standstill since October 1893, were beginning to make serious progress.[4] These reports were in fact quite inaccurate; and they were denied, in perfect good faith, by the Congolese negotiator himself, de Grelle-Rogier.[5] But Anderson not unnaturally preferred to believe the respected veteran statesman Lambermont[6] rather than de Grelle, a man of straw who was often Leopold's mouthpiece for deliberately misleading statements. By March 1894 Anderson was acutely anxious lest Leopold should at any moment come to terms with France and present England with another *fait accompli* on the Upper Nile.

By February 1894 the Upper Nile situation seemed even more critical than in the summer of 1893; but the fate of Uganda still remained obstinately unsettled. Portal had indeed completed his final report as long ago as 18 May 1893, and by 30 August Anderson had read it and found it 'admirable'. Rosebery, for all his careful briefing of Portal, did not agree. Apparently Portal had advocated too close a connection of Christian Uganda with Muslim Zanzibar; and this appeared likely to provoke an outcry among the anti-slavery movement, which had recently been actively campaigning on the Zanzibar front. At all events, Rosebery withheld the report from his colleagues until Portal himself had returned and had been given an opportunity to 'reconsider' it. Portal reached England on 27 November, and was at once interviewed by Rosebery.[7] His report, in a heavily amended

---

[1] I.R.E. No. 23, March 1894.

[2] FO 10/625, Rosebery to Rodd unnumb., 5 Mar. 1894. FO 83/1310, Hill, *loc. cit.*

[3] FO 10/614, Plunkett to Rosebery No. 18, 11 Feb. 1894, minute by Anderson 13 Feb.

[4] FO 10/597, Plunkett to Rosebery Nos. 183 and 187, 23 and 31 Dec. 1893. FO 10/614, same to same No. 18, 11 Feb. 1894.

[5] FO 10/614, Plunkett to Rosebery No. 21, 21 Feb. 1894; Adam to Rosebery No. 23, 7 Mar. 1894.

[6] 'The clearest head of any of the King's advisers': 'There is hardly a more discreet statesman in Europe'—Anderson on Lambermont 17 Oct. 1892 (FO 84/2203); 17 Feb. 1893 (FO 10/595).

[7] Perham, *op. cit.*, pp. 448-50. Cf. James, *op. cit.*, pp. 285-6.

version, was circulated to Ministers on 20 December. It was, as expected, a brief for annexation; and it laid particular emphasis on Uganda's 'strategical position of great natural importance . . . controlling the head waters of the Nile'. If Britain withdrew, some other Power would doubtless intervene on the pretext of protecting 'the Christian country of Uganda' against the Mahdists or the East African Arabs, and would inevitably extend its influence into 'the Nile Valley and the natural highways of the interior'. It pointed out that the evacuation of Uganda 'means, practically, the renunciation of the whole of that vast territory reserved by the Anglo-German Convention [of 1890] for the sphere of British influence'. The report was spiced here and there with appeals to humanitarian sentiment and commercial interest, but the core of its argument was the crucial importance of Uganda for Nile strategy—an emphasis all the more remarkable in that Portal admitted that this was 'a question of wide and general policy which it is outside my province to discuss'.[1] It seems very likely that this element of the report bears the heavy impress of Rosebery's 'suggestions' to Portal for its revision.

It has been stated that the Portal report 'completed the conversion of Sir William Harcourt' and that its submission to the Cabinet in December was 'a mere formality'.[2] But in December 1893 the Cabinet took no action on the report. It was not in fact adopted until 22 March 1894, after Rosebery had become Prime Minister, and with Harcourt still fighting hard in the last ditch.[3] Yet Rosebery accepted this further delay, in spite of the increasingly critical situation on the Upper Nile, without attempting to coerce his colleagues by the threats of resignation with which he had previously been so lavish. By the end of 1893 such threats had in fact lost their coercive power. On 9 September 1893 Gladstone's Home Rule Bill, after passing the Commons, had been contemptuously rejected by the Lords. Gladstone wished to dissolve forthwith and appeal to the electorate on the single issue of Home Rule. This proposal was vetoed by his colleagues; and thereafter Gladstone seems to have become increasingly indifferent whether his government stood or fell.[4] At all events, his strongest motive for conciliating Rosebery had disappeared; and had a resignation now been proffered, it might well have been accepted. Had Rosebery attempted to force the pace on Uganda, he might have found himself faced with the dilemma either of having to accept an unfavourable decision or of leaving the government. Hence his otherwise astonishing remark, in a letter to Gladstone of 27 December 1893, that Uganda was a matter of

---

[1] *Africa No. 2 (1894)*, No. 9, Portal to Rosebery dated (fictitiously) 'November 1, 1893'. Cf. Perham, *op. cit.*, pp. 450-1.

[2] Langer, *op. cit.*, p. 124. Robinson and Gallagher, *op. cit.*, p. 327. The report was not in fact 'brought . . . to the Cabinet' in Dec. 1893; it was merely circulated to Ministers, cf. Perham, *loc. cit.*

[3] L.Q.V. 3, ii, pp. 384-5, 389-90, Rosebery to the Queen 22 Mar. and 7 Apr. 1894.

[4] James, *op. cit.*, pp. 288-93, citing at p. 288 Rosebery to Hamilton, 23 July 1893. Cf. P. Magnus, *Gladstone* (London 1954), p. 414.

no great urgency.[1] Moreover, it was already clear that Rosebery might soon be Prime Minister himself, with Prime Ministerial powers to enforce his policy on Uganda and the Upper Nile. Gladstone was visibly failing; and Harcourt's personal unpopularity, even with colleagues who shared his political views, was rapidly excluding him from the succession. At the beginning of 1894, indeed, it looked as if Rosebery might succeed Gladstone within a matter of days. On 9 January 1894 the G.O.M. found himself in a minority of one among his colleagues in his fanatical opposition to the Admiralty's programme of naval expansion; and even his faithful henchman Morley concluded that 'now is the accepted time for our chief's resignation'.[2]

Gladstone did not think so. He clung to office until March, spending a month at Biarritz and forbidding his colleagues to hold cabinets in his absence. On 3 March he resigned at last.[3] On the 5th Rosebery kissed hands as Prime Minister.[4] Now at last Rosebery had a chance of enforcing his policy on Uganda; now at last he was free, as he had not been in the summer of 1893, to undertake the desperately urgent task of protecting the Upper Nile by some 'reasonable arrangement' with King Leopold, the man who appeared to be in possession. He did not lose a day, scarcely even an hour, in initiating the negotiation. On 5 March 1894 he added the date and his signature to a draft which was ready and waiting in fair copy. This draft contained instructions to Rodd[5] for a secret mission to King Leopold; and its operative part began with the words: 'The time has arrived when British policy [as to] the Great Lakes, which form the sources of the Nile, must be defined'.[6] For Rosebery that time was of course long overdue; as early as August 1893 he had been forced to recognise the apparent impossibility of either ejecting the Congolese or forestalling the French. But then he had been powerless to act except by the very inadequate expedients of secret instructions to Portal and letters to Rabīh Zubair, on which Rabīh was very unlikely to act even if he ever received them.[7] King Leopold was, to all appearances, the key to the situation on the Upper Nile; but the timing of Rosebery's approach to the King was determined, not by events in Africa or by the Franco-German Protocol, nor even by the rumours of an impending agreement between King Leopold and the French, but by the internal politics of the British Liberal Party.

[1] Rosebery to Gladstone, 27 Dec. 1893, cited Perham, *loc. cit.*
[2] James, *op. cit.*, pp. 294-6; Magnus, *op. cit.*, p. 415; Gardiner, *op. cit.* II, pp. 253-4.
[3] For Gladstone's last days of office and the struggle for succession between Rosebery and Harcourt, see: James, *op. cit.*, pp. 297-328; Magnus, *op. cit.*, pp. 417-23; Gardiner, *op. cit.* II, pp. 254-73.
[4] L.Q.V. 3, ii, p. 376, the Queen's journal 5 Mar. 1894.
[5] J. R. Rodd, recently consul at Zanzibar and later Cromer's assistant at Cairo.
[6] FO 10/625, Rosebery to Rodd 5 Mar. 1894. The date on the file copy is in a different hand (and ink) from the body of the draft.
[7] It seems probable that Rosebery's letters did in fact reach Rabīh towards the end of 1895; but there is no trace of any acknowledgment.

H

VI

THE ASCENDANCY OF KING LEOPOLD

II—FRANCE, THE CONGO STATE AND

THE UPPER NILE, 1887–93

ALTHOUGH the French sometimes claimed that they needed 'une ouverture sur le Nil'—through the Bahr al-Ghazal *sudd*—for their non-existent commerce on the upper Ubangi,[1] in fact their interest in the Upper Nile derived almost entirely from its connection with Egypt. By 1894, though perhaps not earlier, the Upper Nile had become for much of French public opinion an integral part of the Egyptian question, and it had therefore acquired a political importance which far transcended that of ordinary African disputes. It was not only that the geography of the Nile waters offered tempting opportunities for challenging the British occupation of Egypt by a *prise de possession* in the southern Sudan. The Egyptian connection implied implacable hostility to any attempt by Britain to settle the fate of the Upper Nile without reference to France. To permit such a settlement would be to permit a second humiliation of France in 'Egypt'; and the humiliation of 1882 was already an almost intolerable affront to French self-esteem.

The eclipse of France as a major political influence in Egypt was in French eyes no ordinary political setback for which compensation might be sought and found elsewhere. Nor was the consequent disturbance of the Mediterranean balance, for all its intrinsic importance, the real source of French bitterness. In July 1879 the American consul at Cairo had remarked that: 'France . . . since the time of the first Napoleon, has considered itself as having rights in . . . Egypt . . . superior to those of the other European Powers. . . . This has been a national idea which has not been affected by the various changes in the form of its government'.[2] But consul Farman's transatlantic matter-of-factness did not tell the whole story. Many Frenchmen believed that since the time of the first Napoleon it had been the destined mission of France, one of her major contributions to world history, to modernise and 'enlighten' Egypt. Jules Cocheris wrote of Egypt in 1903:

[1] E.g. Sadi Carnot's statement to Monteil in May 1893; Paul Cambon during the negotiations of Jan.-Mar. 1899.
[2] Farman to Secretary of State 8 July 1879, quoted Shukry, *Khedive Ismail and Slavery in the Sudan*, Appendix D, p. 28.

La France a été longtemps sa sœur aînée, son soutien, son appui, sa consolatrice dans les mauvais jours. Elle a été l'étoile éclatante qui répandait, sur l'aïeule du vieux monde, la lumière bien-faisante de son génie national. Nos hommes d'action l'ont conquise par leur audace. . . . Elle a fait de Bonaparte un demi-dieu. D'autres l'ont éveillée de sa torpeur et, sous ses yeux alanguis par un sommeil de plusieurs siècles, ils ont ressuscité l'Egypte pharaonique et semé sur les rives du Nil, avec l'étonnante fébrilité de leur race, les germes rapides et féconds de la civilisation occidentale et de l'activité humaine.'[1]

This was no empty boast. Since the days of Muhammad 'Ali Egypt had been served by a large and distinguished company of French scholars, scientists and technical experts; and French civilisation then made upon educated Egyptian society an impression which has still not been effaced, in spite of half a century of British control and the rise of an intransigently 'Arab' nationalism.

It was utterly inadmissible that France, the true centre of Western culture and 'depuis la chute de l'Empire romain . . . le foyer principal des événements qui ont ébranlé l'univers',[2] should permit her mission to be frustrated, and herself to be supplanted, by a rival whose culture was at best provincial compared with her own. Moreover, the circum-stances in which French hegemony had been lost were in themselves humiliating. Fearful of weakening her position in Europe, in particular against Germany, France had shrunk from an operation which the British, second-rate soldiers in French estimation, had carried out with spectacular ease and success. As a recent French historian of the Third Republic candidly admits, 'Les Français . . . pardonnent difficile-ment aux Britanniques de n'avoir pas partagé leur pusillanimité'.[3] Once they had got over their relief that the West had succeeded in crushing Muslim resistance, Tel-el-Kebir began to be felt as a humiliation to French arms second only to Sedan itself. So painful was this feeling that a mythology grew up, and was accepted not only by popular journalists, but by diplomatists and serious historians, that 'Urābi had been bribed by the British to throw away the battle. Indeed, it was sometimes asserted that the 'Urābist movement itself had been engineered and financed by the *Intelligence britannique* as a means of ejecting France from Egypt.[4]

Nevertheless, the official French hostility to Britain over Egypt took some years to harden. The discovery that the London financial convention of 1885 did not after all lead to early evacuation played its part. So did the Drummond Wolff Convention; not because of

---

[1] J. Cocheris, *Situation Internationale de L'Egypte et du Soudan* (Paris 1903), p. 558.
[2] *Ibid.*, p. 560.
[3] Chastenet, *La République des Républicains*, p. 119.
[4] Cocheris, *op. cit.*, pp. 138-40, 144-50. C. Vergniol, 'Fachoda: Les Origines de la Mission Marchand', *Revue de France*, 1 and 15 Aug., 1 Sept. 1936, pp. 416-34, 630-45, 112-8, at pp. 417-8. D.D.F. xiv, No. 305, Geoffray to Delcassé 25 Aug. 1898.

its substance, which was in principle not unacceptable to Paris, but because the French intensely resented any attempt to solve the Egyptian question without their participation. Meanwhile, 'Egyptianist' Anglophobia among the French public seems to have developed side by side with Boulangisme in the years after 1885. Doubtless both movements had similar psychological origins; and, as Salisbury recognised, hostility to England on this issue afforded an outlet to feelings of resentment and frustration which, in their most extreme and outspoken form, it would have been dangerous to direct towards Germany.[1] Symptomatic of this state of mind is E. Chesnel's *Plaies d'Egypte*[2] with its indiscriminate denigration of all British activity in Egypt. The collapse of Boulangisme in 1889, and the recognition that hopes for the early recovery of the Lost Provinces were utterly unfounded, left 'Egyptianist' hostility to Britain as the main vehicle for French chauvinism. During the eighteen-nineties, in France as elsewhere in Europe, an aggressive and self-conscious nationalism was to be in the ascendant. It was encouraged, and given an anti-British twist, by the conclusion of the Franco-Russian entente, which was in itself 'a triumph for the conservative, military, clerical elements' in French society, traditionally hostile to England;[3] and the real strength of this group, behind the studiously 'moderate' façade of French parliamentary politics, was to be shown in its resistance to the 'revision' of Dreyfus' condemnation. Moreover, like the Dreyfus affair, hostility to Britain in Egypt was a platform upon which most of the right-wing sects, otherwise often bitter rivals, could work together harmoniously. It acted as a link between the classical 'sword and altar' Right and the new popular, 'radical' Right, represented by Boulangisme and by Déroulède's *Ligue des Patriotes*, which drew its inspiration from Revolutionary Jacobinism but also foreshadowed twentieth-century Fascism. 'Egypt' and 'Dreyfus' ultimately became war-cries common to a large section of the French Right; indeed, under the impact of Fashoda some of the anti-Dreyfusards became almost more anti-British than they were anti-Dreyfus.[4]

By 1890, however, intransigence on Egypt extended far beyond the Right; indeed, everywhere except on the extreme Left, the Egyptian situation was felt as a stain upon national honour which it was an imperative duty to remove. Even to discuss the question in other terms was to incur the reproach of being a bad Frenchman. By 1894 the Upper Nile was being seen in the same light. In June 1894, when the Chamber debated the Anglo-Congolese Agreement, the colonialist leader Eugène Etienne struck the keynote with the words, 'Messieurs, c'est la question égyptienne qui s'ouvre ainsi devant vous'. The debate was conducted almost entirely in terms of the injury done to French

---

[1] Cecil, *Salisbury* IV, pp. 47-8, citing Salisbury to Baring 11 Feb. 1887.
[2] Paris, 1888. Cf. also O. Borelli in *Le Bosphore Egyptien*.
[3] Cf. Langer, *The Diplomacy of Imperialism*, p. 58.
[4] *Infra*, Ch. XVI, p. 373.

rights in the Nile valley; and when the deputy Delafosse attempted to examine the question in the light of practical possibilities and political expediency, he was greeted by angry murmurs and an interjected reminder that he was not speaking in the House of Commons. After the debate, the Chamber unanimously adopted an Order of the Day drafted by the colonialist leaders, expressing confidence in the Government's determination to defend 'the rights of France'.[1] Such unanimity was unusual in debates on colonial or African topics; it had evidently been achieved by presenting the issue of the Upper Nile as an integral part of the Egyptian question.

Still, until the British in 1894 provoked French opinion by disposing of the Upper Nile as if it was their own property, its identification with Egypt in French minds had not become strong enough to exert a major influence on policy. The Anglo-German Agreement of 1890 had evoked noisy protests in France;[2] but the Quai d'Orsay was able to preserve an official silence though it could not of course even contemplate recognising the Agreement. Similarly, proposals for a French penetration to the Upper Nile were, even in colonialist circles, firmly subordinated to other projects until the beginning of 1893. Such penetration was in any case hardly even a geographical possibility until 1887, when the Congo State ceded to France its territories on the right bank of the river Ubangi.[3] It has been suggested that after 1882 the French consoled themselves for Egypt, and perhaps for the inaccessibility of the Upper Nile, by expansion in West Africa at British expense.[4] But, except in the Gabon-Congo region, 1882 does not seem to have initiated any noticeable forward movement in West Africa.[5] The major initiative here had already taken place in 1879, when de Freycinet's projects for the *Transsaharien* and for the Senegal-Niger railway launched the first serious French campaign into the eastern hinterland of Senegal.[6] The *Transsaharien* was killed by the massacre of the Flatters mission in 1881; a year or two later the Senegal-Niger project was also abandoned as too expensive in lives and money. By 1884 the watchword in Senegal was consolidation and retrenchment; and in September 1885 the Ministry of Marine almost decided to abandon the hinterland conquered between 1880 and 1883.[7] In 1884 Jules Ferry offered no official resistance to the buying-up by Goldie's

---

[1] *J.O.*, Débats, Chambre, 7 June 1894.
[2] *Supra*, Ch. IV, p. 83.
[3] Franco-Congolese Agreement of 29 April 1887 (Hertslet II, No. 156).
[4] Robinson and Gallagher, *Africa and the Victorians*, pp. 163-89, 465-7; and in *New C.M.H.* XI, pp. 602-11.
[5] Cf. J. Stengers, 'L'Impérialisme colonial de la fin du XIXe siècle: Mythe ou Réalité', *J.A.H.* III, 3 (1962), pp. 471-82. In 1883 Jauréguiberry did attempt an advance in West Africa proper; but the results were 'extremely meagre'.
[6] The Senegal-Niger plan originated with Brière de l'Isle, Governor of Senegal 1876-1881: J. D. Hargreaves, *Prelude to the Partition of West Africa* (London 1963), pp. 253-5. Cf. Monteil, *Souvenirs Vécus*, pp. 17-29; A.-L.-C. Gatelet, *Histoire de la Conquête du Soudan Français* (Paris-Nancy 1901), pp. 24-34.
[7] Hargreaves, *loc. cit.*; Monteil, *op. cit.*, pp. 30-2, 36-42; Gatelet, *op. cit.*, pp. 51, 132-5; Chastenet, *op. cit.*, pp. 78-9.

National African Company of the French enterprises established in the Niger delta during 1878 and 1879.[1] In 1886 de Freycinet vetoed, as too dangerously exposed to British interference from Lagos, plans for a northward push to the Middle Niger from Dahomey.[2] Meanwhile, Ferry's acquisitions on the Ivory Coast stagnated until 1887, when the expeditions of Gustave Binger began to link them to the French Niger Soudan.

To this general picture of stagnation and even of retreat there was however one outstanding exception. In spite of the efforts of Paris to call a halt, the French soldiers in Senegal continued to push eastwards. In his first three campaigns, from 1880 to 1883, Colonel Borgnis-Desbordes had encroached upon the militantly Islamic tarīqa-State of Ahmadu Shehu and on the military empire of the Mandingo adventurer Samory Touré, a Rabīh Zubair of the far west. Ahmadu Shehu riposted by jihād; Samory by a more flexible but often aggressive resistance. The commandants supérieurs in the French Soudan felt that the prestige of French arms was at stake, and were themselves no less aggressive. In their quest for a final and decisive action and in their competitive zeal to carry the Tricolour yet further forward, successive commandants seem to have neglected the more humdrum tasks of securing their flanks and pacifying occupied territory. Periodical military emergencies, often in areas far behind the 'front line', caused growing uneasiness in Paris; but 'the colonels' could always find reasons good in their own eyes for disobeying orders to pause and consolidate.[3] By 1890 the officiers soudanais had become quite unamenable to metropolitan control; and fears that a forward policy on the upper Ubangi might similarly get out of hand exercised a powerful negative influence on French policy towards the Upper Nile even as late as 1894.[4]

This collapse of effective control was hardly surprising. Between 1885 and 1889, in the hey-day of the partition of Africa, the sous-secrétariat d'Etat aux Colonies was for a time non-existent; and when it did exist, it was usually held by men of little political weight. Revived by Ferry in February 1883, the sous-secrétariat was suppressed in April 1885. Revived again in May 1887, it was held for a bare six months by the Algerian Eugène Etienne; but it was not until March 1889, when Etienne took over for a second time with quasi-ministerial powers and a seat in the Cabinet, that it became a really effective office. Etienne strove, not without success, to introduce some order and coherence into

[1] Hargreaves, op. cit., pp. 275-8, 310-5, 330. Flint, Sir George Goldie, pp. 34-9, 47-54, 67-8. C. W. Newbury, 'The Development of French policy on the Lower and Upper Niger, 1880-1898', J. Mod. Hist. xxxi, 1 (1959), pp. 18-23. So far from this inertia being a 'mystery', as Robinson and Gallagher suggest (Africa and the Victorians, p. 176), it seems quite consistent with French policy elsewhere in West Africa.

[2] Newbury, ubi supra, p. 24, citing de Freycinet to Aube 10 Mar. 1886.

[3] Gatelet, op. cit., pp. 35-132 (for the campaigns 1880-89). Monteil, op. cit., pp. 30-5. M. Blanchard, 'Français et Belges sur L'Oubanghi', Rev. Hist. Cols. xxxvi (1950), pp. 1-36, at pp. 6, 20.

[4] Blanchard, loc. cit.; Gatelet, op. cit., pp. 208-9, 214.

the haphazard extremes of aggression and stagnation which constituted French colonial activity in Africa. As a good Algerian, Etienne
saw in West Africa south of the Sahara the natural hinterland of the
Mediterranean north; and he recognised that this hinterland could be
extended to the Equator and beyond if France could secure the 'pivot'
—the territories adjacent to Lake Chad.[1] Early in 1890 Etienne
sponsored the first expedition, under Crampel, northwards towards
Lake Chad from the French Congo; he then launched another under
Mizon which was to reach the lake by way of the Niger and the Benue.[2]
But in August 1890 the Foreign Minister Alexandre Ribot sacrificed to
England a comparatively small but rich slice of Etienne's potential
Algerian hinterland. The Anglo-French Agreement of 5 August 1890
recognised a line—not necessarily a straight line—between Say on the
Niger and Barrawa on Lake Chad, as the southern limit of 'the Mediterranean possessions of France'—a formulation which in itself suggests
the influence of Etienne's ideas.[3] The sacrifice was none the less unwelcome to Etienne. A few days after the signature of the Agreement,
he commissioned P.-L. Monteil, an able and experienced *officier
soudanais*, to make a reconnaissance from Senegal to Lake Chad and,
if possible, to deflect in favour of France the very indefinite boundary
which the Agreement had laid down.[4]

Etienne also set himself to popularise colonial expansion, and in
particular to persuade French opinion that it was not merely the
expensive hobby of a few reckless militarists. The *Comité de l'Afrique
française*, which he founded in November 1890, was an essentially
civilian organisation of colonial enthusiasts.[5] Salisbury's notorious
remark about the surrender of 'very light land' in the 1890 Agreement
played into the hands of Etienne's propagandists,[6] in particular the
able journalist Hippolyte Percher, better known by his pen-name
Harry Alis. Harry Alis was Secretary-General of the *Comité* from its
foundation in 1890; and the emphasis of his propaganda was always
very heavily on Lake Chad.[7] By 1894 some colonialists thought that
this propaganda had been even too successful. Henri Dehérain complained that the very word 'Chad' had become 'a talisman which
brings even the dullest lecturer at least one burst of applause'; and that

---

[1] Chastenet, *op. cit.*, pp. 266-73. S. H. Roberts, *History of French Colonial Policy, 1870-1925*
(London 1929), reprint of 1963, pp. 20-1, 303-4. Newbury, *ubi supra*, p. 25.

[2] Flint, *op. cit.*, pp. 167-72; Chastenet, *op. cit.*, pp. 269-70.

[3] Hertslet 11, No. 229. This formulation enabled the French to assert, in Feb. 1894,
that the line had demarcated *merely* the limit of the French *Mediterranean* possessions, and
had left territory to the south *res nullius* pending occupation. (FO 27/3184, enclosure in
Dufferin to Rosebery 10 Feb. 1894; cf. *infra*, Ch. ix, pp. 192-3.)

[4] Monteil, *op. cit.*, pp. 54-9; *idem, De Tripoli à Saint-Louis par le Lac Tchad* (Paris 1894).

[5] Roberts, *op. cit.*, pp. 20-1; Chastenet, *op. cit.*, p. 267. H. Brunschwig, *Mythes et Réalités
de l'Impérialisme Colonial Français, 1871-1914* (Paris 1960), pp. 116-22.

[6] Cf. FO 27/3184, Phipps to Anderson, private, 4 Jan. 1894—'it sticks in their gizzard'.
An apocryphal addition, to the effect that 'the Gallic cock had been left plenty of sand to
scratch in', is still being presented as authentic (Brunschwig, *op. cit.*, p. 108).

[7] Both his book-length publications—*A la Conquête du Tchad* (Paris 1891); *Nos Africains*
(Paris 1894)—deal exclusively with the Lake Chad missions.

the distant gleam of the lake had blinded the French public to the need for action on the Upper Nile, where the 'succession of Egypt' was at stake.[1]

Engrossed with his Grand Design for Lake Chad—and with the systematic insubordination of Colonel Archinard, *commandant supérieur* on the Niger[2]—Etienne had little attention and no resources to spare for the Upper Nile, or even for the upper Ubangi. In November 1893, when the Monteil mission to the Upper Nile had been on the stocks since May, and when Monteil's own departure had already been scandalously delayed, Etienne still thought it more important to send him to Berlin as a negotiator than to send him to Africa as a military explorer.[3] Monteil's task at Berlin was to negotiate a Cameroon hinterland frontier which should preserve French access to Lake Chad from the south. Nothing could indicate Etienne's scale of priorities more clearly. Not that he was entirely indifferent to the Upper Nile; on at least one occasion (December 1892) he intervened to prevent Ribot signing away to King Leopold the independent 'ouverture sur le Nil' which France had obtained in 1887.[4] But here Etienne was merely reserving the future. The Upper Nile was irrelevant to Etienne's dream of a Greater Algeria; it therefore had to wait its turn.

The way to the Nile from the French Congo had been opened by the Franco-Congolese Protocol of 29 April 1887, by which the Congo State had ceded to France its territories on the west bank of the river Ubangi. Within a month of its signature the Foreign Minister Flourens, always combative towards England, had pointed out to his colonial colleague that the right-bank affluents of the upper Ubangi 'pourraient . . . offrir des voies d'accès intéressantes vers le Soudan égyptien'.[5] The Upper Nile was at that time in the news. In March 1887 Stanley had disembarked at Matadi. If Stanley could reach the Upper Nile by way of the Congo and its affluents, why not a French expedition? But Flourens' colonial colleague was Etienne; and no action followed. Late in 1889 or early in 1890 Gabriel Hanotaux, then *Sous-directeur des Protectorats* at the Quai d'Orsay, put up to his Minister a memorandum pointing out 'cette pénétration de flanc que les affluents du Congo enfoncent vers le Moyen-Nil';[6] but Hanotaux' Minister was Spuller, an old Gambettist more concerned to settle quarrels with England than to seek new ones in darkest Africa. In June 1891 the colonialist deputy François Deloncle gave public currency to the 'Upper Nile idea' by reminding the Chamber, though without much emphasis, that France

[1] H. Dehérain, 'La Succession de l'Egypte dans la Province équatoriale', *Revue des Deux Mondes*, 15 May 1894, pp. 345-6.
[2] Cf. Etienne to Governor Senegal 14 April 1891, cited Robinson and Gallagher, *New C.M.H.* xi, p. 610. Gatelet, *op. cit.*, pp. 208-9, 214; Monteil, *op. cit.*, p. 35.
[3] Blanchard, *ubi supra*, pp. 21-2; cf. Monteil, *op. cit.*, pp. 70-2.
[4] *Infra*, pp. 131-2.
[5] Flourens to Aube 16 May 1887, cited M.-A. Ménier, 'La Marche au Tchad de 1887 à 1891', *Bulletin d'Etudes Centrafricaines*, 5 (1953), pp. 6-7. Cf. Blanchard, *ubi supra*, p. 14.
[6] G. Hanotaux, *Fachoda; Le Partage d'Afrique* (Paris 1909), p. 71.

now had 'une ouverture sur le Nil' in the headwaters of the Ubangi.[1]
About a year later, in May and June 1892, the project was for the first
time actively canvassed in colonialist circles. But this agitation—if it
be worthy of the name—evidently owed much to the hidden promptings of King Leopold, who hoped to use it as a means of pressure
on the British.[2] Nor did it have any discernible effect upon French
policy.

Meanwhile, de Brazza's policy as Governor of the French Congo
faithfully reflected the priorities of Etienne. On the strength of a statement made in October 1898 by Victor Liotard, 1890 has often been
taken as the starting-point of the enterprise which was to lead to
Fashoda. Liotard then said that in 1890 he had been commissioned by
de Brazza to occupy the upper Ubangi and to create a French sphere
with an outlet on the Nile.[3] In fact, Liotard was not even posted to the
upper Ubangi until late in 1891; nor was he then the precursor of
Marchand that was implied in his speech of 1898. His real task was to
cover the right flank of yet another northward mission to Lake Chad
under Dybowski, by assuring 'the success of our penetration towards
the north and north-east en pays musulman'; and for this purpose a
certain M. Goujon, an Islamic expert from Algeria, was to be attached
to him.[4] In April 1891 de Brazza explained to Etienne that his plans
for the expansion of the French Congo were primarily directed towards
extending 'our influence in those regions to the north . . . which are
destined to become the Algerian Sudan'.[5] The approaches to Lake
Chad across the Sahara and eastwards from the upper Niger had by
now been recognised as quite impracticable; hence the importance of
the drive to the north from the French Congo. But even here there
were serious difficulties. It was essential to limit German expansion
eastward from the Cameroons by pegging out claims in the Sangha
and Shari basins; while in their direct drive for the lake the French soon
came into collision with the formidable Rabīh Zubair. Indeed, the
Crampel mission had already been almost annihilated by Rabīh's
feudatory al-Sanūsi, the 'sultan' of Dar Banda and Dar Kouti.[6]

Although almost all de Brazza's energies were devoted to linking the
Congo with Etienne's Algerian Sudan, he did not lose sight of the need
to forestall Britain and Germany in the whole of the territory extending
'from the east bank of Lake Chad to the Egyptian Sudan'. He hoped in
1891 that Liotard's north-eastern thrust would lead to the foundation
of an advanced post on the upper Ubangi, as 'a base for operations

---

[1] J.O., Débats, Chambre, 24 June 1891.
[2] Cf. FO 84/2202, Gosselin to Salisbury No. 53, 17 June 1892; and infra, pp. 137-8.
[3] Speech at the Gare Montparnasse 7 Oct. 1898. Cf. Cocheris, op. cit., p. 391; Langer,
op. cit., p. 126.
[4] Blanchard, 'Administrateurs d'Afrique Noire', Rev. Hist. Cols., 1953, p. 398. MC
G.C., I 39a, Chavannes to Etienne 18 Aug. 1891.
[5] MC G.C., I 37a, de Brazza to Etienne 18 April 1891.
[6] For this Sanūsi (not to be confused with his more famous Libyan namesake), see:
S. Santandrea, 'Sanusi, Ruler of Dar Banda and Dar Kuti . . .', S.N.R. xxxviii (1957),
pp. 151-5.

towards the north-east, in order to make contact with the Arab chiefs who dwell in those regions'. De Brazza writes indeed of 'sending explorers as far as the affluents of the Upper Nile'; but it is clear that his objective is not a direct drive towards the Upper Nile itself, but rather penetration towards the Muslim 'Sudanic' regions lying, roughly, to the north of the tenth parallel. De Brazza specifically states that the north-eastern policy is to be adapted to 'the Islamic populations dwelling to the north, north-east and east of the rivers Ubangi and Sangha'.[1] But this north-eastern policy never really emerged from the realms of aspiration. The resistance of Rabīh Zubair compelled the almost exclusive concentration of de Brazza's resources—and those of the *Comité de l'Afrique française*—upon the drive to the north. A constant stream of expeditions—Cholet, Fourneau, Crampel, Dybowski, Maistre, Clozel, as well as those led by de Brazza himself—operated in the Sangha valley or struck directly towards Lake Chad. Meanwhile, Liotard on the upper Ubangi was pitifully starved of men and money.[2] He was scarcely able to hold his own even against the local tribes, much less against the deliberate resistance of King Leopold's agents to any French expansion east or north of the M'Bomu-Uele confluence.

De Brazza did not however entirely neglect the possibility of a direct drive for the Upper Nile. Indeed, in April 1891 he suggested that a French occupation of the Upper Nile 'peut . . . nous donner une situation qui . . . nous permettrait d'entrer avec l'Angleterre en pourparlers au sujet de concessions réciproques dans le règlement de la question égyptienne'; and in July he urged that Congolese encroachments north of the fourth parallel should be checked, so as to keep open French access to the Nile 'en prévision de concessions réciproques avec l'Angleterre'.[3] Here was the germ of the policy that was to lead to Fashoda; but the seed fell on stony ground so long as Etienne and his disciple Jamais were at the *Colonies*. Moreover, de Brazza himself was merely attempting to reserve the future, not suggesting a policy for immediate adoption; this was evidently an even remoter aspiration than the 'north-eastern policy'. Until 1893 the upper Ubangi, whether as a base for a north-eastwards advance towards Wadai and Darfur or for a direct thrust to the Upper Nile, was invariably subordinated to the needs of the Sangha valley and the drive to the north.[4]

Until 1889, however, the French managed to keep pace with their Congolese rivals on the Ubangi; in June and July of that year French

[1] MC G.C., 1 37a, de Brazza to Etienne 18 April 1891, and enclosures: memo. by de Brazza 19 Nov. 1889; de Brazza to Dolisie 5 Feb. and 24 Mar. 1891.

[2] According to Chavannes, Liotard's credits amounted only to 120,000 francs: C. Chavannes, *Le Congo Français* (Paris 1937), p. 315. As late as 1893 Wingate estimated his strength at only 30 Senegalese and 40 locally recruited *miliciens* (Cairint 3/15/299, memo. of 30 Jan. 1893). Cf. Cocheris, *op. cit.*, p. 392.

[3] MC G.C., 1 37a, de Brazza to Etienne 18 April 1891; Monthly Report June-July 1891.

[4] This is clear not only from the numerous expeditions sent northwards, but also from de Brazza's own activities and the emphasis in the Gabon-Congo 'Monthly Reports'.

and Congolese posts were founded at and opposite Bangui. But the French garrison consisted merely of one officer and ten Senegalese seamen; and this attempt to hold a province with a corporal's guard paid the inevitable penalty. In January 1890 the garrison and its commander were massacred by local tribesmen. By October 1891 the French had indeed restored the situation here and founded a post at Les Abiras on the M'Bomu-Uele confluence; but by this time Van Kerckhoven was already well on his way to the Nile watershed and Congolese influence firmly established over the Nzakara and Zande chiefs whose territories extended northwards from the M'Bomu towards the Bahr al-Ghazal.[1]

At Les Abiras the French found themselves immobilised by the persistent obstruction of the Congolese, which was ultimately carried to the point of armed resistance. The Franco-Congolese Protocol of April 1887, which purported to define the frontier in this region, had in fact left it hopelessly indeterminate. By this Protocol the Congo State had bound itself to abstain from political action on the right (or north) bank of the Ubangi upstream of the intersection of that river by the fourth parallel. But by the autumn of 1891 the Congolese were maintaining that the river Ubangi ceased to exist upstream of the point where it was formed by the confluence of the Uele and the M'Bomu. East of this confluence there was therefore, in the Congolese view, no northern limit to their sphere.[2] But the 1887 Protocol had further, and most confusingly, stated that the northern boundary of the Congo State (though perhaps not the limit of its political influence?) was fixed at latitude 4° north. De Brazza and his subordinates therefore regarded as encroachments all Congolese activity north of the fourth parallel.[3] This activity went far beyond mere flag-hoisting expeditions. Every Congolese agent was expected to deliver commodities for export; and this obligation, explicitly enjoined by Leopold's secret circular of 21 September 1891, led to large-scale Congolese ivory-hunts in the disputed area. The region which the French claimed as their sphere was thrown into turmoil by the forcible impressment of porters and by acts of violence on the part of Congolese soldiers and armed irregulars.[4] The pitifully weak French garrisons were tempting targets for the resentment of the local Africans, who could hardly be expected to make the fine distinction between Frenchmen and Belgians. It was inevitable in the circumstances that King Leopold's agents should be

---

[1] B.C.B. II, Hanolet, Vangele; Cocheris, op. cit., p. 454; Vergniol, ubi supra, pp. 426-7. Cf. supra, Ch. v, p. 89.
[2] Hertslet II, No. 156. Blanchard, 'Français et Belges . . .'; p. 17, citing Gov.-Gen. Wahis to Dolisie 17 Oct. 1891. Cocheris, op. cit., p. 392. Lotar, Bomu, p. 26.
[3] MC G.C., I, 37a, de Brazza to Etienne 18 July 1891; Blanchard, ubi supra, pp. 17-18. But even Eetvelde had originally taken this view; cf. Eetvelde to Leopold 3 Nov. 1888, cited D.K. XXVII (1916), p. 138.
[4] Blanchard, ubi supra, pp. 8-12, citing: Dolisie 2 Feb. 1891; de Brazza 7 Nov. 1891; Liotard 10 and 20 Mar. 1892, 12 May 1892; Chavannes 31 Dec. 1892, 10 Sept. and 27 Sept. 1893. MC G.C., I 38c, Dolisie to Chavannes 14 Oct. 1891. Cf. MC G.C., VI 14a, passim; and A. Stenmans, La Reprise du Congo par la Belgique (Brussels 1949), p. 135.

accused not only of arming the natives, but of actively inciting them against the French.[1]

Léopoldville replied to French complaints by pointing out that the Ubangi ceased to exist east of Les Abiras; but up-country the Congolese agents rejected French protests in terms which, as the acting French Governor Chavannes complained, 'remplaçent par la désin-volture des procédés et le sans-gêne des expressions le sérieux et la courtoisie ordinaire des relations diplomatiques'. In September 1891 Vangele wrote in reply to a protest by Dolisie, the French com-missioner at Brazzaville:

> Je vous ferai remarquer que je ne cherche pas à faire croire que c'est uniquement par des moyens pacifiques que je suis parvenu à assurer la sécurité des routes dont vous venez de si largement profiter. . . . Grâce à trois années d'efforts, de luttes et de patience, l'Etat Indépendant du Congo est parvenu à pacifier toute la contrée, et à donner aux routes une sécurité complète. . . . Sans difficulté vous avez pu de la sorte arborer le drapeau français sur de grands territoires.[2]

To these provocations Paris reacted very mildly; indeed, it scarcely reacted at all. Etienne, like not a few of his colonialist contemporaries, seems to have looked upon King Leopold as a pseudo-Power who could in the last resort always be induced or compelled to collaborate with France. If so, his encroachments need not be taken seriously; while his advance to the Upper Nile might perform, for the ultimate profit of France, the task to which Etienne's own scheme of priorities denied all adequate resources. Etienne's only apparent uneasiness about Leopold was that he might be tempted to collaborate with London instead of with Paris; and in May 1891 he did ask the Quai d'Orsay to be on the watch for this danger.[3]

In February 1892 Etienne was replaced at the *Colonies* by Jamais, who seems to have adhered strictly to his predecessor's general lines of policy. The series of missions northwards towards Lake Chad was continued; in Dahomey General Dodds was launched against King Behanzin to create the corridor from the coast to the Middle Niger which Etienne had planned.[4] Jamais also launched a second Mizon mission, again ostensibly 'scientific and commercial', again ostensibly directed towards Lake Chad. But this time Mizon's main objective was to consolidate—with Etienne's approval—the 'new French province of Adamawa', in territory already spoken for by England and Germany and far to the south of the Say-Barrawa line which the Agreement of

---

[1] Blanchard, *ubi supra*, p. 12, citing Liotard 20 Mar. 1892; Lotar, *op. cit.*, p. 40, citing Liotard 6 July 1892.

[2] Blanchard, *ubi supra*, pp. 11-12, citing Chavannes to Delcassé, 10 Sept. 1893; Vangele to Dolisie, 17 Sept. 1891.

[3] MC G.C., 1 37a, minute, 'Extrait à faire pr. les affs. Etrangères', on de Brazza to Etienne 18 May 1891.

[4] Newbury, *ubi supra*, pp. 25-6, citing Jamais to Ribot 2 Dec. 1892; Cocheris, *op. cit.*, p. 454.

August 1890 seemed to have established as the boundary between the British and the French spheres.[1] Mizon's behaviour in Adamawa during his first mission had been, if possible, even more provocative than that of the soldiers in the Niger Soudan.[2] Jamais now had on his hands in Africa alone, Dahomey, Adamawa and the perennial problem of the *officiers soudanais*; and he had no stomach for a forward policy on the upper Ubangi. He recognised indeed that the Congolese seemed, by October 1892, 'trop disposés... à régler, en dehors de nous et d'accord avec l'Angleterre, l'affaire du Soudan égyptien', and that firm action would sooner or later be necessary. 'Mais le moment est-il bien propice pour le tenter, alors que nous sommes engagés à la fois au Dahomey, au Tonkin, au Soudan? Quant à moi je ne le crois point.' In this policy of reserve Jamais was strongly supported by Jacques Haussmann, his *Directeur politique*. For Haussmann French expansion was already far too ambitious. He strongly disapproved of the Adamawa affair as yet another adventure over which Paris had no effective control, and which might end by aligning England and Germany against France in Africa. As late as February 1894, when the Nile project had already been on the stocks for a year, Haussmann could write: 'Se laisser aller au Congo-Oubangui à une entreprise aussi hazardeuse et mal préparée, je dirais volontiers aussi peu réfléchie que celle du Soudan et du Niger, serait une aventure.'[3]

When in November 1891 de Brazza had met Liotard on his way up-country, he had been confident that the French occupation of the upper Ubangi would be 'un véritable succès'. This confidence was quite unfounded. Liotard arrived at Les Abiras in March 1892. His first report was so disquieting that the *Colonies* minuted: 'Signaler les mauvais procédés des agents belges. Dire que nous nous préoccupons de renforcer la mission Liotard.'[4] Then in May the disaster of Bangui was almost repeated at Les Abiras. The commandant de Poumayrac and most of his garrison were ambushed and massacred while out foraging, and Liotard's position at once became very precarious. This news reached Paris in July; and in an unwonted fit of militancy the Quai d'Orsay, presumably moved by Jamais, held Congolese incitement responsible for de Poumayrac's death and protested formally to Leopold.[5] Meanwhile Chavannes at Libreville was attempting to obtain reinforcements from Senegal for Liotard. But to meet the immediate emergency he suggested to Jamais that Liotard might be

---

[1] Flint, *op. cit.*, pp. 172-5. Cf. D.D.F. IX, No. 435, Ribot to Waddington 8 Aug. 1892; and, for the real status of the Mizon Mission, M C Afrique III 16a, 16b, 17a.

[2] Flint, *op. cit.*, pp. 169-72.

[3] Blanchard, *ubi supra*, pp. 16-17, citing Jamais to Ribot 13 Sept. 1892; p. 6, citing Haussmann 24 Feb. 1894. Cf. *eundem*, 'Administrateurs d'Afrique Noire', pp. 380-2, citing Haussmann to M. Lebon 10 Dec. 1893.

[4] Chavannes, *op. cit.*, p. 264, citing de Brazza to Chavannes 3 Nov. 1891. MC G.C., I 39a: Monthly Report, Apr.-May 1892; Liotard to Chavannes 10 Mar. 1892, and minute.

[5] MC G.C., I 40a: Monthly Report, July-Aug. 1892; Chavannes to Jamais 18 Sept. 1892. Cf. FO 84/2202, Monson to Salisbury Nos. 71 and 76, 6 and 12 Aug. 1892. The protest was not however pressed with much vigour.

reinforced by a private mission under the duc d'Uzès which had reached Brazzaville in July. This mission seems to have had no very clearly defined objective, though its second-in-command, a soldier of fortune called Julien, apparently cherished visions of advancing to Fashoda—or even to Khartoum![1] Jamais appeared to concur. On 13 September he telegraphed to Chavannes completely approving the proposals for reinforcing Liotard 'as described in your political report of 16 August', and indeed urging Chavannes to further efforts 'pour augmenter effectif miliciens Liotard'. Chavannes replied that, as suggested in his August report, he had already sent off the d'Uzès mission. He received by return a sharp reprimand for employing a mission over which he had no official control.[2]

Chavannes was very angry; and well he might be.[3] Paris had told the man on the spot to do what he could, and had then reprimanded him for doing it. But Jamais' overriding concern was to avoid becoming involved, by a local excess of zeal, in another Niger on the Ubangi. He had already warned Chavannes that any reinforcement for Liotard from Senegal 'n'a aucun caractère agressif et est destiné seulement à permettre rester sur défensive tout en renforçant notre action pendant négociations en Europe'.[4] He probably guessed that Chavannes and his colleagues were profoundly frustrated by the 'politique de moindre effort' on the upper Ubangi, if only because of the constant humiliations at the hands of the Congolese to which it exposed them. Chavannes himself already cherished projects for a break-through to the Upper Nile, and early in 1893 he was to spend some of his home leave in lobbying for a Nile mission.[5] And just as Chavannes had despatched the d'Uzès mission without awaiting the explicit approval of Jamais, so Dolisie at Brazzaville had already instructed the mission to reinforce Liotard without waiting for orders from Chavannes. Dolisie's instructions to Julien (who had now taken over command of the mission) would have confirmed the apprehensions of Jamais. Julien was indeed warned not to react to Congolese provocation—but with the potentially explosive proviso 'tant que la dignité et l'honneur du pavillon ne seront pas mis en cause'.[6]

Towards the end of 1892 Jamais was evidently torn between the fear of provoking the Congolese and a growing anxiety that the French position on the upper Ubangi might collapse completely. On 21 October 1892 he again urged Chavannes to spare no effort to ensure

[1] Lotar, *op. cit.*, pp. 41-3; MC, *loc. cit.*, Monthly Report, July-Aug. 1892. Many years later Chavannes wrote (*op. cit.*, pp. 295-7) as if he and Dolisie had shared Julien's ideas; but there is nothing of this in the contemporary documents.

[2] MC G.C., 1 40b, Jamais to Chavannes 13 and 16 Sept. 1892.

[3] *Ibid.*, 40a, Chavannes to Jamais 18 Sept. 1892.

[4] *Ibid.*, 40b, Jamais to Chavannes 13 Sept. 1892.

[5] J. Stengers, 'Aux Origines de Fachoda: L'Expédition Monteil', *Rev. Belge Phil. Hist.* XXXVI (1958), pp. 436-50, XXXVIII (1960), pp. 366-404, 1040-65, at pp. 439-41. Cf. Vergniol, *ubi supra*, pp. 633-4; Lotar, *op. cit.*, pp. 44, 60-2.

[6] Lotar, *op. cit.*, p. 41. *B.C.B.* 1, Dolisie, d'Uzès. Vergniol. *ubi supra*, citing Dolisie to Julien 22 Sept. 1892.

the complete safety of Liotard.[1] On 29 September he had even suggested—quite fruitlessly—that de Brazza should take personal charge on the upper Ubangi.[2] In December news was received that the Congolese were more aggressive than ever; and Chavannes pointed out that Liotard, even after reinforcement by Julien, was still in a position of hopeless inferiority. By January 1893 Chavannes had written off the upper Ubangi situation as quite beyond repair by any local action: 'la première chose à souhaiter, c'est que le différend du Haut-Oubangui reçoive une prompte solution en Europe'. And in March 1893, when Julien was known to have reached Les Abiras, Chavannes cabled with laconic gloom: 'conduite des Belges ne pas changer'.[3]

However, Liotard decided to use his reinforcements, scanty as they were, in an attempt to break through to the valley of the M'Bomu. His immediate objective was the village of chief Bangasso, who had been under Congolese protection since June 1890. Liotard's departure on 10 March 1893 was observed by the commandant at Yakoma, the Congolese post immediately opposite Les Abiras. Commandant Hennebert at once warned his colleague Mathieu at Bangasso, and himself hastened to Bangasso with most of his garrison. When Liotard arrived there on 16 March he found a greatly superior Congolese force drawn up in battle order, and Mathieu determined to oppose his advance by force of arms. After a few very tense minutes, Liotard agreed to remain at Bangasso until the arrival of Balat, the Congolese 'Commandant supérieur du Haut-Oubanghi—Bomu'. Liotard's sojourn at Bangasso amounted almost to an internment: he was not allowed to fly the French flag, and his camp was guarded by Congolese soldiers. When after some days Balat failed to appear, Liotard returned crestfallen to Les Abiras.[4] On 2 May he reported to Libreville that he had been forced to retreat by the 'absolutely threatening' attitude of the Congolese at Bangasso.[5] Liotard's ill-advised advance had merely demonstrated, in a most humiliating manner, the complete military superiority of King Leopold.

Of King Leopold indeed; for Mathieu's truculent resistance had not been in any way the indiscretion of a fire-eating junior officer. He was completely supported by Balat, who subsequently wrote to Liotard:

Mon chef de poste de Bangasso, en vous sommant de déposer les armes, a agi dans la plénitude de ses droits établis aux ordres que je lui avais donnés. . . . Je tiens à vous prévenir que les postes nombreux que j'ai établis dans le bassin de l'Oubanghi

---

[1] MC G.C., I 40b, Jamais to Chavannes 21 Oct. 1892; cf. same to same 16 Oct.
[2] *Ibid.*, Jamais to Chavannes 29 Sept. 1892.
[3] *Ibid.*, 40a, Chavannes to Jamais 4 Jan. 1893; to Delcassé 20 Mar. 1893. The d'Uzès-Julien mission achieved little or nothing; by June 1893 both its leaders had been invalided back to the coast.
[4] Lotar, *op. cit.*, pp. 51-60. B.C.B. I, Balat; II, Liotard, Mathieu.
[5] MC G.C., I 41a, A/Gov. Libreville to Delcassé 12 July 1893, transmitting Liotard's report of 2 May.

ont reçu les ordres les plus sévères au sujet de l'approche d'une troupe étrangère armée: je vous rends donc responsable des conflits qui pourraient se présenter. . . .[1]

This intransigence was not prompted merely by the 'âpreté au gain matériel'[2] of which Chavannes complained, but by a deliberate design, undoubtedly conceived by Leopold himself, to seal off completely from the French the territories east and north of the M'Bomu-Uele confluence. Behind this iron curtain which Liotard had failed to penetrate, Leopold launched not only the Van Kerckhoven expedition to Equatoria but also a series of missions to the Bahr al-Ghazal, to southern Darfur and to the Shari basin. In these regions the King was able to operate, not only without interference from the French but in the complete secrecy which enabled him to exploit real or fictitious successes and to suppress all news of failures.

As early as March 1892 the Congolese agent G. Le Marinel had founded a post at Bakuma, to the north of Bangasso at about 5° 30' and a useful jumping-off point for expeditions either north-westwards towards the Shari basin or north-eastwards towards Dar Fertit and southern Darfur. At the beginning of 1893 the approaches to Dar Fertit were reconnoitred.[3] In October 1893 a more ambitious venture was launched. An expedition, ultimately to be commanded by Hanolet, left Bangasso for the Shari basin; and on 4 April 1894 a post was founded at Mbelle on the river Gounda, a sub-affluent of the Shari. One important object of this mission was to make contact with al-Sanūsi, sultan of Dar Kouti, and if possible with al-Sanūsi's overlord Rabīh Zubair. It seems very likely that Leopold, who already saw the difficulties of maintaining a position in strength on the Wadelai-Lado reach of the Nile, hoped to enlist Rabīh as an auxiliary against the Mahdists and open up a route to a point near Fashoda by way of Dar Fertit, the Bahr al-'Arab and Meshra'er Req—a plan rather like the one which Anderson's apprehensions attributed to Monteil. But in August 1894 sickness and shortage of supplies compelled the withdrawal of Leopold's Shari mission before any effective contact with Rabīh Zubair had been made.[4]

Further Congolese expeditions launched northwards from the M'Bomu from the end of 1893 onwards were doubtless intended to secure the more accessible stages of this line of advance. The earliest of these, under Nilis, left Bangasso for southern Darfur in December 1893. Its specific objective was Hofrat en Nahas, where copper had long been worked in primitive fashion and which Leopold believed to be a site of rich mineral wealth. By March 1894 Nilis had reached

[1] Blanchard, 'Français et Belges . . .', pp. 12-13, quoting Balat to Liotard Apr. 1893.
[2] Ibid., p. 11, citing Chavannes, 27 Sept. 1893.
[3] B.C.B. i, Le Marinel G., de la Kéthulle de Ryhove. Lotar, op. cit., pp. 45-51.
[4] B.C.B. i, Inver, Stroobant; ii, Van Calster, Hanolet. Lotar, op. cit., pp. 66-80, 86-91.
A.-J. Wauters, 'Souvenirs de Fachoda et de l'Expédition Dhanis', M. Géog., 1910, No. 20, 15 May, cols. 251-2.

Katuaka on the river Adda, about seventy miles south of Hofrat en Nahas, and had taken under Congolese protection a Kresh chief whom the Belgians called 'Acmed Curcia'. Here the expedition was halted by the early rains; and in October 1894 it was withdrawn under threat of Mahdist attack. The Mahdists under al-Khātim Mūsa had in fact launched an expedition southwards from Kordofan to expel the Europeans, and 'Acmed Curcia' had hastened to re-insure with them as soon as it became clear how little real protection the Congolese could afford to him.[1]

Al-Khātim Mūsa's expedition to the Bahr al-Ghazal also prompted a Congolese advance to Raga in Dar Fertit, where sultan Hāmad Mūsa of the Feroge had been in treaty relationship with the Congo State since September 1892. Early in 1894 Hāmad Mūsa asked for Congolese support against the Mahdists. Fiévez, the Congolese resident at Zemio, was already under orders to push northwards as soon as possible; and in March 1894 he set out for Raga. But on 2 April he was recalled by news of the critical situation on the upper Uele; a Belgian warrant officer (Donckier de Donceel), with one or two African N.C.O.s and a handful of Zande irregulars, was left to carry on to Raga. De Donceel made contact with Hāmad Mūsa in July; but by the end of August the Mahdists were too near for comfort, and he retired towards the Nile-Congo divide to make contact with a Congolese supporting party. In October he returned to Dar Fertit with his reinforcements, only to retreat again when he found private war raging between the Feroge and his Zande auxiliaries, and Sultan Hāmad preparing—naturally enough—to make his peace with the Mahdists. On 9 December, however, de Donceel was joined by a second supporting expedition under Colmant; it was now decided to send one detachment eastwards down the Bahr al-'Arab towards Meshra' er Req, while another watched the Mahdists in Dar Fertit. But these operations were checked at the outset by news of the Franco-Congolese Convention on 14 August 1894, whereby Leopold accepted the M'Bomu as his northern frontier. By February 1895 all Congolese forces within the Nile basin had returned to Zemio.[2]

All these expeditions, like that to the Nile itself under Van Kerckhoven, met with setbacks which were the inevitable result of attempting such grandiose operations with insufficient troops. But these setbacks were not necessarily decisive. By the end of 1894 the doubly reinforced Bahr al-Ghazal expedition may well have been equal to its tasks; it might have been no less successful than the second Nile expedition under Chaltin, which in February 1897 ejected the

[1] B.C.B. I, Gérard A., de la Kéthulle de Ryhove, Nilis. Lotar, op. cit., pp. 80-5. S. Santandrea, 'The Belgians in Western Bahr el Ghazal', S.N.R. xxxvi, 2 (1955), pp.188-91.

[2] B.C.B. I, Donckier de Donceel, Fiévez, Lebègue, Walhousen; III, Faki Ahmed. Lotar, op. cit., pp. 92-116, 123-6. Santandrea, ubi supra. Sanderson, 'Contributions from African Sources . . .', J.A.H. 1962, pp. 79-80. A. Abel, 'Traduction de documents arabes concernant le Bahr-el-Ghazal (1893-4)', Bull. I.R.C.B. xxv, 5 (1954), pp. 1385-1409.

I

Mahdists from Rejaf.[1] Moreover, Leopold's expeditions had by now hoisted the State flag along an immense belt of territory from the Nile almost to the Shari, a belt whose northern limit was in places not far short of the ninth parallel. What Leopold prized was his priority of occupation. So long as the French and everyone else were kept in ignorance by the iron curtain on the upper Ubangi, nobody could contradict the King's claim to 'effective occupation', and he could take his own time in making it really effective. King Leopold's ascendancy on the south-western approaches to the Upper Nile was lost, not in Africa, but in Europe when in August 1894 the French forced him to surrender all but an innocuous fraction of his claims within the Nile basin.

The French diplomatic pressure upon Leopold in the summer of 1894 was ruthless and effective; but it was very belated. Until 1894 the French offered no diplomatic resistance worthy of the name to Congolese encroachments. De Brazza's pleas for action in 1891 went unheard; and when negotiations did begin in April 1892 it was on the initiative of King Leopold, who evidently hoped to use them as a means of pressure on London in the dispute over the Van Kerckhoven expedition and the Mackinnon Treaty.

In a letter of 11 April 1892 Leopold laid formal claim to the territories of the 'lower M'Bomu'—a river carefully distinguished from the upper Ubangi, which did not in his view exist upstream of the M'Bomu-Uele confluence. At the beginning of June he proposed a specific frontier—a line running northward from Hanssen's Falls, on the M'Bomu a little above the confluence, to the Congo-Shari watershed. Such a frontier would have permitted an almost indefinite northward expansion of the Congo State to the east of about the twenty-first meridian, and would of course have completely excluded the French from the Upper Nile. Nevertheless, on the basis of these proposals Ribot deputed Gabriel Hanotaux to negotiate with de Grelle-Rogier, the Foreign Secretary of the Congo State. On 28 June agreement was reached on a frontier rather further to the east and therefore in detail more generous to France, but still retaining the long northward extension which closed the French route to the Nile. Astonishingly, this frontier was a proposal from the French side! Further, Hanotaux agreed that the Congo State should continue to occupy 'pendant une période de plusieurs années à déterminer', the posts which Leopold had already founded in the M'Bomu valley on the French side of the proposed frontier.[2]

An agreement on these lines would of course have transformed out

---

[1] *Infra*, Ch. XIII, p. 307.
[2] The main source for this negotiation is a recapitulatory despatch, de Grelle to Leopold 29 Aug. 1892, printed by R.-J. Cornet, 'A propos de deux dossiers: Le dossier diplomatique de l'Oubangui et le dossier de Grelle Rogier', *Bull. I.R.C.B.* XXIV, 3 (1953), pp. 876-904. Cf. *B.C.B.* III, de Grelle-Rogier; Cocheris, *op. cit.*, p. 393; Stengers, *ubi supra*, pp. 369-70.

of recognition the later diplomatic history of the Upper Nile. But on 30 June Hanotaux repudiated his own proposals, pleading the lame excuse that serious frontier incidents had been reported from the upper Ubangi. Presumably there had been a last-minute intervention by French colonialist interests. But even the frontier now proposed by Hanotaux—roughly, latitude 4° 30' as far as the Nile-Congo divide— would have left the King a free hand within the Nile basin itself.[1] This was not enough for Leopold, who was interested not merely in the Nile basin but in expansion along the whole six-hundred-mile front from the Nile to the eastern affluents of the Shari. He would however accept if he were permitted to occupy for twelve years 'les territoires du M'Bomou appartenant à la France'; he doubtless calculated that it would be virtually impossible for the French to evict him after twelve years' 'effective occupation'.[2] But the French refused this bargain; the negotiation lapsed, and Leopold turned to London with his alarming stories of an imminent French advance and proposals for a delegation of British sovereignty extending into the Nile basin.

In October 1892 a resumption of the negotiation was suggested by Paris. Jamais, if not Ribot, was disquieted by the steady deterioration of the French position on the upper Ubangi and doubtless by the suspicion, already widespread in French colonialist circles, that London was secretly backing the Van Kerckhoven expedition.[3] King Leopold replied by a grandiose project for a Franco-Congolese partition of the Upper Nile. France was to have access to the Nile through the Bahr al-Ghazal; and she was to be permitted to recruit, from the M'Bomu tribes under Congolese protection, a thousand Zande irregulars for her Upper Nile garrison. In return, France was to guarantee Leopold's acquisitions both inside and outside the Nile basin and was to cede to the Congo State, on demand, 'une route de la crête de partage au Nil, sur 20 kilomètres de largeur, et 50 lieues [carrées] sur le Nil à l'ouest [sic, but surely a slip for 'est'?] des postes français et au choix de l'Etat.' So far as can be made out, not only the recruitment of the French garrisons, but also their access to the Bahr al-Ghazal, would in practice have been subject to Congolese control. Moreover, the proposed arrangement was a very thinly disguised combination against Britain; de Grelle was very anxious that London should not get wind of it prematurely.[4]

By the third week of December, as a result of the personal intervention of Ribot, a frontier had been fixed along the river Shinko (a northern affluent of the M'Bomu) to latitude 6° 30', and thence that parallel 'prolongé indéfiniment' into the Nile basin. However, north

[1] Cornet, *ubi supra*; B.C.B., *loc. cit.*
[2] MAE, Mémoires et Documents Afrique 139 (Congo et Gabon 14), Casimir-Périer to Hanotaux and Haussmann 16 Apr. 1894, citing this proposal as having been made by de Grelle 'in July 1892'.
[3] B.C.B. 111, de Grelle-Rogier. MC Afrique 111 24, Jamais to Ribot [ ] Jan. 1893. Blanchard, *ubi supra*, pp. 16-17, citing Chavannes 16 Mar. 1894.
[4] Stengers, *ubi supra*, pp. 370-2.

of this line, France would *cede* to the Congo State, on demand, an enclave on the Nile 'ten square leagues in area'. She would also *occupy temporarily*, on demand, two points in the Congolese sphere to be designated by the Congo State; as a garrison for these posts the State would place five hundred Congolese regulars at French disposal for three years. The Congo State further undertook to 'faciliter par tous les moyens qui seraient en son pouvoir, toute mission d'exploration ou d'occupation qui serait dirigée par la France, soit vers le nord, soit vers le sud, hors des territoires reconnus à l'Etat Indépendant du Congo.'[1] This was not merely, as Hanotaux later called it, 'une grande action commune'[2] for the partition of the Upper Nile. The peculiar arrangements by which France was to occupy temporarily, with Congolese troops, two points in the Congolese sphere to be designated later, suggests very strongly that Leopold intended to trap France, by the bait of 'une ouverture sur le Nil', into fighting the Congo State's battles—and perhaps in no metaphorical sense—against England.

Yet Ribot seems to have at first accepted the arrangement. At all events, by 2 January 1893 Leopold regarded the negotiation as complete and was ready to conclude; and he would certainly not have been willing to sign merely on the basis of the 6° 30' frontier in isolation. But at the very last moment Ribot took alarm. He showed the 'projet de convention' to the colonialist leaders Etienne and d'Arenberg, who condemned it out of hand as 'a snare for France' and threatened to mobilise parliamentary opposition against it. Ribot was well aware of the dangers of 'being denounced in the Chamber for abandoning territory to which France may have a legitimate claim'. On 3 January he torpedoed the negotiation by demanding modifications to the agreed frontier line. On the 8th de Grelle telegraphed 'impossible conclure', and on the following day he returned to Brussels.[3]

Ribot's last-minute decision to consult Etienne and d'Arenberg may have been prompted not only by misgivings about colonialist opinion, but by a desire to share the responsibility for denouncing an arrangement in which he had discerned, almost too late, dangers quite different from those which troubled the colonialists. It passes belief that Ribot, 'anglomane impénitent',[4] should have consciously sought a quarrel with Britain on the Upper Nile at the very time when he was encouraging Waddington to discuss the Egyptian question itself with Gladstone. A Quai d'Orsay memorandum, probably drafted in the last few days of December, drew his attention very clearly to this danger. The memorandum admitted that:

---

[1] Stengers, *ubi supra*, pp. 372-5. Blanchard, *ubi supra*, pp. 18-19. Cf. MC Afrique III 19c, Nébout to *Colonies* 22 Dec. 1893, where this proposal is clearly referred to, but mis-dated by a slip to the 'beginning of 1892'.

[2] Stengers, *ubi supra*, p. 375, citing Hanotaux 19 Apr. 1894.

[3] *Ibid.*, pp. 374-8. Monteil, *op. cit.*, pp. 106-8. Cocheris, *op. cit.*, pp. 395-6. D'Arenberg was President of the *Comité de l'Afrique Française*.

[4] Blanchard, 'Administrateurs d'Afrique Noire', p. 380. Cf. Flourens in *L'Eclair* 2 Jan. 1894.

'L'arrangement nous reconnaît définitivement toutes les voies d'accès vers le haut Nil. Il nous permet de mettre le pied dans le bassin du fleuve, et déchire ainsi indirectement le traité anglo-allemand qui attribue à l'Angleterre le bassin du Nil en entier. Peut-être, dans un avenir plus ou moins éloigné, nos communications avec le Nil par le Bahr-el-Gazal joueront-elles un rôle important dans la solution de la question d'Egypte.'

But it then uttered a grave warning which Ribot of all ministers was unlikely to ignore: 'En déclarant qu'elle met le pied dans le bassin du Nil, [la France] peut soulever un gros conflit qui paraît devoir être particulièrement dangereux en ce moment, étant donné l'état d'esprit en Angleterre relativement à la question de l'Ouganda.'[1]

Ever since 1890 Ribot had persistently refused to quarrel with England about the Upper Nile, lest by so doing he should further complicate the Egyptian question, which he still regarded as not beyond solution by friendly agreement. Although he was well aware that the Anglo-German Agreement would enable Britain to 'régir à son gré la vallée du Nil',[2] he had always avoided an open dispute about it. This was all the easier because Salisbury never officially communicated the Agreement to Paris.[3] Ribot merely refrained from recognising the Agreement; and at the same time obtained compensation which, even if it did not satisfy the advanced colonialists, at least demonstrated that Britain did not confine her favours to Germany alone. In November 1891 Salisbury had replied—reluctantly, for he valued his good relations with Ribot—to the speeches of Gladstone and Morley predicting an early evacuation of Egypt, and had emphasised that 'paper engagements' were an insufficient guarantee for Egyptian security. Waddington had then remarked that this declaration amounted to excluding in advance any diplomatic solution; but Ribot was content to prescribe complete reserve on Egypt 'jusqu'à nouvel ordre'.[4] These 'further orders' had come after the Liberal electoral victory in 1892.

Ribot's original approval of the Franco-Congolese arrangements of December 1892 must surely have been the result of inadvertance and an over-hasty desire to dispose of a tedious and apparently unimportant problem. Ribot's total lack of interest in Africa, and his profound ignorance of African detail, were a by-word in colonialist circles. The Franco-Congolese dispute was no exception: in August 1892 de Grelle told Monson that Ribot was ignorant not only of the particular questions at issue 'but of all geographical details whatever'.[5] In Ribot's

---

[1] Quoted Stengers, *ubi supra*, p. 379. The French also suspected British collaboration with Leopold (*ibid.*, pp. 380-3).   [2] D.D.F. VIII, No. 140, Herbette to Ribot 5 Aug. 1890.
[3] Ribot in the Chamber 7 June 1894. (It had in fact been sent to the Paris embassy for information only.)
[4] Cecil, *op. cit.*, IV, pp. 392-5. D.D.F. IX, No. 62, Waddington to Ribot 10 Nov. 1891; No. 70, Ribot to Waddington 17 Nov. 1891.
[5] Blanchard, 'Français et Belges . . .', p. 15. FO 84/2202, Monson to Salisbury No. 72, 6 Aug. 1892; cf. FO 10/595, Monson to Rosebery No. 15, 20 Jan. 1893.

eyes the successful nursing of the Franco-Russian entente into a full military alliance with its point against Germany took precedence over any African geographical details, however important these might seem to colonialists. Only once in his dealings with the Congo State did Ribot take a really firm stand. This was in June 1890, when the French right of preference under the arrangements of 1884 and 1887 was the disputed issue. In that month there was placed before the Belgian Chambers a Bill providing for a Belgian option on the Congo at the end of ten years. Ribot did not wish to use the French right of preference to exclude Belgium; but he did wish to exact, as the price of French *agrément*, an explicit admission that the right of preference applied to any type of cession or exchange of territory, and would continue to be so interpreted if the Congo fell into Belgian hands.[1] At the outset of the negotiation Ribot took a high and even menacing tone. In this he was probably influenced by his fear lest: 'Monsieur Flourens, backed by Monsieur de Brazza, Monsieur Charmes, and the clique hostile to the Congo State, should seize on any modification of the arrangement of 1884 as a weapon to attack the Government.'[2] But when the controversy began to develop so as to threaten an open dispute with Belgium as well as with the Congo State, Ribot at once backed down and abandoned the discussion without gaining his point.[3] As always with Ribot, African advantages seemed quite unimportant if they carried the slightest risk of complications in Europe.

But neither Etienne's scale of priorities in Africa, nor Ribot's almost exclusive interest in Europe, provides a full explanation for the astonishing complaisance with which France treated a state whose agents in Africa behaved with constant and calculated hostility and at whose door the Quai d'Orsay had officially laid the massacre of a French garrison. In fact, throughout this period Leopold enjoyed the support of an influential body of sympathisers in France. Those who, like Haussmann, always thought it 'plus sage de limiter notre expansion à l'est et de tirer parti des territoires que nous possédons',[4] tended to support Leopold as a lesser evil than risking a possible collision with England. There may have been a few simple souls who still supported 'l'œuvre léopoldienne' as a philanthropic enterprise. There were certainly some—few, but very influential—who had invested heavily in the Congo State and were determined to protect their capital. And behind all these there were the paid secret agents of King Leopold, of whom the most important was none other than Harry Alis, Secretary-General to the *Comité de l'Afrique française*.

[1] D.D.F. viii, Nos. 111 and 119, Ribot to Bourée 12 and 18 July 1890; Nos. 117 and 125, Bourée to Ribot 17 and 19 July. For details, see Sanderson, *Anglo-French Competition...*, pp. 146-58.
[2] FO 84/2024, Vivian to Salisbury Africa No. 52, 9 Aug. 1890, reporting Lambermont.
[3] D.D.F. viii, No. 129, Ribot to Bourée 22 July 1890. Stenmans, *op. cit.*, p. 122. Sanderson, *loc. cit.*
[4] Stengers, *ubi supra*, p. 379, citing Haussmann to Chavannes 31 Dec. 1892.

It was the 'respectable' sympathisers, doubtless often influenced by others less respectable, who were most valuable to Leopold. Their recruitment was not difficult. For some years after the Protocol of 1887 even the most enthusiastic French colonialists seem to have regarded Leopold as a useful collaborator rather than a serious rival. In 1887 the arrangements with the Congo State had included permission for the King to raise a loan on the Paris money-market. It was an open secret that the funds were to be used for the construction of a railway from Matadi to Léopoldville; and if such a railway were constructed, French operations would inevitably come to depend upon it. Yet no opposition was offered by the colonialists; and the loan project was defeated in the Chamber by the Royalist Right, which accused the Ministers of having received 'pots de vin' from Leopold.[1] Even as late as January 1889 de Brazza, soon to be one of Leopold's most bitter opponents, submitted to the *Colonies* a project for a joint Franco-Congolese railway. Nor did Etienne reject this proposal out of hand. In April 1889 he agreed to the formation of a joint *comité d'études*, though he did point to the dangers of becoming 'tributaires d'un chemin de fer étranger'.[2]

In the course of 1889 de Brazza changed his views completely. Others did not; and in August 1890 Vivian at Brussels could still call the French opponents of the Congo State a mere 'clique'. Although in December 1892 Etienne opposed the particular arrangement reached with the Congo State, he was still in favour of negotiating rather than enforcing a settlement.[3] No doubt Etienne's associate Harry Alis did his best to keep him in this frame of mind. J.-L. Deloncle, the *chef du bureau politique* at the *Colonies*, was determined to preserve the 'ouverture sur le Nil'; but even as late as January 1894 he was prepared to buy the 'ouverture' from Leopold by some pretty sweeping territorial concessions.[4] Even Hanotaux, who was in 1894 to be Leopold's most formidable enemy, seems until the end of 1892 to have been quite strongly in favour of conciliation and concession.[5] Another important sympathiser was Bourée, the French Minister at Brussels. Bourée was more than merely conciliatory; he was a strong supporter of 'l'œuvre léopoldienne'. As early as September 1886 Eudore Pirmez had reported to the King his 'excellentes dispositions' on the Congo-Ubangi question.[6] In July 1890, during the dispute on the right of preference, Bourée was an outspoken advocate of the Congolese case and throughout urged Ribot not to insist on the French demands. He harped on the

[1] Stenmans, *op. cit.*, pp. 62-70. J. Stengers, 'Rapport sur le dossier "Léopold II—Strauch"', *Bull. I.R.C.B.* xxiv, 4 (1953), pp. 1199-1200.

[2] Blanchard, *ubi supra*, pp. 31-2, citing: de Brazza to Etienne 11 Jan. 1889; Etienne to de Brazza 20 Apr. 1889. At this time de Brazza was even prepared to allow Leopold to recruit Senegalese for service in the Congo State.

[3] Stengers, 'Aux Origines de Fachoda', pp. 377-8, fn.

[4] Blanchard, *ubi supra*, pp. 22-3, citing J.-L. Deloncle 2 Jan. 1894.

[5] There is at all events no hint of his having opposed the concessions which Ribot proposed to make in June and Dec. 1892.

[6] Cornet, *ubi supra*, pp. 881-2, citing Pirmez to Leopold 1 Sept. 1886.

'odium' which France would incur if her attack on Leopold were to be exploited by the Belgian parliamentary Opposition. He affected to take seriously Leopold's impudent bluff of a possible gratuitous cession of the Congo to England, and warned Ribot against creating 'des complications hors de toute proportion avec l'intérêt spécial qui nous préoccupe'.[1] By 1893 Bourée's Congolese sympathies had become even more outspoken. In November 1893 he refused to formulate a written protest against Congolese proceedings on the upper Ubangi: 'l'on se demande non sans émotion ici pourquoi M. de Brazza cherche à enfoncer une porte qui lui est si largement ouverte'[2]—an astonishing travesty of the real situation at that time.

Other sympathisers, whose activities are less easily traceable, existed in the international world of high finance of which Leopold himself was an important member.[3] One or two close connections are definitely known. The French banker Charles Bunau-Varilla was a director of the Congo Railway Company and of the *Compagnie du Katanga*, both of them indirectly controlled by the King through Albert Thys and the *Compagnie du Congo pour le commerce et l'industrie* (the 'C.C.C.I.').[4] Conversely, some of Leopold's close Belgian associates in Congolese finance were also important figures in French big business. One of these was Alexandre Browne de Tiège, the Antwerp banker who organised the *Société Générale Africaine* on the King's behalf.[5] Another, Baron Edouard Empain, said to have been one of Leopold's very few real confidants, was a major operator of railways and tramways in France—indeed, he was later to be the principal promoter of the Paris *Métro*.[6] Business interests of this type in particular could hardly have been established and maintained without a correspondingly wide network of political contacts. Thanks to the influence of his French financial connections, Leopold was able to evade the obstacles which the Ministry of Finance normally placed against investment in stocks not quoted on the Paris Bourse. The King had failed to obtain the privilege of quotation for Congolese stocks, which he had been promised in April 1887; but between 1887 and 1894, when French governmental control of foreign lending was being very effectively used to stifle the economy of Italy, Congolese loans enjoyed an 'administrative tolerance' of which French capital was not

---

[1] D.D.F. VIII, Nos. 125 and 134 (cited), Bourée to Ribot 19 and 28 July 1890.

[2] Blanchard, *ubi supra*, pp. 15-16, citing Bourée to Develle 27 Nov. 1893.

[3] *Ibid.*, p. 35.

[4] *B.C.B.* II, Daumas; III, Browne de Tiège; IV, Thys. J. Stengers, 'La première tentative de reprise du Congo par la Belgique (1894-1895)', *Bull. Soc. Roy. Belge Géog.* LXIII (1949), pp. 43-122, at pp. 51-76. H. R. Fox-Bourne, *Civilisation in Congoland* (London 1903), pp. 108-9, 120-7, 131. Philippe Bunau-Varilla, an engineer brother of Charles, was also on the board of the Congo Railway Co.

[5] Stengers, *loc. cit.*, and at p. 120. Fox-Bourne, *op. cit.*, p. 140. *B.C.B.* III, Browne de Tiège.

[6] *B.C.B.* II, Empain; III, Browne de Tiège. Blanchard, *ubi supra*, p. 34. For the part played by Empain in the crisis of Congolese finances towards the end of 1894, see: Stengers, *ubi supra*, pp. 47-52; *eundem*, 'Note sur l'histoire des finances congolaises', *Bull. I.R.C.B.* XXV, I (1954), pp. 154, 250-1.

slow to take advantage.[1] Nor was it slow to defend its investments. In October 1889 de Brazza, who was by now at the head of an agitation to prevent the public floating of a Congolese loan in France, complained to Etienne:

> Ce n'est pas amusant d'avoir à me débattre comme je le fais derrière les coulisses pour obtenir le rejet de l'emprunt du Congo en France. . . . Une groupe financière qui a une grande influence sur un certain nombre de journaux, notamment sur le *Figaro*, dont il [*sic*] possède la publicité financière, y a perdu vingt-six millions parce qu'il les avait souscrits ferme. . . . Il m'a fait savoir qu'on serait heureux de mettre à ma disposition deux millions pour le Kiliou pour peu que je me tienne tranquille. Je vous assure qu'il n'est pas amusant d'accumuler sur son dos de pareilles animosités.[2]

De Brazza did not allow himself to be intimidated;[3] but it would be naïve to suppose that such pressure was always unsuccessful—or that evidence of successful pressure would be readily available.

Leopold maintained in Paris a lavishly staffed 'Bureau d'informations' which was later recognised to be a centre of espionage;[4] but his most spectacular achievement at 'boring from within' was the corruption of Harry Alis. Harry Alis became a paid agent of King Leopold at some time after April 1891 and probably before October of that year, when he publicly defended the very suspect merger with a Congolese company of the only French concern providing a transport service between the lower and upper Congo.[5] During the Franco-Congolese negotiations of 1892 he certainly did his best to earn his disreputable salary. He used his influence with Ribot, with Jamais, with Haussmann and with Hanotaux. In May and June 1892, when the French very nearly made a complete surrender to Leopold and were on the point of abandoning their 'ouverture sur le Nil', Harry Alis was particularly active; and in his letters to Camille Janssen, his Brussels connection and paymaster, he boasts of his successes, especially with Hanotaux and Ribot.[6] Harry Alis was after all the official spokesman of the most influential colonialist organisation in France. His views therefore carried considerable weight; and they were made more acceptable by the lingering conviction among perfectly honest Frenchmen that it was possible and desirable to co-operate with Leopold.

[1] Blanchard, *ubi supra*, pp. 30-3.
[2] *Ibid.*, citing de Brazza to Etienne 7 Oct. 1889.
[3] Instead, he tried to launch a French Congo railway company under the (apparently nominal) headship of a Capt. Le Chatellier (Blanchard, *loc. cit.*; Stengers, 'Aux Origines de Fachoda', p. 389).   [4] Cf. Vergniol, *ubi supra*, p. 640.
[5] Stengers, *ubi supra*, pp. 384-5, 393-4. T. Heyse, 'Correspondance Léopold II—Janssen', *Bull. I.R.C.B.* xxiv, 2 (1953), at pp. 480-4 *B.C.B.* iii, Percher *dit* Harry Alis. The French Company was directed by one Daumas, who later became a director of at least two Congolese companies—and a secret agent of King Leopold.
[6] Stengers, *ubi supra*, pp. 386-7; Heyse, *ubi supra*, p. 483. He was also very active in Dec. 1892.

Harry Alis did not confine himself to intrigue behind the scenes. In May and June 1892 he took part in, and was doubtless mainly respons-ible for, the mild flurry of discussion on the Upper Nile project which caused the British, as Leopold had intended, to speculate nervously on 'the design of the French Colonial Party, openly alluded to both in the Chamber and in the Press, to push forward . . . to the Nile basin'.[1] Harry Alis of course always recommended action in collaboration, and not in competition, with the Congo State. In May 1892, and again in October, articles from his pen in the *Bulletin du Comité de l'Afrique Française* emphasised the advantages of such collaboration:

Est-ce à nous de leur barrer la route du nord-est où la place libre, si elle n'est pas prise par eux, risque d'être occupée par les Anglais? Nous ne le croyons pas.

Nous avons intérêt à ce que la marche des Belges vers le nord-est ne soit pas complètement arrêtée par nous et à ce que le prolongement de leurs possessions vers le Haut-Nil, formant tampon entre les Anglais et nous, protège notre expansion contre des voisins plus dangereux et nous facilite du même coup la pénétration dans le Bahr-el-Ghazal.[2]

These effusions did not indeed go unchallenged, and from July 1892 Harry Alis was under attack as 'pro-Belgian' among the small group of convinced opponents of the Congo State. But this was apparently no obstacle to his appointment in 1893 as delegate for the French Congo on the *Conseil supérieur des Colonies*.[3]

In January 1893 the French had just managed to escape subordin-ating themselves completely to Leopold's Nilotic policy and becoming a catspaw in his dispute with London. But that was all. The Upper Nile, thanks to its connection with Egypt, was potentially an issue on which very strong French feeling could be aroused. But in 1893 these passions were still dormant. The Upper Nile had been kept out of the public eye by Etienne's African priorities, by Ribot's refusal to quarrel with London about it and by his complete lack of interest in the dispute with Leopold. Harry Alis, exaggerating Etienne's policy to the point of caricature, had taken care to direct Africanist enthusiasm almost exclusively towards Lake Chad, well clear of King Leopold's interests. No influential personality among the colonialists had come out in strong and consistent support for a drive to the Upper Nile. In 1892 only Chavannes, Dolisie and possibly Liotard felt really strongly on the subject; but their distant voices had little weight in Paris, and their local weakness kept them from reproducing on the Ubangi the behaviour of the *officiers soudanais* on the Niger. In this situation King Leopold's skill in diplomatic manœuvre and backstairs intrigue had completed the stifling of the always rather feeble French aspirations

---

[1] FO 84/2202, Gosselin to Salisbury No. 53, 17 June 1892.
[2] Harry Alis in the *Bull. C.A.F.*, May and Oct. 1892.
[3] Stengers, *ubi supra*, p. 389; B.C.B. III, Percher *dit* Harry Alis.

to make use of their 'ouverture sur le Nil'. Meanwhile, he had decisively defeated Rosebery's attempt to eject him from the Nile basin and was in practice drawing the profits of Salisbury's skill in concluding the Anglo-German Agreement. But he could not leave well alone. Early in 1893 he overreached himself by encouraging for his own purposes a French expedition to the Upper Nile. Thereby he helped to set in motion political forces which he found himself unable to control, and which in the not very long run shattered his grandiose dreams of Nilotic empire.

VII

A FRENCH INITIATIVE AND ITS

FRUSTRATION. *MISSION MONTEIL*

1893–94

IN January 1893 there had been a re-shuffle of the French Cabinet. Ribot was forced by the repercussions of the 'Panama' scandal to take over the Ministry of the Interior; the Quai d'Orsay was entrusted to Jules Develle, an obscure figure who seems nevertheless to have been considerably more combative towards England than his predecessor—perhaps simply because he did less to restrain the traditionally combative tendencies of his officials.[1] At the same time the *Colonies* fell to a man previously untried in office—Théophile Delcassé, a *méridional* from Ariège whose actions at this stage of his career often seem to betray a typically southern impulsiveness. On 3 February Develle, in reply to an enquiry by d'Arenberg, President of the *Comité de l'Afrique française*, declared himself 'prêt à appuyer moralement et même matériellement une mission vers le Bahr el-Ghazal'.[2] On 20 February Delcassé informed Libreville of a decision he had already taken as early as the 10th: 'Suis disposé organiser mission destinée renforcer solidement Liotard et pénétrer région Haut Mbomou afin atteindre le plus rapidement possible bassin du Nil.'[3]

At first sight this looks like a considered decision by the French Government to reply by a coup on the Upper Nile to Rosebery's refusal to discuss the affairs of Egypt. By February 1893 the British reaction to the khedivial crisis of January had made it very clear that Ribot's policy of an amicable arrangement with the Liberals was utterly bankrupt, at any rate so long as Rosebery remained in office. Rosebery's normal intransigence was intensified by his personal dislike of Waddington and by his extreme irritation at the ambassador's earlier attempt to negotiate privately with Gladstone; and in January and February 1893 it was with evident relish that he snubbed all

---

[1] Cf. T. M. Iiams, *Dreyfus, Diplomatists and the Dual Alliance* (Geneva-Paris 1962), p. 26, where Develle is described as 'a deplorable minister [because] he couldn't bear to say no'.

[2] Stengers, 'Aux Origines de Fachoda', *Rev. Belge Phil. Hist.*, 1960, pp. 391-2, citing Harry Alis to Janssen 3 Feb. 1893.

[3] *Ibid.*, p. 444 (1958). MC G.C., 1 40b, Delcassé to Chavannes, 20 Feb. 1893.

Waddington's efforts to discuss the Egyptian situation.[1] Moreover, the French were by now well aware that they could expect no help from their Russian allies in breaking down this resistance. During the khedivial crisis St Petersburg had made no move; and even the French ambassador Montebello, never a severe critic of Russian policy, had to admit that 'la Russie, malgré l'action puissante qu'elle pourrait, si elle le voulait, exercer sur la politique de l'Angleterre en Egypt, est généralement portée à se désintéresser de cette question'.[2] Other French diplomatists[3] suspected that this reserve was deliberately intended to perpetuate the British occupation and with it the estrangement between Britain and France. They were right. In June 1891 the Russian Foreign Minister Giers had remarked: 'Si les Anglais restaient en Egypte cela ne nous ferait pas grand'chose et nous y gagnerions. Cette occupation rend impossible une entente entre la France et l'Angleterre. Ce n'est pas à nous de nous en désoler.'[4] In this situation it was tempting to think of forcing the British to negotiate by French intervention on the Upper Nile; and Develle certainly allowed himself to be tempted, at any rate up to a point. But the temptation came in the first instance not from the officials at the Quai d'Orsay, nor even from Delcassé, but from King Leopold, working through his usual channel of Harry Alis and the *Comité de l'Afrique française*.

In July 1892 Camille Janssen had suggested to Leopold that the *Comité* should offer to subsidise an expedition 'towards' the Bahr al-Ghazal on condition that the Franco-Congolese dispute was first settled. A few days later Harry Alis put precisely this proposal to Hanotaux, adding that 'si on ne s'entend pas avec les Belges, il n'y a rien à essayer de ce côté, le Comité de l'Afrique française ne voulant pas exposer ses envoyés à des difficultés avec les Belges.'[5] In January 1893 Leopold revived this project, hoping thereby to secure the 'grande action commune' which had just so narrowly escaped him; in any case, such a project would increase the pressure on the British. On Leopold's orders, Harry Alis went the rounds of the leading colonialists; and, using the Portal mission to Uganda as a scarecrow, expatiated on his:

désir déjà vieux d'organiser une sérieuse mission qui allât
planter le drapeau français sur le Bahr-el-Ghazal et permît
ainsi à l'influence française de devancer les Anglais et de
s'implanter sur le Nil occidental et peut-être sur le Nil moyen.
J'ai rappelé mon ardente conviction qui est que l'entente entre

---

[1] James, *Rosebery*, pp. 272-3, 277-80. Miller, 'The Egyptian Question . . .', *J. Mod. Hist.*, 1960, pp. 5-6. D.D.F. x, Nos. 153 and 156, Waddington to Develle 31 Jan. and 1 Feb. 1893. L.Q.V. 3, ii, p. 222, the Queen's journal 7 Feb. 1893.

[2] D.D.F. x, No. 142, Montebello to Develle 27 Jan. 1893.

[3] Notably Paul Cambon at Constantinople; cf. *ibid.*, No. 176, Cambon to Develle 25 Feb. 1893. Herbette at Berlin seems also to have been a sceptic.

[4] Staal, *Correspondance*, p. 124, Giers to Staal 16 June 1891; cf. pp. 147-8, Staal to Shishkin 18 Nov. 1891.

[5] Stengers, *ubi supra* (1960), pp. 389-90.

l'Etat Indépendant et la France peut seule leur permettre de tenir tête aux Anglais.

D'Arenberg was persuaded to seek Develle's approval for a project on these lines; and it was in these circumstances that Develle gave his assurance of support.[1]

On about 10 February, a week or so after Harry Alis' campaign of lobbying, Delcassé told d'Arenberg that he had decided to send an expedition 'vers le Bahr-el-Ghazal'.[2] Janssen attributed this decision to the manœuvres of Harry Alis, and congratulated Leopold on the prospect of a very early settlement of the Franco-Congolese dispute 'afin que cette expédition puisse marcher rapidement en restant sur le territoire français et avec notre aide'.[3] But Delcassé's mission was not, even at this early stage, the mission King Leopold had bargained for. Delcassé was already planning to finance it, and therefore to control it, himself;[4] and so far as is known he never asked the *Comité* for a subvention. Perhaps Delcassé was already suspicious of the *Comité*; but however this may be, his decision to be financially independent at once destroyed Leopold's strongest means of influence. Further, it soon became clear that for Delcassé the reinforcement of Liotard—against the Congolese—was just as important as the breakthrough to the Nile basin. From the very outset Delcassé seems to have opposed any arrangement with Leopold, at any rate until France could negotiate from a local position of strength; and if meanwhile the Congolese offered physical opposition, he was quite prepared to meet force with force. Delcassé's decision seems to have been at least as much a response to Liotard's almost desperate position at Les Abiras as to any promptings, direct or indirect, by Harry Alis.

In February Delcassé was reported as having decided on a mission 'vers le Bahr-el-Ghazal'. If this was indeed the original goal of the mission, Delcassé soon modified it. By April at the latest, and probably long before, Delcassé was aiming at the Nile itself, and the Nile near Fashoda.[5] This evolution was almost certainly inspired by the notorious paper 'Soudan Nilotique', delivered on 20 January 1893 before the *Institut Egyptien* by the French hydrologist Victor Prompt. In it Prompt had discussed the project of a storage dam on the White Nile immediately below its confluence with the Sobat; and in a section ominously entitled 'Opérations dans le Haut-Nil dues à la malveillance', he had suggested that such a dam could be operated so as to ruin Egypt either by drought or by untimely flood.[6] Advance (lithographed) copies of this paper were circulating in the Paris ministries early in 1893; and although there is no need to attribute to Delcassé any

---

[1] Stengers, *ubi supra*, pp. 391-2, citing Harry Alis to Janssen 3 Feb. 1893.
[2] *Ibid.*, *loc. cit.*; and (1958), p. 444.
[3] *Ibid.* (1960), p. 393.
[4] This seems clear from *ibid.* (1958), p. 444, citing Janssen to Leopold 12 Feb. 1893.
[5] Monteil, *Souvenirs Vécus*, p. 65.
[6] V. Prompt, 'Soudan Nilotique', *Bulletin de l'Institut Egyptien*, III, 4 (1893), pp. 71-116.

definite project for malicious interference with the Nile waters, it is morally certain that the ultimate objective of the Monteil Mission was to exert pressure upon England, and so 're-open the Egyptian question', by the implicit threat of such interference.[1]

This was African policy on the heroic scale; but it was the policy of Delcassé, not of the French Cabinet nor even of the Quai d'Orsay. Develle was not consulted or even informed, in spite of its grave international implications. In June 1893 he complained that he had been left to learn from the newspapers the appointment of Monteil as commander of the expedition; and at the end of July he had still received 'aucune indication sur la composition et l'objectif de la mission Monteil'.[2] Delcassé doubtless had his reasons for keeping Develle in ignorance. A 'mission vers le Bahr-el-Ghazal', such as Develle had approved, was a comparatively safe way of putting pressure on London; but Develle might have shrunk from a seizure of Fashoda, which would obviously have provoked a severe crisis even as early as 1893. Moreover, Develle was also 'prêt à terminer le différend franco-belge' by negotiation,[3] and Delcassé seems to have distrusted anything short of complete intransigence in dealing with Leopold. Develle was not, however, the only one to be kept in the dark. Delcassé did not reveal the instructions he had given to Monteil even to his own officials. That he should have by-passed Haussmann, now as ever the strongest opponent of a forward policy, is comprehensible enough. But J.-L. Deloncle was also kept in ignorance; and Deloncle was no impassioned advocate of consolidation. But he was also no intransigent enemy of Leopold, and was in January 1894 quite prepared to negotiate a settlement provided that 'la France n'abandonne pas les voies d'accès au bassin du Nil'.[4] Nor did Delcassé after February 1893 consult or inform any of the leading colonialists; at the end of May even Etienne still seems to have had no knowledge of Delcassé's plans.[5] Delcassé is often said to have been secretive by nature; but he may have guessed that secrets revealed to the colonialists did not long remain secrets from Leopold.

Chavannes at Libreville, sourly remarking that Delcassé's proposal was very belated in view of the preponderance gained by the Congolese, had suggested Liotard as leader of the Nile mission.[6] Delcassé ignored this recommendation. He wanted the *officier soudanais* Monteil, who had in December 1892 returned, by way of the Sahara and Tripoli, from his great march to Lake Chad. Monteil was not easy to

---

[1] Cf. MC Afrique III 19a, Monteil to M. Lebon 7 Mar. 1894 (published, in part, D.D.F. XI, No. 65).
[2] Stengers, *ubi supra* (1958), p. 449.
[3] *Ibid.* (1960), p. 392, citing Harry Alis to Janssen 3 Feb. 1893.
[4] *Ibid.* (1958), pp. 448-9. Blanchard, 'Français et Belges . . .', *Rev. Hist. Cols.* 1950, pp. 22-3, citing Deloncle 2 Jan. 1894.
[5] This is at any rate the impression given by the account of Chavannes (cf. Vergniol, 'Fachoda', *Revue de France*, Aug. 1936, pp. 633-4; Lotar, *Bomu*, pp. 60-2).
[6] MC G.C., I 40a, Chavannes to Delcassé 21 Feb. 1893.

persuade. In March and again in April he declined the commission, pleading exhaustion after his recent African exertions and a total ignorance of the geography and local politics of the upper Ubangi. In order to overcome this resistance Delcassé, a mere junior *sous-ministre*, invoked the assistance of the President of the Republic. On 3 May 1893 Delcassé inveigled Monteil into the President's study at the Elysée; whereupon, according to Monteil's own account, Sadi Carnot took the initiative: 'Voyons, Monteil, acceptez!' Monteil replied: 'vous êtes le chef de l'armée, le chef de la marine, donnez un ordre, j'obéirai'—a declaration which was scarcely to be fulfilled by his subsequent conduct. Thereupon the President explained that France must exploit the status of the Sudan as *res nullius* in order to secure for her posts on the upper Ubangi 'un débouché sur le Nil par le Bahr el Ghazal'. The goal of the expedition was to be Fashoda, indicated, said the President, by M. Prompt, 'un de mes camarades de Polytechnique'; and he handed to Monteil a lithographed copy of Prompt's 'Soudan Nilotique'. Then, says Monteil, 'je demandai . . . au Président de préciser s'il s'agissait d'une simple exploration ou d'une occupation. "Il faut *occuper* Fachoda", conclut M. Carnot.'[1]

Monteil does not report Sadi Carnot as having given any detailed reasons why France had to have 'un débouché sur le Nil'; Jules Cocheris, who evidently obtained his material on this episode from Monteil himself, repairs this omission by putting into the President's mouth the declaration 'Je veux rouvrir la question d'Egypte'.[2] However, it is not a matter of very great moment whether these words were actually spoken or not; for the idea was certainly present in the minds both of Delcassé and of the President. Three weeks later Sadi Carnot told the explorer Casimir Maistre that France had to establish herself on the Upper Nile 'de façon à avoir son mot à dire le jour où se poserait la question d'Egypte'.[3] Monteil's own correspondence establishes that the planners of the mission, inspired by M. Prompt's indiscreet hydrological speculations, intended to enable France to 'say her word' in tones of menace.[4] Meanwhile, the Foreign Minister was quite unaware that the President of the Republic was aiding and abetting Delcassé in a private foreign policy whose diplomatic consequences were not easily calculable, but would certainly be very grave.

On 27 May Delcassé cabled Libreville to stand fast on the upper Ubangi and the M'Bomu, and promised early reinforcements under Monteil. An immediate credit of 300,000 francs permitted Monteil's

---

[1] Monteil, *op. cit.*, pp. 65-8.

[2] Cocheris, *Situation Internationale*, p. 426. This statement may however have owed more to Cocheris' historical hindsight that to Monteil's report. In the immediately following passage Cocheris contradicts Monteil by making Sadi Carnot describe the Sudan as 'Egyptian territory'; and makes the President suggest that the ultimate object of the mission was to provoke the intervention of 'Europe' in the Egyptian question. These two ideas were not in fact developed until 1894 and 1895 respectively.

[3] C. Maistre, 'Le Président Carnot et le plan français d'action sur le Nil en 1893', *Afrique Française*, Mar. 1932, pp. 156-7. Cf. Vergniol, *ubi supra*, p. 632.

[4] Cf. MC Afrique III 19a, Monteil to Lebon 7 Mar. 1894.

advance party to leave as early as 10 June.[1] In July Monteil went to Rotterdam to arrange transport on the upper Congo and lower Ubangi with the *Compagnie hollandaise de navigation du Congo* (the 'Greshoff Company'). There he was assured that his boats would be ready at Brazzaville by 1 October. On 10 August the bulk of the expedition's stores were shipped. All that now remained was a small consignment of technical stores—and Monteil himself. The technical stores left on 10 September; but Monteil remained in France, and almost a year later he had still not embarked.[2]

Monteil's protracted delay was a mystery which developed into a scandal; and when he published his memoirs he was at pains to explain it away. During August and September 1893 he was, he says, preoccupied 'à me créer une âme congolaise', in démarches to obtain the appointment of *commandant supérieur du Haut Oubangui*, and in arranging to bring the d'Uzès mission under his official control. However, by 10 October he was quite ready. Indeed, his bags were on the quay at Bordeaux when, out of the blue, a telegram was received from de Brazza advising the postponement of the mission: the Congolese were determined to use force to prevent Monteil leaving Brazzaville, and had already given earnest of their intransigence by 'imprisoning' Liotard. Monteil thereupon consulted Haussmann and, in the absence of Delcassé from Paris, Eugène Etienne. This trio waited upon Develle, who promised to take the matter up with de Grelle-Rogier. A day or two later, Develle reported that de Grelle had been quite 'uncompromising both in his demands . . . and in his general attitude'. When Monteil persisted, Develle replied that he had had little time to spare for African affairs, for until the previous day France had been on the brink of war with Italy as a result of the Aigues-Mortes incident. Monteil then betook himself to Foix for a personal consultation with Delcassé, the upshot of which was that the mission should be strengthened 'pour, au besoin, s'ouvrir passage malgré l'attitude délibérément hostile de l'Etat Indépendant'. Until these reinforcements had been obtained, the Foreign and Colonial ministries saw no point in Monteil's leaving for Africa—'Je m'inclinai devant la décision prise par le gouvernement'.[3]

The provision of the necessary credits was however delayed, first by a general election, then by the festivities which accompanied the visit of the Russian fleet to Toulon. Monteil occupied the time by working

[1] MC G.C., 1 41b, Delcassé to A/Gov. Libreville 8 June 1893, citing a tel. of 27 May. Stengers, *ubi supra* (1958), pp. 448-9, citing J.-L. Deloncle to Lebon 15 Dec. 1893. According to Haussmann, 900,000 francs had been earmarked for the mission for the two years 1893-4 and 1894-5 (Vergniol, *ubi supra*, p. 633, citing Haussmann to Monteil 8 June 1893).
[2] MC Afrique III 19a, *loc. cit.*; Monteil, *op. cit.*, pp. 67-8; Vergniol, *ubi supra*, p. 634, citing Monteil to Chavannes 17 July 1893.
[3] Monteil, *op. cit.*, pp. 68-70. The 'Aigues-Mortes Incident' (17 Aug. 1893) was a riot by French strikers against Italian blackleg labour, in which seven Italians were killed. On 19 and 21 Aug. there were counter-demonstrations by the Roman mob, which attempted to set fire to the French embassy.

K

out plans for his reinforced expedition; but he also devoted some thought to a possible diplomatic arrangement by which, in order to avoid an armed conflict, the Congo State should relinquish territory giving access to the Nile in return for compensation elsewhere. In the course of these studies Monteil became aware of the dangers inherent in the undefined eastern boundary of the German Cameroons. To this he drew Delcassé's attention; as a result he and Haussmann were in December sent to Berlin, where they ultimately concluded the Franco-German Protocol of 4 February 1894.[1]

Meanwhile, at the beginning of December, there had been a change of government at Paris. Jean Casimir-Périer now combined the foreign ministry with the *Présidence du Conseil ;* at the *Colonies* Delcassé had been replaced by Maurice Lebon. These changes, 'quelques intrigues aidant', led we are told to Monteil's credits being dropped from the budget. In January 1894 Monteil complained to Lebon that his mission was being frustrated by the Government's 'deliberate and culpable neglect', and sent to Casimir-Périer a copy of his letter. In March he obtained an interview with Casimir-Périer, in which he emphasised the extreme urgency of a settlement with the Congo State. The minister concurred, and forthwith nominated Monteil and Haussmann as negotiators. Negotiations took place at Brussels in April 1894; but in these Monteil played no part, having been dropped at the last minute in favour of Hanotaux. No agreement was reached—mainly, in Monteil's view, because Monteil had been replaced by Hanotaux; and before any further action could be taken, King Leopold had concluded his agreement with England.[2]

Monteil's explanation is *prima facie* suspect in that some of the events which he adduces as having delayed his departure after 10 October actually occurred before that date. The general election of 1893 took place, not in October, but in August and September.[3] The Aigues-Mortes crisis had been at its height in August, and was by 10 October a closed incident.[4] Negotiations with the Congo State had already reached deadlock before 10 October.[5] Nor can any alarming telegram from de Brazza be traced on or about 10 October; but as early as 9 September Libreville had cabled that strong Congolese reinforcements · were moving up the Ubangi, and that there was talk among Belgian officers of opposing Monteil by force.[6]

But in fact none of these events, whether correctly dated or not, was relevant to Monteil's decision not to leave for Africa. As early as 14 August 1893 Monteil had explicitly stated, in a formal Note to

---

[1] Monteil, *op. cit.,* pp. 70-2.
[2] *Ibid.,* pp. 103, 105-7. Monteil seems to have written to Lebon on 2 Jan. 1894 (Cocheris, *op. cit.,* p. 429).
[3] J. Chastenet, *La République Triomphante* (Paris 1955), p. 52.
[4] Cf. D.D.F. x, No. 382, Billot to Develle, 8 Oct. 1893.
[5] *Infra,* pp. 147-8.
[6] MC G.C., 1 41a, Lippmann to Delcassé 16 Sept. 1893, citing tel. of 9 Sept. Stengers, *ubi supra* (1960), p. 402, cites this tel. from the *Papiers Monteil.*

Delcassé, that he would not start until a Franco-Congolese settlement had been reached: 'Il est à exercer *une action gouvernementale*, soit par la voie diplomatique, soit par la force qui me permette de quitter le Haut Oubanghi sans avoir à entrer en conflit avec une *puissance européenne.*' Monteil backed this demand with a military appreciation which was in itself reasonable enough. His force would not be strong enough to enable him to demand on the spot the evacuation of the disputed territories—though so far as is known Delcassé had never suggested that he should do this. Alternatively, simply to by-pass the Belgian posts and push on to the Nile would be to leave his line of communication at the mercy of the Congolese. Monteil did not however ask for sufficient reinforcements to enable him to mask the Belgian posts while he himself advanced to the Nile, which seems to be the obvious textbook solution to this military problem. Instead he demanded a prior settlement of the Franco-Congolese dispute, and answered with a firm negative his own question 'La pénétration vers le Bahr-el-Ghazal est-elle d'une execution possible, tant que le conflit franco-belge ne sera pas réglé?' Monteil did not indeed exclude a forcible solution; but his own suggestion on these lines—'le blocus de l'embouchure du Congo par la Division navale de l'Atlantique sud'—has two noteworthy characteristics. It involved no action by Monteil himself; and it was so absurdly drastic that its serious consideration was very unlikely. But the main purpose of his note was to press for a prior *diplomatic* settlement; and he concludes: 'L'avis du chef de mission est que mieux vaut un arrangement un peu onéreux que des tiraillements continuels qui n'auraient pour conséquence que d'user en pure perte les efforts de tous.'[1]

Delcassé, in no mood for 'un arrangement un peu onéreux' with King Leopold, actually suggested Monteil's proposed forcible solution to the Quai d'Orsay; 'mais on lui fit comprendre en forme plutôt sèche que c'était là une plaisanterie dont le Département d'Affaires étrangères ne goûtait aucunement le sel'.[2] Meanwhile, in July, Develle had already resumed negotiations with the Congolese. According to Monteil's Note of 7 March 1894, this had been done '*sur ma demande expresse*', which suggests that Monteil had urged this course upon Develle even before he had presented his quasi-ultimatum to Delcassé in August 1893. Develle, who conducted the negotiation himself, seems to have been anxious throughout for a diplomatic solution and was evidently prepared to make considerable sacrifices to obtain it. In July Hanotaux, whose attitude had evidently hardened considerably since the beginning of the year, remarked sourly to de Grelle, 'If you had me to deal with, you would find me less accommodating'.[3] By

[1] Monteil to Delcassé 14 Aug. 1893 (published, with important omissions, Cocheris, *op. cit.*, pp. 427-9). MC Afrique III 19a, Monteil to Lebon 7 Mar. 1894 (the extracts cited are those expressly stated to be recapitulations or summaries of passages in the August note). Cf. Stengers, *ubi supra*, pp. 396-8. The emphases, in these and other citations from Monteil's March Note, are in the original.   [2] Blanchard, *ubi supra*, p. 16.
[3] MC, *loc. cit.* Stengers, *ubi supra*, p. 398. Hornik, *Der Kampf der Grossmächte*, p. 106, citing Lützow (Paris) to Kálnoky 13 July 1893.

the end of September Leopold was demanding a frontier along the M'Bomu, then northwards along the Shinko as far as the seventh parallel. Such a settlement would have destroyed all practicable French access to the Upper Nile; and even for Monteil it was too much, though not apparently for Develle. 'M. Develle a insisté pour savoir si cette concession pouvait être faite. J'ai refusé net.'[1]

Although the negotiations were not formally suspended until 23 October, they had already reached deadlock in the first few days of the month.[2] This time Leopold had not attempted to seduce the French by offering rights of temporary occupation within the Congolese sphere. By October 1893 Leopold had long been aware that his plan for encouraging a French expedition had backfired; and his aim now was simply to keep the French as far as possible from the Upper Nile. As early as 11 May the Parliamentary colonial group had published a resolution demanding action by the Government to secure the evacuation by the Congo State of 'certaines régions qui, aux termes du protocole du 29 avril 1887, appartiennent à la sphère d'influence de la France'; and Le Temps had at once linked this resolution with the rumoured mission of commandant Monteil to the upper Ubangi. By 24 May Leopold had been forced to recognise that his subtlety had overreached itself. On that date he sent to Governor-General Wahis at Léopoldville the first of a stream of peremptory orders to reinforce the upper Ubangi, and especially the key-point of Bangasso.[3] If diplomacy failed to seal off the Nile from the French, Leopold was fully determined to use force.

Monteil's reaction to the breakdown of the negotiations in October was to demand lavish reinforcements from Delcassé. This was reasonable enough, for the threatening attitude of the Congolese was by now well known. But in addition to three more companies of Senegalese, Monteil also asked for the construction of a telegraph line from Loango to Brazzaville, and the procurement of two steam-launches and six other craft for the expedition.[4] If Monteil were going to wait until these latter demands had been fulfilled, he would obviously wait for a very long time.[5] Although Monteil justified his demand for boats by the undesirability of the expedition's being dependent on a foreign concern for its river transport, this stipulation, coming at the time when it did, seems rather suspect. There was never any question of the Greshoff Company's failing to fulfil its obligations. Indeed, by November, Monteil's boats were not merely at Brazzaville, but on their way to Bangui. When Chavannes learned that Monteil was postponing his departure in order to obtain boats, he gave way to bewildered despair:

[1] Stengers, ubi supra, pp. 398-9, citing Monteil to Delcassé 4 Oct. 1893. Cf. Cocheris, op. cit., p. 394.

[2] Stengers, loc. cit., citing Leopold to de Grelle 6 Oct. 1893.

[3] Ibid., pp. 399-401.

[4] MC, loc. cit.; Lotar, op. cit., p. 64, citing Chavannes, 9 Nov. 1893; Stengers, ubi supra, p. 403.

[5] The telegraph did not in fact reach Brazzaville until 1901.

'C'est l'inexplicable, et désormais tout sera inexplicable'.[1] But the whole question of the scale of Monteil's reinforcements is fundamentally irrelevant. In March 1894, when Monteil had been granted credits sufficient to give him the military strength for which he had pleaded, he was still flatly refusing to leave for Africa without prior settlement of the Franco-Congolese dispute—[la] 'solution qui devait me permettre à me *rendre utilement* au Congo pour y accomplir la mission que j'avais accepté de remplir'.[2] However strongly Monteil might be reinforced, he was still determined not even to embark without a previous guarantee that he would not have to fight the Congolese.

According to Monteil's published account, in October 1893 the Government forbade him to depart until his expedition had been reinforced 'de manière à m'ouvrir, au besoin par la force, l'accès de la vallée du Nil'. In his Note of 7 March 1894 he is much less explicit; he simply says 'il fut décidé dans ces circonstances que je ne pouvais partir'. There is no explicit mention of an ultimate breakthrough to the Nile by force of arms; nor does Monteil venture to make Delcassé responsible for his failure to embark.[3] Delcassé must indeed have realised, from the receipt of the August note if not before, that he had caught a tartar in Monteil. There was little that he could do to repair this situation. In 1893 Monteil was very much a hero of the colonialists, and he still enjoyed the protection of the powerful Eugène Etienne—indeed, it was Etienne who insisted, in November 1893, that Monteil, rather than a professional diplomatist, should be sent to Berlin as a negotiator.[4] Monteil was too influential either to be disciplined or to be unceremoniously dropped. All the same, at least one attempt was made, precisely in October 1893, to find an alternative leader. In that month the colonialist deputy François Deloncle approached Charles Chaillé-Long, a strongly francophile American who had served the khedive Ismāʿīl in the southern Sudan. Chaillé-Long was asked to lead a mission, not indeed to Fashoda, but to the Nile somewhere between Lado and Shambe. It is not known whether Delcassé was a party to this approach, which was in fact fruitless.[5] But in October 1893 there were good reasons why Delcassé should have sought an alternative to the Monteil mission, and equally good reasons why he could not undertake this quest in person.

Monteil attributes the delay at the end of 1893 and early in 1894 to the ill-will of Maurice Lebon, whom he spatters with mendacious innuendo. Lebon, a hard-headed Norman, seems at first to have accepted Haussmann's views. In December he let it be known that he was not in favour of a forward policy; and he feared that the operations

---

[1] Chavannes, 9 Nov. 1893, cited Lotar, *loc. cit.* On 25 Oct. de Brazza had written to Chavannes: 'le transport de la Mission est assuré' (Vergniol, *ubi supra*, pp. 634-5).
[2] MC, *loc. cit.*
[3] *Ibid.* Monteil, *op. cit.*, p. 106.
[4] Blanchard, *ubi supra*, pp. 20-1.
[5] C. Chaillé-Long, *My Life in Four Continents* (London 1912), ii, pp. 447-8.

of Monteil's vanguard under Decazes, who had by now reached the upper Ubangi, had 'too pronounced an offensive character'.[1] But the accusation that he dropped Monteil's credits from the budget is simply untrue. On 22 January 1894 he informed Libreville that 800,000 francs—Monteil's full demand—was to be earmarked for the mission from the 1894 budget.[2] Moreover, once he had played himself in, Lebon began to take a more positive interest in the mission. On 16 February 1894 a telegram from Libreville reported that the expected arrival of Monteil had provoked an outburst of extreme hostility from the Congolese on the upper Ubangi. Lebon at once passed the telegram to Casimir-Périer, with the recommendation that Monteil's departure should be hastened and that the Quai d'Orsay, its hand strengthened by this initiative, should then resume the negotiation with Leopold.[3] Casimir-Périer, who was at this time utterly opposed to the Nile expedition and strongly in favour of wholesale concessions to Leopold, ignored this suggestion; and when Lebon received Monteil's note of 7 March he must have discovered that hastening commandant Monteil was not so easy as it might look.

Monteil certainly had a right, and perhaps a duty, to suggest political action which would in his view facilitate the accomplishment of his mission. But Monteil, having accepted command of the mission, then attempted to dictate policy by refusing to act until his political suggestions had been adopted. This behaviour may well have been partly prompted by Monteil's overweening personal vanity. Lionised by the colonialists and entrusted with an important diplomatic mission, he had by the end of 1893 come to regard himself not merely as an able military explorer but as a skilled diplomatist and an influential politician. It is however strange that Monteil should have been so reluctant to come to grips with the Congolese, whose behaviour towards his compatriots on the upper Ubangi had been so unremittingly hostile. His personal courage had been amply proved by his previous career; as an *officier soudanais*, and a Marine at that, he had grown up in a military tradition whose main article of faith was attack at any cost and against almost any odds. The possibility cannot be rejected that Monteil was influenced, doubtless without his realising it, by members of King Leopold's connection in France. Monteil, arrogant, muddle-headed and inordinately vain of his non-existent political and diplomatic expertise, was a character made to be duped and manipulated by cleverer men than himself.[4]

The evidence suggests indeed more than a mere possibility. The

[1] Stengers, *ubi supra*, pp. 403-4; Blanchard, *loc. cit.*

[2] MC G.C., I 43b, Lebon to A/Gov. Libreville 22 Jan. 1894. Cf. Stengers, *loc. cit.*, citing Monteil to Lebon 18 Nov. 1893; MC Afrique III 19a, Monteil to Lebon 7 Mar. 1894.

[3] MC G.C., I 43a, Chavannes to Lebon 16 Feb. 1894, citing Liotard to Chavannes 6 Dec. 1893. MC Afrique III 19c, Lebon to Casimir-Périer 17 Feb. 1894.

[4] These characteristics are clearly discernible in *Souvenirs Vécus* and in Monteil's note of 7 Mar. 1894; and cf. Blanchard, *ubi supra*, pp. 19-20.

diplomatic solution which Monteil demanded as a pre-condition of his departure was precisely that for which Leopold had hoped when he first instructed Harry Alis to agitate for a French expedition to the Nile basin. 'La note que Monteil adressa à Delcassé le 14 août 1893 ... constituait, en matière de chimie politique, exactement la réaction que le Roi avait préparée dans ses éprouvettes bruxelloises.'[1] It is difficult to believe that this exact identity was a mere coincidence. Leopold doubtless worked upon Monteil through the usual Harry Alis network; but he also had another finger on Monteil. When in March 1894 Monteil was pressing his claim to be sent to Brussels as a negotiator, he stated that he had a 'private line' to the King.[2] This 'private line' was presumably Monteil's acquaintance the comte d'Ursel, a Belgian nobleman who combined an entrée into Paris society with secret service work for King Leopold. It seems quite likely that d'Ursel had been specifically detailed by the King to find out all he could about Monteil's activities and intentions. By April 1894 Leopold seems to have regarded Monteil as thoroughly 'reliable' from his own point of view.[3] The King then wished to re-open his line to Paris after the conclusion of his Agreement with England, the existence of which had still not been revealed. D'Ursel was therefore instructed to invite Monteil to undertake private and secret negotiations with the King. Monteil was told that everything could still be put right between France and the King, but only if he would agree to go to Brussels, for Leopold would accept nobody except Monteil as negotiator. Monteil, who himself recounts this episode, declined the invitation;[4] but even after the publication of the Anglo-Congolese Agreement he did not advocate the use of force against the Congolese on the upper Ubangi. He was ready enough to talk big about the French being 'dégagés désormais de toute attitude de réserve qui pourrait être taxée de sentimentale', and to demand that France should 'répondre par des actes à la politique agressive ... de l'Etat Indépendant'. But Monteil's own 'dégagement' inspired him to nothing more militant than a fantastic scheme for reaching the Upper Nile—and by-passing the Congolese— by way of the Niger, the Benue and the Shari.[5]

In the early months of 1894 Casimir-Périer, whom Monteil's published memoirs treat remarkably leniently, was certainly very strongly opposed to the Nile expedition. But he can hardly be said to have halted the Monteil mission. Months before he took office the mission was already at a complete standstill, thanks to the threatened resistance of Leopold and the suspect exigencies of Monteil himself. But the Monteil mission was not the only element in the Delcassé-Carnot plan for the Nile. Both men recognised that if Monteil did get

[1] Stengers, ubi supra, p. 396.   [2] Blanchard, ubi supra, p. 25.
[3] Blanchard suggests that already by April 1894 Monteil was no longer fully trusted in Paris.
[4] Monteil, op. cit., pp. 108-10.
[5] MC Afrique III 19a, Monteil to Delcassé 30 May 1894.

through to Fashoda he would need to be reinforced; to this end they hoped to obtain the co-operation of the Negus Menelik.[1] The prospects of obtaining such assistance seemed not unpromising. Since 1889, when Menelik had become Negus, France had built up a considerable fund of goodwill at Addis Ababa. In February 1893 Menelik had formally denounced the Treaty of Uccialli;[2] and Menelik's need for French support was now perhaps great enough for Paris to be able to put a price on it. Indeed, the efforts to obtain Menelik's co-operation were by early 1894 beginning to produce some tangible results. But at this point the whole enterprise was suddenly and completely abandoned; and Paris almost ceased to interest itself in Ethiopian affairs. This sudden reversal followed immediately upon Casimir-Périer's accession to office in December 1893.

The potential importance of Ethiopia for the political fate of the Nile valley had been indicated to the Quai d'Orsay as early as January 1888. Soumagne, the French Consul at Obock, had then drawn the attention of Paris to the influence which might be exerted by or through Ethiopia: 'soit dans le Soudan oriental, où son action peut être directe et immédiate, soit d'une façon indirecte et réflexe en ce qui concerne l'Egypte et le domaine de la Mer Rouge'. Soumagne considered that French interests would best be served by an independent Ethiopia in close and friendly relations with France; and he added that if Ethiopia were to fall under the domination of an European Power she would become 'mistress of the eastern Sudan' and a force with which Egypt would have to reckon very seriously.[3] In 1889 Italy attempted to fill the role indicated by Soumagne. But in January 1890 the Italians forfeited Menelik's confidence and ruined the work of Antonelli by General Orero's unauthorised advance across the Mareb to Adowa.[4] Thereafter the Italian hegemony was so obviously precarious that the French feared, not its consolidation, but a complete collapse which would have enabled Menelik to dispense with the friendship of France. As Ribot put it in April 1892:

> . . . le plus mauvais tour que pourraient nous jouer les Italiens serait de quitter Massaouah et de nous laisser, seuls européens, en face de Ménélik, dont les bonnes dispositions actuelles à notre égard tiennent évidemment, en majeure partie, au besoin qu'il a de se ménager un appui contre l'Italie.[5]

The French were therefore careful to make no specific demands upon Menelik, and above all to refrain from anything that looked like territorial encroachment. In October 1889 Léonce Lagarde, the Governor of Obock, had suggested that the French might reply to the Treaty of

[1] M C Afrique 111 19a, Monteil to Delcassé 7 Mar. 1894; Maistre, *ubi supra*.
[2] D.D.F. x, No. 278 Annex, Menelik to Sadi Carnot 20 Yakatit 1885/26 Feb. 1893.
[3] MAE, Mémoires et Documents Afrique 138 (Abyssinie 5), Soumagne to Flourens 26 Jan. 1888.
[4] *Supra*, Ch. iv, pp. 75-6. Zaghi, *Crispi e Menelich*, pp. 31-42.
[5] D.D.F. ix, No. 253, minute on Billot's despatch of 2 Apr. 1892.

Uccialli by sending a mission to Harar. The Quai d'Orsay testily vetoed this proposal: 'Le moment paraît singulièrement choisi . . . rechercher si nous n'avons pas déjà eu occasion de signaler aux Colonies l'inopportunité de missions analogues à celle dont il s'agit ici.'[1] Meanwhile, although the French never acceded to Menelik's repeated requests that he should be officially authorised to import arms through Obock,[2] no obstacles were placed in the way of his procuring munitions by that route and from French sources. Menelik's chief purchasing agent was the merchant Léon Chefneux, who also acted as courier for the official correspondence which passed between Paris and Addis Ababa. It was through Chefneux that in 1891 Menelik conferred a high Ethiopian decoration upon the President of the Republic, and received in return the Grand Cordon of the *Légion d'Honneur*. Associated with Chefneux, both as a friend and as a commercial partner, was the Swiss Alfred Ilg. Ilg had originally entered Menelik's service as an engineer, but by 1890 he had become the Emperor's confidential adviser on European relations. Ilg also acted on occasion as Menelik's diplomatic courier; and during his visits to Europe he put his special knowledge of Ethiopia at the disposal of the French Government.[3] Meanwhile, France did not recognise the Treaty of Uccialli; Paris replied directly, and not through Rome, to Menelik's well-known circular of April 1891 'to the Christian Powers', in which he defined, for the information of those who 'come forward to partition Africa', the 'actual' and the 'ancient' frontiers of his realm.[4]

Until 1893 official French policy in Ethiopia had aimed at no more than acquiring the confidence and goodwill of the Negus, and that primarily as a weapon with which to harass Italy. Indeed, in Ribot's eyes the French manœuvres in Ethiopia seem to have had the same fundamental objective as the economic 'war' against Italy in Europe—to convince Rome that membership of the Triple Alliance was dearly bought at the cost of French friendship. For a few weeks in May and June 1891 Ribot was beguiled by di Rudinì's insinuations into believing that Italy might be prepared at least to weaken the links with her Triplice partners; and he was then evidently prepared to buy this advantage by recognising the Italian position in Ethiopia. As he had

---

[1] MAE, *ubi supra*: Lagarde to Spuller tel. No. 2, 23 Oct. 1889; Etienne to Spuller, 23 and 29 Oct., and minute by the Dept.; cf. Lagarde to Spuller 10 July 1889.

[2] *Ibid.*: Menelik to Lagarde 1 June 1887; Menelik to Sadi Carnot (recd. 6 Dec. 1889); same to same 6 Tahsas 1882 / 14 Dec. 1889. To the first of these letters the French made no reply, to the second only a formal acknowledgment. To the third the President replied personally and in cordial terms (*ibid.*, Carnot to Menelik 8 Aug. 1890); but nothing was said about the import of arms. An earlier draft reply, not sent, had admitted Menelik's right to import arms, under the Brussels Act. Cf. MAE, *ubi supra*, Menelik to Carnot 30 Oct. 1890.

[3] For Ilg and Chefneux generally, see: C. Keller, *Alfred Ilg* (Leipzig 1918); H. Le Roux, *Ménélik et Nous* (Paris n.d. (?) 1902), p. 222ff; T. L. Gilmour, *Abyssinia: The Ethiopian Railway and the Powers* (London 1906), pp. 12-13. For some of their activities, see: MAE *ubi supra*, Lagarde to Etienne 23 Feb. and 7 Dec. 1890, 26 Aug. 1891; J.-L. Deloncle to Etienne 8 Aug. 1891. Cf. D.D.F. IX, No. 119 fn.; X, No. 227 fn.

[4] D.D.F. IX, No. 20, Billot to Ribot 21 Sept. 1891.

told his ambassador Billot at Rome a few weeks earlier, the purely African question 'n'a pour nous qu'une importance secondaire'.[1] The part which Ethiopia might play in the politics of the Upper Nile certainly did not interest Ribot. It does however seem to have interested Ilg and Chefneux, who cherished a scheme for the construction of a railway from Obock to Addis Ababa and ultimately to the Upper Nile. This was a project which could be plausibly represented as in Ethiopian interests: the Obock branch would facilitate the import of arms, while the Upper Nile branch might enable the Negus to assert his sovereignty in the region of the Nile-Sobat confluence which was, according to the circular of April 1891, within the 'actual' boundaries of his empire. But the circumstances in which Menelik approved this project strongly suggest that he did so in the belief that it would be pleasing to France. In February 1893 he wrote to Sadi Carnot formally denouncing the Treaty of Uccialli. At the same time he requested the French Government to strike for him a coinage bearing his effigy; a fortnight earlier he had authorised Ilg to set about the promotion of a company to construct the Obock-Nile railway.[2]

Even before these moves were known in Paris, Delcassé and Sadi Carnot were planning to enlist Menelik's support for the Nile project. On 26 May Sadi Carnot interviewed the explorer Casimir Maistre. After discussing the potential importance of the Upper Nile for the solution of the Egyptian question, Carnot pointed out that the problem of Monteil's reinforcement would be solved if Menelik could be induced to occupy the regions on the White Nile which he had already publicly claimed as his territory. Maistre was asked to lead an unofficial French mission, to be supported by the *Comité de l'Afrique Française*, through Ethiopia to the White Nile, where an Ethiopian (or Franco-Ethiopian) post would be set up. Maistre declined this commission, pleading ill-health and a total ignorance of Ethiopian conditions.[3] A more direct approach had also been made to the Negus, through Lagarde at Obock; and on 15 June 1893 Lagarde telegraphed to Delcassé that he had good hopes of inducing Menelik to found a post on the Nile 'pour notre compte'.[4]

With the Nile project apparently launched, French policy towards Ethiopia became in the second half of 1893 more openly, and more officially, cordial than ever before. Here again, almost all the initiative seems to have been taken by Sadi Carnot and Delcassé, not by Develle. Early in September the *Hôtel des Monnaies* agreed to strike Menelik's coinage for him.[5] Much more important, on 22 September, Sadi

[1] D.D.F. viii, Nos. 362, 329, Ribot to Billot 26 May and 2 Apr. 1891. Cf. Sanderson, 'England, Italy, the Nile Valley . . .', *H.J.* 1964, p. 112.
[2] D.D.F. x, No. 278, Annex and footnote. R. Ferry, 'L'Ethiopie et l'expansion européenne en Afrique Orientale', *Ann. Sci. Pol.*, xxv (1910), p. 205.
[3] Maistre, *ubi supra*; Vergniol, *ubi supra*, p. 632.
[4] D.D.F. xi, No. 65 fn.
[5] *Ibid.*, No. 9, fn.

Carnot replied to Menelik's letter denouncing the Treaty of Uccialli in terms which, while committing France to no particular action, seemed almost to imply the existence of an informal alliance with Ethiopia:

La France, qui n'a pour l'Ethiopie que les sentiments d'une amitié très sincère et désintéressée, suit avec une profonde sympathie les efforts constants de Votre Majesté pour développer la grandeur et la prospérité de la fière nation qui, depuis des siècles, défend si courageusement son indépendance et sa foi chrétienne.[1]

To emphasise the solemnity of this communication, it was transmitted officially through Lagarde, not through the usual channel of Chefneux.[2] Menelik's reaction was all that could be desired. In his reply of 5 January 1894 he dwelt upon the joy with which the President's letter had filled him; and early in March he granted to Ilg a charter authorising the formation of the *Compagnie Impériale d'Ethiopie*, whose main function was to be the construction and exploitation, with a ninety-nine-year monopoly, of a railway along the trace Jibuti, Harar, Addis Ababa, Kaffa, White Nile.[3] Meanwhile, in December Lagarde had reported—direct to President Carnot—that Ras Makonnen of Harar had been weaned from his Italian intrigues by subsidies and gifts of arms.[4] If Menelik was to be induced to take action on his far western marches, he must not be distracted by suspicions about his most powerful feudatory in the east—especially as Ras Makonnen's open hostility might threaten the transport of arms from the sea.

At this point, when the fruit seemed almost ripe for picking, Paris suddenly retreated into an attitude of complete reserve towards Ethiopia. On 17 January 1894 Chaillé-Long, who had always looked upon Ethiopia as the key to the Upper Nile, suggested to Casimir-Périer that France should promote an Ethiopian invasion of the Sudan under Chaillé-Long's technical direction.[5] Casimir-Périer of course turned down this visionary scheme; but a few weeks later Monteil himself, in his note to Lebon of 7 March 1894, emphasised the importance of prepared liaison with the Ethiopians in the Fashoda region.[6] Two days later Lagarde at Obock sent home a sensational and highly implausible report alleging that a letter of submission from Menelik to King Humbert had been intercepted at Harar, at the very last moment, thanks to Lagarde's personal intervention with Ras Makonnen: 'Nous avons évité, on peut dire *in extremis*, la reconnaissance par l'Ethiopie du protectorat italien, qui aurait amené la ruine de notre influence.' This report was of course utterly untrue, and

---

[1] Cited *ibid.*, No. 5, fn.　　　　　　　　　　[2] *Ibid.*, No. 56, fn.
[3] *Ibid.*, No. 5, Menelik to Carnot 5 Jan. 1894. Gilmour, *op. cit.*, pp. 63-6, printing Menelik to Ilg 1 Magabit 1886/9 Mar. 1894.
[4] D.D.F. XI, No. 56 fn.
[5] Chaillé-Long, *op. cit.*, pp. 447-9; *idem*, 'England in Egypt and the Sudan', *North American Review* CLXVIII (1899), pp. 578-80.
[6] MC Afrique III 19a, Monteil to Lebon 7 Mar. 1894.

Lagarde must have known it to be untrue. It looks as if Lagarde, always rather a crack-brained diplomatist, was attempting in this extraordinary way to re-awaken the interest of Paris in Ethiopian affairs. He did not succeed. Casimir-Périer took no action except, weeks later, to send the despatch to Rome for comment.[1]

In January 1894 Casimir-Périer had objected to Chaillé-Long's proposal because 'any expedition from the Red Sea, by way of Obock, might cause complications with Italy'.[2] This was not an entirely empty fear. In December 1893 the volatile Crispi had returned to the head of affairs in Italy. In January 1894 Rome had protested against the aid and comfort which France was giving to Menelik, and in particular against the activities of Chefneux.[3] In February Billot at Rome had feared that the unusually large drafts of Italian reserves then being called to the colours might portend a war with France as Crispi's desperate reaction to chronic domestic unrest and an economy on the verge of collapse.[4] Yet in September 1893, when the Aigues-Mortes crisis was still creating really dangerous tension with Italy, France had not shrunk from aligning herself with Menelik much more closely than before. Moreover, by February 1894 the general diplomatic position of France had been greatly strengthened, not only by the Czar's long-awaited approval of the Franco-Russian military convention, but by a marked rapprochement with Germany in the colonial field.[5] Nor did Casimir-Périer's fear of complications with Rome lead him to relax in the slightest the economic sanctions which were the principal and continuing cause of tension between the two countries, and which indeed seem never to have pressed more hardly upon Italy than during Casimir-Périer's premiership.

Casimir-Périer's reversal of French policy towards Ethiopia was undoubtedly inspired by his general attitude to the Nile project, to which he was, according to J. Cocheris, inflexibly hostile 'pour des raisons brûlantes que je ne puis discuter'.[6] These reasons cannot have had much to do with Casimir-Périer's view of the intrinsic merit of the policy; for in November 1894, against the strong opposition of Hanotaux, he moved the French Cabinet to authorise Liotard's advance to the Nile. His main motive in November 1894 is clear enough. He wished, as President of the Republic, to 'faire acte d'autorité' and in particular to snub Hanotaux, who was in Casimir-Périer's view conducting foreign policy without keeping the President adequately informed.[7] It seems to have been for very similar reasons that at the beginning of 1894 he enforced precisely the opposite policy towards the

[1] Cf. D.D.F. xi, No. 106, Billot to Casimir-Périer 18 May 1894, and footnotes, for the whole episode.
[2] Chaillé-Long, North American Review, loc. cit.
[3] D.D.F. xi, No. 9, Note de l'Ambassade d'Italie, 10 Jan. 1894.
[4] Ibid., No. 37, Billot to Casimir-Périer 6 Feb. 1894.
[5] Cf. the Franco-German West African Protocol of Feb./Mar. 1894 (Hertslet ii, No. 198).
[6] Cocheris, op. cit., p. 394.   [7] Cf. infra, Ch. ix, pp. 206-7.

Upper Nile. Casimir-Périer regularly exalted the prerogatives of whatever office he happened to be occupying, and showed an extreme hostility to any tendency to encroach on these prerogatives.[1] In December 1893, when he took office as Foreign Minister and as Prime Minister, he found that policy towards the Upper Nile had been made, in collaboration with a junior *sous-ministre*, by a President of the Republic who seemed to have forgotten his constitutional limitations. Sadi Carnot clearly had to be shown his place.[2] To veto the policy that the President had promoted was an obvious and effective retort. But this was not all. When Maurice Lebon showed signs of interesting himself in the Monteil mission he was dismissed and replaced by one Boulanger, whose invincible ignorance of colonial affairs soon became a by-word;[3] and for Boulanger's benefit the *sous-secrétariat aux Colonies* was raised to the status of a full Ministry. This episode has all the appearance of a calculated snub to the colonialists, and to the Nile enthusiasts in particular.

Casimir-Périer was not only inflexibly hostile to the Nile project; he also showed, in the words of Edmond van Eetvelde, now King Leopold's principal agent for Congolese affairs, 'a more conciliatory spirit [towards the Congo State] than any previous or present French statesman'[4]—Ribot included. This was not at first apparent. Casimir-Périer seems to have taken no personal interest in the Franco-Congolese negotiations which were taking place, without any perceptible progress, in January and February 1894.[5] But about the second week of March, apparently prompted by his interview with Monteil, he privately informed Leopold of his desire for an early and definitive settlement.[6] On 20 March de Grelle concluded at Paris an interim agreement by which the two governments agreed 'à respecter réciproquement leurs positions'.[7] The French thus renounced all action in the disputed area, where they had no positions, only claims which they had so far failed to make good. However, this interim agreement was to be immediately followed by detailed negotiations; and on 13 April Hanotaux and Haussmann travelled for this purpose to Brussels, 'where they were the object, on the part of His Majesty, of a marked and somewhat excessive attention'.[8]

On the previous day King Leopold had concluded the first version of his Agreement with London, by which he became the lessee of

[1] Casimir-Périer seems also to have oscillated between crises of depression and acts of rather uneasy self-assertion. Some light is thrown on his character by: Chastenet, *op. cit.*, pp. 62-3, 75-6; G. Chapman, *The Dreyfus Case* (London 1955), pp. 36, 77, 105-7; D.D.F. XI, No. 345, Herbette to Hanotaux 18 Jan. 1895.

[2] Maistre suggests (*ubi supra*, p. 157) that dissatisfaction with Carnot's proceedings was not confined to Casimir-Périer. This seems likely enough.

[3] Monteil, *op. cit.*, p. 110; Cocheris, *op. cit.*, p. 431.

[4] FO 10/614, Plunkett to Kimberley No. 54, 27 April 1894.

[5] *Ibid.*, Plunkett to Rosebery Nos. 9 and 21, 21 Jan., 21 Feb. 1894.

[6] *Ibid.*, Plunkett to Kimberley Nos. 52 and 57, 24 and 29 Apr. 1894.

[7] Text at MAE, Mémoires et Documents Afrique 139 (Congo et Gabon 14).

[8] FO 10/614, Plunkett to Kimberley No. 40, 15 Apr. 1894. Cf. Blanchard, *ubi supra*, p. 25.

almost the whole western basin of the Upper Nile. He was therefore grossly duping the French; but this could not be helped. The critical phase of his negotiation with London had not begun until 9 April.[1] Until then he had needed the forthcoming negotiations with France as a goad for the British; thereafter it was too late to put the French off. The negotiation with France would now have to be torpedoed after a respectable amount of talk. Perhaps Leopold was already contemplating his later request to London that the Anglo-Congolese Agreement should be post-dated;[2] in this way he could represent it as a painful necessity forced upon him by French intransigence.

Not that Casimir-Périer was in the least intransigent. In an additional instruction of 16 April to Hanotaux and Haussmann, he ruled that if Leopold could demonstrate effective occupation north of the Uele 'nous ne refuserions pas à examiner dans quelle mesure il peut être tenu compte à l'Etat Indépendant des sacrifices qu'il a pu faire de ce chef'; and he suggested as a basis for discussion Leopold's proposal of July 1892 whereby the King was to occupy for twelve years 'the M'Bomu territories belonging to France'.[3] But this instruction was ignored at Brussels, where Hanotaux in particular was already engaged in a bitter struggle to retain independent and unambiguous French access to the Nile. Since Leopold was equally determined to keep 'Zemio's country', northwards from the M'Bomu, as a means of access to his Bahr al-Ghazal leases, deadlock was inevitable.[4] Hanotaux' temper was not sweetened by his growing conviction that the King had already come to terms with England.[5] From the outset of the negotiation he had insisted that 'il ne s'agit pas ici de quelques kilomètres de plus ou de moins; nous envisageons cette question du point de vue européen'.[6] Before he returned to Paris on 23 April he warned Eetvelde in threatening terms that Leopold's 'politique de casse-cou' in Africa 'intervenait dans des questions qui dépassaient de beaucoup l'horizon de différends purement coloniaux', and might lead to serious difficulties not only for the King but for Belgium herself. He threatened 'de mener une campagne de presse qui ferait peut-être sauter la monarchie en Belgique', and to crush Congolese resistance by a Franco-Portuguese blockade of the Congo mouth. Reminding Eetvelde that the Congo State was a creation of the Powers, which the Powers could also destroy, he concluded: 'Si vous persévérez dans cette voie, prenez garde d'être écrasé entre les lourdes machines qui finiront par s'ébranler.'[7]

---

[1] *Infra*, Ch. VIII, p. 164.

[2] FO 10/614, Plunkett to Kimberley No. 51, 24 Apr. 1894.

[3] MAE, *loc. cit.*, Casimir-Périer to Hanotaux and Haussmann No. 2, 16 Apr. 1894.

[4] For details, see *ibid.*: Hanotaux to Casimir-Périer 21 Apr. 1894 (tel. and desp.); same to same No. 3, 22 Apr.; Hanotaux, 'Note très confidentielle', 2 May. Cf. FO 10/614, Plunkett to Kimberley Nos. 52 and 57, 24 and 29 Apr. 1894, for Eetvelde's account of the negotiation.   [5] MAE, *ubi supra*, Hanotaux' Note of 2 May 1894.

[6] FO 10/614, Plunkett to Kimberley No. 52, 24 Apr. 1894.

[7] Blanchard, *ubi supra*, pp. 26-7. FO 10/614, *loc. cit.* FO 10/615, Plunkett to Kimberley No. 80, 26 May 1894.

Leopold attempted to calm this storm by privately informing Casimir-Périer, on 28 April, that he now held certain leases from Britain within the Nile basin; he was careful not to specify either the extent of the leases or the date of the Agreement. Early in May Casimir-Périer replied, in non-committal terms which however contained no shade of reproach or protest.[1] For the next few days Leopold seems to have been quite confident that the Quai d'Orsay would not take matters to extremes; evidently, as Lambermont confided to Plunkett, he had great faith in 'the calming personal influence of Monsieur Casimir-Périer'.[2] It was not until the second week of May, when Casimir-Périer's parliamentary position suddenly became very precarious, that Leopold's apprehensions revived.[3] Meanwhile, Casimir-Périer kept the King's letter secret even from his senior departmental officials; in the first week of May Hanotaux still did not know whether an Anglo-Congolese Agreement really existed or not.[4]

On 22 May the Anglo-Congolese Agreement, in its second version which had been concluded on 12 May, was published in London. Casimir-Périer could no longer avoid taking some action. But he did not act in haste. Only on the 26th was Bourée instructed to protest at Brussels, and not until the 28th did London receive a Note embodying 'the most express reserves'.[5] And beyond these merely formal gestures Casimir-Périer flatly refused to go, on the grounds that since his defeat in the Chamber on the 21st he had been a *ministre démissionnaire*. Herbette at Berlin urged him to respond to the German offers of collaboration, inspired by their grievance against the 'Corridor Clause' which 'encircled' German East Africa. The Germans were indeed for a few days very pressing; they recalled that in the Franco-German Protocol of February 1894 both Powers had concerted their policy on the Niger navigation question, and suggested that the Anglo-Congolese Agreement offered an opportunity for carrying this collaboration into a wider sphere. But Casimir-Périer was content to reply: 'Il ne m'appartient pas d'engager mon successeur et je ne puis que lui laisser le soin de choisir la voie qui pourra le mieux sauvegarder les intérêts de la France.'[6]

Casimir-Périer's excessive complaisance towards King Leopold doubtless sprang from several sources. He seems to have been quite genuinely innocent of all colonialist enthusiasm. Early in March 1894 he had even attempted—albeit rather half-heartedly—to restrain the extreme combativeness of his department towards England on the

---

[1] MAE, *ubi supra*, Leopold to Casimir-Périer 28 Apr. 1894; Casimir-Périer to Leopold dated 'Mai (?) 1894'.
[2] FO 10/615, Plunkett to Kimberley No. 63, 6 May 1894.
[3] Cf. *infra*, Ch. VIII, pp. 168-70.
[4] MAE, *ubi supra*, Hanotaux' Note of 2 May 1894.
[5] D.D.F. XI No. 109, Casimir-Périer to Bourée 26 May 1894; No. 113, *Note pour le Gouvernement britannique*, 28 May.
[6] *Ibid.*, No. 109; No. 110, Herbette to Casimir-Périer 26 May 1894, and footnote citing Casimir-Périer to Herbette 29 May.

question of the Say-Barrawa line.[1] Again, a more or less complete surrender to Leopold would punish the promoters of the Nile project for their improper conduct and at the same time dispose of a tedious and—to Casimir-Périer—a trivial dispute. The sulky inertia, disguised as an ostentatiously correct refusal to bind his successor, with which Casimir-Périer greeted the Anglo-Congolese Agreement seems to have been part of his normal reaction to loss of office. The attitude of outraged self-righteousness which was implicit in May 1894 became explicit in February 1895, when Casimir-Périer resigned the Presidency of the Republic.[2] But these considerations may not suffice to explain Leopold's confident initiative in writing privately to Casimir-Périer, nor Casimir-Périer's very mild and non-committal reply. Casimir-Périer was the Chairman and controlling shareholder of a great coal-mining concern at Anzin (Valenciennes), in the region where Leopold's friend and financial associate Baron Empain held a virtual monopoly of goods and mineral transport.[3] Casimir-Périer and Empain must at least have had close and constant business dealings; and with King Leopold and his circle the boundary between business and politics is not always easily discernible.

The reconstruction of the French Government at the end of May 1894 brought Hanotaux, rather unexpectedly, to the head of the Ministry where he had been for so many years a career official; it also brought Delcassé back to the *Colonies*, this time as a full Minister. This was an ominous combination for King Leopold. Delcassé, almost alone among the colonialists, seems never to have contemplated collaboration with the King; and his Nile project had from the outset been as much anti-Congolese as it was anti-British. Hanotaux was by now a bitter opponent of the Congo State on principle; and he also had the personal humiliation of the Brussels negotiations to avenge. According to his own account he accepted office, in spite of misgivings, because he felt that he was the only man with sufficient expert knowledge to rectify the situation created by the Anglo-Congolese Agreement.[4] In any case, he certainly could not afford to begin his career as minister by tamely accepting so sharp a diplomatic defeat. But the new ministry did not necessarily imply a direct physical challenge to Britain on the Upper Nile. Hanotaux was not in 1894, nor indeed perhaps at any time, a convinced supporter of the Nile project. In a memorandum of 28 May 1894 Hanotaux explained why the Quai d'Orsay had not forestalled the Anglo-Congolese Agreement by accepting the offers of partition made by Leopold in 1892. One reason was indeed suspicion of Leopold's relations with London; but another, not less cogent to

[1] As a result of a personal appeal from Phipps, Casimir-Périer prevailed upon Hanotaux to agree—momentarily—to a draft recognising the bilateral character of the Say-Barrawa line (FO 27/3184, Phipps to Anderson, private, 7 and 8 Mar. 1894; Dufferin to Rosebery No. 68, 8 Mar.).
[2] Cf. Chastenet, *op. cit.*, pp. 75-6; Chapman, *op. cit.*, pp. 105-7.
[3] Chastenet, *op. cit.*, pp. 54, 76; *B.C.B.* II, Empain.
[4] Iiams, *op. cit.*, pp. 24-5.

Hanotaux, was that a French incursion into the Nile basin would enable Britain to pose as the defender of Ottoman and Egyptian rights. It would be a glaring contradiction for France to violate Egyptian rights on the Upper Nile, 'quand elle proteste sans cesse contre les actes d'occupation ou autres analogues qui sont une violation constante du droit dans ces régions'.[1]

But the views of Hanotaux were not the only, nor perhaps the most important factor in the situation. The Anglo-Congolese Agreement did more than force the Quai d'Orsay to break its prudent four years' silence and to challenge publicly the hegemony which Britain claimed on the Upper Nile. It made the Anglo-French dispute a matter of heated public debate, into which were at once injected the very strong feelings with which Frenchmen looked upon the Egyptian question. 'Messieurs, c'est la question égyptienne qui s'ouvre ainsi devant vous!' —these fateful words, spoken in the Chamber by Etienne on 7 June 1894, marked the transformation of the Upper Nile question. So far as official policy went, and so far as the public knew, the Upper Nile affair had since 1890 been both for London and Paris a matter of territorial dispute with King Leopold. In that guise it had been a purely African question, and a minor one at that. Leopold's aggressive enterprise in the Nile basin had cushioned the potential conflict between Britain and France. The Anglo-Congolese Agreement brought London and Paris into head-on collision; in the dispute which followed, the essential connection of the Upper Nile with Egypt was demonstrated with increasing clarity. On both sides of the Channel national prestige and public feeling became ever more completely engaged; and the question of the Upper Nile rapidly developed into a major issue of Great-Power diplomacy. If Hanotaux was to achieve his ambition of a satisfactory settlement, he would have to fight a hard battle not only against London but also against the colonialist and 'Egyptianist' *enragés* who would now be satisfied with nothing less than direct action on the Upper Nile.

[1] MAE, *ubi supra*, Hanotaux, memo. of 28 May 1894.

L

VIII

COUP MANQUÉ

THE ANGLO-CONGOLESE

AGREEMENT AND ITS DESTRUCTION

MARCH–AUGUST 1894

ROSEBERY'S instructions to Rodd, signed on 5 March 1894, empowered him to discuss with Leopold a lease of territory west of the White Nile to the Congo State 'for fixed renewable periods of a limited number of years to be agreed on, but in any case terminable at H.M.'s death'. In return Leopold was to recognise the British sphere as defined in the Anglo-German Agreement; and to relinquish all claims in the Nile basin including those under the Mackinnon Treaty, to which (it was said) 'Lord Salisbury has distinctly denied that he gave the sanction attributed to him by misunderstanding'. The Foreign Office also asked for 'powers of telegraphic communication', through Congolese territory, between Uganda and 'Rhodesia';[1] Rhodes himself, who had in October 1892 pressed Rosebery to ask for similar facilities through German East Africa, doubtless inspired this request.[2]

Rodd was told to cover his tracks, and undertook a pointless journey to Berlin so as to be able to stop off at Brussels.[3] Leopold was equally coy, and evaded a direct meeting with Rodd; but on 17 March he communicated his counter-proposals through Eetvelde. The King wished the lease to subsist, not for his lifetime only, but: 'as long as these Congo regions remain as an Independent State or a Belgian Colony under the sovereignty of the King or his direct descendants— to terminate, that is, only in the case of Belgium becoming a republic or the Congo territories passing into other hands.' Leopold also made a number of minor demands, of which only two were followed up. One was simply that the northern frontier of the Congo State should be pushed forward to the Nile-Congo divide so as to give easy access to his leases. The other was a request for access to Lake Albert.[4]

[1] FO 10/625, Rosebery to Rodd 5 Mar. 1894.
[2] *Africa No. 1 (1893)*, No. 33, Rhodes to Rosebery Oct. 1892. Cf. B. Williams, *Cecil Rhodes* (London 1938), pp. 181, 309-10.
[3] FO 10/625, Rodd to Anderson, private, 17 Mar. 1894. Cf. Rodd, *Social and Diplomatic Memories*, I, pp. 345-6. [4] FO 10/625, Rodd to Rosebery 19 Mar. 1894.

Meanwhile, Anderson was on tenterhooks. Early in March he had sent Lugard, who was still rather under a cloud as a result of his controversial proceedings in Uganda, to pump Monteil in Paris. Lugard 'cleverly passed as an officer out of place and with rather a grievance' and 'did his work with tact and adroitness'.[1] On 10 March Lugard submitted his report; and Anderson forthwith concluded that 'Monteil means to march on Lado or Fashoda with an exceptionally well-organised expedition'.[2] He also feared that Rodd's failure to see Leopold might indicate that the King had already aligned himself with France. On 14 March Anderson privately asked Rodd to investigate whether Leopold was already 'playing into the hands of France'; Rodd replied that the King did not as yet seem to have committed himself, but might do so at any moment 'if we do not anticipate such a combination by a very definite agreement'.[3] This was some comfort to Anderson; but he was still tormented by the fear that after months of delay and frustration he might still lose the game by a matter of days or even hours.

Rodd's official report, containing Leopold's counter-proposals, reached London on 22 March. Sir Clement Hill of the African Department minuted, not very enthusiastically, 'there are at least possibilities of further negotiations'.[4] But by the 25th, when the report reached Anderson, the Franco-Congolese interim Agreement had been published. Anderson believed that the King had 'never had a better chance of success' in playing off Britain and France against one another, and he pressed for immediate action. He feared, indeed, that the King's proposed formula for the lease might involve 'Gt. Britain in delicate dynastic or internal struggles' in Belgium; but he was quite prepared to extend the lease beyond Leopold's lifetime. Nor did he object to the lease of a port on Lake Albert so long as Britain retained the ultimate sovereignty; but he suggested, 'as a natural equivalent' for this concession, that Britain should ask for a port 'on the north end of Lake Tanganyika'. Kimberley concurred; and Rosebery, when he saw the papers on 27 March, was no less impatient than Anderson: 'I think it *essential* to proceed without delay'.[5] But Kimberley always tended to move deliberately; and he had still not taken action by 2 April, when a report from Brussels indicated, not only that Monteil's departure was imminent, but that Decazes on the upper Ubangi might already have been ordered to begin the advance to the Nile. This report was a deliberate 'plant' by Leopold, who was also getting impatient. It should have been suspect, not only from de Grelle's extreme anxiety to

---

[1] FO 27/3258, minute by Anderson 10 June 1895; FO 83/1310, minute by Anderson 12 Mar. 1894.
[2] FO 27/3207, memo. by Lugard 10 Mar. 1894; FO 83/1310, Anderson, *loc. cit.*
[3] FO 10/625, Rodd to Anderson 17 Mar. 1894, citing Anderson to Rodd 14 Mar.
[4] *Ibid.*, minute by Hill on Rodd to Rosebery 19 Mar. 1894.
[5] *Ibid.*, memo by Anderson 25 Mar., on Rodd's report of 19 Mar.; minutes by Kimberley (26 Mar.) and Rosebery (27 Mar.). The Franco-Congolese Standstill Agreement had been published in the *Indépendance Belge* on 24 Mar.

volunteer it, but because it flatly contradicted de Grelle's own conclusion, stated four days earlier, that 'France, for the moment, had no designs upon the Upper Nile' and intended devoting all her energies to the drive for Lake Chad. But even Hill now took alarm— 'the presence of the French in force seems to be beyond doubt'; and Anderson pointedly minuted: 'Rodd has not yet received our answer'.[1] The success of this ruse reflects the atmosphere of almost panic-stricken urgency with which everyone at London (apart from Kimberley) conducted the negotiation.

On 27 March Rosebery had concurred in a proposal by Leopold that a special Congolese envoy should be sent to London;[2] and on 9 April Eetvelde began the detailed negotiation with Anderson. Anderson now offered to extend the lease as far north as the tenth parallel, which was more than Leopold had originally asked for; he had been convinced by Lugard that anything less might still leave a loophole for Monteil. He explained the difficulty about the 'dynastic' lease; Eetvelde suggested that this might apply only in the regions to the west of the thirtieth meridian. To the east, in the region immediately adjacent to the Nile, the lease should be for the King's reign as Sovereign of the Independent Congo State. This compromise did nothing to remove Anderson's original objection[3]; but it did avoid installing the Congo State or its successor in perpetuity as a riparian Power on the Nile itself. It was accepted on 10 April; and Anderson thereupon 'broached the question of the lease to us of a port on Tanganyika with a road from Lake Albert Edward . . . as a natural equivalent for a port on Lake Albert'. 'A road' now meant a territorial lease, and not a mere wayleave. The 'Corridor Clause' was fully-fledged and, after reference to Brussels, Eetvelde agreed to it on 12 April. He then pressed for immediate signature, 'saying that the King . . . would never forgive him if he were to sign on Friday the 13th'.[4] Leopold of course wanted the Agreement in his pocket before he began his negotiations with the French; and it was duly prepared and signed on 12 April. It was in principle to 'be kept secret for three months, unless H.M. Govt. should find it imperative to divulge [it], in which case due notification will be made'.[5]

Anderson was jubilant. Even if the French still 'continued to neglect' the Anglo-German Agreement it would, he thought, 'be difficult even for French chauvinists, after the publication of its recognition by the Congo State, to send an armed expedition to the Nile'. However, Anderson relied on stronger obstacles than this rather

[1] FO 10/614, Plunkett to Kimberley Nos. 32 and 35, 28 and 31 Mar. 1894; minutes by Hill (n.d.) and Anderson (2 Apr.).
[2] FO 10/625, minute, 27 Mar., on Rodd's report of 19 Mar.
[3] However, the final draft referred to Leopold's 'successors', not to his 'direct descendants'.
[4] Ibid., Anderson, 'Notes on the Belgian Negotiations', 15 Apr. 1894.
[5] FO 10/613, Kimberley to Plunkett No. 29, 18 April 1894. The text of the April Agreement (which has never been published) was enclosed.

doubtful piece of argumentation. Eetvelde had revealed that Leopold had posted on the upper Ubangi a force of eight hundred men with Krupp guns. This detachment already had orders to offer forcible resistance to a French expedition; but the King had naturally been 'nervous as to the course which the French would take' and anxious 'for the support of an arrangement with us'. 'This fear', concluded Anderson, 'has been our opportunity . . . It was evident, from the first, that we had hit on exactly the right moment for our negotiation.'[1] By April 1894 it seemed indeed that the whole problem of the Upper Nile was well on its way to solution. On 22 March Rosebery had extorted the agreement of his Cabinet to the proclamation of a protectorate over Uganda—though not to the construction of the Mombasa railway, which Harcourt was able to frustrate for another year and more.[2] On 5 May, by a secret agreement with Italy, Harar was recognised as in the Italian sphere, but Britain was authorised to occupy and administer it until Italy was ready to take over.[3] Here was a threat to the link between Addis Ababa and Obock and a possible means of scotching a French advance to the Nile through Ethiopia.

The Anglo-Italian Agreement of May 1894 was also intended as a gesture of general solidarity with Italy, whose naval assistance in the Mediterranean perhaps no longer seemed so superfluous as it had in 1891. With Rosebery thus at pains to align one of the Triplice Powers in the defence of the Upper Nile against France, it is the more remarkable that he should have gone out of his way to offend Germany by including the 'corridor clause' in an Agreement which was already sure to arouse the intense opposition of Paris. The practical uselessness of a Central African corridor was by 1894 even more obvious than in 1890 when Salisbury had publicly derided it. Anderson, who has so much to say about the general significance of the Agreement, is silent about Clause III; nor do the documents give the slightest hint of any pressure from Cape-to-Cairo enthusiasts either inside or outside the Office. On the face of it, Clause III was simply the result of Anderson's insistence that England must have an exact equivalent for the concession of a port, with a road to it, on Lake Albert.[4]

At the end of June 1894 Rosebery found it necessary to explain to Berlin that the corridor clause was not inspired by deliberate ill-will. He pleaded inadequate information; Salisbury's record of the 1890 negotiations gave no hint of the strong German objection to 'ein Durchgang längs der Kongogrenze'.[5] Salisbury's reporting of the Anglo-German negotiations was indeed very sketchy, but in the simultaneous discussions on the Mackinnon Treaty he had recorded

[1] FO 10/625, *loc. cit.*
[2] L.Q.V. 3, ii, pp. 384-5, 516, Rosebery to the Queen 22 Mar. 1894 and 28 May 1895.
[3] 'Note Officieuse' and 'Déclaration Secrète' attached to the Agreement of 5 May 1894. The French soon learned of these secret annexes.
[4] FO 10/625, Anderson's memoranda of 25 Mar. and 15 Apr. 1894.
[5] G.P. VIII, No. 2071, Hatzfeldt to Caprivi 30 June 1894.

his conviction that the Germans were 'quite uncompromising' about their common frontier with the Congo State. Anderson was of course fully aware of this; indeed, he had been the first to point out that the proposed 'Mackinnon corridor' would be 'very irritating' to Berlin.[1] In 1900, after Anderson was safely dead, Rosebery volunteered quite a different explanation. He had, he said, asked Anderson in 1894 'whether German rights would be in any way affected' by the corridor clause; and Anderson, 'in an inconceivable fit of forgetfulness', had expressly stated that they would not.[2] In June 1894 the Germans alleged a violation of their rights under the German-Congolese treaty of 8 November 1884 which, in the view of Berlin, subjected to German approval any cession of Congolese territory adjacent to the German sphere.[3] If Rosebery's question to Anderson was in fact framed in the terms reported, Anderson might well have replied that strictly speaking German *rights* would not be infringed, since the arrangement contemplated was not a cession but a lease. He may also have recalled— he can indeed hardly have forgotten—that in 1890 Salisbury had evaded a rather similar difficulty by insisting that the 'Mackinnon corridor' should not be ceded in full sovereignty.

Anderson must of course have recognised that Berlin would object just as strongly to an indefinite lease as to an outright cession; but if in April 1894 it were believed that Germany would have no *legal* ground for complaint, this opportunity of giving the Germans tit-for-tat for their stab in the back on the Niger may not have been unwelcome at the Foreign Office. This was not indeed Anderson's policy; his very wise advice was 'to take no notice of the treachery, be careful not to quarrel and wait for an anti-French reaction' at Berlin.[4] But not even Kimberley, usually so placable and easy-going, could stomach the Franco-German Protocol of 1894. It was not only the cession of Bifara and French access to the navigable Niger. On 16 March, when the Protocol was published, the British got another slap in the face. By Article 3 France and Germany bound themselves 'd'appliquer et de faire respecter' the provisions of the Berlin Act relating to the freedom of navigation *and of trade* on the Niger. This was an explicit Franco-German challenge to the British position.[5] The lengthy and argumentative *Denkschrift* with which the published Agreement was prefaced was hardly necessary to show plainly, as Kimberley noted, 'that the Benue concession . . . has been deliberately made in order to combine with France against the Niger Compy.'.[6] On 21 March Kim-

---

[1] FO 84/2082, minute by Salisbury 4 June 1890; FO 84/2086, minute by Anderson 27 May 1890. Cf. *supra*, Ch. v, p. 91.

[2] G.P. viii, No. 2071, footnote citing Metternich to A.A. 20 Feb. 1900.

[3] Cf. *ibid.*, Nos. 2034, 2038, 2040, 2043, 2045, 27 May–12 June 1894.

[4] FO 64/1333, minute by Anderson 13 Mar. 1894, on Malet's Nos. 28, 29 and 30, all of 7 Mar.

[5] The Anglo-German Agreement of Nov. 1893 had bound the parties to respect freedom of *navigation* only.

[6] FO 64/1333, minute by Kimberley 22 Mar. 1894, on Malet's No. 34, 16 Mar.

berley minuted ominously: 'this combination against us of Germany with France is not at all a friendly action, and it should be borne in mind in our dealings with Germany about African matters elsewhere'.[1] A man slow to anger, Kimberley was slow to be appeased. In May, when the German press pointedly speculated whether the corridor had received the prior approval of Berlin, he commented, significantly enough: 'the Germans did not consult us when they gave the French access to the Niger'.[2] And on 11 June, nettled by the tone of a German Note on the corridor clause, Kimberley told Hatzfeldt to his face that London had looked upon the Franco-German Protocol as 'eine Un-freundlichkeit'.[3] The implication was obvious; and when the Austrian ambassador in London described the Anglo-Congolese Agreement as 'a sort of revenge' for the Franco-German Protocol,[4] he can hardly have been very wide of the mark.

The satisfaction of the Foreign Office with the Anglo-Congolese Agreement was not shared by Sir William Harcourt. On 3 March 1894 Harcourt had demanded, as a condition of his serving under Rosebery, that 'in relation to foreign affairs he must stand in the same position of communication and consultation beforehand upon all important decisions before they are adopted as that which belongs to the Prime Minister'. On the following day Harcourt receded a little from this claim to a co-Premier's authority; but he believed Rosebery to have agreed that 'the Foreign Secretary should communicate as fully and freely with the Leader of the House of Commons as he did with the Prime Minister'. With both the Prime Minister and the Foreign Secretary in the Lords, this was not an unreasonable demand; it was obviously desirable, as Harcourt pointed out, that 'the Leader of the House of Commons should have notice not only when foreign affairs reached a crisis, but *ab initio* when affairs were beginning to "creak" '.[5] Kimberley was aware that an agreement on these lines had been reached, and on 27 March he reminded Rosebery that Harcourt ought to be informed of the negotiation with King Leopold.[6] On the following day Kimberley wrote to Harcourt explaining that the ob-jects of the negotiation were 'to prevent the French, who are about to send an expedition [to the Upper Nile], from establishing them-selves there, and to settle with the Belgians, who are there already'.[7] Harcourt expressed his doubts of this policy; but he was engrossed with his Death Duties budget, which had generated a most enjoyable dis-

---

[1] *Ibid.*, minute of 21 Mar. on Malet's No. 33 of 14 Mar.
[2] *Ibid.*, minute of 29 May on Gosselin's No. 63, 26 May 1894. Malet used similar language in reply to Marschall's complaints: *ibid.*, Malet to Kimberley No. 70, 9 June 1894; G.P. viii, No. 2042, memo. by Marschall, 8 June.
[3] G.P. viii, No. 2044, Hatzfeldt to A.A. 11 June 1894; cf. FO 64/1332, Kimberley to Malet No. 86, 11 June.
[4] G.P. viii, No. 2068, Eulenburg to Caprivi 18 June 1894.
[5] Gardiner, *Harcourt* ii, pp. 269-72, 627-8, citing memoranda by Harcourt, 3 and 4 Mar. 1894. Cf. James, *Rosebery*, pp. 326, 330-2.
[6] Crewe, *Lord Rosebery* ii, p. 447, citing Kimberley to Rosebery 27 Mar. 1894.
[7] Gardiner, *op. cit.* ii, p. 313, citing Kimberley to Harcourt 28 Mar. 1894.

pute with Rosebery, and he made no further enquiries.[1] Nor did he receive any further information. Kimberley, far from communicating with him 'as fully and freely . . . as with the Prime Minister', did not communicate with him at all. Harcourt remained in complete ignorance, even of the introduction of the Central African corridor, until on 22 April he received a copy of the Agreement 'as a concluded affair in a circulation box ten days after [its] signature'.[2]

There followed an explosion of awesome dimensions, which for once was thoroughly justified. Harcourt roundly accused Kimberley of a breach of faith, denounced the Agreement as likely to provoke 'the united hostility of France and Germany', refused to regard himself as committed to defend it in the Commons and demanded an immediate Cabinet to consider it. At the Cabinet on the 23rd, a majority of ministers supported Harcourt; and it was suggested—Harcourt seems for a time to have thought it had been agreed—that Anderson should go to Brussels 'to see if the King of the Belgians can be induced to give [the Agreement] up'.[3] But Anderson never went to Brussels, and the Agreement was maintained. It was now essential to Rosebery's authority as Prime Minister that it should be maintained. It is difficult to believe that Rosebery never had second thoughts about the Agreement, as the passage of time revealed its embarrassing consequences with growing clarity. But the head-on collision with Harcourt had precluded him from using the opportunities of altering the Agreement which did in fact arise. The very weight of the opposition mustered by Harcourt made it impossible for Rosebery to yield anything of substance without abdicating as an effective Prime Minister.

On 23 April the Franco-Congolese negotiations at Brussels broke up with 'relations between the . . . delegates more than strained'.[4] Impressed by the open threats of Hanotaux, Leopold at once enquired whether his Agreement with London could be post-dated. Kimberley refused to consider this course, and indeed made it clear that he intended to publish the Agreement almost at once[5]—an obvious precaution against any attempt by the King to re-insure with Paris. Leopold then begged that publication should not take place before 7 May—a delay evidently intended to enable him to communicate privately with Casimir-Périer.[6] But until Leopold had got his answer from Paris he was very uneasy indeed. He repeatedly prompted Lambermont to warn Plunkett of the danger that Belgium might become involved; and Eetvelde hinted more than once that the King

---

[1] Gardiner, pp. 313-4, citing Harcourt to Kimberley 22 Apr. 1894. Cf. James, *op. cit.*, pp. 341-7.
[2] Gardiner, *loc. cit.*
[3] *Ibid.*, p. 315, citing L. Harcourt's journal. James, *op. cit.*, pp. 348-9.
[4] FO 10/614, Plunkett to Kimberley Nos. 50 and 52, 24 Apr. 1894.
[5] *Ibid.*, Plunkett to Kimberley No. 51, 24 Apr. 1894. FO 10/618, Kimberley to Plunkett, tels. unnumb., 25 and 26 Apr.
[6] FO 10/614, Plunkett to Kimberley No. 54, 27 Apr. 1894. Cf. FO 10/618, same to same, tel. unnumb., 27 Apr.

would welcome a radical alteration, or perhaps even an abandonment, of the Agreement.[1] To these hints Rosebery did not and could not respond. Moreover, there were signs that unless Leopold were kept firmly tied down, he might yet slip through British fingers and come to terms with Paris. The Foreign Office guessed that he had communicated with Casimir-Périer; and on 28 April de Grelle told Plunkett, in flat contradiction of earlier reports, that there had been no rupture of negotiations with the French, only an indefinite postponement. On the previous day, for reasons which remain obscure, Hanotaux had told Phipps that although de Grelle had shown 'little elasticity as a negotiator . . . nothing had disturbed the harmony of the proceedings at Brussels', and that the negotiations might soon be resumed. Rosebery was necessarily impressed by this sinister coincidence of reports.[2]

However, on 4 May Rosebery agreed, under heavy pressure from his colleagues, that to 'remove the grounds of [the King's] apprehension . . . the existing agreement should be cancelled and replaced by another to be made public at once'.[3] Even Rosebery was now beginning to see that it would hardly do for the Agreement to bear its original date;[4] and if this concession of mere form would help to pacify the Cabinet, so much the better. But although this proposal was put to Leopold as the only alternative to almost immediate publication, he received it very coolly. He was, he said, perfectly happy with the original Agreement; all he asked of London, 'as a favour', was twenty-four hours' notice of publication. However, since London was thinking along these lines, he ventured to suggest an improvement in the drafting of Clause IV, which defined the King's political status in the leased territories.[5] Leopold's amendment was designed to exclude even more firmly than before any French claim that Leopold had ignored the right of preference by ceding to England rights which he had acquired in the Nile basin. It also protected England even more completely from any Congolese claim arising out of the Mackinnon Treaty or prior occupation; it was therefore willingly accepted by London.[6] Then on 9 May Eetvelde suddenly informed Plunkett that Leopold wished to sign the new Agreement forthwith; and when Plunkett asked the reason for this sudden haste, he received the meaningless reply that the King 'disapproved very much of any pro-

---

[1] FO 10/614, Plunkett to Kimberley Nos. 54 and 55, 27 Apr. 1894; same to same No. 57, 29 Apr.; Plunkett to Anderson, private, 29 Apr.
[2] *Ibid.*, Plunkett to Kimberley No. 59, 29 Apr. 1894, and minute by Rosebery. FO 27/3185, Phipps to Kimberley No. 123, 27 Apr.
[3] James, *op. cit.*, pp. 349-51. FO 10/618, Kimberley to Plunkett tel. Africa No. 2, 5 May 1894.
[4] L.Q.V. 3, ii, p. 396, Rosebery to the Queen 4 May 1894.
[5] FO 10/615, Plunkett to Kimberley Nos. 62 and 65, 6 May 1894; Plunkett to Anderson, private, 6 May.
[6] FO 10/618, Plunkett to Kimberley tel. No. 2, 9 May 1894; Kimberley to Plunkett tel. Africa No. 4, 10 May. Cf. FO 10/615, Plunkett to Kimberley No. 66, 9 May, enclosing note by Eetvelde.

longed discussion'.[1] In fact, on the previous day Casimir-Périer had escaped defeat in the Chamber only with the support of the anti-Republican Right; given the growing unpopularity of his government even among Moderates of a Radical tinge, this was a clear portent that his 'calming personal influence' might very soon disappear.[2]

The new Agreement was signed on 12 May and published on the 22nd. For over a week after its publication events seemed to falsify Harcourt's prediction that it would provoke 'the united hostility of France and Germany'.[3] Casimir-Périer closed his ears to the siren voices of Berlin and exploited his status as *ministre démissionnaire* to avoid taking any but the most purely formal action. Marschall at the Wilhelmstrasse, perhaps because he failed to elicit any response from France, was for several days content to demand simply that the corridor should be situated not less than twenty kilometres from the German-Congolese frontier.[4] For Leopold, however, the appointment of Hanotaux was, in Lambermont's words, 'a very grave symptom'.[5] Hanotaux' speech in the Chamber on 7 June was indeed militant in substance, though studiously moderate in tone. Hanotaux' analysis of the legal status of the leased territories threw a flood of unwelcome light upon the juridical weakness, not only of the Anglo-Congolese Agreement but of the whole British claim to a sphere in the southern Sudan.[6] In particular, it destroyed London's favourite thesis that Paris, by failing to protest against the Anglo-German Agreement, had permitted Britain to acquire a prescriptive right valid even against France.[7] Basing himself on the continued survival of Ottoman and Egyptian rights, Hanotaux had no difficulty in throwing grave doubt on the legal validity of the Anglo-Congolese Agreement; he would therefore consider it, 'jusqu'à plus ample informé, comme nulle et de nulle portée'. Turning to practical measures, he announced the early departure of commandant Monteil to safeguard French rights on the spot—Monteil's precise destination was left conveniently unspecified. The Chamber responded by the unanimous adoption of an Order of the Day, drafted by Etienne and Deloncle, which pledged the Government to safeguard the rights of France. Two days later Delcassé asked for a credit of 1,800,000 francs 'for the defence of French interests in Africa'; and on 20 June this sum was voted.[8]

Necessarily militant in public, Hanotaux was conciliatory in private. He could not of course for a moment accept the Anglo-

[1] FO 10/615, *loc. cit.*
[2] *Annual Register*, 1894, pp. [225-6]. Chastenet, *La République Triomphante*, pp. 57-9. Cf. FO 10/615, Plunkett to Kimberley No. 63, 6 May 1894.
[3] Gardiner, *op. cit.*, II, p. 317.
[4] G.P. VIII, No. 2032, Marschall to Alvensleben (Brussels) 25 May 1894.
[5] FO 10/615, Plunkett to Kimberley No. 95, 2 June 1894.
[6] *J.O.*, Débats, Chambre, 7 June 1894.
[7] FO 27/3185, minute by Rosebery on Dufferin to Kimberley No. 162, 13 June 1894. Cf. FO 10/625, Anderson, 'Notes on the Belgian Negotiations', 15 Apr. 1894.
[8] *J.O.*, *loc. cit.* Cocheris, *Situation Internationale*, pp. 407-10. Hanotaux, *Fachoda*, pp. 73-6. Vergniol, 'Fachoda', *Revue de France*, Aug. 1936, p. 638.

Congolese Agreement, but he offered to co-operate with London in 'finding a solution'.[1] Indeed, he regarded the crisis, not as an opportunity for a new and bitter quarrel with England, but rather as the starting-point for hard but friendly bargaining upon a number of troublesome African questions which might if neglected poison Anglo-French relations. He was encouraged in this course by Lord Dufferin's conciliatory attitude at Paris and by the laconic and unprovocative answers given in London to Parliamentary Questions about the extent of the British sphere and the suspected plans of the French.[2] On 5 June Kimberley offered to the French Ambassador Decrais a negotiation on 'all African questions pending between the two governments', including the Anglo-Congolese Agreement but excluding Egypt as 'un trop gros morceau'.[3] It was on the strength of this offer that Hanotaux had moderated the tone of his Chamber speech on the 7th; and its moderation stood out well against the fulminations of MM. Etienne and Deloncle. On the 9th he accepted Kimberley's offer;[4] but it soon became clear that London intended, not to negotiate seriously, but to spin out time until the storm had blown over. Nevertheless, Hanotaux continued to pursue his original objective and did not abandon it, even temporarily, until the middle of July. The crisis with France was therefore delayed; and it was Germany with whom Leopold and Rosebery had first to contend.

The Germans fired the first shot at Brussels on 25 May, when they demanded that the corridor should be at least twenty kilometres from their frontier. The Foreign Office had no objection; Anderson minuted 'it should be an interior road'.[5] However, when Leopold pleaded that he must first consult London, the demand was repeated as an ultimatum and with threats such that Kimberley doubted whether he should 'quietly . . . acquiesce in this demand'; however, he concluded that Leopold was exaggerating the violence of the German language.[6] On 29 May de Grelle-Rogier handed to the German Minister Alvensleben a note complying with Berlin's request.[7] The Wihelmstrasse did not acknowledge this note; but on 31 May Marschall wrote to Hatzfeldt in London in terms which suggest that he was still mainly concerned to avoid 'eine etwaige englische Grenznachbarschaft',

---

[1] D.D.F. xi, No. 123, note du Ministre, 2 June 1894.
[2] Cf. FO 10/625: minute by Grey 21 May 1894, on a P.Q. by Ashmead-Bartlett; draft of an answer to Labouchere 28 May. FO 27/3208, drafts of answer to Ashmead-Bartlett 14 June. Dufferin had been posted from Rome to Paris in 1892.
[3] D.D.F. xi, loc. cit.; No. 129, Decrais to Hanotaux 5 June 1894; No. 133, Dufferin to Hanotaux 6 June. Cf. FO 27/3182, Kimberley to Dufferin No. 187a, 5 June.
[4] FO 27/3185, Dufferin to Kimberley No. 152, 8 June 1894. D.D.F. xi, No. 136, Hanotaux to Dufferin 9 June.
[5] G.P. viii, No. 2032. FO 64/1333, Gosselin to Kimberley No. 63, 26 May 1894, and minute by Anderson.
[6] G.P. viii, No. 2033, Alvensleben to A.A. 26 May 1894; No. 2034, Marschall to Alvensleben 27 May. FO 10/618, Plunkett to Kimberley tels. No. 6 and 7, 28 May; Kimberley to Plunkett tel. No. 5, 29 May. FO 10/615, minute by Kimberley 29 May, on Plunkett's No. 86, 28 May.
[7] FO 10/615, Plunkett to Kimberley No. 90, 31 May 1894, enclosing Congolese Note.

and admitting that the Congo State seemed prepared to comply with German wishes, though he did not state precisely what these wishes were.[1]

Hitherto the German demands had been presented verbally; but on 1 June Marschall drafted a note reserving Germany's full freedom of action until her consent had been obtained to the corridor clause. When Leopold made enquiries, he was bluntly told that the mere shifting of the corridor would no longer satisfy Berlin.[2] Marschall seems to have deliberately kept open the possibility of such a change of line by previously confining himself to purely verbal, if extremely minatory, communications and by concealing from Hatzfeldt the precise nature of his demands; when the British later complained that Germany had changed her ground, Marschall replied that in her first note to Leopold she had reserved complete freedom of action.[3] No doubt Casimir-Périer's failure to respond to German suggestions of collaboration had discouraged Marschall from committing himself completely before 1 June. But when Casimir-Périer was replaced by an able and ambitious African expert with his spurs to win as Minister, Marschall evidently felt able to take the stronger line which the German public—and the Emperor—were already beginning to demand.

The increased pressure on Brussels was coupled with an offensive at London. On 4 June Hatzfeldt delivered a note protesting against the unilateral alteration of the German-Congolese frontier as defined in the treaty of 1884.[4] On 8 June Marschall swept aside as mere evasions the British ambassador's explanations that a lease was not a cession and that the shifting of the corridor would leave the German frontier undisturbed. The real point, he told Malet, was that Germany would never have concluded the Agreement of 1890 but for her firm belief that England had renounced all aspiration to a Central African corridor.[5] Marschall was also incensed by Sir Edward Grey's Commons statement that 'complete and unqualified assurances' had been given to Germany;[6] and he had already told Kayser of the *Kolonial-abteilung* to draft a note which should make Germany's position absolutely clear. The result was so pure a distillation of Dr Kayser's unpleasing personality that even Caprivi, when he saw the note, thought it less than civil. It asserted unequivocally that Article III was

---

[1] G.P. VIII, No. 2037, Marschall to Hatzfeldt 31 May 1894. On 26 May Marschall had told the Austrian ambassador that German interests were not seriously affected: Szögyenyi to Kálnoky 26 May, cited M.P. Hornik, 'The Anglo-Belgian Agreement of 12 May 1894', *E.H.R.* LVII, 226 (1942), p. 236.

[2] G.P. VIII, No. 2038, Marschall to de Grelle Rogier 1 June 1894. FO 10/615, Plunkett to Kimberley No. 98, 3 June.

[3] G.P. VIII, No. 2045, Marschall to Hatzfeldt 12 June 1894; cf. No. 2044, Hatzfeldt to A.A. 11 June.

[4] *Ibid.*, No. 2040, Hatzfeldt to Kimberley 3 June 1894.

[5] *Ibid.*, No. 2042, memo. by Marschall 8 June 1894. FO 64/1333, Malet to Kimberley No. 70, 9 June.

[6] FO 10/625, Grey, draft answer to P.Q. by Dilke 8 June 1894. FO 64/1332, Kimberley to Malet No. 85a, 9 June. Cf. G.P. VIII, No. 2045, Marschall to Hatzfeldt 12 June.

invalid pending German consent; and it imputed bad faith by the remark that 'the attempt is made to realise, to the detriment of Germany, the object which was not attained in 1890'.[1]

The German note of 11 June touched London on the raw. It caused Kimberley to blurt out that the Franco-German Protocol had been 'an unfriendly act'; Rosebery found it 'insufferable'—'a tone which she might properly use in addressing Monaco'.[2] Rosebery encouraged Leopold to go on temporising with the Germans, although Berlin had already contemptuously rejected the Congolese reply to the German note of 1 June.[3] On the 13th, Rosebery went over to the offensive himself. He told the Austrian ambassador, for relay to Berlin, that 'if Germany continues to show herself so hostile . . . I shall feel obliged to take back the assurances which I have given on the subject of Constantinople'; and on the following day he threatened to abandon altogether the Mediterranean Agreements of 1887.[4] But the German pressure on Brussels did not relax; indeed, Berlin returned, in most menacing tones, to a theme she had opened even before the end of May —the threat to Congolese neutrality inherent in the Agreement with London. Then on 15 June Alvensleben refused even to accept Leopold's reply to the latest German note; more, he now demanded the immediate cancellation of the whole Agreement, and not merely of Article III. Failing a satisfactory answer within forty-eight hours Germany would cease to regard the Congo State as neutral and 'would take whatever other steps she might think proper'. On the same day Hatzfeldt was instructed to warn London that the total abandonment of the Agreement, 'and that without delay', was the only means of avoiding a European conference on the Egyptian question itself.[5]

This second fundamental change of ground, which looks at first sight blatantly aggressive, was in fact forced upon Marschall by the difficulties of his own situation. In the first few days of June he had discovered that collaboration with France was not so easy as it looked. The French ambassador Herbette had indeed made overtures; but Marschall had been forced to make it clear that Germany's objections had a much narrower basis than those of France, and in particular that Berlin was not prepared to raise the question of 'the integrity of

---

[1] G.P. VIII, No. 2043, Marschall to Hatzfeldt 9 June (delivered as a Note to Kimberley 11 June).
[2] *Ibid.*, No. 2044, Hatzfeldt to A.A. 11 June 1894. FO 64/1332, Kimberley to Malet No. 86, 11 June. L.Q.V. 3, ii, p. 405, Rosebery to the Queen 14 June.
[3] FO 10/618: Kimberley to Plunkett tel. No. 21, 14 June 1894; Plunkett to Kimberley tels. No. 10 and 14, 6 and 12 June; Kimberley to Plunkett tel. No. 12, 6 June. FO 10/615, Plunkett to Kimberley Nos. 100 and 119, 6 and 12 June.
[4] Deym to Kálnoky tels. No. 29 and 31, 13 and 14 June 1894, quoted in H. W. V. Temperley and L. M. Penson, *Foundations of British Foreign Policy* (Cambridge 1938), pp. 490-2. Hornik, *ubi supra* p. 239; *idem, Der Kampf der Grossmächte*, pp. 114-5. Cf. L.Q.V. 3, *loc. cit.*
[5] G.P. VIII, No. 2050, Marschall to Alvensleben 13 June 1894; 2053, Marschall to Hatzfeldt 15 June; 2057, Alvensleben to A.A. 15 June. FO 10/618, Plunkett to Kimberley tels. No. 16 and 17, 15 and 16 June. FO 10/616, same to same Nos. 130 and 131, and Plunkett to Anderson, private, all of 15 June.

the Ottoman Empire' in the remote wilderness of the Upper Nile. Herbette soon saw that Marschall had no intention of turning Britain into an open enemy by actually *using* the *bâton égyptien*. He warned Hanotaux to be wary; Marschall would welcome French assistance in winning a minor diplomatic victory over England, but was certainly not prepared to 'faire de l'incident une affaire de politique générale'. Hanotaux therefore refrained from pressing the instructions which he had just sent asking Herbette to raise the question formally.[1]

Marschall was therefore left in isolation; and before the middle of June he was finding this isolation very uncomfortable indeed. Unless he could enforce his demand of 1 June for the total abandonment of Article III, he might just as well resign forthwith; by this time neither the Emperor nor German opinion would have stomached a humiliation on this scale. The Congo State he could of course bully to his heart's content; but all this minatory pressure had not brought—and could not bring—any concrete result, so long as London stood firm. To threaten war would be absurd; moreover, Rome and Vienna were already beginning to point out, if a little timidly, that Germany's inflexible attitude might have unfortunate consequences in the field of general diplomacy.[2] The only solution was to exhibit the scarecrow of Franco-German collaboration; but Marschall now knew that he would have to take great care not to allow himself to be carried, via the Egyptian question, much further than he wanted to go in hostility towards Britain. At the same time, the British would not be much impressed unless they could be induced to believe that the Franco-German collaboration would in fact extend to Egypt. Moreover, and not least unfortunate, the continued silence of Hanotaux meant that Marschall would have to solicit French co-operation, not graciously accept it. On 12 June, in the face of London's continued resistance, he brought himself to do this. On the 15th, to give his offer of collaboration greater verisimilitude, he demanded the total cancellation of the Agreement and told Herbette that he had done this. He later admitted to Herbette that he had never intended to insist on this demand, and explained it away as simply an additional means of pressure.[3]

Marschall's bluff worked. Rosebery's resistance collapsed on 16 June, just in time to release Marschall from the very awkward problem of defining the precise scope of his collaboration with Paris. Hatzfeldt's threat of a conference on Egypt drove home the point of Sir Edward Malet's repeated warnings from Berlin that the abandonment of Article III was the only way to escape very serious difficulties. Indeed, Malet thoroughly sympathised with the German complaint that they

[1] D.D.F. xi Nos. 128, 130, Herbette to Hanotaux 5 and 6 June 1894; cf. footnote to No. 130.
[2] G.P. viii, Nos. 2054, 2068, Eulenburg to A.A. 15 and 18 June 1894; No. 2063, Bülow to A.A. 17 June.
[3] D.D.F. xi, Nos. 140, 147, Herbette to Hanotaux 12 and 15 June 1894. G.P. viii, No. 2046, Marschall to Münster 12 June; No. 2053, Marschall to Hatzfeldt 15 June; No. 2057, fn. Cf. *infra*, pp. 178-80.

had been jockeyed by a *de facto* violation of the 1890 Agreement.[1] On 14 June the Austrian ambassador had asked Rosebery incredulously whether he really intended to turn his whole foreign policy upside-down for the sake of a strip of wilderness in darkest Africa. Two days later, after news had been received of Alvensleben's ultimatum to Leopold, Rosebery confessed to Deym that he now had second thoughts. The German note of 11 June was not perhaps so insulting after all; and he had admittedly made a mistake in not consulting Berlin before concluding with Leopold. He was indeed now ready to sacrifice Article III, though he did not think it was for him to make this suggestion to Leopold.[2]

Nevertheless, at 12 noon on 16 June, not many minutes after Rosebery's conversation with Deym, the Foreign Office telegraphed to Plunkett: 'You may tell the King that if he likes to ask for withdrawal of article three we shall consent'.[3] The same afternoon Eetvelde sent to Plunkett an official request for withdrawal; and de Grelle told Alvensleben what had been done and enquired whether the withdrawal would satisfy Germany. In the course of the day Malet made a similar enquiry of Marschall; meanwhile, Deym's news that Rosebery was ready to withdraw Article III was being transmitted to Berlin through Hatzfeldt.[4] Thus by the evening of the 16th Marschall knew that Leopold had asked for the withdrawal of Article III, and he had every reason to believe that the King's request would be granted. Marschall's main anxiety now was to disentangle himself from collaboration with the French. This he did on 17 June, tacitly dropping his demand for the complete cancellation of the Agreement.[5] However, he did not at once admit to London that he was completely satisfied with the withdrawal of Article III.[6] He suspected, correctly, that the unstable Rosebery might veer again and try to put Berlin off with something less than withdrawal pure and simple. To meet this contingency he needed at least to be able to talk as if Franco-German collaboration were still a possibility. However, by 21 June London had abandoned its rather feeble efforts to fob off Berlin with a mere suspension of Article III.[7]

---

[1] L.Q.V. 3, ii, pp. 405-7, Malet to the Queen 15 and 16 June 1894. G.P. VIII, Nos. 2047, 2052, the Emperor to Caprivi 11 and 14 June. FO 64/1335, Malet to Kimberley tel. No. 9, 11 June.

[2] Deym to Kálnoky tels. No. 31 and 32, 14 and 16 June, cited Temperley and Penson, *loc. cit.* Hornik, *E.H.R.*, *ubi supra; Der Kampf der Grossmächte*, *loc. cit.*

[3] FO 10/618, Kimberley to Plunkett tel. No. 23, 16 June 1894. The Cabinet was not consulted; and Harcourt protested, adding ominously: 'Do you really believe that after Hanotaux' speech he will allow you to refuse to France what you have been compelled to yield to Germany?' (to Kimberley 16 July [*sic*—? June] 1894, cited Harcourt, *op. cit.* II, p. 319).

[4] FO 10/616, Plunkett to Kimberley No. 133, 17 June 1894. G.P. VIII, No. 2056, Hatzfeldt to A.A. 16 June; No. 2058, Alvensleben to A.A. 16 June; No. 2059, memo. by Marschall 16 June. FO 64/1335, Malet to Kimberley tel. No. 13, 16 June.

[5] *Infra, loc. cit.*

[6] G.P. VIII, No. 2065, memo. by Marschall 18 June 1894.

[7] FO 64/1335, Kimberley to Malet tel. No. 24, 21 June 1894. FO 64/1332, Kimberley to Malet Nos. 92, 93 and 97a of 17, 18 and 21 June. FO 10/618, Kimberley to Plunkett tel. No. 30, 21 June; Plunkett to Kimberley tel. No. 20, 21 June.

On 22 June a Declaration satisfactory to Berlin was signed by Eetvelde and Plunkett, and the incident was closed.[1]

It has been suggested that the German opposition to Article III was in some way artificial or spurious, and that Marschall's real motive was 'to blackmail the British into renewing their support of Austria-Hungary and Italy in the Mediterranean'. Marschall is supposed to have declared himself satisfied, and to have evaded further collaboration with France, not because of the 'trivial British concession' of withdrawing Article III, but because of Austrian alarm at Rosebery's threats to 'take back' his assurances on Constantinople.[2] The case for regarding the African issue as spurious and irrelevant relies heavily on the fact that, although London did not officially announce its willingness to withdraw Article III until 18 June, Marschall had already on the 17th flatly turned down the detailed French proposals for collaboration, and had indeed made it clear that collaboration no longer interested him even in principle.[3] But already on the 16th Marschall was fully aware of London's intentions;[4] he had no need—and, when he saw the details of the French proposals, certainly no desire—to await official confirmation before escaping with relief from an entanglement which was already proving even more embarrassing than he had feared. Trivial or not, the British concession in Africa cannot therefore be dismissed as irrelevant. It also seems very doubtful whether Rosebery's threats had any effect other than to increase Marschall's determination to gain his point. On 15 June he scornfully defied these 'geschmacklose Drohungen' and declared himself ready 'to carry through to the end' the conflict forced upon Germany.[5]

Marschall's bitter opposition can only be understood against his general assessment of Rosebery's policy both in Europe and in Africa. Until July 1893 Marschall was prepared to accept—though not with complete confidence—Hatzfeldt's view that Rosebery intended to follow Salisbury's policy of 'leaning towards' the Triple Alliance, but could give no more than 'personal assurances' of this because of the danger of a head-on collision with his colleagues.[6] But Rosebery's conduct during the Siam crisis converted Marschall's doubts about Rosebery's policy into active distrust. Prompted by Holstein, he interpreted Rosebery's request for German diplomatic support as an attempt 'to cover the retreat of Britain by the interposition of a third Power';

[1] FO 10/618, Plunkett to Kimberley tel. No. 21, 22 June 1894. The Declaration was officially communicated to Hatzfeldt on 26 June.
[2] Taylor, The Struggle for Mastery, pp. 349-52; idem, 'Prelude to Fashoda', E.H.R. LXV, 254 (1950), pp. 52-80, at p. 62.
[3] G.P. VIII, No. 2065; No. 2061, Marschall, memo. of conversation with Herbette 17 June 1894. Cf. D.D.F. XI, No. 153, Herbette to Hanotaux 17 June.
[4] By 17 June both Marschall and Hatzfeldt regarded the withdrawal of Art. III as all but a fait accompli: cf. G.P. VIII, No. 2062, Marschall to Hatzfeldt 17 June 1894; FO 64/1332, Kimberley to Malet No. 92, 17 June.
[5] G.P. VIII, No. 2055, Marschall to Eulenburg 15 June 1894.
[6] Cf. G.P. VIII, Nos. 1739 and 1740, Hatzfeldt to Caprivi 7 and 11 Sept. 1892.

England was looking, not for allies, but for 'lightning-conductors'.[1] Marschall's worst suspicions were confirmed when in February 1894 Rosebery told Vienna that his promises of assistance at Constantinople depended on his being able 'to count on the Triple Alliance to prevent France from taking part in the struggle'. In other words, thought Marschall, Germany was to bind herself to fight France while Britain could always escape on the grounds that it had been only Rosebery's 'personal view' that she would fight.[2] By the spring of 1894 Marschall regarded Rosebery's 'personal assurances' as a deliberate snare for Germany; and he certainly then held the view of British policy which he was to state explicitly in November:

> H.M. the German Emperor is to pledge himself to intervene on behalf of British interests—for instance, in the Mediterranean. England as such undertakes no engagement, but the sound sense of the English people will certainly recognise the suitable moment to leap to the side of a Germany already fighting for British interests. So long as Germany fails to conclude this *pactum claudicans*, she will meet with underhand opposition in both major and minor questions.[3]

'Underhand opposition in . . . minor questions'—here was the crux of the German grievance. To Berlin, Article III of the Anglo-Congolese Agreement was the culmination of a long series of malicious pinpricks which went back to December 1892—for Marschall had still not forgotten the British opposition to German railway concessions in Asia Minor. In 1893 London had shamefully grudged what little co-operation she gave in facilitating the repression of Henrik Witboi in South-West Africa; she had even created absurd difficulties about the procurement of Singapore coolies for German New Guinea.[4] In December 1893 she had attempted, by a confidence trick of the most impudent kind, to meddle in the German sphere of Bagirmi. For this Germany had indeed silently retaliated; but for the public affront of the Anglo-Congolese Agreement public reparation must be made. Whether or not Marschall guessed that the British might be retaliating in their turn, he certainly felt that Germany was being treated, as in the Rabīh Zubair episode but this time in public, either with deliberate malice or with an off-hand lack of consideration which was an insult to her status as a Great Power.[5] At the beginning of June Hatzfeldt had

---

[1] *Ibid.*, No. 1750, Memo. by Holstein 27 July 1893; Nos. 1756, 1757, Marschall to Hatzfeldt 2 and 4 Aug. (both drafted by Holstein); No. 1762, same to same 24 Oct. 1893.

[2] Temperley and Penson, *op. cit.*, pp. 480-7, citing Deym to Kálnoky 31 Jan. and 26 Feb. 1894. G.P. IX, No. 2149, Deym to Kálnoky 27 Feb. 1894; No. 2152, Memo. by Caprivi 8 Mar.; No. 2153, Marschall to Hatzfeldt 28 Mar. 1894.

[3] G.P. IX, No. 2162, Marschall to Hatzfeldt 16 Nov. 1894.

[4] For these incidents, here presented from the German point of view, see G.P. VIII, Nos. 2017-20, June-Sept. 1893. British documentation at FO 64/1301, 1311, 1316, 1317. As late as Nov. 1894 Marschall still recalled the Asia Minor incident with resentment (G.P. IX, No. 2162).

[5] Cf. Alvensleben's remarks to Plunkett, FO 10/615, Plunkett to Kimberley No. 105, 7 June 1894.

suggested that Germany might use the Anglo-Congolese imbroglio as means of exacting concessions in Samoa. Marschall ignored this recommendation. Once he had taken his stand on 1 June, he adamantly insisted that no bargain or compensation was admissible; Britain must withdraw Article III unconditionally. The main object of Marschall's policy was to extort this public confession of wrong-doing; hence his insistence that Germany's legal rights had been violated, as well as her interests injured.[1] He may have hoped, at any rate at the outset, to obtain as a by-product some modification of British policy in Europe; he certainly ended up with the conviction that Germany had little to hope for here so long as British policy was controlled by such a weathercock as Rosebery.

Even if Marschall's personal views had been less intransigent than they were, his hand would certainly have been forced, both by the German public and by the Emperor. No doubt Alvensleben was exaggerating somewhat when he told Plunkett that 'any delay in withdrawing Article III would have caused the Government in Germany to be run away with. The only chance for Baron Marschall to calm the storm was to get that concession *at once*'.[2] But Malet told the Queen that the Emperor himself was being 'unwillingly drawn along by the strong stream of public feeling'; and in fact even the Progressive *Vossische Zeitung*, normally friendly to England, joined the general chorus of denunciation.[3] No doubt the German press could to some extent be managed; but by 1894 it was certainly very much easier to turn on the tap of 'Africanist' agitation than to turn it off again. Marschall, too, as a mere Badener, had to show that in the defence of German interests he could be just as militant as the most rigid Prussian.[4] Then there was the Kaiser, who believed that it had been his personal intervention which had preserved the common frontier with the Congo State in 1890, and who therefore, as Malet emphasised, took it as a personal affront that the Foreign Office should have broken the promise about the Central African corridor made to him by Salisbury.[5] The Kaiser's attitude, like that of the German press, hardened in the course of June. At the beginning of the month he had concurred in Hatzfeldt's suggestion that the dispute should be used to secure concessions in Samoa; but by the 10th he was solemnly warning Malet that the only way to avoid 'incalculable complications' in Europe was for London to withdraw Article III unconditionally and at once.[6]

[1] G.P. VIII, No. 2039, Hatzfeldt to Caprivi 1 June 1894; Nos. 2045, 2051, Marschall to Hatzfeldt 12 and 14 June.   [2] FO 10/616, Plunkett to Anderson, private, 24 June 1894.
[3] L.Q.V. 3, ii, p. 406, Malet to the Queen 16 June 1894. FO 64/1333, Gosselin to Kimberley No. 63, 26 May; cf. D.D.F. xi, No. 111, Herbette to Casimir-Périer 27-29 May 1894.
[4] After the Russo-German trade Agreement of Feb. 1894, he became 'the Badener who had betrayed the agricultural interests of Prussia'; and he was also personally out of favour with the Emperor at this time. Cf. J. A. Nichols, *Germany after Bismarck* (Cambridge, Mass. 1958), pp. 306-7; Rich and Fisher, *The Holstein Papers*, iii, pp. 498-9, Eulenburg to Holstein 19 Feb. 1895.
[5] L.Q.V. 3, ii, pp. 404-7; G.P. VIII No. 2047, the Emperor to Caprivi 11 June 1894.
[6] G.P. VIII, No. 2039, minute by the Emperor; No. 2047.

Marschall has been reproached for the unceremonious manner in which he withdrew from collaboration with the French on and after 17 June. This was not indeed a very creditable episode; but the faults were not all on one side. On 12 June Marschall offered collaboration in principle; on the 13th he made a definite proposal for joint action in favour of 'the *status quo* as to the legal position created by the Congo Act', and suggested, as a possibility, a conference of the Powers.[1] Encouraged by Hanotaux, Herbette saw Marschall again on the 15th. Marschall announced that he was now demanding the entire abrogation of the Agreement, but poured cold water on his own idea of a conference. It was, he said, just an idea; it would in any case probably not be necessary, as he fully expected Leopold to yield. At both these interviews Herbette insisted on talking about Egypt: even if the present crisis was brought to a satisfactory solution, surely the best way of preventing any repetition of such British misconduct was for Germany to align herself with France on this question? But Marschall made no reply—or, at least, none that Herbette cared to report to Paris.[2]

Hanotaux evidently suspected, especially from Marschall's eloquent silences, that Germany hoped to use France as a means of pressure while committing herself to the very minimum of common action. It was only after twenty-four hours' reflection, and a conversation with the German ambassador Münster, that Hanotaux sent Herbette specific proposals; and Herbette was told to test the ground carefully before submitting them. Hanotaux' proposals were doomed from the outset. He had already been misled by Herbette, who had carelessly misreported Marschall as pledging support for 'le *statu quo* légal africain' and not merely for 'the situation created by the Congo Act'. Hanotaux now spelt out the practical consequences of 'le *statu quo* légal africain' with a precision and lack of reserve which smacks more of the *sous-directeur* briefing his Minister than of the Minister himself initiating a delicate negotiation. The Congo State was to be restricted once and for all to the boundaries detailed in the Berlin Act, and in particular to the fourth parallel and the thirtieth meridian. The State was to renounce all leases or other forms of occupation outside these limits, and to accept that the French right of preference applied to all territorial cessions or exchanges of any type whatsoever. France and Germany were to act jointly to secure these aims, and neither Power was to conclude any agreement until both were satisfied.[3]

On 17 June Herbette made no attempt whatever to feel his way with Marschall; he simply submitted, as an *aide-mémoire*, an almost verbatim transcript of Hanotaux' bill of particulars.[4] Marschall promptly tore the proposals to pieces. He had never offered support for 'le *statu quo*

[1] *Ibid.*, No. 2046, Marschall to Münster, 12 June 1894; No. 2049, Memo. by Marschall 13 June. D.D.F. xi, Nos. 140, 142, Herbette to Hanotaux, 12 and 13 June.
[2] D.D.F. xi, No. 147, Herbette to Hanotaux 15 June 1894; and footnote.
[3] *Ibid.*, Nos. 151, 152, Hanotaux to Herbette 17 June 1894; cf. No. 142.
[4] Cf. D.D.F. xi, No. 151 with the French *Aide-memoire* printed at G.P. viii, No. 2061.

légal africain'; he did not agree that the Berlin Act, which had designated the Congolese territory which the Powers had agreed to regard as neutral, had at the same time forbidden all extension of the Congo State. He bluntly indicated that Germany was not going to fight the French battle against King Leopold on the upper Ubangi question; nor had Germany any interest in the French right of preference, except to point out that it must not be interpreted as applying to all cessions to other Powers, for Germany held special rights under her treaty of November 1884. Having already for all practical purposes secured the withdrawal of Article III, Marschall of course also rejected the proposal that neither Power should conclude until both were satisfied. The French proposals were indeed so crude, and so clumsily submitted, that Marschall had some excuse for his hasty withdrawal; indeed, he suspected that the French had deliberately put forward impossibilities, and wrecked the negotiation, in order later on to be able to deny that there had ever been any concerted action.[1] Thereafter, the most that Marschall would do for the French was to permit Münster to say that in the opinion of the Wilhelmstrasse the British leases to Leopold were contrary to the Berlin Act.[2] Hanotaux then attempted to transmit an agreed *aide-mémoire* establishing that the limitation of Germany's explicit objections solely to Article III did not imply the view that the Anglo-Congolese Agreement was otherwise a legally valid instrument. But of this document Marschall refused to 'accuser réception', on the grounds that this would constitute an exchange of declarations; and he then clinched the matter by going off on holiday.[3]

Marschall's conduct brought about the prompt demise of the 'Franco-German entente in Africa' which the Wilhelmstrasse had so assiduously puffed in February and March. This was in itself of no great importance; Paris had always suspected that this whirlwind courtship was merely a tactical weapon against Britain. But the French were left with the bitter conviction that they had been used; and to later German offers of collaboration in Africa they responded either with extreme caution or not at all. Hanotaux had certainly hoped that the Anglo-Congolese Agreement might modify, if only slightly, German policy towards the Egyptian question;[4] he was now forced to recognise that Germany intended, as before, to keep Egypt 'jammed like a wedge' between France and Britain.[5] Meanwhile, Hanotaux found no help at all at St Petersburg. The Russians had of

[1] D.D.F. xi, No. 153, Herbette to Hanotaux 17 June 1894; G.P. *loc. cit.*, Memo. by Marschall 17 June.
[2] G.P. viii, No. 2069, Münster to Caprivi 25 June 1894. Cf. D.D.F. xi, Nos. 159, 172, Hanotaux to Herbette 19 and 22 June.
[3] D.D.F. xi, Nos. 174, 175, Herbette to Hanotaux 24 and 26 June 1894; No. 179, footnote. The published German documents give a misleading impression of this episode: cf. A. J. P. Taylor, 'Les premières années de l'alliance russe', *Rev. Hist.*, cciv, 415 (1950), p. 66.
[4] D.D.F. xi, No. 152.
[5] Cf. G.P. viii, No. 1851, Rotenhan to Heyking (Cairo) 5 July 1894.

course no interests whatever in the Upper Nile, but an expression of opinion in London would have cost them nothing. But, although Hanotaux had written to St Petersburg on 1 June, it was not until the 9th that Giers had even expressed the personal opinion that the attitude of France 'était bien celle qu'exige la situation'; and when pressed for further action he staged one of his diplomatic relapses.[1] This was more than mere indifference. The Russians looked with great suspicion upon the 'fréquentations douteuses' implied in any Franco-German rapprochement; and they indicated their displeasure, not only by an almost complete reserve on the Anglo-Congolese Agreement, but by their coldly formal and almost scandalously belated condolences on the assassination of Sadi Carnot on 24 June.[2]

Hanotaux' position in the third week of June was far from enviable. The German success had greatly reduced his own freedom of man-œuvre in dealing with London. He would now be expected to produce for France a diplomatic success not less complete than that of Germany, and it was all too clear that neither Berlin nor St Petersburg would lift a finger to help him. Meanwhile, his discussions with London, after a promising start, were making no progress whatever. Yet Hanotaux persisted in seeking a genuine settlement with England rather than a merely showy triumph over the Congo State; and it was only when London repeatedly evaded Hanotaux' attempts to engage in serious negotiation that he at last decided to destroy the Anglo-Congolese Agreement by a direct assault at Brussels.

Dufferin, at his first interview with Hanotaux on 1 June, had abounded in conciliatory platitudes, and had not rejected out of hand a hint that the May Agreement might as a provisional solution be 'held in suspense'. On the 5th Kimberley had offered a negotiation to Decrais and had confirmed in writing his desire for discussions on Africa 'for the purpose of . . . plac[ing] the relations of the two countries in that continent on a more satisfactory footing'. On the following day Dufferin had repeated this written invitation, with the apparently insignificant verbal amendment that the discussions were to apply to 'Central and West Africa'.[3] But when on 11 June Dufferin and Hanotaux got down to business, the interview was completely sterile. There was indeed an almost comic failure to communicate. Dufferin appealed throughout to purely practical considerations— the need to reach a settlement with Leopold, the highly theoretical nature of Ottoman rights in a region subject to 'the sinister tyranny of the Mahdi', the British fears of a Mahdist invasion of Uganda. Hanotaux delivered a lecture on international law which covered the

[1] D.D.F. XI, No. 122, Hanotaux to Montebello 1 June 1894; Nos. 138, 143, 169, Montebello to Hanotaux 10, 14 and 21 June.
[2] *Ibid.*, No. 182, Montebello to Hanotaux 2 July 1894, and footnote; No. 223, Herbette to Hanotaux 20 Aug., warning against 'fréquentations douteuses'. Cf. G.P. VIII, No. 2069.
[3] D.D.F. XI, No. 123, *Note du Ministre* 2 June 1894; No. 129, Decrais to Hanotaux 5 June; No. 133, Dufferin to Hanotaux 6 June. FO 27/3182, Kimberley to Dufferin No. 187a, 5 June.

integrity of the Ottoman Empire, the inextensibility of neutral states, and the right of the French, under their right of preference, to intervene whenever there was a change in the 'primordial structure' of the Congo State. Dufferin however made it clear that there was little prospect of the Agreement being even modified; and asked Hanotaux to put his views on paper, evidently so as to start a slow-motion battle of Notes. He concluded, though there was little in Hanotaux' actual words to warrant the conclusion, that 'the real desire of the French is to prevent us from establishing ourselves ... on the Bahr el Gazal and in the valley of the Nile, and perhaps to anticipate us in the occupation of those districts'.[1]

Rosebery thought he saw a way out of the impasse. On 17 June he suggested, to meet the French view that the Upper Nile was an integral part of Egypt, that the boundaries of 'Egypt' should be defined and Britain authorised to occupy the Sudanese provinces until Egypt herself was able to take them over. This arrangement, which was evidently modelled on the status of Kassala under the 1891 Agreement with Italy, might in Rosebery's view be brought about by an international conference, which he believed France to desire and in which he was sanguine enough to hope for German support. On 18 June Kimberley sounded Hatzfeldt about a conference. The ambassador confined himself to the ominous observation that Germany at any rate had nothing to fear from such a proceeding; nevertheless on the 19th Kimberley told Dufferin that if Hanotaux should 'suggest a conference with a limited scope ... you should not discourage it, but declare that you must refer home for instructions'.[2]

By this time Hanotaux was becoming impatient. It was now clear that Berlin had failed him; and on the 18th Dufferin was still without instructions. Hanotaux still hoped for a 'règlement amiable', but he could not afford to wait indefinitely. He urged Decrais at London to press for early action as the only alternative to 'les polémiques les plus dangereuses'.[3] Meanwhile, Kimberley, who claimed to be 'in some perplexity' at not having received a written French statement, had indeed authorised Dufferin to discuss with Hanotaux, but had given him no specific instructions other than the warning not to discourage a conference.[4] Dufferin and Hanotaux met again on 20 June, and Hanotaux touched upon the idea of a conference; but Dufferin, who seems to have treated his instructions in very cavalier fashion, 'n'a pas paru vouloir entrer dans cet ordre d'idées'. The only definite outcome

[1] D.D.F. xi, No. 139, *Note du Ministre* 11 June 1894. FO 27/3185, Dufferin to Kimberley Nos. 162 and 163, 13 June.
[2] Crewe, *op. cit.* ii, p. 448. FO 64/1332, Kimberley to Malet No. 93, 18 June 1894; cf. G.P. viii, No. 2067, Hatzfeldt to A.A. 18 June. FO 27/3188, Kimberley to Dufferin tel. No. 33, 19 June.
[3] D.D.F. xi, No. 160, Hanotaux to Decrais 19 June 1894.
[4] FO 27/3188, *loc. cit.* In fact Hanotaux had already explained to Phipps that he was unwilling to deprive the negotiation of flexibility by a premature written statement (FO 27/3185, Phipps to Anderson 14 June 1894).

of the meeting was to make it clear that the mere suspension of the leases would no longer satisfy Hanotaux—'il fallait en finir tout de suite'.[1] After the success of Berlin, Hanotaux could not indeed demand less.

For reasons which are not apparent from his record of it, Hanotaux regarded this conversation of the 20th as an important step forward.[2] But then day followed day without any sign of life from London, and at last Hanotaux invited Dufferin to call. The interview, on 29th June, began with Dufferin's refusal to admit either that he was engaged in a negotiation or that the phrase 'Central Africa', in his letter to Hanotaux of 6 June, could refer to the Upper Nile. 'Central Africa', he said, meant the Lake Chad region; one should look at the map of Africa from east to west, not from north to south. Hanotaux ignored this pitiful quibble and calmly recapitulated the legal arguments to which, as he said, Dufferin had never attempted to reply and which led inexorably to the conclusion that the leases must be cancelled. Dufferin, still without instructions and evidently ill at ease with an antagonist of much heavier intellectual calibre, complained that Hanotaux' attitude amounted to an ultimatum and rose as if to take his leave. Then, perhaps ashamed of his bad temper, he made a friendly appeal to Hanotaux to drop his lectures on international law and to talk business. Whereupon Hanotaux, after safeguarding himself in every possible way, expressed the personal opinion that if the leases were cancelled agreement might be reached upon 'questions soulevées par les actes antérieurs'. Dufferin greeted this statement as 'les premiers mots de véritable *négociation* que j'entends sortir de votre bouche'; and well he might, for in this context 'actes antérieurs' could only mean the Anglo-German Agreement of 1890.[3]

Dufferin then asked, rather rashly, whether France would in fact recognise this Agreement. Hanotaux refused to commit himself; Dufferin then referred to press reports that France intended to occupy the Bahr al-Ghazal and asked for 'an assurance that no such outrageous step was about to be hazarded'. Receiving no reply, he warned Hanotaux in so many words that 'if Monsieur Monteil attempted to act the part of a second Mizon in the Nile Valley it would simply mean war between the two countries'.[4] Hanotaux retorted that the instructions to be given to Monteil would greatly depend upon London's reply to the French observations on the Anglo-Congolese Agreement. But when Dufferin remarked that this statement would be regarded by London as a menace Hanotaux, evidently wearying of this rather

[1] D.D.F. xi, No. 163, *Note du Ministre* 20 June 1894. FO 27/3185, Dufferin to Kimberley No. 169, 21 June.
[2] D.D.F. xi, No. 165, Hanotaux to Decrais 20 June 1894.
[3] *Ibid.*, No. 178, *Note du Ministre* 29 June 1894. FO 27/3185, Dufferin to Kimberley No. 173a, 30 June.
[4] FO 27/3185, *loc. cit.* This passage scandalised Harcourt, and Kimberley was forced to refer it back to Dufferin for re-drafting. The full story (from the Kimberley Papers) is told by Stengers, 'Aux Origines de Fachoda', *Rev. Belge Phil. Hist.*, 1960, pp. 1044-51.

puerile exchange of discourtesies, 'held up both his hands and said "Oh! for Heaven's sake do not let it have that character" '. Indeed, in spite of all these high words, the interview seems to have closed on quite a cordial note. Dufferin gained the impression that Hanotaux was anxious to come to terms and would be 'very large' in meeting the views of England. This impression was confirmed in a further conversation on 4 July, after which Dufferin reported that if the leases were cancelled Hanotaux would probably recognise the Anglo-German Agreement—in fact, if not in form.[1]

Hanotaux had however insisted throughout that any negotiation would have to begin with a genuine British offer to abandon the leases as the basis of a wider settlement. But this was more than Rosebery could stomach, not least for domestic reasons; and Kimberley therefore continued to deal in the vaguest of generalities. On 11 July he discussed African questions 'incidentally' with Decrais; but the Upper Nile was not even explicitly mentioned, being concealed under a general 'delimitation of our spheres in east and west'. On this topic, Kimberley expressed himself as willing to negotiate, since he understood that M. Hanotaux wished it; and he also mentioned a few other African issues, all of which were either moribund, or trivial, or both.[2] Hanotaux now begun to lose patience with this persistent evasion of the point. He told Decrais to warn Kimberley that 'le temps n'arrangera rien et qu'il envenimera tout'. If the British persisted in their negative attitude, Hanotaux could find other ways of nullifying the Anglo-Congolese Agreement—but only at the expense of much bad blood which he for one wished to avoid.[3] Thereupon, on 17 July, Kimberley agreed that so long as the Anglo-Congolese Agreement were not completely segregated, this difficulty might indeed be considered first. But he still insisted on a written statement from Hanotaux; and he added that forthcoming negotiations between France and the Congo State might well affect the questions at issue.[4]

Hanotaux provided the written statement on 6 August. It was another legal dissertation—a 'note de jurisconsulte', as he himself called it—for Hanotaux did not intend to be the first officially to propose a bargain.[5] Meanwhile, however, he had given up London as hopeless and had towards the end of July launched a direct attack on King Leopold. He had originally demanded a negotiation on 22 June;[6] but Leopold, like the British, evaded action. It was only when Hanotaux began to use 'rude, violent and menacing language' that on 16 July the King appointed de Volder and Goffinet as his plenipoten-

[1] D.D.F. XI, Nos. 178, 184, *Notes du Ministre* 29 June and 4 July 1894. FO 27/3185, *loc. cit.*; FO 27/3186, Dufferin to Kimberley No. 178, 5 July.
[2] D.D.F. XI, No. 190, Decrais to Hanotaux 12 July 1894.
[3] *Ibid.*, Nos. 193, 194, Hanotaux to Decrais 15 July 1894.
[4] *Ibid.*, No. 196, Decrais to Hanotaux 17 July 1894. FO 27/3183, Kimberley to Dufferin No. 260, 17 July; cf. same to same No. 275A, 1 Aug. 1894.
[5] D.D.F. XI, No. 209, Note, 6 Aug. 1894; No. 210, Hanotaux to Decrais 7 Aug.
[6] *Ibid.*, No. 170, Hanotaux to Bourée 22 June 1894.

tiaries. The King had indeed only acted when he discovered, with unconcealed disappointment and irritation, that London had no intention of grasping the French nettle for him.[1] Nor did he comply with Hanotaux' demand that his representatives should have full powers and that the discussions were to be completely secret. On matters relating to the Anglo-Congolese Agreement de Volder and Goffinet were instructed to act as mere reporters; and Leopold had promised Rosebery that nothing would be settled which 'might in any way affect' the Agreement, without prior consultation with London.[2]

When discussions began at Paris on 25 July, Hanotaux at once sent de Volder and Goffinet back to Brussels to obtain full powers.[3] They returned, properly equipped, on the 27th; and for the next few days Leopold struggled to keep his leases by conceding to France a frontier on the M'Bomu, or even on the fourth parallel. Hanotaux would have none of it. By 2 August it was clear that the King would be granted a frontier on the M'Bomu only if he completely relinquished the leases; and on the 6th, after consultation with Leopold, the delegates accepted this *Diktat* in principle.[4] On the 7th Hanotaux made a small concession: the King would be permitted to occupy that portion of his leases situated to the south and east of the lines 5° 30' N and 30° E—the future 'Lado Enclave'. This concession seems to have been prompted by pressure from French investors in the Congo State. Leopold was threatening, not for the first or the last time when in a difficulty, to 'throw up the whole concern'; and representations were made that he should not be driven to despair.[5] But this was the last word. By 9 August Hanotaux looked upon the matter as settled, and had already begun the task of restoring the line to London by a 'most conciliatory' overture to Phipps, the African expert at the Paris Embassy.[6]

Leopold's difficulty now was to settle with Paris without quarrelling with London. On 7 August Eetvelde had insinuated that England might be prepared to release the King from the May Agreement, but Plunkett, on his own authority, rejected this suggestion in almost menacing tones. On the following day Eetvelde revealed the terms which Hanotaux was demanding, though not the fact that Leopold had accepted them, and he now openly begged that London should

---

[1] FO 27/3186, Dufferin to Kimberley No. 178, 5 July 1894; FO 10/616, Plunkett to Kimberley Nos. 164, 166, 13 and 15 July; D.D.F. xi, No. 195, Leopold to Hanotaux 16 July.
[2] FO 10/613, Kimberley to Plunkett No. 76, 28 June 1894. FO 10/616, Plunkett to Kimberley Nos. 144, 149, 164 and 166, of 25 and 28 June, 13 and 15 July. Cf. D.D.F. xi, No. 170.
[3] FO 10/616, Plunkett to Kimberley No. 176, 26 July 1894.
[4] FO 27/3186, Phipps to Kimberley No. 195, 2 Aug. 1894; FO 27/3188, same to same tels. No. 20, 21 and 22, 7 Aug. FO 10/616, Plunkett to Kimberley Nos. 179 (28 July); 190, 191A (4 Aug.); 191B (5 Aug.); 194, 195 (7 Aug.); memo. by Anderson 8 Aug. 1894. FO 10/618, Plunkett to Kimberley tels. No. 29 (1 Aug.); 29a (4 Aug.); 30 (7 Aug.).
[5] FO 10/616, Plunkett to Kimberley No. 197, 8 Aug. 1894. Stengers, 'La première tentative de reprise . . .', *Bull. Soc. Roy. Belge Géog.*, 1949, p. 76, citing Thys to Eetvelde 10 Aug. 1894. The banker Bunau-Varilla acted as intermediary.
[6] FO 27/3188, Phipps to Kimberley tel. No. 23, 9 Aug. 1894.

release the King.[1] On the 9th the Congolese delegates in Paris admitted to Phipps that they had been forced to surrender 'with the knife at their throats'; but Rosebery had already warned the King that no modification of the May Agreement was permissible 'without the privity and consent of Great Britain'.[2] For two days the unfortunate Leopold floundered, transmitting to Plunkett a series of complicated untruths about the negotiation while his delegates in Paris did not attempt to conceal from Phipps that they had made a complete surrender.[3] But Hanotaux, who already regarded his Agreement with Leopold as a *fait accompli*, now gave another turn to the screw. On 11 August Eetvelde made a clean breast of the situation to Plunkett, and urgently requested British permission to comply with Hanotaux' demand for immediate signature:

> The knife was . . . again placed at the throat of the Congo State.
> . . . If H.M. Govt. make [the King] refuse . . ., he must in view
> of Belgian exigencies request that H.M. Govt. will inform French
> Govt. that he is acting in compliance with their wishes and that
> they assume the responsibility towards France of this action.[4]

Rosebery was prepared to assume this responsibility; but almost all his colleagues were not. Harcourt had pointed out from the first that the Anglo-Congolese Agreement might ultimately mean war with France. Early in June, he had been alarmed and incensed by an enquiry from Leopold whether London would treat a French trespass into the leased regions as 'an attack on British territory'—in other words, as an act of war.[5] In July he had successfully insisted that Dufferin's despatch threatening war if Monteil entered the Nile valley should be referred back to Paris for re-drafting in less minatory language. At the Cabinet of 13 August Harcourt won again, and Rosebery was overruled by his colleagues. At about noon Kimberley drafted a telegram on '10 Downing Street' notepaper, informing Plunkett that the Government did 'not feel called upon to oppose the King's desire to sign this arrangement with France'.[6] It was at once communicated to Eetvelde, who remarked, 'Cela veut simplement dire que nous pouvons signer cet arrangement sans risque de nous brouiller avec l'Angleterre?' 'Yes', replied Plunkett.[7] The Congolese signed on the

[1] FO 10/616, Plunkett to Kimberley Nos. 194 and 195, 7 Aug. 1894; No. 197, 8 Aug. FO 10/618, Plunkett to Kimberley tels. No. 32 and 33, 8 Aug.
[2] FO 27/3188, Phipps to Kimberley tels. No. 24 and 25, 9 Aug. 1894. FO 10/618, Sanderson to Plunkett tel. unnumb., 8 Aug.; Kimberley to Plunkett tel. No. 41, 9 Aug.
[3] FO 10/616, Plunkett to Kimberley No. 198, 9 Aug. 1894; FO 10/617, same to same No. 200, 10 Aug.; FO 10/618, same to same tels. No. 34 and 35, 10 Aug. Cf. FO 27/3186, Phipps to Kimberley No. 201, 10 Aug.
[4] FO 10/618, Plunkett to Kimberley tels. No. 36 and 37, 11 Aug. 1894; FO 10/617, same to same No. 201, 11 Aug. Cf. FO 27/3186, Phipps to Kimberley Nos. 202 and 203, 11 Aug.
[5] Harcourt to Kimberley 12 June 1894, quoted Gardiner, *op. cit.* 11, pp. 317-8.
[6] *Ibid.*, p. 320. James, *op. cit.*, p. 352. FO 10/618, Kimberley to Plunkett tel. No. 45, 13 Aug. 1894.
[7] FO 10/618, Plunkett to Kimberley tel. No. 39, 13 Aug. 1894; FO 10/617, same to same No. 207, 13 Aug.

following day, 14 August 1894. All that now remained of Rosebery's master-stroke for the solution of the Upper Nile question was a right of telegraphic communication through Congo territory—in the sardonic words of Baron Marschall, 'des poteaux télégraphiques'.[1]

The knife which Hanotaux had placed at King Leopold's throat had been one which London was quite powerless to blunt or to deflect. Hanotaux had threatened to call upon Belgium, in accordance with her obligations of neutrality, to withdraw her officers from the service of a state unfriendly to France. The Congolese *Force Publique* was by 1894 very largely officered by Belgian regulars who were retained on the strength of, and paid by, the War Ministry at Brussels. Mérode-Westerloo, the Belgian Foreign Minister, was well aware of the very grave dangers inherent in this situation; and in the summer of 1894 the Belgian ministers as a body were aghast at Leopold's recklessness in quarrelling simultaneously with Belgium's two mighty neighbours.[2] Moreover, a general election was impending, in which it was feared that the Socialists would show embarrassing strength. Westerloo and his colleagues appear to have presented the King with an ultimatum: unless his differences with France were settled before the election, they would take no responsibility for the consequences, either for Leopold personally or for the institution of monarchy in Belgium.[3] Hence the reference to 'Belgian exigencies' in Leopold's last desperate appeal to London; an appeal, not to support him against the French, but to permit him to settle with them. 'Ça n'a pas été une négociation. . . . Il n'y avait pas à discuter, il fallait se soumettre',[4] wrote the Belgian minister in Paris. Rosebery saw even deeper when he told the Queen that the collapse of Leopold's position was 'inherent in the fact that he is attempting to combine the position of a second-rate Power in Europe with a first-rate Power in Africa'.[5] But this was a consideration which Rosebery should have pondered before signing the Anglo-Congolese Agreement. Apparently it took the complete destruction of his Upper Nile policy to bring Rosebery to recognise the obvious.

[1] D.D.F. xi, No. 232, Herbette to Hanotaux 29 Aug. 1894.
[2] Stengers, 'Aux origines de Fachoda', pp. 1056-61. Cf. FO 10/616, Plunkett to Kimberley No. 143, 24 June 1894.
[3] Stengers, *ubi supra*, pp. 1061-4. The pressure from the Belgian Ministers, and the threat used by Hanotaux, were admitted to Plunkett by Eetvelde (FO 10/616, Plunkett to Kimberley Nos. 195 (7 Aug.), 197 (8 Aug.); FO 10/617, same to same No. 201, 11 Aug.). Cf. also Lambermont's remarks reported in Plunkett's 205 of 12 Aug. (FO 10/617).
[4] Beyens to Lambermont 18 Aug. 1894, cited Stengers, *ubi supra*, p. 1064. On and after 8 Aug. Leopold begged, not for British support, but for 'l'autorisation de capituler' (Stengers, *loc. cit.*).
[5] L.Q.V. 3, ii, p. 420, Rosebery to the Queen 15 Aug. 1894.

IX

THE FAILURE OF DIPLOMACY

ANGLO-FRENCH NEGOTIATIONS

AUGUST–DECEMBER 1894

THE Anglo-Congolese Agreement was not the only casualty of Hanotaux' settlement of accounts with King Leopold. Another, and unexpected, casualty was the Monteil mission. The revival of this mission had been announced, with great *éclat*, by Hanotaux in his Chamber speech of 7 June. The revived mission had inspired Leopold with fears that the French were contemplating a direct attack upon Léopoldville;[1] it had prompted Dufferin to utter an open threat of war. Towards the end of August it was suddenly withdrawn from the French Congo, and Monteil and most of his men were sent to fight Samory in the Ivory Coast hinterland. At first sight this looks like a deliberate gesture of conciliation towards London, and a sign that Hanotaux had used 'rude, violent and menacing' methods with Leopold only because these were forced upon him. Hanotaux was indeed ready to persevere in the search for a 'règlement amiable', which he quite genuinely desired; but to Hanotaux the sudden recall of the Monteil mission came as a complete surprise, and an unpleasant surprise at that.

On 8 June 1894, the day after Hanotaux' speech, Delcassé cabled Libreville: 'commandant Monteil, renforts et approvisionnements quitteront France fin juin'.[2] In fact, Monteil did not leave France until 16 July. But this time Monteil cannot be blamed for the delay, for until 13 July his instructions had not been signed.[3] This delay was almost certainly due to the insistence of Hanotaux, against the opposition of Delcassé at the Pavillon de Flore, that these instructions should be radically modified. The new instructions completely abandoned Delcassé's original objective of the Nile; Monteil's utmost goal was now to be N'Doruma, a village just—but only just—on the Congo side of the Nile-Congo divide. As against the Congolese, the instructions

[1] FO 10/615, Plunkett to Kimberley No. 121, 12 June 1894.
[2] MC G.C., 1 45b, Delcassé to Governor Libreville 8 June 1894; cf. same to same 23 June.
[3] Monteil, *Souvenirs Vécus*, p. 113; D.D.F. xi, No. 191, Delcassé to Monteil 13 July 1894.

were still fairly combative: the use of force was of course deprecated, but Monteil was ordered 'à vous opposer...à toute opération de la part de nos voisins qui tendrait à améliorer leur situation à notre détriment'. He was however categorically forbidden to enter the Nile valley, 'de façon à ce que la question du Soudan égyptien reste entière et complètement réservée'. This prohibition was certainly the work of Hanotaux; for to make doubly sure he personally interviewed Monteil on 12 July and, after explaining the need to avoid any action 'contraire à notre thèse sur l'intégrité de l'empire ottoman', he obtained Monteil's word of honour that 'il n'enverrait jamais une troupe ou même un homme dans le bassin du Nil'.[1]

On 24 August, when Monteil at Loango was just about to march into the interior, he received a telegram despatched by Delcassé on the 14th. Monteil was told that in view of the Franco-Congolese Agreement his mission had now lost its point. He was to detach one company as a reinforcement for Decazes, and proceed forthwith with the rest of his troops to Grand Bassam on the Ivory Coast.[2] Although Monteil's July instructions had warned him to expect revised orders if a satisfactory settlement with the Congo State were reached, he was evidently reluctant to obey this directive, for on 31 August Delcassé had to send a further telegram peremptorily insisting that Monteil comply with 'la décision définitive du gouvernement'.[3] Whether Monteil would have kept, or had ever intended to keep, his word 'never to send even a man into the Nile basin' is a matter for conjecture. What is certain is that he made a sinister mystery of his recall by suppressing, in his memoirs, all mention of the radical alteration in the object of his mission which had taken place in July. Of his recall in August, he writes 'Ainsi, tous les grands projets étaient abandonnés' —clearly implying that the 'grands projets' still meant the Nile. Poor in facts, Monteil is rich in innuendo: 'Quels intérêts, ou quelles intrigues entrèrent en jeu, je l'ignore encore, je n'ai jamais voulu m'en préoccuper'.[4] In March 1895 the *Colonies* did explain to the Chamber that with the conclusion of the Franco-Congolese Agreement the Monteil mission had become superfluous; but as the alteration in Monteil's instructions was not revealed, this explanation was treated with the derisive contempt which it seemed to deserve. Even as late as the nineteen-thirties, quite serious French writers attributed Monteil's mysterious recall variously to the hidden hand of the *Intelligence britannique* or to the blandishments of certain ladies who were, it seems, unofficially attached to King Leopold's 'Bureau d'informations' at Paris.[5]

---

[1] D.D.F., *loc. cit.*; and footnote (minute by Hanotaux 12 July 1894).
[2] Monteil, *op. cit.*, pp. 113-4. MC Afrique III 19b, Delcassé to Monteil 14 Aug. 1894.
[3] MC, *ubi supra*, same to same tel. No. 4, 31 Aug. 1894. Cf. D.D.F., *loc. cit.*
[4] Monteil, *op. cit.*, p. 114.
[5] J. Delebecque, *Vie du général Marchand* (Paris 1936), pp. 67-8. Vergniol, 'Fachoda', *Revue de France* Aug. 1936, pp. 639-40.

The despised official explanation is now known to be after all correct. But it may yet not contain the whole of the story. Among the writers who later discussed the Monteil mission was Hanotaux himself; and Hanotaux, writing in 1909, comments upon Monteil's recall in terms which clearly imply that the goal of the mission was still Fashoda: 'Si le colonel Monteil eût été sur les lieux dès 1895, trois ans avant Marchand, alors qu'aucune action par l'Egypte n'était même prévue, n'est-il pas évident que les événements eussent tourné autrement?'[1] The memory of Gabriel Hanotaux was undoubtedly the weakest element in an otherwise excellent mental equipment; but it is certainly odd that a mere fifteen years later he should have forgotten the dramatic scene in which he exacted Monteil's 'engagement formel' not to enter the Nile basin.

It is moreover known that Delcassé recalled Monteil without consulting Hanotaux, who protested vigorously against this decision. The motives for Delcassé's impulsive action are obscure; perhaps it would be unwise to look beyond the perfectly genuine crisis in the Ivory Coast hinterland. Hanotaux, however, explained his motives for objection—or some of them—in a letter of 21 August, in which he complains of the failure of the *Colonies* to occupy territory secured for France by the exertions of the Quai d'Orsay: 'Nous avons réparé, au risque de complications graves, les fautes d'inertie commises par l'administration des Colonies depuis sept ans. Une fois le conflit diplomatique arrangé, vaille que vaille, on va s'endormir de nouveau. . . .'[2] In fact, with the company detached to him by Monteil, Decazes was able to take over the Congolese posts on the upper Ubangi without any serious hitch.[3] But Hanotaux' complaint is plausible enough, and would indeed close the question but for a very curious passage in a private letter which he wrote on 7 August to Decrais in London. Deploring that the Foreign Office had forced upon him the dilatory technique of exchanging formal notes, Hanotaux goes on to remark: '*Et comme, en attendant, nos agents opèrent dans le terrain contesté*, je pense que les Anglais finiront bien par comprendre, sans qu'il soit utile de leur dire, qu'ils ne gagnent rien à tous ces retards.'[4]

This was evidently a warning to be passed on, at some suitable moment if not immediately, to the Foreign Office; for the only possible meaning of 'terrain contesté', in this context, is the Nile basin and in particular the regions leased to Leopold. But as Hanotaux very well knew, in August 1894 there was not a single French agent operating in this disputed territory; and the warning must therefore refer—if it means anything at all—to the future operations of Monteil. This does not of course mean that Hanotaux 'really' wished to launch Monteil to

[1] Hanotaux, *Fachoda*, pp. 78-9.
[2] MAE, Congo et Gabon 14, Hanotaux to an unnamed official (probably Nisard) 21 Aug. 1894.
[3] See the correspondence at MC G.C., VI 13.
[4] D.D.F., XI, No. 210, Hanotaux to Decrais, private, 7 Aug. 1894. (Emphasis supplied.)

Fashoda and that his July instructions were some sort of elaborate hoax. Ever since March 1894 Hanotaux had been, both in public and in private, the defender of 'our thesis on the integrity of the Ottoman Empire'. He had been determined not to destroy this thesis, and thereby to present London with a very sound legal and moral case, by a French incursion into the Nile basin; and this determination had doubtless been strengthened by Dufferin's threat to treat such an incursion as an act of war. Indeed, within a day or two of sending this warning to Decrais, Hanotaux was assuring Phipps that France did not intend to enter the Nile valley. On 10 August he told Phipps, 'with some vehemence that there was no question of France advancing to the Bahr el-Ghazal'; and when Phipps asked whether he would take an engagement to this effect, Hanotaux replied that this was

> a matter to be discussed hereafter, but I have already told you we do not dream of going there. Do you imagine that two such nations as England and France contemplate for one moment going to war on account of Sierra Leone, *or any other corner of Africa*?[1]

On the following day he even admitted to Phipps that French recognition of the Anglo-German Agreement 'might eventually legitimately form part of the comprehensive settlement of African questions which would, he hoped, take place'.[2] And between 13 and 15 August several Paris newspapers not usually noted for their friendship to England looked forward to a general Anglo-French settlement in Africa.[3]

Hanotaux, who during his ministerial career was a member neither of the Chamber nor the Senate,[4] more than once gave Phipps to understand that as a professional diplomatist he could afford to take a long-term view, and not strive for merely showy successes in order to impress the electorate.[5] Hanotaux liked to think of himself as a *grand commis* in the tradition of Richelieu and Vergennes; and at least in the formulation of major diplomatic strategy, Hanotaux was not unworthy of his models. For Hanotaux, a rapprochement with England would bear fruit both in greater security against the Triplice and in the more equitable sharing of the profits of the Franco-Russe; it was therefore well worth a few sacrifices in Africa. In Africa, including even the Upper Nile, Hanotaux certainly wanted a 'règlement amiable'. His problem was to get it. To do so, he would have to fight off the colonialist and 'Egyptianist' *enragés*; and he was soon to find that the professional and non-political status of which he was so proud was a

---

[1] FO 27/3186, Phipps to Kimberley No. 202, 11 Aug. 1894 (emphasis supplied).

[2] *Ibid.*, same to same No. 203, 11 Aug. 1894. It was typical of Phipps' tendency to oversanguine reporting that in the first draft of the passage quoted he wrote 'would' instead of 'might . . . form part'.

[3] *Ibid.*, same to same Nos. 205, 13 Aug. 1894; 206, 14 Aug.; 207, 15 Aug. Even *Le Gaulois* and François Deloncle were almost cordial.

[4] Iiams, *Dreyfus, Diplomatists and the Dual Alliance*, pp. 24-6.

[5] For an explicit statement, see FO 27/3186, Phipps to Kimberley No. 202, 11 Aug. 1894.

severe handicap to him in this struggle.[1] Another difficulty, hardly less severe, would be to bring London to the point of serious negotiation. Since January 1893 the British had relied upon silence, evasion and procrastination to wear down the opposition of France in the Nile valley. The collapse of the Anglo-Congolese Agreement was now forcing them to talk, but would they really talk business? It would in any case have been naïve for Hanotaux to suppose that could ever obtain a settlement even marginally acceptable to French opinion unless he could bring some form of pressure to bear upon London. A commandant Monteil, steadily advancing towards the Nile-Congo divide but strictly forbidden to cross it, would have provided the necessary pressure without provoking the explosion with which Dufferin had threatened Hanotaux. The letter of 7 August to Decrais looks very like the first ranging shot in a battle of nerves with London—a battle at once cut short, to the chagrin of Hanotaux, by Delcassé's precipitate recall of Monteil.

On 16 August, two days after Monteil's recall, Dufferin communicated London's proposals to Hanotaux. Phipps had told Hanotaux on the 13th that the Foreign Office would assume an 'extremely conciliatory attitude',[2] but Dufferin produced a very meagre bill of fare; it could hardly have been more unappetising had the British known—which at that time they did not—that Monteil had already been recalled.[3] The British offered £10,000 compensation for the French missionaries whose property had been damaged during the Uganda civil war, a 'favourable rectification' in Sierra Leone, and the cession of so much of Borgu as should ensure geographical connection between Dahomey and the French territories in the Niger basin. In return, they asked for the recognition of the British sphere as defined in the Anglo-German Agreement; but the Foreign Office was willing, rather illogically, to undertake that

> any temporary [British] occupation within that sphere . . . of territory belonging to the former Equatorial Provinces of Egypt, shall be on the same footing as that of Italy at Kassala, and that the rights of Egypt shall only be in suspense until the Egyptian Government shall be in a position to re-occupy the territory in question.[4]

But London had a second major demand. In February 1894 the Quai d'Orsay had replied to British complaints of Mizon's proceedings in Adamawa by the argument that, according to the Anglo-French Agreement of 1890, the Say-Barrawa line was the southern limit, not of the French possessions, but of the French *Mediterranean* possessions. The line was therefore not in any way an international boundary, and

---

[1] Cf. *infra*, pp. 206-8; Ch. XII, pp. 280-4; Ch. XIII, pp. 293-4, 313.
[2] FO 27/3188, Phipps to Kimberley tel. No. 33, 13 Aug. 1894.
[3] It is worth noting that Hanotaux' angry letter to Nisard about Monteil's recall was written after Dufferin had communicated the British proposals.
[4] FO 27/3183, Kimberley to Dufferin Nos. 300 and 300a, 14 Aug. 1894.

III Gabriel Hanotaux

IV Lord Rosebery

territory to the south of it not effectively occupied was *res nullius* and open to French enterprise.[1] Now, in August, the Foreign Office attempted to insist not only that the French should 'recede from their preposterous contention,'[2] but that the Say-Barrawa line should be drawn as a *straight* line, apart from an undefined deflection to the north so as to include in the British sphere 'all that fairly belongs to the kingdom of Sokoto'.[3] As Anderson explained, this last demand was Goldie's price for permitting the Foreign Office to offer a slice of Borgu in return for the French recognition of the Upper Nile sphere.[4] But it was certainly less than wise to link this question, steeped as it was in all the bitterness of the Mizon affair, so directly with the major interest of the Upper Nile.

Anderson, who was throughout 1894 completely hoodwinked by Goldie's fraudulent claim to have already occupied well-nigh all the disputed territory in the Niger sphere, thought that 'M. Hanotaux would be surprised and gratified' by the Borgu offer.[5] Hanotaux was of course completely unimpressed, and told Dufferin that he could make no reply until 30 August, when the next Council of Ministers would be held. Dufferin replied, in accordance with his instructions, that pending an agreement, London reserved full freedom of action.[6] But this was an empty threat. After the collapse of the Anglo-Congolese Agreement, Rosebery urgently needed a success in the Soudan; and the only success he could now hope for was a recognition of the British sphere by Paris. Harcourt would certainly veto any northward movement from Uganda. An advance from the north, under the Egyptian flag, would probably take years to reach the Upper Nile; and it would come under fire not only from Harcourt but from Cromer, still determined as ever not to permit 'this abominable Soudan question' to wreck the solvency and stability of Egypt. Moreover, a northern advance would involve embarrassment with Italy; Crispi, ensconced in Kassala since July 1894, had renewed his campaign for 'parallel action'. The Austrian minister at Brussels might indeed believe that a joint 'Anglo-Egyptian-Italian' advance was 'die einzig richtige Antwort Englands'; but this was a total misreading of the situation.[7]

The Anglo-French discussions were resumed, with Phipps as the British negotiator, on 5 September. Meanwhile, they had already been complicated by mutual suspicions of activities in Africa. The Foreign

---

[1] FO 27/3184, Dufferin to Rosebery No. 37, 10 Feb. 1894.
[2] Cf. *ibid.*, minute by Anderson on Dufferin to Kimberley No. 89, 29 Mar. 1894.
[3] FO 27/3183, No. 300a; cf. Anglo-French Agreement of 5 Aug. 1890 (Hertslet II, No. 229).
[4] FO 27/3183, *loc. cit.*; FO 27/3208, Goldie to Anderson 10 July 1894, and minute by Anderson.
[5] FO 27/3208, *loc. cit.*
[6] FO 27/3186, Dufferin to Kimberley No. 209, 16 Aug. 1894. D.D.F. xi, No. 218, Hanotaux to Decrais 17 Aug.
[7] Kinsky (Brussels) to Kálnoky 27 Aug. 1894, cited Hornik, *Der Kampf der Grossmächte*, p. 121.

N

Office had got wind of a French expedition under Decoeur to Nikki, the capital of Borgu; and Phipps was told to warn Hanotaux that a settlement would be difficult unless Decoeur were stopped.[1] The French were no less disturbed by Colvile's major offensive against Kabarega of Bunyoro,[2] which naturally appeared to them as the first step to an occupation of the southern Sudan. Indeed, long after the British had been stopped in their tracks by Kabarega's tenacious resistance, and even after Colvile himself had been invalided home, the ghost of a mythical 'Colvile mission' continued to haunt the Quai d'Orsay and the Pavillon de Flore.[3]

After his conversation on 5 September, Phipps reported by telegram that Hanotaux was 'undoubtedly prepared to arrive at an arrangement with regard to the British sphere in the Nile watershed', if only the Foreign Office would be a little more generous with its compensation. Even Anderson thought that 'the real difficulty will probably now be found in M. Delcassé's greediness as to other parts of Africa'.[4] But the despatch which expressed Phipps' second thoughts was, as too often happened in his reporting, more than a shade less sanguine than his telegram. Hanotaux had pointed out that he was being asked to make two major concessions, one in the Upper Nile and another on the Say-Barrawa line; and that, in return for these concessions, he could not see 'any bait offered to France at all in proportion with what had been granted' to Germany and Italy in 1890 and 1891. He had added that he would have to do something to 'conciliate the aspirations of the Colonial party'; he himself would have to act as a go-between, and it would be worse than useless to conclude an Agreement only to have it thrown out by the Chambers. Finally, he asked Phipps, à propos of the Anglo-German Agreement, a question to which Dufferin had never replied: 'Where are "the confines of Egypt"?' To this Phipps did not know the official answer, because London had always been careful never to formulate one. Guessing from the Anglo-Congolese Agreement, Phipps replied that the northern boundary of the British sphere was 'the parallel crossing Fashoda', but that 'we considered the rights of Egypt as being merely in suspense as regarded the whole of that sphere'.[5] This answer was not perhaps very lucid; but as an impromptu reconciliation of 'the British sphere' with 'Egyptian rights' it did Phipps no discredit.

The Foreign Office received Phipps' despatch of 5 September with a long sceptical silence; it did not reply until the 14th, after Phipps

---

[1] FO 27/3183, Kimberley to Phipps No. 315, 3 Sept. 1894.

[2] For the apprehensions of the French press, see FO 146/3408, Phipps to Kimberley Nos. 213, 220, 26 and 31 Aug. 1894. Colvile had 'declared war' on Kabarega on 5 Dec. 1893: cf. *Africa No. 7 (1895)* [C.-7708].

[3] Cf. *infra*, Ch. xii, p. 274.

[4] FO 27/3188, Phipps to Kimberley tel. No. 38, 5 Sept. 1894; and minute by Anderson. However, knowing his man, Anderson added: 'we cannot judge until the messenger brings Phipps' despatch'.

[5] FO 27/3186, Phipps to Kimberley No. 223, 5 Sept. 1894. Cf. D.D.F. xi, No. 234, *note du Ministre*, 5 Sept.

had urgently requested further instructions.[1] Phipps' language was approved, and his guess about the boundary of the British sphere confirmed as correct; but Anderson thought he needed 'reminding' that neither Germany nor Italy had received compensation in 1890 and 1891. Not even Kimberley could quite swallow this tale, and he deleted most of the material on Germany and Italy from Anderson's draft despatch. But Kimberley refused to commit himself in any way until Hanotaux had discussed the questions, as he had promised to do, with his Colonial colleague; and the despatch as sent to Phipps contained not the slightest hint that London would consider raising its bid.[2] Meanwhile Hanotaux, pleading inability to interfere with the Colonial Ministry's *fait accompli*, had refused to stop Decoeur. The Foreign Office, playing tit-for-tat, thereupon refused to stop Lugard, who had left for Nikki in July under Goldie's orders.[3]

Before Phipps had received a reply to his first despatch, he had already seen Hanotaux again on 12 September. Hanotaux had not yet consulted the *Colonies*; he was, he said, still trying to work out the broad lines of an arrangement which could ultimately be presented to his Cabinet as a single package. He asked once again—ostensibly to avoid any danger of 'entrenching on the Egyptian Question'—for a precise definition, not of the northern boundary of the British sphere but of the southern confines of Egypt. He still complained that the British offer was inadequate and suggested that France might be given access to the navigable lower Niger below Say. Phipps refused to entertain this proposal; but, impressed presumably by the tone rather than the substance of the interview, he privately assured Kimberley that an agreement seemed in sight if only the Office would be a little less stingy in West Africa.[4] However, at the next meeting on 22 September Hanotaux went straight to the awkward question of 'the confines of Egypt'. Phipps confirmed that the tenth parallel was the northern boundary of the British sphere; whereupon Hanotaux retorted that this view seemed to treat 'a portion of the possessions of Egypt as constituting a British sphere of influence and thus enter upon the Egyptian Question'. Phipps made the standard reply, as convincingly as he could, that Egyptian rights 'over the sphere [were] merely in abeyance until Egypt was in a position to assert them'. Hanotaux then expressed his willingness in principle to recognise a British sphere, provided that its boundaries were properly negotiated and that it was not merely 'an arbitrary one conceived by H.M.G.'. On Borgu, too, he was hopeful of a settlement, but still considered it 'premature' to put forward his own proposals; and he again insisted on his position as a go-between

[1] FO 27/3188, Phipps to Kimberley tel. No. 42, 12 Sept. 1894.
[2] FO 27/3186, minute by Anderson 8 Sept. 1894, on Phipps' No. 223. FO 27/3183, Kimberley to Phipps No. 330, 14 Sept.
[3] FO 27/3188, Phipps to Kimberley tel. No. 40, 6 Sept. 1894; and minutes by Anderson and Kimberley. Cf. Perham, *Lugard* I, p. 493.
[4] FO 27/3186, Phipps to Kimberley No. 232, 13 Sept. 1894; Phipps to Kimberley, private, 14 Sept. FO 27/3188, Phipps to Kimberley tel. No. 42, 12 Sept.

and on the futility of reaching a settlement unacceptable to the French Chambers.[1]

Hanotaux had admitted that he had now consulted Delcassé and Haussmann; and this made Anderson more suspicious than ever of his continued reserve: 'I am afraid that Phipps is playing out every card in his hand while Hanotaux is holding his up'.[2] Hanotaux was in fact awaiting the return from leave of M. Benoît, his *sous-directeur des Protectorats*, before revealing to Phipps the demands of the *Colonies*. But Benoît was not likely to do much to moderate these demands; he was an extreme and aggressive expansionist and was indeed the author of the 'preposterous contention' about the Say-Barrawa line.[3] At the next meeting with Phipps on 29 September Hanotaux, evidently under heavy colonialist pressure, went back on his repeated unofficial promise to recognise an exclusive British sphere on the Upper Nile. He now suggested that the recognition of a British sphere should be 'compensated', 'either by "partition", by a self-denying agreement, or by some formula which should secure equal rights to France'. Phipps expressed surprise at a proposal to partition Egyptian territory and once again trotted out the thesis that 'we intended to respect Egyptian rights, which we regarded as merely in abeyance'. Hanotaux replied rather vaguely that there were some portions of the British sphere to which Egyptian rights did not extend. He did not say where these were; but he did insist very strongly that it was impossible to go any further without first establishing, on a basis of historical geography, 'qu'est-ce que c'est que l'Egypte?'[4]

At this meeting on the 29th Hanotaux also revealed the demands of the *Colonies* in West Africa. These were an even greater shock. It was to be expected that the French would ask for much more of Borgu than the Foreign Office—or rather, Goldie—was prepared to give them. But it was another matter for Paris to exhume its original 'monstrous . . . pretension' about the Say-Barrawa line, to challenge the British claim to Bornu, and even to bring forward, as *matière d'échange*, Mizon's 'treaty rights' in Adamawa. Even Phipps thought it 'a good thing [that] these notions were put before me instead of Lord Dufferin'.[5] However, Hanotaux admitted that these were the most extreme claims of the *Colonies*, which he himself did not intend to press; and having thus demonstrated just how extreme the *Colonies* could be, on 3 October he offered London a reasonable bargain in West Africa. In Borgu he would split the difference between the French demand and

---

[1] FO 27/3186, Phipps to Kimberley No. 247, 22 Sept. 1894. FO 27/3188, Phipps to Kimberley tel. No. 44, 22 Sept.
[2] FO 27/3188, *loc. cit.*, minute by Anderson. 'Little can be made of this summary' was Anderson's contemptuous verdict on this tel.
[3] FO 27/3186, Phipps to Kimberley Nos. 255, 257, 29 and 30 Sept. 1894. Cf. FO 27/3184, Phipps to Anderson, private, 8 Mar. 1894.
[4] FO 27/3186, No. 255; and Phipps to Anderson, private, 30 Sept. 1894. D.D.F. xi, No. 237, *note du Ministre*, 29 Sept.
[5] FO 27/3186, Phipps to Kimberley No. 256, 29 Sept. 1894; to Anderson, private, 30 Sept. Cf. D.D.F., *loc. cit.*

the original British offer. The Say-Barrawa line would be recognised as fully bilateral, and would be drawn so as to leave Bornu, and of course Sokoto, in the British sphere—though it might perhaps be slightly deflected in favour of the French elsewhere.[1] Anderson referred these terms to Goldie, who approved provided that the Say-Barrawa line was to be 'a straight line deflected northwards to include Sokoto possessions but not deflected southwards'. This approval was communicated to Phipps in a telegram beginning, significantly enough, 'Niger Co. would accept . . .'; and even Anderson for once showed a guarded optimism: 'If Phipps has correctly reported this will mean a settlement of the Niger question'.[2]

But the major object of the negotiation was of course not the Niger, but the Nile; and on 4 October the Foreign Office asked Phipps: 'What are we to understand as regards recognition of our sphere in Nile Basin if we conclude an arrangement as regards Niger on basis indicated . . .?'[3] Phipps himself did not know the answer to this; but he thought that Hanotaux' passing mention, on 29 September, of 'a self-denying agreement' might lead to an answer. He therefore asked Hanotaux what he had meant by this phrase; and on 5 October Phipps was able to reply to Kimberley's enquiry:

France would engage not to advance beyond the watershed of the Congo; we on our side engaging not to advance beyond the posts actually occupied by us [i.e. in Uganda and Unyoro], into the sphere under discussion—over which we declare Egyptian rights only to be in suspense—without previous negotiation with the French Government.

As Hanotaux had pointed out, this arrangement would evade the difficult questions of Ottoman rights and 'the confines of Egypt'; and now that King Leopold's encroachments had been checked, there was no longer any urgent need for a definitive settlement.[4]

Meanwhile Phipps had been authorised to accept, subject to the proviso about the Say-Barrawa line, the proposals of Hanotaux for West Africa if a satisfactory settlement could be obtained on the Upper Nile.[5] Thereupon, on 6 October, Phipps telegraphed privately to Anderson urging that the proposed self-denying arrangement offered at least 'an indication' of such a settlement. 'Is there not something anomalous in asking for the recognition as a British sphere of a territory admittedly accruing to Egypt?'[6]—a question which Anderson must have found very irritating, for it was precisely this bare fact which the

[1] FO 27/3188, Phipps to Kimberley tel. No. 48, 3 Oct. 1894; to Anderson, tel. private, 4 Oct. FO 27/3187, Phipps to Kimberley No. 260, 4 Oct.
[2] FO 27/3209, memo. by Anderson 4 Oct. 1894. FO 27/3188, Kimberley to Phipps tel. No. 58, 5 Oct.
[3] FO 27/3188, Kimberley to Phipps tel. No. 57, 4 Oct. 1894.
[4] Ibid., Phipps to Kimberley tel. No. 49, 5 Oct. 1894; FO 27/3187, Phipps to Kimberley No. 263, 5 Oct.
[5] FO 27/3188, Kimberley to Phipps tel. No. 58, 5 Oct. 1894.
[6] Ibid., Phipps to Anderson tel. personal, 6 Oct. 1894.

African Department had always done its best to conceal. On the following day, without waiting for the views of Anderson or Kimberley, Phipps read to Hanotaux the text of the self-denying proposal which he had sent to London. Hanotaux would commit himself 'ni sur le fond ni sur la forme', but was personally inclined to think that agreement could be reached along these lines. But he contended that this project must now be regarded as a proposal from the British side. Phipps 'en avait eu l'initiative et . . . je n'avais fait que le suivre dans la voie ouverte par lui'.[1] This remark Phipps did not report to London. He probably feared that he was going too fast, for his account of this conversation on 7 October consisted mainly of generalities about Hanotaux' 'earnest desire for a comprehensive and speedy agreement'.[2]

Although he had still received no reply from London about the self-denying proposal for the Nile, on 8 and 9 October Phipps plunged into detailed discussions on West Africa with Hanotaux and with Haussmann of the *Colonies*. The French wanted Nikki in Borgu, and the town of Say itself. They accepted a Say-Barrawa line leaving Sokoto and Bornu in the British sphere, but wished to add the potentially dangerous proviso: 'cette ligne serait toujours tracée de manière à ne pas diviser les tribus'. Nevertheless, on 9 October Phipps submitted both to Hanotaux and to the Foreign Office a first draft of bases, in which the paragraph relating to the Upper Nile was still left in blank.[3] At the meeting on the 9th the Upper Nile had however been discussed; and Phipps jubilantly reported that Hanotaux had 'repeated that he was ready to engage that France would not advance eastwards from the Congo watershed into the Nile Valley district . . .'. By now Phipps was so anxious to impress this fact upon the Office that he completely omitted to state that this engagement was of course dependent on a similar undertaking by London.[4]

By this time Phipps was beginning to lose the confidence not only of Anderson but of Rosebery. On 8 October Rosebery had asked Anderson:

1. Whether there was any *quid pro quo* which would justify our giving way about our sphere [on the Nile].
2. Whether it would be advisable to conclude the proposed Niger arrangement as an isolated settlement.

Anderson admitted that to 'keep France entirely off the Nile would be a triumph for British diplomacy, and might justify a surrender elsewhere'. But he never suggested where that surrender might be. Nor was he content merely to keep the French behind the Nile-Congo divide. They must also be kept well away from Darfur lest they should

---

[1] D.D.F. xi, No. 240, *note du Ministre* 7 Oct. 1894.
[2] FO 27/3188, Phipps to Kimberley tel. No. 50, 7 Oct. 1894.
[3] *Ibid.*, same to same, tels. No. 52 and 53, 8 Oct. 1894. FO 27/3187, Phipps to Kimberley No. 266, 9 Oct. D.D.F. xi, No. 243, Phipps to Hanotaux 9 Oct.
[4] FO 27/3187, *loc. cit.*

'launch [Rabīh Zubair] into Darfur and Kordofan, and reap the advantage of his successes'. The furthest that Anderson would go in self-denial was 'an engagement . . . under which, without obtaining French recognition of our sphere, we should retain it, but give an assurance that we would not directly administer it'—Anderson was careful, as his later minutes confirm, to keep open the loophole of *indirect* administration through Egypt. Blindly following Goldie, Anderson utterly rejected the isolated Niger settlement:

> We are now almost impregnable by occupation, if there were no agreement. . . . Why then, [Goldie] asks, should we give up half Borgu? . . . I had no idea, till he fully explained yesterday, how strong our position is. An isolated Niger arrangement seems out of the question.

Goldie had also made it clear that only if the French were kept completely off the Nile would he accept, 'in the interest of the Empire if not that of the Niger Co., . . . the Hanotaux line and give up half Borgu'. But if this result were to be achieved 'a different tone would have to be used . . . from Phipps' apologetic, almost supplicatory language'.[1]

Kimberley concurred; and he thought that Phipps had 'got to the length of his tether' and that Dufferin should take over.[2] But on 10 October Rosebery asked for clarification of the 'self-denying proposition':

> On the face of it [it] appears to be an attempt to debar us from entering our own sphere on the condition that the French do not enter it. This seems a somewhat one-sided arrangement . . . But it would be well at any rate to ascertain exactly what it is that M. Hanotaux does mean.[3]

To this question Phipps made no direct reply. Instead, on 11 October he asked whether London would 'be contented if France declared the territory East of Congo watershed as absolutely outside the sphere of French influence? We declaring that we will not advance into that Egyptian territory from the South without previous understanding with France.'[4] Meanwhile, the Foreign Office had received Phipps' project of bases drawn up on the 9th. Anderson's reaction was to treat the self-denying arrangement as already a dead letter, and therefore to reject the whole project as 'one-sided'.

> Goldie would not give away half Borgu in return for such a lame settlement of the Say-Barrawa line. . . . There is no compensation except the withdrawal of claims which can only be realised, as against us, by force. But the scheme, unsatisfactory as it is, is so imperfect from the want of a settlement of the Nile question, that it seems only necessary to point out its weaknesses.[5]

[1] FO 27/3209, memo. by Anderson 9 Oct. 1894.
[2] *Ibid.*, minute by Kimberley 10 Oct. 1894.
[3] FO 27/3188, Rosebery to Phipps tel. No. 60, 10 Oct. 1894.
[4] *Ibid.*, Phipps to Rosebery tel. No. 55, 11 Oct. 1894.
[5] FO 27/3187, minute by Anderson 10 Oct. 1894, on Phipps' No. 266 of 9 Oct.

It was however in his despatch enclosing these 'bases' that Phipps had emphasised Hanotaux' renewed promise not to enter the Nile basin, but had quite forgotten to state that this depended on a similar promise by Britain. Rosebery spotted this omission, and minuted: 'If Phipps has correctly reported H's language about the Nile watershed —wh. I doubt—there is hope of a settlement.' He therefore asked Phipps directly:

> Are H.M. Govt. to understand that in your 266 you correctly report M. Hanotaux as having said that he was ready to engage that France would not advance eastwards from the Congo watershed into the Nile Valley district but that he did not ask for any counter-declaration from us?[1]

To this question Phipps made the astonishing reply (11 October): 'There was certainly no question of any such counter-declaration from us.'[2] Phipps had allowed himself to become badly confused. He evidently thought that Rosebery's enquiry related not to the despatch of the 9th, but to his earlier telegram of 11 October, in which he had suggested that, while both London and Paris would agree not to advance, Hanotaux might be induced to declare that the Upper Nile was outside the French sphere without asking for a 'counter-declaration' that it was outside the British sphere.[3] Phipps made this clear in a private letter to Anderson a few days later;[4] but his error was a bad one, for Rosebery's enquiry had quoted the serial number of the Paris despatch of 9 October.[5]

On 12 October, the day after Phipps had blundered, the Foreign Office received another of his despatches, enclosing a letter written by Hanotaux on the 10th. This letter made it crystal clear that the proposed arrangement was 'un désistement réciproque'—neither party was to advance into the Nile basin. It also brought up further reservations about the Say-Barrawa line.[6] Anderson refrained, perhaps out of charity, from pointing out the flat contradiction between Hanotaux' letter of the 10th and Phipps' reply to Rosebery's enquiry of the 11th, and was content to minute:

> Hanotaux stands out for concessions which he cannot have east and west of the Niger. . . . As regards the Nile he speaks merely of a self-denying arrangement pending further negotiations. I fear Phipps has been much too sanguine—and that he had much better not have put in his draft of bases.[7]

[1] FO 27/3187, loc. cit., minute by Rosebery. FO 27/3188, Rosebery to Phipps tel. No. 61, 11 Oct. 1894.
[2] FO 27/3188, Phipps to Rosebery tel. No. 56, 11 Oct. 1894.
[3] Ibid., Phipps' tel. No. 55—but even here the arrangement contemplated was merely implied rather than explicitly stated.
[4] FO 27/3187, Phipps to Anderson, private, 15 Oct. 1894.
[5] It is difficult to believe that Phipps looked at his desp. No. 266 before sending his tel. No. 56.
[6] FO 27/3187, Phipps to Kimberley No. 270, enclosing Hanotaux to Phipps 10 Oct. 1894. Cf. D.D.F. XI, No. 245.
[7] FO 27/3187, loc. cit., minute by Anderson 12 Oct. 1894.

But Anderson was now quite determined to stop Phipps, although Kimberley gave no definite instruction. However, on 11 October Kimberley had minuted 'The matter cannot now be carried further by Phipps'.[1] Chancing his arm a little, for since the 10th Rosebery's personal intervention had kept Phipps in play, Anderson now telegraphed privately to Paris: 'I understand it to be Lord Kimberley's wish that you should not have further interviews without special instructions'. Kimberley thoroughly approved: 'Quite right. We will do no good by further interviews at present.'[2]

By 13 October Kimberley had discovered for himself the glaring discrepancy in Phipps' reporting. Complaining to Anderson that he was 'utterly unable to understand Phipps' reports about Hanotaux' language on the Nile basin question', he asked Anderson to draw up a précis of the negotiation 'with your own observations on the different points'.[3] Anderson's observations amounted to a root-and-branch condemnation of all Phipps' proceedings. The object of the self-denying proposal, Anderson explained, was to place Britain and France 'on the same footing' in the Upper Nile:

. . . Our present claim is extinguished. There is no recognition of any part of our sphere. The Anglo-Congolese Agreement is torn up. France is not restricted to a fixed sphere. The concession required from us is not balanced by compensations elsewhere; it is additional to other concessions, for whereas, on the Niger, we are expected to retire from a large portion of Borgu which we actually occupy, we are offered in return nothing, beyond the partial abandonment of extravagant pretensions which we are well able to resist.[4]

Anderson then put forward a counter-proposal which he had already sketched a few days earlier.[5] France should declare 'her sphere bounded by the Nile and Congo watershed'. England and France should both agree to respect the rights of Turkey in the 'Four Provinces'—Nubia, Darfur, Kordofan and Sennar—mentioned in the Sultan's *Hatti-Sherif* of February 1841 to Muhammad 'Ali. 'This engagement would be invaluable to us, as it would keep France out of Darfur and Kordofan. It would not affect our sphere. . . .' Further, both Powers should agree to recognise 'any *equitable* claims of Egypt to territory not specified in the *Hatti-Sherif*, when she should be in a position to enforce them. This would cover our sphere . . . while it would not tie us to any definite admission as to how far the claims of Egypt may subsequently be admitted.' As the meagre sugar for this pill, Anderson offered an engagement not to administer *directly*

---

[1] *Ibid.*, minute by Kimberley 11 Oct. 1894, on Phipps' No. 266.
[2] FO 27/3188, Anderson to Phipps, private, 12 Oct. 1894; minute by Kimberley.
[3] FO 27/3209, Kimberley to Anderson 13 Oct. 1894.
[4] *Ibid.*, Anderson to Kimberley 16 Oct. 1894 (printed for the Cabinet 20 Oct.).
[5] FO 27/3188, minute by Anderson on Phipps' tel. No. 56 of 11 Oct. It will be seen that, for Anderson, even a unilateral French self-denial was not enough.

(his emphasis) any territory on the *west* bank of the Nile north of lat. 5° 30'.[1]

Anderson wanted to force on France some formula by which she should recognise, in practice, that the British and Egyptian spheres taken together covered the whole Nile basin; and at the same time to avoid the definition of any boundary between these two spheres. One useful by-product of such an arrangement would be to banish Anderson's persistent nightmare of Rabīh Zubair's hordes sweeping to the Nile with the Tricolour aloft. But the real point of the proposal was to use the 'rights of Egypt' as an absolute barrier to other Powers while leaving London free to help itself to as much Egyptian territory as might later seem convenient. Anderson seems to have believed that Hanotaux could be brought to swallow this if Phipps would only abandon 'supplicatory language' and bully him a little, and if the proposals were sufficiently wrapped up in obscure references to a *Hatti-Sherif* of 1841. This was a complete delusion. From the very outset of the negotiation Hanotaux had been on his guard against precisely this deliberate confusion of British and Egyptian claims—hence his constantly reiterated question about 'the confines of Egypt'. Kimberley and Rosebery, little as they sympathised with Phipps, were at least aware of this; and none of Anderson's ingenious formulations was ever transmitted to Paris.

Not that this much troubled Anderson. From the outset he had evidently much preferred no settlement at all to a settlement which was not to his own satisfaction. Moreover, as the constant raven's croak of his minutes shows, he had little confidence in Phipps. And with reason. Phipps' excess of zeal, his over-sanguine reporting and above all his tendency to become emotionally involved in the success of his negotiation,[2] were the very antithesis of Talleyrand's classic watchword for young diplomatists. Phipps was moreover a personal friend of Hanotaux, for whose charm and brilliance he had a perhaps rather uncritical admiration. In September even Harcourt had remarked that '*vis-à-vis* of the wily Hanotaux [Phipps] is like a mouse affording cruel sport to the cat'.[3] Anderson would have heartily endorsed this judgment; and the way in which Phipps was inveigled into pushing the self-denying arrangement demonstrates its essential truth. When Phipps blundered on 11 October Anderson did not wait for Kimberley to tell him what to do; he pounced at once and stopped Phipps in his tracks. On 15 October Phipps explained to Anderson what he had really meant to say in his confused telegram, and begged that the negotiation be resumed. He admitted that Hanotaux was 'a very tough nut to crack', but pointed out that he was the only possible Foreign Minister with sufficient authority to put through a reasonable

---

[1] FO 17/3188, *loc. cit.* FO 27/3209, memo. by Anderson, 16 Oct.
[2] As early as August he had spoken to Hanotaux of the forthcoming Agreement being 'our special offspring'; and cf. his personal letters to Anderson and Kimberley, *passim.*
[3] Harcourt to Kimberley 12 Sept. 1894, quoted Gardiner, *op. cit.* ii, pp. 321-3.

settlement. But Anderson would have no more of Phipps as a negotiator. Phipps had specifically stated in a covering note that his letter
of October 15 was to be regarded as semi-official—and therefore for
Kimberley's eye. But Kimberley never saw it.[1] Not that it mattered,
for throughout the negotiation Kimberley had been a faithful if rather
muted echo of Anderson's forthright tones.

Vigorously prompted by Anderson, Kimberley had rejected the
self-denying arrangement. Yet a settlement on these lines would have
afforded complete security to the Nile waters; and Kimberley was well
aware of this. As recently as June 1894 he had remarked to the Austrian
ambassador that Britain's only serious interest in the Upper Nile was
'to prevent any foreign Power from gaining a foothold there and so
being in a position to threaten Egypt'. He had even added that if the
Powers agreed to keep out, the practical object of the Anglo-Congolese
Agreement would have been achieved.[2] But by October 1894 defensive
strategy on the Nile had ceased, at any rate for the time being, to be
the critical factor in British policy. A study of Anderson's minutes on
the Phipps-Hanotaux negotiation leaves little doubt about the motives
to which strategy had taken second place. Anderson says nothing
explicit about the security of the Nile waters. No doubt he thought this
point too obvious to be worth making, but the omission still seems
significant. Instead, he invokes 'the interest of the Empire', insists
adamantly on 'the recognition of our sphere' and is anxious not to be
tied down 'to any definite admission as to how far the claims of Egypt
may subsequently be admitted'. Kimberley's views are very elusive.
Kimberley has never passed for an enthusiastic imperialist; but he
never wrote a word of objection to Anderson's swashbuckling minutes.
But Phipps, who did oppose Anderson, and who persisted in thinking
that the main object of the negotiation was to protect the Nile waters
by keeping out the French, was soon to be punished for his obsolete
ideas by a posting to Buenos Aires.

Anderson was just as intransigent on the Niger as on the Nile. It
has been stated that the Foreign Office was 'ready to go as far in West
Africa as the most chauvinist of Frenchmen could have desired',[3] if
only France would keep off the Nile. It would be much nearer the
truth to say that Anderson, without the slightest interference by either
Kimberley or Rosebery, wrecked whatever chances there were of a
satisfactory Nile settlement by his inordinate appetite on the Niger.
Prompted at every move by Goldie, in whose mythical occupations he
had an unquestioning belief, he insisted throughout on the most
extreme British interpretation of the Say-Barrawa line. He even
bowed to Goldie's decree that the offer of 'half Borgu' must be used
solely to buy French recognition of the Upper Nile sphere, and in no

[1] FO 27/3187, Phipps to Anderson, private, and covering note 15 Oct. 1894. Kimberley's initial does not appear on either of these papers; and he was a conscientious initialler.
[2] Deym to Kálnoky 28 June 1894, cited Hornik, *op. cit.*, pp. 118-9.
[3] Robinson and Gallagher, *Africa and the Victorians*, p. 333.

circumstances as an equivalent for the British Say-Barrawa demand.[1] Phipps once tried to soften Anderson by explaining how difficult it was for Hanotaux to make West African concessions which would force 'the French Colonial party to resign many of the most cherished objects of their ambition'. Anderson's comment on this was a cry of triumph: 'The French Colonial party may have "ambitions", but we have possession'.[2] For Anderson, even a fully satisfactory Nile agreement would have been dearly bought by any substantial sacrifice of these supposed possessions in West Africa. Anderson's slogan— 'possession'—is symbolic of the spirit in which the negotiation was carried on by London—a spirit already very different from that of Salisbury's negotiations with Germany in 1890.

Rosebery, who believed in 'pegging out claims' as a matter of national prestige,[3] was not the man to oppose Anderson's ideas; but mere acquisitiveness was not of course Rosebery's only motive for rejecting the self-denying arrangement. No British Government in the eighteen-nineties would have found it easy to accept, or to bring the public to accept, so lame a settlement, with its *de facto* renunciation of an internationally recognised sphere. In Rosebery's precarious position any such attempt might well have meant political suicide. It was not only that a ferocious hue and cry would be raised by those whom Hanotaux once called 'les Deloncle d'outre-Manche', the Chamberlains and the Ashmead-Bartletts. Rosebery had hitherto carried his imperial policy—notably on Uganda—through the Commons with Conservative aid against his own Radical wing.[4] Such support would not have been forthcoming for self-denial; and even if the Radicals had approved the arrangement, a few abstentions by Liberal Imperialists would have been enough to bring down the Government. Yet in spite of these grave risks Rosebery showed more interest in the self-denying arrangement than Kimberley. He was at least prepared to learn more about it, though in October 1894 he could hardly have seriously considered accepting it. But the unacceptability of self-denial was in itself a strong argument for trying to obtain French recognition by increasing the British offer in West Africa. Rosebery seems to have completely failed to distinguish priorities as between West Africa and the Nile valley; he certainly never attempted to impose any priorities upon Anderson, whose policy hardly went beyond maintaining the maximum British claims everywhere and all the time.

Hanotaux of course had his own Deloncles to deal with, many of whom had no more love for self-denial than Anderson himself; but he still hoped for a settlement. He soon saw that something had gone wrong with the negotiation; and when on 17 October Phipps, in his

[1] FO 27/3208, Goldie to Anderson 10 July 1894. Cf. FO 27/3209, memo. by Anderson 9 Oct. 1894; FO 27/3187, minute by Anderson 10 Oct., on Phipps' No. 266.
[2] FO 27/3187, *loc. cit.*
[3] Cf. his speech to the Royal Colonial Institute 1 Mar. 1893.
[4] Robinson and Gallagher, *op. cit.*, pp. 326-7, 329-30.

capacity as *Chargé d'ambassade*, attended the Minister's weekly reception, Hanotaux attempted to set things right. He offered to persuade the *Colonies* to relinquish Nikki, and he mentioned that he had succeeded in stopping an expedition to the middle Niger under Toutée. He warned Phipps that if the negotiation failed he would be powerless to restrain the 'strong party in France [which] sought to sow, as agents provocateurs, discord between France and England'. The Foreign Office replied that Hanotaux must await the return of Dufferin to Paris.[1] A week later Dufferin had still not returned. Hanotaux repeated his warnings to Phipps, adding that the 'psychological moment' was fast slipping by and that the experts of the Colonial Ministry were getting completely out of hand.[2]

Dufferin saw Hanotaux at last on 31 October. The interview was quite sterile. When Hanotaux began to outline the course of the negotiation, Dufferin interrupted to accuse him of attempting to settle West Africa in favour of France while evading a settlement on the Nile. Hanotaux retorted that he had merely been complying with Kimberley's express desire for a comprehensive negotiation; as for the Upper Nile, how could France recognise a sphere before its limits had been officially defined?[3] On 3 November Rosebery sent new instructions to Dufferin, but these did not re-open the negotiation; they closed it. Rosebery flatly rejected self-denial, 'which would amount practically to the abandonment . . . of a large portion of the British sphere'. However, if:

the French Government display an insurmountable reluctance
to formally recognise our sphere but should be disposed to give
an assurance that they would not advance beyond the watershed
of the Nile, we on our part might then take act of such an assurance and thus arrive at a practical settlement.

As for the West African questions, London would consider these in isolation 'in a friendly spirit', but on the distinct understanding that the original British offer no longer held good. Dufferin was also furnished with an official definition of the British sphere, on the lines of Phipps' original statement.[4] When Dufferin next saw Hanotaux on 7 November he volunteered this definition, explaining that it was based upon the Anglo-Congolese Agreement. Hanotaux retorted that in French eyes this Agreement had no existence. When Dufferin asked whether Hanotaux saw any practical solution, the Minister replied that he saw none except the 'proposition de désintéressement ou désistement provisoire réciproque' which Phipps had formulated.

[1] FO 27/3188, Phipps to Kimberley tel. No. 57, 18 Oct. 1894; Kimberley to Phipps tel. No. 62, 19 Oct. Cf. FO 146/3409, Phipps to Kimberley, private, 19 Oct.
[2] FO 27/3187, Phipps to Kimberley No. 280, 24 Oct. 1894. Cf. D.D.F. xi, No. 257, Hanotaux to d'Estournelles de Constant 28 Oct.
[3] FO 27/3188, Dufferin to Kimberley tel. No. 58, 31 Oct. 1894. D.D.F. xi, No. 263, *note du Ministre* 1 Nov.
[4] FO 27/3183, Kimberley to Dufferin No. 390, 3 Nov. 1894. Much of this despatch was drafted by Rosebery.

Dufferin hotly denied that Phipps had in fact formulated it; in any case it was utterly unacceptable. He then asked point-blank whether France would agree not to extend her sphere beyond the Congo basin. Hanotaux replied that he could give no such undertaking and that France reserved full freedom of action. Then, to soften the blow, he suggested that as King Leopold's encroachments had now been checked, 'the matter might very well be allowed to go to sleep again'; and in this Dufferin 'expressed a certain amount of acquiescence'.[1]

From his conversations with Hanotaux Dufferin drew the conclusion that 'the desire of the French Government is to connect their Congo possessions with the Nile if they can possibly manage it'.[2] Hanotaux had of course no such desire; but his warning to Phipps that he could no longer control the *Colonies* was perfectly genuine. As early as 15 October Haussmann had warned Hanotaux that the Pavillon de Flore could no longer accept the 'projet de désistement réciproque'; there seem to have been suspicions that Phipps' over-eager acceptance of this idea was intended to lull France into a false security while London acted through the 'Colvile mission'.[3] On 20 October Delcassé appointed Liotard, who was on leave in France, 'Commissaire du Gouvernement dans les territoires limités à l'ouest par une ligne tracée de Bangui à El Facher'—these territories had, it appeared, no specific *eastern* limit.[4] Three days later Delcassé was disquieted by a Libreville report that 'une vingtaine officiers anglais sont Léopoldville pour aller Bahr el Ghazal'—apparently the British already had two irons in the fire on the Upper Nile. On 30 October, five days after Liotard had sailed for Africa, Delcassé confirmed his Ministry's rejection of the self-denying arrangement, on the grounds that Liotard could reach the Upper Nile before the 'mission Colvile'.[5]

The Liotard mission to the Nile was approved on 17 November 1894 by a Cabinet at which Casimir-Périer took the Chair as President of the Republic.[6] Delcassé, as was his habit, said little; the project was pressed, against the opposition of Hanotaux, by Casimir-Périer himself, who had only a few months earlier been so resolutely hostile to any action on the Nile. Casimir-Périer seems to have regarded the question simply as a means of asserting his Presidential authority against a Foreign Minister who had failed to keep the Elysée adequately in the picture. As Hanotaux told him to his face a few months later: 'vous avez voulu faire acte d'autorité; vous l'avez fait; je me suis incliné'. But Hanotaux' opposition, as he himself admits, was not over-

[1] FO 27/3187, Dufferin to Kimberley No. 293, 7 Nov. 1894. D.D.F. xi, No. 272, *note du Ministre* 7 Nov.
[2] FO 27/3187, *loc. cit.*
[3] D.D.F. xi, No. 260, *note du Ministre* 30 Oct. 1894.
[4] Vergniol, *ubi supra*, p. 640; Cocheris, *op. cit.*, p. 414.
[5] MC G.C., 1 45a, Governor Libreville to Delcassé tel. No. 75, 23 Oct. 1894. The file copy is heavily underscored in blue pencil—presumably Delcassé's. D.D.F. xi, No. 260; cf. No. 285, *note du Ministre* 17 Nov. 1894.
[6] D.D.F. xi, No. 285; cf. No. 305, Hanotaux to Delcassé 5 Dec. 1894.

vigorous.[1] It could not be. The only argument he could use was that Liotard's mission would wreck a possible agreement with England. But he dared not push this too hard, for with the London negotiation in utter ruin a Cabinet directive to resume it would have been embarrassing indeed.

The mission to the Upper Nile had now at last become, although in a rather fortuitous way, the official policy of the French Government. More important, it had become the official policy of the *bureaux* at the Pavillon de Flore, who were now fully informed, and was no longer merely Delcassé's personal maggot. But as a drive for the Nile, it was still a little half-hearted. Delcassé, who had passed over Liotard for the Nile mission in 1893, must by the end of 1894 have known enough about this conscientious but rather pedestrian administrator to recognise that he was not the man for an epic operation in the Peters-Stanley style. Moreover, Liotard was given no reinforcements, though it was well known that his strength was barely adequate to garrison the regions just ceded by the Congo State. No doubt, as usual, suitable troops were in short supply. But this was a matter of priorities; troops were found for the numerous Niger missions which were already launched, or soon to be launched. Nor did Delcassé make any serious attempt to revive the Ethiopian side of the project; all he did was to instruct Lagarde, very tentatively, to ask the Negus for safe-conduct for any messengers 'venant du centre africain'.[2] Somewhere there must be a link between the aggressive filibustering Delcassé of 1893, eager to strike England at her most vulnerable point, and the sober Delcassé of 1898 who, although a badly frightened man, was also quite genuinely anxious for an all-round improvement in Anglo-French relations.[3] The facts do not forbid the speculation that by November 1894 Delcassé was thinking in terms of merely staking a claim in the Upper Nile basin before it was all occupied by the British, rather than of a dash for the Nile and the re-opening of the Egyptian question under the threat of 'opérations dues à la malveillance'.

For Hanotaux, the Cabinet decision of 17 November was a serious defeat. In September he had been forced by colonialist pressure to abandon his original plan of recognising *a* British sphere (if not *the* British sphere) in return for compensation. His authority as minister was now shaken by the formal rejection of his Upper Nile policy. London had given Hanotaux no help at all in this struggle for power. In its early stages, as Phipps correctly emphasised, the British had not provided nearly enough 'bait' in West Africa; later on, when Hanotaux most needed to keep the negotiation in being, they had turned their backs on him. Hanotaux' authority in African affairs never recovered from these initial set-backs. His non-political status deprived

[1] G. Hanotaux, *Carnets* (selections published by G.-L. Jaray, *Revue des Deux Mondes*, 1 April 1949, at p. 402).
[2] M C C.F.S., Correspce. générale 1892-5, Delcassé to Lagarde 6 Oct. 1894.
[3] Cf. *infra*, Ch. xv, p. 342; Ch. xvi, p. 378.

him of a French minister's strongest weapon: the threat to bring down the Government by taking into opposition one of the parliamentary groups upon whose precarious co-operation the life of a French Cabinet depended. Moreover, it would always be less dangerous to drop Hanotaux than to persevere, on his insistence, in a policy likely to be unpalatable to the Chambers. As Dufferin remarked in March 1896, Hanotaux, although 'undoubtedly a strong and most intelligent man', became in African questions 'more of a mouthpiece than a free agent'.[1]

The collapse of the Phipps-Hanotaux negotiations led to an immediate deterioration in relations between England and France. Anderson was alarmed and infuriated by the unauthorised navigation of the lower Niger by a French gunboat, the *Ardent*: 'It is a repetition of the Mizon affair, secret orders from Delcassé, denied by the Minr. for Foreign Affairs'.[2] So poisonous was the atmosphere that it even endangered the trivial Sierra Leone delimitation, which it had been agreed to salvage from the wreck of the Phipps-Hanotaux discussions.[3] Early in 1895 the expeditions of Decoeur and Toutée appeared not only in Borgu but on the lower Niger below Boussa.[4] Goldie's claims to effective occupation were shown up for what they were worth, and the Foreign Office soon discovered that through trusting Goldie's word they had rejected the Sibylline Books. Before the end of 1895 the British would have been very glad to get the 'isolated Niger settlement' which they had so contemptuously rejected in October 1894—a proposition which the French now dismissed with scarcely concealed amusement. The Niger question remained to bedevil Anglo-French relations—and incidentally to obstruct serious discussion of the Upper Nile—until June 1898. Even then, after the dispute had sharpened to a point where war seemed a not improbable outcome, London still obtained less than Paris had offered in 1894.[5]

In December 1894 Kimberley made a well-meaning but ineffectual attempt to stop the rot when the new French ambassador, Alphonse de Courcel, asked him to explain the Upper Nile difficulty. Kimberley replied that the root of the problem lay in the refusal of British opinion to abandon any part of the Upper Nile sphere; but that a practical solution might be reached if France, without formally recognising the sphere, would agree not to enter it. This was of course the proposal that Hanotaux had flatly rejected a few weeks earlier; and Kimberley hastened to add that he was merely thinking aloud, not making a demand or even a request—'ce sont de ces choses qu'on ne dit pas à

[1] FO 27/3274, Dufferin to Salisbury No. 41, 3 Mar. 1896.
[2] FO 27/3256, minute by Anderson 9 Feb. 1895. This affair was already causing friction by Dec. 1894 (cf. FO 27/3187).
[3] 'This S. Leone business is a real nightmare'—Phipps to Hill, private, 14 Dec. 1894 (FO 27/3187). Cf. FO 27/3188, minute by Rosebery on Dufferin's tel. No. 58, 31 Oct. 1894.
[4] See the correspondence at FO 27/3257, especially Hill's memo of 6 May 1895 on the whole Niger situation. Cf. Perham, *op. cit.*, pp. 532-5.
[5] *Infra*, Ch. x, p. 231; Ch. xiv, pp. 317-23.

une grande nation amie'. He also pointed out that Britain was prepared to recognise Egyptian rights and to hand over the Upper Nile to
Egypt as soon as she could cope with it. This was of course the 'Kassala
clause' again; and Courcel at once asked: 'You promise not to annex,
but does that mean you won't occupy?' But Kimberley evaded this
question; and Courcel could only report that 'sur la question spéciale du
Bahr el-Ghazal, je crains que nous ne soyons bien loin d'une entente'.[1]

Meanwhile, Hanotaux had been trying to re-open the line to London. On 22 November d'Estournelles de Constant, the French *Chargé
d'ambassade*, had reported a conversation with Cecil Rhodes. Rhodes,
with his usual bluntness and vehemence, had remarked that while the
French hostility to the British in Egypt was no more than a 'passive'
grievance, any French trespass into the Upper Nile would be an
'active' grievance, 'qui produira l'explosion'; and the more d'Estournelles protested, the more strongly Rhodes insisted that 'c'est là le point
noir'.[2] Now that Liotard had been authorised to go ahead, this was
anything but good news for Hanotaux; and he asked d'Estournelles,
'au sujet de la question de l'Egypte et du Soudan, d'essayer de dégager les points précis par lesquels on pourrait les régler l'une par
l'autre, en se plaçant principalement au point de vue de l'opinion
publique anglaise'.[3] Hanotaux seems here to have been glancing at
some solution by which England might be granted her sphere (or *a*
sphere) on the Upper Nile in return for an agreement on the evacuation
of Egypt. To the specific question put to him d'Estournelles made no
very clear reply; but he did write what Hanotaux justly called a
'brillant exposé'[4] of the British interest in the Upper Nile and the
development of British opinion on this subject.

D'Estournelles considered that the Sudan had by the end of 1894
become even more important in British eyes than Egypt itself, and was
now the main preoccupation of British policy in Africa. Even Harcourt
now admits, with a sigh, that 'we must have our sphere of influence in
the Sudan'. It was absurd to suppose that Britain could ever evacuate
Egypt and give up her Sudan aspirations into the bargain—'ce serait
un effondrement'—and Rhodes' warning about 'le point noir' ought
to be taken very seriously indeed. Of course France wants to have her
finger in the Sudan pie; so too do other Powers. But when it comes to
the point no British Government, Liberal or Conservative, will be
permitted by public opinion to make serious concessions to anybody.

Car, personne ne s'y trompe, cette question du Soudan fixe
l'attention générale: la solution qu'elle recevra ne sera pas
seulement importante en elle-même, elle sera significative,
décisive peut-être: elle donnera la juste mesure de la puissance

---

[1] D.D.F. xi, No. 319, Courcel to Hanotaux 19 Dec. 1894. FO 27/3183, Kimberley to
Dufferin No. 434a, 18 Dec.
[2] D.D.F. xi, No. 290, d'Estournelles de Constant to Hanotaux 22 Nov. 1894.
[3] *Ibid.*, No. 303, footnote citing minute by Hanotaux.
[4] *Ibid., loc. cit.*

O

britannique. C'est la grandeur même de l'Angleterre peut-être qui se trouve en jeu, c'est une question par conséquent de vie ou de mort.

D'Estournelles concludes that in the cause of Anglo-French friendship, which France so badly needs and which England is perfectly willing to offer, 'il est temps maintenant de nous arrêter, de borner notre champ d'action, de peur d'en faire à la longue, bientôt peut-être, un champ de bataille . . .'.[1]

In this remarkable despatch d'Estournelles squarely faced the fact that at any time after the summer of 1894 a French advance to the Upper Nile carried with it a grave risk of war. More remarkable still, d'Estournelles' despatch stands alone; until the actual outbreak of the Fashoda Crisis no other French diplomatist seems to have been able—or willing—to see the situation as it was. D'Estournelles saw with great clarity that the prestige of England as a Great Power was now fully engaged in her claim to a 'sphere' on the Upper Nile; and that public opinion, even comparatively moderate public opinion, was likely to be even more intransigent in the defence of British 'rights' than the Government itself. He wrote off in advance 'the intervention of Europe', that *deus ex machina* which was to be so uncritically invoked during and after the launching of the Marchand mission. He saw in particular that it was in Russia's interest to encourage rather than resist the establishment of Britain in the Sudan, so as to distract her from the Straits and the Far East and to drive the Egyptian wedge yet more firmly home between London and Paris. Hanotaux for his part seems to have concurred in d'Estournelles' analysis; his minute indicates no shade of dissent, and he reminds himself to ask Courcel to seek a practical basis on which the Upper Nile discussion could be resumed.[2] But he must have ruefully reflected that it was easy for d'Estournelles, always an incorrigible Anglophile, to talk of 'restraint' and 'sacrifices'; not so easy for a minister in Hanotaux' position to enforce such restraint upon the colonialists, who were rapidly entrenching themselves in positions of almost unassailable influence.

By the end of 1894 the aggressive, 'imperialistic' approach of Anderson at the British Foreign Office had its exact counterpart in Paris. In sharp contrast to the situation of 1893, the 'experts' of the Colonial Ministry were now in the van of the forward policy. Although Haussmann had not yet been kicked upstairs to the *Haute Direction des Finances*, his influence was already being overshadowed by the 'Young Turks' of colonialism—Ernest Roume[3] at his own Ministry and Benoît at the Quai d'Orsay. By October 1894 the *politique de moindre effort* was obsolete. So was Haussmann's concept of the Colonial Ministry's function as a drag-chain on local fire-eaters. Secret orders

[1] D.D.F. xi, No. 303, d'Estournelles de Constant to Hanotaux 3 Dec. 1894.
[2] *Ibid., loc. cit.*; and minute by Hanotaux.
[3] For Roume cf. *infra*, Ch. xii, pp. 271-5.

to advance—not merely denied by, but actually concealed from, the Minister of Foreign Affairs—were soon to be a commonplace at the Pavillon de Flore.[1] At both London and Paris, convinced imperialists were now not merely moving in the corridors of power; they were sitting behind the desks at which policy was made. This parallel development can hardly have been fortuitous; and it seems to have coincided pretty closely with the emergence of 'imperialism' as an influence, powerful in France and dominant in England, upon those sections of public opinion which seriously interested themselves in foreign policy. D'Estournelles' estimate of British public opinion was soon to be fully borne out by the way in which the 'Grey Declaration' was regarded, even in quite moderate circles, as a statement of unquestionable British 'rights' in the Nile valley. And if colonial imperialism was in general less popular in France than in Britain, the particular question of the Upper Nile had in June 1894 been linked to the high-voltage circuit of French sentiment on Egypt, and had so become a matter of acute and widespread public concern. The Upper Nile question had reached deadlock between Britain and France at the very time when—and surely partly because—the merely strategic manœuvres of the diplomatists had been dangerously reinforced by less rational and less calculable motives.

[1] *Infra*, Ch. xiii, p. 293; Ch. xiv, pp. 321-2.

X

ENGLAND, FRANCE, THE UPPER NILE
AND EUROPE, 1895–96

AT the turn of the year 1894-5 the Upper Nile, as a cause of the intense mutual irritation at London and Paris, was overshadowed by the sensational developments on the Niger. But it soon resumed the centre of the stage. Towards the end of 1894 the *Comité de l'Afrique française* had at last been converted to a more active policy on the upper Ubangi, to which in December it subsidised a mission under a certain M. Grimaux. This mission was very modest in scale and completely abortive in upshot;[1] but the public announcement of the *Comité*'s change of line had consequences of greater importance. In January 1895 Harry Alis demanded, in the *Bulletin du Comité*, that France should at once 'prendre position sur le Nil, de manière à empêcher de nouveaux empiètements des Anglais'.[2] Harry Alis was by now a somewhat discredited figure; on 1 March 1895 he was to be killed, by one of de Brazza's henchmen, in a duel arising out of accusations of pro-Congolese treachery.[3] Nevertheless, his words evoked a wide and lively response. In the Chamber on 1 February Flourens urged that France should make haste to advance now that her diplomacy had re-opened the route to the Nile. On 12 February de Brazza declared that an advance to the Upper Nile was the only way to settle the Egyptian question; a thesis which was elaborated by François Deloncle in a speech in the Chamber on the 28th:

> Aujourd'hui . . . nous sommes en bonne posture pour prendre à revers certaine position de nos rivaux et fournir ainsi à notre diplomatie des éléments nouveaux pour la négociation . . . que je considère comme indispensable dans un bref délai en vue d'aboutir enfin à l'évacuation tant promise des territoires du Khédive.[4]

[1] MC Afrique III 25, Mission Grimaux. The file closes with a certificate of Grimaux' embarkation at Marseilles; nothing further is heard of him.

[2] *Bull. C.A.F.*, Jan. 1895, p. 83. Cf. P. Renouvin, 'Les origines de l'expédition de Fachoda', *Rev. Hist.*, CC, 408 (1948), p. 186.

[3] The duel was with Capt. Le Chatellier of the French Congo Railway Co. Cf. Stengers, 'Aux Origines de Fachoda', *Rev. Belge Phil. Hist.* 1960, p. 389; *B.C.B.* III, Percher *dit* Harry Alis.

[4] D.D.F. XI, No. 404, footnote. Cocheris, *Situation Internationale*, p. 414. Langer, *Diplomacy of Imperialism*, p. 263.

Early in March *The Times* asked what action the British Government was taking about the threat to the Nile revealed by these pronouncements and by reports of French activity on the upper Ubangi.[1] The War Office Intelligence Division was indeed already interesting itself in the activities of Decazes, although he was doing no more than take over the posts ceded by Leopold.[2] On 11 March Sir Ellis Ashmead-Bartlett asked in the Commons whether, in view of recent statements by de Brazza and Deloncle, the Government would 'now clearly state that the whole Nile waterway is within the British sphere and that no Foreign occupation of the Nile will be permitted'. Sir Edward Grey, Kimberley's Under-Secretary, attempted a non-committal reply, but allowed himself to be pressed, in a supplementary question, to the admission that 'the Egyptian and British spheres together do cover the whole Nile waterway'.[3] Towards the end of March news of the spectacular French successes on the Niger began to give colour to fears of a similar *fait accompli* on the Nile; and Ashmead-Bartlett put down for the 28th a question on each of these rivers. He asked whether it was true that the French had occupied Bajibo and Boussa on the Niger; and whether there was any news of 'the French expedition which left the upper Ubanghi for the Nile waterway some nine months ago'.[4] This was evidently a reference, not to the Liotard mission, but to the Monteil mission; Ashmead-Bartlett seems to have overlooked the fact of Monteil's recall.

Grey evaded both these questions. On the Niger, he merely said that certain information had been received, as a result of which enquiries were being made at Paris. On the Nile, his answer was: 'We do not know that any French expedition has left for the Nile waterway'.[5] This was the strict truth, although Rosebery for one strongly suspected that the French were 'trying to occupy some place on the Nile within our "sphere of influence" '.[6] However, later in the day Ashmead-Bartlett was able to return to the charge in the debate on the Foreign Office vote. Rather unexpectedly, in view of recent events, he said little about the Niger and much about the Nile. There was, he said, 'a race for Transafrican dominion' between France working east and west and Britain working north and south. Britain must win this race, if only because 'any European Power holding the Upper Nile would hold Egypt at its mercy'. He urged the Government to act before it was faced with the *fait accompli* 'of a French occupation of some portion of the Nile, which would render our position in Egypt untenable or which would oblige us to undertake a tremendous struggle in order to

---

[1] Cocheris, *op. cit.*, p. 415; Langer, *op. cit.*, p. 264.
[2] FO 27/3257, memo. by Everett (I.D.) 6 Mar. 1895.
[3] Hansard (Commons), Fourth Series, xxxi, p. 782; cf. xxxii, p. 394. D.D.F. xi, No. 404, d'Estournelles de Constant to Hanotaux 12 Mar. 1895.
[4] Hansard, *ubi supra*, xxxii, pp. 349-50, 352-3.
[5] *Ibid., loc. cit.* Cf. FO 27/3257, drafts of replies by Grey; Gardiner, *Harcourt* ii, p. 335, citing Harcourt to Kimberley 29 Mar. 1895.
[6] L.Q.V. 3, ii, pp. 490-1, Murray to Bigge 29 Mar. 1895.

maintain it'. Britain ought already to have gunboats on the Upper Nile, patrolling 'as far as Lado, and even Fashoda'; they could be usefully employed in looking for the French expedition. Ashmead-Bartlett was followed by Major Darwin, who made much the same points in less combative language; and by J. W. Lowther, who reminded the House that Monteil had in fact been recalled, and doubted whether 'a friendly Power like France would send an armed expedition into a territory which we claimed under such circumstances'.[1]

Grey then replied to the debate. The British claim, he said, had been formally recognised by Germany, Italy and the Congo State. It was 'well known to all the other Powers', and had 'not been disputed during five years'—a strange assertion in view of Hanotaux' repeated refusal to admit it. Then there was the claim of Egypt, which France herself had recently not only admitted, but emphasised. Taken together, 'the British and Egyptian spheres of influence covered the whole of the Nile waterway'. He urged that rumours about French expeditions to the Nile should be treated with great reserve; the Foreign Office had 'no reason to suppose' that they were true. Grey then continued:

> I cannot think it possible that these rumours deserve credence,
> because the advance of a French expedition under secret
> instructions, right from the other side of Africa, into a territory
> over which our claims have been known for so long, would not
> be merely an inconsistent and unexpected act, but it must be
> perfectly well known to the French Government that it would be
> an unfriendly act, and would be so viewed by England.

Grey concluded by remarking that 'during the last two years no provocation whatever . . . has come from our side', and by appealing for French co-operation and goodwill. 'We rely now, as we have relied not unsuccessfully hitherto, on the sense of justice and fairness of the French Government and the French people.'[2]

Such, in its context, was the 'Grey Declaration'. In October 1898 Rosebery claimed to have been 'personally and Ministerially responsible' for it;[3] which means, if it means anything, that he told Grey more or less exactly what to say. Indeed, in March 1895 Courcel thought it 'une mise en scène concertée avec le Premier Ministre', and attributed it to Rosebery's 'nervosité maladive', racked to breaking-point by the precarious and humiliating situation of his government.[4] But Rosebery's claim and Courcel's explanation were alike unfounded. Rosebery's private secretary wrote on 2 April:

> If [the declaration] had been premeditated, it could scarcely
> have been made without the express sanction of the Cabinet;
> and I shudder to think of what the feelings of that august body

---

[1] Hansard, *ubi supra*, pp. 388-403.
[2] *Ibid.*, pp. 403-7.
[3] Speech at Epsom 12 Oct. 1898.
[4] D.D.F. xi, Nos. 420, 432, Courcel to Hanotaux 30 Mar. and 3 Apr. 1895.

would have been, if they had been asked to take such a step in cold blood. As it was, neither they—nor indeed anybody else— knew anything about it beforehand. . . .[1]

Of course, the declaration faithfully reflected Rosebery's views, and once it had been made he thoroughly approved of it, not least as committing his colleagues to 'a policy of which . . . none of them cordially approve, and to which not a few are violently opposed'.[2]

Nor did Kimberley 'premeditate' the declaration. When Harcourt accused him of launching a prepared attack upon France, Kimberley replied that he did indeed give Grey 'some general instructions', but 'did not tell him to use any particular phrase, neither "the phrase of unfriendly action" nor any other'. He added that Grey was not reading a prepared statement, but had 'a few rough notes' only.[3] Grey himself states that on the morning of the 28th Kimberley had authorised him to 'use pretty firm language' about the *Niger*, but gave him no specific instructions about the Nile.[4] It is evident that Grey expected the evening's debate to turn, not on unofficial French speeches about the Nile, but on apparently official French acts on the Niger. So did Kimberley. On the morning of the 28th he had laid before Courcel a budget of complaints about the Niger. He also mentioned that the Nile would probably 'be referred to in the House of Commons to-night'; but apparently in so casual and unemphatic a way that Courcel, normally a careful and accurate reporter, made no mention of the Nile in his despatch to Hanotaux.[5] When, in the event, the debate turned almost entirely on the Nile, Grey was forced to improvise. Precisely because the French had not *acted* on the Nile, but only talked about it, Grey could not transfer unchanged to the Nile the language he had prepared for the Niger. He himself explains that what he did do was to transfer 'to the subject of the Nile *the firmness* which I had been authorised to show about competing claims in West Africa'.[6] Grey's declaration has been described as heralding the age of 'diplomacy by public warning';[7] if so, this age seems to have been inaugurated more by chance than by deliberate policy.

It has also been called a 'strident declaration . . . the first note of the hysteria which was to overwhelm foreign policy towards the end of the century'.[8] These judgments rest on the use of the phrase 'unfriendly

---

[1] Murray to Bigge 2 Apr. 1895, quoted James, *Rosebery*, p. 374.
[2] Same to same, 29 Mar. and 2 Apr. 1895, quoted L.Q.V. 3, *loc. cit.* and James, *loc. cit.*
[3] Kimberley to Harcourt 31 Mar. 1895, cited Gardiner, *op. cit.* ii, p. 336.
[4] E. Grey, *Twenty-Five Years* (London 1925), i, pp. 18-19.
[5] FO 27/3229, Kimberley to Dufferin Nos. 111 and 111a, 28 Mar. 1895. D.D.F. xi, Nos. 412 and 413, Courcel to Hanotaux 28 Mar. Cf. *ibid.*, No. 420, same to same 30 Mar.
[6] Grey, *op. cit.* i, pp. 19-20 (emphasis supplied). This explanation has often been scouted (e.g. by Langer, *op. cit.*, pp. 264-5, and by James, *op. cit.*, p. 375). But both these writers create an unnecessary difficulty by confusing Grey's answers to Ashmead-Bartlett's questions with his reply to the debate later in the day. Nor do the well-known factual inaccuracies of Grey's account necessarily invalidate his main thesis—that he was improvising in a debate which had taken an unexpected turn.
[7] Robinson and Gallagher, *op. cit.*, p. 335.
[8] *Ibid.*, p. 336.

act', which is generally held to have been, in 1895, a technical term of diplomacy and to have implied 'a definite threat of war'.[1] It is however possible to doubt whether in 1895 the implications of this phrase were either so definite or so grave as they later came to be. If the phrase 'unfriendly act' was, as early as 1895, a term of art in diplomacy, it is strange that there should have been no exact equivalent for it in French. 'Acte', or 'procédé', 'peu amical', 'inamical', 'anti-amical', can all be found; and most French writers, including Hanotaux, confess defeat by citing the English word 'unfriendly'.[2] Again, in diplomatic reporting and even in diplomatic dialogue during the years immediately before 1895, the phrase 'unfriendly act'—or 'action'—is not infrequently used in contexts where it would be absurd to suppose that even the remotest threat of war was implied.[3] It seems indeed to have been Rosebery who, in a public speech of October 1898, gave currency to the doctrine that 'unfriendly act' was a technical term with implications of the utmost gravity. Looking back on the Grey Declaration from the height of the Fashoda Crisis, he defined an 'unfriendly act' as 'an act which may lead two countries directly to war', and added that to declare an act 'unfriendly' was a final warning, to be followed if necessary by an ultimatum.[4]

In March 1895 Grey was at pains to deny that he had used 'the language of menace'. Later on in the debate he declared that he had made a plea for a friendly understanding, but had accompanied it by a warning that 'there was a point of view strongly held in this country that would be adhered to with the tenacity which in such cases this country always manifested'.[5] But whatever Grey had meant by his phrase 'unfriendly act', its gravity was increased by the use which the Opposition speakers at once made of it. Chamberlain pounced on it, and used it three times, without any of Grey's courteous qualifications,

---

[1] H. Nicolson, *Diplomacy* (London 1939), p. 228. Cf. *ibid.*, pp. 248-9—'When a State wishes to warn other States that certain actions on their part might lead to war, it is usual to state that that action would "be regarded as an unfriendly act".'

[2] Hanotaux used 'anti-amical (*unfriendly*)'—*Fachoda*, p. 92.

[3] In Jan. 1893 Marschall described the British attitude towards the Asia Minor railway concession as 'an inimical act towards Germany'; in June 1894 he told Malet that Art. III of the Anglo-Congolese Agreement was 'an unfriendly action' (FO 64/1296, Malet to Rosebery tel. No. 1, 6 Jan. 1893; FO 64/1333, Malet to Kimberley No. 70, 9 June 1894). Kimberley on his side complained to Hatzfeldt that the Franco-German West African Protocol of Feb./Mar. 1894 was 'eine Unfreundlichkeit' (G.P. VIII, No. 2044, Hatzfeldt to A.A. 11 June 1894.)
When in Jan. 1895 Courcel protested in advance against any grant to the Italians of landing facilities at Zeila, Kimberley remarked, in a perfectly friendly and matter-of-fact tone: 'Vous considéreriez comme un procédé peu amical tout appui qui pourrait leur être donné de notre part' (D.D.F. XI, No. 359, Courcel to Hanotaux 1 Feb. 1895).
In May 1893 the Colonial Office was reluctant to permit the Germans to land artillery at Walfisch Bay for use against Witboi; Rosebery minuted: 'I think C.O. must be told that it would be an unfriendly act to refuse this.' (FO 64/1316, minute on Loch to C.O. 17 May 1893).
In none of these examples does the phrase 'unfriendly act' or its analogue carry the slightest threat of an ultimatum or of warlike action.

[4] Speech at Epsom 12 Oct. 1898. Evidently Rosebery's views on the significance of the phrase 'unfriendly act' had changed radically between May 1893 and Oct. 1898.

[5] Hansard, *ubi supra*, p. 426.

in a brief but highly offensive speech. Sir R. Temple distorted Grey's statement into an 'unanswerable . . . claim to a British sphere of influence from end to end of the Nile'; he added that 'France would know that when we had made a declaration we would stand by it'. Labouchère's contribution, from the other extreme, was if anything even more mischievous than those of the imperialists. He repeatedly accused Grey of uttering 'a speech of menace addressed to France'; indeed, of making 'a *quasi*-declaration of war against France'.[1]

Courcel, too, used the word 'war'. He complained to Kimberley that France had been provoked at a time when 'je ne voyais pas de question actuellement posée qui valût une guerre entre la France et l'Angleterre'.[2] But even Courcel admitted that Grey's remarks were courteous in form; though, believing as he did that the declaration was a 'coup de théâtre' stage-managed by Rosebery, he dismissed the courtesy as 'presque une ironie'.[3] But Courcel, although of course genuinely angry, deliberately made it his business 'de récriminer et de faire la grosse voix, pour tâcher qu'on ne recommence pas', and so that Hanotaux would appear more conciliatory by contrast.[4] Hanotaux too talked about a 'menace'; but he added, 'je sais qu'il faut en prendre et en laisser', and announced from the outset that he intended to avoid a noisy quarrel. The burden of his protest was not so much that Grey's words were a threat as that they were an unscrupulous attempt to assert by parliamentary demonstration a claim which France still hotly contested: 'Je ne puis admettre que des points qui sont livrés à la contestation des diplomates soient déclarés *incontestables* en plein Parlement anglais.' Recalling that Phipps, when asked to differentiate between the British and the Egyptian spheres, had always hedged, Hanotaux complained that these tactics of deliberate obfuscation had now been transferred from the diplomatic to the parliamentary arena. But Paris would resist none the less strongly—'Nous ne nous laisserons pas faire'.[5]

Although the high-handed British claim had to be resisted, Hanotaux' need for a détente in Anglo-French relations was by now considerably more urgent than it had been in the autumn of 1894. Because France was so friendless elsewhere, the Franco-Russian alliance was, in Courcel's words, beginning to deprive French policy of all elasticity.[6] Worse, the Russians showed a disquieting tendency to use the alliance as a means of guaranteeing to Berlin the good behaviour of France in Europe; in return they obtained security on their western frontier and a freer hand at the Straits and in the Far East. The point of the Franco-

[1] *Ibid.*, pp. 407-9, 416-20.
[2] D.D.F. xi, No. 429, Courcel to Hanotaux 2 Apr. 1895.
[3] *Ibid.*, No. 420, same to same 30 Mar. 1895.
[4] *Ibid.*, No. 432, same to same, private, 3 Apr.
[5] *Ibid.*, No. 416, Hanotaux to Courcel, private, 29 Mar.
[6] Courcel to Hanotaux, private, 17 June 1895, quoted in 'France et Angleterre en 1895', *Rev. Hist.*, ccxii, 431 (1954), pp. 47-8. Cf. D.D.F. xii, No. 32, Hanotaux to Montebello 24 May 1895.

Russe was in fact being turned ever more decisively away from Berlin and against London. Nor did the Russians spare even the tenderest susceptibilities of their allies. In March 1895 the French Cabinet was given almost a direct order by the Czar to send a naval squadron to the ceremonial opening of the Kiel Canal, although in January the Kaiser had proclaimed 1895 as the 'Jubilee Year' of the Franco-Prussian War.[1]

The Germans were happy enough to see France thus neutralised, but they wanted more. As in Bismarck's time, they wanted above all to keep the peace at the Straits. Shaken by Rosebery's 'unreliability', the Wilhelmstrasse had in the second half of 1893 warned Vienna not to hope for German assistance if Russia moved against Constantinople.[2] But it was one thing to give this warning and to reiterate it, quite another to be sure that Germany could really escape involvement, especially if Rosebery justified Marschall's fears by deserting Austria. When Berlin had uttered this warning the Near East had been quiet; by 1895 the consequences of the Armenian insurrection were stirring it up again. Could not Russian attention be diverted elsewhere? In the Far East Japan had just defeated China; France, Russia and Britain had from time to time discussed intervention in this struggle, but had taken no action. Russia was however strongly opposed to any extension of Japanese influence in northern China; and on 23 March 1895 the Germans, who had hitherto held aloof from all projects of intervention, secretly asked St Petersburg to accept them as partners in any joint démarche against Japan.[3] Lobanov, the new Russian Foreign Minister, saw here an opportunity not only to scotch the rising power of Japan but also to undermine the British hegemony of influence in the maritime regions of China. He accepted at once, without consulting or even informing his French ally.[4] The Germans had thus given Russian policy a useful deflection away from the Straits and towards the Far East, where Berlin had at that time no competing interest; they had also prevented the Franco-Russe from receiving its 'baptism of fire' by an intervention in which only Paris and St Petersburg would take part.

On 2 April 1895 Hanotaux learned, indirectly, of the German offer to St Petersburg; two days later he knew that it had been accepted.[5] France could not avoid making a third in the 'Triple Intervention' which was to humiliate Japan by insisting on the retrocession of the Liaotung Peninsula. To act side by side with Germany in rescuing Russia's Far Eastern chestnuts was, from the French point of view, a

[1] D.D.F. xi, No. 384, Montebello to Hanotaux 2 Mar. 1895; No. 394, Herbette to Hanotaux 5 Mar. Cf. D.D.F. xii, *loc. cit.*
[2] G.P. ix, No. 2138, Eulenburg to Caprivi 20 Dec. 1893, minute by the Emperor. Langer, *The Franco-Russian Alliance*, pp. 368-71.
[3] G.P. ix, No. 2228, Marschall to Tschirschky 23 Mar. 1895.
[4] *Ibid.*, No. 2229, Tschirschky to A.A. 25 Mar. 1895. D.D.F. xi, No. 422, Courcel to Hanotaux 1 Apr.; No. 426, Hanotaux to Vauvineux 2 Apr. 1895.
[5] D.D.F. xi, No. 422; No. 431, Vauvineux to Hanotaux 3 Apr. 1895.

complete perversion of the Franco-Russe. But if Britain would make a fourth to this sudden Far Eastern Triplice and thereby give it the appearance of an European Concert, at least the face of France would be saved. Unfortunately for Hanotaux the British, hitherto the leading advocates of intervention, began at this very moment to hesitate and draw back. Hanotaux' policy, as he himself admitted not long after, was in a perfect mess—'Comme imbroglio, c'est parfait'.[1]

The almost desperate desire of Hanotaux to keep London in the Far Eastern concert certainly moderated his reaction to the Grey Declaration; but even before he got wind of the intrigue between Germany and Russia he was determined to avoid a serious crisis.[2] Indeed, as an olive-branch to Britain Hanotaux had already in the early months of 1895 been behaving with studious moderation on questions affecting the Nile. He had encouraged Courcel to discuss Egypt tactfully with Kimberley; no practical result had been achieved, but the tone of the conversations had been so friendly that Courcel did not despair of ultimately removing 'this great stumbling-block'.[3] When in January 1895 the Khedive 'Abbās had once more attempted to assert himself against Cromer, Hanotaux had given him no support whatever and had indeed sharply rebuked Cogordan at Cairo for not having more firmly discouraged the Khedive's 'boutade'.[4] And when on 1 February Flourens demanded in the Chamber a French advance into the Bahr al-Ghazal, Hanotaux in his reply had ventured publicly to doubt the wisdom of this move.[5]

London, too, had made a gesture of conciliation. In January Rome had asked, with the strong support of Berlin, for the lease of Zeila as the base for a campaign against Ras Makonnen of Harar, who had now come out in active support of Menelik. Kimberley had refused, pleading the need not to alienate France when London and Paris were co-operating on the Armenian question.[6] A few days later Courcel warned Kimberley that France would regard as 'un procédé peu amical' any British assistance to Italian operations on the Somali coast or in the Harar region. Kimberley replied that any such operation would in the view of London be 'très peu sage'. Hanotaux grumbled at the vagueness of this assurance; but once he realised that London had in fact turned the Italians down, he paid in cash.[7] On 12 March 1895 Hanotaux, while maintaining in principle his reserves upon the

---

[1] *Ibid.*, No. 422; Nos. 438, 441, Courcel to Hanotaux 9 and 10 Apr. 1895; No. 483, Hanotaux to Montebello 25 Apr.
[2] *Ibid.*, No. 416, Hanotaux to Courcel 29 Mar. 1895.
[3] Cf. *ibid.*, Nos. 333, 396, Courcel to Hanotaux 10 Jan. and 6 Mar. 1895.
[4] *Ibid.*, No. 386, Cogordan to Hanotaux 2 Mar. 1895, and minute by Hanotaux.
[5] Cocheris, *op. cit.*, p. 414.
[6] F. Curato, 'Il rifiuto inglese di cedere Zeila all'Italia nel 1894-96', *Gerarchia*, Nov. 1935, pp. 948-9. G.P. VIII, Nos. 1999, 2001, 2002, 2005, Bülow to Berlin 3, 4 and 13 Jan. 1895; No. 2003, Marschall to Bülow 8 Jan.; Nos. 2004, 2011, Hatzfeldt to A.A. 12 and 30 Jan. 1895.
[7] D.D.F. XI, No. 359, Courcel to Hanotaux 1 Feb. 1895, and minute by Hanotaux. Cf. G.P. VIII, Nos. 2013, 2014, Hatzfeldt to A.A. 6 and 7 Feb.; Curato, *loc. cit.*

Secret Declaration attached to the Anglo-Italian Agreement of 5 May 1894, nevertheless withdrew all practical objection to the British provisionally treating Harar as part of their own sphere.[1]

Hanotaux' desire to smother the crisis caused by the Grey Declaration was met more than half-way by Kimberley. Uneasily aware that Grey's warning had exploded with embarrassing violence at Paris, Kimberley was even more than usually lavish with vague but soothing words in which to wrap up the sharp point of the dispute. Courcel had made it clear that the Grey Declaration was resented as an affront which France had done nothing to deserve. He also pointed out that London had deliberately destroyed any possibility of a diplomatic solution by this public and unilateral 'prise de possession'; surely this was a far more unfriendly act than the possible appearance in the Nile basin of 'a wandering column of explorers'?[2] Kimberley replied, in a conversation of 1 April, that there had been no 'prise de possession'; Grey had merely given public utterance to a claim which had already been privately conveyed to the French Government. The object of this announcement was not to rule out further diplomatic discussion, but rather to make it clear that Britain would 'have just ground for complaint if, whilst the negotiation was still pending, a French expedition entered the territory which was the subject in discussion'. Britain for her part had no intention of disturbing the *status quo*; no advance whatever had been authorised northwards from Unyoro. 'I attached much more importance to action than to words, and I hoped that the French Government would be guided by the same principle.'[3] Kimberley evidently meant that so long as neither party actually entered the Nile basin, there need be no dangerous quarrel. He was in fact hinting that as neither Britain nor France desired such a quarrel both Powers should, as a matter of practical policy, practise self-denial in the Nile basin. But having flatly rejected this solution in November 1894, Kimberley could hardly say this outright.

Courcel, who was not familiar with the 1894 negotiations, reports Kimberley with a rather different nuance: 'Dites à M. Hanotaux de s'attacher à nos actes plutôt qu'à nos paroles, parce que celles-ci sont toujours réparables'. Moreover, according to Courcel Kimberley explicitly admitted that France was free to reject the British 'prétention' and that 'la question restait donc sujette à débat'. But Courcel was well aware that these modifications, even in the form in which he reported them, had done little to compromise the position taken up by Grey; and above all that mere private explanations would not eradicate from the British public mind the conviction, implanted by Grey, that England claimed the Nile valley as of right. Warning Hanotaux of this, Courcel added that the British public, 'une fois son

---

[1] D.D.F. xi, No. 403, Hanotaux to Dufferin 12 Mar. 1895.
[2] *Ibid.*, Nos. 429, 423, Courcel to Hanotaux 2 Apr. 1895.
[3] FO 27/3229, Kimberley to Dufferin No. 112a, 1 Apr. 1895.

amour-propre national engagé . . ., ne reculera plus d'une semelle dans la défense de ce qu'il croit être son droit acquis'.[1] Hanotaux nevertheless replied that Kimberley's explanations were 'évidemment de nature à atténuer sensiblement la portée des paroles de Sir Edward Grey'. If Kimberley would accept as correct Courcel's version of their conversation on 1 April, Hanotaux would be as conciliatory as possible in his forthcoming Senate speech. Hanotaux also suggested that non-military expeditions into the Upper Nile should be considered 'comme n'engageant pas la politique des deux pays'.[2] Here he was evidently thinking of Liotard—who was a civilian—and trying to insure against his turning up in the Nile basin at an awkward moment.

Kimberley acknowledged the 'friendly intention' of the latter proposal, but set it aside; and he would accept Courcel's version only subject to certain reserves. The most important of these was that, while Britain had no present intention of entering the Bahr al-Ghazal, she must not be held to have bound herself to refrain.[3] With the 'Colvile mission' still haunting the French ministries, this cannot have been very reassuring to Hanotaux. But by now Hanotaux had learned of the Far Eastern intrigue between Germany and Russia. He swallowed Kimberley's reserves whole; and his speech on 5 April was so con-ciliatory that *The Times* hailed it as 'temperate and carefully-worded', while Dufferin was instructed to express official satisfaction.[4] It was indeed so 'carefully worded' that it afforded scarcely any clue to the future direction of French policy. Hanotaux of course deprecated Grey's unilateral assertion of claim; he explained that France could do nothing to meet British wishes on the Upper Nile so long as London persistently refused to define the boundary between the British and Egyptian spheres; and he made much of the rights of the Sultan and the Khedive. Beyond that, he said no more than Kimberley was reported to have done, that the matter remained open to debate. In particular, Hanotaux's peroration, designed to suit everybody—the British, the colonialists, and his own declared policy of supporting Egyptian and Ottoman rights—was an elegant exercise in multiple ambiguity:

Personne . . . ne peut prétendre entraver l'initiative des hommes courageux qui vont à la découverte de ces pays nouveaux. Mais, quand l'heure sera venue de fixer les destinées définitives de ces contrées lointaines, je suis de ceux qui pensent qu'en assurant le respect des droits du Sultan et du Khédive, en réservant à chacun ce qui lui appartiendra selon son œuvre, deux grandes nations sauront trouver les formules propres à concilier leurs

[1] D.D.F., *loc. cit.*
[2] *Ibid.*, No. 424, Hanotaux to Courcel 2 Apr. 1895. Cf. Hanotaux, *Fachoda*, pp. 91-5.
[3] D.D.F. xi, No. 430, Courcel to Hanotaux 3 Apr. 1895. Cf. FO 27/3229, Kimberley to Dufferin No. 113a, 3 Apr.
[4] FO 27/3234, Dufferin to Kimberley tel. No. 11, 5 Apr. 1895, and minute by Hill; Kimberley to Dufferin tel. No. 10, 8 Apr.

intérêts et à satisfaire leurs communes aspirations vers la civilisation et le progrès.[1]

On 6 April, in the more friendly atmosphere created by Hanotaux' speech, Kimberley suggested the possibility of 'un *modus vivendi* . . . excluant tout acte unilatéral pouvant préjudicier aux titres et aux prétentions de l'une ou de l'autre'. This move was an attempt to revive the self-denying arrangement in a less formal guise; but again Courcel seems to have missed the reference. He merely reported the suggestion, without attempting to explore it, as evidence that the Foreign Office seemed ready to 'transiger'. Courcel next saw Kimberley on the 9th. By this time it was known in Paris that Liotard was making very slow progress, and Courcel was authorised to say that no French expedition was at all likely to appear on the Upper Nile in the near future. He also pointed out that the Mahdists had recently expelled from the Upper Nile a Congolese force very much larger than the French upper Ubangi column. Why then all this bad blood over so remote and inaccessible a region, especially when there was a major crisis in the Far East?[2]

Within a few minutes of asking this question, Courcel learned that London had finally decided not to take any part in Lobanov's 'friendly démarche' to Japan.[3] Rosebery had in fact wished to participate; but his colleagues, as was by now almost their habit, overruled him.[4] Until 5 May it was very doubtful whether the Japanese would give way without at least a show of armed resistance. Hanotaux was now face to face with the probability of having to commit French battleships to action side by side with the Germans. Worse, he had to choose between either violating the Constitution by engaging in an act of war without parliamentary authority, or provoking a debate which might well have shattered the Franco-Russian alliance.[5] With a characteristic inability to appreciate the feelings of others, Rosebery chose the first week of May as a suitable moment to reconsider the self-denying arrangement. On 6 May he asked Anderson to define the area which might be covered by such a project. Tenacious to the last, Anderson produced a plan by which full mutual self-denial would apply only to the region west of the Nile and south of Darfur and Kordofan. East of the Nile it would not apply at all; and a loophole was left for the administration through Egypt of 'Darfur and Kordofan, the government of which was conferred by a *firman* . . . upon Mehemet Ali, and has been continued to his successors'. This was justified by the supposed

[1] Cocheris, *op. cit.*, pp. 421-3. Cf. Hanotaux, *op. cit.*, pp. 95-6.
[2] D.D.F. xi, Nos. 435, 443, Courcel to Hanotaux 6 and 10 Apr. 1895. Cf. Renouvin, *Rev. Hist.*, *ubi supra*, p. 189; and *infra*, Ch. xii, p. 269.
[3] D.D.F. xi, No. 443.
[4] James, *op. cit.*, p. 377.
[5] D.D.F. xi, No. 483, Hanotaux to Montebello 25 April 1895. For this crisis in general, see Langer, *The Diplomacy of Imperialism*, pp. 180-7. Hanotaux' difficulties, and his last-minute attempts to moderate the Russians and win over the British, are well illustrated in D.D.F. xi.

need to cover 'the approach to the Nile through Darfur and Kordofan' —the old nightmare about Rabih Zubair.[1] Anderson's idea of self-denial was to close the Bahr al-Ghazal, which was now certain to become a French prize if there were a race for the Nile, while reserving all other regions for Britain, to be administered either directly or through Egypt.

Whatever the shortcomings of Rosebery and Kimberley as diplomatists, they at least did not share Anderson's robust faith in the gullibility of Hanotaux. Kimberley made no mention of Anderson's 'self-denying' project when on 10 May he asked Courcel whether the Nile discussions might profitably be resumed. Courcel, usually so courteous and conciliatory, was by now, very pardonably, out of patience with the British. He coldly replied that any overtures would doubtless be received in a friendly spirit, but that the whole question had become much more complex since Grey's 'fameuse manifestation' had established a necessary connection between the Upper Nile and Egypt. Kimberley disclaimed 'any wish or intention to enter upon the subject now', but he did not see why the Upper Nile might still not be settled without trenching on the Egyptian question. Courcel grudgingly admitted that sooner or later 'an exchange of friendly explanations' might take place; but he added that France must not be expected to accept definitions of the British sphere based upon treaties with other Powers. Kimberley insisted no further.[2]

Grey's 'fameuse manifestation' had merely made public, rather than in any way created, the necessary connection between Egypt and the Upper Nile; but even the superficial exchange of views which followed it had at one point shown with great clarity why France found it difficult to discuss the Upper Nile without bringing in Egypt. When on 1 April Kimberley had assured Courcel that the ultimate reconquest of the Sudan would be undertaken by Egyptian troops, and would be followed by an Egyptian administration, the ambassador at once retorted: 'Qu'importe . . . si ces troupes et cette administration sont dirigées du Caire et que l'Angleterre soit au Caire'.[3] Courcel had put into words the silent reservation with which Hanotaux had always qualified his support for Egyptian rights on the Upper Nile. So long as Britain controlled Egypt itself, the French thesis on the rights of the Sultan and the Khedive could easily become a weapon in British hands. Anxious as Hanotaux was not to quarrel seriously with London, his fundamental thesis on the Upper Nile was worthless to France unless he could also secure the evacuation of Egypt.

An attempt was nevertheless made to keep the Upper Nile negotiations in being. Dufferin, presumably with Kimberley's blessing, suggested to Hanotaux a general discussion of African questions in

[1] FO 27/3257, memo. by Anderson 6 May 1895.
[2] FO 27/3229, Kimberley to Dufferin No. 151, 10 May 1895; D.D.F. xii, No. 3, Courcel to Hanotaux, 11 May.
[3] D.D.F. xi, No. 429, Courcel to Hanotaux 2 Apr. 1895.

which the Upper Nile would be handled personally by Hanotaux and himself. This was not a very hopeful proposition; whatever Dufferin's virtues as an ambassador—and they were many—a taste and capacity for detailed negotiation were not among them. But the negotiation in fact never took place. When on 12 June Hanotaux reminded Dufferin of this proposal, the ambassador explained with some embarrassment that this had been his own personal initiative, and that London had not supported it.[1] Perhaps Rosebery, weary of the Upper Nile as he was certainly weary of office, had interposed his veto. Less than a fortnight later he seized the opportunity to resign on a snap defeat in the Commons.

Rosebery's failure, not only in foreign affairs but also as a Prime Minister and a party leader, was not due to lack of intelligence, though he was not of course the superior intellect that he sometimes fancied himself to be. It was rather a failure in the field of human relations. Rosebery seems to have been quite incapable of looking at any question from any point of view but his own, or even of clearly realising that there *was* any point of view but his own.[2] Here, and not merely in unfamiliarity with diplomatic technique, lies the root of Rosebery's total inability to 'understand the importance and significance of his own actions and words [or] of his omissions'. These actions, too, were all too often dictated, not by objective considerations but by 'his vanity [and] especially an excessive personal touchiness'[3]—and by a quick temper under very uncertain control. Although personally far more sympathetic to Germany than Salisbury ever was, Rosebery ruined Britain's credit with Berlin. Marschall and Holstein, unable to believe that any Foreign Minister could really be as incompetent as Rosebery appeared, concluded that his extraordinary behaviour concealed some sinister design against Germany.[4] At the same time Rosebery allowed Anglo-French relations to become much more unfriendly than they had been even in the days of Salisbury's closest collaboration with Berlin after 1890. Of course, both as Foreign Secretary and as Prime Minister Rosebery was severely handicapped by sharp differences with his colleagues. But some of his more disastrous initiatives— for instance, the Rabīh Zubair episode and the Corridor Clause—were those which he deliberately concealed from the Cabinet. And on more than one occasion when Rosebery was overruled by his colleagues one can only applaud their wisdom in doing so.

Salisbury's return to office brought to bear on foreign policy a coldly analytical mind and a massive patience. In July 1895 his hand

---

[1] D.D.F. xii, No. 62, *note du Ministre* 12 June 1895.

[2] Cf. James, *op. cit.*, pp. 488-9. He has also been described as 'always craving for sympathy which he never knew how to get' (Robinson and Gallagher, *op. cit.*, pp. 311-2).

[3] The citations are from Hatzfeldt to Holstein 29 Nov. 1893 (Rich and Fisher, *The Holstein Papers*, iii, p. 447). In March 1893 Hatzfeldt had described Rosebery as 'extremely resentful and sensitive personally' (to Holstein 22 Mar. 1893: *ibid.*, p. 433).

[4] 'You over-estimate Rosebery when you take him for a cunning knave'—Hatzfeldt to Holstein 29 Nov. 1893 (*ibid.*, p. 447).

was strengthened by a spectacular victory at the polls. The division between Conservatives and Liberal Unionists had by now become a matter of form rather than reality; and their combined majority now supported a government stronger than any since the Reform Bill of 1884. But Salisbury's control of foreign and imperial policy was not to go unchallenged. The African Department he could of course put in its place; Sir Percy Anderson was at once deprived of the quasi-dictatorship over detailed African policy which he had exercised in 1894. Moreover, in the autumn of 1896 Anderson died. His successor Sir Clement Hill, a less positive personality and perhaps more old-fashioned in his ideas, had little of Anderson's craving for 'possessions'. But Salisbury's control of African affairs was to be challenged, far more effectively than by any mere departmental official, by his Colonial Secretary Joseph Chamberlain. Chamberlain could not indeed intervene directly in the Upper Nile. Here the writ of the Colonial Office did not run, because of the historical accident that the British sphere in East Africa had grown out of the old relationship with an independent Zanzibar; and Salisbury was able to keep Chamberlain from poaching on the preserves of the Foreign Office African Department. But by July 1895 an isolated settlement of the Upper Nile dispute seemed already out of the question; and by 1897 Salisbury was hoping to buy a settlement by satisfying France in West Africa, much as he had done in 1890. In this policy Chamberlain refused to co-operate; and Salisbury had to yield, as the only means of keeping in the Cabinet a minister whose popularity made him an indispensable member of it.[1]

But the Upper Nile question was for the time being dormant. The French, by ejecting Leopold, had unwittingly rescued Salisbury from his embarrassment over the Mackinnon Treaty; and it was now clear that they themselves had no immediate intention of disturbing the *status quo*. Salisbury therefore turned from the Upper Nile to the task of repairing the disarray in which Rosebery had left British foreign policy as a whole. Berlin hoped, and Paris feared, that Salisbury would revive his previous policy of collaboration with the Triplice and support for Austria at the Straits.[2] But Salisbury now doubted whether this policy was either possible or desirable. Turkey, more decrepit than ever, seemed inevitably destined to become not merely the janitor of Russia but a fully dominated Russian 'protectorate'. The Fleet was still not strong enough to guarantee Constantinople; the increases authorised in 1894 might provide for the future, but in 1895 a Russian *coup* seemed imminent.[3] Above all, Salisbury no longer trusted the Germans. They had threatened to combine with France to destroy the

---

[1] *Infra*, Ch. xiv, pp. 317-21. As early as Nov. 1895 Salisbury had become very uneasy at Chamberlain's aggressive and bellicose outlook (Robinson and Gallagher, *op. cit.*, p. 339).

[2] L.Q.V. 3, ii, p. 535, the German Emperor to the Queen 12 July 1895. D.D.F. xii, Nos. 69, 75, Courcel to Hanotaux 17 and 27 June 1895. Cf. same to same 30 June, quoted *Rev. Hist.* 1954, *ubi supra*, pp. 50-1.

[3] Cf. Marder, *The Anatomy of British Sea-Power*, p. 245.

P

Anglo-Congolese Agreement; they had in fact combined with France and Russia to injure British interests in the Far East. In southern Africa their growing interest in the Transvaal and their unconcealed ambition to acquire Delagoa Bay[1] seemed to portend a threat to British strategic interests potentially at least even more dangerous than that of Russia at the Straits; for the Cape of Good Hope, as the key to the emergency route in time of war, was more critical for Ocean strategy even than the Mediterranean.[2] The Germans were moreover falling into the habit of demanding concessions as the price of their merely refraining from active opposition to England; a form of 'blackmail' which Salisbury had suffered under Bismarck and to which he was afterwards always very sensitive. In December 1894 Hatzfeldt had warned Holstein of the folly of this behaviour, and had predicted that 'in the end [the English] will join in the general chorus against the wicked Germans, and Salisbury will be able to do nothing to counter that when he returns to office'.[3] Hatzfeldt's prediction was more than fulfilled; by July 1895 Salisbury's distrust of the Germans was if anything stronger than that of the general public.

Faced with the necessity of 'coping, practically alone, with the alliance of France and Russia', Salisbury turned away from the Triple Alliance and towards the improvement of relations with both these Powers, particularly Russia. Salisbury believed that the ending of the permanent Anglo-Russian estrangement would provide 'the best chance for something like an equilibrium of Europe';[4] and the Anglo-Russian Pamir Agreement of November 1894—Rosebery's one real success in foreign policy—had suggested that the Russians were not completely intractable. The ruinous Ottoman Empire, its weakness inviting Russian intervention, was a permanent threat to peace; but its very decrepitude might permit an orderly liquidation in which competing interests could be peacefully adjusted and, in particular, one of the main causes of Anglo-Russian tension abolished. Salisbury could not of course make a direct approach to Russia. Such a move, quite apart from committing him far too deeply at the outset, would have evoked deep suspicion and resentment in both Paris and Berlin; and St Petersburg would doubtless have seen in it a ruse to distract Russia from the Far East by embroiling her with Austria at the Straits. Salisbury therefore attempted to approach Russia indirectly, through

[1] On Delagoa Bay, see: FO 64/1301, Rosebery to Malet No. 45, 5 Dec. 1893; FO 64/1332, Kimberley to Gosselin No. 174a, 13 Oct. 1894; Gardiner, *op. cit.*, II, p. 325, citing Kimberley to Harcourt 7 Dec. 1894.

[2] Cf. Rosebery's remarks to Deym, reported in Deym to Kálnoky No. 35B, 1 Nov. 1894; and quoted in L. M. Penson, 'The New Course in British Foreign Policy, 1892-1902', *Transactions of the Royal Historical Society*, 4th series, XXV (1943), at pp. 127-8.

[3] Hatzfeldt to Holstein 22 Dec. 1894 (Rich and Fisher, *op. cit.* III, p. 486). Cf. same to same 19 Dec. 1894 (*ibid.*, p. 483).

[4] The citations are from Salisbury to Iwan-Muller 31 Aug. 1896 (B.D. VI, Appx. IV, p. 780). But they doubtless represent his views a year earlier. Cf. his remarks to Courcel in June 1896 (D.D.F. XII, No. 410, Courcel to Hanotaux 20 June 1896); his Guildhall speech of 9 Nov. 1896; and his more famous ('staked our money on the wrong horse') speech of 19 Jan. 1897.

both Paris and Berlin. Almost simultaneously, on 9 and 12 July, he spoke to Hatzfeldt and to Courcel about the dangers inherent in trying to preserve the Ottoman Empire—'n'importe quelle combinaison serait préférable au maintien de ce qui existe actuellement'. To both he hinted that he would be prepared to pay for a more stable situation by making extensive concessions to Russia. To Courcel in particular Salisbury insisted that an Anglo-Russian entente was by no means out of the question; as 'an old Tory' he himself had no prejudices against a close and friendly relation with the Czar.[1]

These hints fell on stony ground. Courcel at once told Salisbury that the overriding interest of France was to shore up Turkey so as to preserve the *status quo* in the Near East; and France could indeed have hardly contemplated a policy which would have destroyed the Ottoman buffer between her own aspirations and those of Russia in the Levant.[2] At Berlin, Holstein at once concluded that Salisbury would attempt to embroil St Petersburg with the Triple Alliance by denying Russia her fair share of the spoils. An unguarded suggestion by Salisbury that Italy might seek compensation in Albania was magnified by Holstein's pathological suspicion into an attempt to disrupt the Triplice by fomenting a quarrel between Italy and Austria.[3] On 5 August Salisbury repeated his hints, this time to the German Emperor at Cowes. According to Holstein, the Kaiser 'turned him down flat'. But by this time Hatzfeldt had convinced the Wilhelmstrasse that Salisbury's concessions might include Constantinople 'avec tout ce qui s'ensuit', and so make Russia's alliance with France 'dispensable' (*entbehrlich*). Salisbury was therefore invited to meet the Emperor again on 6 August. He failed to keep the appointment. Perhaps he resented the snub of the previous day; more probably, he was, on second thoughts, reluctant to confide at all in a monarch whom he considered indiscreet and two-faced. But the Germans naturally now became more suspicious than ever.[4]

Meanwhile, St Petersburg had firmly rejected a direct British suggestion for joint action in the Armenian question;[5] and Salisbury

---

[1] G.P. x, No. 2396, Hatzfeldt to Hohenlohe 10 July 1895. D.D.F. xii, No. 88, Courcel to Hanotaux 12 July. *Rev. Hist.*, *ubi supra*, pp. 53-5, Courcel to Hanotaux 15 July. The precise significance of these hints has been much debated (guides to the literature at Robinson and Gallagher, *op. cit.*, p. 341; and Hinsley, *C.H.B.E.* iii, pp. 491-2). The standard account in English is by Langer (*op. cit.*, pp. 197-201). A recent revision by J. A. S. Grenville (*Lord Salisbury and Foreign Policy* [London 1964], pp. 24-37) suggests that Salisbury's remarks were scarcely even hints, and have been given an exaggerated importance owing to 'misrepresentation and . . . downright falsification' on the part of Hatzfeldt. All the same, Courcel seems to have gained much the same impression as his German colleague—cf. especially his private letter to Hanotaux of 15 July (*Rev. Hist.*, *loc. cit.*).

[2] D.D.F., *loc. cit.* Cf. *infra*, p. 235.

[3] G.P. x, Nos. 2373, 2374, Rotenhan to Hatzfeldt 1 and 2 Aug. 1895; No. 2377, Holstein to Hatzfeldt 3 Aug.; No. 2379, Rotenhan to Hohenlohe 5 Aug.

[4] G.P. x, Nos. 2381-6, 5 Aug.-8 Aug. 1895. Cf. Holstein's memoir of 13 Jan. 1909, in Rich and Fisher, *The Holstein Papers I-Memoirs and Political Observations* (Cambridge 1955), at p. 161; *ibid.* iii, pp. 537-9, Kiderlen-Wächter to Holstein 7 Aug. 1895, enclosing Salisbury to Hatzfeldt 6 Aug. For a different interpretation, cf. Grenville, *op. cit.*, pp. 37-9.

[5] Langer, *op. cit.*, p. 201.

now turned to France. As early as 12 July he had indeed hinted to Courcel that the Siam question might be ripe for solution;[1] but by the middle of August, with the Russians obstinately aloof and the Germans thoroughly disgruntled and suspicious, a rapprochement with France had become a matter of some urgency for Salisbury. No real entente was of course possible so long as the 'great stumbling-block' of Egypt still lay in the path. But certain minor disputes might be settled; and the very fact that some of them had loomed disproportionately large in Anglo-French polemics would itself enhance the value of their settlement. It was easy to guess that Hanotaux would co-operate, if only to loosen the Russian fetters upon French policy. Indeed, on 13 August Courcel himself suggested that the time was ripe for an airing of these minor issues; whereupon Salisbury at once plunged into substantive discussion of the Siam-Mekong question.[2]

Hanotaux was at first sceptical of success, and uneasy at Salisbury's readiness to see 'sick men' everywhere and to dwell upon 'la curée des mourants'.[3] But by the end of September he was convinced that a bargain was possible and that France ought to work for it, if only 'pour montrer . . . au monde qu'entre les Anglais et nous, des arrangements raisonnables sont toujours possibles'.[4] Courcel was by this time so impressed by the improvement in relations that he did not despair of making progress even on the Egyptian question, especially if Hanotaux persevered in his policy of refraining from constant administrative pin-pricks in Egypt itself—'un système de vexations quotidiennes, aussi irritantes . . . que stériles'.[5] By 23 October 1895, just before Hanotaux relinquished office on the fall of the Ribot government, the main lines of the Siam-Mekong arrangement had been settled, though the Agreement was not formally signed until 15 January 1896.[6] Immediately afterwards, the Foreign Office rejected an unusually generous German proposal for the settlement of the Gold Coast-Togo hinterland. Berlin had for some time been attempting to use this question, and its Togo-Dahomey analogue, as a means of frustrating the disquieting improvement in Anglo-French relations.[7] But Salisbury was on his guard; and he had already agreed with Hanotaux that the Anglo-French West African negotiations should be resumed.[8] The moment was propitious; in this region of all too active rivalry there had recently been a lull. The French had sent out no new expeditions; and

---

[1] D.D.F., loc. cit.   [2] D.D.F. xii, No. 128, Courcel to Hanotaux 14 Aug. 1895.
[3] Ibid., Nos. 136, Hanotaux to Courcel 22 Aug. 1895; 144, Courcel to Hanotaux 29 Aug.; 157, Hanotaux to Courcel 27 Sept. 1895. On 29 Aug. Salisbury had particularly dwelt upon the decrepitude of Morocco.
[4] Ibid., No. 157.   [5] Ibid., No. 161, Courcel to Hanotaux 29 Sept. 1895.
[6] Ibid., No. 181, Courcel to Hanotaux 23 Oct. 1895; Nos. 273, 274, Courcel to Berthelot 15 Jan. 1896. For a detailed account of this negotiation, see: J. D. Hargreaves, 'Entente Manquée; Anglo-French Relations 1895-1896', C.H.J., xi, 1 (1953), pp. 69-75.
[7] Hargreaves, ubi supra, pp. 67-8, 72-3, 76-7. Cf. D.D.F. xi, No. 372, Herbette to Hanotaux 19 Feb. 1895; xii, No. 291, Berthelot to Herbette 31 Jan. 1896; No. 294, Herbette to Berthelot 3 Feb. 1896.
[8] D.D.F. xii, No. 179, Hanotaux to Courcel 21 Oct. 1895. FO 146/3421, Salisbury to Dufferin No. 508, 23 Oct.

as early as May Howard, who had replaced Phipps at Paris, could report that Benoît 'no longer seems to think it is a huge joke to occupy all we claim'.[1] In August the *Ardent* incident, which had so incensed Anderson, was closed by the recall and reprimand of the ship's commander. In September the Foreign Office reciprocated by notifying Paris that they had refused to enter into relations with Samory so long as he was at war with France.[2]

This was by no means the limit of British conciliation. In December 1895 Salisbury refused to the Italians the use of Zeila in circumstances which were, as the German Chancellor complained, 'ein Hohn für Italien und eine Ermutigung für Frankreich'.[3] Almost as soon as Salisbury had returned to office, Crispi had revived his request for the lease, or even the cession, of Zeila; but all that Salisbury would offer was the admission of an Italian consular agent.[4] This Crispi disdainfully refused; but the threatening situation in Ethiopia forced him to ask again in November 1895. Salisbury replied that in the opinion of his military advisers the Italian situation in Ethiopia gave no cause for alarm. This prognosis was at once belied by the rout of Toselli at Amba Alagi on 7 December; and on the 13th, under heavy pressure from the Italian Ambassador Ferrero and from Hatzfeldt, Salisbury withdrew his objections to the passage of Italian troops through Zeila.[5] But a week later Berthelot, who had succeeded Hanotaux at the Quai d'Orsay, threatened to drop the Siam-Mekong negotiation if the Italians were given access to the Harar region. On 23 December Salisbury promised Courcel that he would 'advise' the Italians to take no action at Harar without prior agreement with France; and on 2 January 1896 he notified Ferrero of these 'restrictions and conditions' which, in his own words, 'detracted considerably from the value of the concession'.[6]

A few days later Berthelot flatly rejected an invitation from Berlin to co-operate in 'limiting the insatiable appetite of England' in the Transvaal and elsewhere. The German proposal was not in itself very attractive: the Transvaal would obviously be the first sphere of co-operation, and here France had no interests. But Marschall put himself completely out of court by excluding Egypt in advance.[7] He was

---

[1] D.D.F. xii, No. 157, Hanotaux to Courcel 27 Sept. 1895. FO 27/3231, Howard to Anderson 14 May 1895.

[2] FO 27/3232, Howard to Salisbury No. 216, 16 Aug. 1895. D.D.F. xii, No. 156, Howard to Hanotaux 26 Sept.

[3] G.P. xi, No. 2689, Hohenlohe to Radolin 24 Feb. 1896.

[4] Curato, *ubi supra*, pp. 949-50. G.P. x, No. 2369, Bülow to Hohenlohe 15 July 1895; No. 2371, Hatzfeldt to Holstein 30 July; No. 2387, Hatzfeldt to A.A. 14 Aug. 1895. Cf. *History of 'The Times'*, iii, pp. 251-6.

[5] Curato, *loc. cit.* G.P. xi, No. 2748, footnote; Nos. 2750, 2751, 2753, Hatzfeldt to A.A. 13, 15 and 18 Dec. 1895.

[6] D.D.F. xii, No. 240, Courcel to Berthelot 18 Dec. 1895; No. 242, Berthelot to Courcel 20 Dec.; No. 245, Courcel to Berthelot 23 Dec. Curato, *loc. cit.*, citing Salisbury to Ferrero 2 Jan. 1896; cf. FO 45/747, Salisbury to Ford (Rome) No. 65, 20 May 1896.

[7] D.D.F. xii, Nos. 254, 255, 257, Herbette to Berthelot 1, 2 and 3 Jan. 1896; No. 262, Berthelot to Herbette, 7 Jan. Cf. G.P. xi, No. 2641, Hohenlohe to Münster 1 Jan. 1896.

asking France to incur British hostility for a purely German interest in the Transvaal, and at the same time safeguarding Germany by firmly retaining the *bâton égyptien*. Berthelot was not seeking quarrels with Britain; indeed, his zeal to compose such quarrels was warmer—and more naïve—than that of Hanotaux. As a Radical, he was an anglophile *a priori*; as an outsider in diplomacy, he did not share the Quai d'Orsay's 'extremely combative' office tradition towards England.[1] Meanwhile, Salisbury's repudiation of the Zeila concession must have seemed to him a long step towards an Anglo-French entente.

To the Germans, however, it appeared as evidence that the entente might already be on the point of consummation; and the Kruger Telegram was among other things a clumsy and almost panic-stricken attempt to harass Britain out of her new alignment.[2] But the explosion of wrath with which British opinion greeted the attempted German intervention in the Transvaal merely hastened the rapprochement with France. On 11 January Salisbury emphasised to the Queen how important it was 'in the present state of things to settle as many questions with France as possible'.[3] The Siam-Mekong Agreement, published a few days later, had on the whole a good press in England; some newspapers even hinted that an agreement on Egypt was not impossible.[4] Berthelot was indeed already urging Courcel to attempt a negotiation on Egypt. Courcel objected, correctly, that the time was not yet ripe; but early in February his hand was forced when the French got wind of overtures to London by the Sultan for a negotiation on the evacuation of Egypt.[5] On 19 February 1896 Courcel, having previously prepared the ground with the Permanent Under-Secretary Sir Thomas Sanderson, opened the Egyptian discussion with Salisbury.

Courcel suggested that the question had been 'artificiellement grossie d'une quantité d'appendices hétérogènes'; if, like the Siam-Mekong dispute, it could be 'dégonflée', it might not prove so difficult after all. France desired neither a French occupation, nor a practical restoration of Ottoman authority, nor a condominium of the Powers, nor, least of all, a simple abandonment of Egypt to the Egyptians. This would lead simply to the early revival of revolutionary nationalism and militant xenophobia—'anarchy' which would hurt France perhaps even more than it hurt Britain. Indeed the practical British concessions need not be very far-reaching, so long as they were presented in the right spirit. What France really needed was a spontaneous *beau geste* which should heal the wound to her national self-

[1] Cf. FO 27/3455, Monson to Salisbury No. 48, 27 Jan. 1899.
[2] Cf. G.P. xi, Nos. 2758, 2759, Marschall to Bülow 25 and 28 Dec. 1895; No. 2650, Münster to Hohenlohe 16 Jan. 1896; No. 2651, Marschall to Radolin 19 Jan. 1896.
[3] Hargreaves, *ubi supra*, p. 75, citing Salisbury to the Queen 11 Jan. 1896.
[4] Langer, *op. cit.*, pp. 251-2; Hargreaves, *loc. cit.*
[5] D.D.F. xii, No. 306, Courcel to Berthelot 19 Feb. 1896 (at p. 464). Courcel to Berthelot 11 Jan. 1896 (mentioned in No. 295); cf. No. 301, Paul Cambon to Berthelot 7 Feb. Hargreaves, *op. cit.*, p. 82.

respect.[1] Courcel suggested in passing that King Leopold might be installed as a neutral custodian—a suggestion which Salisbury did not take seriously, though it may have been meant seriously.[2] Failing that, France would be satisfied with the withdrawal of all troops 'under the British flag', and the employment of more French officials in the Egyptian administration. Courcel also begged Salisbury not to take any major step in Egyptian policy 'sans entente confiante avec nous'. This was a hint that he knew of the negotiation with Constantinople; as a further hint he reminded Salisbury that France had objected to the Drummond Wolff Convention not so much because of its substance but because it had been concluded behind her back.[3]

It seems doubtful whether these moderate proposals would have gone far to satisfy the doctrinaire anglophobes of the Right who did most to keep the Egyptian question alive in France. At the same time, as Cromer pointed out, their adoption would have made the orderly administration of Egypt very difficult. The military evacuation Cromer would accept at a pinch, given the right of re-entry and a permanent garrison in Cyprus; but the employment of numerous senior French officials would in practice involve all the notorious inconveniences of a condominium. As for Courcel's plea for prior consultation, Cromer sardonically remarked that this would be more acceptable 'if French governments were composed of anything but Frenchmen'. But even Cromer was prepared at least to consider these proposals if he could obtain in return 'full financial freedom' for his Egyptian administration.[4]

Courcel for his part was by no means dissatisfied with Salisbury's reception of his opening play. At least, the dialogue had been engaged and the British could no longer 'cheminer dans leur mutisme'.[5] He was therefore the more perturbed when further progress of the Anglo-French reconciliation was compromised by a deadlock in the Niger negotiations, which had begun at Paris on 8 February. The Foreign Office hoped to get the 'isolated Niger settlement' which Phipps had obtained for them, and which they had rejected, in October 1894. The French negotiators, MM. Roume and Benoît, scouted this naïve notion. Their claims were now based on the treaties of French explorers in the middle of Goldie's imaginary occupations. Worse, they returned to the 'monstrous French pretension' about the Say-Barrawa line and even seemed disposed to revive the Mizon claims in Adamawa. Salisbury was, for once, very angry indeed. 'If', he fumed, 'our agreements are not to be interpreted according to the plain meaning of their words, any further agreement . . . would be useless.'

[1] D.D.F. xii, No. 306, Courcel to Hanotaux 19 Feb. 1896: SP Egypt, Salisbury to Cromer 20 Feb. 1896.
[2] D.D.F., loc. cit. Cf. infra, Ch. xii, pp. 269-70.
[3] SP, loc. cit.; D.D.F., loc. cit.
[4] SP Egypt, Cromer to Salisbury 29 Feb. 1896.
[5] D.D.F., loc. cit.

In a personally drafted despatch of 21 February 1896 he pointed out that the French contention about the Say-Barrawa line amounted to the imputation to Waddington of deliberate bad faith during the 1890 negotiation.[1]

When Dufferin communicated the contents of this despatch to Berthelot, the Minister evaded discussion on a plea of unfamiliarity with the details. Commenting acidly on Berthelot's general incapacity as a diplomatist and total 'inability to grasp the first elements of the question', Dufferin concluded that he would 'undoubtedly continue to screen himself behind his Commissioners, who themselves probably take their orders from the French Colonial Office'. It was, Dufferin said, one of the great difficulties in African negotiations with the French that 'one never feels oneself face to face with the real persons who are determining ... policy'.[2] Dufferin was not far wrong. The Africanists entrenched in the French ministries had in their own field been able completely to reverse the general trend of foreign policy. Courcel sought a solution to this problem by taking the negotiation out of the hands of the 'experts' with their extreme views. On 11 March he suggested to Sanderson that the two of them should try to work out together 'some broad lines which would enable the matters under discussion to advance a little'. But on the following day Courcel learned to his astonishment and consternation that the London Cabinet had authorised an Egyptian advance into the northern Sudan; and on the 13th he sadly admitted that 'it would be best to let the [Niger] Commission continue its work'.[3]

Courcel did not however intend to abandon the Anglo-French rapprochement without a struggle. To most Frenchmen the Sudan advance seemed yet another example of English arrogance in the Nile valley; to those who understood the recent drift of Anglo-French relations it might well seem perfidious into the bargain. Courcel knew better. Deprecating the tunnel-vision of French public opinion, which hardly looked beyond the Egyptian question in its narrowest form, Courcel was at pains to explain to his minister that the origins of the British move lay in Europe rather than in the Nile valley. Salisbury had evidently been constrained, for reasons of general policy, to re-insure with the Triple Alliance by making a gesture of solidarity with Italy in Africa. It would be foolish for France to push him yet further in this direction by adopting a hostile and purely negative attitude.[4] On 16 March Dufferin raised with Berthelot the question of the release by the *Caisse de la Dette* of half a million pounds for the Sudan

[1] FO 27/3274, Dufferin to Salisbury No. 22, 15 Feb. 1896; minutes by Anderson and Salisbury. FO 27/3273, Salisbury to Dufferin No. 56, 21 Feb.
[2] FO 27/3274, Dufferin to Salisbury No. 41, 3 Mar. 1896.
[3] FO 27/3273, Salisbury to Dufferin No. 91, 20 Mar. 1896. D.D.F. XII, No. 318, Courcel to Berthelot 12 Mar.
[4] D.D.F. XII, Nos. 320, 341, 349, Courcel to Berthelot 13, 21 and 24 Mar. 1896; No. 384, Courcel to Hanotaux 9 May 1896. Paul Cambon took the same view: cf. No. 362, Cambon to Berthelot 31 Mar.

operation. Berthelot, in 'language . . . characterised throughout by extreme lucidity, moderation and suavity of expression', hinted that France would comply if London would propose the discussion of 'some arrangement respecting Egypt that might be satisfactory to France'. Courcel, who was now in Paris, had coached his minister well.[1]

On the following day, however, *Le Temps* carried an *Havas* communiqué stating that Berthelot had discussed the Sudan decision with Dufferin and had drawn the ambassador's attention to 'the gravity of its consequences'. Berthelot repudiated all responsibility for this communiqué and disclaimed any intention 'to use language with the faintest breath of menace in it'.[2] Nevertheless, there was an immediate and marked stiffening of the French attitude; Berthelot was under heavy pressure from his colleagues and particularly from his Prime Minister Léon Bourgeois, who was probably responsible for the release of the 'Havas Note'.[3] On 19 March Berthelot formally notified Dufferin that he could not consider the British proposals except as part of a general discussion of the Egyptian question by a conference of the Powers; and he announced in the Chamber that in the view of France a unanimous, and not merely a majority, vote of the *Caisse* would be necessary for the release of the funds requested by Cairo and London.[4]

Courcel, now back at his post, begged Berthelot not to close the discussion in this purely negative way. Salisbury was willing to give an assurance that the Sudan expedition did not imply a decision to remain permanently in Egypt, and that the present application to the *Caisse* would not be treated as a precedent.[5] Salisbury, no less anxious than Courcel to save the rapprochement from total shipwreck, gave the ambassador time to work upon his 'embarrassed and divided' government by instructing Cromer to postpone the meeting of the *Caisse*.[6] On 22 March he permitted Courcel to take away (without formally 'accepting') an unsigned draft in which Salisbury repeated his previous assurances and added that he did not 'think there is the slightest possibility of our wishing to carry [the] advance further South than Dongola'.[7] This was the kind of quasi-promise which the French had good reason not to trust too far; but Courcel continued to urge that an absolute negative by Paris would, 'dans l'état actuel de

---

[1] FO 27/3268, Dufferin to Salisbury tel. No. 7, 16 Mar. 1896. FO 27/3264, Dufferin to to Salisbury No. 90, 17 Mar. D.D.F. xii, No. 325, *note du Ministre* 16 Mar. Cf. Hargreaves, *ubi supra*, pp. 86-91.

[2] FO 27/3264, Dufferin to Salisbury No. 91, 21 Mar. 1896. D.D.F. xii, No. 329, *note du Ministre* 18 Mar.

[3] The origins of the 'Havas Note' are discussed at: FO 27/3264, *loc. cit.*, and Dufferin to Salisbury No. 96, 29 Mar. 1896; FO 78/4892, same to same tel. No. 8, 18 Mar.; G.P. xi, No. 2706, Münster to Hohenlohe 19 Mar.; Vergniol, 'Fachoda', *Revue de France*, Sept. 1936, pp. 121-5.

[4] FO 27/3264, Dufferin to Salisbury No. 83, 19 Mar. 1896; No. 86D, 20 Mar. D.D.F. xii, No. 331, Berthelot to Courcel 19 Mar.; No. 334, Berthelot to Dufferin 19 Mar.

[5] D.D.F. xii, Nos. 335, 341, Courcel to Berthelot 20 and 21 Mar. 1896.

[6] FO 78/4892, Salisbury to Cromer tels. No. 35 and 36, 20 Mar. 1896; tel. No. 40, 22 Mar.

[7] D.D.F. xii, No. 346, Courcel to Berthelot 22 Mar. 1896. A copy of the draft (dated 21 Mar.) is at FO 78/4892.

l'Europe', have very disadvantageous consequences. France would do far better to consider what price she should demand for her acquiescence, especially as 'en tout état de cause . . . les Anglais ont résolu l'expédition'.[1] This plea crossed with an instruction from Berthelot authorising Courcel to accept only that portion of Salisbury's draft containing the assurance on the future of Egypt. The remainder he was to refuse. From this decision all Courcel's pleas failed to budge Berthelot, though the Minister's reasons for this intransigence were not very convincing: the Egyptian bondholders in France were protesting; an unnamed British official in Cairo had been heard to say, 'It's not to Dongola, but to Khartoum that we're going'.[2]

To Courcel's surprise, Salisbury readily signed and communicated, on 25 March, the acceptable portion of his draft.[3] The 'mutilated letter' did not however commit England to anything new; and it did keep the line to Paris still open. But the line did not stay open for many more hours. Berlin closed it by the threat to oppose Britain on the *Caisse* if the meeting were further delayed.[4] The Germans had rejoiced at the Sudan expedition as bringing to an abrupt end the 'flirtation' with France;[5] if Salisbury could not see the logic of this, the Wilhelmstrasse knew how to enforce it. The *Caisse* met on 26 March. The French and Russian Commissioners, having asserted the principle of unanimity, walked out of the meeting. Two days later the conciliatory Berthelot had been forced out of office, and the negotiation with Paris was dead.[6]

Salisbury did not attempt to revive it; indeed, he evaded all discussion of Egypt for many months, doubtless fearing that it could lead only to useless recriminations. He did indeed allow Courcel to discuss Egypt with Cromer in August 1896, perhaps merely to introduce them to one another's point of view. But the interview was abortive even as an essay in political education, for the two men almost completely failed to communicate. Courcel complained that Cromer, with his 'very narrow view, purely local and so to say provincial', completely failed to grasp the international implications of the Egyptian question. Cromer was no less scandalised at Courcel's failure to take seriously the practical problems of administering Egypt: he concluded that Courcel was anxious somehow or other to get a negotiation started, when 'he would trust to luck and adroit diplomacy to turn matters to French advantage'.[7]

---

[1] D.D.F. xii, No. 349, Courcel to Berthelot 24 Mar. 1896.

[2] *Ibid.*, No. 347, Berthelot to Courcel 24 Mar. 1896; No. 350, Courcel to Berthelot 25 Mar.; No. 351, Berthelot to Courcel 25 Mar.

[3] *Ibid.*, No. 350; No. 352, Courcel to Berthelot 25 Mar. 1896. Berthelot had done his best to be conciliatory in form: cf. FO 27/3263, Salisbury to Dufferin No. 105, 25 Mar.

[4] Hargreaves, *ubi supra*, p. 90, citing Cromer's tels. of 23 and 24 Mar. 1896. G.P. does not throw any light on this episode.

[5] G.P. xi, No. 2713, minute by the Kaiser on Radolin to A.A. 21 Mar. 1896. Cf. Münster to Holstein 19 Mar. (Rich and Fisher, *op. cit.* iii, p. 599).

[6] For the circumstances of Berthelot's fall, cf. *infra*, Ch. xii, p. 279.

[7] D.D.F. xii, No. 442, Courcel to Hanotaux 13 Aug. 1896. S P Egypt, Cromer to Salisbury 9 Aug.

Once the Sudan campaign had got under way, any early solution of the Egyptian question in isolation was obviously impossible; but Salisbury on more than one occasion suggested that France might 'disinterest herself' in Egypt if she were compensated elsewhere—a broader version of the solution which he was later to attempt for the special problem of the Upper Nile. It was doubtless with this idea in mind that Salisbury had in August 1895 dwelt so emphatically on the decrepitude of Morocco. But Salisbury did not now confine himself to such indirect hints. In June 1896 he returned to his old theme of the impending collapse of the Ottoman Empire and the need to anticipate it by a peaceful partition; and he suggested that France might be interested in acquiring Syria. Courcel retorted that for France Syria would be more trouble than it was worth—just as Egypt was for England; and he warned Hanotaux, who more than concurred, that there was no surer way of disrupting the Franco-Russe than by instigating a French 'prise de possession' in the Levant.[1] Salisbury was not abashed. In August 1896 he was contemplating an arrangement by which France might acquire Crete;[2] and in October, referring to the critical situation in the Near East, he remarked to Courcel that 'the solution of the drama which is being played at Constantinople may facilitate the solution . . . in Egypt'.[3] In December 1896 Monson, the new ambassador at Paris, suggested that Hanotaux was becoming resigned to the Egyptian situation, and that certain influential sections of French opinion, particularly in financial and commercial circles, were really very satisfied with the *status quo*.[4] Perhaps encouraged by this report, in January 1897 Salisbury twice tempted Courcel with the rich spoils which France might gain from a partition of the Ottoman Empire—Syria, the Holy Places, perhaps a slice of Asia Minor. When Courcel protested that France had no wish to be a buffer between England and Russia, Salisbury replied unperturbed that if these compensations were unsuitable, 'il entrevoyait d'autres moyens de nous désintéresser'—evidently a veiled reference to Morocco, upon the attractions of which Salisbury had dilated a few days earlier.[5]

But Courcel continued to insist that the Egyptian question in isolation contained 'sufficient elements of agreement'; and after January 1897 Salisbury abandoned these attempts to liquidate the whole Nile imbroglio by 'disinteresting' France in Egypt. At best, they were very long and speculative shots, and were far too dependent upon the project of Ottoman partition which had been so stormily received in July 1895. Meanwhile, on the special problem of the Upper Nile,

[1] D.D.F. xii, No. 410, Courcel to Hanotaux 20 June 1896; cf. No. 418, Hanotaux to Paul Cambon 1 July 1896. Hanotaux feared that an Ottoman collapse might *ipso facto* destroy the Russian alliance.
[2] S P Egypt, *loc. cit.*
[3] D.D.F. xii, No. 468, Courcel to Hanotaux 3 Oct. 1896.
[4] FO 27/3267, Monson to Salisbury No. 388, 11 Dec. 1896.
[5] D.D.F. xiii, Nos. 68, 77, Courcel to Hanotaux 18 and 27 Jan. 1897.

complete silence prevailed; and in the course of 1896 decisions were taken in both London and Paris which could only lead, at an early but otherwise unpredictable date, to a direct collision in this disputed sphere—unless meanwhile the Khalifa succeeded in ejecting one or other of the 'enemies of God' who were invading his realm.

XI

FROM HALFA TO OMDURMAN

BRITISH POLICY IN THE SUDAN, 1895-98

ON 1 April 1895 Kimberley had asked Courcel for an assurance that the rumours of a French Nile expedition were unfounded. The ambassador replied that communications were so precarious that a mission might indeed turn up in the Nile basin 'malgré vous et malgré nous'; upon which Rosebery minuted, in anger and alarm: 'It appears . . . that the French do not even profess to have any knowledge of the position or objective of the large armed expeditions that they appear to launch at hazard in Africa! No wonder there are complications.'[1] Within the next few days Rosebery asked Cromer whether he and the Egyptian ministers took seriously the French threat to the Upper Nile and whether they would approve of a forward movement, at any rate as far as Dongola.[2]

Cromer's views on Sudan policy had changed little since 1891, when the shock of Tokar had convinced him that even partial reconquest was neither possible nor desirable 'for some long time to come'. By 1895 Cromer's Egypt had accumulated a handsome little financial surplus; but the more money he saved, the less inclined he was to spend it on reconquering the Sudan. Cromer now aspired, in his smaller sphere, to endow his satrapy with the productive public works which were the pride of the Indian *Raj*. The Asswan dam project was already in his mind, and towards the end of 1894 he was more than ever afraid of 'having this abominable Soudan question forced on us prematurely'.[3] Yet he admitted that 'sooner or later the Egyptians should go back —so far, at least, as Khartoum'.[4] Challenged directly in April 1895, Cromer for the first time admitted that the Upper Nile, as well as the northern and central Sudan, was vital to Egypt. There was, he felt, good reason for disquiet at possible French encroachments, and it would 'not be possible or desirable to maintain a purely passive attitude much longer. . . . The only question is . . . when and how we shall move forward.' But this question Cromer did not answer. Instead,

[1] FO 27/3229, Kimberley to Dufferin No. 112a, 1 Apr. 1895; minute on the draft by Rosebery. Cf. D.D.F. XI, Nos. 429, 432, Courcel to Hanotaux 2 and 3 Apr.
[2] Zetland, *Lord Cromer*, p. 213.
[3] Cromer to Kimberley 8 Nov. 1894, cited *ibid.*, p. 221.
[4] Same to same 29 Mar. 1895, cited *ibid.*, p. 222.

he pointed out that a situation had now been reached where if Britain took any decisive step forward she would 'risk a very serious quarrel' with France. Indeed, in Cromer's view, war with France was 'a not improbable solution of the whole mess'. If Rosebery would accept this risk, Cromer would abandon his public works and stifle his fears of 'bankruptcy and extremely oppressive taxation'.[1]

This was cold comfort for the leader of a government rent by internal schism and tottering on the brink of collapse; but the scare which had evoked the Grey Declaration was by now dying away. As early as 9 April Courcel had assured Kimberley that there was no immediate prospect of the French reaching the Nile. A month later he added that Liotard had no more than about fifty men available for 'exploration'; 'leur petit nombre était une garantie suffisante de leur conduite pacifique, quelle que fût la région où ils se dirigeraient'.[2] On 14 June Chamberlain attempted to trouble the waters by claiming to have authentic knowledge of the progress of the French; but Grey and Harcourt joined forces to denounce his language as dangerous, inept and provocative.[3] Rosebery's enquiry to Cromer had been the last phase of an old scare, not the beginning of a new policy.[4]

In April 1895 Kimberley had been at pains to assure Courcel that the British had no intention of pushing northward from Unyoro;[5] and he was as good as his word. In 1894 there had indeed been two more flying visits to the Wadelai region by British officers. The first of these had taken place in June;[6] it appears to have been a reconnaissance linked with the campaign which Colvile had launched against Kabarega—the campaign which was the germ of the French apprehensions about the 'Colvile mission'. However, at the end of 1894 Colvile, presumably still acting under Rosebery's secret instructions of August 1893, sent a small party to reconnoitre 'down the Nile to its furthest navigable point'. This party was given a hostile reception at Wadelai; but it pushed on northwards past Dufilé and Nimulé to the Fola Falls, 'the furthest navigable point'. On 15 January 1895 they made a treaty with the Dufilé chief, and planted a Union Jack on both sides of the river.[7] But by the spring of 1895 the Foreign Office was no longer encouraging these operations, and was looking coldly even on the campaign against Kabarega.[8] Kimberley never brought himself actually to countermand this campaign; but Kabarega's tenacious

---

[1] FO 633/6, No. 205, Cromer to Rosebery 12 Apr. 1895. Cf. Zetland, *op. cit.*, pp. 213-6
[2] D.D.F. xi, No. 443, Courcel to Hanotaux 10 Apr. 1895; xii, No. 3, same to same 11 May 1895. Cf. FO 27/3229, Kimberley to Dufferin No. 151, 10 May.
[3] Cocheris, *Situation Internationale*, p. 432. Cf. D.D.F. xii, No. 161, footnote.
[4] As early as the end of April Rosebery had concluded that the Sudan question 'had better be allowed to rest': cf. FO 633/6 No. 207, Cromer to Rosebery 4 May 1895.
[5] D.D.F. Nos. 429, 430, 432, Courcel to Hanotaux 2 and 3 Apr. 1895.
[6] For this reconnaissance see: *Africa No. 7 (1895)*, No. 42, Hardinge to Kimberley 20 Oct. 1894, and enclosures. Cf. A. B. Thruston, *African Incidents* (London 1900), pp. 194-7.
[7] FO 27/3368, Gleichen, *Précis of Events on the Upper Nile . . . to March 1898*, p. 12. S. Vandeleur, *Campaigning on the Upper Nile and Niger* (London 1898), pp. 23-36. F. I. Maxse, *Seymour Vandeleur* (London 1905), pp. 48-50.
[8] Cf. *Africa No. 7 (1895)*, No. 61, Anderson to Jackson (Uganda) 6 Apr. 1895.

resistance was sufficient guarantee against any excess of zeal in pushing to the north. On 28 May 1895, a fortnight before his fall, Rosebery did indeed extort his Cabinet's consent to the construction of the Mombasa railway.[1] But the immediate importance of this mere decision of principle was perhaps less for Nile strategy than for Rosebery himself —as a demonstration that he could still win a victory over Harcourt.

Meanwhile, the French also seemed to be observing this unofficial and unavowed 'désistement mutuel'. By June 1895 even the suspicious Anderson was easy in his mind. Captain Decazes had recently lectured on the situation on the upper Ubangi; his account made it, in Anderson's view, 'extremely improbable that there can be any French advance on the Nile'.[2] In August Anderson was further cheered by reports of Liotard's anxiety at the Mahdist concentration in Dar Fertit, on his left flank.[3] In the same month Wingate refused to be impressed by a Congolese suggestion that a French expedition of two officers and fifty men could establish itself at Fashoda. Wingate confidently reported that the difficulties of 'the worst road in Africa', the 'pestilential climate' and the opposition of the Mahdists would deny success to anything less than 'a properly organised expedition with commanders who could raise and combine the Bahr el Ghazal tribes'. Evidently, thought Anderson, Leopold had gone back to his old game of trying, for London's benefit, 'to magnify the risk of a French advance'.[4]

The Marchand Mission was approved in principle by the Foreign Minister Berthelot on 30 November 1895.[5] On 5 December the journal *Politique Coloniale* announced that a Captain of Marine Infantry was to be posted to the upper Ubangi as Lieutenant-Governor. But of this appointment the journal strongly disapproved; military recklessness might compromise Liotard's 'prudent and wise' policy and perhaps provoke hostilities with the Mahdists. The watchword on the upper Ubangi should be not expansion, but consolidation, for which indeed the whole of the 1896 budget had been earmarked. This article was the first shot in a regular campaign against the Marchand Mission conducted by the *Politique Coloniale*; the reasons for this hostility, quite untypical of the colonialist press, are unknown. But Sir Thomas Sanderson, naturally taking this article as representative of colonialist opinion, minuted: 'This does not look like any immediate move forward by the French'.[6] The War Office I.D. was inclined to identify the captain of Marines with a certain Vermot, who had served in the

[1] L.Q.V. 3, ii, pp. 515-6, Rosebery to the Queen 27 and 28 May 1895.
[2] FO 27/3231, minute by Anderson 24 June 1895, on Dufferin to Kimberley No. 174.
[3] Cf. FO 27/3232, Dufferin to Salisbury No. 222, 22 Aug. 1895.
[4] FO 27/3258, memo. by Anderson 20 Aug. 1895.
[5] D.D.F. xii, No. 219, Berthelot to Guieysse 30 Nov. 1895; cf. *infra*, Ch. xii, pp. 275-6.
[6] FO 27/3233, minute by Sanderson on Dufferin to Salisbury No. 317, 6 Dec. 1895. The development of this polemic by the *Politique Coloniale* can be traced in: FO 27/3275, Dufferin to Salisbury Nos. 95, 107, of 5 and 16 June 1896; FO 27/3276, same to same No. 177, 11 Sept. 1896.

upper Ubangi and was then in France on leave. In any case, the I.D. thought the French forces on the upper Ubangi 'too small and too scattered to have any sinister designs at present'.[1]

Nothing further seems to have been heard until early April 1896, when Howard at Paris learned from a journalist that the captain of Marines was in fact Marchand. Recalling Marchand's brilliant exploits as a military explorer in West Africa, Howard suggested that his latest posting might well imply a French push to the Nile; but he pointed out that there was no provision for expeditions in the current upper Ubangi budget.[2] Howard's report was sent to the I.D., but their observations do not seem to have been preserved. But the I.D. remained completely unperturbed when on 11 May 1896 the *Politique Coloniale* announced that Marchand was to sail in five days time to lead an exploring mission on the upper Ubangi. Their comfortable verdict was that Marchand's movements were of little real import-ance, for there was: 'no reason to suppose that he would be accom-panied by any Expeditionary Force, and the present strength of the French on the upper Ubanghi would not allow of any active opera-tions to the North or the North-West'.[3] The argus-eyed *Intelligence britannique* had been caught napping; Marchand's first two échelons had sailed on 25 April and 10 May.

The I.D. produced this optimistic appreciation on 18 May 1896; yet already on 11 March the British had decided to take action in the northern Sudan. Whatever the reasons for this decision, apprehensions about the security of the Upper Nile can hardly have been among them. Indeed, in November 1895 Salisbury had explained to Cromer that any British move in the north would at once *provoke* 'a French forward movement on the Upper Nile' to which Britain could make no effective reply until the Mombasa railway had been completed.[4] With this railway Salisbury was indeed pushing ahead as fast as possible. Immediately on his return to office he had obtained a token initial grant of £20,000. But this was only the top of the iceberg. So urgent was the railway in Salisbury's eyes that he was prepared to throw Gladstonian finance overboard and build it with public money, and even to begin construction on the strength of Macdonald's very sketchy preliminary survey.[5] 'If I could command such a result', he told Cromer on 8 November 1895, there should be 'no forward move-ment in Egypt till our railway has reached the lake'. Equally, and for precisely the same reason, there must be no immediate action in the south. Here, too, 'our only chance is to keep the thing quiet until our railway is sufficiently far advanced'.[6]

---

[1] FO 27/3259, D.M.I. to Sanderson 13 Dec. 1895. For Vermot's activities, see MC, G.C., VI 13.
[2] FO 27/3275, memo. by Howard enclosed in Dufferin to Salisbury No. 63, 9 Apr. 1896.
[3] *Ibid.*, Dufferin to Salisbury No. 80, 12 May 1896; FO 27/3300, I.D. to F.O. 18 May.
[4] SP Egypt, Salisbury to Cromer 8 Nov. 1895.
[5] Cecil, *Salisbury* IV, pp. 315-6. Robinson and Gallagher, *Africa and the Victorians*, pp. 350-1.   [6] SP, *loc. cit.* L.Q.V. 3, ii, p. 578, Salisbury to Bigge 5 Dec. 1895.

In the south, Salisbury was well able 'to keep things quiet' so far as British action was concerned; but on the northern front he had inserted the proviso 'if I could command such a result'. Here, as Salisbury recognised, he was not fully his own master. The increasingly desperate plight of Italy in Ethiopia, and at Kassala in the eastern Sudan, could not leave Salisbury completely unmoved. The fate of Italy in Africa would not perhaps have been a matter of major importance when Salisbury had left office in 1892. The pattern of European alignments had then been reasonably stable. The Triple Alliance dominated Europe. Britain, while contriving to maintain tolerable relations with France, secured German goodwill by supporting Italy in the Mediterranean and Austria at the Straits, thereby reinforcing the weak points in the armour of the Triplice. By the end of 1895, without any formal change in official alignments, this pattern had dissolved. The maturing of the France-Russe, combined with the German distrust of Rosebery, had brought Berlin to desert Austria at the Straits and informally to re-insure with Russia. The Russians thereupon embarked on a series of threatening gestures at the Straits which were almost as unwelcome to the French as to the British, while at the same time treating their French ally as little more than a milch cow for loans. Meanwhile, German opposition to Britain in Africa and Oceania estranged London and Berlin to a point which reached outright hostility in January 1896. Salisbury, by now profoundly suspicious of the Germans and rebuffed in his attempts to reach an understanding with Russia, had turned away from the Triple Alliance and had sought a rapprochement with France; a move welcome to Paris as an escape from total dependence on an ally who, in addition to her other shortcomings, seemed far too ready to play Germany's game. Out of this very fluid situation—the so-called 'fluctuation of alliances'—new alignments might well crystallise; and for this process the total collapse of Italy in Africa could quite conceivably be, if not the cause, at least the catalyst. Italy was still mainly of value to Berlin because she brought with her the prospect of British naval support in the Mediterranean. But if, as the Germans increasingly feared, Britain had deserted Italy for France, Italy was well-nigh worthless as an ally. And if London allowed Italy to collapse completely in Africa, without making even a gesture of assistance, how could the conclusion be escaped that Britain had in fact deserted her?—especially when Salisbury had just shown himself so reluctant to support Austria at the Straits.[1] Would Italy, feeble as she was, even wish to remain a member of the Triplice if the total wreck of her imperial ambitions strengthened the irredentist, francophile Italian Left? Salisbury could hardly look

---

[1] In fact, Salisbury had not only refused to extend British obligations under the Second Mediterranean Agreement, but had let it be known that he no longer regarded this Agreement as binding (B.D. viii, No. 1, memo. by Sanderson 1 July 1902). But the Austrians seem to have concealed from Berlin the full extent of their disappointment—cf. G.P. xi, Nos. 2659-69.

upon these prospects without foreboding. It was impossible to predict the detailed outcome if the Triple Alliance collapsed; but one strong possibility, and a particularly dangerous one for England, seemed already foreshadowed by the warm informal friendship between Germany and Russia.

In November 1895 such speculations may still have seemed rather remote; four months later they were to be much less so. Indeed, even before the old year was out Italy had begun to cast her shadow on policy towards the northern Sudan. After the Italian defeat at Amba Alagi on 7 December, Cromer became anxious about their position at Kassala; if the Italians were expelled by the Mahdists, the local effects would be unfortunate. He suggested that a couple of Egyptian battalions might be sent from Suakin to Kassala; but his recommendation was far from enthusiastic, and he warned Salisbury that the German Consul in Cairo was suspiciously eager to involve Egypt in military collaboration with Italy.[1] Salisbury did not authorise action; but on 11 January 1896 he asked Cromer whether 'a demonstration in the neighbourhood of Wadi Halfa would be useful to create a diversion' in favour of the Italians.[2] After the unpleasant Zeila affair, Salisbury needed some gesture to prove that he was not completely indifferent to Italy's fate; and perhaps a mere demonstration in the extreme north would not trigger off the French advance in the south. But Cromer vetoed a demonstration: the ultimate withdrawal of the Egyptians would be regarded, not only in Omdurman but throughout the Near East, as a major victory for the Khalifa. He suggested instead an advance up the Nile, perhaps even as far as Dongola; or an advance from Suakin towards Berber. The latter would be cheaper and of more practical help to the Italians. But Salisbury, doubtless fearing that operations on this scale would provoke the French to action in the south, decided on 14 February to await further developments at Kassala.[3]

On 24 February 1896 Ferrero told Sanderson unofficially that Italy would be forced to evacuate Kassala unless she received assistance.[4] Cromer now strongly advised an immediate advance towards Kassala from Suakin. He recognised that such an advance might involve expenditure so heavy as to put his beloved Egyptian administration 'more or less at the mercy of the French'. But for the sake of relations 'with the Italians and indirectly with the Germans', he thought it impossible for Britain to 'stand completely aside while [the] Italians are beaten as I greatly suspect they will be'. 'On the whole I would stand the risk and go on.'[5] But Wolseley, the Commander-in-Chief,

[1] SP Egypt, Cromer to Salisbury 18 Dec. 1895.
[2] Shibeika, British Policy in the Sudan, p. 352, citing Salisbury to Cromer tel. No. 1, 11 Jan. 1896.
[3] Ibid., pp. 352-3, citing Cromer to Salisbury tel. No. 1, 14 Jan. 1896; Salisbury to Cromer tel. No. 2, 14 Jan.
[4] Ibid., p. 353, citing: memo. by Sanderson 24 Feb. 1896; Salisbury to Cromer tel. No. 10, 24 Feb.; Cromer to Salisbury tel. No. 17, 26 Feb.
[5] SP Egypt, Cromer to Salisbury tel., 26 Feb. 1896.

condemned Cromer's proposals as likely to lead to an expedition to rescue the rescuers. More important, on 29 February Salisbury made up his mind that the loss of Kassala by the Italians did not justify the military and the political hazards of intervention. 'The power of the Khalifa tends steadily to diminish, *and a waiting game is the obvious policy.* Whenever we are masters of the valley of the Nile Kassala will be easily dealt with. Till then it has little value.'[1] Salisbury was still determined to avoid all piecemeal advance in the north, with its danger of provoking a French thrust in the south. When Salisbury wrote of being 'masters of the Nile valley' there is no need to suppose that he was referring exclusively to the *northern* Sudan.

On the following day, 1 March 1896, General Baratieri, goaded into action by Crispi's insulting telegrams, led the Italian forces in Ethiopia to a catastrophic defeat at Adowa. On 5 March Crispi resigned, to the accompaniment of violently hostile popular demonstrations in most of the large Italian cities. For a day or two the demonstrators were masters of the streets. For a moment it seemed that Adowa had put a match to all the combustible material generated by Italy's chronic social and economic discontents, and had precipitated a revolutionary situation. Italy might be driven not only out of Africa— as the demonstrators were demanding—but out of the Triplice as well. Meanwhile, until 10 March, Italy was still without a Cabinet.[2] Salisbury was perforce deaf to Ferrero's unofficial requests, on 6 and 8 March, for 'Anglo-Egyptian' military intervention;[3] in the circumstances these represented little more than the personal wishes of the ambassador. But in the purely diplomatic sphere Salisbury was already moving to underpin the Triple Alliance. On 4 March he went out of his way to explain to Hatzfeldt that the recent negotiations with France had related to colonial details only and did not imply any general rapprochement; in particular, there had never been any question of the evacuation of Egypt. Hatzfeldt, impressed, compared this conversation to those he had enjoyed with Salisbury in the early nineties, when the two men had been able to discuss even the most delicate questions with complete frankness and cordiality. Salisbury also spoke to the Austrian ambassador in a similar vein; and Hatzfeldt confidently concluded that England had abandoned any idea of an entente with France directed against the Triple Alliance.[4]

But re-insurance with the Triplice would, unfortunately, require

---

[1] Shibeika, *op. cit.*, p. 354, citing Salisbury to Cromer tel. No. 11, 29 Feb. 1896 (emphasis supplied).

[2] Langer, *The Diplomacy of Imperialism*, pp. 277-81. Bourgin, 'Francesco Crispi', pp. 145-51. FO 45/751, Ford to Salisbury tels. No. 10, 13, 15 of 7, 9 and 10 Mar. 1896. Cf. D.D.F. XII, No. 362, Paul Cambon to Bourgeois 31 Mar. 1896; C. Giraudeau, 'Après Adowa, Avant Dongola', *Revue Politique et Littéraire* 21 Mar. 1896, pp. 362-4—a very shrewd appreciation.

[3] G.P. XI, Nos. 2774, 2776, Hatzfeldt to A.A. 6 and 8 Mar. 1896. Cf. FO 45/747, Salisbury to Ford No. 65, 20 May 1896.

[4] G.P. XI, No. 2693, Hatzfeldt to A.A. 4 Mar. 1896; No. 2694, Hatzfeldt to Hohenlohe 5 Mar.

deeds as well as words. By 10 March, when the popular unrest in Italy had died down and a reliably Tripliste government under di Rudinì had been installed at Rome, Salisbury could no longer avoid action. On that day Ferrero submitted to Sanderson an aide-mémoire requesting a diversion in favour of Italy 'du côté du Nil'; he was doubtless aware of Salisbury's previous refusal to act in the eastern Sudan.[1] On 11 March the Cabinet approved an advance up the Nile 'as far—and no farther—than we can [go] without any undue effort on the part of Egypt'. Above all, no risks were to be taken. The Gordon disaster still cast its long shadow over Sudan policy; even Chamberlain feared that 'the Government would be deserted by its own followers' if a British force had to be sent to the rescue of the Egyptians.[2] Indeed, at the Cabinet on 12 March, which was to settle military policy in consultation with Wolseley, ministers seemed afraid of their own temerity. Lansdowne, the War Minister, was inclined to favour a mere demonstration rather than an advance, so as not to 'expose Kitchener to temptation'. Salisbury, too, seems to have thought a demonstration a lesser evil than too ambitious an advance.[3] The final decision of the Cabinet was an odd blend of timid advance and unprovocative demonstration. There were to be two separate operations: first, 'the immediate occupation of Akasheh', an obscure hamlet only thirty miles or so beyond the Egyptian advance post at Sarras; second, a 'demonstration towards Abu Hamed', across the Nubian Desert from Halfa. How far towards Abu Hamed was at first obscure; but it later transpired that the troops should at least go beyond Murrat Wells (already occupied by friendly 'Abābda tribesmen) and 'ultimately retire again'. It was 'most important that [these operations] should be carried out at once'.[4]

Such were the orders which the War Office sent to Egypt on 12 and 13 March 1896. But they were not sent to Cromer or to Kitchener; these orders for a purely Egyptian advance were sent to General Knowles, the commander of the British Army of Occupation.[5] However, Cromer was informed, on the night of 12-13 March, in a telegram intended for publication, that in response to an Italian request for a diversion in favour of Kassala, it had been decided

> that the occupation of Dongola would be the most effective demonstration.... It will also tend to repel any disposition to attack

---

[1] FO 170/504, Ferrero to Sanderson 10 Mar. 1896. Cf. Hargreaves, 'Entente Manquée', *C.H.J.* 1953, pp. 84-5.
[2] Chamberlain to Salisbury 11 Mar. 1896, quoted in J. L. Garvin, *Life of Joseph Chamberlain*, III (London 1932), pp. 169-70. Cf. FO 45/747, *loc. cit.*, which makes it quite clear that *two* cabinets were held, on 11 and 12 Mar.
[3] Salisbury to Chamberlain 12 Mar. 1896, quoted Garvin, *op. cit.* III, pp. 170-1.
[4] FO 78/4892, War Office to Knowles tel. unnumb., 13 Mar. 1896; Salisbury to Cromer tel. No. 23, 16 Mar.
[5] This attempt to work through Knowles was evidently due to Wolseley; on the 12th Lansdowne had assumed that Kitchener would be in charge (Garvin, *loc. cit.*). Cf. G. C. A. Arthur, *Life of Lord Kitchener*, I (London 1920), p. 188; E. W. C. Sandes, *The Royal Engineers in Egypt and the Sudan* (Chatham 1937), p. 150.

Egypt which the recent victories of Africans over Europeans may have created among the Dervishes. Of course, it is intended to keep Dongola. . . . No secrecy at all is necessary.[1]

Simultaneously, the Queen, Dufferin and Sir Clare Ford at Rome were informed that an advance had been authorised 'as far as Dongola'[2]—a less precise formulation, on which the most illuminating commentary is the closing passage of the War Office telegram to Knowles: 'As to contemplated advance on Dongola, confine yourself for present to collection of supplies at Wady Halfa. . . . Avoid all action which might lead to a belief that we may not go to Dongola.'[3]

Salisbury explained some of these apparent contradictions to Cromer in a private telegram of 13 March. The main object of the operations was to help the Italians; but the Nile rather than the eastern Sudan had been chosen as their theatre partly because they would thus be more profitable to Egypt, but also to avoid the risk of crossing swords with the Abyssinians 'which might take us far'. It might indeed; even after Omdurman had been fought and won, fears of a clash with the Ethiopians continued to weigh heavily on military planning in the Sudan.[4] But the Italians would not be helped much unless the Khalifa thought that a genuine invasion was being mounted. It was therefore necessary to state 'an objective, however conditional and contingent'.

> For this reason publicity was essential—and indeed would have to be carried even to a certain amount of bluffing . . . I have told the Ambassadors that we have sanctioned an advance to Dongola. We do not hold ourselves bound to go so far . . . if our object can be obtained with a less advance.

Salisbury lamented that the Italian 'capacity for being beaten' had made action necessary two or three years before 'we were quite ready in the valley of the Nile'. 'But it would not have been safe, either from an African or European point of view, to sit quite still while they were being crushed.'[5]

It has been suggested that the 'deliberations of the Cabinet must have been singularly confused. Several purposes were kept in view, but the plan adopted served none of them efficiently.'[6] The only purposes actually 'kept in view'—as opposed to those invented later to impress the public[7]—were to help the Italians and 'to plant the foot of Egypt rather further up the Nile'.[8] Clearly, 'the foot of Egypt' was to take only

---

[1] FO 78/4893 (print), Salisbury to Cromer tel. No. 17, 12 Mar. 1896. According to Rodd, it came 'like a bolt from the blue' (Rodd, *Social and Diplomatic Memories*, II, p. 86).

[2] FO 78/4893, Salisbury to Dufferin tel. No. 30, to Ford tel. No. 24, both of 12 Mar. 1896. L.Q.V. 3, iii, p. 33, Salisbury to the Queen 12 Mar.

[3] FO 78/4892, W.O. to Knowles 13 Mar. 1896.

[4] Cf. *infra*, Ch. xv, p. 332.

[5] SP Egypt, Salisbury to Cromer 13 Mar. 1896.

[6] Hargreaves, *ubi supra*, p. 85.

[7] The story was put out, both for foreign and domestic consumption, that the advance was necessary to forestall a Mahdist invasion of Egypt. Unfortunately, Cromer's 1895 report (published, by a deplorable coincidence, on 12 Mar. 1896) had emphasised the 'strictly defensive attitude' of the Mahdists.

[8] SP Egypt, *loc. cit.*

a very short step; and the operations planned would give very little, if any, practical military help to Italy. But what Italy needed was not so much military help—her position in Ethiopia was already past praying for, and her continued occupation of Kassala of no intrinsic importance—but rather a gesture of solidarity and goodwill, as some proof that her old friend England had not deserted her in the hour of need. Far from being confused, Salisbury, Balfour, Lansdowne and Chamberlain all seem to have understood pretty clearly that the policy was to make 'a successful feint in the interests of Italy', without engaging in serious military operations. The confusion, such as it was, arose almost entirely out of the Cabinet's attempt to hit on some non-existent compromise between a mere demonstration, which after Adowa would have been inadequate even as a gesture; and a genuine advance, which carried risks of different kinds in both the northern and the southern Sudan.[1] Indeed, Salisbury evidently feared that the operations authorised—or, rather, the operations announced —would be enough to start the French moving in the south. Immediately after the March decision he asked his Chancellor of the Exchequer for a cool three million for the Mombasa railway. Hicks Beach resisted, like Goschen in 1891; but 'Black Michael', formidable though he was, did not enjoy Goschen's independent political influence and was forced to give way. In July 1896 the Commons voted the funds.[2] Meanwhile, in June, the proclamation of a protectorate over Unyoro had given the 'southern base' a legal existence.

Salisbury had gone to considerable lengths to achieve the 'essential publicity' for his advance in the northern Sudan. On 13 March *The Times* had announced it 'in a telegram purporting to come from Cairo, really written in London', before Cromer could even go through the formality of consulting the Khedive. Cromer thought the advance 'mainly . . . in Italian interests' and 'from the English and Egyptian point of view . . . certainly premature'. Nevertheless, and in spite of the fact that it had been sprung upon him in so unceremonious a manner, Cromer had 'no wish to deprecate' the decision. 'I can well understand that from the point of view of general policy it may be absolutely necessary, whatever be the local objections.' But he did beg Salisbury to bear in mind the implications of what he was doing. There might be a diplomatic crisis: 'If once Dongola is occupied the whole Soudan question will possibly be raised.' There would 'almost certainly' be an internal Egyptian crisis, which even Cromer doubted his power to control unless the Khedive and his ministers could be convinced that Egyptian interests were being taken seriously and that Egypt was not being merely used as a pawn in England's diplomatic game. Cromer agreed with the Khedive (a rare phenomenon) that 'the whole affair

---

[1] S P Egypt, F O 78/4892. *loc. cit.* Garvin, *loc. cit.* (Salisbury to Chamberlain 12 Mar.) Lansdowne to Salisbury, S P Cabinet Memoranda, 24 Mar. 1896.

[2] Robinson and Gallagher, *op. cit.*, pp. 350-1. It is noteworthy that Salisbury increased the pressure on Hicks Beach on 6 Apr., *after* the launching of the northern advance.

[was] a move to help [the] Italians'. He therefore pleaded that, if advance there must be, it at least should not stop short of Dongola. Any less advance 'would be impossible to justify to the Khedive and the Egyptian ministers'.[1]

With these warnings before him, Salisbury began to have second thoughts. When on the morning of 14 March the Italians decided to abandon Kassala, he telegraphed to Cromer countermanding the operation; it might now be possible to 'sit still' without incurring quite such grave suspicion of deliberately abandoning Italy in order to curry favour with France. But later in the day Rome changed its mind again and decided to hold on at Kassala after all, and Salisbury had no alternative but to reinstate the advance.[2] Meanwhile Cromer had learned not only that the published objective of Dongola was largely a bluff, but that the Egyptian Army was to be placed through Knowles under the orders of the War Office, with Cromer himself—to say nothing of the Khedive—completely outside the chain of command. On 14 March he permitted himself an almost minatory protest which hinted pretty clearly that a resignation might be proffered unless matters were mended. 'Control of the whole machine here', he complained, 'has passed out of my hands.' Orders were being given, and expenditure incurred, for which Cromer could take no responsibility, since there was not even a pretence of consulting the Egyptian Government. Finally, he repeated that it was utterly impossible for him to justify an advance merely to Akasha.[3]

On 15 March Salisbury called a Cabinet to consider Sudan policy in the light of Cromer's telegrams. Cromer was granted the authority he demanded: Kitchener was to be responsible direct to Cromer, and Cromer himself was to take his orders not from the War Office but from the Foreign Office. Wolseley's ill-advised attempt to side-track Cromer and Kitchener had in fact cost him all effective influence on the campaign. Towards the end of March Cromer announced his intention to treat War Office directives 'not as instructions, but simply as views of H.M.G.'s military advisers, for careful consideration'. Salisbury did not challenge this; and Cromer also successfully resisted Wolseley's attempt to saddle Kitchener with a 'War Office Liaison Officer'.[4] He had less cause for satisfaction with the Cabinet's deliberations on Dongola policy. Salisbury explained once more that the move had two objects. The first was 'to keep the Dervishes off the Italians'. This, Cromer was solemnly told, would be achieved by the demonstra-

---

[1] FO 78/4892, Cromer to Salisbury tels. No. 26, 27, 28, 29 and 30, all of 13 Mar. 1896.
[2] FO 78/4893 (print), Salisbury to Cromer tels. No. 20 and 21, 14 Mar. 1896. Cf. ibid., Ford's tels. No. 18 and 19, 14 Mar.
[3] Ibid., Cromer to Salisbury tel. No. 31, 14 Mar. 1896.
[4] FO 78/4892, tels.: Salisbury to Cromer No. 23, 16 Mar. 1896; Cromer to Salisbury No. 66, 27 Mar.; Salisbury to Cromer No. 49, 26 Mar.; Cromer to Salisbury No. 65, 27 Mar. Cromer was however forced to accept an Italian liaison officer, in spite of his warning that this would be a further provocation to the Khedive (FO 78/4893, tels. Cromer-Salisbury 6-16 Apr. 1896).

tion 'beyond Murrat Wells'. The second object was 'to restore a portion of her lost territory to Egypt', and to this end there would be an advance to Akasha 'with an avowed intention of going to Dongola'. 'But we are not bound to go there in haste'—indeed, it would be a good idea to go there as slowly as possible, so as to give the Mahdists plenty of time to reinforce Dongola and so 'take the strain off the Italians'.[1]

It was perfectly clear that Egyptian interests were being ruthlessly subordinated to considerations of European policy—precisely as Cromer had feared all along. But still he stuck to his guns. Time and again during the next few weeks he urged that the advance *must* reach Dongola 'whatever may be the difficulties and objections'; and he warned Salisbury that 'native Anglophobe opposition' was very strong, and that any open expression of disapproval by the Khedive would have a disastrous effect on the Egyptian troops.[2] Salisbury turned a deaf ear; while Wolseley attempted to crab Kitchener's campaign by abounding in objections to any but the most timid of advances—unless, of course, British troops were to be employed, a policy for which Wolseley was now pushing very hard as part of his manœuvres to regain control of the operations.[3] It was not until 8 May that Cromer received even a clear directive on Dongola, and this was couched in a forbiddingly negative form: Kitchener must not go to Dongola until his railhead had reached Firka.[4] But on 7 June Kitchener routed and dispersed the Mahdist garrison at Firka. This impressive military success was an unanswerable argument; and on 11 June, in a telegram seen and approved by Lansdowne at the War Office, Salisbury at last gave Cromer a free hand as far as Dongola.[5]

Cromer's prolonged struggle to ensure that Egyptian interests should even *seem* to be taken seriously is sufficient commentary on the alleged objective of 'planting the foot of Egypt rather further up the Nile'. In the course of this debate Salisbury did indeed draw Cromer's attention to the possible French threat to the Upper Nile and the recent signs of renewed activity by King Leopold. 'In short, the Nile valley is in the diplomatic market and considering how much Egypt depends on the Nile we can hardly keep her from bidding at the sale.'[6] But the date of this letter (1 April 1896) suggests that Salisbury was casting around rather desperately for almost any argument which might convince the aggrieved Cromer that Egyptian interests were not

[1] FO 78/4892, Salisbury to Cromer tel. No. 23, 16 Mar.
[2] *Ibid.*, Cromer to Salisbury tels. No. 39, 40, 41, 44 and 76 of 17, 18, 19 and 31 Mar. 1896; Cromer to Sanderson, private, 1 Apr. FO 78/4893, same to same, private, 21 Apr.; Cromer to Salisbury tel. No. 132, 5 May. SP Egypt, Cromer to Salisbury 27 Mar. Meanwhile, Cromer had the difficult task of keeping up Kitchener's morale by promising an ultimate advance to Dongola while forbidding any immediate movement beyond Firka.
[3] FO 78/4893, Salisbury to Cromer tel. No. 50, 26 Mar. 1896; D.M.I. to F.O. 9 Apr.; Salisbury to Cromer tel. No. 72, 1 May. SP Egypt, Salisbury to Cromer 1 Apr. and 1 May. Cf. Wolseley to Lansdowne 2 Apr. 1896, quoted F. Maurice and G. Arthur, *The Life of Lord Wolseley* (London 1924), II, p. 301.
[4] SP Egypt, Salisbury to Cromer 8 May 1896.
[5] FO 78/4894, Salisbury to Cromer tel. No. 94, 11 June 1896.
[6] SP Egypt, Salisbury to Cromer 1 Apr. 1896.

being entirely neglected. It was of course absurd to suggest that an advance which might not even reach Dongola could in any way safeguard the Upper Nile, and Cromer told Salisbury so pretty bluntly: 'When we get to Dongola we shall be little nearer the exercise of a real control over the Nile valley than we are at present.'[1] Salisbury did not in fact believe his own argument: on 2 September 1896, when Kitchener was well on his way to Dongola, he told the Queen that the protection of British interests on the Upper Nile was still entirely dependent on the completion of the railway. 'For the next two years there is no remedy. We must trust to our luck.'[2] Indeed, Salisbury's remark in his telegram of 13 March that Britain had been forced to act two or three years before she was ready,[3] probably refers not to the training state of the Egyptian Army but to the estimated period for the completion of the Mombasa railway.

There is no doubt a sense in which 'the ultimate aim' of the March advance was the reconquest of the Sudan. Some ministers—Chamberlain, it seems was one—flattered themselves that the Khalifa might collapse at the first blow.[4] But Salisbury, though he believed the Khalifa's power to be on the decline, had never subscribed to the fashionable belief that the Mahdist State lived on in a perpetual agony of dissolution. Action in the northern Sudan had been forced upon him by the Italian collapse. It had therefore better be taken on the Nile itself as a first step, however short and tentative, towards ultimate reconquest. But in March 1896 Salisbury was no more able than Cromer had been in April 1895 to predict when Kitchener would reach Khartoum—to say nothing of Fashoda. It was still a matter of 'sooner or later'; and, in the minds of the whole Cabinet including even Chamberlain, very much later if the Mahdists put up any sort of fight.[5] It passes belief that Salisbury in March 1896 launched a reconquest of the Sudan on the off-chance that an unexpectedly quick success might forestall the French occupation of the Upper Nile which it was in his view almost certain to provoke. But then, in March 1896 Salisbury did not launch a reconquest of the Sudan. He authorised, not without grave misgivings, an advance to Akasha and a demonstration 'beyond Murrat Wells'.

The Upper Nile situation certainly did not prompt Salisbury's decision, but tended on the contrary to discourage it. Egyptian interests in the northern Sudan played a minimal part. Salisbury acted, certainly to prevent a further disintegration of the Triple Alliance, and quite probably to prevent a thoroughly disgruntled Germany from drawing yet closer to Russia. Courcel remarks with great insight that if Salisbury had succeeded in reaching a satisfactory

---

[1] *Ibid.*, Cromer to Salisbury 24 Apr.
[2] L.Q.V. 3, iii, pp. 72-3, Salisbury to Bigge 2 Sept. 1896.
[3] S P Egypt, Salisbury to Cromer 13 Mar. 1896.
[4] Chamberlain to Salisbury 11 Mar. 1896 (Garvin, *op. cit.* iii, pp. 169-70).
[5] *Ibid.*, *loc. cit.*

modus vivendi with Russia 'il eût peut-être fait bon marché du maintien de la Triple Alliance'.[1] As a move in European politics Salisbury's decision certainly had the desired effect. The Russian ambassador in London perhaps put it too highly when he wrote of the Triplice being 're-born from its ashes'; but Salisbury certainly restored to health an alliance which had become gravely, perhaps dangerously, sick.[2] In so doing he had however not merely re-insured with the Triple Alliance. He had committed himself to it, and more particularly to Berlin. As early as 13 March Lascelles had read to Marschall a confidential letter announcing Salisbury's intention of 'leaning towards' the Triplice in future.[3] Salisbury, who in March 1896 had by no means lost his fears of an excessive dependence on Berlin, at the same time made strenuous efforts to keep the Anglo-French rapprochement alive. But this was an impossible task, in spite of Courcel's hearty co-operation. A few weeks later, Courcel himself told Salisbury, 'Vous avez fait votre choix!'.[4]

In reality, the 'choice' was hardly a choice at all. However Courcel might wrap up the fact in fair words, the price of a genuine entente with France was still the evacuation of Egypt to be followed by an Anglo-French condominium of influence. Even Salisbury's great authority could hardly have made this sacrifice acceptable to his country and his party; and this was doubtless in itself enough to enforce the rejection of the French 'choice'. Moreover, Egypt now seemed to be more indispensable strategically than ever before. Precisely in February 1896, the naval experts had reached the conclusion that there was no way of preventing a Russian seizure of the Straits which would give their Black Sea Fleet the run of the Levant. To meet this danger, Britain must herself have a naval base in the Levant; Malta was inconveniently remote. The Admiralty therefore recommended that Alexandria be developed as a base; and this of course implied 'the absolute and permanent occupation of Egypt, and the determination to hold it against all comers! ... By taking Egypt absolutely, we should secure what we have so long sought to maintain by keeping Russia out of Constantinople.'[5]

Of course, Russia was formidable in the Mediterranean only in combination with France. But the bare statement of this fact reveals yet another obstacle to an Anglo-French entente—the French dilemma of choice between England and Russia in the Levant and at the Straits.

[1] D.D.F. XII, No. 384, Courcel to Hanotaux 9 May 1896. Cf. *ibid.*, No. 320, Courcel to Berthelot 13 Mar. 1896; No. 362, Paul Cambon to Bourgeois 31 Mar.
[2] Staal, *Correspondance*, p. 313, Staal to Lobanov 1 Apr. 1896. Rich and Fisher, *The Holstein Papers*, III, p. 601, Holstein to Radolin 22 Mar. 1896. Cf. Giraudeau, *ubi supra*, p. 362.   [3] G.P. XI, No. 2779, memo. by Marschall 13 Mar. 1896.
[4] D.D.F. XII, No. 383, Courcel to Hanotaux 7 May 1896.
[5] Hatzfeldt reported that Salisbury had 'seen that he must pay too high a price for [an] understanding [with France], and has admitted this to me' (Rich and Fisher, *op. cit.* III, p. 607, Hatzfeldt to Holstein 28 Apr. 1896). Cf. Marder, *The Anatomy of British Sea-Power*, pp. 244-50, citing D.N.I. memoranda of 12 Nov. 1895 and 29 Feb. 1896; and Appx. IV, D.N.I. memorandum of 28 Oct. 1896.

The entente might become possible if Britain and Russia could settle their differences here by the partition of the Ottoman Empire; but Salisbury did not confuse this boldly speculative flight with the practical exigencies of day-to-day policy. Again, an entente with England was for France a question of domestic as well as foreign policy. The 'conservative, military, clerical elements' in France had welcomed the Franco-Russe not least because of their traditional hostility to Britain. It was absurd to believe that Berthelot could over-come these powerful forces when he was unable to prevent his own officials from reversing in the Niger negotiations the trend of his policy towards England. For Salisbury to have thrown over the Triplice in order to seek an entente with France would evidently have been to exchange the substance of security for its shadow. Nor would the entente be worth much, even if it could be achieved on paper, if Russia and Germany decided to work for a Continental League against England.[1] Meanwhile, the Eastern Question was smouldering, South Africa was still inflamed, and the potentially very dangerous Vene-zuelan dispute with the United States was still unsettled. March 1896 was no time for Salisbury to embark on an experimental foreign policy.

Salisbury's fears of committing himself to Germany may have been somewhat appeased by the Kaiser's effusive offers of friendship at the beginning of March. The Emperor's remarks were, characteristically, not without a spice of the absurd: he 'could not understand how Britain should wish to quarrel with him [sic] about so unimportant a matter as the Transvaal', and his bloodcurdling tales of the aggressive *Welt-politik* of the Franco-Russian group were almost pure fantasies.[2] Nor did Salisbury put much trust in German words, least of all in those of Wilhelm II. But the Kaiser's behaviour, and indeed that of the Wilhelmstrasse itself,[3] at least showed a recognition that the Kruger Telegram had been a gross blunder, and that there was more to be gained from Britain by friendly offers of co-operation than by kicks and curses. All the same, Salisbury committed himself with the great-est reluctance; and it was not only for Egyptian and African reasons that he countermanded the Sudan operation when the Italians an-nounced their intention of abandoning Kassala. Never was Salisbury more sensitive to real or imaginary German 'blackmail' than between 1896 and 1898.[4]

The British decision of 11-12 March had been taken for European reasons and was indeed an event of some importance in the diplo-

[1] Cf. Holstein's famous memorandum of 30 Dec. 1895 (G.P. xi, No. 2640).
[2] FO 64/1376, Lascelles to Salisbury Nos. 59 and 61, of 4 and 6 Mar. 1896; memo. by Col. Grierson 3 Mar. (enclosed in 61).
[3] *Ibid.*, Lascelles to Salisbury Nos. 47 and 49, of 26 and 29 Feb. 1896; memo. by Col. Swaine (enclosed in 49).
[4] Cf. *infra*, p. 252. FO 78/4895, Salisbury to Cromer tels. No. 112, 125, of 5 Oct. and 5 Dec. 1896. Salisbury to Balfour 9 Apr. 1898, cited B. E. Dugdale, *Arthur James Balfour* (London 1936), pp. 257-8.

matic history of Europe. Unless, *per impossibile*, the Mahdist State crumbled into dust at the first very tentative blow, it was intended by Salisbury to create the least possible disturbance of the *status quo* in the Nile valley. But no sooner had the 'European' decision for a minimal advance been taken than it began to be profoundly modified by African factors which had not been foreseen. Even as Colonel Hunter was making his little military promenade from Sarras to Akasha—a place which turned out to be completely devoid, not only of a Mahdist garrison, but even of inhabitants[1]—Cromer was moving Heaven and Earth to ensure that the advance should not stop short of Dongola, lest Egyptian indignation erupt in a crisis which even the strongest of proconsuls would be unable to contain. Kitchener's early military successes enabled Cromer to get his way; and these successes were soon to carry action in the Sudan much further than even Cromer had intended.

Dongola fell to Kitchener on 23 September 1896. Cromer 'thought to stop two or three years at Dongola before making any further advance', and on 24 September he telegraphed to Salisbury that 'the Soudan campaign [was] virtually over'.[2] Kitchener thought differently. His initial successes had convinced him, quite erroneously, that the Mahdist State presented no great military problem; and he pressed hard for permission to go on.[3] By 27 September Cromer had been converted. A further advance would be popular with the Egyptian ministers, and he could see 'no insuperable military objections'. The difficulty was purely financial. Egypt had expended the half-million from the *Caisse*; but 'if . . . H.M.G. are willing to pay, question solves itself'.[4] But Salisbury shrank from further demands on Hicks Beach and the Commons. Moreover, he was very uneasy at the attitude of Germany.[5] There had recently been recriminations about German volunteers in the Transvaal, bickerings about frontier violations in West Africa and some gratuitously arrogant German behaviour at Zanzibar.[6] None of these disputes had any serious consequences; they seem to have been simply demonstrations that Germany could afford to assert herself now that Salisbury had been forced to break with France. But Salisbury seems to have feared that they were the prelude to a campaign of 'blackmail' for which any setback in the Sudan would provide Berlin with an admirable opportunity.

Cromer did not take no for an answer. Coached by Kitchener, who

---

[1] W. S. Churchill, *The River War* (London 1899; 3rd Edn. 1933), p. 108.
[2] S P Egypt, Cromer to Salisbury 30 Oct. 1896. F O 78/4894, same to same tel. No. 242, 24 Sept. 1896.
[3] P. Magnus, *Kitchener, Portrait of an Imperialist* (London 1958), pp. 101-2.
[4] FO 78/4894, Cromer to Salisbury tel. No. 245, 27 Sept. 1896.
[5] FO 78/4895, Salisbury to Cromer tels. No. 111 and 112, 5 Oct. 1896. Cf. L.Q.V. 3, iii, p. 85, Salisbury to the Queen 29 Sept. 1896.
[6] FO 64/1402, *passim*. L.Q.V. 3, iii, pp. 71, 87: Salisbury to Bigge 31 Aug. 1896; to the Queen 2 Oct. Hollingsworth, *Zanzibar under the Foreign Office*, pp. 125, 128-30.

was now in Cairo, Cromer pointed out on 30 October that with the expenditure of another half-million the reconquest might well be completed in the course of 1897. Kitchener was confident that he could take Berber; as for Khartoum, its fall could not be long delayed once the Egyptian gunboats had reached Berber. Cromer supplied the financial arguments. The Egyptian Mixed Courts would probably declare the *Caisse* advance illegal in that the Commissioners had not been unanimous. Britain would then have to find half a million to enable Egypt to repay the *Caisse*. Why not find another half million and finish the job in the Sudan? Cromer himself greatly preferred to incur a debt for a definite lump sum, rather than face the unpredictable expense of delaying the operations.[1] In November Kitchener went to England on leave, and was able to put his case personally to Hicks Beach, Balfour and Salisbury. He did not, in the end, get the half million that he and Cromer had asked for; but he did get enough to procure more gunboats and to build a railway from Halfa to Abu Hamed.[2] Salisbury raised no objection; the 'alienation from Germany', which he had feared in September, had not materialised after all. The objective of Kitchener's new advance was to be Berber. Here, Salisbury ruled, the army would halt 'for some little time', unless perchance its march had to be 'hastened by the advance of some other Power towards the Upper Nile'.[3]

A few weeks earlier, on 2 September, Salisbury had told the Queen that there was 'no remedy' for the Upper Nile until the Mombasa railway was complete.[4] He was now evidently so impressed by the optimistic appreciations of Cromer and Kitchener that he began for the first time to look upon the advance from the north as a possible 'remedy'. He was to be disappointed, for the military appreciations of Cairo were fundamentally unsound. Kitchener's victories so far had been over forces that were little more than outposts; and this weakness of the Khalifa's northern garrisons was not fortuitous. The slender thread of cultivation along the Nile could support only a strictly limited number of men; and the Khalifa was never able to organise a transport system capable of victualling this northern defensive screen from the granaries of Omdurman.[5] Kitchener, a great quartermaster if he was great at all, won the Sudan campaign by minute personal concentration on his problems of supply and transport. Intensely preoccupied with finding his own solutions, he never seems to have reflected that his adversary, too, might be faced with very similar

[1] SP Egypt, Cromer to Salisbury 30 Oct. 1896; cf. FO 78/4895, Cromer to Salisbury tel. unnumb., 21 Oct. The Cairo Mixed Court had already (6 June) found for the bondholders against the Egyptian Government and the Caisse. The defeated parties had then appealed to the Mixed Court of Cassation at Alexandria.

[2] Magnus, *op. cit.*, pp. 102-4. FO 78/4895, Salisbury to Cromer tel. No. 138, 20 Dec. 1896. Hicks Beach had after all raised objections (SP Egypt, Hicks Beach to Salisbury 9 Dec. 1896).

[3] SP Egypt, Salisbury to Cromer 16 and 27 Nov. 1896.

[4] L.Q.V. 3, iii, pp. 72-3, Salisbury to Bigge 2 Sept. 1896.

[5] Cf. Sanderson, 'Contributions from African sources . . .', *J.A.H.* 1962, pp. 70-6.

problems. Had he ever done so, he could hardly have failed to notice the obvious strategic implications. The Sudan campaign, and quite possibly the diplomatic history of the Upper Nile, would then have taken a different course.

By February 1897, however, Cromer had realised that the main Mahdist forces were very much more formidable than he had supposed. If they were to move northwards and concentrate at Berber, the advance along the Nile to the projected railhead at Abu Hamed would be a quite unacceptably hazardous operation. So apprehensive was Cromer that he begged the Sirdar to give very early warning if he felt that the military situation was getting out of hand.[1] These fears were as groundless as Cromer's earlier optimism. The Khalifa was unable to move any large force very far north of Omdurman, where it would face precisely the same difficulties of victualling which had kept the northern garrisons so weak. Meanwhile the desert railway was going forward; but for some months the river campaign was at a standstill. In March Salisbury began to doubt whether Kitchener would reach Khartoum by the end of the year; by May he was doubtful whether even Abu Hamed could be taken in the course of 1897.[2]

By the spring of 1897 this delay was most unwelcome to Salisbury. He had now become convinced that the French were indeed going ahead in the southern Sudan; he even began to suspect that they might already have reached the Upper Nile. The I.D. and the African Department had gained their first inkling of the French advance in June 1896, largely through the very circumstantial reports which a Mr Dennett, a British resident at Loango, was able to compile from the indiscretions of the French officers whom he entertained.[3] Shortly afterwards, obviously authentic news was received of Liotard's arrival at Tambura, just within the Nile basin; while the *Politique Coloniale* was already treating Marchand's destination as an open secret.[4] By August 1896 the I.D. was seriously disquieted and had begun to press for an accelerated advance on Khartoum so as to forestall the French; confirmation of the French movements in the Bahr al-Ghazal had meanwhile been received from Congolese sources.[5] In October the Suakin authorities arrested a Hungarian adventurer called Karl Inger, who had been unofficially encouraged by the Quai d'Orsay to make diplomatic contact with the Khalifa. Inger's actual proceedings had been farcically incompetent.[6] But the motives behind his mission

[1] FO 78/4895, Cromer to Salisbury tel. No. 25, 17 Feb. 1897. Cf. I.R.E. No. 51, Jan. 1897.   [2] SP Egypt, Salisbury to Cromer 12 Mar. and 7 May 1897.
[3] FO 27/3301, Cawston to F.O. 16 June and 12 Aug. 1896, enclosing Dennett to Cawston 30 Apr. and 2 July.
[4] FO 27/3276, Howard to Salisbury No. 142, 3 Aug. 1896, and minute by Hill. FO 27/3275, Dufferin to Salisbury No. 107, 16 June 1896; minute by Anderson (20 June) reporting the views of the I.D.
[5] FO 27/3301, Everett (I.D.) to Bertie (F.O.) 31 Aug. 1896. Cf. *ibid.*, F.O. to India Office 15 Sept. 1896.
[6] G. N. Sanderson, ' "Emir Suleyman ibn Inger Abdullah" ', *S.N.R.* xxxv, 1 (1954), pp. 22-71. Cf. *infra*, Ch. xiii, pp. 300-1.

seemed serious enough, in view of Wingate's reports from Sudanese sources of a rapprochement between Menelik and 'Abdallāhi, and Lagarde's forthcoming diplomatic mission to the Negus.[1] And in December 1896, when the French Chamber debated the upper Ubangi budget, inopportune enquiries about its inflated size had been silenced by the demand for 'une vote nationale'.[2]

In November 1896 the D.M.I., Sir John Ardagh, had personally repeated his department's demand for an accelerated advance in the Sudan. *A propos* of the Inger episode, he thought it quite possible that the French might gain the Khalifa's goodwill, as they appeared to have gained that of Menelik, by gifts of arms and ammunition.[3] Indeed, the I.D. thought the French activities in Ethiopia even more dangerous than their advance from the west, though Cromer and Wingate were always more sceptical, pointing to the well-known inability of Ethiopian highlanders to support the climate of the Upper Nile swamps. On 4 February 1897, however, the D.M.I. submitted to the Foreign Office a complete survey of the situation in the upper Ubangi, the Upper Nile and Ethiopia. He concluded that it was morally certain that Marchand was 'going in', and that he was very unlikely to meet with any insuperable obstacle. It was very probable that Menelik was collaborating actively with the French; and quite possible that Paris had also secured the co-operation of King Leopold, who had recently launched a very powerful expedition, under Baron Dhanis, in the direction of the Upper Nile. The D.M.I. did not this time demand an accelerated advance from the north. Given the state of the campaign in February 1897, this seemed impossible without the employment of British troops; and to ask for this was still to court a certain refusal. Instead, Ardagh recommended that a force of Indian troops should at once be sent 'from Uganda down the Nile to make treaties and assert sovereignty'.[4]

From this recommendation the African Department dissented. Sir Clement Hill's objections were partly based on the same old difficulty —sufficient railway had not yet been built 'to find the carriage which a body of Indian troops requires'. But he also hinted that in any case 'a race against France with a sufficient force to maintain even a semblance of effective occupation would be a costly and hazardous operation'. The only solution Hill could offer was, as he himself admitted, a woefully inadequate one. An officer with a small local escort might perhaps 'get down the Nile for some distance safely and make treaties; but it would be a dangerous mission, and treaties without occupation would meet with scanty respect'. The force of this

---

[1] I.R.E., Nos. 50 and 51 (Aug.-Dec. 1896, Jan. 1897). FO 27/3301, D.M.I. to F.O. 6 Nov. 1896, enclosing letter by Wingate 27 Oct.; Fairholme to D.M.I. 18 Nov. Cf. *infra*, Ch. XIII, pp. 293-300.
[2] Cocheris, *op. cit.*, pp. 490-1. FO 27/3276, Monson to Salisbury No. 222, 9 Dec. 1896, and minute by Hill.
[3] FO 27/3301, D.M.I. to F.O. 6 Nov. 1896.
[4] FO 27/3368, same to same 4 Feb. 1897.

remark was obvious from the repeated British futilities at Wadelai, and on a larger scale in West Africa. Towards the end of February the D.M.I.'s report, with Hill's dissenting minute, was placed before the Cabinet.[1] Impressed by all the difficulties, the ministers took no positive decision.

Salisbury still felt that something must be done; and it obviously could not be done from the north. By the last week of March his private secretary Barrington was in correspondence with J. R. L. Macdonald, formerly of the Mombasa railway survey, about a mission from Uganda to the Upper Nile on the lines suggested by Hill. On 30 March Salisbury minuted on this correspondence that the matter could not 'be pushed further without reference to the Cabinet'.[2] But the Cabinet seems still to have been hostile, for Macdonald was now told that the project was 'suspended for the moment'. However, he was still encouraged to submit a plan for it.[3] Reports were now beginning to circulate in Paris that Marchand had indeed reached the Nile, even that Liotard had joined hands with de Bonchamps from Ethiopia.[4] For all their origin in the minds of irresponsible journalists, these fantasies seemed credible enough in their context. On 2 April 1897 the I.D. reminded the African Department of its February appreciation; pointing to the well-attested presence of Liotard, at any rate, in the Bahr al-Ghazal, it recalled and emphasised an earlier warning by Ardagh that 'if nothing is done we may soon have a belt of French Treaties from the Ubanghi across the Nile Valley to Abyssinia'.[5] Salisbury now made up his mind to go ahead without the approval of the Cabinet. On 8 April Macdonald was told in effect that his mission was on again. When on the 10th Macdonald submitted his plan, Barrington minuted: 'This letter must form the basis of a draft to the Treasury . . . but there must be no reference to the Upper Nile in it.'[6] On 25 April Salisbury asked Hicks Beach in strict secrecy to provide £35,000 for 'sending an expedition to the east bank of the Nile to make friends with the tribes before the French get there from the west . . . the ostensible reason for despatch will be to explore the source of the Juba'.[7] Macdonald's real instructions and his 'cover' instructions were both signed on 9 June 1897; but only the 'cover' instructions were revealed to the Cabinet.[8]

Macdonald was to confine his operations to the territory to the east

[1] FO 27/3368, minute by Hill 23 Feb. 1897.
[2] FO 2/144, Macdonald to Barrington 27 Mar. 1897; minute by Salisbury 30 Mar. Macdonald hoped to take Fashoda within a year.
[3] *Ibid.*, Macdonald to Barrington 10 Apr. 1897.
[4] FO 27/3337, Monson to Salisbury No. 75, 19 Mar. 1897 (reporting a speech by Richard Waddington in the Senate). FO 27/3338, Gosselin to Salisbury No. 95, 1 Apr. (reporting *Politique Coloniale*).
[5] FO 27/3368, I.D. to F.O. 2 Apr. 1897.
[6] Barrington to Macdonald 8 Apr. 1897, cited Robinson and Gallagher, *op. cit.*, p. 363. FO 2/144, minute by Barrington on Macdonald to Barrington 10 Apr. 1897.
[7] Hicks Beach, memo. of 25 Apr. 1897, cited Robinson and Gallagher, *op. cit.*, p. 362.
[8] FO 2/144, Salisbury to Macdonald Nos. 1 and 2, 9 June 1897; minutes on the draft by Hill and Salisbury. Cf. FO 2/175, minutes by Bertie and Salisbury 1 July 1898.

v *above*: J.-B. Marchand; Evelyn Baring (Earl of Cromer)
below: H. H. Kitchener; Théophile Delcassé

VI *above*: the final assault by the Mahdists at Omdurman;
from a sketch by Corporal Farquharson, 1st Seaforth Highlanders
VII *below*: the gunboat *Malik* in action at Omdurman
(both pictures from the *London Illustrated News*, October 1898)

of the Nile and south of the tenth parallel. There he was to stake claims by means of treaties, to 'secure the allegiance of the Chiefs by presents and the grant of the British flag' and in general 'effectually to secure the territories in question against other Powers'. If he encountered a rival European expedition he was to continue with his programme, 'disregarding any claims or pretensions which may be advanced on the ground of prior treaties or occupation'.[1] But the timing of Macdonald's mission was thrown completely awry, and its effective strength greatly reduced, by the outbreak of the Uganda Mutiny in September 1897. The original mutineers were the remnants of Emin's troops whom Lugard had in 1891 settled as a garrison in north-western Uganda. These Sudanese—the 'Nubies' as they were called in Uganda —whose refusal to fall in with the schemes of Emin and Stanley had in 1888 helped to ring up the curtain on the international struggle for the Upper Nile, were now to play a part of some importance in the final act. The Nubies had plenty of material grievances: their minuscule pay was disgracefully in arrears, and their clothing and necessaries were in rags. But the spark that lit the mutiny was the rumour that Macdonald was going to lead them to fight their fellow-Muslims in the Sudan.[2] Once again Africa had stepped in to make nonsense of European calculations.

The Nubies were soon joined by all the discontented in Uganda; among these were Kabarega, and also Mwanga, who had fled to German territory after an abortive rising in July 1897. Not until April 1898 was the situation sufficiently restored for Macdonald even to begin his mission.[3] In that month he announced his intention of making a direct push for Lado and, if possible, Fashoda.[4] Salisbury approved; but then, on the ground that his party was not strong enough for this mission, Macdonald decided to make for Lake Rudolf instead. Salisbury utterly disapproved this decision as irrelevant to Macdonald's proper mission and as likely to bring on the dreaded clash with the Ethiopians.[5] Macdonald was now beyond the reach of instructions from London; but in August 1898 Salisbury learned that he had now decided to split his force, which seemed quite nonsensical if it was already too weak. One party, under Macdonald's subordinate Austin, would reconnoitre the Lake Rudolf region; the other, Mac-

[1] FO 2/144, Salisbury to Macdonald No. 2, 9 June 1897.
[2] For the Uganda Mutiny, see: H. R. Fox-Bourne, 'The Uganda Protectorate and its relation to the Sudan', *Asiatic Quarterly Review*, Third Series, VII (April 1899), pp. 322-37; A. F. Mockler-Ferryman, 'The Story of the Uganda Mutiny', *Macmillan's Magazine*, LXXVIII, 466 (1898), pp. 308-20; H. H. Austin, *With Macdonald in Uganda* (London 1903), pp. 36-114, 134-68.
[3] Macdonald's only reliable troops were twenty-seven Sikhs. His 'loyal' Sudanese could not be relied upon against the scattered bands of mutineers who were still at large.
[4] FO 2/175, Berkeley to F.O. No. 37, 20 Apr. 1898, enclosing Macdonald to Berkeley No. 4, 18 Apr.; minutes by Hill and Salisbury.
[5] *Ibid.*, Berkeley to Salisbury tels. No. 7 and 8, 4 June 1898, transmitted by Craufurd (Mombasa) 27 June; Salisbury to Craufurd (for Berkeley) tel. No. 10, 1 July 1898. Cf. *ibid.*, Berkeley to Salisbury Nos. 60 and 61, 4 June 1898 (received 15 Aug.).

R

donald himself would lead to Lado.[1] Austin got to Lake Rudolf—
luckily without colliding with the Ethiopians, who were very much on
the look-out for him;[2] but Macdonald never got anywhere near Lado.
In November 1898 lack of provisions—which was doubtless the real
reason for his apparently irrational decision to split his force—compelled him to return to Uganda from Tirrangole near Torit.[3] Salisbury blamed Macdonald for this complete fiasco: 'He might repeat
the General Confession to us with much propriety.'[4] Macdonald had
indeed been an irresolute and vacillating leader; his movements were,
as Salisbury complained, 'always wholly unexpected', and he made
matters worse by quarrelling bitterly with his British colleagues in
Uganda.[5] But the task he had been given was not far short of a physical
impossibility. When it had appeared in July 1898 that Macdonald was
going only to Lake Rudolf, Berkeley, the Commissioner in Uganda,
had improvised an Upper Nile expedition of his own under Major
Martyr.[6] By November 1898 Martyr had reached Rejaf and joined
forces with the Congolese; a joint expedition then moved on Bor, the
headquarters of the depleted Mahdist garrison under 'Arabi Dafa'-
allāh.[7] 'Arabi and his men retreated across country to Darfur; but the
road to Fashoda was guarded by an obstacle more formidable than the
Mahdists. The Bahr el-Jebel *sudd* proved to be quite impenetrable,
and Martyr made no further progress whatsoever.[8] Railway or no railway, the approach from the south was utterly impracticable.[9]

Some of the fears which had led to the launching of the Macdonald
mission also prompted British diplomatic intervention in Ethiopia,
where since the battle of Adowa the French, and increasingly the
Russians, had been steadily consolidating their influence. In December 1896 Cromer suggested a mission to the Negus, to counteract
Lagarde and to allay Menelik's suspicions that Kitchener's operations
might ultimately be directed against Ethiopia.[10] Rodd, accompanied
by Wingate, arrived at Addis Ababa in April 1897.[11] On 14 May Rodd

[1] FO 2/174, Macdonald to Salisbury unnumb., 18 July 1898; same to same No. 2,
20 July, transmitted by Hardinge (Zanzibar) 9 Sept.
[2] Austin, op. cit. G. N. Sanderson, 'The Foreign Policy of the Negus Menelik, 1896-98',
J.A.H. v, 1 (1964), pp. 87-97.
[3] FO 2/174, Macdonald to Salisbury No. 40, 7 Nov. 1898. Austin, op. cit., pp. 155-61.
[4] SP Private Secretary, minute on a memo. by Barrington 5 Apr. 1899.
[5] FO 2/175, minute by Salisbury on a memo. by Bertie 1 Nov. 1898; Berkeley to Salisbury Nos. 61, 133, 4 June and 7 Oct. 1898. Austin, op. cit., pp. 113-20.
[6] FO 2/175, Berkeley to Martyr 7 July 1898; Berkeley to Salisbury No. 88, 8 July.
[7] Ibid., Berkeley to Salisbury tel. No. 17, 11 Oct. 1898. Flament et al., La Force Publique
de sa Naissance à 1914 (Brussels 1952), pp. 337-9. Hill, Biographical Dictionary, s.v. Martyr.
[8] Flament, loc. cit. Hill, op. cit., s.v. 'Arabi Dafa' Allāh, Martyr.
[9] Contact between Uganda and the Sudan was not established until 19 Jan. 1900. On
that date, Bimbashi Peake, in charge of an elaborately equipped sudd-cutting expedition
from Khartoum, rescued from death by starvation an Anglo-Congolese expedition which
was attempting, with inadequate resources, to penetrate the sudd from the south. Cf.
S.I.R. No. 67 (Jan.-Mar. 1900); Gage, 'Sudd-Cutting', S.N.R. 1950, pp. 7-20; Anon, 'Le
Commandant Henry sur le Haut-Nil', M. Géog., Feb. 1900, cols. 61-3.
[10] SP Egypt, Cromer to Salisbury 5 Dec. 1896. Cf. Sanderson, J.A.H., loc. cit.
[11] For this mission generally see: FO 1/32, FO 1/33; and the War Office confidential
print, Précis of Information obtained by the British Mission to Abyssinia.

obtained a treaty by which the Negus declared the Mahdists to be 'the enemies of his empire' and promised to prevent their receiving arms through Ethiopia. In conversation with the British, Menelik showed a pleasing readiness to fulminate against the Mahdists: 'it was inconceivable that he could ever give them aid or countenance'; 'he could never, under any circumstances, enter into any form of understanding with them'; indeed, 'he would not be unprepared for common action against them'.[1] Neither Wingate nor Rodd had the remotest suspicion that Menelik had just consummated a friendly entente with the Khalifa. They had indeed heard rumours of negotiations; but had concluded, quite erroneously, that all the initiative had come from Omdurman and that Menelik's response had been, at most, 'one of disinterested neutrality'.[2]

The Lion of Judah was however less easily tamed, even in appearance, when it came to negotiating his frontier with the Sudan. Confident of his own strength and of French diplomatic support, Menelik put forward as a basis of negotiation his Circular of April 1891, in which he claimed 'ancient frontiers' extending to Khartoum and Lake Albert.[3] Faced with this, Rodd thought it pointless even to mention the modest concessions on the Blue Nile which he had been authorised to make.[4] He also became convinced, rather uncritically, that Menelik's effective occupation already extended almost to the White Nile; and he forbore to express any explicit reserves lest this act should 'urge the King to push on with greater energy the progress of his effective occupation'. He therefore merely observed that the Ethiopian claims were incompatible with the Anglo-German Agreement of 1890; and requested that, pending a settlement, the debatable lands should not be ceded to any third Power. Menelik replied that he had never heard of the Anglo-German Agreement, and that he would make 'no cession to any Government, whoever it may be'. With this double-edged reply Rodd had to be content. He recommended that the negotiation be postponed until the time when, with 'a fleet of powerful steamers' on the White Nile, 'we should have behind us that moral [sic] force . . . which is wholly wanting now'.[5] Rodd had in fact been completely outmanœuvred. When J. L. Harrington arrived in Addis Ababa as British Representative a year or so later, he was dismayed to find the Negus 'under [the] impression that, no protest having been made, we accept [the] proclamation [of] 1891'.[6]

[1] FO 1/32, Rodd to Salisbury Nos. 20, 21 and 26, of 13, 14 and 15 May. 1897. Treaty printed at Hertslet II, No. 99.
[2] FO 1/32, memo. by Wingate enclosed in Rodd to Salisbury No. 18, 9 May 1897. *Précis of Information*, pp. 71-2. Cf. *infra*, Ch. XIII, pp. 296-8.
[3] FO 1/32, Rodd to Salisbury No. 15, 4 May 1897. Cf. *supra*, Ch. VII, p. 153.
[4] FO 1/32, Salisbury to Rodd, instructions, 27 Feb. 1897. The limit of concession extended to Karkoj, downstream of Roseires.
[5] *Ibid.*, Rodd to Salisbury No. 15, 4 May 1897; same to same No. 21, 14 May, and enclosures: Wingate, memo. of 9 May; Rodd to Menelik 14 May; Menelik to Rodd 6 Genbot 1889/14 May 1897.
[6] FO 1/35, Harrington to Salisbury tel. No. 2, 2 May 1898. Sanderson, *J.A.H., loc. cit.*

The mission to Menelik had in fact been even less successful than the British imagined; but it was in any case clear that the Negus would have to be handled very carefully. Elaborate precautions were taken against a 'premature collision' with the Ethiopians in the Nile valley; Salisbury personally assured Menelik in January 1898 that the despatch of British troops to the Sudan implied no hostile intent; Queen Victoria even recorded a message of goodwill to be played to the Negus on a phonograph.[1] As a means of avoiding all complications, Kitchener suggested a very generous territorial settlement; Cromer went further, and would concede any frontier which secured 'the right of Egypt to the free navigation of the Nile throughout its whole length'.[2] Salisbury was unwilling to go so far, and in March 1898 Harrington was told to say, if asked, that England supported the rights of Egypt 'in the Nile valley generally'. But Harrington was not to raise the subject, nor was he to enter into negotiation; the Foreign Office had abandoned hope of influencing Menelik by diplomatic representations.[3] This unsatisfactory situation was completely transformed by the victory at Omdurman, the Anglo-Egyptian occupation of Fashoda and the discovery, by reconnaissance up the Sobat, that Menelik's 'effective occupation' was a pure bluff. All that Harrington now had to do was to 'lay on the agony . . . as much as possible'.[4] But diplomatic intervention in Ethiopia had done no more to solve the problem of the Upper Nile than the ill-starred Macdonald mission. Indeed, the British difficulties in Ethiopia were themselves overcome as a by-product of the military victory at Omdurman and the diplomatic victory at Fashoda. The advance from the north, which in February 1897 had seemed to be indefinitely held up, finally turned out to be the 'remedy' on the Upper Nile, and not such a very belated remedy after all.

From February to May 1897 there had seemed little prospect of Kitchener's reaching Berber, or even Abu Hamed, in the near future. But in June Cromer's hopes began to revive. Evidently encouraged by the Khalifa's failure to despatch any large force to the north, he now thought 'the Soudan nut . . . less difficult to crack than I had supposed'. Abu Hamed would be taken without difficulty in August; by October the railway would be complete. If, as seemed likely, Berber then fell, the power of the Mahdists might well collapse; but if it did not, Kitchener could stand fast and 'await events'.[5] For a few weeks all went well. Abu Hamed fell on 7 August; Berber, well in advance of the pro-

---

[1] S P Cabinet Memoranda, Cromer to Salisbury 5 Nov. 1897. FO 141/336, FO 78/5049, Salisbury to Cromer tels. No. 4 and 5, 12 Jan. 1898; Cromer to Salisbury tel. No. 48, 8 Feb. 1898. L.Q.V. 3, iii, p. 263, the Queen's journal 8 Aug. 1898.

[2] Cairint 3/218/1, memo. by Kitchener 28 Jan. 1898. FO 141/336, Cromer to Salisbury tel. No. 77a, 5 Mar. 1898. FO 1/35, same to same No. 40, 5 Mar.

[3] Cf. Sir T. Sanderson's deletions from Cromer's draft instructions for Harrington, at FO 1/35, loc. cit.; FO 141/336, Salisbury to Cromer tel. No. 24, 6 Mar. 1898.

[4] FO 1/35, Harrington to Rodd, private, 29 Sept. 1898; same to same 6 Oct., 13 Nov. Sanderson, J.A.H., loc. cit.

[5] S P Cabinet Memoranda, Cromer to Salisbury 5 and 6 June 1897.

gramme and almost without a fight, on 31 August.[1] But the Khalifa's power did not collapse; indeed the fall of Berber seemed rather to have stiffened the Mahdist resistance. The true dimensions of the military problem now began to dawn on Kitchener. On 11 October he admitted that he was 'now for the first time face to face with the real Dervish force'. This was the force under Mahmūd Ahmad camped at Metemma opposite Shendi; and it was not in fact the main Mahdist army. All the same it was, as Kitchener said, 'a force of dervishes of better fighting qualities and far greater numerical strength than we have ever met before'. The more he looked at it, and at his own very vulnerable line of communication, the less he liked it. Meanwhile, the Egyptian Treasury had refused him funds to take over Kassala, which the Italians were about (after all!) to abandon. This seems to have been the last straw, and on 18 October 1897 Kitchener tendered his resignation. His latest biographer says that he 'was not far removed from a nervous collapse'. Cromer himself said that Kitchener's 'nerve had gone'.[2]

Cromer patched up the Kassala affair and succeeded in persuading Kitchener to carry on.[3] But he fully agreed that:

There is not the smallest question of any further advance at present. . . . It is abundantly clear that the reconquest of Khartoum is beyond the military and financial resources of the Egyptian Government. In moments of retrospection I tear my hair over the hurried decision of March 1896. It has upset all my calculations.

All that could now be done was to 'hold our present line and nothing more . . . for some while—it may be for some years'. Pressure from the War Office for the despatch of British troops and an early advance should be firmly resisted: 'no sufficiently important English interest is involved to justify the loss of life and money'. Only if the Egyptian position at Berber itself became dangerous should British reinforcements be sent.[4] This necessity could not be escaped. The domestic, local and international repercussions of yet another Sudan disaster hardly bore thinking about.

The expected War Office pressure was soon forthcoming. In May 1896, nettled by his failure to regain control of the Sudan operations, Wolseley had disclaimed all responsibility, and all intention to intervene further, in a letter reeking with innuendo against Kitchener's competence for command.[5] The setback at Berber gave him an op-

---

[1] The Khalifa had withdrawn almost all the Berber garrison, fearing its isolation by an Anglo-Egyptian advance across the Bayuda desert (Shibeika, *op. cit.*, p. 379).

[2] Arthur, *op. cit.* I, pp. 213-20, Magnus, *op. cit.*, pp. 108-9, citing Kitchener to Grenfell, 14 Oct. 1897; to Cromer, 18 Oct. SP Cabinet Memoranda, Cromer to Salisbury 22 Oct.; SP Egypt, Salisbury to Cromer 23 Oct.

[3] Magnus, *op. cit.*, pp. 109-12.

[4] SP Cabinet Memoranda, *loc. cit.*

[5] FO 78/4894, Wolseley to Lansdowne 8 May 1896; cf. SP Egypt, Cromer to Barrington 5 June 1896.

portunity for the intervention which he professed to have repudiated; and in October 1897 he pressed both Lansdowne and the Queen
for the despatch of British troops and an immediate push to Khartoum.
The argument he most emphasised was that 'the French are now working hard to forestall us on the Upper Nile, and if they do so we may
have serious complications with them when we attempt the job in the
autumn of 1898'.[1] Lansdowne, Salisbury and Cromer in turn considered and rejected this proposal, never seriously mooted before, that
the pace of the Sudan campaign should be set not by the capabilities
of the Egyptian Army but by the situation on the Upper Nile.[2]
Lansdowne doubted whether the early arrival of Kitchener at
Khartoum would really do much to prevent complications with the
French. Salisbury concurred. If ever Britain 'put into execution the
claim of the Anglo-German Agreement of 1891' (sic), there would of
course be 'a very lively protest from the French'. But Salisbury doubted
whether this protest would be 'any the louder, or seriously louder,
because upon some spot in the Nile valley a French explorer may have
succeeded in inducing some chief to accept a treaty'.[3]

But such a situation would obviously provoke a British demand for
the removal of the French flag; and it is strange that Salisbury should
have thought that this would produce no more serious a crisis than the
mere occupation of their sphere by the British. Discussing Lansdowne's memorandum with Cromer, Salisbury used some even odder
arguments. Ignoring recent and very circumstantial reports of the
movements of Marchand and Liotard,[4] he told Cromer that 'we have
heard of no force moving up the Ubanghi . . . still less of food and
munitions'. He did not believe that the French had 'moved any force,
even a small one, into the Nile valley'; but if they had, the Mahdists
would crush them as they had crushed the Congolese at Rejaf. (In fact
the Congolese had in February 1897 taken Rejaf, after defeating 'Arabi
Dafa'allāh in a pitched battle.) But even if the French did reach the
Nile, Salisbury still did not 'believe that any adventure of Liotard
or Brazza would affect our title to whatever, in the valley between
Lado and Khartoum, is not Egyptian'. A French occupation would
be legally irrelevant because the Anglo-German Agreement had been
'duly communicated to Paris' (it had not) without evoking any expression of reserves—but throughout 1894 and 1895 Hanotaux had
explicitly and repeatedly refused to recognise it. 'Moreover Edward
Grey's bellicose protest . . . was conveyed to Paris in due diplomatic

---

[1] Maurice and Arthur, op. cit. II, p. 304, citing Wolseley to Lansdowne Oct. 1897.
L.Q.V. 3, iii, p. 206, Wolseley to the Queen 25 Oct. 1897.
[2] Salisbury's remarks in Nov. 1896 (supra, p. 253) had assumed that there was no serious
military obstacle to an advance.
[3] Salisbury to Lansdowne 22 Oct. 1897, quoted Lord Newton, Lord Lansdowne (London
1929), p. 148.
[4] In June 1897 there had been reports that the Marchand Mission was concentrated at
Les Abiras; in Sept., that Liotard had occupied Deim Zubeir: FO 27/3338, Gosselin to
Salisbury No. 192, 25 June 1897; FO 27/3371, I.D. to F.O. 20 Sept.

form.'[1] But, as Monson remarked a few weeks later, 'Lord Kimberley hardly communicated anything at all, except . . . some indefinite watering down of Grey's declaration'.[2]

Cromer was by no means so confident as Salisbury that the presence of the French on the Upper Nile would be irrelevant to the scale of the ultimate crisis. Nevertheless, he did not think that the political value of forestalling the French justified reinforcing Kitchener by British troops. He pointed out that the attempt to forestall the French might lead to the unnecessary acquisition in the southern Sudan of 'large tracts of useless territory which it would be difficult and costly to administer properly'. Moreover, Cromer correctly judged that Khartoum, and not Fashoda, was the real military key to the strategic centre of the Upper Nile immediately to the north of the *sudd*; and 'we can always get to Khartoum before anyone else whenever we choose to send [a British] expedition there'. He concluded that, at any rate so long as the French were not certainly known to be on the Nile, the Government 'should not allow themselves to be hurried by fears of French activity'. No British reinforcements should be sent—unless of course it became clear that the Egyptians at Berber were in danger.[3]

Salisbury's almost perverse scepticism in October 1897 about the movements of the French may well have been a reaction against what he now saw to have been his excessive credulity earlier in the year. By October the very precision with which Wingate's Sudanese informants indicated the presence of the Congolese at Rejaf added point to their complete silence about other Europeans on the Nile.[4] But Salisbury's other conclusions were—one can only say intuitively—very much sounder than the arguments with which he sought to buttress them. The strategic crux of the Upper Nile situation lay in the extreme difficulty of reaching the all-important Fashoda region from any direction except the north. The problem for the French was not merely to occupy Fashoda; but to occupy it in strength sufficient to resist the crushing riposte from Omdurman which would be a mere routine operation for any power—Mahdist or Anglo-Egyptian—which had a few steamers at its disposal. Cromer recognised this; and Salisbury had at least an inkling of it when he looked to the Mahdists to deal with the French, and used as one of his arguments against an advance the consideration that 'by destroying the Dervish power we are killing the defender who holds the valley for us now'.[5]

Again, Salisbury's argumentation about the legal irrelevance of 'any adventure of Liotard or Brazza' was well-nigh worthless; but he went to the heart of the matter when he predicted that the clash on the Upper Nile would be 'something to remember', a full-scale trial of

[1] S P Egypt, Salisbury to Cromer 29 Oct. 1897.
[2] F O 27/3341, Monson to Bertie, private, 10 Dec. 1897.
[3] S P Cabinet Memoranda, Cromer to Salisbury 5 Nov. 1897.
[4] I.R.E. No. 56, Oct. 1897.
[5] Salisbury to Lansdowne 22 Oct. 1897 (Newton, *loc. cit.*).

strength in which 'the technical considerations will not go for very much'.[1] In this naked contest of power the minutiae of local treaties and prior occupation would indeed be irrelevant—as in fact they turned out to be. In October 1897 Salisbury was evidently not anxious to hasten a crisis on this scale, for which at that time his diplomatic preparations were far from complete. Once Kitchener had reached Khartoum there could no longer be any question of tolerating 'a French principality at Fashoda'.[2] If the French then turned out to be in possession the challenge would have to be met whatever the consequences.

A few days after Salisbury had so strongly expressed his disbelief in the French advance, *La Dépêche Coloniale* published an obviously authentic letter from Liotard at Deim Zubeir; and on 30 November Monson was told to warn Hanotaux that the Salisbury government 'adhered to' the Grey Declaration.[3] It was now perfectly clear that the French were 'going in', and equally clear that Macdonald could not possibly forestall them. Nevertheless, Salisbury adhered to the policy agreed at the beginning of November, and there was no question of the despatch of British troops because of 'French activity'. But doubts were growing about the Sirdar's position at Berber. On 11 November the best Kitchener himself could say of it was that it was risky but not untenable. Grenfell, the commander of the British Army of Occupation and, as a former Sirdar, Kitchener's chief until 1892, was asked for an appreciation. On 19 November he reported that 'should the enemy undertake offensive operations in almost any direction, no one could view the situation without disquiet'.[4] These fears were groundless. Mahmūd's army at Metemma was now a rapidly deteriorating force, crippled by shortage of food; for even at this comparatively short range the Khalifa's efforts to organise an effective victualling service had been unsuccessful. But in mid-December it was learned that the Khalifa was concentrating a large force at Kerreri, just north of Omdurman, apparently in preparation for a northward advance by the entire Mahdist army.[5] By the last week in December Cromer was thoroughly alarmed. He begged Kitchener to ask for British reinforcements 'whilst there is yet time', and complained to Salisbury of the Sirdar's procrastination.[6] Kitchener was in a difficult position. He feared supersession by Grenfell, a senior officer with Egyptian experience whom Wolseley had posted to Cairo, behind the back of Salisbury, with precisely this object in

[1] Salisbury to Cromer 29 Oct. 1897 (SP Egypt, *loc. cit.*).
[2] *Ibid.*
[3] FO 27/3373, D.M.I. to F.O. 10 Nov. 1897. FO 27/3341, Monson to Salisbury No. 385, 22 Nov. 1897, and minute by Salisbury. FO 27/3336, Bertie to Monson, private, 30 Nov.
[4] SP Cabinet Memoranda, Cromer to Salisbury 11 Nov. 1897. FO 78/4895, Grenfell to W.O. 19 Nov.
[5] Sanderson, 'Contributions from African Sources . . .', *J.A.H.* 1962, pp. 72-5. I.R.E. No. 57, Nov.-Dec. 1897. Churchill, *op. cit.*, pp. 211-3.
[6] FO 78/4895, Cromer to Kitchener 22 Dec. 1897; to Salisbury tel. No. 155, 22 Dec.

mind.[1] Very reluctantly, and under heavy pressure from both Cromer and Wingate, Kitchener telegraphed for British reinforcements on the last day of 1897.[2]

Cromer was now anxious to finish the campaign, so as to bring back the British troops in particular as quickly as possible; and on 26 January 1898 the Cabinet authorised the Sirdar to advance to Khartoum.[3] Meanwhile, the Khalifa had dispersed the concentration at Kerreri. A report on the Metemma situation by his chief clerk and seal-bearer seems to have convinced him that to send his main army north would be merely to expose it to the privations which were already ruining the efficiency and morale of Mahmūd Ahmad's force.[4] But the supposed Mahdist threat may well have advanced the fall of Khartoum by a year, for when it came to the point Kitchener was unwilling to advance on Khartoum except at the season when the Nile flood permitted his gunboats and transports to pass the Sixth Cataract at Sabaloka. Had Kitchener missed the 1898 flood, which he might well have done but for the despatch of British troops early in the year, the French at Fashoda and in the Bahr al-Ghazal would have had another twelve months in which to consolidate their position and above all to improve their communications. The local situation, which in September 1898 was not in fact to be quite so unimportant as Salisbury had supposed, would by that time have been much more favourable to the French.

Even with his British reinforcements, Kitchener did not err by impetuosity. When Mahmūd advanced to the Atbara—a desperate course which the Khalifa had permitted only as a lesser evil than the army's continued disintegration at Metemma—Kitchener was bewildered by the failure of the Mahdists to attack. It was only after prolonged indecision and much agitated telegraphing to Cairo that Kitchener successfully assaulted Mahmūd's *zarība* on 8 April 1898.[5] Never suspecting that his adversary was the most expendable of forlorn hopes, the Sirdar complained that 'the defeat of Mahmud . . . has not more fully cleared up the situation in the Sudan'.[6] Deliberately and methodically he began his preparations for the major battle which evidently still lay ahead. It was fought at Kerreri on 2 September 1898. It brought about not only the total collapse of the Mahdist state but the almost complete annihilation of the Mahdist army. Salisbury could devote himself, untroubled by local distractions, to the European complications on the Upper Nile.

[1] S P Egypt, Salisbury to Cromer 8 July, 11 July 1897. Magnus, *op. cit.*, pp. 107, 112-3, 116.

[2] FO 78/5049, Cromer to Salisbury tel. No. 1, 1 Jan. 1898. R. Wingate, *Wingate of the Sudan* (London 1955), pp. 113-4, citing F. R. Wingate's diary. Salisbury is said to have replied to a last-ditch W.O. attempt to oust Kitchener by a threat of resignation (Arthur, *op. cit.* I, p. 222).

[3] Shibeika, *op. cit.*, p. 382. FO 141/336, Salisbury to Cromer tel. No. 8, 26 Jan. 1898.

[4] Sanderson, *J.A.H.* 1962, *loc. cit.*

[5] *Ibid.*, pp. 75-6. Shibeika, *op. cit.*, pp. 382-7. Arthur, *op. cit.* I, pp. 223-5. Magnus, *op. cit.*, pp. 119-21. Cromer, *Modern Egypt*, II, pp. 98-102.

[6] Kitchener, covering minute to I.R.E. No. 59, 24 June 1898.

After Kitchener's victory on the Atbara, a bloody soldiers' battle which dispelled any lingering doubts about the fighting qualities of the Egyptian troops, it was time to think about the future status of the reconquered Sudan. On 1 November 1897 Hicks Beach had remarked: 'But suppose [Khartoum] taken . . ., what then? Can we stop there? I think not . . .'.[1] By the spring of 1898 Salisbury was thinking very differently. Now that a merely defensive Nile strategy had given place to total reconquest, it no longer seemed so easy merely to restore the northern Sudan to Egypt, even though as late as October 1897 Salisbury had evidently regarded the valley, north of Khartoum at least, as a purely Egyptian sphere.[2] It was not only that the re-introduction into the Sudan of the international institutions which functioned in Egypt would be an intolerable handicap to its future administration. The British now found themselves actively coveting the northern Sudan,[3] especially as the South—the British sphere so long and so tenaciously defended as a matter of strategy, of prestige, or of both—had turned out to be the whitest of white elephants. The British public, increasingly excited by the dramatic closing stages of the Khartoum campaign, was unlikely to be satisfied with this completely negative reward for British financial and military participation in the reconquest. Then there was the awkward problem of Egyptian rights in the south, which London had always affected to respect. In law and logic they were after all just as good—or just as bad—at Fashoda as they were at Dongola.

On 3 June 1898 Salisbury cut all these knots. He suggested to Cromer that the whole Sudan, 'from Halfa to Wadelai' should be treated, not as *de jure* Egyptian territory temporarily dominated by rebels, but as an independent and sovereign 'Mahdi state'.

> We might treat Khartum as the capital of the Mahdi state:
> and the capture of Khartum would deliver by right of conquest
> the whole of the Mahdi state from Halfa to Wadelai into the
> power of the capturing army. That army consists of two allied
> contingents. . . .[4]

The claim to a separate British sphere was tacitly abandoned; but at Khartoum the British and Egyptian flags would fly *side by side* as a symbol of the complete juridical equality of the two conquerors.[5] Each would have a right of conquest and neither would have any other right;

---

[1] Hicks Beach to Salisbury 1 Nov. 1897, quoted Robinson and Gallagher, *op. cit.*, pp. 363-4.

[2] S P Egypt, Salisbury to Cromer 29 Oct. 1897—'whatever, in the valley between Lado and Khartoum, is not Egyptian'.

[3] As early as Oct. 1896 Cromer had suggested that in return for the British loan, Britain should 'control the administration . . . of the reconquered provinces' (FO 78/4895, tel. unnumb., to Salisbury 21 Oct. 1896). In December Hicks Beach wished to announce that Britain would retain Dongola as a 'pledge' for the loan. Cromer and Salisbury concurred; but Salisbury, for diplomatic reasons, would not act unless Cromer could first obtain the consent of the Khedive. This condition Cromer rejected as quite impracticable, and no action was taken. Cf. Shibeika, *op. cit.*, pp. 374-5.

[4] FO 78/5050, Salisbury to Cromer tel. No. 47, 3 June 1898.

[5] *Ibid.*—emphasis in Salisbury's holograph draft.

the claims of Egypt based on sixty-odd years of undisputed ownership, before the Mahdia, would be completely extinguished. In these circumstances, juridical equality between Britain and Egypt implied complete British predominance in practice; no wonder Salisbury suggested that the size of the British contingent be increased.[1] In the north, the British would be masters; in the south they could, while safeguarding the Nile waters, escape the responsibility and expense of administering 'large tracts of useless territory'. Cromer was not at first happy with the 'two flags' policy. He feared that Salisbury's reference to 'the whole . . . Mahdi State from Halfa to Wadelai' implied operations for the acquisition of 'useless territory' at the cost of a politically dangerous increase in Egyptian taxation.[2] In January 1898 Cromer had grudgingly admitted that 'sooner or later we shall have to put up an Egyptian flag at Fashoda'; but throughout 1898 he was determined to keep operations south of Khartoum to the 'absolutely necessary' minimum.[3] However, on 11 June he wrote to Salisbury: 'I have been thinking over the two-flag idea and the more I think over it the more I like it.' Four days later Cromer had formally accepted the two-flags policy, though he still insisted that occupation south of Khartoum should be restricted 'mainly to the banks of the White Nile and a portion of the Blue Nile'.[4] In an instruction to Cairo of 2 August 1898, which Cromer himself had drafted, the 'two flags' policy became the official symbol of the British Government's 'predominant voice in all matters connected with the Sudan'.[5]

The advantages of the 'right of conquest' doctrine and of the 'two flags' policy were not confined solely to Anglo-Egyptian relations.[6] As Salisbury remarked, they would enable him to 'shake free of a good deal of diplomatic hamper'.[7] There was more to this than the mere abolition in the Sudan of 'obligations such as capitulations, and treaties, and Khedivial decrees, [which] have been submerged and swept away by the flood of two conquests passing over the land'.[8] The thesis that 'the Mahdi state' had been independent and sovereign, and no longer in any sense a part of Egypt or the Ottoman Empire,

[1] *Ibid.*

[2] SP Cabinet Memoranda, Cromer to Salisbury 15 June 1898. Cf. FO 78/5050, same to same tel. No. 163, 4 June.

[3] Zetland, *Lord Cromer*, pp. 260–1, citing Cromer to Salisbury 28 Jan. 1898. FO 141/336, Salisbury to Cromer tel. No. 8, 28 Jan. SP, *loc. cit.*

[4] Zetland, *op. cit.*, p. 238, citing Cromer to Salisbury 11 June 1898. SP, *loc. cit.*

[5] Cromer attended the cabinet of 25 July, at which his draft was considered. Cf. L.Q.V. 3, iii, pp. 260–1, Salisbury to the Queen 25 July 1898; FO 78/5050, Salisbury to Cromer No. 109, 2 Aug. 1898 (draft in Cromer's hand).

[6] However, the right-of-conquest thesis had emerged, significantly enough, within a few days of a threat by Salisbury to assert a similar right over Egypt itself. Salisbury argued that in 1882 the khedive Tawfīq had lost his sovereign rights to 'Urābi, from whom they had been 'wrested by . . . British victory at Tel-el-Kebir . . . England has never parted with the rights over Egypt which she won at that battle'. Salisbury also threatened to reconsider 'whether we should give back to [the Khedive] the reconquered Soudan at all'. (FO 141/336, Salisbury to Cromer tels. No. 41 and 43, of 15 and 25 May 1898. Cf. D.D.F. xiv, No. 197, Cogordan to Hanotaux 22 May 1898.)

[7] FO 78/5050, Salisbury to Cromer tel. No. 47, 3 June 1898.

[8] SP Private Secretary, Salisbury to the Law Officers of the Crown 30 June 1898.

destroyed the claim of any Power except the two conquerors to have the slightest say in the settlement of its future status. This was the position that Salisbury was determined to establish; and it did not worry him that the French too could claim a right of conquest for Marchand at Fashoda and, even more convincingly, for their occupation in the Bahr al-Ghazal.[1] Salisbury was quite uninterested in the legal, or even the logical, value of the arguments to be used against the French. The French were simply to be shown the door, by force if necessary; and their ejection would merely be an incident on the way to Salisbury's ultimate diplomatic objective: the acceptance by the Powers of the *de facto* British control throughout the Sudan implicit in the 'right of conquest', and soon to be spelled out in the Condominium Agreement. The Anglo-French conflict on the Upper Nile would of course be by far the most important and probably the crucial incident in this development—not least because any weakening towards the French might encourage other Powers to question the very doubtful legality of the Condominium Agreement.[2] Since the challenge to British hegemony everywhere in the Sudan had come in the south, in the south it had to be met. In order to safeguard their *de facto* acquisition of the northern and central Sudan, the British found themselves threatening France with war over one of the more unhealthy and unattractive spots of the worthless and unwanted south—the 'miserable and small object'[3] of Fashoda.

[1] Salisbury's assumption that the conquest of a capital city gives a right to the whole territory of which it is capital finds no support in international law. Cf. Oppenheim's *International Law* (7th Edn., ed. H. Lauterpacht, London 1952), pp. 435, 600; and *infra*, Ch. xv, p. 345.

[2] Cf. *infra*, Ch. xvi, pp. 366-9.

[3] L.Q.V. 3, iii, p. 305, the Queen to Salisbury 30 Oct. 1898.

XII

MISSION MARCHAND

1895–98

IN November 1894 Delcassé had promised the French Cabinet that
Liotard would be on the Nile within about a year.[1] In fact, by
February 1896 Liotard had only just reached, at Tambura, the
outer rim of the Nile basin.[2] As early as April 1895 Paris had begun to
receive reports from the upper Ubangi which emphasised Liotard's
difficulties and relegated his arrival on the Nile to an indefinite future;
and in May Hanotaux had been able to put this information to good
use in patching up his relations with London.[3] Indeed, Hanotaux
seems to have been sufficiently impressed by the Grey Declaration to
contemplate, unofficially, a project for 'neutralising' the whole Nile
valley under an international commission, with King Leopold as
the commission's executive officer in the central and southern Sudan.
This idea was already attracting Leopold; in June 1895 he wrote to
d'Anethan in Paris: 'Tâchez insensiblement . . . de faire naître en
[Hanotaux] le sentiment spontané que nous pourrions être un facteur
dans la solution de neutralisation à trouver pour le Haut-Nil'.[4] Perhaps
as a result of d'Anethan's hints, in July 1895 François Deloncle, acting
(so he said) with the concurrence of Hanotaux, turned up in Brussels
with a project for a 'neutral solution' on these lines. Deloncle would do
his best to prepare French opinion for this proposal; but Leopold himself must try to secure the good will of England.[5]

Leopold tried. On three separate occasions (August and December
1895, January 1896) he fruitlessly suggested to a highly suspicious
Salisbury that he should be installed as a neutral custodian of 'a considerable portion of the Nile valley'.[6] Meanwhile, he had sent through

[1] D.D.F. xi, No. 285, note du Ministre (Hanotaux) 17 Nov. 1894.
[2] Anon., 'De l'Oubangui au Nil', Bull. C.A.F. Oct. 1898, p. 327. Cocheris, Situation Internationale, p. 456.
[3] Renouvin, 'Origines', Rev. Hist. 1948, p. 189. Cf. supra, Ch. x, p. 222; Ch. xi, p. 238.
[4] Leopold to d'Anethan 16 June 1895, cited in Stengers, 'La première tentative de reprise', Bull. Soc. Roy. Belge Géog. 1949, pp. 109–10. Cf. FO 10/641, Plunkett to Salisbury 30 June 1895.
[5] L. Ranieri, Les Relations entre l'Etat Indépendant du Congo et l'Italie (Brussels, I.R.C.B., 1959), pp. 78–82.
[6] Stengers, ubi supra, pp. 119–22, quoting memo. by Salisbury 13 Aug. 1895 (FO 10/646). L.Q.V. 3, ii, pp. 577–9, Salisbury to Bigge 5 and 7 Dec. 1895; ibid., iii, pp. 24–5, same to same 17 Jan. 1896.

Eetvelde a favourable reply to Deloncle, together with advice on the tactics to be followed in France: 'Dites à M. Deloncle de ne pas se faire conciliant dans ses articles, mais de continuer à être menaçant. C'est moi qui dois être le conciliateur.' Deloncle forwarded this reply, together with its enclosures containing Leopold's detailed stipulations, to the Quai d'Orsay—a fact which suggests that his activities had indeed been countenanced by Hanotaux.[1] But there are no minutes on these papers, and no action followed. Courcel's suggestion to Salisbury in February 1896 of King Leopold as a neutral custodian for Egypt[2] itself may however be evidence that the idea was not entirely forgotten. But the whole affair was at most one of those very long shots through unofficial agents to which Hanotaux seems at this time to have been rather addicted.[3]

Meanwhile, throughout the summer of 1895 Liotard's plight had left the Colonial Ministry unmoved, and nothing was done to reinforce him. Delcassé had been dropped at a change of government in January 1895; in June there had been a strong parliamentary move to make him the scapegoat for the disastrous failure of Monteil's expedition against Samory in the Ivory Coast hinterland.[4] His successor Chautemps, a competent and hard-headed administrator, was also a Radical and a Mason with a reputation for hostility to unregulated colonial expansion.[5] No doubt he also noticed how badly Delcassé had burned his fingers by being too enterprising. Chautemps reined in the 'colonels' on the Niger,[6] and cut the upper Ubangi down to a care-and-maintenance budget. In September 1895 he was still following a 'politique d'expectative' here, posting to the upper Ubangi reliefs only and not reinforcements.[7] Ironically, the 'Grey Declaration' had been made just at the moment when Paris was apparently putting the Nile project into indefinite cold storage. In the following months Liotard struggled slowly northward. He reached Deim Zubeir, but not until April 1897; and at Deim Zubeir the devastation and depopulation of the country to the north-east compelled him to abandon all hopes of a further advance.[8] As Renouvin has very justly remarked: 'Pour que les difficultés soulevées par "l'avertissement Grey" s'apaisent, il suffirait de laisser les événements suivre leur cours.'[9]

[1] MAE, Congo et Gabon 14, Eetvelde to Deloncle 20 July 1895, with undated enclosures.
[2] Cf. supra, Ch. x, p. 231. There were in fact further discussions between Eetvelde and Deloncle in Dec. 1895 (Ranieri, loc. cit.).
[3] Cf. his feelers to Berlin in the summer of 1896 through the journalist Morre and the Franco-Danish confidential agent Jules Hanssen (G.P. xi, Nos. 2837-43).
[4] C. W. Porter, The Career of Théophile Delcassé (Philadelphia 1936), pp. 92-8.
[5] Vergniol, 'Fachoda', Revue de France Sept. 1936, p. 113.
[6] C. W. Newbury, 'The Formation of the Government-General of French West Africa,' J.A.H. i, 1 (1960), pp. 114-7.
[7] D.D.F. xii, No. 152, Chautemps to Hanotaux 21 Sept. 1895.
[8] Anon., 'Dans le Bahr al Ghazal. L'occupation de Dem Ziber', Bull. C.A.F., Nov. 1898, p. 367. D.D.F. xiii, No. 365, Annex ii, Liotard to Marchand 8 Apr. 1897. Delebecque, Vie du général Marchand, pp. 100-1, citing Liotard to Germain 15 Mar. 1897.
[9] Renouvin, loc. cit.

But events were not allowed to take their course. By September 1895 their course was already being changed; and the occasion, if not the cause, of this change was the activity of a young captain of Marine Infantry, Jean-Baptiste Marchand. Marchand was already a veteran at thirty-one. He had seen seven years' active service in West Africa, had been twice wounded, and enjoyed a brilliant reputation both as a fighting soldier and as a military explorer.[1] He is said to have interested himself in the Nile project as early as August 1893; and this interest was certainly reinforced when in 1894 he served under Monteil in the ill-fated campaign against Samory.[2] When he came to France on leave in June 1895 it was evidently his major preoccupation. According to his own account he obtained an interview with Hanotaux on 14 June 1895; Hanotaux is said to have advised him to 'mûrir son projet' and to submit it in writing to the *Colonies*.[3] Marchand then saw Chautemps, who commissioned him to study 'l'extension plus large de notre sphère d'influence, en particulier dans la direction du Nil'. On 11 September Marchand submitted to Chautemps a detailed project; this document has not survived, but its salient features are preserved in the lengthy extracts from it which Marchand incorporated in a later memorandum.[4] On 21 September Chautemps reported to Hanotaux the receipt of Marchand's project. He pointed out that his Ministry was following a 'politique d'expectative'; he had, he said, told Marchand to go and talk about his project to Hanotaux. After this interview, the Quai d'Orsay would doubtless make known its views 'sur une question qui touche plus encore à la politique générale extérieure qu'à des intérêts purement coloniaux'.[5]

Chautemps was behaving cautiously, responsibly and correctly—behaviour which was becoming increasingly unusual at the Pavillon de Flore. All the same, he had been brought at least to consider a complete and very radical departure from his 'politique d'expectative'. It is very difficult to believe that this was the unaided work of a mere junior officer on leave from Africa, and an officer who, for all his distinguished local reputation, cut no figure whatever in the political society of Paris. What little evidence there is points all in one direction —that Marchand and his project were strongly supported by the senior officials at the Pavillon de Flore. Of these Ernest Roume,[6] the head of the administrative and commercial section (and in 1896 one of the Niger Commissioners whose intransigence was to be so deplored by the British), is the only one who can be positively identified. During

---

[1] Delebecque, *op. cit.*, pp. 24-60.

[2] *Ibid.*, p. 69. Monteil, *Souvenirs Vécus*, pp. 115-6, 121.

[3] Marchand in *Le Matin* 20 June 1905.

[4] *Ibid.* D.D.F. xii, No. 152; No. 192, *note du capitaine Marchand* 10 Nov. 1895. Some of the critical passages of this note are in quotation marks, and are presumably reproduced from the September memorandum.

[5] D.D.F. xii, No. 152.

[6] Roume became in 1902 Governor-General of French West Africa (Newbury, *ubi supra*, p. 124).

the interregnum between the departure of Haussmann and the appointment of Gustave Binger as *Directeur des affaires d'Afrique* towards the end of 1896, Roume was the Ministry's principal African expert. Binger himself, a very influential figure though not yet in the Office, may also have supported Marchand. Binger was in Paris towards the end of 1895;[1] he knew Marchand, who had served under him when he was Governor of the Ivory Coast; and Marchand certainly thought very highly of Binger.[2] At all events, Binger would not be the man to discourage Marchand or his scheme; as *Directeur* he was to be, if anything, even more aggressively combative towards England than Roume himself.[3] Beyond these speculations it is impossible to go. All the papers relating to the incubation of the Marchand Mission were removed, in the course of 1938 and in June 1939, from the Colonial Ministry files by the then Minister, Georges Mandel; and they have not been recovered.[4] This loss, and a weeding of the Quai d'Orsay papers carried out by Delcassé in May 1904,[5] also make it impossible to trace in detail how the project came later to be approved by Berthelot, at a time when this most anglophile of French Foreign Ministers was actively and successfully pursuing a rapprochement with England.

However, in September 1895 the decision still lay with Hanotaux. He interviewed Marchand, probably towards the end of September. Marchand asserted that given two hundred men and 600,000 francs he could reach the Bahr al-Ghazal—there is no mention of the Nile or of Fashoda—'sans être inquiété outre mesure par les Mahdistes, qui laisseraient, selon lui, facilement passer une troupe peu nombreuse'.[6] This robust faith in the benevolent neutrality of the Mahdists, which remained uncontradicted for far too long and vitally affected the whole planning of the Marchand Mission, sprang from the widespread French idea that Mahdism was in some way factitious, something indeed which the *Intelligence britannique* had probably encouraged for its own nefarious ends.[7] Like the legend of 'Urābi's corruption by English gold,[8] these ideas were part of the bizarre political mythology which, for too many Frenchmen, replaced all serious thought on the Egyptian question. Hanotaux, however, was not so sure of the

---

[1] FO 27/3233, Howard to Anderson, private, 26 Nov. 1895.

[2] M.-A. Ménier, 'Lettres du commandant Marchand à Guillaume Grandidier', *Rev. Hist. Cols.* XLV (1958), pp. 61-108, Marchand to Grandidier 1 Feb. 1897, at p. 93. Marchand describes Binger as 'plus sage et intelligent que tous'.

[3] Cf. *infra*, Ch. XIV, p. 322.

[4] D.D.F. XIV, *Avant-Propos*, p. ix. The *Colonies* file Afrique III 32, which probably contained this documentation, can no longer be traced at all. Mandel also removed (8 June 1939) a large number of pieces from Afrique III 33 and 34a (cf. the notes on these files). These are briefly indexed on the file covers; they related to the Fashoda crisis itself.

[5] D.D.F. XIV, *Avant-Propos*, p. viii.

[6] D.D.F. XII, No. 153, undated minute by Brice, of Hanotaux' secretariat.

[7] In Feb. 1895 François Deloncle had told the Chamber, without contradiction, that 'c'est assurément l'intrigue britannique . . . qui a suscité, entretenu et fortifié le Mahdisme' (*J.O.*, 28 Feb. 1895). The character of 'M. Fardet', in A. Conan Doyle's *The Tragedy of the Korosko* (London 1898), is evidently intended as a caricature of this attitude.

[8] Cf. *supra*, Ch. VI, p. 115.

VIII Marchand in Africa with members of his mission

ıx The Negus Menelik ıı

Mahdists: an undated note by one of his secretaries recalls that in 1894 the Congolese, seven hundred strong, had been thrown neck and crop out of the Bahr al-Ghazal.[1] In any case Hanotaux can hardly have found Marchand's project very welcome at a time when he too was attempting to improve relations with England and was indeed actively negotiating on the Siam-Mekong question. Some ten years later Marchand stated that Hanotaux was 'ready to sign' when in October 1895 he quitted office on the fall of the Ribot Government.[2] In fact Hanotaux' only action was to arrange for a conference with his Colonial colleague.[3] When the Ribot government fell this had still not taken place; nor is there any evidence that either Hanotaux or Chautemps had attempted to hasten it.

Hanotaux was asked to stay on in the succeeding Radical cabinet of Léon Bourgeois; but he refused, evidently fearing to compromise his political respectability by associating with revolutionaries who wanted to introduce Income Tax. The Quai d'Orsay was finally taken over, very reluctantly, by the distinguished chemist Marcellin Berthelot. Berthelot, well aware of his own unsuitability, nevertheless worked conscientiously at his unfamiliar task and on occasion asserted himself both forcefully and wisely.[4] But his colleague at the *Colonies*—another scholar, the Egyptologist Guieysse—seems to have been content to allow himself and his ministry to be managed by the permanent officials. No sooner had Guieysse taken office than the *bureaux*, released from the hampering presence of Chautemps, took the bit in their teeth on the Marchand Mission. On 8 November, just a week after the new government had been installed, a departmental (as opposed to ministerial) note from the Pavillon de Flore pressed the Quai d'Orsay for a decision as a matter of the utmost urgency. At the same time it suggested that the proposed inter-departmental conference be convened forthwith.[5] At the Quai d'Orsay, this note would certainly have been passed for action to Benoît; and Benoît was not the man to discourage a project like the Marchand Mission.

On 10 November 1895 Marchand submitted a second memorandum on his project, doubtless as an agenda paper for the forthcoming conference. The political object of the mission is described, in a passage copied from Marchand's September note, as follows:

En dernière analyse, c'est par des moyens pacifiques, mais sûrs, 'de mettre l'Angleterre dans la nécessité d'accepter, sinon de provoquer elle-même la réunion d'une conférence européenne au sein de laquelle serait discuté et fixé le sort réservé au Soudan égyptien, c'est-à-dire à la vallée du Nil. En outre de l'intérêt que l'obtention d'un pareil résultat présente pour la colonisation

[1] D.D.F., *loc. cit.*   [2] Marchand in *Le Matin* 20 June 1905.
[3] D.D.F. XII, No. 197, *note pour le Ministre* 13 Nov. 1895.
[4] Notably in defining French policy at the Straits during the crisis of Dec. 1895—Jan. 1896.
[5] D.D.F. XII, No. 190, *note du Ministère des Colonies* 8 Nov. 1895.

S

française en Afrique, dont l'avenir est si gravement menacé par les ambitions anglaises, n'est-il pas permis d'espérer que la question de l'évacuation de l'Egypte découlerait tout naturellement de celle du Soudan égyptien et s'imposerait avec une force nouvelle aux délibérations de la conférence?'[1]

To avoid any violation of the rights of the Sultan and the Khedive, which Marchand acknowledges as 'le plus solide argument . . . pour résister aux prétentions britanniques', the points to be occupied by the mission would not be annexed, but merely held as pledges: 'des gages de restitution collective à l'Egypte des territoires ayant formé le Soudan égyptien et momentanément occupés . . . par une ou plusieurs Puissances européennes'. The mission would attempt to reach the Nile 'après entente avec les Derviches'; it would be completely non-military and indeed almost unofficial, 'une espèce de visite anonyme . . . sans pavillon et sans mandat'. Only if the expedition encountered a European rival, violating by its very presence the rights of the Sultan and the Khedive, would Marchand hoist the Tricolour and reveal the true character of his mission. Marchand's arguments in support of this course seem to be simply a variant on the theme that two wrongs make a right; but he was very anxious to emphasise that no conflict could possibly arise from such an encounter. The two missions, treating one another 'avec toute l'urbanité et la correction désirables' would simply report one another's presence to their governments 'pour la suite à donner'.[2]

Such an upshot would indeed have been likely enough had Marchand encountered a mission analogous to his own: the Macdonald mission or the mythical Colvile mission, whose ghost was still being made to walk thanks not least to Colvile's own indiscretions.[3] Marchand can be forgiven for neglecting the possibility that he might encounter an officially Egyptian expedition; even in the Paris ministries this possibility does not seem to have been discussed until the astonishingly late date of July 1898. It is not so easy to excuse the professional diplomatists who uncritically accepted a junior officer's views on the upshot of a crisis which was to explode at some unpredictable date in the future. In particular, the idea of using the mission to provoke an international conference was an entirely new one,[4] due to Marchand himself or, more probably, to his mentors at the Pavillon de Flore. Yet it escaped all critical examination, although at the best of times it would have been the merest crystal-gazing to attempt to

[1] D.D.F. xii, No. 192, *note du capitaine Marchand* 10 Nov. 1895.
[2] *Ibid., loc. cit.*
[3] In Apr. 1895 Colvile had publicly stated that the British could advance from Uganda into the southern Sudan whenever they pleased; and *Bull. C.A.F.* had noted his remarks (Langer, *The Diplomacy of Imperialism*, p. 267). As late as Aug. 1896 Marchand was still worried about the advance of the 'Mission Coolville' (letter to Grandidier, printed Ménier, *Rev. Hist. Cols., ubi supra*, p. 67).
[4] Cocheris (*op. cit.*, p. 426) does indeed attribute this idea to Sadi Carnot in May 1893. But this statement should be treated with great caution, for Cocheris is here unsupported by (and indeed contradicted by) his source Monteil. Cf. *supra*, Ch. vii, p. 144, footnote.

forecast the outcome of a conference to be held many months, even years, ahead. And the later months of 1895, with 'the fluctuation of alliances' in full swing, were very far from the best of times.

Meanwhile, at the Quai d'Orsay, Benoît had not been idle. On 13 November the *Direction Politique* submitted to Berthelot a memorandum on the Marchand Mission. The object of the mission was defined in a quotation from Marchand's September memorandum; but the quotation had been carefully chosen. It gave the impression that the mission was designed simply to secure for France a ticket of entry to a forthcoming European conference on the partition of the southern Sudan:

> Nous voulons obtenir prudemment, d'une façon plutôt indirecte,
> parmi les populations indigènes de la vallée du Nil par le Bahr
> el Ghazal, une influence suffisante pour que la France puisse
> être admise d'une façon légitime, le jour où le sort de ces pro-
> vinces sera discuté, à faire partie de la conférence européenne
> qui pourra être réunie à ce sujet.[1]

Not a word about Egypt. Just a harmless little mission to the Bahr al-Ghazal, of which the graver implications would be far from obvious to a beginner in diplomacy like Berthelot. The *Direction's* memorandum of 13 November also pressed for the inter-departmental meeting, which had not yet been held.[2] Indeed, it is not known whether it was ever held; but by 21 November Guieysse evidently regarded the matter as settled in principle. At a Cabinet meeting on the 21st he passed to Berthelot a chit urgently requesting a formal letter of approval for 'the new mission'. Berthelot replied verbally that he was ready to sign; whereupon Roume importuned the *Direction Politique* at the Quai d'Orsay for very early action in preparing the draft.[3] All this desperate haste is very suspect; the *Colonies*, having obtained the Foreign Minister's approval, did not produce even the first version of Marchand's instructions until 24 February 1896.[4] It seems pretty obvious that the great point was to commit Berthelot before he should bethink himself to make enquiries which might prove embarrassing.

On 30 November 1895 Berthelot signed the letter of approval for the Marchand Mission. Whoever drafted it—presumably Benoît—was even willing to transfer all responsibility from the Colonial Ministry to the Foreign Ministry. The letter explicitly stated to Guieysse that 'en se plaçant au point de vue purement colonial, votre Département serait porté à restreindre au strict nécessaire les effectifs qui seraient envoyés sur le Haut-Oubangui'. This was an almost verbatim quota-

---

[1] D.D.F. XII, No. 197, *note pour le Ministre* 13 Nov. 1895. The passage here cited is printed in quotation marks; as it does not appear in Marchand's November note, the missing September memo. seems to be the obvious source.

[2] *Ibid., loc. cit.*

[3] D.D.F. XII, No. 210, *note de M. Guieysse* 21 Nov. 1895; footnote citing Roume to Affaires Etrangères 22 Nov.

[4] André Lebon, *La Politique de la France en Afrique, 1896-1898* (Paris 1901), p. 3. Cf. D.D.F. XII, No. 312, Guieysse to Liotard 24 Feb. 1896.

tion from Chautemps' letter of 21 September; but the subsequent hot campaign of the Colonial Ministry for a speedy and favourable decision on the proposed mission was passed over in complete silence. This letter, like the *Direction*'s earlier memorandum to Berthelot, omitted the 'Egyptian' implications of the mission and indeed restricted its activities to the Bahr al-Ghazal, where its presence 'nous permettrait d'intervenir utilement pour le règlement de la question du Soudan égyptien et pourrait avoir pour effet de hâter ce règlement'. However, the political safeguards originally suggested by Marchand were maintained. The mission was to be strictly non-military; further, 'la mission ne ferait pas acte d'occupation, elle ne chercherait même pas à passer des traités politiques'. To the project thus conceived, Berthelot gave his 'entire adhesion'.[1] Whatever he thought he was approving, it cannot have entered his mind that he was launching an enterprise which three years later was to seem a deliberate challenge to British hegemony throughout the Nile valley[2]

The political safeguards were even feebler than they looked. The British were unlikely to have much patience with subtleties about Marchand's precise mandate, unless he were reduced to the status of a mere private traveller or at most—to use a phrase later famous—of 'an emissary of civilisation'.[3] But in the event these safeguards were simply ignored, and Marchand did all the things which he had stated that his mission ought not to do. He flew the Tricolour throughout; he made treaties of protection, notably with the *Reth* of the Shilluk at Fashoda; he styled himself 'Commissaire du Gouvernement français dans le Haut Nil et le Bahr el Ghazal'; he hoisted the flag of the Republic over a former Egyptian headquarters, christened it 'Fort St Louis du Nil', and refused to evacuate it at the personal summons of the commander-in-chief of the Egyptian Army. These were not the indiscretions of a fire-eating junior officer. They were acts fully authorised by later instructions from the Pavillon de Flore, issued in flat defiance of Berthelot's directive and never communicated to, much less approved by, the Quai d'Orsay. The mission which reached Fashoda was not the mission which Marchand himself had originally proposed.

After all the fuss and bustle in November 1895, the Colonial Ministry produced no instructions for Marchand until 24 February 1896. This delay has never been satisfactorily explained. Marchand himself simply blames bureaucratic inertia; but he gives the interesting hint that the *Colonies* tried to excuse the delay by pleading that serious discussion with Britain on Egypt seemed at last to be in sight.[4] This

---

[1] D.D.F. xii, No. 219, Berthelot to Guieysse 30 Nov. 1895; cf. No. 152.

[2] The part (if any) played by the *Directeur politique* Nisard in these transactions is completely obscure. But Nisard seems to have been a rather ineffectual figure—even Berthelot over-ruled him without difficulty on occasion. In Dec. 1898 Monson described him as 'timid and very fearful of responsibility . . . also exceedingly deaf' (FO 27/3398, Monson to Salisbury No. 703, 23 Dec. 1898).

[3] Delcassé's description, according to Monson (FO 78/5050, Monson to Salisbury No. 441, 8 Sept. 1898).   [4] *Le Matin*, 20 June 1905.

might imply that Berthelot had woken up to some of the implications of the project he had approved, and was pressing Guieysse to delay its execution. If so, his efforts must have failed just at the moment when Courcel had opened the Egyptian discussion and was hopeful of continuing it fruitfully. Courcel spoke to Salisbury on 19 February 1896;[1] on the 24th Marchand's instructions were at last signed. In view of this coincidence the hypothesis of Berthelot's belated resistance might appear implausible; but in fact towards the end of February the Foreign Minister's influence must have been particularly weak. On 3 March 1896 Dufferin reported that Berthelot, 'enfeebled by bad health and lately unnerved by domestic affliction', seemed quite unable to cope with his duties.[2] There was however a controversy within the Colonial Ministry itself between those who wished to retain Liotard's well-established policy of supporting the Azande against the Mahdists; and those who believed with Marchand that a *modus vivendi* with the Mahdists, and if necessary the sacrifice of the Azande, was indispensable to the success of the mission.[3] This evidently led to a prolonged wrangle, for it was not finally settled until Guieysse had been replaced by the more experienced and authoritative André Lebon.[4] It may in itself have generated enough internal friction to account for the delay; if so, the timing of the instructions was purely fortuitous.

At all events, their timing did not depend on any foreknowledge or intelligent anticipation of the Anglo-Egyptian advance in the northern Sudan. This hypothesis was first put forward in 1904 by J. Darcy, who goes on to explain that at the end of 1895 Salisbury confidentially informed Courcel of his intention to move on Dongola and offered not to advance further 'sans nous être au préalable entendus avec vous'.[5] This looks very like a misdating of the abortive Salisbury-Courcel negotiations which actually took place in March 1896, after the Sudan expedition had been announced.[6] However, Hanotaux himself seemed to authorise this report by including it in his book *Fachoda*; and he added that Berthelot had been willing to treat on this basis but was overborne by his colleagues—a statement which is almost certainly correct, but again for March 1896, not December 1895.[7] In 1936 this report was repeated by C. Vergniol, who however made an addition of his own: on 9 February 1896 Salisbury is supposed to have approached Courcel a second time, and to have offered not to go beyond *Khartoum* 'sans avoir l'agrément de la France'. For Vergniol, the decision to set Marchand in motion followed naturally from the

[1] D.D.F. xii, No. 306, Courcel to Berthelot 19 Feb. 1896.
[2] FO 27/3274, Dufferin to Salisbury No. 41, 3 Mar. 1896.
[3] D.D.F. xii, No. 312, Guieysse to Liotard 24 Feb. 1896, makes it clear that the Zande-Mahdist problem was regarded as a very real difficulty.
[4] *Ibid.*, No. 411, Lebon to Liotard 23 June 1896.
[5] J. Darcy, *France et Angleterre: Cent Années de Rivalité Coloniale* (Paris 1904), pp. 400-2.
[6] Cf. *supra*, Ch. x, p. 233.
[7] Hanotaux, *Fachoda*, pp. 101-2.

refusal of Paris to negotiate on this basis.[1] Once again, the report is not completely false; but once again its significance has been completely distorted by an error of dating. Vergniol's account is in fact a crude but recognisable version of discussions which took place, not in February 1896, but a year later in February 1897.[2] Of course, neither the British nor the French documents bear the slightest trace of Salisbury's supposed offers in December 1895 and February 1896, which would indeed have been quite incompatible with Salisbury's policy towards the Sudan at that time. And Marchand himself bears witness that the Pavillon de Flore was as much taken aback as everyone else by the British move in the Sudan.[3]

Two sets of instructions were signed by Guieysse on 24 February 1896: one for Liotard, and one for Marchand. The full text of Marchand's instructions has now disappeared; but extracts published by André Lebon show that on most points of importance these instructions were identical with those addressed to Liotard.[4] Liotard's instructions, for the first time in any surviving document, name Fashoda as the goal of the Marchand Mission. Both sets of instructions define the political object of the mission as that of creating for France 'dans la région du Nil blanc des alliances sérieuses et des titres indiscutables pour le jour où viendra à être réglé le sort de ces provinces'.[5] The mission was thus no longer confined to the Bahr al-Ghazal; and 'alliances sérieuses et . . . titres indiscutables' were already a long way from Marchand's 'politique des gages' and Berthelot's prohibition of political treaty-making. An attempt was however made to assert the non-military character of the mission by firmly subordinating Marchand to the civilian Liotard, who was indeed authorised to cancel the whole operation if he thought it 'a priori impossible'. But Liotard was told that the Government 'tient essentiellement à ce que le "raid" . . . soit exécuté'. The use of this English word was doubtless an echo of Dr Jameson's recent exploit—not the happiest of auguries, but a useful clue to the way in which minds were working at the Pavillon de Flore. Great emphasis was laid on the need to achieve good relations with the Mahdists, and if possible their active co-operation; if the Mahdists showed 'une hostilité marquée', the expedition was to retire. The Zande-Mahdist problem was discussed at some length, but inconclusively; the hope was expressed that Marchand and Liotard would themselves be able to reach an amicable solution.[6]

On 24 February Guieysse was still unable to state, even approximately, the date of Marchand's departure.[7] According to Marchand the Ministry persisted in its dilatory ways until, precisely as Salisbury had feared, it was shaken out of its lethargy by the Anglo-Egyptian advance. Thereupon, writes Marchand, 'changement de vue au

---

[1] Vergniol, ubi supra, pp. 117-8.   [2] Infra, Ch. xiv, p. 316.
[3] Le Matin, 20 June 1905.
[4] Lebon, op. cit., pp. 3, 9-10. D.D.F. xii, No. 312.
[5] D.D.F., loc. cit.; Lebon, loc. cit.   [6] D.D.F., loc. cit.   [7] Ibid.

Pavillon de Flore. M. Guieysse et la direction me supplient de pré-
cipiter mon départ. Si j'avais écouté je serais parti dans les quarante-
huit heures, sans préparation.'[1] This was not the only way in which the
progress of the Marchand Mission was promoted by the 'Dongola
expedition'. At the end of March 1896, as a result of this development,
St Petersburg suddenly offered to Paris active support in Egypt and on
the Red Sea littoral. In April the Prime Minister Léon Bourgeois, who
had now taken over Foreign Affairs from Berthelot, began to interest
himself personally in the mission; and the belief that France was
now assured of Russian support in the Nile valley doubtless weighed
strongly with him when he gave the Marchand Mission his unqualified
approval.

It was not the Anglo-Egyptian advance in itself that the Russians
objected to; secretly they welcomed it. What worried St Petersburg,
especially against the background of the recent Anglo-French rapprochement, was the very mild reaction of the Quai d'Orsay to the
British 'provocation'. Lobanov profoundly distrusted the anglophile
tendencies of a government of Radicals; and the Russian Ambassador
Mohrenheim was daily at the Quai d'Orsay, attempting to fan the
flame of the very moderate French resentment.[2] When Berthelot
accepted Salisbury's assurances about the future of Egypt, Lobanov
lost patience. On 27 March he upbraided Montebello on the failure
of the French to seek Russian approval before accepting a document
which, even in its curtailed form, 'paraît clore l'incident de la façon
la moins satisfaisante'. If the French were going to abandon their
Egyptian interests so tamely, they must not expect Russia to come to
the rescue.[3] By this time Berthelot had 'gone back to his science', his
position having been made impossible by Russian pressure and the
intrigues of Bourgeois against him. Bourgeois, now Foreign Minister,
replied to St Petersburg in almost grovelling terms: France could
never for a moment have contemplated a settlement not previously
approved by Russia.[4] Having got rid of Berthelot by threats, Lobanov
now decided to egg Bourgeois on by promises. On 29 March he
announced to Montebello that Russia had, after all, an interest of
first-rate importance in Egypt—the neutralisation of the Suez Canal.
He had already sent combative instructions in this sense to Staal at
London; now he offered to France 'l'appui le plus énergique' in this
question. Montebello was jubilant. For years France had been complaining of Russian apathy on Egypt: 'aujourd'hui le revirement est
complet, et nous pouvons compter sur elle'.[5] For a time Lobanov

---

[1] *Le Matin*, 20 June 1905.
[2] G.P. XI, Nos. 2706, 2721, Münster to Hohenlohe, 19 and 31 Mar. 1896. Cf. D.D.F.
XII, No. 353, Herbette to Berthelot 25 Mar. 1896.
[3] D.D.F. XII, No. 355, Montebello to Berthelot 27 Mar. 1896.
[4] *Ibid.*, No. 356, Bourgeois to Montebello 28 Mar.
[5] *Ibid.*, Nos. 361, 365, Montebello to Bourgeois 31 Mar. and 2 Apr. 1896. The instructions to Staal were in fact less combative than Lobanov made out; cf. Staal, *Correspondance*,
p. 316, Lobanov to Staal 6 May 1896.

seemed as good as his word. On 4 April he told the British Ambassador at St Petersburg, in a tone that was 'not pleasant' that the neutrality of the Canal would remain illusory until the British had evacuated Egypt, and he demanded 'a full enquiry . . . into the whole Egyptian situation'.[1]

Léon Bourgeois had already been hankering after a more spirited response to the British intervention in the Sudan. On 29 March he had asked his ambassador at Constantinople whether he could suggest, as a riposte to London, any demonstration or 'prise de possession' in the Levant. Paul Cambon replied pointing out the dangers, both to peace and to the Franco-Russe, inherent in any independent French action here.[2] A few days later the Prime Minister's attention was drawn to the Marchand Mission; Bourgeois' son was, as it happened, a personal friend of Marchand.[3] Here was a 'prise de possession' already in active preparation, and one that at first sight seemed far less risky than French action in the Levant. On 18 April Bourgeois interviewed Marchand, who estimated that he could be on the Nile at or near Fashoda by the end of 1897. April 1896 was perhaps the latest date at which the Marchand Mission could have been called off without arousing a major political storm. Instead, Bourgeois, encouraged by the new-found enthusiasm of the Russians for Egypt, gave it his personal blessing—and at that in its new form as a 'raid' for the seizure of Fashoda.[4] Exactly a week later, on 25 April, Marchand's advance party sailed for Africa.

On 29 April the Bourgeois government was replaced by that of Jules Méline, with Hanotaux back at the Quai d'Orsay and André Lebon at the *Colonies*. Hanotaux was hungry for office and contemptuous of the amateur fumblings of his predecessors.[5] He was at once confronted with the Marchand Mission, now doubly a *fait accompli*. Any attempt to countermand it would have been political suicide: this is the one clear impression to emerge from the fog of half-truths and special pleadings with which Hanotaux attempts to bemuse the reader of his apologia *Fachoda*. André Lebon, in his own apologia, insists on the political impossibility of calling off the Mission.[6] The Méline government was to have an unusually long innings, but during its first months of office it seemed anything but secure.[7] Rather than face a storm in the Chamber it would doubtless have decided to sacrifice Hanotaux—a non-political minister who was insisting on an unpopular policy could always be dropped without penalty. Moreover, the recent interregnum had shown that Hanotaux was perhaps not quite so indispensable

---

[1] FO 78/4892, O'Conor to Salisbury No. 21, 4 Apr. 1896.
[2] D.D.F. xii, No. 357, Bourgeois to Paul Cambon 29 Mar. 1896; No. 362, Cambon to Bourgeois 31 Mar.
[3] Vergniol, *ubi supra*, pp. 126-7.   [4] Renouvin, *ubi supra*, p. 194.
[5] Cf. D.D.F. xii, No. 382, Hanotaux to Montebello, private, 7 May 1896.
[6] Hanotaux, *op. cit.*, pp. 106-8; Lebon, *op. cit.*, pp. 12-14.
[7] G. Chapman, *The Dreyfus Case* (London 1955), p. 115. FO 27/3267, Monson to Salisbury No. 388, 11 Dec. 1896.

after all. If Hanotaux were dropped now, he might quite well never come back; and he aspired to be the 'permanent' Foreign Minister whose tenure would be unaffected by changes of government.[1]

Moreover, Marchand's mission had from Hanotaux' point of view certain redeeming features. Numerically it was very weak. Marchand had deliberately kept its numbers down, partly to avoid provoking desperate resistance by eating the country bare as the Congolese had done, and partly in the belief that the Mahdists would take more kindly to a small expedition.[2] Perhaps Marchand would not get to Fashoda. Perhaps he would get just far enough to cause London disquiet, but not to precipitate a really serious crisis; he might then be used as Hanotaux seems to have hoped to use Monteil in August 1894. Such a means of pressure on England, although a little risky, may not have been unwelcome to Hanotaux in May 1896. It was becoming very clear that unless the Egyptian question could somehow be opened the influence of France at Cairo was likely to decline even further. In February Cogordan, the French Agent at Cairo, had reported that Egyptian nationalist circles were beginning to resent French administrative obstruction of projects which, like the Asswan dam, were of obvious material benefit to Egypt; and that France would lose face disastrously if the current Near Eastern crisis blew over without any progress having been made in the Egyptian question. In April he had reported that Egyptian opinion was beginning to see in a French occupation of the Bahr al-Ghazal the only hope of putting pressure on England. In this view Cogordan, always a pretty enthusiastic 'Egyptianist', heartily concurred. When the British 'asked for explanations', 'notre réponse serait facile, car sans doute il nous coûterait peu . . . d'évacuer ces lointaines provinces, du jour où les troupes anglaises quitteraient le Delta'.[3]

This was an even cruder version of the scheme originally hatched by Marchand, and it is not suggested that Hanotaux' approach was so *simpliste*. Indeed, it seems likely that Hanotaux never did have a very clear idea of exactly what he hoped to get from the Marchand Mission. More than once during 1897 and 1898 President Félix Faure asked Hanotaux just what he was about with the Mission; but the question was always brushed aside with the banal reply, 'si Marchand est à Fachoda, il nous fournira une monnaie d'échange'.[4] But Hanotaux certainly felt in May and June 1896 that *something* had to be done about the Nile valley—his repeated attempts to engage the Russians are evidence enough of this. Moreover, the Marchand Mission must have seemed all the more attractive as events demonstrated the

[1] FO 27/3267, *loc. cit.*

[2] A.-E.-A. Baratier, *Souvenirs de la Mission Marchand: Au Congo* (Paris 1914), pp. 8-12. D.D.F. XII, Nos. 153, 192.

[3] D.D.F. XII, No. 305, Cogordan to Berthelot 15 Feb. 1896; No. 373, Cogordan to Bourgeois 16 Apr. 1896.

[4] Félix Faure, memorandum 'Affaires d'Angleterre', printed under the title 'Fachoda (1898)', *Rev. Hist. Dip.* LXIX (1955), pp. 29-39 (at p. 30).

complete uselessness of the Sultan as a weapon against England. In March 1896 Paris instigated the Sultan to protest against the Egyptian invasion of the Sudan. 'Abd al-Hamīd thereupon sent to the Khedive 'Abbās a Note, as from Sultan to *wāli*, 'tantamount to an order to desist' from hostilities against fellow-Muslims. But when the Khedive pointed out that the Mahdists ought not to be considered orthodox Muslims, the Sultan accepted this lame explanation in an almost cordial telegram.[1] On 14 April the Ottoman ambassador told Bourgeois that the Sultan now intended to follow 'une ligne de conduite sérieuse', and suggested that France and Turkey should concert their policy in Egypt and the Red Sea. This proposal, if seriously intended, would have been far from welcome to Russia, and Bourgeois answered evasively.[2] In the event the Sultan merely protested against the proposed garrisoning of Suakin by Indian troops; the British retorted that in case of military necessity they proposed to do as they pleased.[3] Well might Hanotaux lament on 7 May: 'nous nous appuyons sur un roseau si nous comptons sur la diplomatie turque'.[4]

There was of course still Russia; but Hanotaux probably had less confidence in Russia than Montebello and Bourgeois. Other diplomatists, notably Herbette at Berlin, were less impressed by Lobanov's sudden interest in the Suez Canal, and were quite sceptical of Russian assistance in securing the evacuation of Egypt, 'vu la froideur avec laquelle le Cabinet de Pétersbourg envisage une entente franco-anglaise'.[5] Hanotaux, with his experience and intelligence, must have shared these doubts; but there was nothing to be done but take Lobanov's offer at its face value and press for action. Hanotaux pressed hard, but he did not get any action. On 13 May he suggested that if British troops disembarked at Suakin, France and Russia should invite Germany and the Ottoman Empire to stage a counter-demonstration by a four-power landing elsewhere on the Sudan coast. This was of course a rather chimerical scheme, especially as Hanotaux insisted that Germany should take part; but Lobanov's reply was the feeblest of anti-climaxes. He suggested that the Sultan should be induced to protest—as if the utter futility of the Sultan's protests had not already been adequately demonstrated; meanwhile, Lobanov would canvass the views of Berlin, Rome and Vienna on the preservation of the *status quo* in the Red Sea.[6] In the first week of June the

---

[1] D.D.F. xii, No. 345, Berthelot to de la Boulinière 22 Mar. 1896. FO 78/4893, Currie to Salisbury tels. No. 112, 113, of 24 Mar.; Salisbury to Currie No. 55, 25 Mar.; Cromer to Salisbury Nos. 61 and 62, 25 Mar.; No. 69, 28 Mar.; No. 74, 30 Mar.; No. 81, 1 Apr. 1896. Shibeika, *op. cit.*, pp. 359-61.
[2] D.D.F. xii, No. 371, Bourgeois to Vauvineux 14 Apr. 1896.
[3] Shibeika, *op. cit.*, pp. 368-9.
[4] D.D.F. xii, No. 382, Hanotaux to Montebello 7 May 1896.
[5] *Ibid.*, No. 353, Herbette to Berthelot 25 Mar. 1896; Nos. 367 (cited), 369, Herbette to Bourgeois 3 and 6 Apr. G.P. xi, Nos. 2721, 2730, Münster to A.A. 31 Mar. and 25 Apr. 1896.
[6] D.D.F. xii, No. 377, Hanotaux to Vauvineux 29 Apr. 1896; Nos. 386, 388, Hanotaux to Montebello 13 and 15 May; footnote to No. 388,

Indian troops landed at Suakin and the Cairo Mixed Court condemned as illegal the advance from the *Caisse de la Dette*. Hanotaux pleaded that in this 'changed situation' Paris and St Petersburg should concert their policies. He was still without a reply when on 15 June he was greatly alarmed by a report that England was about to cede Kassala to the Germans, in return for the active support of Berlin in the Nile valley. Hanotaux now begged Lobanov for 'immediate decisions' to prevent the complete disappearance of French and Russian influence on the Red Sea littoral. Lobanov, who had helped to start this utterly baseless scare, was content to reply that it would be sufficient to watch events and to avoid giving any impression of uneasiness.[1] At this point Hanotaux seems to have abandoned his efforts in despair.

Meanwhile Lobanov continued to talk to the British in vaguely threatening terms about their occupation of Egypt, but he never of course explicitly demanded evacuation.[2] He did not even make a formal demand for the neutralisation of the Suez Canal, though he gave Paris to understand that he had done so.[3] However, early in April Lobanov did make serious efforts to persuade the Germans to act with France and Russia on the Egyptian question.[4] The object of this manœuvre was probably not so much to secure the actual evacuation of Egypt as to embroil both France and Germany in a common quarrel with England, thereby giving Russia an enviably free hand at the Straits and in the Far East. The Germans of course saw the trap, and were not gulled by Lobanov's explicit offer to guarantee the peaceful behaviour of France in Europe; they declined to change their policy on the rather feeble pretext that the refusal of France to cooperate against England in the Transvaal had 'proved' her obsession with *revanche*.[5] Lobanov continued his attempts to persuade the Germans until his sudden and untimely death in August 1896; but he meanwhile evaded all joint action with France. He had after all achieved his primary object of destroying an Anglo-French negotiation on Egypt which might have rescued the earlier rapprochement between London and Paris.

On 13 May 1896 Hanotaux had told Montebello that his proposal for a demonstration on the coast of the Sudan was absolutely dependent on the participation of at least two other European Powers. The question of the Nile valley, he insisted, interested Europe as a whole, not merely France; and Europe as a whole must co-operate to solve it.

[1] *Ibid.*, Nos. 404, 408, Hanotaux to Montebello 12 and 15 June 1896. No. 408 fn., citing Montebello to Hanotaux 17 June.
[2] D.D.F. xii, No. 380, Montebello to Hanotaux 3 May 1896. Staal, *Correspondance*, p. 317, Lobanov to Lessar 18 June. Cf. Salisbury to Howard 15 July, cited B.D. i, No. 380.
[3] L.Q.V. 3, iii, pp. 102-3, Salisbury to the Queen 29 Oct. 1896. Cf. D.D.F. xii, No. 442, Courcel to Hanotaux 13 Aug. 1896.
[4] D.D.F. xii, No. 354, Montebello to Berthelot 25 Mar. 1896; No. 442, Courcel to Hanotaux 13 Aug. Staal, *Correspondance*, pp. 313-6: Osten-Sacken to Lobanov 20 Mar. 1896; Lobanov to Osten-Sacken 21 Apr. G.P. xi, No. 2732, Rodolin to Hohenlohe 5 May 1896. [5] G.P. xi, No. 2734, memo. by Marschall 15 May 1896.

Isolated action by France had brought, and could bring, nothing but an unnecessary increase in British hostility, and it was time to abandon this self-sacrificing and self-defeating policy. It was for Europe to act: 'si elle veut me laisser tout le fardeau, je m'abstiens'.[1] These were considerations which applied supremely to the Marchand Mission itself, and in a world of pure diplomacy they would have far outweighed the real or imagined advantages of allowing the mission to proceed. But no diplomatist ever operates in a world of pure diplomacy—least of all Hanotaux, who had his own position to think of. According to his own later account, however, Hanotaux' attitude to the Marchand Mission was not merely passive and permissive. He claims to have inspired a new set of instructions, signed by André Lebon on 23 June 1896, which brought about 'une atténuation très caractérisée' in the whole nature of the mission. He asserts in particular that by insisting on the subordination of Marchand to the civilian Liotard he had ensured that the mission should have 'un caractère exclusivement pacifique'.[2]

The instructions of 23 June certainly did emphasise very strongly the subordination of Marchand to Liotard. They were indeed addressed to Liotard, now promoted to Governor, as Marchand's political chief.[3] But the February instructions of Guieysse had insisted no less firmly on Marchand's subordinate status. As for Hanotaux' having given the mission 'un caractère exclusivement pacifique', the very passage which he cites in support of this claim is presented in the June instructions as a paraphrase from 'la dépêche de mon prédécesseur du 24 février dernier'.[4] It is moreover clear from the context that this 'pacific character' relates exclusively to relations with the Mahdists, with whom Liotard is now instructed to 'établir, sinon une alliance véritable, tout au moins de bons rapports'—even, if necessary, at the cost of strained relations with the Azande.[5]

All the same, Hanotaux' claim to have introduced 'une atténuation très caracterisée' is probably not unfounded, although the 'atténuation' was not the one for which he sought credit and perhaps not one to which he would have cared to admit, even when he published his book. There was in the June instructions a distinct watering-down of the political objectives which had been prescribed for the mission in February 1896. There is no mention whatever of Fashoda, which had in February been declared the goal of the mission; the June instructions talk vaguely of 'the Nile basin'. Again, there are no references to the 'alliances sérieuses' and 'titres indiscutables' upon which the February instructions had insisted. The political objective of the mission is defined—or rather, left undefined—in a single woolly sentence: 'Il s'agit ... de maintenir strictement la ligne politique que,

---

[1] D.D.F. xii, No. 386, Hanotaux to Montebello 13 May 1896.
[2] Hanotaux, *op. cit.*, pp. 108-9. D.D.F. xii, No. 411, Lebon to Liotard 23 June 1896.
[3] D.D.F., *loc. cit.*
[4] Hanotaux, *loc. cit.*; D.D.F. xii, Nos. 312, 411. Cf. Renouvin, *ubi supra*, pp. 194-5.
[5] D.D.F. xii, No. 411.

depuis près de deux années, vous suivez avec persévérance et dont notre établissement dans le bassin du Nil doit être le couronnement.'[1] Seeing that Liotard, for all his perseverance, had been making so little progress and hardly hoped to reach the Nile itself in the near future, this directive 'strictly to maintain' his existing policy might almost be paraphrased: 'Forward into the Nile valley! But not too fast or too far!'[2] Indeed, Marchand himself seems to have interpreted the directive in this sense. When in the autumn of 1897 Marchand received further and very different orders from the Pavillon de Flore, he reacted with great excitement, as if to a completely new development.

> Ordre très grave pour marche en avant, provenant du Gouvernement. J'ai reçu une lettre du plus haut protecteur de la mission. [presumably the Colonial Minister, André Lebon] . . . Enfin! Occupation Fachoda par France décidée. Il faut que j'y sois en décembre.[3]

All this strongly suggests that Hanotaux attempted to transform the Marchand Mission from a 'raid' for the seizure of Fashoda to a mere 'presence' in the Bahr al-Ghazal, and that his efforts were at first not unsuccessful. Such an attempt would also explain his insistence, in his apologia, on the otherwise incomprehensible thesis that the true object of the Marchand Mission 'n'était pas même un objet d'échange, un gage ou une matière à négociation, c'était la négociation elle-même'.[4]

Not that Marchand had any need artificially to delay his march: Africa took care of that. On 24 July 1896 he disembarked at Loango to find the French Congo almost in a state of insurrection and its porterage system dislocated to the point of non-existence. On 18 August he obtained from de Brazza, by the threat to return immediately to France, full powers to restore order. By January 1897 this task had been completed, though it had required a full-dress campaign by Marchand and his subordinate Mangin. Marchand now concentrated all his men and stores at Brazzaville; but the French had not enough boats to carry them, and Marchand was forced to beg the loan of the Congolese steamer *Ville de Bruges*. Marchand had always intended to march by way of Deim Zubeir, southern Darfur and southern Kordofan; but in April 1897 he was informed by Liotard that this route was impracticable, and instructed to follow an almost all-river route by the M'Bomu, by a southern affluent of the Bahr al-Ghazal and then by the Bahr al-Ghazal itself.[5] To Marchand, these instructions seemed to condemn the Mission to almost certain failure. It was, in

[1] *Ibid.*
[2] The instructions lay considerable emphasis on caution and careful consolidation; and as late as June 1897 Liotard was in fact still wedded to a policy of deliberate, cautious advance. Cf. D.D.F. xiii, No. 365 Appx. ii, Liotard to Marchand 8 Apr. 1897, enclosed in Liotard to Lebon 15 June.
[3] Cited Delebecque, *op. cit.*, pp. 109–10. The letter is undated; but the 'December' must be Dec. 1897.
[4] Hanotaux, *op. cit.*, p. 137.   [5] D.D.F. xiii, No. 365, Appx. ii.

the first place, more than doubtful whether the M'Bomu was navigable at all. From Hanssen's Falls to its confluence with the Shinko it was known to be a mere series of cataracts and rapids; beyond the Shinko it was unexplored, the Belgians having written it off as very unlikely to show any improvement. Another difficulty was that the expedition had not enough boats of its own; but Marchand, 'la mort dans l'âme', nevertheless decided to try the river route. He commandeered all the boats he could lay hands on, including the upper Ubangi post-boat, a thirty-foot steam-launch called the *Faidherbe*. Although the *Faidherbe* was not a *bateau démontable*, Marchand's mechanics took out its machinery; and then Marchand began the perhaps interminable series of portages around the M'Bomu cataracts. He now had his one real stroke of luck. Had the M'Bomu turned out to be entirely unnavigable, three to four hundred miles of portages would probably have broken even Marchand's iron will. But above the Shinko confluence he found a magnificent unencumbered reach nearly three hundred miles long. By September 1897 the flotilla had reached a point only about 125 miles from the head of possible navigation on the Sueh, an affluent of the Bahr al-Ghazal. The *Faidherbe* was now completely dismantled and its pieces carried by porters with the other boats to the Sueh. But the *Faidherbe*'s boilers were too heavy for this treatment. They were therefore transported in improvised carts along an improvised track cut through the virgin bush.[1]

By the end of November 1897 Marchand and his flotilla were on the Sueh at Wau. The *Faidherbe* had been reconstructed and was under orders to raise steam. Marchand now thought himself already as good as at Fashoda. On 25 November he wrote that the *Faidherbe* could take him 'en 15 jours à mon choix à Khartoum si je veux, ou à Lado si ça me plaît, ou . . . n'importe où sur le Nil'.[2] But Africa still had a few surprises in store. Early in December the waters of the Sueh began to fall; and it was not until the beginning of June 1898 that the mission was able to set out on its final stage through the Bahr al-Ghazal *sudd*. During the next five weeks it often seemed as if the mission would be forced to a standstill almost within reach of its goal. There were times when a few hundred yards seemed a satisfactory day's march. Marchand was sometimes reduced to building little mud dams in front of his boats so as to give them the necessary few inches' draught of water. He himself wrote: 'Je n'ai jamais eu le soupçon d'un travail pareil. Rien ne peut en donner une idée même lointaine et j'aurais refusé d'en croire le récit.'[3] But Marchand reached Fashoda at last—

---

[1] For the progress of the Mission, see: Baratier, *Souvenirs de la Mission Marchand, Au Congo* (Paris 1914); *Vers le Nil* (1923); *Fachoda* (1941); J. Emily, *Mission Marchand* (Paris 1913); Marchand's letters to Grandidier, *Rev. Hist. Cols.* 1958, pp. 61-108; C.-M.-E. Mangin, *Regards sur la France d'Afrique* (Paris 1924), pp. 236-56; *eundem*, 'Lettres de la Mission Marchand', *Revue des Deux Mondes*, 15 Sept. 1931, pp. 241-83; Delebecque, *op. cit.*, pp. 84-119.

[2] Marchand to Grandidier, from Wau, 25 Nov. 1897 (*Rev. Hist. Cols.*, *ubi supra*, p. 102).

[3] Emily, *op. cit.*, pp. 89-110. Baratier, *Fachoda*, pp. 43-54.

at 5 p.m. on 10 July 1898. The *Faidherbe*, which had been left behind at Wau to await a further rise in the Sueh waters, did not begin her battle with the *sudd* until 19 July. She reached Fashoda on 29 August, having spent just six weeks on a voyage of less than 450 miles.

On 12 July 1898, in the presence of the *Reth* and notables of the Shilluk, Marchand ceremonially hoisted the French flag and took possession of Fashoda in the name of France; at the climax of the ceremony the halyard snapped and the Tricolour fluttered to the ground.[1] This ill-omened gesture was however Marchand's only act of occupation on the Nile itself before the arrival of Kitchener. Relative to his own line of communication through the Bahr al-Ghazal *sudd* and the M'Bomu cataracts, Marchand was isolated at the end of the world;[2] but he was well aware that Fashoda was only a few days' easy sail from Omdurman. He therefore kept his troops in strict defensive concentration and pushed ahead with the reconstruction of the ruinous Egyptian fort at Fashoda.[3] His precautions were wise. On 25 August the two Mahdist steamers *Safia* and *Tawfiqia* appeared off Fashoda. Their commander, Sa'īd al-Sughaiar, had been sent to Fashoda to collect grain from the Shilluk, not to fight the French. Nevertheless, he improvised a vigorous assault; but it cost him so many casualties that he withdrew discomfited to Omdurman.[4] Marchand profited by this victory to conclude, on 3 September, a formal treaty of protection with *Reth* Kur 'Abd al-Fadīl of the Shilluk.[5] On 15 September he issued an Order of the Day announcing that 'le double but de la mission [était] de faire l'occupation du Bahr el Ghazal et d'établir la domination française à Fachoda'; and at the famous 'encounter' on the 19th he officially notified Kitchener that he had occupied both the Bahr al-Ghazal and the Shilluk country 'par ordre de mon Gouvernement'.[6]

He was making no false or empty claim. All the far-reaching political acts of Captain J.-B. Marchand, 'Commissaire du Gouvernement français dans le Haut Nil et le Bahr el Ghazal',[7] were carried out in obedience to direct and peremptory orders from the Pavillon de Flore. The documents embodying these orders to perform acts of occupation and make political treaties have now disappeared; but their existence can be quite clearly inferred, and their date can be established with fair precision as within the first three months of 1897

[1] Emily, *op. cit.*, pp. 133-4.
[2] Letters between Paris and Fashoda took from eight to nine months en route.
[3] Apart from reconnaissances by the *Faidherbe*. Cf. D.D.F. xiv No. 445, transmitting Marchand to *Colonies* tel. No. 14, 20 Aug. 1898.
[4] Statement of Sa'īd al-Sughaiar, 15 Sept. 1896 (S.I.R. No. 60, Appx 46).
[5] Printed at D.D.F. xiv, Appendix I, Annex to No. v.
[6] Order by Marchand, 15 Sept. 1898 (selected for publication, but not published, in D.D.F. xiv). FO 78/5051, Marchand to Kitchener 19 Sept. 1898 (original), enclosed in Rodd to Salisbury No. 153, 29 Sept.
[7] The letters from Marchand to Kitchener and other British officers, as published in D.D.F. xiv, Appendix I, bear the style 'Chef de la Mission Congo-Nil'. But in the originals (all of which are at Khartoum except that of 19 Sept.) Marchand invariably styles himself 'Commissaire du Gouvernement français dans [or 'sur'] le Haut Nil et le Bahr el Ghazal'.

—February or March seems the most likely. It was in March 1897 that the Colonial Ministry revived the old project of persuading the Ethiopians to join hands with the French on the White Nile.[1] Early in March 1897 André Lebon's letters begin to refer to 'our possessions in the Bahr al-Ghazal' and to assert that the Nile was the frontier between the French and the Ethiopian possessions.[2] A date of despatch in or about February 1897 is consistent with Marchand's having received in the autumn of that year the orders which caused him to exclaim: 'Enfin! Occupation Fachoda par France décidée'.[3] However, the only surviving shred of direct evidence is a telegram from Lebon dated 8 January 1898:

> Prévenez Liotard et Marchand nécessaire conclure traités avec chefs toutes populations avec lesquelles sont en contact. En vue revendications ultérieures autres Puissances, est de toute importance que limites indiquées par ces traités se correspondent, et laissent entre elles aucune solution [?] continuité dans territoires Bahr el Ghazal et rive gauche Nil.[4]

But Lebon states elsewhere that this was merely an urgent reminder of earlier instructions;[5] and when in November 1898 Marchand was ordered to evacuate Fashoda, he angrily referred Delcassé to the 'ordres formels que j'ai reçus du Gouvernement *en 1897* et 1898'.[6] Nor did the Pavillon de Flore confine itself to mere verbal instructions. In the course of 1897 it began to follow up the spearhead of the Marchand Mission by a systematic occupation of the Bahr al-Ghazal and of the west bank of the Nile, which was ultimately reached not only at Fashoda but at Shambe. By the autumn of 1898 about a dozen points, other than Fashoda, had been occupied within the Nile basin.[7] And as early as 26 April 1898 a decree by Liotard, as Governor of the upper Ubangi, had created for the 'French Bahr al-Ghazal' an administrative structure consisting of three districts (*cercles*) with their headquarters at Tambura, Jur Ghattas and Ayack.[8]

Meanwhile, the elaborate mystification of Marchand's subordination to Liotard was quietly dropped. In the summer of 1898 Liotard went to France on leave, and nobody has ever suggested that Marchand then became the subordinate of Liotard's deputy, a certain Dr

---

[1] *Infra*, Ch. XIII, pp. 293-4.
[2] D.D.F. XIII, No. 137, Lebon to Hanotaux 5 Mar. 1897; No. 169, Lebon to Lagarde 27 Mar. In Feb. 1897 Lebon had received a despatch from Liotard explaining his plans for the penetration of the Bahr al-Ghazal (D.D.F. XIII, No. 99, Lebon to Hanotaux 11 Feb. 1897, enclosing Liotard to Lebon 9 July 1896).
[3] Delebecque, *op. cit.*, pp. 109-10.
[4] D.D.F. XIV, No. 4, Lebon to Lamothe (Congo) 8 Jan. 1898.
[5] Lebon, *op. cit.*, pp. 38-9.
[6] D.D.F. XIV, No. 490, Marchand to Delcassé 5 Nov. 1898.
[7] MC Afrique III 36a, *Rapport confidentielle, Organisation et Renforcement de la Mission Marchand*, 10 Oct. 1898. E. Roulet, *La Mission Roulet* (Paris 1933). Cf. Gage, 'Sudd-Cutting', *S.N.R.* 1950, pp. 7-20; S.I.R. No. 67 (Jan.-Mar. 1900); FO 78/5051, D.M.I. to F.O. 4 Oct. 1898.
[8] Roulet, *op. cit.*, p. 23; Anon., 'De l'Oubangui au Nil', *Bull. C.A.F.*, Oct. 1898, pp. 328-30; H. Bobichon, 'Le Haut-Oubangui', *La Revue Forézienne*, 1902, pp. 392-6, 400.

Cureau.[1] Marchand himself has stated that he did not regard this relationship as being in force after January 1898.[2] It was doubtless then that Marchand put away his official stamp which read 'Commandant des Troupes, Haut-Oubangui', and took out another with which he had been provided—and which he invariably[3] used in his correspondence with Kitchener and other 'Anglo-Egyptian' officers. This second stamp bore the proud legend 'Afrique Centrale Française: Mission du Congo-Nil'. Such stamps are not supplied by accident. The Pavillon de Flore had evidently made up its mind early in 1896 about the real objective of the Marchand Mission—and from that objective it did not intend to be diverted, even though instructions might have to be temporarily modified at the behest of the Quai d'Orsay.

[1] Cocheris, *op. cit.*, pp. 485-94.
[2] *Le Matin*, 20 June 1905.
[3] Almost invariably. One or two letters bear both stamps—presumably the first had been used inadvertently.

T

XIII

ETHIOPIA, THE UPPER NILE AND
THE POLICY OF HANOTAUX, 1895–98

MANY years after his exploits on the Upper Nile, Marchand stated that he would never have undertaken his mission had he not been given firm assurances of support from Ethiopia, both by French missions and by the Ethiopians themselves.[1] In fact the project of assistance from Ethiopia had played no part whatever in the original planning of the mission; and the first indication that Marchand himself was counting on it occurs in a letter to Gentil of 15 April 1897.[2] By this time the Pavillon de Flore was indeed making strenuous efforts to secure Ethiopian co-operation; but until the end of 1896 it seems to have pinned its faith completely, as did Marchand himself, to 'sinon une alliance véritable, tout au moins de bons rapports avec les Derviches'. Partly for this very reason, Marchand had kept the numbers of his mission low, and as late as 1 January 1898 he was still asking, not for reinforcements, but merely for reliefs.[3]

However, the closer Marchand got to the Mahdists, the less he liked the look of them. Already by the end of January 1898 he had changed his tune. In a private letter of 30 January he girds at the Government for having arbitrarily restricted his force to a size unequal to its military and political tasks. 'Après cette mission il ne restera plus . . . qu'à me confier quatre hommes et un caporal, avec l'ordre de prendre Berlin de vive force, à la baïonette. . . .'[4] By June, when he was about to pass through the protective screen of the Bahr al-Ghazal *sudd*, he had no more illusions. On 4 June, the day on which he left Wau, he wrote: 'Situation actuelle d'indécision et d'incertitude ne peut se prolonger. Envoyez les moyens d'occuper ou l'ordre d'évacuer.'[5] A fortnight later, at Meshra' er Req, Marchand was almost distracted by the military weakness of his position. He con-

[1] Delebecque, *Vie du général Marchand*, pp. 77-8, reporting a statement by Marchand.
[2] M.-A. Ménier, 'Une lettre inédite de Marchand à Gentil', *Rev. Hist. Cols.* XL (1954), pp. 431-40.
[3] MC Afrique III 36a, *Organisation et Renforcement de la Mission Marchand* 10 Oct. 1898; and undated annexes thereto. Cf. *ibid.*, 36b, Binger to Lebon 31 May 1898.
[4] Marchand to an unnamed correspondent, 30 Jan. 1898, published in *Le Gil Blas*, 27 Oct. 1898.
[5] Marchand to Lebon tel. 4 June 1898; cf. D.D.F. XIV, p. 683, footnote 2. (This tel. was seen among material for publication in D.D.F. XIV, but was not in fact published.)

fesses 'je ne sais trop qui ni quoi je vais trouver à Fachoda', and goes on to blame the Government for his plight:

Devant l'attitude d'une certaine presse, il n'ose pas me donner les moyens d'accomplir la tâche formidable qu'il me demande.

. . . Aussi la conduite étrange que l'on tient avec moi ici m'a-t-elle complètement écœuré, découragé. . . . C'est lâche, lâche . . . je pleure de rage . . .—

and more in a similar vein.[1] By this time Marchand was relying very heavily on assistance from Ethiopia. Within forty-eight hours of his arrival at Fachoda he had sent a message to the 'Chef de la Mission française venant de la Côte Somalis', of which the burden was 'il n'y a pas une heure à perdre'.[2] His messages were returned undelivered; and when the *Faidherbe* returned from a reconnaissance up the Sobat without having made any contact, Marchand was 'atterré'.[3]

After Kitchener's arrival had guaranteed him against the Mahdist danger, Marchand sent three successive parties overland in search of Ethiopian support.[4] The last of these, under Mangin, did make contact with *Dejazmach* Dimissi, the Ethiopian Governor of the Bani Shanqūl region; but not until 17 December 1898. The *dejazmach* was however equally innocent of any knowledge of the French objectives and of any instructions to co-operate with Marchand; Mangin was mortified to find himself treated as a spy—exact nationality unknown, but probably English or Italian.[5] Mangin's plight neatly exemplifies the fact that Menelik was no more ready to play the French game on the Upper Nile than he was the British. In 1897 and 1898 Menelik had indeed been lavish in promises of assistance to the French, but these were as empty as the verbal thunderbolts which he hurled at the Mahdists for the benefit of Rodd and Wingate. Menelik's policy served purely Ethiopian interests, which he was quite shrewd enough to safeguard without any prompting from Europeans with ulterior motives.[6]

In October 1894 Delcassé had, with the concurrence of Hanotaux, resumed the dialogue with Menelik which Casimir-Périer had broken off.[7] In March 1895 Menelik had offered, in return for the formal

---

[1] Marchand to Grandidier, from Meshra' er Req 17(?) June 1898: Ménier, 'Lettres du commandant Marchand . . .', *Rev. Hist. Cols.*, 1958, pp. 106-8.

[2] This letter, of 12 July 1898, with a postscript dated 1 Sept., fell into the hands of the British and is now at Cairint 1/61/323. Cf. D.D.F. xiv, No. 445, transmitting Marchand to *Colonies* tel. No. 13, 12 July 1898.

[3] D.D.F. xiv, No. 445, transmitting Marchand to *Colonies* tels. No. 14, 20 Aug. 1898; No. 18, 1 Sept.; No. 19, 15 Sept. *Ibid.*, Appendix i, No. x, Marchand to Lagarde 27 Sept. 1898. *Ibid.*, p. 903 footnote, citing Marchand's log 14 Sept.

[4] Under Baratier 28 Sept.; under Germain 9 Oct.; under Mangin 11 Nov.: Baratier, *Fachoda*, pp. 178-81; Emily, *Mission Marchand*, pp. 194, 197, 213.

[5] Mangin, 'Lettres de la Mission Marchand', *Revue des Deux Mondes* Sept. 1931, letters of 18 Dec. 1898; 18 Feb., 6 Mar. 1899 (pp. 277-82). *Idem, Regards sur la France d'Afrique*, p. 255.

[6] Cf. MC Afrique iii 34b, Mangin to *Colonies* 14 Dec. 1898: 'Situation Fachoda-Sobat semble inconnue chefs abyssins, qui marchent seulement vers frontière Sennaar et ignorent coopération française Nil ou Abyssinie . . .'.

[7] MC C.F.S., Correspondance Générale, Hanotaux to Delcassé 6 Oct. 1894; Delcassé to Lagarde, 6 Oct. On the same day Hanotaux replied formally to Menelik's letter of 5 Jan. 1894 to Casimir-Périer. Cf. *supra*, Ch. vii, pp. 154-5; MAE, Abyssinie 5, Menelik to Hanotaux 5 Magabit 1887 / 13 Mar. 1895, acknowledging Hanotaux' letter of 6 Oct. 1894.

recognition of his independence and the free passage of arms through Obock, not to cede any territory to a third Power without 'friendly consultation' with France.[1] But by July 1895, when these proposals were received in Paris, Hanotaux was reluctant to commit himself so fully to Menelik. A decisive struggle in Ethiopia was evidently imminent; but its outcome was unpredictable, and it would be awkward to have backed the loser. 'Le mieux serait évidemment le maintien du *statu quo*'; failing that, a protracted struggle 'pour dégager d'autant la politique européenne'.[2] Moreover, on 8 April 1895 Rome had warned Hanotaux that to permit the free passage of arms to Menelik would be 'un acte peu amical'. Hanotaux' temper exploded at this provocative echo of the Grey Declaration, but he could not ignore the warning.[3] On the other hand he fully recognised that 'refuser à Ménélik le passage des armes, c'est pour ainsi dire rompre avec lui'.[4] Hanotaux decided to hedge. In September 1895 the import of arms through Obock was officially prohibited, but the prohibition had a gaping loophole in that caravans were allowed to carry arms and ammunition 'for their own protection'. It was the Italians, not Menelik, who complained of the situation which resulted.[5]

After Menelik's victory at Adowa, the French became a little more enterprising in Ethiopia. The Ethiopian railway project, dormant since early in 1894, was now revived. On 27 April 1896, in the last hours of the Bourgeois government, Guieysse authorised the construction of the line from Obock to the Ethiopian frontier. On 9 August the *Compagnie Impériale des chemins de fer éthiopiens* was constituted, with Léon Chefneux as its Chairman.[6] Meanwhile, on 3 June, President Félix Faure had written to the Negus offering to negotiate on the basis of Menelik's proposals of March 1895.[7] Menelik had now no great need of the French, and was in no hurry to reply. In September, however, the *Colonies* began to press for the immediate recognition of Ethiopian independence, lest France should lose the fruits of a policy matured over many years. On 30 September 1896 Hanotaux replied very non-committally to this suggestion; but on that very day his own *Direction* minuted strongly in favour of a firm entente with a sovereign who could influence the fate of the Upper Nile, 'où peuvent, à bref délai, se poser des questions politiques d'une haute importance'.[8] The project of Ethiopian assistance to the Nile mission had implicitly been revived.

[1] MAE, *loc. cit.*; D.D.F. XIII, No. 76, Menelik to Félix Faure 1 Magabit 1887/9 Mar. 1895.
[2] D.D.F. XII, No. 99, *Note du Ministre*, Question du Harrar et Obok 23 July 1895.
[3] D.D.F. XI, No. 462, Hanotaux to Billot 17 Apr. 1895.   [4] D.D.F. XII, No. 99.
[5] *Ibid.*, No. 155, Menelik to Félix Faure 14 Maskaram 1888 / 24 Sept. 1895; No. 289, Berthelot to Billot 28 Jan. 1896; No. 309, Berthelot, circular despatch, 22 Feb. 1896.
[6] Gilmour, *The Ethiopian Railway*, pp. 15, 71-2, printing Guieysse to Chefneux 27 Apr. 1896. Cf. R. Ferry, 'L'Ethiopie et l'expansion européenne en Afrique orientale', *Annales des Sciences Politiques*, XXV (1910), p. 205.
[7] D.D.F. XIII, No. 35 footnote. Cf. MC C.F.S., Lagarde to Menelik 3 June 1896.
[8] MC C.F.S., Lebon to Hanotaux 6 Sept. 1896; Hanotaux to Lebon 30 Sept. D.D.F., *loc. cit.*, footnote citing Departmental minute of 30 Sept.

Hanotaux was still reluctant to act. Having failed in his attempt to engage Russia in Egypt and the Red Sea littoral, he now hoped to gain her co-operation in Ethiopia. In October 1896, when the Czar visited Paris, Hanotaux agreed with the acting Russian Foreign Minister, Shishkin, that the two countries 'feraient en commun les plus sérieux efforts pour s'attacher Ménélik'.[1] Hanotaux seems to have been unwilling to engage himself deeply in Ethiopia without Russian support; but the declaration of October 1896 remained a mere vœu, in spite of his strenuous attempts to make it a reality.[2] Meanwhile, the pressure from the Colonies was maintained. On 1 November André Lebon pointed out that a favourable answer had now been received from Menelik, and explicitly stated that: 'C'est . . . en grande partie par le souverain éthiopien que nous devrons chercher à faire sentir l'influence française dans [le Haut Nil], si nous voulons qu'elle devienne un jour un facteur important du règlement de la question du Soudan et du Nil.'[3] On 24 November the Cabinet authorised Lagarde to negotiate; on 3 December his instructions from the Pavillon de Flore, after modification, were counter-signed by Hanotaux. These instructions represented a very weak dilution of the ideas of the Colonies. Lagarde was to confine himself to discussing frontier details with Ras Makonnen at Harar; he was not even to proceed to Addis Ababa without further orders.[4] These orders were however soon forthcoming. On 18 December the Colonies sent him a 'Note spéciale d'instructions' which was not counter-signed, and presumably not seen, by Hanotaux. Lagarde was to push the railway project—Menelik had in fact already on 5 November authorised the construction of the first Ethiopian section. Further, Lagarde was given funds to finance two French expeditions to the White Nile: one under Clochette, who was already in Ethiopia; another under Bonvalot, who would leave France in January 1897. It was essential that these expeditions should reach the Nile in time to assist Marchand.[5] The Pavillon de Flore had evidently by now reinstated Fashoda as Marchand's goal.

Early in March 1897 there was a direct conflict between Hanotaux and the Colonies on Ethiopian policy. Lebon now demanded that Menelik be encouraged to push his western frontier to the White Nile, which would thus become the boundary between Ethiopia and the 'French possessions'. This completely novel suggestion was stated by Lebon to have 'always been the policy of the French Government'. Hanotaux seems to have shrunk from raising objections of principle; instead, he objected on the very unconvincing ground that it would be premature to take such action in Ethiopia until the results of the

[1] D.D.F. xii, No. 474, note du Ministre . . . entretiens avec M. Chichkine 14 Oct. 1896; xiii, No. 16, Hanotaux to Vauvineux 5 Nov. 1896.
[2] Infra, pp. 302-4.   [3] MC C.F.S., Lebon to Hanotaux 1 Nov. 1896.
[4] D.D.F. xiii, No. 35, Hanotaux to Lebon 30 Nov. 1896. MC C.F.S., draft instructions countersigned by Hanotaux 3 Dec. 1896.
[5] MC C.F.S., Note spéciale d'instructions pour M. Lagarde 18 Dec. 1896. Gilmour, op. cit., p. 67, printing Menelik to Ilg and Chefneux 27 Teqemt 1889 / 5 Nov. 1896.

Marchand Mission were known. But he allowed himself to be over-ruled at a Cabinet on 11 March; and on the 14th Lebon instructed Lagarde that Menelik's advance to the White Nile was 'indispensable'.[1] But the battle in the Cabinet seems to have been fought only to obtain cover for secret instructions already sent by the *Colonies* to Lagarde. On 20 March 1897, far too early for Lebon's telegram of the 14th to have reached him,[2] Lagarde concluded with Menelik an Agreement for the partition of the Upper Nile basin. By this 'Convention pour le Nil Blanc' the French promised to assist Menelik in establishing his authority on the east bank south of the fourteenth parallel, while the Negus promised to support to the best of his ability the French missions on the west bank. The east bank was recognised as Ethiopian territory, but the French were authorised to operate there 'sous la protection de sa Majesté'.[3]

The missions in Ethiopia got off to a very bad start. Lagarde, a childishly vain man, was incensed that his instructions had expressly forbidden him to exercise any operational control over the missions. He ignored his orders to use his good offices with the Negus, and left Addis Ababa before Bonvalot had arrived. On his way down to Obock he met Bonvalot coming up; the result of the meeting was a violent quarrel.[4] Lacking Lagarde's support, Bonvalot made so little headway with the Negus that he returned to France.[5] His deputy, de Bonchamps, persevered. Menelik at last provided guides and a letter of introduction to *Dejazmach* Tassama, the Governor of Goré on the upper Sobat.[6] De Bonchamps arrived at Goré in July 1897 to find Clochette a dying man and Tassama not merely unhelpful, but actively obstructive. It was clear that he could get no farther, and in September he sent two of his party back to Addis Ababa to solicit the personal intervention of the Negus. By September Lebon had learned of de Bonchamps' plight at Goré, and was impatiently cabling, 'nous devrions être solidement établis Nil déjà' and Menelik must at all costs be persuaded to support the French by founding his own posts on the White Nile.[7] Lagarde, now back in Addis Ababa, bestirred himself a little. In October Menelik vouchsafed a curt note—very unlike the usual elaborate productions of his Chancery—authorising de Bonchamps 'de planter notre drapeau éthiopien et de soumettre les

---

[1] D.D.F. xiii, No. 137, Lebon to Hanotaux 5 Mar. 1897; footnote, minute by Nisard recording Hanotaux' opinion. *Ibid.*, No. 149, Lebon to Lagarde 14 Mar. 1897; footnote, minute recording Cabinet decision.

[2] There was at that time no telegraph between Jibuti and Addis Ababa, and the transmission of a tel. never took less than a fortnight.

[3] D.F.D. xiii, No. 159, *Convention pour le Nil Blanc* 20 Mar. 1897.

[4] For these missions in general, see: C. Michel, *Vers Fachoda* (Paris 1900), *passim*; G. N. Sanderson, 'Emir Suleyman . . .', *S.N.R.* 1954; *eundem*, 'Contributions from African Sources . . .', *J.A.H.* 1962; *eundem*, 'The Foreign Policy of the Negus Menelik', *ibid.*, 1964.

[5] Cf. D.D.F. xiii, No. 281, Bonvalot to Hanotaux 24 July 1897.

[6] Michel prints a French translation, *op. cit.*, p. 137.

[7] Michel, *op. cit.*, pp. 217-8, 166, printing de Bonchamps to Menelik 2 Sept. 1897; to André Lebon 27 July 1897. D.D.F. xiii, Nos. 325, 334, Lebon to Lagarde 15 and 27 Sept. 1897.

habitants', and drafted a rather more positive letter for *Dejazmach* Tassama.[1] Lagarde ordered the mission to establish a French and an Ethiopian post, the one on the west, the other on the east bank of the Nile. However, the mission was ordered to march on the south bank of the Sobat, the bank remote from Fashoda and a route obstructed by the flooded or swampy mouths of several large tributaries. André Lebon was bewildered: 'ne m'explique pas que [les missions] se dirigent rive gauche'.[2]

When Menelik's instructions reached Goré, Tassama became less actively unhelpful. All the same, when the mission once again tried to move off, most of its Ethiopian escort deserted. A very depleted party struggled on down the Baro (or upper Sobat) until on 29 December 1897 hunger, disease and the flooding of the country forced it to turn back at the Baro-Pibor confluence. Two of de Bonchamps' party, accompanied by Colonel Artamanov, a member of the Russian mission to the Negus, later joined more or less as guests an expedition under *Dejazmach* Tassama into the Kaffa country on the south-western marches of Ethiopia. They persuaded Tassama to permit them to accompany a reconnaissance which was pushed out down the Sobat. This party reached the Nile-Sobat confluence on 22 June 1898, sixteen days before Marchand passed the same point. Here the Europeans planted a French flag; the Ethiopians, not to be outdone, hoisted their own colours. Then, ignoring the pleas of the Europeans for a longer stay, the party at once hastened back to re-join Tassama.[3] The swamps of the Sobat were no place for Ethiopian highlanders. Quite apart from the ravages of disease, no Ethiopian force could establish itself in country which provided so little to live off. When Marchand passed the Sobat mouth the flags were no longer there.

Although Menelik more than once professed to Lagarde his desire for French military collaboration in the Sobat region,[4] he did nothing to ensure the success of the French missions and much to ensure their failure. As far as he could, he affected to regard the French as simple 'travellers'. It was thus that de Bonchamps was originally introduced to *Dejazmach* Tassama, in a letter which did not so much recommend de Bonchamps as warn Tassama against him.[5] At the end of his adventures, de Bonchamps' deputy Michel received a polite note from the Negus thanking him for 'the journey he had made'. There was no reference to the political objects or results of the 'journey' although de Bonchamps had concluded treaties on Menelik's behalf with

[1] Michel, *op. cit.*, pp. 250-3, printing a translation of Menelik to Tassama 20 Oct. 1897.
[2] *Ibid.*, pp. 253-5, printing Lagarde to de Bonchamps 10 Oct. 1897. D.D.F. xiii, No. 347, Lebon to Lagarde 30 Oct. 1897.
[3] Michel, *op. cit.*, pp. 257-461. Lagarde later gave Delcassé to understand (D.D.F. xiv, No. 583, Lagarde to Delcassé 28 Dec. 1898) that the Frenchman Faivre had led this expedition; but this was completely misleading.
[4] D.D.F. xiii, No. 386, Lagarde to Hanotaux 24 Dec. 1897; xiv, No. 70, Lebon to Hanotaux 2 Mar. 1898. MC C.F.S., Lagarde to Lebon 8 Feb. 1898.
[5] It concluded, in the French translation: 'Mais toi [i.e. Tassama], viens vite, nous parlerons de cela lorsque tu seras ici'. (Michel, *op. cit.*, p. 137.)

several of the Sobat chiefs.[1] The guides provided by Menelik for de Bonchamps' original journey to Goré misled the French in vast detours along the worst roads. During the first phase of de Bonchamps' sojourn at Goré, Tassama immobilised the expedition by impounding its transport animals (as he had already impounded Clochette's), and by winking at strikes and wholesale desertion among its Ethiopian escort. When the expedition nevertheless tried to move off, one of Tassama's subordinates halted it by a very serious show of force. Later, when new instructions from the Negus had been received, Tassama could not be so openly obstructive. All the same he did not intervene when, once again, most of the Ethiopians deserted. In any case, Menelik had now condemned the expedition to almost certain failure by insisting that it should march on the south bank of the Sobat.[2] Meanwhile, the Negus humoured the French by showing them his treaty with Rodd;[3] by creating Lagarde 'Duke of Entoto'—a comic-opera title which Lagarde was silly enough to take very seriously; and by appointing Frenchmen to high-sounding but purely ornamental posts in the Ethiopian administration.[4]

The Negus was unwilling to allow these missions to succeed, and above all determined that the 'Convention pour le Nil Blanc' should remain a dead letter, because of his anxiety not to disrupt the friendly entente with the Khalifa which he had achieved early in 1897. By this remarkable feat of diplomacy he had not only prevailed over the indiscriminate Mahdist hostility towards 'enemies of God'; he had overcome a long history of particular hostility to Ethiopia, the traditional foe of Islam in north-east Africa. Such a rapprochement was obviously precarious, and doubly so because of the Khalifa's suspicious nature. Any semblance of Ethiopian encroachment on the Sudan, above all in collusion with Europeans, would destroy it forthwith.

In the spring of 1895, when war with Italy had already been declared, Menelik had sent an Ethiopian Muslim as an envoy to 'Abdallāhi with a plea for more friendly relations. The Khalifa, uneasy at the fall of Kassala to the Italians and rumours of European encroachments in the South, replied, though with no excess of courtesy, requesting proposals in writing.[5] Menelik did not answer until 25 April 1896, after his victory at Adowa; and he then had no specific proposals to make. He merely assured the Khalifa of his desire for peace with all Powers, whether his immediate neighbours or not;

---

[1] Menelik to Michel 27 Genbot 1890 / 3 June 1898 (Michel, op. cit., facsimile between pp. 420-1).
[2] Ibid., pp. 93-275, passim.
[3] D.D.F. xiii, No. 387, Lagarde to Hanotaux 28 Dec. 1897.
[4] Camille Mondon-Vidailhet became Minister of Posts and Public Instruction (the former function was nearly non-existent, the latter completely so); Léon Chefneux became Councillor for Railways.
[5] Mahdia 1/34/12, 'Abdallāhi to Menelik, Safar 1313/July-Aug. 1895. For details of Sudanese-Ethiopian relations see Sanderson, S.N.R. 1954; J.A.H. 1962 and 1964.

and he pointedly added that any future aggressor against Ethiopia would meet the same fate as the Italians.[1] This confident mood did not last. Menelik's victory at Adowa had brought an even more formidable Power into the military arena in north-east Africa; and he soon began to fear that Kitchener's operations might ultimately be directed against Ethiopia. In June and July 1896 he sent further messages to Omdurman offering co-operation against all Europeans but against 'the red English' in particular. The French, for all their promises of diplomatic support, were evidently unable to stop Kitchener; 'Abdallāhi at least might do so. So long as Kitchener continued to advance the Khalifa was bound to go on fighting; whereas the French, who had sat elegantly on the fence during the climax of Menelik's struggle with Italy, would almost certainly do so again if he came to blows with the British.[2] In a letter to the Khalifa of 17 July 1896 Menelik specifically stated that the British were just as much his enemies as 'Abdallāhi's: 'Your enemy is our enemy and our enemy is your enemy, and we should stand together as firm allies'. This letter, written on Menelik's behalf by his senior 'Court Ras' and official confidant, Ras Bitwatid Mangasha, begins with a most elaborate and respectful Islamic salutation—a delicate mark of courtesy, but not one which the Lion of Judah could personally offer.[3]

With Kitchener bowling over his northern outposts, the Khalifa could not ignore this offer.[4] About the time of the fall of Dongola he sent to Addis Ababa a senior and trusted envoy, Muhammad 'Uthmān al-Hajj Khālid. Still, as Muhammad 'Uthmān himself noted, it was Menelik who made all the cordial advances while 'Abdallāhi's response remained distinctly cold and grudging. However, Menelik offered to supply the Khalifa with arms and ammunition; and, doubtless to convince Omdurman that his policy of co-operation enjoyed general support in Ethiopia, he introduced Muhammad 'Uthmān to some of his most powerful Rases.[5] No written alliance seems ever to have been concluded; but by February 1897 Menelik was causing his principal Rases to write fulsome letters congratulating the Khalifa on the establishment of cordial relations.[6] In a letter of December 1897 Menelik addressed 'Abdallāhi as 'our superior, venerable, dear friend';[7] and when in the spring of 1898 an Ethiopian diplomatic mission reached Omdurman, it was given the most cordial of receptions. It was greeted by an official firework display; arrangements were made for its meat to be slaughtered by

[1] Mahdia 1/34/16, Menelik to 'Abdallāhi, 8 Miyazya 1888 / 25 Apr. 1896.
[2] Sanderson, *J.A.H.*, *ubi supra.*
[3] Mahdia 1/34/16, Ras Bitwatid Mangasha to 'Abdallāhi 6 Safar 1314/17 July 1896. This Mangasha, an old henchman of Menelik's, is not to be confused with Mangasha of Tigre, son of Yohannes.
[4] He tried however to insist that Menelik should expel all Europeans from Ethiopia (Mahdia 1/34/12, 'Abdallāhi to Menelik, Rabi' al-Akhir 1314 / Sept.-Oct. 1896).
[5] Mahdia 1/34/15, Statement of Muhammad 'Uthmān al-Hajj Khālid 15 Sept. 1898.
[6] Sanderson, *S.N.R.*, *ubi supra*; *J.A.H.* 1962. The letters are at Mahdia 1/34/16.
[7] Mahdia 1/34/16, Menelik to 'Abdallāhi 7 Kiyahk 1890 / 15 Dec. 1897.

Christians; even the Islamic prohibition of alcohol was relaxed, so as to provide date wine for its refreshment.[1]

Menelik hoped that his entente with Omdurman would play a major part in solving Ethiopia's 'European Problem'. But if it were to do so, the Khalifa must not be distracted by the slightest apprehension about the security of his eastern frontier—the whole point of the entente was to enable 'Abdallāhi to concentrate all his military resources against 'the red English'. Menelik was therefore at pains to smother all controversy about the debatable lands between the Sudan and Ethiopia. The gold-bearing region of the Bani Shanqūl he did indeed occupy; but only after the Khalifa had expressly approved— according to some sources, even invited—Ethiopian action against its ruler 'Abd al-Rahmān Khōjali, who had been in practice independent of both Addis Ababa and Omdurman. Menelik also coveted other territories: notably the Gallabat district and the region on the Blue Nile around Roseires, both of which he regarded as *Ethiopia Irredenta*. But in spite of his overwhelming local superiority of force, the Negus took no action in these regions until, in the summer of 1898, they were abandoned by their Mahdist garrisons and administration. Even then, he confined himself to the despatch of peaceful diplomatic missions bearing the Ethiopian flag and an offer of Ethiopian protection, and abstained from all military occupation. In this way, should 'Abdallāhi after all be victorious, Menelik could represent his action as an insurance against prior occupation by the common enemy—which indeed it was—and not as in any way a hostile act against the Khalifa.[2]

When Menelik's action was so circumspect in territories which he eagerly coveted, it is inconceivable that he could have authorised the irresponsible gesture, at once futile and provocative, of planting and immediately abandoning an Ethiopian flag at the Nile-Sobat confluence, in territory which the Negus well knew to be worthless and indeed uninhabitable by Ethiopians. In fact, Menelik took particular care to explain to the Khalifa that *Dejazmach* Tassama's operations were directed solely against the Europeans who 'intended to enter between my country and yours and to separate and divide us'; and he explicitly begged the Khalifa not to misunderstand his intentions. The main object of the reconnaissance to the Sobat mouth was evidently to observe and if necessary resist any encroachments by the Belgians from Rejaf or, in particular, by the Macdonald mission.[3] Just as Salisbury had feared, Macdonald's movements were causing the liveliest apprehension at Addis Ababa. To Menelik, suspicious that Kitchener's operations would also ultimately be directed against Ethiopia, they

[1] Holt, *The Mahdist State*, p. 209.
[2] Sanderson, *J.A.H.* 1964. Cf. Wingate in S.I.R. No. 60, p. 20: 'Menelik's object was to strengthen the Khalifa against the Government troops, whom he feared as neighbours, preferring the dervishes.'
[3] Mahdia 1/34/16, unsigned Ethiopian Note attached to Menelik to 'Abdallāhi, 7 Kiyahk 1890 (a translation is printed by Sanderson, *J.A.H.* 1964).

must indeed have looked sinister. The sources of the river Juba were after all not so very far south of Addis Ababa itself.[1]

Thanks to Lagarde's fatuously over-sanguine reporting, the French had no inkling of the true situation until de Bonchamps returned to France in the summer of 1898. De Bonchamps then bluntly stated that 'les Abyssins n'ont pas aidé la mission; ils ont fait tout leur possible pour empêcher son départ vers le Nil'; and Gustave Binger ruefully noted 'combien il paraît aléatoire de compter sur l'appui effectif de Ménélik'.[2] But Lagarde himself had been anything but helpful to the missions. He neglected to send up from Jibuti the *bateau démontable* which had been sent out for the expedition's use and which offered the one real hope of successfully using the Sobat route. He refused to detach to de Bonchamps a few disciplined Senegalese from his ceremonial escort.[3] Such conduct was not far short of outright sabotage; and it is not surprising that the received account has always blamed Lagarde, and not Menelik, for the French failure.[4] Lagarde's behaviour was indeed often influenced by petty spite and professional jealousy. Yet even when, in September 1897, André Lebon placed the de Bonchamps mission under Lagarde's personal control,[5] his support remained less than lukewarm. In 1897 Lagarde, particularly through his close acquaintance Alfred Ilg,[6] may have known more than he cared to admit to Paris about Menelik's relations with the Khalifa, of which there were rumours enough in Ethiopian Court circles. Such knowledge would doubtless have brought home even to Lagarde that the Negus was now unlikely to give any serious support to French expeditions to the Nile. By January 1898 at the latest, Lagarde was certainly aware of the entente between Addis Ababa and Omdurman; but he did not care to report to Paris a development which made waste paper of his own diplomatic masterpiece, the 'Convention pour le Nil Blanc'. Instead, he attempted, on his own initiative and to the consternation of Hanotaux, to use this entente as a means of offering French protection to the Khalifa.

Lagarde evidently believed that the alliance was directed exclusively against the English; and Menelik did not discourage this belief. Early in 1898, in the presence of Lagarde, Menelik handed a small French Tricolour to his envoy Muhammad al-Tayyib. 'Menelik said ... "Take this flag ... and give it to the Khalifa, and tell him that if the

---

[1] Cf. Sanderson, *ubi supra*.
[2] MC Afrique III 36a, No. 2, undated memo. (July-Aug. 1898) by de Bonchamps, 'Causes d'impossibilité de jonction avec Marchand'; minute by Binger.
[3] Michel, *op. cit.*, pp. 243-53.
[4] E.g. that of Michel himself, who even attributes Menelik's unhelpfulness to his having been deliberately misled by Lagarde. Cocheris also indicts Lagarde; Langer is more cautious.
[5] So that it was no longer, in Lagarde's words, 'entachée du péché originel' (Michel, *op. cit.*, p. 245).
[6] Who had been created Councillor of State by Menelik in Mar. 1897 (Keller, *Alfred Ilg*, p. 118). Cf. D.D.F. XIII, No. 169, Lebon to Lagarde 27 Mar. 1897, where Lebon proposes that Ilg be decorated.

English advance against him he is to fly it at the head of his army. When they see it they will do him no harm, and this will be the same if the French advance against him." ' But Muhammad al-Tayyib was also told, more privately, to impress upon the Khalifa that 'it was not desirable that either French or English should come into the Sudan'.[1] The envoy also took with him an unsigned note ('an Abyssinian *Note Verbale*', as Rodd was to call it), warning 'Abdallāhi to be on his guard against *all* Europeans; and a formal sealed diploma accrediting him as the bearer of an important confidential message.[2] Just as Menelik had avoided difficulties with the Khalifa by never effecting the mythical occupation which had fooled the British, so now he spared no pains to prevent 'Abdallāhi from being disquieted by his successful deception of the French. But if after all the Khalifa did use the flag, and the flag did stop Kitchener, Menelik would not be the loser.

The Khalifa, in public at least, rejected the flag with correct Mahdist intransigence, declaring that 'if Heaven and Earth together should advance against him he would not accept the protection of a European Power'.[3] With this message Muhammad al-Tayyib was sent back to Addis Ababa; and on 18 June Lagarde reported the failure of the démarche which had, as he supposed, been made by Menelik and himself 'de concert'.[4] He did so in the words: 'le Mahdi [*sic*] repousse de nouveau tout arrangement avec nous', which seems to imply a previous overture. Of such an overture nothing is known; but in 1896 and 1897 Lagarde had in fact been involved in two abortive attempts to make contact with the Khalifa through the intermediary of the Hungarian ex-officer Karl Inger.

This odd fish had been wandering about North Africa and the Near East, without visible means of support, for some eighteen months when in August 1896 he turned up in Paris. To Lagarde, and to Hanotaux' *sous-chef de Cabinet* Hippolyte Borel, Inger suggested that the Khalifa might be persuaded to seek, with French diplomatic support, recognition 'by the Sultan of Turkey as Sultan of Nubia'. Inger himself would lead a diplomatic mission to 'Abdallāhi and could guarantee its favourable reception. In August 1896 hopes of 'good relations with the Dervishes' were at their rosiest in Paris. Here was a definite proposal for initiating those good relations; if one forgot all about the religious and ideological basis of Mahdism (which the French habitually did), it did not seem on the face of it absurd. More-

[1] Mahdia 1/34/15, Statement of Muhammad 'Uthmān. FO 141/333, statement of Muddāththir Ibrahīm al-Hajjāz (Chief Clerk and *custos sigilli* to the Khalifa), enclosed in Rodd to Salisbury No. 165, 13 Oct. 1898.
[2] This was the unsigned Note attached to the letter of 7 Kiyahk (Mahdia 1/34/16). Cf. Menelik to 'Abdallāhi 9 Ter 1890 / 16 Jan. 1898 (*ibid.*).
[3] Mahdia 1/34/15, statement of Muhammad 'Uthmān, who also asserts that the flag was returned to Addis Ababa. But Yūsuf Mikhā'īl, usually a well-informed witness, states that the Khalifa secretly conveyed the flag to his own house and seriously considered using it. Cf. for details Sanderson, *J.A.H.* 1962.
[4] D.D.F. xiv, No. 227, Lagarde to Hanotaux 18 June 1898.

over, Inger called himself 'Sulaimān', professed to be a Muslim and had some knowledge of Arabic; it may well have seemed not impossible that he was in some way in touch with Omdurman. The French would not give Inger any money; but they were prepared to assist him, as far as possible, to make his way to Omdurman by way of Jibuti and Addis Ababa. But when on his return to Cairo Inger dropped this plan in favour of a landing on the Sudan coast near Suakin, the French hastily dropped him, doubtless fearing that he would fall into the hands of the British.[1]

They were wise. Inger made his landing on 26 October 1896; but he could then think of nothing better to do than to give himself up to the British at Suakin. It was at first proposed to try him by court-martial as a spy, for he had been arrested wearing a Mahdist *jibbah*, but inside-out so as to conceal the patches. But Cromer thought him 'probably half-witted',[2] and was content to deport him to Trieste. In March 1897 Inger obligingly announced in the *Courrier d'Egypte* his intention of making a second attempt to reach the Khalifa. Suakin was duly alerted; but this time Inger tried the Jibuti-Addis Ababa route, presumably with the connivance of Lagarde. Poor Inger had no luck. On 6 June 1897, on the trail between Jibuti and Harar, he found himself face to face with the redoubtable Wingate himself, who was returning to the coast with the Rodd Mission. Inger got no further than Harar, whence he was sent back to the coast by Ras Makonnen at Rodd's request.[3]

Inger's activities were both farcical and completely negligible; but the 'Inger Legend' which grew up around them, though equally farcical, was not quite so negligible. In October 1897 Inger gave an interview to the newspaper *L'Eclair*. He expounded his views on Sudan policy; more, he now claimed to be an accredited representative of the Khalifa, with the rank of Amir. He had, he said, reported to Omdurman in September 1896 the favourable dispositions of the French, and had requested the Khalifa to treat Marchand as a friend. He had then intended to return to Omdurman 'to place myself at the head of the army against England'. The British at Suakin had frustrated this; but his message had got through to the Khalifa, and thereafter 'Marchand was well received and could freely advance to the Nile'.[4] Inger's grip on reality, never very strong, seems to have deserted him completely after his Suakin ordeal, when he had faced the prospect of court-martial on a capital charge. These absurd fantasies were the result.[5]

[1] Cairint 1/45/263, *Arrest of Karl Inger at Suakin* Oct. 1896. Sanderson, *S.N.R.* 1954, pp. 22-39, 54-62.
[2] FO 78/4763, Cromer to Salisbury No. 139, 16 Nov. 1896.
[3] Cairint, *ubi supra*; Sanderson, *S.N.R.*, *ubi supra*, pp. 39-45. Cf. W.O. Confidential Print, 'Précis of Information . . .', pp. 17, 133; Rodd, *Social and Diplomatic Memories*, 11, pp. 183-4.   [4] Sanderson, *ubi supra*, pp. 34-5.
[5] By 1898 Inger was claiming that he had served the Khalifa in the rank of Amir; in 1914 and 1917 he signed himself (in letters to the Austro-Hungarian War Ministry) as 'Emir Suleyman ibn Inger Abdullah'; and before his death in 1935 he was claiming to have ruled an Ethiopian province as a Mahdist Viceroy (Sanderson, *ubi supra*, pp. 24-5, 46-50).

By the end of 1897 all confidence in the benevolence of the Mahdists had ebbed away at the Pavillon de Flore.[1] But the will-o'-the-wisp of the Dervish alliance had no sooner flickered out in the *bureaux* than it began an even wilder career in the Press. By December 1897, Jean Hess in *Le Figaro* and Pierre Marceau in *Le Gaulois* were asserting that it was a *fait accompli*, thanks to the good offices of 'Soliman Inger'; they called upon their readers to admire the masterstroke of diplomacy which had created a coalition of the 'Mahdi', the Negus, the Sultan and the Khedive under the auspices of France and, of course, Russia.[2] By February 1898 the Inger Legend had even reached the more austere pages of *Questions Diplomatiques et Coloniales*; an article by Paul Bourdarie, though it does not mention Inger by name, nevertheless hints very strongly that a formal alliance had been, or shortly would be, concluded between Paris and Omdurman.[3] Yet the Pavillon de Flore, which best understood the utter falsity of the Inger Legend and the appreciations based upon it, never seems to have issued a *caveat*, much less a contradiction. The sudden revelation of the truth at the moment of crisis doubtless added its quota to the stunning shock which Fashoda administered to the French public.

Another and much more competent adventurer who played some part in French policy towards Ethiopia and the Upper Nile was the Russian nobleman Nicolai Stepanovitch Leontiev. This 'buccaneer in the grand style' was between 1895 and 1898 the unofficial Russian representative at Addis Ababa.[4] Hanotaux profoundly distrusted him; and even Mohrenheim, the Russian ambassador, warned the Quai d'Orsay against him. When Muraviev, the new Russian Foreign Minister, visited Paris in January 1897, Hanotaux obtained from him a promise to send to Ethiopia an official envoy who would co-operate with the French and counteract Leontiev's influence.[5] However, in the summer of 1897 Leontiev joined forces with Prince Henri d'Orléans, whose 'unofficial' mission to Ethiopia was strongly backed by the Pavillon de Flore. In June Leontiev obtained from the Negus a vaguely worded grant appointing him 'Governor-General of the Equatorial Provinces of Ethiopia'. These territories were supposed to comprise Menelik's paper claims, south of what he actually occupied, as far as the Bahr el Jebel, the second parallel of north latitude, and the Indian Ocean! When in August 1897 Prince Henri returned to France, stating quite inaccurately that he was co-governor with Leontiev and that Menelik would provide the necessary troops for occupation, the

---

[1] D.D.F. xiii, No. 325, Lebon to Lagarde 15 Sept. 1897; No. 388, Lebon to Hanotaux [ ] Dec. 1897.
[2] *Le Figaro*, 8 and 9 Dec. 1897; *Le Gaulois*, 12 Dec.
[3] P. Bourdarie, 'Les Missions Liotard—Marchand—de Bonchamps et la Question du Nil', *Q.D.C.* iii (15 Feb. 1898), pp. 231-3.
[4] For his career see C. Jesman, *The Russians in Ethiopia* (London 1958), pp. 110-25. Cf. D.D.F. xii, Nos. 98, 121, Montebello to Hanotaux 22 July and 7 Aug. 1895.
[5] D.D.F. xiii, No. 66, Hanotaux to Lebon 16 Jan. 1897; Nos. 87, 128, Hanotaux to Montebello, 31 Jan. and 25 Feb. 1897. Cf. MC C.F.S., Lebon to Lagarde 1 Nov. 1896.

colonialists hailed a 'complete and tangible success'. Leontiev and the Prince would establish a buffer-state which, together with the territory occupied by Marchand, would completely exclude the British from the Upper Nile.[1]

In fact, Menelik would not give Leontiev 'a single soldier or sou'; and Leontiev's main motive for inviting Prince Henri to share his spoils seems to have been the hope of attracting French capital. In this he did not succeed; nor did he fare any better when he approached Sir George Cawston of the British South Africa Company.[2] He ultimately obtained financial backing in Brussels, at the price of ceding all but the barest political rights to a syndicate which was—of course—King Leopold under a very thin disguise.[3] These manœuvres were still unknown in Paris when in March 1898 Prince Henri was given a farewell banquet attended by most of the leading colonialists, including François Deloncle, Etienne, Flourens and Monteil. 'Toasts' delivered by Etienne and Monteil suggested that the French Government confidently expected the New Order in the Ethiopian Equatorial Provinces to be 'un puissant élément d'équilibre' on the Upper Nile. Indeed, the Pavillon de Flore promised to lend a company of Senegalese *tirailleurs* to the Prince Henri—Leontiev partnership.[4]

In May 1898 the Paris banker Nicolas Notovitch informed Hanotaux of Leontiev's dealings with the Belgians; he also suggested, erroneously, that British capital and perhaps even the British Foreign Office were also involved.[5] Hanotaux at once cabled Lagarde for advice and asked him to remain at Addis Ababa to watch the situation. Lagarde, who was now at Harar on his way to France, refused to turn back. Nor had he any advice to give, except that Paris should have allowed him to take up the 'Governorship of the Nilotic Provinces' which Menelik, surely with his tongue in his cheek, had offered to Lagarde in December 1897. Meanwhile, Hanotaux had been pressing Muraviev for a joint démarche to deter Menelik from ratifying Leontiev's arrangements. Muraviev was content to reply that he would warn the Negus against the danger of English financial penetration; he added soothingly that Leontiev's influence at Addis Ababa appeared to be on the wane. Perhaps indeed it was. On 30 June 1898 Leontiev was severely wounded, apparently by accident, by an Ethiopian

[1] FO 141/332, Cawston to Barrington 15 Mar. 1898 (copy), enclosing French translation of Menelik's grant dated 12 Sanne 1889 / 18 June 1897; cf. *ibid.*, Monson to Salisbury No. 102, 21 Feb. 1898. D.D.F. xiii, No. 291, Boutiron to Hanotaux 5 Aug. 1897. P. Bourdarie, 'La Mission du Prince Henri d'Orléans en Ethiopie', *Q.D.C.* i, 15 Aug. 1897, pp. 68-70. Cf. FO 1/34, Harrington to Salisbury No. 6, 30 Apr. 1898.
[2] FO 1/35, Harrington to Sanderson, private, 22 Sept. 1897. FO 141/332, Cawston to Barrington (copy) 15 Mar. 1898.
[3] E. D. Morel, 'The Congo State and the Bahr-el-Ghazal', *The Nineteenth Century*, Aug. 1901, pp. 211-2. N. Ascherson, *The King Incorporated* (London 1963), pp. 227-8.
[4] Henri Pensa, 'La Question du Nil', *Revue Politique et Parlementaire*, xvi, May 1898, pp. 171-5. G. de la Genardière, 'Les Provinces Equatoriales de l'Ethiopie', *Q.D.C.* iv (1 May 1898), pp. 12-19. Ješman, *op. cit.*, pp. 115-23.
[5] D.D.F. xiv, Nos. 190, 200, Notovitch to Hanotaux 12 and 24 May 1898.

soldier during a machine-gun demonstration at Harar.[1] Leontiev recovered, and by the end of 1898 was back in Ethiopia again; but his further adventures do not concern this narrative.

Muraviev's behaviour during the Leontiev affair was typical of Russian policy towards the French in Ethiopia. In October 1896 collaboration had been promised by Shishkin, in January 1897 by Muraviev.[2] Shishkin, a mere permanent official, had no power to fulfil this promise; Muraviev, probably no intention of doing so. A few days after his conversation with Hanotaux, Muraviev told the Italian ambassador in Berlin that he no longer intended to support the chauvinistic tendencies of France; in particular, previous Russian policy in Ethiopia had been grossly mistaken.[3] In October 1897, after his visit to Cronstadt with the French fleet, Hanotaux attempted to elicit some genuine co-operation in the cordial atmosphere created by the *Pothuau* toasts. But his careful memorandum on Ethiopian policy went unanswered for over three weeks, and the answer, when it came, was the most formal of acknowledgments: the memorandum had been laid before the Czar, and instructions would be given to Vlassov in due course.[4] Vlassov was the official Russian representative whose appointment had been promised by Muraviev in January 1897. He did not arrive in Addis Ababa until February 1898; and his credit with Menelik was ruined from the outset by the fact that he was married to an Englishwoman. At the same time the officially disavowed Leontiev arrived bearing the Czar's personal gift of 30,000 rifles to the Negus.[5] In January 1897 Muraviev had warned Hanotaux that Leontiev had very strong support at St Petersburg,[6] and this support seems to have included a Court camarilla very close to the Czar. The Russian Foreign Ministry therefore had only a limited control of policy; and the Slavophile, ultra-Orthodox Russians who were most interested in Ethiopia[7] were the last people to co-operate willingly with representatives of the French Republic.

It has sometimes been suggested that in spite of Hanotaux' failure to secure the co-operation of the Negus or the goodwill of the Khalifa, he had nevertheless firmly aligned himself with King Leopold; and that the local position would have been much more favourable to France but for the disaster which befell the great Congolese Nile

---

[1] D.D.F. xiv, No. 204, Hanotaux to Lagarde 29 May 1898; No. 217, Lagarde to Hanotaux 7 June; No. 229, Hanotaux to Geoffray 18 June. Cf. D.D.F. xiii, No. 386, Lagarde to Hanotaux, private, 24 Dec. 1897. The offer was renewed in Feb. 1898; cf. MC C.F.S., Lagarde to Lebon 28 Feb. 1898; D.D.F. xiv, Nos. 70, Lebon to Hanotaux 2 Mar.; 79, Hanotaux to Lebon 11 Mar. Jeśman, *op. cit.*, p. 117.

[2] D.D.F. xii, No. 474, Hanotaux, note of conversations with Shishkin 14 Oct. 1896; xiii, No. 87, Hanotaux to Montebello 31 Jan. 1897.

[3] D.D.I., 3rd Series, i, No. 346, Lanza to Visconti Venosta 2 Feb. 1897.

[4] D.D.F. xiii, No. 321, Hanotaux to Vauvineux 10 Sept. 1897; footnote citing Vauvineux to Hanotaux 3 Oct. 1897.

[5] D.D.F. xiii, No. 386. MC C.F.S., Lagarde to Lebon private, 20 Feb. 1898. Vlassov and Leontiev were on the worst of terms (Jeśman, *op. cit.*, pp. 116-7).

[6] D.D.F. xiii, No. 87.

[7] Cf. Jeśman, *op. cit.*, *passim*; esp. pp. 126-33.

expedition under Baron Dhanis in February 1897.[1] In September 1895, when Marchand's project was being incubated, Leopold visited Paris and held conversations with, among others, Félix Faure, Hanotaux and André Lebon. At the same time Hanolet, one of the Congolese Upper Nile experts, visited Paris on a secret mission. Far-reaching conclusions have also been drawn from chronological co-incidences in the movements of Marchand, Hanolet and Dhanis.[2] In these conclusions there is the grain of truth that during 1896-7 there was some limited collaboration between Leopold and the French. Marchand was permitted to borrow the steamer *Ville de Bruges*, and Leopold allowed French reinforcements for the Bahr al-Ghazal to travel on the completed section of the Matadi-Léopoldville railway.[3] Moreover, in September 1898 Delcassé let slip the remark that the Marchand Mission had been 'undertaken in virtue of an understanding with the Congolese Government.'[4]

This 'understanding' was doubtless prompted, on Leopold's side, by hopes of ultimately gaining French support for the 'neutral solution'. But whatever its details may have been, it amounted to far less than an alliance, or even a serious rapprochement; nor did it exclude a very strong suspicion of Leopold's military preparations in the Nile valley. As early as March 1896 the Quai d'Orsay was suspicious that these might have been concerted with the 'Anglo-Egyptian' advance in the northern Sudan.[5] When in September 1896 Leopold suggested to Paris that he should be permitted to send his troops beyond the Lado Enclave in order to forestall the British, Hanotaux was so alarmed that he contemplated reviving his old threat to call upon Belgium to withdraw her officers from the Congolese *Force Publique*.[6] In London, Salisbury was no less suspicious of Leopold's hints about a possible neutral custodian for the Nile valley: 'He is at some mischief. . . . I suspect he is making some arrangement to sell to France the succession of the Congo State, together with any rights of ours which he can lay hold of in the Valley of the Nile'.[7] London and Paris continued to suspect one another of intriguing with Leopold; in fact he had completely forfeited the confidence of both Salisbury and Hanotaux, and neither would now willingly collaborate with him.

At the end of 1894 the Belgian Ministers had wished to annex the Congo State, as an insurance against any repetition of the hazards to which the Anglo-Congolese Agreement had exposed Belgium. On 2 January 1895 Leopold had indeed initialled a deed of cession to

[1] A.-J. Wauters, 'Souvenirs de Fachoda et de l'expédition Dhanis', *M. Géog.*, May 1910, Nos. 20-22. Cf. Hornik, *Der Kampf der Grossmächte*, pp. 162-3. Ascherson, *op. cit.*, pp. 221-2.
[2] Wauters, *ubi supra*, cols. 253-4, 259-61.
[3] Fox-Bourne, *Civilisation in Congoland*, p. 244. D.D.F. XIII, No. 27, Montholon to Hanotaux 23 Nov. 1896. Cf. FO 78/5051, Plunkett to Salisbury No. 201, 8 Oct. 1898.
[4] FO 78/5050, Monson to Salisbury No. 441, 8 Sept. 1898. Cf. Hanotaux, *Fachoda*, p. 129.
[5] D.D.F. XII, No. 320, Courcel to Berthelot 13 Mar. 1896; No. 326, Montholon to Berthelot 16 Mar.; No. 359, Montholon to Bourgeois 29 Mar., and minute thereon.
[6] *Ibid.*, No. 451, Courcel to Hanotaux 9 Sept. 1896; No. 458, Hanotaux to Courcel 25 Sept.   [7] L.Q.V. 3, ii, pp. 578-9, Salisbury to Bigge 7 Dec. 1895.

U

Belgium.[1] But Belgian public opinion proved so hostile to annexation that the Belgian Ministers were by June 1895 glad to buy themselves out of their predicament by paying off Leopold's Congo deficit—which included at least one totally fictitious debt deliberately arranged by Leopold for the purpose of milking the Belgian Exchequer.[2] With his coffers thus replenished to the tune of nearly seven million francs, Leopold gave free rein to ambitions which had by now become those of a megalomaniac. He would be 'the neutral solution' for the Upper Nile; nay, he would 'be Pharaoh' of the whole Nile valley. He would administer Nilotic Ethiopia and secure a lease of Eritrea; the latter project was in fact discussed quite seriously with the Italians in the course of 1897. Leopold even hoped to secure from London, through the good offices of the German Emperor, a lease of the eastern Sudan between Kassala and Sennar.[3]

Leopold's trump card in this game was to be an enormous Nile expedition under Dhanis, the conqueror of the Congo Arabs. This was to push as far as it could to the north, to Khartoum if possible. The British sphere, the King held, extended no further north than Wadelai, for here were 'the confines of Egypt'. But Egypt had lost her rights in these Sudanese territories, which were now therefore *res nullius* and open to the first occupant.[4] Eetvelde tried to recall his royal master to the world of reality: he was told to mind his own business and 'de bien vouloir suivre mes instructions'. By the end of 1895 Eetvelde was confiding to Plunkett that the King's plans were 'little short of insanity', and suggesting that London should definitely cancel the 1894 leases in order to save Leopold from himself.[5] But in September-October 1896 Dhanis, at the head of three thousand men, marched eastwards out of Stanleyville. He had been ordered to follow, not the now well-trodden road along the water-parting between the Uele and the M'Bomu, but Stanley's old Emin Pasha relief route through the rain-forest of the Aruwimi valley. The deadly hazards of this road were notorious; it seems to have been adopted in order to conceal the strength and operations of Dhanis from the outside world and particularly from the French, who were given explicit assurances that in no circumstances would the expedition advance beyond Lado.[6]

---

[1] Stengers, 'La première tentative de reprise . . .', *Bull. Soc. Roy. Belge Géog.*, 1949, pp. 52-65. Cf. FO 10/617, Plunkett to Kimberley Nos. 205, 210, 219, 224, 251 and 257, Aug.-Dec. 1894.

[2] Stengers, *ubi supra*, pp. 48-52, 77-109. *Idem*, 'Note sur l'histoire des finances congolaises', *Bull. I.R.C.B.* xxv, 1 (1954), pp. 154, 250-1. Ascherson, *op. cit.*, pp. 186-94.

[3] Ranieri, *Les relations entre l'Etat Indépendant du Congo et l'Italie*, pp. 82-108. T. Simar, 'Léopold II et l'Erythrée', *Congo*, 1924, No. 2, pp. 319-25. Cf. D.D.I., 3, 1, Nos. 335, 399, 407, Jan.-Apr. 1897; Wauters, *ubi supra*, cols. 271-4; Ascherson, *op. cit.*, pp. 224-7.

[4] R.-J. Cornet, 'Rapport sur les dossiers: Création, administration et gouvernement . . . de l'E.I.C.', *Bull. I.R.C.B.* xxv, 2 (1954), pp. 581-5, and correspce. there cited. Wauters, *ubi supra*, col. 262.

[5] Stengers, *Bull. Soc. Roy. Belge Géog.* 1949, pp. 109-14, citing Plunkett's despatches from FO 10/640, 641, 642. B.C.B. 11, van Eetvelde.

[6] Wauters, *loc. cit.* Flament *et al.*, *La Force Publique*, pp. 383-7. D.D.F. xiii, No. 27, Montholon to Hanotaux 23 Nov. 1896.

King Leopold had however still to re-occupy the Lado Enclave itself. His time-table had been badly thrown out by Zande resistance, which was not fully overcome until April 1896.[1] Chaltin, the Congolese commandant on the upper Uele, was then ordered to push forward to the Nile. On 17 February 1897 Chaltin defeated 'Arabi Dafa'allāh in a pitched battle at Bedden, and entered Rejaf on the following day. 'Arabi fell back on Bor, whence he launched a strong counter-attack in June 1898. But this time the Belgians were not to be dislodged from the Nile.[2] Meanwhile, however, the Dhanis expedition had foundered in total disaster. On 14 February 1897, at Ndirfi just within the Nile basin, the vanguard mutinied, exasperated by the hardships of the march, by the inhuman severities of its commander and above all by semi-starvation. As the mutiny swept back into the rear échelons the expedition dissolved, Dhanis himself barely escaping with his life.[3]

In spite of this crushing disaster, King Leopold still continued to hanker after his 'neutral solution', flying kites through inspired newspaper articles and on occasion by more or less direct diplomatic suggestion.[4] It seems very unlikely that Leopold would have achieved his ambition even had the Dhanis expedition succeeded; but Dhanis' success might perhaps have paved the way for an Anglo-French settlement of the Upper Nile at Leopold's expense. Had the mutiny at Ndirfi not taken place, Dhanis would have forestalled the French by many months on the west bank of the Nile and perhaps in the Bahr al-Ghazal. Salisbury and Hanotaux would have been equally anxious to eject him; imperialist chauvinism on both sides of the Channel could have been conveniently diverted to Leopold's address. The obvious Anglo-French bargain, probably acceptable to both statesmen in the circumstances, would have been a recognition of the British sphere in return for moderate territorial concessions in the Bahr al-Ghazal. The alternative, the alignment of Leopold with either Britain or France, would have generated a crisis which neither Power could have contemplated without dismay, for it might soon have involved the question of Belgian neutrality. The mutiny of Dhanis' Batetela soldiers may have destroyed the only chance after October 1894 of settling the Upper Nile dispute with reasonable satisfaction to England and without the humiliation of France.

'Vous allez tirer un coup de pistolet sur le Nil; nous en acceptons toutes les conséquences.' These, according to Baratier, were Hanotaux' parting words to Marchand.[5] To one element at least in this

---

[1] Flament, *op. cit.*, pp. 308-18.
[2] *Ibid.*, pp. 318-38. L. Lotar, 'Redjaf', *Congo*, 1932, No. 1, pp. 54-76, Cf. Mahdia 1/34/1, 'Arabi Dafa'allāh to the Khalifa, 12 Rabi' al-Awwal 1316 / 30 July 1898.
[3] Flament, *op. cit.*, pp. 389-402. Ascherson, *op. cit.*, pp. 223-4.
[4] Wauters, *ubi supra*, cols. 271-2, citing *Belgique Coloniale*, 4 May 1898. J. Stengers, 'Rapport sur les dossiers relatifs aux territoires cédés à bail', *Bull. I.R.C.B.* xxiv, 2 (1953), pp. 580-2. FO 141/332, Plunkett to Salisbury No. 191, 8 Sept. 1898, citing *L'Indépendance Belge*, 7 Sept. D.D.F. xiv No. 372, Gérard to Delcassé 24 Sept. 1898.
[5] Baratier, *Fachoda*, p. 133. For a slightly different wording, cf. Mangin, letter of 6 Nov. 1898, 'Lettres de la Mission Marchand', *Revue des Deux Mondes*, 1931, p. 277.

'pistol-shot' Hanotaux was openly opposed—the invocation of Ethiopian assistance. Hanotaux doubtless suspected, even if his own *Direction* did not, that even for moderate British opinion a 'plot' to call in Menelik's 'warlike hordes' against Kitchener's 'civilising mission' would be 'devilry' fully justifying a war of retaliation. 'Could anyone wonder', said Campbell-Bannerman on 24 November 1898, 'that even the quietest amongst us were filled with hot indignation?'[1] But even on the Marchand Mission itself Hanotaux' diplomatic correspondence from 1896 to June 1898 preserves a remarkable reticence; and its scanty references to Egypt and the Nile valley disclose a policy which is the very antithesis of 'a pistol-shot on the Nile', though not perhaps of a French 'presence' in the Bahr al-Ghazal.

In January 1897 Hanotaux wrote to Cogordan in Cairo a despatch which was explicitly intended to dissipate the 'découragement que laisse percer le ton de votre télégramme'. In it he mentions, as one of the more encouraging factors in the Egyptian situation, 'marche sur le Bahr el Ghazal'—not, be it noted, 'sur le Nil' or 'sur Fachoda'. Nor does Hanotaux expatiate on this theme.[2] Just a month later, on 10 February 1897, the *Direction Politique*—Benoît again?—formally recommended to Hanotaux a complete revolution in French policy towards the Nile valley. Egypt, whose southern frontier was to be arbitrarily extended to the Fifth Cataract just north of Berber, would be evacuated and 'internationalised'. South of this line the rights of the Sultan and the Khedive, for so long the sheet-anchor of French policy, would disappear, and the Sudan would be partitioned between France and England. England would thus be compensated for this evacuation of an enlarged Egypt by annexing what remained of the Sudan after the Bahr al-Ghazal, west of the Nile and south of the tenth parallel, had been 'attribué à la France'.[3] The coincidence of this suggestion with the more openly aggressive policy of the Pavillon de Flore early in 1897 suggests that the Quai d'Orsay was not really, as opposed to officially, ignorant of this development. Nor can Hanotaux himself have been ignorant of it, in view of the battle he was fighting over Ethiopian policy.[4]

Hanotaux did not however accept his *Direction*'s proposal. Nor was

---

[1] 'Devilry' was Grey's epithet, in a letter of Jan. 1897, cited Robinson and Gallagher, *Africa and the Victorians*, p. 337. The other citations are from Campbell-Bannerman's speech, cited by Garvin, *Chamberlain*, III, pp. 233-4. For a still more violent British reaction, see: Anon., 'France, Russia and the Nile', *Contemporary Review*, LXXIV, Dec. 1898, pp. 761-78. Cf. *infra*, Ch. XV, p. 351.

[2] D.D.F. XIII, No. 61, Hanotaux to Cogordan 10 Jan. 1897.

[3] D.D.F. XIV, No. 258, *note du Département* 18 July 1898, reproducing proposals of a similar note dated 10 Feb. 1897.

[4] Hanotaux was of course notified of the operational plans for penetration into the Bahr al-Ghazal towards the Nile; but there is no evidence that the Quai d'Orsay was ever officially informed of the change from a 'policy of pledges' to a 'policy of annexation'. Lebon seems to have confined himself to forwarding Liotard's despatches with formal covering notes. Cf. D.D.F. XIII, No. 99, Lebon to Hanotaux 11 Feb. 1897, enclosing Liotard's desp. of 9 July 1896; No. 365, same to same 22 Nov. 1897, enclosing Liotard's desp. of 15 June 1897.

he moved by a despatch from Cairo of March 1897, in which Cogordan emphasised the part which a French occupation of Fashoda might play in the settlement of the Egyptian Question.[1] His policy in the Sudan, in so far as he had one at all, was still based, as he told Cogordan in November 1897, on maintaining the inalienable rights of the Sultan and the Khedive in 'the provinces of Nubia, Darfur, Kordofan and Sennar, *with all their dependencies*'. As a solution to the Egyptian question, and its increasing Sudanese complications, Hanotaux still pinned his faith to international action—sooner or later:

> N'est-il pas permis de penser que d'autres Puissances en viendront à leur tour à reconnaître la communauté de leurs intérêts et des nôtres dans cette partie de l'Orient et qu'ainsi les questions relatives à l'Egypte se poseront un jour, *dans leur ensemble*, devant l'Europe entière?[2]

Meanwhile there must be no pistol shots. The correct policy in Egyptian and Sudanese affairs was 'la politique, non cassante, mais vigilante, que [la France] a suivi jusqu'ici'.[3] In January 1898 Hanotaux' policy was still unchanged; indeed, he minuted more strongly than ever against any isolated French action which might provoke a crisis in Egyptian affairs: '. . . il me paraît évident que notre intérêt n'est pas de pousser les choses à l'extrême; la continuation de l'état de choses actuel est ce que nous devons désirer, aussi longtemps que l'Europe n'aura pas ouvert les yeux. . . . Donc, prolongeons et négocions.'[4]

When Hanotaux wrote these words the latest news from Marchand was that he was working his way up the M'Bomu.[5] But a day or two later, on 24 January 1898, Hanotaux learned that Marchand was in the Bahr al-Ghazal near Rumbek and that the *Faidherbe* was with him: 'quand vous lirez ceci, il aura porté, à allure 14 nœuds, pavillon au Nil là où il doit être planté'.[6] To this clear indication that Marchand was probably already at Fashoda Hanotaux showed not the slightest reaction. Indeed, on 17 February he wrote to André Lebon of the 'règles de prudence et de réserve' which had guided French action in the affairs of the Upper Nile, although admittedly in this letter he was protesting against Lagarde's offer of the French flag to the Khalifa.[7] In May 1898 a further report, despatched on 1 January from the river Sueh, reached Paris from Marchand.[8] It revealed that the mission was

---

[1] D.D.F. XIII, No. 154, Cogordan to Hanotaux 17 Mar. 1897.
[2] *Ibid.*, No. 360, Hanotaux to Cogordan 16 Nov. 1897 (emphasis supplied).
[3] D.D.F. XIII, No. 343, *note du Ministre* (of a conversation with Mohrenheim) 23 Oct. 1897.
[4] D.D.F. XIV, No. 11, minute by Hanotaux (c. 20 Jan. 1898) on Cogordan 13 Jan.
[5] MC Afrique III 36b, Marchand to Lebon 10 May 1897 (received 29 Aug.) An advanced party had however already reached Tambura.
[6] D.D.F. XIV, No. 28, Lebon to Hanotaux 24 Jan. 1898.
[7] *Ibid.*, No. 55, Hanotaux to Lebon 17 Feb. 1898.
[8] MC Afrique III 36a, Rapport Confidentiel 10 Oct. 1898, and annexes. Cf. *ibid.* 36b, Binger to Lebon 31 May 1898. Marchand's report itself has disappeared; but it is summarised in D.D.F. XIV, No. 246, Trouillot to Delcassé 4 July 1898.

held up at Wau until the Sueh waters rose again, but that Marchand expected to be at Fashoda by May 1898. Still no reaction from Hanotaux.[1] But on 21 June 1898, a week after the fall of the Méline government and after Hanotaux had become *ministre démissionnaire*, he suddenly put forward a quite revolutionary Nile policy in which the Marchand Mission was to play a leading part—a departure so unexpected that it came as a complete and unpleasant surprise to President Félix Faure himself.[2]

This policy was embodied in a despatch to Cogordan at Cairo,[3] the gist of which is well given in Faure's own summary:

> ... Le Ministère avait fait savoir que Marchand allait incessamment arriver à Fachoda, que son arrivée concorderait avec diverses actions venant de l'Est et du Sud-Est et que cette arrivée marquerait la date de la réouverture de la question d'Egypte, que notre agent au Caire avait pour devoir de réunir déjà tous les éléments des négociations qui fatalement s'ouvriraient ainsi.[4]

In these negotiations, Cogordan was told, 'toutes les Puissances qui ont des intérêts en Egypte auront également à prendre part'. The frivolous irresponsibility of this despatch is shown by one of the other 'favourable' factors which Hanotaux adduced. The recent peace between Greece and Turkey would, he said, 'free the Sultan from the fetters which have trammelled his action in Egyptian affairs'—as if the action of the Sultan, at peace or at war, could have had the slightest effect on the fate of the Nile valley in June 1898. It also appeared from this despatch that while some parts of the Sudan were 'placés sous l'autorité de droit du Sultan et du Khédive', others were *res nullius* and were indeed already the subject of negotiations between France and Ethiopia 'pour la possession des deux rives du Nil'.[5] A hint as to the dividing-line between these two zones was contained in an inspired article published in *Le Matin* on 19 June, two days before the despatch to Cogordan. The fall of Khartoum was to be 'le signal d'un effort diplomatique pour replacer les rapports de l'Angleterre avec l'Egypte dans une position légale'. It was also stated that Khartoum was situated at 'les dernières limites égyptiennes'.[6] Apparently Egypt, including the northern Sudan which Kitchener had just reconquered, was to be evacuated by the British, while the Sudan south of Khartoum was to be partitioned between France and Ethiopia. As a 'position légale', this proposition would be hard to beat.

[1] It is just possible that Hanotaux was ignorant of these facts, as they were not *officially* communicated to the Quai d'Orsay until 4 July (D.D.F., *loc. cit.*, which refrains from stating when Marchand's report had been received).

[2] Félix Faure, 'Fachoda (1898)', *Rev. Hist. Dip.* 1955, p. 30.

[3] D.D.F. xiv, No. 236, Hanotaux to Cogordan 21 June 1898.

[4] Faure, *ubi supra*.   [5] D.D.F., *loc. cit.*

[6] FO 141/332, Monson to Salisbury No. 298, 19 June 1898, enclosing the article. At this time *Le Matin* seems regularly to have expressed the views of the Quai d'Orsay: cf. R. Arie, 'L'opinion publique en France et l'affaire de Fachoda', *Rev. Hist. Cols.* xLI, (1954) pp. 329-67, at p. 350.

If this visionary nonsense has any significance at all, it can only be that 'the indispensable Foreign Minister' was deliberately trying to queer the pitch for his successor, who would necessarily have to abandon these absurdities and could then be accused of betraying the interests of France. Hanotaux' undoubted if sometimes calculated charm certainly concealed a streak of feline malice; and he is known to have looked upon Delcassé rather as Lord Curzon looked upon Stanley Baldwin—'a person of the utmost insignificance'. At any rate, during the Fashoda Crisis itself Hanotaux was singing a very different tune. On 25 October 1898 he told Wilfrid Blunt that war would be absurd 'for such a trifle as Fashoda'.

> M. Hanotaux maintained that no war would be popular in France, that nobody knew where Fashoda was, or cared three straws about the Marchand Mission. He even considered the Egyptian question itself one of small importance to France. As for the Bahr el Gazal, it was 'a country inhabited by monkeys and by black men worse than monkeys'.[1]

Blunt was perhaps the man to make a good story better; but his reports of conversations, where they can be checked, are usually accurate enough[2]—and in any case he can hardly have reported exactly the opposite of what Hanotaux said.

Delcassé was faced with the legacy of Hanotaux within a few days of taking office. On 4 July 1898 the new Colonial Minister Trouillot sent Delcassé a situation report on the Marchand Mission. He pointed out that the time was drawing nigh when France would have to 'légitimer' her action on the Upper Nile. 'La question va se trouver posée, avec une certaine acuité sans doute, dès que l'armée du Sirdar se sera rapprochée de Fachoda. . . .' The Marchand Mission might be presented as simply a defensive operation intended to forestall a Mahdist invasion of the upper Ubangi; but it would be better still if the Quai d'Orsay could obtain from the Sultan, 'suzerain du Khédive' a mandate permitting France to act on his behalf for the restoration of 'order, security and the normal development of civilisation' on the Upper Nile.

> Il serait naturel, dans ce cas, de lui demander que, dans cette entreprise délicate où nous nous trouvons substitués à l'autorité ottomane, il témoignât envers la France d'égards tout particuliers. Il serait peut-être possible d'obtenir du Sultan . . . qu'il nous reconnaisse officiellement soit une souveraineté déléguée, soit un simple droit de bail à long terme. Ce serait là pour nous le moyen de nous acheminer insensiblement dans l'avenir, en ce qui concerne ces régions, vers un protectorat effectif.'[3]

[1] W. S. Blunt, *My Diaries* (London, edn. of 1932), p. 303,
[2] Cf. *ibid.*, p. 220, where Blunt's record of conversations with Lady Cromer and with the Khedive on the origins of the Dongola expedition records very accurately what his interlocutors were in a position to know.
[3] D.D.F. xiv, No. 246.

Delcassé was not in the happiest position to savour the rich comedy of these proposals; but he was baffled to find a policy of his own. His *Direction Politique* took out of its pigeon-hole the project of February 1897 for the 'internationalisation' of an enlarged Egypt and an Anglo-French partition of the central and southern Sudan. This it presented to Delcassé on 18 July, complacently remarking that with Marchand at Fashoda 'nous pourrons attendre, munis d'un excellent gage, l'heure des pourparlers'.[1] Delcassé knew better than that; but what to do he did not know. For week after week he procrastinated, deaf to repeated reminders both from the *Colonies* and from his own *Direction*[2] and perhaps hoping against hope that the Khalifa might still check Kitchener. At last on 7 September he could procrastinate no longer—rumour had it that Kitchener had already left Omdurman for Fashoda. He ruled that Marchand, if challenged, should represent his presence as part of a defensive operation against the Mahdists and should leave all questions of right and sovereignty for discussion in Europe. The *Colonies*' suggestion of a mandate from the Sultan he rejected for the nonsense that it was, pointing out that such a mandate, to be valid, would require the assent 'des Puissances garantes de l'intégrité de l'empire ottoman'.[3] Indeed, the best Delcassé could hope for now was that the encounter would pass off without an actual armed clash.[4] As for the Pavillon de Flore, its main preoccupation was to wriggle out of a tight corner by transferring all responsibility to the Quai d'Orsay. On 15 September Trouillot pointed out that in 1895 'mon Département, en se plaçant au point de vue purement colonial, aurait été "porté à restreindre au strict nécessaire" notre occupation du Haut-Oubangui'; but that it had modified this policy at the express desire of the Foreign Minister. 'L'action de la France dans le Soudan égyptien, vous ne l'ignorez pas, n'a été qu'une des manifestations de notre politique générale.'[5]

If this were so, it was a pity that it had never been properly under the control of the Foreign Minister. It was not only that the Pavillon de Flore, at any rate from the beginning of 1897, had pursued a private foreign policy on the Upper Nile and in Ethiopia. In January 1899 Monson complained that in France 'questions of serious international moment' were far too often 'dependent upon the manipulation . . . of irresponsible officials'.[6] Unknown to Monson, the Marchand Mission was a glaring example of this dangerous practice. Between November 1895 and April 1896 the permanent officials of both the Pavillon de

---

[1] D.D.F. xiv, No. 258, *note du Département* 18 July 1898.
[2] *Ibid.*, No. 296, Trouillot to Delcassé 19 Aug. 1898; No. 302, *note du Département* 23 Aug.; No. 323, Trouillot to Delcassé 4 Sept.
[3] *Ibid.*, No. 329, Delcassé to Trouillot 7 Sept. 1898.
[4] He feared that Kitchener might have been ordered to eject Marchand by force: A. Maurois, *King Edward and His Times* (English edn., London 1933, p. 70, citing Delcassé's diary, 19-26 Sept. 1898).
[5] D.D.F. xiv, No. 352, Trouillot to Delcassé 15 Sept. 1898.
[6] FO 27/3455, Monson to Salisbury No. 48, 27 Jan. 1899.

Flore and the Quai d'Orsay had manœuvred their inexperienced Ministers into launching a mission the full significance of which those Ministers probably—in Berthelot's case, certainly—did not understand. The practice was all the more dangerous when these officials even at the Quai d'Orsay were not only, as Monson complained, narrowly departmental in their outlook, but also apparently blind to the realities of international politics.[1] The *Direction Politique* was playing with fire when it supported the *Colonies*' project of encouraging Ethiopian intervention on the Upper Nile; and its proposed Sudan settlement of February 1897, revived in July 1898, was arrant nonsense unless Britain allowed herself to be treated as a negligible quantity or unless some diplomatic miracle secured for France the support both of Russia and of Germany.

Hanotaux, faced with the Marchand Mission as a *fait accompli* on his return to office in April 1896, had attempted, with some success at first, to modify its objectives to suit more closely his own ideas of the correct policy for the Upper Nile. But he was in a false position from the outset; and his inherent weakness as a 'non-political' Minister forced him into repeated concessions. After his defeat on Ethiopian policy in 1897 he seems to have abandoned the struggle, and he doubtless preferred not to be officially aware of all that was going on. He may well have been reduced to hoping, as Bonvalot in October 1898 publicly accused him of hoping, that 'Marchand n'arriverait pas'[2]—or at least that Marchand would not get far enough to cause a major explosion. Hanotaux never seems to have attempted to enforce his views by a threat of resignation. No doubt he feared to be taken at his word. With his vanity, his calculated charm, his calculated petulance and his occasional genuine hysteria, there was in Gabriel Hanotaux something of the *prima donna*. And a *prima donna* needs, above all, to be in the centre of the stage.

[1] Or, as Monson put it (*loc. cit.*), addicted to proceedings 'more characteristic of low-class pettifogging than of dignified and businesslike frankness'.
[2] Bonvalot, 'Les Affaires du Nil', *Le Matin*, 23 Oct. 1898.

XIV

FASHODA : THE DIPLOMATIC SETTING

OF THE CRISIS, 1897–98

IN 1897 and 1898 the French colonialist press frequently asserted that Hanotaux would never have 'sent Marchand to Fashoda' 'sans avoir préparé son jeu sur l'échiquier de la politique génér-ale'[1]—in plain language, without having secured the support of Russia. In fact Hanotaux, doubtless fearing a direct refusal, never directly asked St Petersburg for support on the Upper Nile. Even on Egypt itself, his confidence in Russia's 'New Course' of March 1896 was probably extinct before Lobanov's death in August. Although Hanotaux sometimes encouraged Cogordan by suggesting that he had obtained Russian support,[2] he was really well aware that he had nothing to hope for in this quarter. During Hanotaux' conversation with the Czar in October 1896, Egypt was apparently not even mentioned; in his conversation with Shishkin at the same time it was merely agreed that the two Powers should continue their policy of financial obstruc-tion.[3] In January 1897, the sole Egyptian fruit of his conversation with Muraviev was that the Russian representative on the *Caisse de la Dette* should always vote with his French colleague; but this had already been agreed as early as March 1895.[4]

It was difficult for Hanotaux to ask very much of the Russians in the Egyptian department of the Eastern question when France was at the same time consistently refusing her support at the Straits—the depart-ment that interested Russia. In December 1895 Lobanov had told Montebello that he intended to seize Constantinople if Britain forced the Dardanelles, and had asked for French support. President Faure himself had replied:

Aller au delà d'une action diplomatique ne se comprendrait pas en France, à moins que la question dont nous souffrons depuis vingt-cinq ans ne soit sérieusement envisagée. Comment com-

---

[1] The citation is from *Bull. C.A.F.*, Nov. 1897. Many others could be given.
[2] E.g. D.D.F. XIII, Nos. 61, 360, Hanotaux to Cogordan 10 Jan. and 16 Nov. 1897.
[3] D.D.F. XII, Nos. 467, 472, 474, Hanotaux' notes of conversations with the Czar and with Shishkin 2, 12 and 14 Oct. 1896. V. Khvostov has however stated (*Istorik Marksist*, XX, 1930, cited Langer, *Diplomacy of Imperialism*, p. 332) that Hanotaux persuaded the Czar 'to accept a far-reaching French programme' involving the recognition of the British occupation in return for the neutralisation of the Suez Canal and compensation for France on the Upper Nile. If this statement be correct (and it is utterly unsupported by Hanotaux' record), the Czar's agreement, as on other similar occasions, led to no practical result.
[4] D.D.F. XIII, No. 87, Hanotaux to Montebello 31 Jan. 1897.

prendrait-on que la France s'engageât militairement dans une affaire en Orient, l'Allemagne restant l'arme au pied. . . .[1]

France would not fight except for the Lost Provinces. More, she would not even enter any formal diplomatic combination of which Germany was a member, unless Russia accepted in advance 'le principe d'un règlement de la question d'Alsace-Lorraine'. Berthelot, who prompted the President's letter, was not only avoiding war on Russia's behalf in an area where French and Russian interests conflicted; he was also demanding a guarantee against the Franco-Russe being emasculated by the admission of Germany as a partner.[2] These refusals were re-iterated by Hanotaux in December 1896 and April 1897. At the end of 1896 he told Mohrenheim bluntly that 'la France ne se con-sidérerait nullement comme engagée dans un conflit qui viendrait à éclater pour la question de la mer Noire et des Détroits'.[3] When in March 1897 Hanotaux received a peremptory Russian demand to define his attitude in the case of isolated British action in Crete or at the Straits, he simply repeated the answers given by Berthelot and the President in December 1895.[4] The Czar professed himself content with this attitude of 'defensive reserve';[5] but it was obviously not the answer he would have liked.

Courcel, with his usual penetration, indicated a major contradiction in French policy when in January 1897 he admitted to Salisbury that the French had to avoid being 'poussés par la considération puissante, mais accessoire, de nos idées sur l'Egypte à prendre parti au jour de la liquidation ottomane dans un sens peut-être préjudiciable à nos intérêts généraux'.[6] A month later, when the Cretan insurrection seemed likely to touch off the explosion in the Near East, Hanotaux was even prepared to attempt a partial accommodation with Britain over Egypt as a demonstration that France was not forced to follow wherever Russia might lead. The circumstances were not at first sight auspicious. On 5 February 1897 Hicks Beach had accompanied his announcement of the British loan to Egypt by the remark that the French themselves, who had challenged the authority of the *Caisse*, would be responsible for any lengthening of the occupation which this loan might entail. There was great excitement in Paris, while the French community in Egypt apparently expected that 'war would be declared instantaneously' in reply to this demonstration. Instead, Hanotaux instructed Courcel to seek some gesture of conciliation, 'qui

---

[1] *Ibid.*, No. 193, citing Félix Faure to Montebello 25 Dec. 1895.

[2] D.D.F. xii, No. 292, Berthelot to Montebello 31 Jan. 1896. He was not impressed by a conditional Russian promise to take up the Egyptian question 'avec la dernière énergie' (*ibid.*, No. 288, note du Ministre 27 Jan. 1896). Cf. Hargreaves, '*Entente Manquée*', *C.H.J.* 1953, pp. 79–80.

[3] D.D.F. xiii, No. 54, *note du Ministre* 30 Dec. 1896; cf. No. 87. Chastenet, *La République Triomphante*, pp. 143, 362. Langer, *op. cit.*, pp. 330–48.

[4] D.D.F. xiii, No. 193, Hanotaux to Montebello 10 Apr. 1897.

[5] D.D.F. xii, No. 302, Montebello to Nisard 7 Feb. 1896; xiii, No. 241, Montebello to Hanotaux 27 May 1897.

[6] D.D.F. xiii, No. 77, Courcel to Hanotaux 27 Jan. 1897.

serait particulièrement précieuse dans les circonstances que nous traversons'.[1]

Salisbury, always ready to mend the line to Paris as a precaution against too great a dependence on Berlin, met Courcel by suggesting that the *Caisse* might advance to Egypt a sum equal to the British loan. He undertook to furnish as to its expenditure 'any information which would not compromise military operations'. Hanotaux replied by the counter-proposal that the *Caisse* should *lend* the money, and that Salisbury should recognise that any further loan for Sudan operations would be 'une question d'ordre politique, nécessitant l'adhésion de tous les commissaires'. Courcel added that France would then be morally bound to consider any such application 'sans hostilité de parti-pris . . . et sans esprit d'obstruction systématique'.[2] These were fair words, but the arrangement would still have made the progress of the Sudan campaign dependent upon French goodwill. Yet Salisbury was so anxious 'to enable Hanotaux to boast in the Chamber that his diplomacy has extorted a satisfaction from the English Govt.', that he told Cromer: 'I wish to gratify the French Govt. and Chamber to this extent unless you can show that real practical inconvenience would result.'[3] Cromer did not object to the possible hamstringing of the campaign. Perhaps he calculated, as Salisbury may also have done, that the French would not seriously oppose an advance as far as Khartoum for fear of alienating Egyptian opinion; and in February 1897 the situation of the campaign did not seem to justify the faintest hope that it could be a factor in the settlement of the Upper Nile. Cromer's objection, to which Salisbury bowed, was that *any* acceptance of the principle of unanimity on the *Caisse* would sooner or later make Egyptian finances unworkable.[4]

When Salisbury failed to refer to the project again, Hanotaux also allowed it to drop. Nor was the proposal revived when Salisbury visited Hanotaux in Paris in March 1897. Salisbury's dislike of these 'summit conferences' was normally so great that it has been conjectured that this meeting represented an attempt by personal interview to dissipate the gathering storm on the Upper Nile. In fact, Hanotaux' very full account of the conversation contains no reference either to the Upper Nile or to Egypt. There was however a passing reference to West Africa, where a new crop of open and embittered disputes was again pushing the Nile controversy into the background.[5] Salisbury still hoped to use West Africa as he had used it in 1890, to

---

[1] *A.R.*, 1897, pp. [36-7]. FO 27/3314, Monson to Salisbury No. 88, 11 Feb. 1897. FO 27/3312, Salisbury to Monson No. 67, 11 Feb. SP Egypt, Salisbury to Cromer 12 Feb. Zetland, *Lord Cromer*, p. 260, citing Cromer to Salisbury 18 Feb. 1897. D.D.F. xiii, No. 93, Hanotaux to Courcel 9 Feb.; No. 100, Courcel to Hanotaux 11 Feb.

[2] D.D.F. xiii, Nos. 100, 121, Courcel to Hanotaux 11 and 22 Feb. 1897. FO 27/3312, *loc. cit.*

[3] FO 78/4895, Salisbury to Cromer tel. No. 30, 4 Mar. 1897; cf. same to same tel. No. 27, 1 Mar.   [4] *Ibid.*, Cromer to Salisbury tel. No. 39, 8 Mar. 1897.

[5] D.D.F. xiii, No. 166, *note du Ministre* 26 Mar. 1897; No. 167, communication from Courcel 26 Mar.

disinterest France in the Nile valley. Given the state of opinion in France in 1897-8 this would have been a very difficult goal to reach. But it was made quite impossible by the exigencies of Salisbury's Colonial Secretary Joseph Chamberlain.

The Niger negotiations begun in February 1896 had been suspended three months later in May. Hanotaux had rejected a British offer in Borgu rather more generous than the Phipps-Hanotaux line of October 1894; his counter-proposal was so exorbitant that Salisbury concluded that Hanotaux wanted 'a noisy breach with us for some Parliamentary purpose'.[1] Between the middle of 1896 and the spring of 1897 there was vigorous local action on both sides. Goldie conducted a successful campaign against the Amir of Nupe; the French overran Borgu and reached the navigable lower Niger at Boussa, where Goldie had a treaty, but no occupation. In March 1897 Monson protested verbally against the occupation of Boussa; in spite of repeated reminders, no answer was received until June. This reply was quite unsatisfactory, and Salisbury minuted wearily, 'we shall have to make a formal protest'.[2] Sir Clement Hill was indeed in favour of 'allowing Sir G. Goldie to enforce our rights'.[3] But Goldie had no intention of doing this. The advance of the French had exposed not only the falsity of Goldie's claims to occupation, notably in Borgu, but also the hollowness of his military bluster. Goldie expected the Government to protect his paper claims against European trespassers, and in July Chamberlain had to warn him that 'there can be no question of going to war with France on account of Boussa'.[4] On 2 September 1897 Goldie was officially reprimanded for his failure to make good his Company's claims, which 'had greatly complicated the position and embarrassed H.M.G. in their dealings with the French Govt.'. Goldie blustered about 'what the Company could do if they were given a free hand'; but Salisbury minuted, 'he is hardly sane', and Chamberlain was already prepared to 'expropriate him at once, lock, stock and barrel'.[5]

As Goldie faded out, Chamberlain took over. Chamberlain was not content with 'a formal protest' as an answer to the French occupation of Boussa. In June, apparently without consulting Salisbury, he authorised the Governor of the Gold Coast to retaliate by treating with Samory, in breach of repeated assurances to France; and by occupying disputed territory including, if constrained by military necessity, a place called Bonduku on the French side of a frontier settled in July

[1] FO 27/3274, passim. FO 27/3275, Dufferin to Salisbury Nos. 69, 75, of 30 Apr. and 8 May 1896; minute by Salisbury on No. 75.
[2] Flint, Sir George Goldie, pp. 226-57, 264-8. FO 27/3337, 3338, Mar.-June 1897, passim. FO 27/3338, Monson to Salisbury No. 187, 19 June 1897; minute by Salisbury.
[3] FO 27/3338, loc. cit., minute by Hill.
[4] Flint, op. cit., pp. 268-74. Perham, Lugard I, pp. 632-4. FO 27/3368, Niger Co. to F.O. 9 Mar. 1897. FO 27/3370, F.O. to Niger Co. 23 July 1897; Goldie to F.O. 27 July; Goldie to Colonial Office 19 July. Ibid., C.O. to F.O. 26 June 1897, enclosing draft of letter to Goldie (sent 1 July).
[5] FO 27/3371, memo. by Bertie (who administered the rebuke) 2 Sept. 1897; minute by Salisbury. Flint, op. cit., pp. 274-8, citing (p. 277) Chamberlain to Selborne 22 Sept. 1897.

1893.[1] Both Hill and Sanderson deprecated these instructions, Sanderson hinting pretty clearly that they could be justified only as a prelude to war. But Salisbury had to give way, if he was to keep Chamberlain in the Cabinet. On 5 August 1897 he minuted 'I think the C.O. may play the game their own way . . .'.[2] Chamberlain soon extended his game. He insisted that 'by making a stand and retaliating on [the French] . . . we shall convince them that we are in earnest, and so induce them to agree to an early settlement'.[3] The instrument of retaliation was to be a regular military force, to the formation of which Salisbury agreed in the course of August. The technique of retaliation was to be the very dangerous 'Chessboard Policy' of planting posts behind and between those of the French and 'sitting on' their communications.[4] On 2 September the Foreign Office agreed that in this way Boussa was to be made 'untenable without collision'. Not that Chamberlain cared if there were a collision; on 28 September he told Selborne that the Niger and Gold Coast hinterlands must be saved 'even at the cost of war'.[5]

Already by the end of August protests were being bandied back and forth between London and Paris almost weekly, and Hill had minuted, 'the position is becoming very unsatisfactory, almost dangerous'.[6] Monson in Paris was pressing for a resumption of negotiations. He pointed to Hanotaux' vague but conciliatory hints of a general settlement in Africa; he feared that the Franco-German Dahomey-Togoland treaty of 23 July 1897 might portend a rapprochement which would find a field of action in the Nile valley.[7] Goschen and Hicks Beach—neither of them timid men—begged Salisbury to curb Chamberlain.[8] He would have been only too glad to do so; but before he could even start negotiations he had to fight two major battles: to persuade Chamberlain to withdraw from Bonduku, and to persuade him to give up his idea of making the French 'eat dirt publicly' by evacuating Boussa before the discussions began.[9]

---

[1] F O 27/3370, C.O. to F.O. 26 June 1897, enclosing Chamberlain to Maxwell 4 June. Cf. D.D.F. xii, No. 156, Howard to Hanotaux 26 Sept. 1895; FO 27/3335, Salisbury to Monson No. 60, 25 Mar. 1897.

[2] F O 27/3371, minutes by Hill, Sanderson and Salisbury 5 Aug. 1897, on C.O. to F.O. 4 Aug.

[3] *Ibid.*, C.O. to F.O. 14 Aug. 1897.

[4] *Ibid., loc. cit.*; F.O. to C.O. 19 Aug.; C.O. to F.O. 25 Aug. Cf. Perham, *op. cit.*, pp. 638-42, 659-63. Chamberlain had already begun his 'Chessboard Policy' in both the Lagos and the Gold Coast hinterlands: cf. FO 27/3370, C.O. to F.O. 23 July and 26 June 1897, enclosing Chamberlain's instructions to the Governors of these colonies.

[5] F O 27/3371, Hill, minutes of the first Niger Conference, 2 Sept. 1897. Garvin, *Chamberlain* iii, p. 208, citing Chamberlain to Selborne 28 Sept. 1897. Cf. Perham, *op. cit.*, p. 641.

[6] F O 27/3335, despatches Aug. 1897, *passim*. FO 27/3357, Geoffray to Salisbury 17 Aug.; minute by Hill.

[7] F O 27/3339, Monson to Salisbury No. 202, 2 July 1897; No. 223, 23 July; to Bertie, private, 20 Aug.; to Salisbury Nos. 261, 262, 5 Sept.; No. 273, 17 Sept.

[8] Goschen to Salisbury 19 Sept. 1897; Hicks Beach to Salisbury, 1 Oct. and 1 Nov. 1897: cited Robinson and Gallagher, *Africa and the Victorians*, p. 406.

[9] F O 27/3335, Salisbury to Monson No. 265, 10 Sept. 1897. FO 27/3336, minutes by Wingfield, Chamberlain, Sanderson and Salisbury 22-25 Oct. 1897; Salisbury to Monson No. 328a, 27 Oct. FO 27/3371, minute by Salisbury on C.O. to F.O. 14 Aug.

The negotiations opened at the end of October. The British commissioners soon found that the pretensions of the Niger Company could not possibly be maintained. Monson agreed, and emphasised that a quick settlement was the only alternative to war, or at best a chronic hostility from which the Germans would ultimately profit. Hanotaux was, he thought, anxious for a peaceful solution, but 'I do not well see how Hanotaux *can* give us what we want . . . without running the risk of being turned out of office'.[1] But Chamberlain refused to budge an inch. The watchword was to be 'Stand firm Moses!', until Lugard and his new West African Frontier Force had 'occupied places in their hinterland . . . then we shall be ready for a deal'.[2] Salisbury too wished to 'spin out the discussions', but for a different reason. Salisbury's object was 'to force [the French] to propose the basis of a general settlement of all controversies at issue between the Governments. We must not propose it ourselves.'[3]

Thus Salisbury on 25 November 1897. Two days later Hanotaux took what seemed to be a step in this direction by putting forward a scheme of general bases which included the claim to a French sphere east and north of Lake Chad.[4] Indeed, Hanotaux afterwards asserted that in this way 'la France posait indirectement la question Marchand'.[5] Whether or not this is so, Hanotaux' bases were certainly intended to rescue the West African negotiations from the morass of contentious detail in which they were floundering. But by this time the mere mention of regions east of Lake Chad aroused intense suspicion at the Foreign Office. Francis Bertie minuted that Hanotaux was 'hankering after a French band [of territory] from Lake Tchad to the Nile'.[6] Hanotaux was therefore informed that 'if other questions are adjusted' London would not contest the French claim north and east of the lake; but that England 'must not be understood to admit that any other European Power than Great Britain has any claim to occupy any part of the valley of the Nile'.[7]

This statement, drafted by Salisbury himself, was much the most extreme formulation of the British position so far communicated to Paris. It called upon Hanotaux to forget his objections to the 'British sphere', to abandon all hope of compensation in the Bahr al-Ghazal where he could already claim prior occupation, and indeed to

---

[1] FO 27/3340, Monson to Hill, private, 26 Oct. 1897. Cf. Monson's despatches Oct.-Nov. 1897, in FO 27/3340 and 3341; and Chamberlain's comments in FO 27/3372 and 3373.

[2] FO 27/3336, Chamberlain to Wingfield 22 Oct. 1897. FO 27/3373, minute by Chamberlain 11 Nov. 1897, on report of the Niger Commissioners 10 Nov.

[3] FO 27/3336, Bertie to Gosselin, private, 2 Nov. 1897; FO 27/3343, Salisbury to Monson tel. No. 15, 25 Nov. 1897.

[4] FO 27/3341, Monson to Salisbury No. 394, 27 Nov. 1897.

[5] Hanotaux, *Fachoda*, pp. 118-9. Cf. D.D.F. xiv, No. 413 (footnote citing minute by Nisard 15 Oct. 1898).

[6] FO 27/3343, minute by Bertie on Monson to Salisbury tel. No. 42, 27 Nov. 1897. Hanotaux' motives seem in fact to have been conciliatory; cf. FO 27/3341, *loc. cit.*

[7] FO 27/3336, Salisbury to Monson No. 406, 9 Dec. 1897 (delivered to Hanotaux as a Note, 10 Dec.).

recognise the British occupation of Egypt; and it did not deign to support any of these demands by reasoned argument. This uncompromising tone was doubtless the result of Salisbury's belated recognition that the French were, after all, moving towards the Nile; but such a statement was hardly the way to open the negotiation desired by Salisbury for 'a general settlement of all controversies at issue'. The British willingness to recognise French rights between Lake Chad and the Nile basin was in French eyes hardly a compensation at all. London had no valid grounds for opposing the French claim here, since in November 1893 she had relinquished to the Germans any conceivable claim of her own.[1] Whether or not Hanotaux had originally intended to 'poser la question Marchand', he was now content to reply to the British demand by recalling his public and private rejoinders to the Grey Declaration, and by deprecating the introduction of an issue alien to the negotiations in progress.[2]

Gosselin, the British negotiator in Paris, concluded that 'Hanotaux is clearly anxious to keep the question of the Nile outside the present discussions';[3] and for Salisbury there was now no longer any point in 'spinning out the discussions', especially as the local situation in West Africa was becoming dangerously tense. On 30 December he sent off to Paris a project of West African bases.[4] He had long been convinced that the clue to the West African labyrinth was to offer to the French access to the navigable Niger below the Boussa rapids. He had indeed suggested this idea as early as March 1896, much to the dismay of Anderson. Now that Anderson was dead, and Goldie discredited, Salisbury put forward this solution.[5] But Chamberlain was at the height of his power and he flatly vetoed the proposal, complaining that Salisbury wanted 'to give away everything and get nothing'.[6] The most that Salisbury could offer in his bases of 30 December 1897 was 'non-political' access to the Niger. But Gosselin was warned not to 'lay down an abstract negative' in reply to French requests for full territorial access.[7]

By January 1898 Hanotaux was at least as anxious for a settlement as Salisbury. He may still have hoped to raise the question of the Nile when the Niger was clear; if so, time was getting very short. But West Africa was in itself incentive enough; as early as January he told Monson that the local situation could 'hardly endure much longer

---

[1] By the Anglo-German Agreement of 15 Nov. 1893.
[2] FO 27/3342, Gosselin to Salisbury No. 454, 26 Dec. 1897, enclosing Note by Hanotaux.
[3] *Ibid.*, Gosselin to Salisbury No. 458, 27 Dec. 1897.
[4] FO 27/3336, Salisbury to Gosselin No. 438, 30 Dec. 1897.
[5] FO 27/3300, minutes by Anderson and Salisbury 12 Mar. 1896. FO 27/3341, Monson to Salisbury No. 400, 28 Nov. 1897; minute by Salisbury. FO 27/3343, Salisbury to Monson tel. No. 16, 29 Nov. 1897.
[6] FO 27/3374, F.O. to C.O. 30 Nov. 1897, minute by Chamberlain. Garvin, *op. cit.* III, pp. 212-3, citing Chamberlain to Salisbury and Chamberlain to Selborne 1 Dec. 1897.
[7] B.D. I, No. 157, Salisbury to Gosselin 30 Dec. 1897; No. 159, minute by Salisbury 11 Jan. 1898.

without a collision', and he was later to be very apprehensive at fancied British attempts to slow down the negotiations by extending their scope.[1] In January Notes were exchanged disclaiming 'responsibility for the consequences' of a French occupation of Nikki in Borgu.[2] In February and March news of a French incursion into Sokoto seemed for a time actually to threaten war.[3] By the end of May, when Lugard had put the 'Chessboard Policy' into full operation, the peace in Borgu depended on the restraint shown by European junior officers and African N.C.O.s in the face of every provocation short of powder and shot.[4] Chamberlain meanwhile fought tenaciously to delay a settlement until Lugard had established 'posts all over . . . the Dahomey hinterland'. He vilified the British negotiators as 'excellent men to arrange an unconditional surrender . . . not enough stiffening in the lot to hold up a paper collar'. He ignored Monson's warning that France might turn to war as an escape from the racking agony of the Dreyfus Affair, now working up to its crisis.[5] On 2 June, having just received Lugard's 'hundred-pound telegram' explaining just how and why flash-point had been reached, Chamberlain refused to concur with Salisbury in conceding the village of Illo to the French: 'I think that we shall not be the greatest losers even if the present negotiations fall through'.[6]

For all Salisbury's difficulties with Chamberlain, he at least knew what his Colonial colleague was doing. But Hanotaux, on his side, was sometimes kept really, and not merely officially, in the dark by the Pavillon de Flore, which on occasion did not scruple secretly to modify the text of instructions previously agreed with the Quai d'Orsay. This was indeed the origin of the French 'invasion of Sokoto', perhaps the most critical incident in the whole West African imbroglio. The invader of Sokoto was a certain Captain Cazemajou, who had in October 1896 been entrusted with a mission to Lake Chad.[7] In December 1896 Hanotaux had insisted, successfully as he thought, that Cazemajou 'demeurerait au nord de la ligne conventionelle Say-Barroua'.[8] But on 22 February 1897 the Pavillon de Flore merely forbade Cazemajou to 'pénétrer dans les territoires qui, au sud de

---

[1] Hanotaux, op. cit., pp. 122-6. Lebon, La politique de la France en Afrique, p. 46. B.D. 1' No. 164, Monson to Salisbury 31 Jan. 1898. D.D.F. xiv, No. 35, Hanotaux to Courcel 1 Feb. 1898; No. 236, Hanotaux to Cogordan 21 June 1898.

[2] B.D. 1, No. 158, Monson to Salisbury 10 Jan. 1898. D.D.F. xiv, No. 32, Courcel to Hanotaux 28 Jan.

[3] For this episode see A.R., 1898, pp. [32-3], 14; Perham, op. cit., pp. 672-4. Salisbury threatened to expel the intruders by force: B.D. 1, No. 169, Salisbury to Monson 21 Feb. 1898.

[4] Perham, op. cit., pp. 677-97.

[5] Ibid., p. 698, citing minutes by Chamberlain 25 and 28 May 1898; pp. 670, 685.

[6] Ibid., pp. 695, 699-701. Garvin, op. cit. iii, pp. 218-20, quoting Salisbury to Chamberlain 2 June 1898; Chamberlain to Salisbury 2 June.

[7] He was also instructed to offer a treaty of protection to Rabïh Zubair, and if possible to make contact with the Marchand Mission (MC Afrique iii 25, Lebon to Cazemajou 22 Feb. 1897).

[8] MC Afrique iii 25: Hanotaux to Lebon, 21 Dec. 1896; Lebon to Hanotaux 5 Feb. 1897; Hanotaux to Lebon 12 Feb. 1897.

X

la ligne Say-Barroua, "font équitablement partie" du royaume de Sokoto'.[1] Cazemajou did not observe even this diluted prohibition. In January 1898 he turned up at Argungu, certainly within 'the kingdom of Sokoto' and indeed to the south of Sokoto city; and there he made a treaty and distributed French flags.[2] On 28 April 1898 Hanotaux complained to Lebon of the recent irresponsible proceedings of the Colonial Ministry and its agents in a bitter letter of recrimination, of which the Cazemajou affair was the centre-piece. But there were no signs of contrition at the Pavillon de Flore. Gustave Binger drafted, and André Lebon signed, an aggressively polemical reply. It concluded with the insolent reflection that should Hanotaux fail to make good the claims of France by diplomacy, 'mon Département sans doute ne manquerait pas de le déplorer, mais avec le sentiment certain de n'avoir rien négligé, quant à lui, pour sauvegarder les intérêts de la France dans l'Afrique occidentale'.[3]

By April 1898 Hanotaux was a badly frightened man; and no wonder. With the Pavillon de Flore in this frame of mind not only on the Niger but, as Hanotaux must have known, also on the Nile, a catastrophe was sooner or later inevitable—all the more so because acts like the 'invasion of Sokoto' appeared to the British as sheer perfidy. It was not only that Hanotaux was anxious to settle the Niger before the Nile exploded; he thought that in London 'l'on désire un éclat pour en finir'. He saw in the British stiffness on West Africa a means of temporising until London's military preparations were complete[4]—and he was not far off the mark so far as Chamberlain was concerned. For the first time in his career, as a result of Chamberlain's sabre-rattling, Hanotaux was more afraid of the British than of the Pavillon de Flore. This was a salutary development, in spite of the imprudence of the 'Chessboard Policy' and Chamberlain's irrational conviction that the cession of obscure villages was an intolerable humiliation. Had Hanotaux not been so alarmed, he would undoubtedly have continued, in spite of his anxiety about the Nile, to defer to his Colonial colleague's ideas of a satisfactory settlement on the Niger. The result, when the Nile crisis came to a head, would almost certainly have been war. Salisbury saw the danger of the two disputes becoming entangled: on 3 June 1898 he warned Chamberlain that 'it will be a pity if we break off the negotiations, for it will add to our difficulties in the Nile valley'.[5] On the Upper Nile Salisbury by this time needed, and needed badly, a resounding success, and he was prepared if necessary to go to war to get it.[6] But he hoped for a peaceful success, if

---

[1] M C Afrique III 25; Lebon to Cazemajou 22 Feb. 1897.
[2] D.D.F. XIV, No. 59, footnote; No. 84, Lebon to Hanotaux 14 Mar. 1898. M C Afrique III 25, same to same 18 Apr. 1898.
[3] M C Afrique III 25, Hanotaux to Lebon 28 Apr. 1898; Lebon to Hanotaux 9 May.
[4] D.D.F. XIV, No. 32, Courcel to Hanotaux 28 Jan. 1898; No. 35, Hanotaux to Courcel 1 Feb.; No. 80, Courcel to Hanotaux 12 Mar.
[5] Salisbury to Chamberlain 3 June 1898, cited Garvin, op. cit. III, p. 220.
[6] Cf. infra, p. 324; Ch. XVII, p. 400.

only because war with France would have given Germany opportunities for the 'blackmail' which he so dreaded. If the issue were limited to the Upper Nile there was at least a chance that it might be settled peacefully by a French surrender. But if the Upper Nile were to be complicated by the West African tangle, the only alternative to war would be a protracted detailed negotiation.[1] This neither Salisbury nor British opinion could have tolerated once it was known that the Tricolour was flying at Fashoda.

The West African Convention was at last signed on 14 June 1898;[2] but West Africa was not the only international complication which Salisbury wished to remove, or at least to evade, before the Nile question came to a head. From about January 1898, when the final advance on Khartoum was authorised, Salisbury seems to have consciously worked to keep his hands as free as possible for the impending crisis with France. In February 1898 Milner in South Africa was 'inclined to work up to a crisis', but he was sharply reined in. Chamberlain, probably coached by Salisbury, warned him in March of the impending explosion on the Nile and of the existing 'difficulties of the most serious character with France, Russia and Germany'. And in July 1899, when all these 'difficulties' except that of the Upper Nile had been settled or at least postponed, Chamberlain administered another cold douche to Milner and insisted on his maintaining the pacific South African policy 'which the whole Unionist Cabinet knew to be imperative.'[3]

In South Africa the British could choose their own moment for 'working up to a crisis'. But in the Far East the 'difficulties with Russia' forced a crisis upon them. In March 1898 the Russians occupied Port Arthur as a naval base. Salisbury's Cabinet was as fully committed to resist this action as any government could be. On 17 January Hicks Beach had promised that the 'open door' in China would be maintained 'if necessary, at the cost of war'; on 1 March the Government had accepted Ashmead Bartlett's resolution that 'the independence of Chinese territory' was 'of vital importance for British commerce and influence'.[4] But on 25 March it was decided simply to protest to St Petersburg in comparatively moderate terms and to seek 'compensation' at Wei-Hai-Wei.[5] This decision was enforced, from his sick-bed, by Salisbury himself. Most of his colleagues wanted to give Russia notice to quit; but Salisbury insisted that a conflict with Russia 'might

---

[1] 'We cannot afford to have more than a limited area of heather alight at the same time'—Salisbury to Hardinge 15 July 1898, cited Grenville, *Lord Salisbury and Foreign Policy*, pp. 122–3.
[2] Hertslet ii, No. 241.
[3] Garvin, *op. cit.* iii, pp. 366–9, citing Chamberlain to Milner 16 Mar. 1898. Cf. J. S. Marais, *The Fall of Kruger's Republic* (Oxford 1961), pp. 205–10.
[4] B.D. i, No. 36, Salisbury to O'Conor 22 Mar. 1898; No. 37, O'Conor to Salisbury 23 Mar.; No. 38, Salisbury to O'Conor 24 Mar. Cf. *A.R.*, 1898, pp. [7], [36–7]; Langer, *op. cit.*, p. 474.
[5] L.Q.V. 3, iii, p. 238, Balfour to the Queen 26 Mar. 1898. B.D. i, No. 41, Salisbury to O'Conor 28 Mar.

clash awkwardly with our French policy'. This rather dark saying was glossed by Salisbury himself, in a remark made to his daughter as he rejected a draft despatch whose transmission would probably have meant war: '. . . I don't think we carry enough guns to fight [the Russians] and the French as well. . . . In six months' time . . . we shall be on the verge of war with France; I can't afford to quarrel with Russia now.'[1]

The 'climb-down' over Port Arthur was bitterly resented by British opinion and cost Salisbury much of his popularity. Indeed Port Arthur and Salisbury's frail health combined to generate a whispering campaign that Salisbury was a senile invalid who had quite lost his grip on affairs and whose retirement was overdue.[2] But Salisbury had not only avoided war with Russia. He had also avoided the alternative— of humiliating Russia so deeply that she would have sought her revenge anywhere and at almost any cost.[3] Salisbury could now be morally certain that Russia would not intervene on the Upper Nile except conceivably as a member of a Continental League. The indispensable member of any such combination was however Germany; and at the end of 1897 relations between England and Germany had for some time been marked by mutual irritation. Except for Samoa, no open disputes existed; but the Germans still felt that they should ask a price for not opposing Britain. The price was usually colonial concessions or assistance in obtaining them from others. Salisbury resented these importunities; the Germans were irritated by their failure to obtain the favours they asked. Meanwhile, the press of both countries was finding material for polemic in the German programme of naval expansion.[4]

In November 1897 the situation suddenly changed to Salisbury's advantage. The Emperor and Tirpitz, without informing the Wilhelmstrasse, seized the Chinese port of Kiao-Chow.[5] This, if ever there was one, was the act of 'unmitigated noodles'. The Russian reaction was so hostile that Holstein thought it 'hardly necessary to advise the Emperor. He alone will know whether he wants war with Russia or not'.[6] It was not quite so bad as that; but the unofficial Russo-German entente, which had been so useful to both countries since the beginning of 1895, was now at an end. The Russians 'compensated' themselves by the seizure of Port Arthur in March 1898; by April even

---

[1] B.D. i, No. 34, minute by Salisbury 22 Mar. 1898. Memorandum by Lady G. Cecil, quoted in A. L. Kennedy, *Salisbury 1830-1903* (London 1953), p. 276. Cf. Langer, *op. cit.*, pp. 488-9; L.Q.V. 3, *loc. cit.*

[2] Langer, *op. cit.*, pp. 485-8. Z. F. Steiner, 'The Last Years of the Old Foreign Office, 1898-1905', *H.J.* vi, 1 (1963), pp. 59-90. Cf. *A.R.*, 1898, pp. [57-8], [71-8]; D.D.F. xiv, No. 176, Geoffray to Hanotaux 30 Apr. 1898; *infra*, Ch. xvii, pp. 399-400.

[3] Cf. Balfour's speech in the Commons 29 Apr. 1898.

[4] Cf. G.P. xiii, Ch. lxxxiv, 'Das Deutsch-Englische Verhältnis, 1897'.

[5] Rich and Fisher, *The Holstein Papers*, i, pp. 178-81, Holstein's memorandum of 1 Feb. 1909. Cf. G.P. xiv/i, Nos. 3686-3691.

[6] G.P. xiv/i, Nos. 3692-3711, 8-22 Nov. 1897. E. Eyck, *Das Persönliche Regiment Wilhelms II* (Zürich 1948), pp. 198-200.

the Kaiser had recognised that it was 'nicht ganz gefahrlos' to be face-to-face with Russia in the Far East, and he welcomed the British occupation of Wei-Hai-Wei.[1] Indeed, as always when relations with Russia became strained, Germany had been forced to turn to England; and in January 1898 Bülow had promised Salisbury that Kiao-Chow should remain 'open to the commerce of the world'.[2] In January 1898 Salisbury had been attempting to interest the Russians in a demarcation of 'spheres of preponderance' in China; but his approach to St Petersburg was not exclusive, and he was soon able to profit by the new situation.[3] Bülow's declaration enabled Salisbury to maintain that the 'open door' had not been closed by Germany; and in March 1898 he was able to arrange a joint Anglo-German loan to China. Salisbury on his side assured Berlin that the occupation of Wei-Hai-Wei did not imply any intention to compete with Germany in Shan-Tung.[4] Meanwhile, he had succeeded in inducing the British press to moderate its tone towards Germany, and towards the Emperor in particular.[5] Some indication of the improvement in relations is given by the cordial informality of the Kaiser's congratulations on Kitchener's victory at the Atbara in April: 'So glad! Best congratulations to Lord Salisbury and Sirdar.'[6]

Meanwhile, with Salisbury's knowledge, Chamberlain had begun his discussions with Hatzfeldt on the possibility of an Anglo-German alliance. He made it very clear that the point of such an alliance would be against Russia in the Far East. Berlin was not averse from incidental co-operation here; but the Germans saw no reason to carry a mainly British burden and above all did not wish to divert Russian energies westward.[7] As the Kaiser once remarked, 'Je weiter die Russen in Asien sich engagieren, desto stiller sitzen sie in Europa'.[8] What Berlin wanted was re-insurance in the west. The British alliance would be of value to Germany if it led to an Anglo-Russian appeasement under German auspices and a consequent loosening of the link between Paris and St Petersburg.[9] There was here, as Salisbury saw, no basis for an alliance. When in May 1898 Berlin suggested that the problem would be simplified if German opinion were first wooed with colonial concessions, Salisbury replied by a polite but firm refusal.[10] At the end of

---

[1] G.P. XIV/I, Nos. 3760, 3761; No. 3768, the Kaiser to A.A. 8 Apr. 1898. Cf. W. Becker, *Fürst Bülow und England* (Greifswald 1929), p. 60.

[2] G.P. XIV/I, Nos. 3747, 3748, Bülow to Hatzfeldt 5 and 7 Jan. 1898.

[3] B.D. I, Nos. 5-24. A. W. Palmer, 'Lord Salisbury's Approach to Russia, 1898', *Oxford Slavonic Papers*, 1955, pp. 102-14.

[4] B.D. I, No. 21, Macdonald to Salisbury 1 Mar. 1898; No. 47, Balfour to Lascelles 2 Apr.; No. 52, Lascelles to Bülow 20 Apr.

[5] L.Q.V. 3, iii, pp. 224-5, Sir T. Martin to the Queen 13, 14 and 16 Jan. 1898.

[6] FO 78/5049, Lascelles to Salisbury tel. No. 16, 9 Apr. 1898.

[7] The most recent discussion is in Grenville, *op. cit.*, pp. 148-76.

[8] Cited Becker, *op. cit.*, p. 72.

[9] G.P. XIV/I, No. 3792, Bülow to Hatzfeldt 24 Apr. 1898. Cf. S. E. Lewis, 'Anglo-German Diplomatic Relations, 1898-1902', *Bull. I.H.R.* IX (1931-32), pp. 123-7.

[10] G. S. Papadopoulos, 'Lord Salisbury and the projected Anglo-German Alliance of 1898', *Bull. I.H.R.* XXVI (1953), pp. 214-8. G.P. XIV/I, No. 3798, Hatzfeldt to Hohenlohe 20 May 1898. L.Q.V. 3, iii, pp. 262-3, Salisbury to the Queen 4 Aug. 1898.

May the German Emperor learned, through trying to intimidate the Czar by the prospect of an Anglo-German alliance, that Russia had recently rejected far-reaching proposals from London.[1] Bülow concluded that any alliance with Britain, however carefully it might be drafted, would necessarily have its point against Russia; the correct policy for Germany was therefore to treat with London only on definite individual questions.[2] But in spite of the failure of the Chamberlain-Hatzfeldt conversations and the unpleasant surprise from St Petersburg, Anglo-German relations remained reasonably friendly.

The Germans themselves soon raised an 'individual question'— that of the Portuguese colonies, in which they had been interested since 1893. In June 1898, his hand strengthened by an expression of interest from the French ambassador,[3] Bülow intervened in the Anglo-Portuguese loan negotiations. He offered to abandon opposition to an ultimate British acquisition of Delagoa Bay, and to withdraw support from the South African Republic, in return for an option on most of Portugal's colonial empire. He insisted, however, that much more was at stake than mere territorial acquisition, or even the balance of power in southern Africa. The negotiation was to be a test of British intentions towards Germany. Its success might well be the first step to a more general understanding. But if it failed Germany would co-operate against Britain overseas with Russia and above all with France; and southern Africa would certainly not be the only theatre of this co-operation. Although the word 'Egypt' does not appear to have been uttered by Hatzfeldt in his conversations with Salisbury, Bülow had in his instructions specifically mentioned Egypt as the means by which the collaboration of France and Russia would be obtained.[4] Doubtless he counted upon the impending crisis on the Upper Nile to weaken Salisbury's resistance;[5] and it must have been clear to Salisbury that France was very unlikely to support Germany in southern Africa unless she received her *quid pro quo* in the Nile valley. But Salisbury was inclined, quite correctly, to dismiss as a bluff the threatened Franco-German collaboration; and it was the misgivings of his colleagues, notably Chamberlain and Balfour, which constrained him to the distasteful task of 'cutting up Portugal while still alive'.[6] All the same, the existence of the Agreement on the Portuguese colonies may well have had some influence on the attitude of Germany during the Fashoda crisis.

The visible improvement in Anglo-German relations in the course of

[1] W. Goetz, *Briefe Wilhelms II an den Zaren* (Berlin 1920), pp. 309-11, the Kaiser to the Czar 30 May 1898. G.P. xiv/1, No. 3803, the Czar to the Kaiser 3 June.
[2] G.P. xiv/1, No. 3804, Bülow to Hatzfeldt 8 June 1898; No. 3805, memo. by Bülow 11 June; No 38.06, Bülow to Hatzfeldt 8 June.
[3] *Infra*, p. 330. When Bülow revealed his terms to London on 22 June, both the German and the French Minister at Lisbon had already protested to Portugal.
[4] G.P. xiv/1, No. 3818, Bülow to Hatzfeldt 22 June 1898.
[5] Cf. *ibid.*, No. 3783, Bülow to Hatzfeldt 30 Mar. 1898.
[6] Grenville, *op. cit.*, pp. 188-98. Nor did the threat of collaboration with France made the F.O. uneasy; cf. B.D. I, No. 81, memo. by Bertie 10 Aug. 1898.

1898 aroused the fears of French diplomatists, especially in London, that Salisbury was clearing the decks for a *coup* against France which should restore his political credit, damaged by the Port Arthur climb-down and by difficulties with the House of Commons.[1] Just where the blow would fall was, rather surprisingly, not always clear to the French, although as early as 9 February Courcel had recognised that one of Salisbury's major objectives was 'l'affermissement définitif de la puissance anglaise en Egypte et sur tout le cours du Nil'.[2] But it seemed clear enough that France would be the target. Throughout the first half of 1898 the prolonged West African wrangle continued to poison Anglo-French relations; the potentially calming effects of its settlement on 14 June were largely nullified by the decision of the French Chamber to postpone ratification. By August 1898 Geoffray, the *Conseiller d'ambassade* at London, thought that British hostility to France was, if anything, sharper than ever. The British press was raking up all the old quarrels—Newfoundland, Madagascar, even the wretched Warina affair of December 1893.[3] War with France was not exactly desired in England, but it would be accepted without hesitation if the occasion arose.[4]

France, for her part, faced the looming crisis on the Upper Nile in depressing isolation. It was already clear that she could expect no support whatever from St Petersburg in Africa, and no positive support in Egypt. But Russia soon announced her indifference to French interests even more unmistakably. On 24 August, the very eve of the crisis, without consulting or even forewarning his French ally, the Czar communicated to the Powers his proposal for a conference on the limitation of armaments.[5] Monson for one thought the report of this proceeding 'almost incredible'.[6] But it was true none the less; and the Czar's action probably did more than the promises of Mura-viev to dispel British fears that the conference might lend itself to the discussion of 'existing causes which might lead to hostilities, e.g. . . . Egypt'.[7]

From time to time between 1896 and 1898 Hanotaux attempted to break down this isolation by investigating whether the support of Berlin on extra-European questions was available at a price which France could afford to pay. In the summer of 1896 Hanotaux suggested through the Franco-Danish confidential agent Jules Hanssen that

[1] D.D.F. xiv, No. 9, Geoffray to Hanotaux 12 Jan. 1898; No. 15, Nisard to Noailles 14 Jan.; No. 26, Noailles to Hanotaux 23 Jan.; No. 193, Geoffray to Hanotaux 17 May; No. 232, Noailles to Nisard 19 June 1898.

[2] *Ibid.*, No. 176, Geoffray to Hanotaux 30 Apr. 1898; No. 47, Courcel to Hanotaux, 9 Feb.

[3] The 'Warina incident', an accidental armed clash with fatal casualties on both sides, had occurred in the hinterland of Sierra Leone. Both countries were usually happy to forget it.

[4] D.D.F. xiv, No. 283, Geoffray to Delcassé 9 Aug. 1898.

[5] *Ibid.*, No. 303, Montebello to Delcassé 24 Aug. 1898; No. 304, Russian circular despatch 24 Aug.; No. 306, Delcassé to Montebello 27 Aug.

[6] B.D. i, No. 262, Monson to Salisbury 1 Sept. 1898.

[7] *Ibid.*, No. 261, Balfour to Scott 30 Aug. 1898.

French opinion might ultimately be reconciled to the Treaty of Frankfurt if Germany gave sufficient proof of her goodwill to France. But the Germans were not prepared to do business on such highly speculative terms.[1] At about the same time, in June and July 1896, Courcel openly suggested to Hatzfeldt that the two countries should collaborate on Egypt; he contended that Egypt was inseparable from other African questions in which, as the Wilhelmstrasse had often pointed out, French and German interests found a common adversary in England.[2] But Courcel was careful to qualify his proposal by the warning that collaboration must go no further than ostensibly spontaneous 'parallel action', for no French government could survive the reproach of open and cordial co-operation with Germany so long as the Alsace-Lorraine question remained unsolved.[3] It is not surprising that in January 1897 Courcel received a completely evasive reply when he again suggested to Hatzfeldt that France and Germany should follow 'parallel' policies in the 'Eastern Question'.[4]

The general state of Franco-German relations in these years did not provide a fertile soil for the very tender plant of collaboration. Both countries seem to have found Alsace-Lorraine a more active irritant than in the earlier eighteen-nineties. To this irritation the Kaiser's 'Jubilee' celebrations, conducted with a characteristic lack of tact and consideration,[5] undoubtedly contributed; on the French side, the Cronstadt celebrations and the *Pothuau* toasts fanned the flickering ashes of old hopes and released a flood of rhetoric about the Lost Provinces. Jules Méline, to the intense annoyance of Berlin, found it necessary publicly to acclaim the 'ardent patriotism' of an Alsatian delegation which had hailed Cronstadt as the first step to liberation.[6] As if this were not enough, from early in 1898 German policy at the Vatican and in the Near and Far East seemed to aim at supplanting France as the protecting Power of Roman Catholics *in partibus infidelium*;[7] while the revival of the Dreyfus Affair, and in particular the Zola trial, evoked an outburst of anti-French sentiment in the German press.[8]

Even had relations been much easier than they were, the French quest for German support in the Nile valley would have been fruitless. The overriding objective of German policy towards France in these years was to convince the French that the loss of Alsace-Lorraine

---

[1] G.P. xi, Nos. 2837-2842, June-Sept. 1896. The published French documents are silent on these overtures.

[2] *Ibid.*, Nos. 2739, 2744, Hatzfeldt to Hohenlohe 22 May and 18 June 1896.

[3] D.D.F. xii, No. 435, Courcel to Hanotaux 31 July 1896.

[4] D.D.F. xiii, No. 68, Courcel to Hanotaux 18 Jan. 1897.

[5] D.D.F. xii, No. 223, Herbette to Ricard 5 Dec. 1895; No. 414, Noailles to Hanotaux 24 June 1896.

[6] D.D.F. xiii, No. 323, Soulange-Bodin to Marcel 13 Sept. 1897.

[7] D.D.F. xiv, (e.g.) No. 39, Hanotaux to Poubelle 3 Feb. 1898; No. 182, Paul Cambon to Hanotaux 10 May.

[8] *Ibid.*, No. 60, Noailles to Hanotaux 21 Feb. 1898; Appendix ii, No. vii, same to same 26 Feb.

was irreversible. During 1896 in particular Berlin strongly hinted to the Russians that they should persuade or constrain their ally to close the question; to this end the Germans harped on the danger to European peace inherent in the alleged French 'obsession' with *la revanche*.[1] Similarly, at no less a price would Germany sell to France her support in the Nile valley. Berlin hoped, by holding this co-operation always just out of reach—'en nous tenant la dragée haute', as Courcel put it[2]— that the French would sooner or later be brought to make the great sacrifice. This result, if it could be achieved, would indeed have been worth waiting for. The Franco-Russe itself would then become pointless, for no material question other than the Lost Provinces separated France and Germany. German hegemony in Europe would be as unassailable as at the height of Bismarck's career. In the Kaiser's words: 'Wenn das je käme! . . . dann "wehe denen die uns Feind sind".'[3]

The price which Germany demanded was, however, one which no French statesman could have paid even if he would. In January 1897 Hanotaux told Muraviev that any French government rash enough to attempt a serious rapprochement with Germany, before the 'vital and most important interests' of France had been secured, would not 'last half an hour before it would be overthrown by the feeling of complete and unanimous indignation of the entire French people'.[4] Indeed, Courcel had said as much to Hatzfeldt in July 1896, and Hanotaux had approved his language.[5] The Germans were well aware that French opinion was still not prepared for the definitive abandonment of the Lost Provinces. The Wilhelmstrasse was therefore determined to restrict current collaboration to minor questions on which there was a clear balance of tangible advantage to Germany; but collaboration on these terms did not attract Paris. The Kaiser, who took a less narrow view than Bülow of the limits of collaboration, did indeed attempt in the spring of 1897 to interest France in the fate of the Portuguese colonies. But Hanotaux kept cautiously aloof; he doubtless feared being drawn into a dangerously compromising intimacy with Berlin.[6] By the end of 1897 all prospect of collaboration appeared to be dead. Courcel himself admitted to Hatzfeldt that even on minor questions it would be unacceptable to French opinion.[7]

However, on 16 June 1898 the French ambassador in Berlin, on his

---

[1] G.P. xi, No. 2651, Marschall to Radolin 19 Jan. 1896; No. 2734, memo. by Marschall of conversation with Osten-Sacken 15 May 1896; Nos. 2735, 2844, Hohenlohe to Radolin 20 May and 8 Dec. 1896.

[2] D.D.F. xiii, No. 106, Courcel to Hanotaux 13 Feb. 1897. Cf. D.D.F. xii, No. 464, Barère to Hanotaux 30 Sept. 1896; and G.P. xi, No. 2844.

[3] G.P. xiii, No. 3561, minute on Münster to Hohenlohe 4 Feb. 1899.

[4] Langer, *op. cit.*, p. 346, citing F. V. Kelyin in *Krasnyi Arkhiv*, xlvi (1931), pp. 71-89. Cf. D.D.F. xiii No. 87, Hanotaux to Montebello 31 Jan. 1897.

[5] D.D.F. xii, No. 435, Courcel to Hanotaux 31 July 1896, and minute by Hanotaux.

[6] D.D.F. xiii, Nos. 197, 198, Noailles to Hanotaux 13 Apr. 1897; No. 224, same to same 4 May. Cf. G.P. xi, p. 328, footnote citing minute by the Emperor 19 Aug. 1896.

[7] G.P. xiv/i, No. 3709, Hatzfeldt to Holstein 18 Nov. 1897.

own initiative, drew the attention of Bülow to the dangerous possibilities for both France and Germany inherent in the Anglo-Portuguese loan negotiation. The Marquis de Noailles was an aristocrat and an anglophobe to whom the Potsdam Court was much more congenial than it had been to the bourgeois and conscientiously Republican Herbette. Noailles had always regretted the very brusque way in which his predecessor had in January 1896 brushed aside Marschall's proposals for collaboration in Africa.[1] He had now taken the initiative, so he told the Quai d'Orsay, lest Britain, having absorbed the Portuguese colonies, should by the twentieth century have as her frontiers 'les frontières du monde'.[2]

Bülow received this approach evasively (*ausweichend*), mainly because he believed that he could make a better bargain by dealing with England in isolation.[3] However, on 18 June he discussed the matter with Noailles at length, but in his most rambling and ambiguous style. He suggested that Germany's interests in the Far East were more important to her than Africa, and that moreover he hesitated to injure his relations with London. But he also hinted that this sacrifice was not perhaps entirely out of the question. At least, France and Germany should cease to behave to one another like 'chiens de faïence'; even if formal co-operation was impossible, there was nothing to prevent 'un parallélisme spontané' in defence of common interests.[4] Noailles urged Paris not to rebuff Berlin by a purely negative reply; Bülow was interested enough to ask Münster to find out whether 'practical collaboration' was still excluded in principle at the Quai d'Orsay, as it had seemed to be in January 1896.[5]

Münster's démarche at Paris on 19 June went far beyond the 'parallélisme spontané' of which Bülow had talked to Noailles. He submitted a *note verbale* which, after establishing the identical interests of France and Germany, declared:

> Il faudrait donc faire savoir au Gouvernement portugais que les
> Gouvernements français et allemand . . . se voient obligés
> d'examiner immédiatement la question, par quelles représailles
> économiques ou autres, l'organisation d'un contrôle financier
> international pourrait être amenée pour le Portugal.[6]

Here was Germany proposing, by joint action of a most minatory kind, an infringement of Portuguese sovereignty which could hardly have been enforced without an ultimatum; it is difficult to imagine anything more likely to have aroused Portuguese national pride than this proposal to treat Portugal like Egypt or Turkey. This was just the kind of action which on Hanotaux' own showing would be fatal to any

---

[1] D.D.F. XIII, No. 73, Noailles to Hanotaux 24 Jan. 1897.
[2] D.D.F. XIV, No. 228, Noailles to Hanotaux 18 June 1898; No. 232, to Nisard 19 June.
[3] G.P. XIV/1, No. 3812, Bülow to Hatzfeldt 17 June 1898.
[4] D.D.F. XIV, No. 232.
[5] *Ibid., loc. cit.* G.P. XIV/1, No. 3813, Bülow to Münster 18 June 1898.
[6] D.D.F. XIV, No. 238, footnote.

French government. Indeed, only four days earlier he had told President Faure that French public opinion would utterly forbid joint action with Germany against England on this question.[1] Hanotaux must also have been well aware that if France hoped to obtain German assistance on the Upper Nile she would have to do more than help to defy Britain in southern Africa and bully Portugal. Luckily for himself, Hanotaux was now *ministre démissionnaire*; and he took refuge in this status to avoid all action on the German proposal.[2] Perhaps with a certain sardonic satisfaction, he passed the problem to Delcassé, with the remark:

> On croit superflu de signaler au Ministre l'importance de cette initiative, prise auprès de nous par le Gouvernement allemand dans une question de cette nature, et les conséquences éventuelles de l'antagonisme d'intérêts qui paraît s'être ainsi révélé sur un point déterminé entre l'Allemagne et l'Angleterre.[3]

Delcassé took no action at all. Münster never returned to the subject; and in the second week of July Salisbury agreed in principle to an arrangement with Germany.[4] It is not known whether Delcassé's inaction was deliberate, or whether he merely hesitated until the apparent opportunity had gone by. His conduct was severely judged, not least by Hanotaux,[5] in the years following Fashoda; and between the wars men like Charles Maurras and Ernest Judet made it their business to preach that if Delcassé had troubled to 'read his files' he could have secured German support in the Fashoda crisis.[6] This belief was doubly fallacious. Bülow was throughout convinced that he could get a better bargain by a direct deal with Salisbury; and he valued the French approach only as an additional means of pressure on England.[7] Moreover, Delcassé's critics were naïve in their belief that German support on the Nile could be bought at the bargain price of mere collaboration in African affairs. It was not Delcassé's fault that France was isolated at Fashoda.

[1] Faure, 'Fachoda (1898)', *Rev. Hist. Dip.* 1955, p. 31.
[2] D.D.F. xiv, No. 238, Hanotaux to Noailles 22 June 1898. G.P. xiv/1, No. 3814, Münster to A.A. 19 June. Hanotaux congratulated himself 'qu'il avait ainsi sauvé la France du piège que lui tendrait l'Allemagne' (Faure, *loc. cit.*).
[3] D.D.F. xiv, No. 245, *note pour le Ministre* 30 June 1898.
[4] G.P. xiv/1, No. 3814, footnote. B.D. i, Nos. 74, 75, 77, 9-19 July 1898.
[5] Hanotaux, *Fachoda*, p. 132. Cf. Cocheris, *Situation Internationale*, pp. 469-71.
[6] Iiams, *Dreyfus, Diplomatists and the Dual Alliance*, p. 45.
[7] G.P. xiv/1, Nos. 3812, 3818, Bülow to Hatzfeldt 17 and 22 June 1898.

XV

FASHODA : THE CRISIS

SEPTEMBER–NOVEMBER 1898

IN June 1898 Cromer, while still as anxious as ever to restrict the occupation of the southern Sudan to the 'absolutely necessary' minimum, pointed out to Salisbury that after the fall of Omdurman it would be necessary to reconnoitre the Blue and White Niles. If the French were encountered, the 'Anglo-Egyptian' commander would have to protest and formally lay claim to the territory. 'But is he to lay claim . . . in the name of the English Government, or of the Khedive, or of both combined? Definite instructions should be issued on this point.'[1] This question was settled in principle within the next few days by the official adoption of the 'two flags' policy; the detailed instructions were drafted by Cromer himself after a Cabinet on 25 July at which he was present by invitation.[2] Kitchener was to command the White Nile flotilla in person. If he met with 'any French or Abyssinian authorities' he was not to say or do anything which might imply any recognition of their title anywhere within the Nile valley. If the intruders were French, he should 'endeavour to convince' them that their presence 'in the Nile valley is an infringement of the rights both of Great Britain and of the Khedive'. However, the Sirdar might not only encounter French or Ethiopian 'authorities' but also French and Ethiopian 'forces'. He was to avoid, 'by all possible means, any collision with the forces of the Emperor Menelek'. But should the 'force' turn out to be French, 'the course of action to be pursued must depend so much on local circumstances that it is neither necessary nor desirable to furnish Sir Herbert Kitchener with detailed instructions'.[3] Salisbury was evidently prepared to accept an armed collision with the French, which might bring on an European war; but not a clash with the Ethiopians. He was confident that if it came to war with the French, England would be quickly victorious; but hostilities with Ethiopia might well jeopardise the fruits of Kitchener's victory over the Khalifa.

[1] SP Cabinet Memoranda, Cromer to Salisbury 15 June 1898.
[2] *Supra*, Ch. XI, p. 266; L.Q.V. 3, iii, pp. 260-1, Salisbury to the Queen 25 July 1898.
[3] FO 78/5050, Salisbury to Cromer No. 109, 2 Aug. 1898 (B.D. 1, No. 185). References in this form will hereafter be given to documents printed in the British or French official collections. Other printings—e.g. in Blue Books or Yellow Books—are ignored.

Immediately after the fall of Omdurman Kitchener began his organisation of the White Nile force. His preparations were almost complete when on 9 September the Mahdist steamer *Tawfiqia* arrived at Omdurman from Fashoda bearing the scars of her encounter with Marchand on 25 August. Her company did not know the nationality of the 'whites' whom they had fought; but Kitchener had no real doubt about who was at Fashoda. On 10 September Kitchener sailed for Fashoda on the steamer *Dal*, escorted by the gunboats *Sultan*, *Fattah*, *Nasir* and *Abu Klea*. Also embarked were two Sudanese battalions, a battery of Egyptian field artillery and a company of Cameron Highlanders. On 15 September, at Renk, the flotilla encountered the second Mahdist steamer—the *Safia*—which had been involved in the engagement with Marchand. The *Safia* was badly damaged; but her commander Sa'īd al-Sughaiar offered resistance, which was quickly overcome. Sa'īd al-Sughaiar was taken prisoner; but his captors were still unable to learn the nationality of the whites at Fashoda. At mid-day on 18 September the flotilla hove to off Fabiu, a village some fifteen miles north of Fashoda. From Fabiu, in order to avoid an accidental outbreak of hostilities, Kitchener despatched a message in French to the 'Chief of the European Expedition at Fashoda'. He announced that, having destroyed the Mahdist army and 're-occupied the country', he was now proceeding in force to Fashoda, where the presence of 'des Européens quelconques' had been reported.[1]

At Fabiu orders were drafted for the encounter itself. Unless the 'Europeans' at Fashoda themselves commenced hostilities, their commander would be invited to call upon the Sirdar. If, after discussion, the commander refused to withdraw the garrison, the signal 'Hoist Flag' would be made. Thereupon Colonel Smith-Dorrien, O.C. Troops, would disembark his force from the *Fattah* and the *Nasir* 'sufficiently far away from the French position to avoid bringing on an action', erect a flagstaff, and report completion to the Sirdar. These prudent dispositions were almost certainly Wingate's work. The decision to hoist one flag only—the Egyptian—at Fashoda was quite certainly the result of Wingate's prompting, to which Kitchener, *more suo*, yielded with a bad grace—'Damn it, have it your own way'.[2] But the wisdom of this decision is now obvious. It may well have been the main factor in preventing an immediate armed clash, for Marchand

[1] FO 141/336, Rodd to Salisbury tels. No. 231, 10 Sept. 1898; No. 244, 25 Sept., enclosing Kitchener to Rodd tel. of 24 Sept. (B.D. 1, No. 193—hereafter cited as: Kitchener, Fashoda Tel.). FO 141/333, Rodd to Salisbury No. 153, 29 Sept. 1898, enclosing Kitchener to Rodd 21 Sept.—hereafter cited as: Kitchener, Fashoda Desp. *Ibid.*, Kitchener to Marchand 18 Sept. 1898 (D.D.F. xiv, Appendix I, No. 1). S.I.R. No. 60, pp. 8-9 and Appdx. 46. Sandes, *The Royal Engineers in Egypt and the Sudan*, pp. 278-80. H. Smith-Dorrien, *Memories of Forty-Eight Years' Service* (London 1925), pp. 121-4.
[2] Cairint 1/61/323, Orders for O.C. Gunboats 18 Sept. 1898. R. Wingate, *Wingate of the Sudan* (London 1955), pp. 118-9, 141. The only Union Jack to make its appearance at Fashoda was worn, together with the Egyptian flag, by the gunboat in which the Cameron Highlanders were embarked. Smith-Dorrien, *op. cit.*, pp. 124-5.

would almost certainly have believed it his duty to make at least token resistance against the hoisting of the Union Jack in what was since 3 September in his eyes a French protectorate. The decision was not perhaps strictly in accordance with the spirit of Kitchener's instructions; but this isolated deviation from the 'two flags' policy could hardly compromise Salisbury's determination to compel, rather than persuade, the French to withdraw.

On the morning of the 19th the flotilla steamed dead slow upstream towards Fashoda; Kitchener was anxious not to get there before he had received Marchand's answer to his message of the previous day. At about 9 a.m. a small boat arrived bearing Marchand's reply. Marchand, styling himself 'Commissaire du Gouvernement français sur le Haut Nil et Bahr el Ghazal', informed Kitchener that he had by order of his Government occupied the Bahr al-Ghazal and the Shilluk country; the latter had been brought under French protection by a treaty of 3 September. He would be happy to welcome the Sirdar to Fashoda 'au nom de la France'. This was more than Kitchener had bargained for; and he was, in Wingate's words, 'rather staggered'. Wingate 'begged him to be firm and to stick absolutely to what we had arranged'; but Kitchener remained nervous and uneasy until the actual meeting with Marchand, when he 'pulled himself together and spoke well'.[1]

Complying with Kitchener's invitation, Marchand with his second-in-command, Germain, went aboard the *Dal* at Fashoda at about 10.30 a.m. Kitchener made a formal protest against Marchand's 'infringement of the rights of Egypt and Great Britain'. Marchand replied that he had occupied Fashoda at the orders of his Government and had therefore no alternative but to remain there pending further orders from Paris. Recognising the danger of an immediate deadlock, Kitchener now said no more about 'the rights of Great Britain'; instead, he played the Egyptian card for all it was worth. He had, he said, been ordered 'to re-establish Egyptian authority in the Fashoda Mudirieh'; drawing attention to his superior force, he asked whether Marchand 'was prepared . . . to resist the execution of those orders'. Marchand replied that if Kitchener proceeded to extremities, he and his companions could only 'die at their posts'; but:

> he begged . . . that I would . . . allow the question of his remaining at Fashoda to be referred to his Government as, without their orders, he could not retire from his position or haul down his flag; at the same time, he felt . . . sure that, under the circumstances, the orders for his retirement would not be delayed. . . .

Kitchener then asked whether Marchand considered himself 'authorised by the French Government to resist Egypt in putting up its flag

[1] Kitchener, Fashoda Tel., Fashoda Desp. FO 78/5051, Marchand to Kitchener 19 Sept. (D.D.F., *ubi supra*, No. 11). Smith-Dorrien, *loc. cit.* Wingate, *op. cit.*, pp. 119-21, citing F. R. Wingate to his wife.

and reasserting its authority in its former possessions—such as the Mudirieh of Fashoda? M. Marchand hesitated and then said that he could not resist the Egyptian flag being hoisted.'[1]

Kitchener had placed Marchand in a dilemma. It was not merely that Marchand could in fact have made no effective resistance; this would not necessarily have restrained him from vindicating military honour by force of arms. But Marchand was well aware that the Quai d'Orsay's policy in the Nile valley had long been based on 'respect for the rights of the Sultan and the Khedive'; and it is unlikely to the point of impossibility that even the Pavillon de Flore could have instructed him forcibly to defend the 'rights of France' against *Egypt*. Marchand therefore yielded, but on condition that the hoisting of the Egyptian flag should not pre-judge the political status of the country, which was to be referred to Europe for settlement.[2] Kitchener however also reports Marchand as having said that he expected the mission soon to be withdrawn and that Marchand himself would welcome this withdrawal. Marchand's later behaviour throughout the crisis makes it incredible that he could really have said this. It seems likely that Kitchener misunderstood references by Marchand to the *relief* of his personnel, which Marchand had in fact requested on medical grounds in January 1898.[3] The point is important because Marchand's supposed anxiety 'to get away' had some influence on later events.

Kitchener and Wingate at first tried to insist that the Egyptian flag should be hoisted within the perimeter of the old Egyptian post now occupied by the French. But this was obviously impracticable; and the Sirdar finally pitched his camp some six hundred yards to the south, by the hamlet of Kodok. The Egyptian flag was ceremonially hoisted at 1 p.m. *Qa'immaqām* H. W. Jackson was appointed 'Mudir of Fashoda and the surrounding districts', with instructions to avoid friction with Marchand but in the event of 'aggressive action by French troops [to] use the force at your disposal to repel it'. Jackson's force consisted of one Sudanese battalion (the XIth), four guns and the gunboat *Abu Klea*. Early in the afternoon Kitchener paid a courtesy call on Marchand, reviewed the French garrison resplendent in new uniforms, and accepted a present of fresh vegetables and flowers. He then sailed for the Sobat mouth; but just as he embarked, as if as an afterthought, he reminded Wingate to hand a written protest to Marchand. On 20 September Kitchener installed a garrison at the Sobat mouth, and then steamed direct for Omdurman in the *Dal*, passing Fashoda without stopping on the afternoon of the 21st. Of the three remaining

---

[1] Sandes, *op. cit.*, p. 282; Smith-Dorrien, *op. cit.*, p. 126; Wingate, *loc. cit.* Baratier, *Fachoda*, pp. 144-6; Emily, *Mission Marchand*, p. 182. Kitchener, Fashoda Tel., Fashoda Desp. (citations from the latter). Cf. Marchand in *Le Figaro*, 26 Aug. 1904.

[2] Marchand to Kitchener 20 Sept. 1898—not delivered (D.D.F., *ubi supra*, No. v, Annexe I). Cf. Baratier, *op. cit.*, pp. 148, 160-1.

[3] Kitchener, Fashoda Desp. Cf. FO 141/336, Rodd to Salisbury tel. No. 245, 25 Sept. 1898 (B.D. 1, No. 194); same to same tel. No. 248, 26 Sept. D.D.F. xiv, No. 246, citing Marchand's desp. of 1 Jan. 1898.

gunboats, the *Fattah* and the *Nasir* remained with Smith-Dorrien to complete the occupation of the Sobat mouth; but the third, the *Sultan*, was sent to Fashoda with a further protest from Kitchener to Marchand. This second protest was not to be delivered until the Sirdar had passed Fashoda on his way back to Omdurman.[1]

Kitchener's first written protest, handed to Marchand by Wingate on the 19th, asserted that with the hoisting of the Egyptian flag 'the Government of the country had been formally resumed by Egypt'. Marchand, in his turn, at once drafted a written protest against this infraction of the *status quo* to which he believed the Sirdar to have agreed. But this reply never reached Kitchener. Cowan, the commander of the *Sultan*, did indeed accept it for delivery when on the late afternoon of the 21st he handed to Marchand Kitchener's second written protest. But Cowan could not deliver it himself, for the *Sultan* had been detailed for duty as guard-ship at the Sobat. He therefore tried to transmit it through Smith-Dorrien, who had now completed his duties at the Sobat and was on his way back to Omdurman with the two remaining gunboats. But Smith-Dorrien had received explicit orders to hold no communication whatever with Marchand, since Kitchener 'wished the French and British Governments to consider his own reports . . . before any representations from Marchand could reach them'. Smith-Dorrien therefore refused to transmit Marchand's reply, and Cowan had to hand it back to Marchand with a lame excuse.[2] Kitchener had thus virtually isolated Marchand from the outside world, for the French line of communication by way of the Bahr al-Ghazal and the M'Bomu was now some nine months long; and Kitchener's description of the situation at Fashoda held the field almost until the end of the crisis.

Kitchener's second protest to Marchand, delivered by Cowan on 21 September, recalled an alleged verbal notification by the Sirdar that the country had been placed under military law and that the movement of 'munitions of war' was forbidden. Kitchener pointed out that the Egyptian commanders had been ordered rigorously to enforce this prohibition, and requested Marchand to issue to his own officers 'les ordres qui comportent'. Kitchener had in fact given orders in these terms on 20 and 21 September. Against this prohibition Marchand now protested 'avec la dernière énergie'. He denied that the Sirdar had ever informed him that the country had been placed under military law; there seems no reason to doubt his word, for Kitchener's own reports of his conversation with Marchand do not mention his having

---

[1] Kitchener, Fashoda Tel., Fashoda Desp. FO 78/5051, instructions for Jackson 19 Sept., enclosed in Rodd to Salisbury No. 167, 14 Oct. FO 141/333, Kitchener to Marchand 19 and 21 Sept., enclosed in Fashoda Desp. (D.D.F. xiv, Appendix i, Nos. iii and iv). Sandes, pp. 282-5; Smith-Dorrien, pp. 126-8; Wingate, *loc. cit.* Baratier, pp. 144, 148-9, 153-8; Emily, pp. 182-9.
[2] FO 141/333, Kitchener to Marchand 19 Sept. D.D.F. xiv, Appendix i, No. v, Annexe i, Marchand to Kitchener 20 Sept. Cairint 3/15/243, note by Jackson 22 Sept. (Appdx C to Intelligence Diary). Smith-Dorrien, pp. 128-9. Baratier, pp. 161-3; Emily, pp. 190-1.

made such a declaration. Marchand also pointed out that he had no means of communicating with the *Faidherbe*, now on its way back to Fashoda after a trip to Meshra' er Req; responsibility for the consequences would lie with the Sirdar.[1] This letter, together with his reply to Kitchener's first protest which Smith-Dorrien had refused to deliver, Marchand now attempted to transmit to Omdurman through Jackson. It was the same story. Jackson returned the letters, 'having received at present no instructions from Hd. Qrs. Omdurman on this subject'. Jackson did however agree to transmit a letter from Marchand to the commander of the *Faidherbe*. He also agreed, on his own responsibility, that on this voyage the normal armament of the *Faidherbe* and her crew should not count as 'munitions of war'. This derogation from the Sirdar's orders was evidently indispensable if an immediate conflict were to be avoided; very wisely, Jackson did not notify it to Omdurman.[2]

Meanwhile, on the *Dal*, Kitchener and Wingate were drafting their report. This took two forms; a telegram despatched from Omdurman on 24 September and received in London on the same day; and a despatch dated 21 September, of which a summary was telegraphed from Cairo to London on the 29th.[3] Internal evidence suggests that the despatch was drafted first. Its closing passage was devoted to the demonstration that 'Marchand's position at Fashoda is as impossible as it is absurd'; and the existence at Khartoum of numerous fragmentary and heavily amended drafts of this passage are some indication of the care taken to paint a vivid and convincing picture.[4] The telegraphic version runs:

He is short of ammunition and supplies . . . he is cut off from the interior and his water transport is quite inadequate. He has no following in the country and had we been a fortnight later in crushing the Khalifa nothing could have saved him and his expedition from being annihilated by the Dervishes. Marchand quite realises the futility of all their efforts and he seems quite as anxious to return as we are to facilitate his departure.[5]

In another telegram Kitchener stated that he was 'quite sure that no one would be more pleased than Marchand and his officers to receive . . . release from their present unpleasant position'.[6] Marchand's state-

[1] FO 141/333, Kitchener to Marchand 21 Sept. FO 78/5051, orders to Jackson 19 and 20 Sept.; orders to O.C. Gunboats 21 Sept. D.D.F., *ubi supra*, No. v, Annexe ii, Marchand to Kitchener 22 Sept.

[2] Intel. 5/4: Marchand to Jackson No. 3; Jackson to Marchand No. FSD 1; Marchand to Jackson No. 4; Jackson to Marchand No. FSD 2: all of 22 Sept. (D.D.F., *ubi supra*, Nos. v, vi, vii, viii). *Ibid.*, Marchand to Jackson, No. 6, 23 Sept. Cairint 3/15/243, Jackson, Intelligence Diary, 22 Sept. Cf. Baratier, pp. 164-8; Emily, p. 192.

[3] FO 141/336, Rodd to Salisbury tel. No. 251, 29 Sept.

[4] Cairint 1/61/323 contains three early drafts of the despatch, in all of which the concluding portions have been heavily amended. Cairint 1/62/324 contains three fragmentary drafts, all of the concluding passage of the despatch. Two early drafts of the tel., at Cairint 1/61/323, are much more 'finished' than any of the early drafts of the desp.

[5] Kitchener, Fashoda Tel.

[6] FO 141/336, Rodd to Salisbury tel. No. 245, 25 Sept. 1898.

Y

ment, in his first letter to Kitchener, that he would welcome the Sirdar to Fashoda 'au nom de la France', was evidently felt to strike a jarring note. It appears in the early drafts, but not in the final version, of the main 'Fashoda' telegram.[1]

In the despatch,[2] Kitchener's reflections on the absurdity of March-and's position were spiced with the jibe that the French claims to effective occupation were 'more worthy of Opéra-Bouffe than the out-come of the maturely considered plans of a great Government'. As propaganda, Kitchener's reporting was a brilliant success. British opinion, from the Queen down to the cartoonists of *Punch*, saw in the Marchand Mission a band of destitute explorers marooned in darkest Africa and saved from massacre only by the Sirdar's timely arrival. However, 'these broad effects are capable of refinement'. That Marchand was 'cut off from the interior' is doubtful, but was in any case of little moment in a country where communication was almost entirely by water. The *Faidherbe*, his 'inefficient steam launch' (which Kitchener had never seen),[3] was on Jackson's admission a faster and above all a much handier craft than any of the Egyptian gunboats. Nor was the French water transport so inadequate as Jackson's. Marchand's small boats gave the French a mobility which Jackson, who had no such craft, found it impossible to counter.[4] The only shortage experienced by the French was of fresh meat—after Jackson had discouraged the Shilluk from supplying it. Their kitchen-garden provided them with fresh vegetables; four months' European supplies had been brought up by the *Faidherbe* on 29 August; and when March-and left Fashoda he handed over to Jackson fifteen *tons* of local flour for which he had no further use.[5] The equipment of the French was also much better than that of their rivals. Every man had his groundsheet and mosquito-net; not even the officers of Jackson's garrison had mosquito-nets until Marchand generously presented a bale of material from which to make them.[6] In spite of Marchand's trek across Africa, the morale of his Senegalese was certainly higher than that of Jackson's troops. In fact, the XI Sudanese, diluted by 250 Mahdist prisoners whom Jackson 'did not trust a yard', was anything but a reliable force. The men were aggrieved at being posted to a notorious penal station, where there were no available women and the mosquitos bit 'through coat and trouser', while their comrades en-joyed the flesh-pots of Omdurman. They and their Egyptian officers, apparently unknown to Jackson, strongly sympathised with the French

[1] Cf. the Fashoda Tel. with the early drafts at Cairint 1/61/323.
[2] Kitchener, Fashoda Desp.
[3] *Ibid.* The *Faidherbe* was en route from Meshra' er Req to Fashoda between 19 and 21 Sept.
[4] Cairint 3/15/243, Jackson to Maxwell (Omdurman) 4, 16 and 28 Nov. 1898.
[5] *Ibid.*, Jackson to Wingate 20 Nov. Cairint 1/61/323, Marchand to Maxwell 11 Dec. 1898. Cf. D.D.F. xiv, No. 445, Marchand to *Colonies* tel. No. 16, 30 Aug. 1898; Emily, *op. cit.*, pp. 201, 206, 215-6.
[6] H. W. Jackson, 'Fashoda 1898', *S.N.R.* iii, 1 (1920), pp. 2-3. Cairint 3/15/243, Jackson to Wingate 24 Sept. 1898. Cf. Emily, *op. cit.*, p. 200.

and fraternised wholesale with them. One very disquieting symptom was a crop of desertions with arms, though Jackson managed to prevent this from becoming epidemic.[1]

Kitchener's assertion that Marchand was doomed to early annihilation by the Mahdists is at least doubtful. The key to Marchand's security was his small-arms ammunition stock, of which he had expended very nearly a third—12,000 rounds—in the battle of 25 August. But four days later, with the arrival of the *Faidherbe*, his stock rose to 90,000, enough to cope with anything short of a full-scale siege.[2] The Khalifa, with only two barely serviceable steamers at his disposal, would have been quite unable to mount such a siege. But Marchand, who knew nothing of the Khalifa's situation, was acutely apprehensive lest the attack of 25 August be renewed in greater force. As Kitchener drew near to Fashoda, the local Shilluk, through ignorance or malice, reported his approach to Marchand as that of a Mahdist flotilla. Marchand's intense relief betrayed itself when he wrote to Kitchener on 19 September that he had feared 'une seconde attaque des Derviches plus forte que la première et que j'attendais vers le 25 courant. Votre arrivée l'a empêchée.'[3] Kitchener was quick to take this hint; but well before he arrived at Fashoda he had made up his mind that it should be his role to 'rescue' Marchand. Neither he nor Wingate, when they got to Fashoda, seem to have been able or willing to see anything that conflicted with their preconceived idea of a destitute band of explorers in the last extremity of privation.[4] For all its value as propaganda, Kitchener's account was grossly misleading as a factual appreciation.

This was the picture from which, until he received Marchand's own report on 22 October, even Delcassé had to work. But Delcassé had already opened the diplomatic dialogue as early as 7 September, perhaps prompted by the premature report that Kitchener had left Omdurman for Fashoda. Remarking to Monson that Marchand might be found there, Delcassé then stated, according to Monson, that Marchand had been warned not to take any action which might cause a conflict and 'had been distinctly told that he is nothing but an "emissary of civilisation" '. Delcassé's version does not go quite so far

[1] Cairint 3/15/243, Jackson to Wingate, 24-25 Sept., 6 Oct., 20 Nov. 1898. Cf. Emily, pp. 199-212; Baratier, 171-4, 224.
  Some idea of the difficulties may be gained from Jackson's description to Wingate (24-25 Sept.): 'Another d—able night, heaviest rain yet, all drenched to the skin and all tukls [circular thatched huts] down, camp ankle-deep in mud and water. . . . Up best part of night . . . wading about and hauling men out of debris of fallen *tukls*, no catch Fashoda in rainy season . . . Rain or *millions* of mosquitoes by night. . . . They bite *through coat and trouser*, so you can imagine what men suffer. No women whatever for men, and Shilluks and Denkas are most particular. Something will have to be thought out. . . .'
[2] D.D.F. xiv, No. 445, Marchand to *Colonies* tels. No. 15 and 16, 26 and 30 Aug. 1898. Cf. Emily, *op. cit.*, p. 162.
[3] FO 78/5051, Marchand to Kitchener 19 Sept. 1898.
[4] FO 141/336, Rodd to Salisbury tel. No. 240, 21 Sept. 1898, transmitting Kitchener from Renk 15 Sept. At Cairint 1/62/324 there is a fragment of a draft which begins (in the middle of a sentence) '. . . shall reach Fashoda in a few hours with a flotilla of gunboats . . .' and then goes on to describe how hopeless Marchand's position must be.

in disavowing Marchand; but he pointed out that it was neither for Marchand nor for Kitchener 'de tirer les conséquences politiques des expéditions qu'ils ont eu à diriger', and remarked that the exploits of both the Sirdar and Marchand were 'au profit également de la cause de la civilisation'. Delcassé was evidently concerned to minimise, for the moment at least, the political significance of the Mission; and for this Berthelot's letter of 30 November 1895 gave him ample warrant. He certainly feared that Kitchener might have orders to eject Marchand by force, and he begged that the Sirdar would be given 'such instructions as would prevent a collision by reserving all questions of principle for direct discussion at home'. Monson found Delcassé's calm and cordial manner a pleasant change after the 'petulance and hysterical susceptibilities' of Hanotaux. He seems indeed to have been deceived by it into believing that Delcassé would admit the British pretensions without much fuss, so long as his hand was not forced by press or Parliament.[1]

On 9 September Salisbury instructed Monson to 'point out that all the territories which were subject to the Khalifa pass by the military events of last week to the British and Egyptian governments by right of conquest. We do not consider this right is open to discussion.' However, 'any territorial controversies in those regions which are not affected by this assertion' could still be settled by negotiation.[2] This formula did not exclude the possibility that there were territories in the Upper Nile basin which, not having been 'subject to the Khalifa', could be the subject of discussion. Salisbury probably left this loophole open deliberately. But Monson always read these instructions in the light of the Grey Declaration and of the British Note of December 1897, denying that 'any other European Power than Great Britain has any claim to occupy any part of the valley of the Nile';[3] he therefore interpreted them as precluding any discussion at all. On 10 September Monson handed to Delcassé a French paraphrase of Salisbury's telegram, in which, presumably by an oversight, there was no phrase corresponding to 'by right of conquest'. But Delcassé saw the point, and at once pounced on the weakness in the British argument. 'Si Marchand est à Fachoda, ses "droits" sont exactement de même sorte que ceux de Kitchener à Khartoum'.[4] On 18 September Delcassé attempted to impress this argument on Monson, during the one interview to take place in the uneasy pause while news was awaited from Fashoda. Monson simply referred him to the Grey Declaration

[1] FO 78/5050, Monson to Salisbury No. 441, 8 Sept. 1898 (with omissions, B.D. 1, No. 188). FO 141/336, Monson to Salisbury tels. No. 127, 128, 7 Sept. D.D.F. xiv, No. 331, Delcassé to London and Cairo, 8 Sept. Cf. D.D.F. xii, No. 219, Berthelot to Guieysse 30 Nov. 1895.
[2] FO 141/336, Salisbury to Monson tel. unnumb., 9 Sept. 1898 (B.D. 1, No. 189).
[3] FO 27/3341, Monson to Salisbury No. 413, 10 Dec. 1897.
[4] FO 141/336, Monson to Salisbury tel. No. 131, 10 Sept. 1898 (B.D. 1, No. 190). FO 78/5050, Monson to Salisbury No. 449, 12 Sept. D.D.F. xiv, No. 338, *Télégramme de Lord Salisbury* 9 Sept., and minute by Delcassé, 10 Sept.

and to Salisbury's telegram. Delcassé then suggested that there was really no such thing as the Marchand Mission; Marchand was merely the subordinate of Liotard, whose mission had been launched in 1893 (*sic*), long before the British had made known their uncompromising views on the Upper Nile. When Monson refused to discuss this consideration, Delcassé appears to have thought that he found it 'embarrassing', although Monson warned him that 'the situation on the Upper Nile is a dangerous one' and that 'on ne consentira jamais à transiger sur ce point'.[1]

On 25 September Salisbury saw Kitchener's Fashoda telegram. His impression is summed up in his report to the Queen: Marchand was 'short of ammunition and supplies and anxious to get away'.[2] Monson was instructed to read the Sirdar's telegrams to Delcassé and was later permitted to communicate an aide-mémoire. This described Kitchener's proceedings at Fashoda (or some of them), and asserted that 'si la défaite des Derviches . . . avait eu lieu quinze jours plus tard l'expédition française aurait été totalement détruite'.[3] Delcassé's first reaction was of relief that no armed clash had taken place;[4] but on the 27th, after consulting the French Cabinet, he informed Monson that he could not proceed until he had received information from Marchand and that he therefore requested facilities to communicate with Fashoda. Monson asked, in menacing tones, whether this request implied that Delcassé refused to withdraw Marchand until his report had been received. Delcassé begged Monson 'not to drive him into a corner', and suggested that preliminary discussions might begin forthwith; he was again referred to Salisbury's prohibition of all discussion on Fashoda. Delcassé retorted that in this situation a rupture seemed inevitable. Why would not London make a clear statement of its claims within the Nile basin? And why was the French title at Fashoda worse than that of the Belgians at Lado, or of the British themselves at Wadelai? When Monson persisted in his refusal to discuss these issues, Delcassé flattered himself that the ambassador's silence betrayed an inability to meet his arguments, and that agreement might yet be possible: 'Difficile, très difficile, mais je crois aussi qu'on pourra s'entendre. Il n'a pas trouvé un mot à redire à mon exposé et à notre droit d'être à Fachoda comme les Anglais à Ouadelaï, les Belges à Lado, etc.'[5]

[1] FO 78/5050, Monson to Salisbury tel. No. 137, 18 Sept. (B.D. 1, No. 191). FO 78/5050, same to same No. 471, 22 Sept. D.D.F. xiv, No. 358, *note du Ministre* 18 Sept.; No. 361, Delcassé to Geoffray 20 Sept.
[2] FO 78/5051, Salisbury to the Queen tel., 25 Sept.
[3] *Ibid.*, minute by Salisbury 25 Sept.; cf. B.D. 1, No. 195. *Ibid.*, Salisbury to Monson tel. No. 202, 26 Sept.; Monson to Salisbury No. 483, 27 Sept. Cf. D.D.F. xiv, No. 383, Delcassé to Geoffray 27 Sept.
[4] Maurois, *King Edward and his Times*, p. 70, citing Delcassé's diary 22 and 26 Sept. Cf. FO 78/5051, Monson to Salisbury tel. No. 148, 26 Sept.; same to same No. 480, 27 Sept.
[5] FO 78/5051, Monson to Salisbury tel. No. 151, 27 Sept. (B.D. 1, No. 196). D.D.F. xiv, No. 384, *note du Ministre* 27 Sept.; No. 386, Delcassé to Geoffray 28 Sept. Monson states, in a separate tel. (FO 78/5051, No. 152, 28 Sept.) that he 'opposed an explicit demurrer' to Delcassé's argument about Lado and Wadelai. Evidently it was not explicit enough.

Monson grudgingly transmitted to London Delcassé's request to communicate with Marchand; and Salisbury condescendingly agreed 'to convey a message . . . to a French explorer who finds himself in a difficult position on the Upper Nile'. Meanwhile Delcassé was beginning to see more clearly the full dimensions of the crisis. On 28 September he told Monson that he would go very far to secure a friendly settlement and even added that he would prefer to be the friend of England rather than of Russia. But he must not be faced with impossible demands, or there might be an explosion of French resentment which he would be powerless to control. Monson retorted that British opinion was already quite determined not to compromise; and to Delcassé's direct question, 'You surely would not break with us over Fashoda?' he replied 'that it was exactly that which I feared'. Delcassé then remarked: 'In that event we shall not stand alone, but I repeat I would rather have England for our ally than [Russia].'[1] Delcassé feared that London's next step would be a formal demand for Marchand's withdrawal, to be followed if necessary by an ultimatum; and in the hope of forestalling this demand he warned Monson unofficially on 30 September that it could have but one result—France would go to war rather than swallow 'such an insult to the national honour'. Monson maintained his blank wall of negation: 'H.M.G. had already . . . signified their point of view, and . . . I did not see how they could possibly retreat from it.' But he warned Salisbury that Delcassé was almost certainly not bluffing; indeed, with the Dreyfus Affair now rising to its climax, Monson did not think that any French government could survive such a climb-down.[2]

By agreeing to transmit Delcassé's message to Marchand, Salisbury had to some extent precluded himself from using the extremes of diplomatic pressure until Delcassé had received a reply from Fashoda. On 3 October he told the Queen: 'We . . . are doing nothing, but only waiting, and we cannot do anything else.'[3] But this was not strictly true. Salisbury, while maintaining the diplomatic pressure, was now attempting a turn of the screw on the Upper Nile itself. On 27 September Kitchener had stated that the French at Fashoda 'must collapse' unless they were 'quickly removed'. Sanderson minuted: 'I do not think it will be a great calamity if Marchand is left a fortnight or so on short commons, in order to demonstrate how helpless and illusory the supposed occupation is.'[4] Salisbury concurred, and on 1 October he told Cairo that Marchand's 'position should be made as untenable as

[1] FO 141/336, Salisbury to Monson tel. No. 206, 28 Sept.; cf. B.D. 1, No. 197. FO 78/5051, Monson to Salisbury tel. No. 154, 28 Sept. (B.D. 1, No. 198). D.D.F. xiv, No. 387, *Télégramme de Lord Salisbury* 28 Sept.; No. 390, Delcassé to Geoffray 29 Sept. Cf. Maurois, *op. cit.*, pp. 70-1.
[2] FO 78/5051, Monson to Salisbury tel. No. 160, 30 Sept. (B.D. 1, No. 200). *Ibid.*, Monson to Salisbury No. 491, 1 Oct. D.D.F. xiv, No. 400, *note du Ministre* 30 Sept. Maurois, *op. cit.*, p. 71, citing Delcassé's diary 1 Oct.
[3] L.Q.V. 3, iii, pp. 289-90, Salisbury to the Queen 3 Oct.
[4] FO 141/336, Rodd to Salisbury tels. No. 250, 27 Sept.; No. 252, 29 Sept. (B.D. 1, No. 199). FO 78/5051, minute by Sanderson.

possible' by the denial of all supplies 'except in extreme necessity'. On 7 October Salisbury went further. After having been assured by Kitchener that there would be 'no great practical difficulty in obliging [Marchand] to capitulate by cutting off all supplies', he authorised orders which required Jackson practically to blockade the French and to intern them, as an armed force, in Fashoda and its immediate vicinity.[1]

This attempted turn of the screw had unfortunate, and very nearly disastrous, consequences. Literally interpreted, the new orders required Jackson to forbid the French all communication with their post at Meshra' er Req;[2] any attempt to enforce this would have provoked an immediate conflict. The orders did not in fact reach Fashoda until 24 October, when the crisis in Europe had little more than a week to run; thereafter, they were a major factor in creating a very dangerous crisis at Fashoda itself. On 25 October Marchand had left Fashoda for Cairo in order to communicate directly with his government.[3] Relations between the two garrisons at once deteriorated, partly because Germain, Marchand's deputy, was much less congenial to Jackson as a person,[4] partly because it was only now that Jackson began to get wind of the reconnaissances which the French were sending out eastwards in search of the Ethiopians. The crisis had begun before the end of October; intensified by Jackson's new orders —even though Jackson applied them as leniently as he dared—it persisted with deepening gravity until 4 December.[5] Not until 29 November had Cromer released from Omdurman the steamers which were to carry Marchand back to Fashoda, and with him, at long last, news of the settlement which had been reached in Europe nearly a month earlier.[6] On 2 December Dr Emily, perhaps the coolest head among the French, had written: 'Allons! Pourvu que cela dure encore quelques jours, les fusils partiront tout seuls ici!' Jackson, for his part, was overwhelmed with relief when on 4 December the steamers at last arrived: 'THANK THE LORD, as the situation with Germain had been *very* strained of late and he had been doing all possible to provoke matters.'[7]

Cromer's protracted delay in informing Fashoda that Delcassé had agreed to withdraw Marchand was inexcusable. It was based partly on an extreme suspicion of Marchand, and a consequent determina-

[1] FO 141/336, Salisbury to Rodd tel. No. 92, 1 Oct. (B.D. 1, No. 201); Cromer to Salisbury tel. No. 260, 7 Oct.; Salisbury to Cromer tel. No. 106, 7 Oct. (B.D. 1, No. 205).
[2] Cairint 1/62/342, Kitchener to Maxwell 17 Oct. Intel. 5/4, Maxwell to Jackson 18 Oct.
[3] Cairint 3/15/243, Jackson's I.D. 24 and 25 Oct.
[4] Jackson thought Marchand 'a perfect gentleman'; but Germain was 'a French bounder, a man one cannot trust out of sight, or believe a word of his "plausible talk" ' (Cairint 3/15/243, Jackson to Maxwell 28 Nov. 1898).
[5] This local crisis is very fully documented in the Khartoum archives, Cairint 3/15/243 and Intel. 5/4. A detailed account is being prepared for publication in *S.N.R.*
[6] Cairint 1/62/324, Cromer to Maxwell 29 Nov. 1898.
[7] Emily, *op. cit.*, p. 221. Cairint 3/15/243, Jackson's I.D. 4 Dec. 1898. The French lowered their flag at Fashoda at 8.20 a.m. on 11 Dec. An Egyptian officer was detailed to take over their post; and not until 5 p.m. was the Union Jack hoisted beside the Egyptian flag.

tion not to let him loose in the Upper Nile again until he had worked out with Omdurman plans to frustrate Marchand's every possible and impossible movement.[1] But it was also based on complete confidence in the harmlessness and helplessness of the French so long as they were at Fashoda—the impression created by Kitchener's despatches. Similarly, the orders which so dangerously complicated the crisis were based upon Kitchener's utterly misleading appreciation. Salisbury, who after all did not want to precipitate a conflict, would hardly have authorised such orders had he realised that they would do nothing significant to weaken the French; but much to increase the tension of a situation where both the English and the French commanders claimed to be the legally constituted authority in the Fashoda district.[2] Jackson attempted to explain to Omdurman what was going on; unluckily his steamer broke down at a critical moment,[3] and the reports that did get through seem at first to have been discounted[4]—Jackson had a reputation as a fusser and a worrier.[5] But if in December 1898 an armed conflict at Fashoda had shattered the diplomacy of Salisbury and Delcassé, the responsibility would not have lain with Jackson or Germain, both of whom had on the whole behaved with commendable restraint in an almost impossible situation.

Salisbury's attempted pressure at Fashoda itself was also unnecessary. As early as 3 October Delcassé had convinced his ministerial colleagues that Fashoda would have to be given up as the only alternative to a pointless war; and that this could be done without injury to national honour if France could obtain a territorial sop in the Bahr al-Ghazal. But there was obviously nothing to be done with Monson on these lines; and on 4 October Courcel, who was on leave pending retirement, was sent to London to tackle Salisbury personally. Delcassé's asking price for the evacuation of Fashoda was the whole region bounded by the Bahr al-'Arab, the Bahr al-Ghazal and the Upper Nile itself.[6] Wisely, Courcel did not reveal this at his first conversation with

[1] FO 141/336, Cromer's telegrams to London 30 Oct.-25 Nov.; Cairint 1/62/324, his correspondence with Omdurman 30 Oct.-29 Nov.

[2] This is brought out very clearly in the correspondence between Jackson and Germain (at Cairint 3/15/243 and Intel. 5/4) during the final and sharpest phase of the crisis at the beginning of Dec. 1898.

[3] Jackson's reports of the tension caused by the new orders were sent to Omdurman on 8 Nov. by the steamer *Abu Klea*. But the *Abu Klea* broke down and did not reach Omdurman until the night of 24/25 Nov. Meanwhile, Jackson was completely isolated and without information. By 28 Nov. he was so disquieted that he despatched his own guardship *Tamai* with further reports, replacing it by the *Sultan* from the Sobat. The *Sultan* was ordered to report to Fashoda 'ready for any emergency' and carrying a fighting-party of thirty men.

[4] Even when Jackson's ominous reports down to 8 Nov. were belatedly received on the 24th/25th, Cromer agreed that a steamer ready to leave Omdurman for Fashoda should be held 'pending further instructions' (FO 141/336, Cromer to Salisbury tel. No. 331, 25 Nov. 1898).

[5] Cf. Cairint 1/62/324, Maxwell to Wingate 28 Oct.: 'I enclose letters and papers received from Jackson . . . —he seems happier!!; but wants a great deal more than I can give him. He has not yet asked for bathing-machines but I expect he will.'

[6] D.D.F. xiv, No. 412, Delcassé to Courcel 4 Oct. 1898. FO 78/5051, Monson to Salisbury tel. No. 163, 4 Oct.

x Kitchener and Wingate (in topee) on the *Dal* watching the
arrival of Marchand's messenger, 19 September 1898

xi Kitchener's flotilla bombarding the Mahdist steamer *Safia* and camp
near Renk, 15 September 1898

Salisbury on 5 October. He began by suggesting that in April 1895 Kimberley had admitted that France, as well as England, had claims in the Upper Nile; but that it had then been agreed to leave the question in suspense so long as the practical situation remained unchanged. This situation had now been modified by two events, the British occupation of Omdurman and the French occupation of Fashoda; and these two occupations had a precisely similar legal status.[1]

With his own 'right of conquest' argument thus turned against him, Salisbury apparently did not care to put forward the very doubtful doctrine which he had formulated in June—that the taking of a capital city gives a title by right of conquest to the whole territory of the State concerned. Instead he tried to supplement the right of conquest by appealing to the earlier rights of Egypt in the Sudan; a stranger doctrine still, for any attempt to combine these two types of 'right' must surely result in their mutual cancellation. He told Courcel that the Egyptian title had 'been rendered dormant by the military successes of the Mahdi; but that the amount of right, whatever it was, which by those events had been alienated from Egypt, had been entirely transferred to the conqueror'. Until the battle of Omdurman, it seemed, Egypt did after all have a right, or some quantitative fraction of a right, in the Sudan. Therefore, as Salisbury had already told Delcassé through Monson, 'the region in which Marchand was found has never been without an owner'; and French intervention had been illegal *ab initio* and now had 'no political effect or significance'. Salisbury also contrasted Kitchener's strength with Marchand's weakness and supposed vulnerability: 'but for the arrival of the British [*sic*] flotilla, M. Marchand's escort would have been destroyed by the Dervishes'. The French occupation was therefore ineffective as well as illegal. Finally, Salisbury complained that if France intended to challenge the British claim on the Upper Nile 'she was bound to have broken silence'; she could not now expect to negotiate on the basis of 'a secret expedition into territory already owned and occupied'. Courcel replied that as France was now quite willing to evacuate Fashoda in return for access to the navigable Nile system, agreement might emerge from a discussion of the geographical point to which Marchand was to retire. According to Courcel, Salisbury declined to engage in detailed geographical discussion but promised to consult his colleagues on this proposal. Salisbury's report makes no mention of such a promise and states specifically that he 'gave no countenance' to any suggestion that France might be compensated in the Bahr al-Ghazal.[2]

However, Courcel's report of this conversation strengthened Del-

[1] D.D.F. xiv, No. 414, Courcel to Delcassé 6 Oct.

[2] *Ibid., loc. cit.*; and No. 410, Delcassé to Courcel 4 Oct. FO 78/5051, Salisbury to Monson No. 355A, 6 Oct. (B.D. I, No. 203). FO 141/336, Salisbury to Monson tel. No. 213, 3 Oct. (B.D. I, No. 202).

cassé's hopes of a serious discussion. On 7 October he thought the situation distinctly easier. *Le Matin*, which throughout the crisis reflected Delcassé's views, had on 5 October carried the headline: 'NON! La Seule Réponse Digne de la France'; but on the 7th and 8th it was explaining that the evacuation of Fashoda was perfectly compatible with national honour, since all that France desired was access to the Nile system. The practical task was therefore to indicate a frontier by determining the point to which Marchand should retire.[1] On 11 October, after deploring the repeated failure of London to respond to his friendly advances, Delcassé attempted to move Monson in the direction indicated in Courcel's despatch; he promised that if England 'would make things easy for him in form he would be conciliatory in substance'. Once again Monson declined all discussion; but he emphasised to Salisbury that Delcassé, who was under severe strain both politically and personally, was 'prepared to retreat . . . if we can build him a golden bridge'.[2]

Salisbury was perhaps impressed by this report; for in his conversation with Courcel on 12 October he showed, for the first and last time, some sign of willingness to make concessions. He once more brought forward his own special compound of previous Egyptian title and right of conquest; and he emphasised the 'impossible position' of Marchand at Fashoda. Courcel did not contest this latter assertion, and Salisbury then suggested that Marchand should retire beyond the Nile watershed, the French meanwhile protecting their interests by a declaration that this withdrawal did not prejudice any existing controversy. To this Courcel replied that Marchand would indeed be withdrawn if Britain would concede 'pour les territoires français du bassin du Congo la possession de leur débouché naturel sur le Nil, qui était la vallée du Bahr el Ghazal'; or, in Salisbury's words: 'such a territorial delimitation as would place France upon the navigable portion of the Bahr al-Ghazal, so that no frontier would intervene between her commerce and the [navigable system of the] Nile'. Salisbury agreed to think about (*réfléchir à*) these proposals, and to bring them before his colleagues; but he thought it 'better to wait until they were submitted . . . in a more precise and tangible form, rather than enter upon a discussion which under the circumstances would have been fruitful of misapprehension'. He therefore suggested that Courcel should make a written communication about 'the means of M. Marchand's retreat and any other stipulations which it was his object to suggest'.[3]

Here, after a month of blank negation, was at last the hope of a discussion on more or less equal terms; but Courcel himself at once

[1] Maurois, *loc. cit.*, citing Delcassé's diary 7 Oct. D.D.F. xiv, No. 419, Delcassé to Courcel 8 Oct. FO 78/5051: Monson to Salisbury Nos. 499, 5 Oct.; 500, 7 Oct.; 504, 9 Oct.; 505, 10 Oct. (The last three are printed: B.D. i, Nos. 204, 206, 208.)

[2] FO 78/5051, Monson to Salisbury tel. No. 169, 11 Oct. (B.D. i, No. 209). *Ibid.*, same to same No. 517, 14 Oct. D.D.F. xiv, No. 428, Delcassé to Courcel, 11 Oct.

[3] FO 78/5051, Salisbury to Monson No. 369, 12 Oct. FO 141/336, same to same tel. No. 223, 12 Oct. D.D.F. xiv, Nos. 433, 437, Courcel to Delcassé 13 and 15 Oct.

destroyed it. Immediately after the interview he informed Salisbury by personal letter that France claimed the whole of the region bounded by the Nile, the Bahr al-Ghazal and the Bahr al-'Arab. Presumably Courcel feared that in his conversation with Salisbury he had not fully carried out Delcassé's instructions; but it was surely unwise to be so forthright when the very possibility of a negotiation still hung in the balance. Salisbury at once replied that but for the information contained in Courcel's letter, he would have quite misunderstood the effect of their conversation. The pretension now put forward was completely new to him, and in declining for the moment to discuss it he was not 'in any degree admitting its validity'.[1] Courcel afterwards realised his mistake, and tried to explain that his letter was merely intended to show that the French claims on the Upper Nile had 'historic roots'.[2] But the damage had been done. The prospect of negotiation, and perhaps of token compensation, vanished and never re-appeared.

On 13 October Courcel returned to Paris. There was now a pause in the diplomatic dialogue, for Salisbury had nothing more to say to the French until they themselves took the initiative on the basis of the Marchand report,[3] which Salisbury doubtless expected to reveal the growing desperation of the French position at Fashoda. However, on 10 October Salisbury had taken the unusual, and somewhat minatory, course of issuing a Blue Book in the midst of an unsettled dispute.[4] This publication released a flood of political oratory in England. Whatever the concessions Salisbury may have been contemplating when he promised to 'think about' Courcel's proposals, they were swept into limbo by the vehemence of the speakers, particularly the Liberal Imperialists. Rosebery's speech at Epsom on 12 October, which attracted great attention, set the key-note. Rosebery claimed to have been 'personally and Ministerially responsible' for the Grey Declaration, dwelt on the 'exceptional weight and gravity' of the term 'unfriendly act', and asserted that no government which showed signs of yielding would last a week. A fortnight later, at Huddersfield, Grey himself declared that 'the rights of Egypt, the necessity of Egypt, and our obligations' to safeguard Egyptian rights on the Upper Nile 'make it imperative for the Government to take the position they occupy and make it impossible for them to recede from it'. Support for the Government was strongly expressed as far to the Left as Asquith, Bryce and Harcourt; while Hicks Beach, as government spokesman, declared with his usual brutal candour that 'this country has put its foot down' and would go to war rather than yield.[5]

---

[1] FO 78/5051, Courcel to Salisbury 12 Oct.; Salisbury to Courcel 13 Oct. (B.D. I, Nos. 210 and 211).
[2] D.D.F. XIV, No. 446, Courcel to Geoffray 21 Oct.
[3] FO 141/336, Salisbury to Cromer tel. No. 112, 15 Oct.
[4] Egypt No. 2 (1898) [C.-9054].
[5] A.R., 1898, pp. [162-8] gives a useful summary of the speeches.

Meanwhile, the British popular press indulged in an orgy of scurrility. The French at Fashoda were 'mere tourists', sometimes even 'scum of the desert'. The *Daily Mail* called openly for war; even among Liberal newspapers only the *Manchester Guardian* was by the third week of October still persevering in its moderation. On 22 October the tasteless witticisms of *Punch* culminated in the notorious 'organ-grinder' cartoon, doubly offensive in that the organ-grinder's monkey wore the uniform of a French soldier. In France, the more serious newspapers confined themselves to dignified protest against this provocative behaviour; but in the 'boulevard press' Déroulède, de Rochefort and de Cassagnac wrote with a chauvinistic virulence that matched the flippant arrogance of their British counterparts. The tone of the English press in particular had by about 20 October become a powerful psychological preparation for war.[1]

Marchand's long-awaited report, telegraphed from Cairo by his colleague Baratier, reached Paris early on 22 October. It was a perplexing document. It consisted merely of the telegrams for Paris which Marchand had drafted between his arrival at Fashoda in July and the end of September. The encounter with Kitchener was described in a few laconic sentences; and Baratier transmitted neither the correspondence with the Sirdar, nor the undelivered letters of protest. Nor did Marchand give any general appreciation of his situation at Fashoda, though the tone of his telegrams left little doubt that Kitchener's picture was exaggerated.[2] Before all the telegrams had come through, Delcassé summoned Baratier to Paris to elucidate them.[3] But Delcassé now cared little for the local situation at Fashoda, except in so far as it might provide a respectable excuse for withdrawing Marchand. On 22 October he confided to his diary: 'The problem is, how to combine the demands of honour with the necessity of avoiding a naval war which we are absolutely incapable of carrying through, even with Russian help.'[4]

On the 23rd he clutched at the possibility that the arrangement suggested by Courcel to Salisbury on the 12th might still be a solution: 'My line is decided upon, and I have let it be known—"Recognise an outlet for us on the Nile and I shall order Marchand's withdrawal".' But Monson's response to this suggestion was as frigidly negative as ever; and by 24 October Delcassé had recognised that nothing would

[1] T. W. Riker, 'A Survey of British Policy during the Fashoda Crisis', *Political Science Quarterly*, XLIV, 1 (1929), pp. 65-70. Arie, 'L'opinion publique . . .', *Rev. Hist. Cols.*, 1954, pp. 350-3.

[2] D.D.F. xiv, No. 445, Lefèvre-Pontalis to Delcassé, transmitting Marchand's tels., 21/22 Oct. Marchand was conscious of the meagreness of this 'report'; and he attempted to excuse it by alleging that Jackson had insisted on despatching the post-boat from Fashoda to Omdurman before his report was complete. Jackson's circumstantial rebuttal of this allegation (Cairint 1/62/324, Jackson to Maxwell 24 Oct.) suggests that Marchand may have had reasons of his own for telling Paris as little as possible. But what these reasons may have been it is not easy to conjecture.

[3] FO 141/336, Monson to Salisbury tel. No. 176, 21 Oct.

[4] Maurois, *op. cit.*, p. 72, citing Delcassé's diary 22 Oct. Cf. D.D.F. xiv, No. 445, Marchand to *Colonies* tel. No. 22, 27 Sept.

satisfy London short of a withdrawal which should be unconditional in form at least. On 24 October, seizing upon a statement by Marchand that the health of his men must suffer unless they were soon relieved, Delcassé wrote: 'If England does not accept my proposal, I publish Marchand's journal and recall the heroic little band. I will not murder them out there with no gain to the country.' But this was not quite the total surrender that it seemed. Courcel was sent back to London to offer a 'spontaneous' withdrawal from Fashoda, in return for which Salisbury would 'spontaneously' offer a discussion of frontiers, it being understood that French commercial access to the navigable Nile system would be preserved.[1]

25 October 1898, the day Courcel arrived in London, was in Paris a day of acute domestic crisis—indeed very nearly a revolutionary *journée*. The Brisson government, stabbed in the back by the unheralded resignation of its War Minister General Chanoine—its third since the beginning of September—was deserted by the Moderate Republicans in the Chamber and threatened by an anti-Dreyfusard mob in the streets. The rioters were dispersed by the police; but the Government fell, and Monson thought that its fall might well be the signal for a military coup d'état. A government of generals, he feared, might even welcome a war with England if they could in this way stave off the 'revision' of the Dreyfus case, with all its explosive possibilities for the French military Establishment.[2] The British, who had already ordered the manning of the Reserve Fleet,[3] now began to intensify their naval preparations. On 26 October war orders were drafted for the Home, Mediterranean and Channel Fleets, and the First Sea Lord demanded the concentration of the Home Fleet.[4] Meanwhile, it looked as if Courcel's journey to London had been in vain; Salisbury refused to see him until after a Cabinet to be held on the 27th. Courcel feared that the result of this Cabinet would be an ultimatum; and in this emergency he communicated to Salisbury through an intermediary the proposal for a 'spontaneous' evacuation of Fashoda coupled with a 'spontaneous' invitation to discuss a frontier which should:

tenir compte, dans toute la mesure compatible avec les intérêts de l'Egypte et ceux de l'Angleterre, de la nécessité impérieuse pour les possessions françaises de pouvoir obtenir un débouché commercial dans la vallée du Bahr-el-Ghazal, et par conséquent, par le Nil et l'Egypte.[5]

---

[1] Maurois, *loc. cit.*, citing Delcassé's diary 23 and 24 Oct. D.D.F. xiv, No. 449, *note du Ministre* 23 Oct.; No. 455, Courcel to Delcassé 26 Oct.

[2] Chapman, *The Dreyfus Case*, pp. 236-8. FO 27/3397, Monson to Salisbury No. 546, 25 Oct.

[3] On 24 Oct.: Marder, *The Anatomy of British Sea Power*, pp. 321-2. Cf. Riker, *ubi supra*, p. 71.

[4] Marder, *op. cit.*, pp. 322-6.

[5] D.D.F. xiv, No. 455. B.D. i, No. 216, Sanderson to Salisbury 25 Oct., and minute by Salisbury. SP Cabinet Memoranda, Papers communicated by M. de Reuter 27 Oct.

It is very likely that Salisbury communicated these proposals to the Cabinet,[1] and that he himself was not unwilling to grant France a commercial outlet to the Nile. He may have recalled how, in the summer, the concession to France of commercial 'enclaves-with-wayleaves' had helped to cut through the inextricable tangle on the Niger. But the Cabinet would not hear of the slightest concession on the Nile. Most of Salisbury's colleagues seem to have felt that 'the row would have to come, and that it might as well come now as later'. Chamberlain and possibly Goschen went further, and were positively in favour of war. Only Salisbury seems to have set real store by a peaceful outcome; but he had behind him the whole-hearted support of the Queen, who shrank from war 'for so small and miserable an object'.[2] The decision of the Cabinet seems to have been a compromise between an immediate ultimatum and a settlement somewhat on the lines suggested by Courcel. Marchand must be withdrawn unconditionally, and no promises could be given about 'access to the Nile and such like'. After Marchand's withdrawal it would be possible to consider whether the French claims admitted of discussion. If Marchand were not withdrawn he would not be physically molested; but no reinforcements would be permitted to reach him, and it would be for the French 'to adopt any active measures that would precipitate a conflict'.[3] Meanwhile, the Navy was put on a complete war footing. On 28 October the war orders drafted on the 26th were signalled to the Mediterranean Fleet, and on the 29th the Channel Fleet was ordered to Gibraltar.[4]

Immediately after the Cabinet of the 27th Salisbury told Courcel that there could be no compromise or negotiation whatever so long as the French flag flew at Fashoda, and that he could neither give nor imply any promise of British concessions after its removal. He even evaded Courcel's attempt to extract from him an admission that negotiations must necessarily begin as soon as Marchand had been withdrawn. Courcel was well aware that Salisbury's colleagues would not allow him to go further, and that this was the final word of the British. He therefore now devoted himself to bringing about the evacuation of Fashoda with the minimum loss of face for France. At Courcel's request, Salisbury communicated an 'unofficial' aide-mémoire establishing that 'whatever was at present abnormal in the diplomatic relations between the two countries would cease' once Marchand had been ordered to withdraw. The French claims would

---

[1] Courcel's proposals are filed in S P as a Cabinet Memo.

[2] M. V. Brett (ed.), *Journals and Letters of Reginald Viscount Esher*, I (London 1934), pp. 221-2. Garvin, *Chamberlain* III, pp. 229-30. G.P. XIV/2, No. 3898, report by Capt. Coerper 25 Oct.: No. 3908, Metternich to Richthofen 6 Nov. L.Q.V. 3, iii, pp. 298-9, 305.

[3] S P Cabinet Memoranda, cutting from the *Pall Mall Gazette*, 28 Oct. This newspaper was well-informed; it also reproduced almost *verbatim* Monson's Most Secret tel. No. 185 of 25 Oct.

[4] Marder, *op. cit.*, pp. 323, 326. Brett, *loc. cit.* D.D.F. XIV, No. 468, *note d'un agent de renseignements* 29 Oct.

then be considered without prejudice; but Salisbury 'could not give or imply any kind of pledge as to the conclusions to which we should be willing to come'. Courcel also obtained from Sir Thomas Sanderson a written statement confirming that London had never formally demanded the evacuation of Fashoda. Armed with these documents, he advised Delcassé on 29 October that France should quit Fashoda at once, while she could still do so 'avec honneur et la tête haute'. The withdrawal could be explained by adducing the difficulties of the local situation.[1] While awaiting an answer from Paris Courcel opened unofficial discussions with Sanderson on Marchand's probable evacuation route. Courcel favoured Khartoum-Berber-Suakin, for this route could not give rise to any suspicion of a junction with the Ethiopians. He had already told Delcassé, as a self-evident truth, that if the Fashoda garrison 'se joint aux Abyssins, soit volontairement, soit entraînée par eux, c'est naturellement la guerre avec l'Angleterre'.[2]

Courcel's letter to Delcassé of the 29th crossed with a suggestion by Delcassé that Courcel should seek an undertaking that on Marchand's withdrawal an Anglo-French commission would be set up, with the task of completing those provisions of the June West African Convention relating to the territories east and north of Lake Chad. The Nile settlement would thus be smuggled in as an annex to the West African question; and this formulation gave Salisbury the opportunity, if he wished to take it, of making a promise without formally infringing the principle of 'no promises in the Nile valley until Marchand is under orders to withdraw'. This procedure would also be less unpalatable to public opinion in France. But at 5.45 p.m. on 30 October Delcassé suddenly abandoned his own ingenious proposal. Cancelling his earlier instructions to Courcel, he wrote 'je crois qu'il est inutile, au moins pour le moment, de pousser plus loin'.[3] Meanwhile, Courcel received no reply to his suggestion of the 29th that France should go while the going was good.

On 31 October, however, Courcel received from Geoffray, his *Conseiller d'ambassade* who was at the time in Paris, a letter which threw him into utter consternation. Geoffray's letter has disappeared; but it is clear from Courcel's reply that Delcassé was under pressure, doubtless from the Parliamentary colonial group and its fellow-travellers, to refuse the evacuation of Fashoda and damn the consequences. Courcel wrote:

> Cela me semble de la folie pure, de la folie dangereuse. Faites, je vous en supplie, tout ce qui dépendra de vous pour réveiller ces visionnaires. Ne les abandonnez pas. Retournez rue de Constantine. Si vous ne pouvez voir et éclairer M. D[elcassé]

---

[1] D.D.F. xiv, No. 459, Courcel to Delcassé 28 Oct.; No. 465, same to same, private, 29 Oct.; No. 465, Annex ii, unofficial memo. by Salisbury 27 Oct. B.D., i, No. 220, Sanderson to Courcel 28 Oct.

[2] D.D.F. xiv, No. 476, Courcel to Delcassé 1 Nov. Cf. No. 465.

[3] *Ibid.*, Nos. 464, 469, Delcassé to Courcel 29 and 30 Oct.

voyez du moins N[isard] itérativement, et jusqu'à ce que vous ayez mis la conviction dans son esprit. . . . Au besoin, je vous demanderais d'aller de ma part à l'Elysée. Ne laissez pas les choses dormir, je vous en prie.[1]

Meanwhile, Courcel warned Delcassé that while the British had not yet decided on war and were indeed appreciative of Delcassé's efforts for peace, they were now completely ready. The moment they believed that war was inevitable, they would strike at once with their maximum force. Courcel was also scarcely less alarmed by talk in France of using the crisis to re-open the Egyptian question. In a single devastating sentence Courcel castigated this irresponsibility, and at the same time ruthlessly dissipated the cloudy hopes that had gathered round the Nile project ever since 1893.

> Ceux qui lancent au moment actuel un semblable brûlot ignorent absolument la situation de l'Europe, et oublient, volontairement ou non, qu'une nation qui veut préparer une campagne de cette envergure doit y songer des années à l'avance; être assurée non seulement de ses forces propres, mais de ses alliances, de la capacité et de l'intensité d'effort de ses alliés, et avoir réussi à disposer tout l'échiquier européen d'une manière favorable.[2]

This sudden change in Delcassé's attitude at the end of October was not entirely unheralded. By now he was finding the strain almost intolerable, and on 27 October he became, almost for the first time, excited during his discussions with Monson. Complaining bitterly of the rejection of all his conciliatory overtures, he declared that if England insisted on the humiliation of France he could not remain in office. Two days later, on the 29th, he told Monson that he now saw no other course than resignation. France must either humiliate herself or go to war with England; his patriotism rejected the first alternative, his political convictions the second. Delcassé was on this occasion particularly distressed, for he had just heard of Marchand's departure from Fashoda for Cairo.[3] Marchand had taken this step in all good faith, without realising that it would be widely interpreted, both inside and outside France, as the first move towards evacuation. Delcassé complained that Marchand's 'incredible and unpardonable' conduct in thus apparently deserting his post was provoking accusations that the Quai d'Orsay had sent him secret orders to retire.[4] However, in spite of these complications, Delcassé was on 29 October still ready to withdraw Marchand, at any rate if he could get the promise of a mixed commission.

His despairing 'je crois qu'il est inutile . . . de pousser plus loin',

---

[1] D.D.F. xiv, Nos. 473, 474, Courcel to Geoffray 31 Oct.
[2] Ibid., No. 476.
[3] FO 78/5052, Monson to Salisbury No. 554, 28 Oct. (B.D. i, No. 221); same to same tel. No. 194, 29 Oct.; same to same No. 558, 29 Oct. (B.D. i, No. 222).
[4] FO 78/5052, No. 558. Men as diverse as Count Münster and Wilfrid Blunt thought that Marchand's departure was the first step towards withdrawal. Cf. G.P. xiv/2, No. 3901, Münster to A.A. 29 Oct.; Blunt, My Diaries, p. 306.

La Silhouette, Paris.]

[Oct. 2.

MAJOR MARCHAND'S MISSION.

COCK-A-DOODLE DOO!

LORD SALISBURY: "Ah, you may crow, but the spirit of Wellington remains with us yet!"

on the 30th, and the developments which so alarmed Courcel on the 31st, may have been the result of a démarche by the colonialists which Baratier claims to have instigated. Baratier had arrived in Paris on 26 October, and had seen Delcassé on the 27th. He was shocked to discover that Delcassé still accepted, in its essentials, Kitchener's account of the situation at Fashoda. He was even more distressed to find that the Minister seemed to look upon the occupation of Fashoda itself as a mere embarrassment. The interview ended stormily; when Delcassé let fall the words, 'vous ne comprenez pas bien l'honneur de la France', Baratier stalked from the room. On the following day he again attempted to convince Delcassé that the situation at Fashoda was perfectly satisfactory. This was cold comfort to Delcassé, who was hoping to use the distress of the French at Fashoda as the publishable reason for Marchand's withdrawal. He brushed aside these local details with the remark 'vous ne pouvez vouloir que nous nous mettions mal avec un Etat aussi puissant que l'Angleterre, quand nous sommes saignants sur la frontière de l'Est', and began to discuss Marchand's possible evacuation routes. Baratier then appealed to Etienne; and on 29 October the newspapers carried a declaration, drawn up by Etienne and signed by a number of Deputies, protesting against the conclusion of any settlement without prior discussion in the Chambers.[1]

Monson probably had this incident in mind when in his despatch of 30 October he referred for the first time to the attitude of the Colonialists. The Colonial group was, he said, 'not so strong in the Chamber as formerly; but it still numbers in its ranks a few Deputies with influence enough to excite an angry debate on any Colonial question in which there is friction with England'. The Colonialist press had also become increasingly violent towards the end of October; on the 28th *La Dépêche Coloniale* had openly demanded war rather than humiliation.[2] The new Cabinet, now being painfully constructed by Dupuy, would at once have to grapple with the apparently insoluble Dreyfus crisis. If to this were to be added a parliamentary storm over Fashoda, the new government was likely to die before it had started to live. At this point the President of the Republic himself intervened, perhaps with decisive effect. He persuaded Delcassé to stay on in the new Cabinet, and to order the evacuation of Fashoda.

> Cette décision . . . coûtait beaucoup [à Delcassé], tous ses amis étant du parti chauvin et lui-même ayant toujours eu une attitude très ardente. Pour vaincre ses scrupules, je dus lui dire que je le couvrais absolument et que dès la constitution du nouveau Cabinet, je le dégagerais de cette action.

He also acted through Dupuy to persuade the Colonialists to withdraw their threatened interpellations.[3] In the end only two remained on

[1] Baratier, *op. cit.*, pp. 206-13.
[2] FO 78/5052, Monson to Salisbury Nos. 566, 567, 30 Oct.
[3] Faure, 'Fachoda (1898)', *Rev. Hist. Dip.* 1955, pp. 36-8.

the Order Paper; neither was by an active Colonialist and both were withdrawn—amid applause—before they could be debated.[1]

The new government was formed on 1 November; on the 2nd, Delcassé notified Courcel of his *disposition* to send Marchand back to Fashoda to lead his detachment 'sur un autre point'.[2] On 3 November, the French Cabinet, under strong pressure from President Félix Faure, officially confirmed this decision. Monson was at once informed. Courcel, who had already told Sanderson that the decision was 'imminent', was instructed to inform Salisbury.[3] The proposal to set up a joint Anglo-French commission was abandoned. Both Delcassé and Courcel, on second thoughts, felt that it would be embarrassing officially to discuss with England what were, however much disguised, still in French eyes the frontiers of 'Egypt'. Courcel was to do no more than cautiously sound Salisbury about the resumption of discussions; if Salisbury agreed, 'les deux Gouvernements pourraient constater cet accord par une formule commune'.[4] But even this miserable shred of agreement was to be denied to Delcassé. On 4 November Salisbury suggested to Courcel that discussion should be postponed until the public excitement had died down. Courcel agreed, in the belief that Salisbury was still prepared to make concessions in the Bahr al-Ghazal, but could not do so while the fighting words of Rosebery and Grey were still fresh in the public mind. It was agreed to consider the question again after Salisbury's Mansion House speech on 9 November.[5] Salisbury's words at the Mansion House were moderate and conciliatory; but the public reaction to all that related to Egypt was so aggressively jingoistic that on the 10th Salisbury refused to enter into discussions, pleading the need for further geographical information. On the following day Courcel left London; and the negotiation did not begin until his successor Paul Cambon took the initiative on 11 January 1899.[6]

The withdrawal of Marchand had been inevitable from the outset unless France was prepared to fight. Delcassé recognised this; but he permitted himself to hope—not quite unreasonably—that France would be spared the humiliation of an unconditional withdrawal without even the promise of a negotiation to follow. Such a climb-down, politically dangerous at the best of times, was doubly so when all the most anglophobe elements in French society were already excited to frenzy by the threatened 'revision' of the Dreyfus case. Delcassé therefore played for time, protested, doubtless sincerely, his fundamental

---

[1] One was by the Comte de Mun (Constitutionalist Right); the other by Brunet (Radical Socialist).

[2] D.D.F. xiv, No. 477, Delcassé to Courcel 2 Nov.

[3] FO 78/5052, Monson to Salisbury tel. No. 200, 3 Nov. (B.D. i, No. 226). D.D.F. xiv, No. 480, Delcassé to Courcel 3 Nov. Faure, *loc. cit.*

[4] D.D.F. xiv, No. 482, Courcel to Delcassé 3 Nov.; No. 485, Delcassé to Courcel 4 Nov.

[5] *Ibid.*, Nos. 488, 491, 496, Courcel to Delcassé 4, 5 and 7 Nov. FO 78/5052, Salisbury to Monson tel. No. 262, 4 Nov. (B.D. i, No. 227).

[6] D.D.F. xiv, No. 506, Courcel to Delcassé 10 Nov. *Infra,* Ch. xvi, p. 369.

goodwill towards Britain, and hinted that Salisbury, rather than push his intransigence to the point of war, should buy that goodwill at the bargain price of a sop for France in the Bahr al-Ghazal. Courcel's unwonted clumsiness on 12 October made a possible discussion on these lines abortive. But it is clear that in any case the intransigence of British opinion from the Cabinet downwards would have prevented Salisbury from making any real concession. On 22 October, when the possibilities of delay had been exhausted by the arrival of the March-and report, Delcassé was brought back to the bare bones of the problem: how to avoid a hopeless war without incurring intolerable humiliation.[1]

In April 1895 Cromer had predicted that naval strength would be the deciding factor in the ultimate solution of the Sudan and Upper Nile questions. Delcassé's reference to 'a naval war which we are absolutely incapable of carrying through' is sufficient vindication of Cromer's prophecy.[2] In 1898 British naval superiority over France alone was overwhelming. The Spanish-American War had just demonstrated the fate that lay in store for the weaker force in a modern naval conflict; and Delcassé himself admitted that if the French Fleet challenged the British on the high seas, it would be at the bottom of the ocean within a fortnight.[3] The British Navy had by 1898 begun to benefit from the increases planned (and so tenaciously resisted by Gladstone) in 1894. The French Fleet, on the other hand, was caught by the crisis of 1898 at an awkward moment when it was a collection of prototypes old and new rather than a homogeneous force. There were doubtless some excellent individual vessels; but no strong squadrons of sister-ships capable of manœuvring and delivering their broadsides together. Of this and other deficiencies the French Ministry of Marine was well aware; while the British on their side were serenely confident that the French would not have 'a ghost of a chance'.[4] The Admiralty was confident that even if Russia intervened it could frustrate a raid on Port Said or Alexandria and at the same time prevent a junction between the Toulon squadron and the Russian Black Sea Fleet. In March 1898 Salisbury had declared that he did not 'carry enough guns' to fight both France and Russia; seven months later he accepted this prospect with equanimity. The season itself had something to do with this: from early November to early April the Gulfs of Bothnia and Riga are ice-bound, and the Russian Baltic Fleet would therefore have been immobilised until long after the issue at sea had been decided. Moreover, had England gone to war with Russia in March 1898, the

[1] Maurois, op. cit., p. 72, citing Delcassé's diary for 22 Oct.
[2] FO 633/6, No. 206, Cromer to Rosebery 13 Apr. 1895; Delcassé's diary Oct. 1898, cited Maurois, loc. cit.
[3] Marder, op. cit., pp. 320-36. G.P. XIII, No. 3558, von Huhn to A.A. 5 Dec. 1898 (citing Delcassé).
[4] Marder, loc. cit. E. Lockroy, La Défense Navale (Paris-Nancy 1900), pp. 3-10, 29; cf. Faure, ubi supra, p. 35. D.D.F. XIV, No. 454, note d'un agent de renseignements 25 Oct. (The 'agent', who was evidently himself an Englishman, cites in English the phrase quoted.)

British China squadron, numerically at least weaker than the combined Franco-Russian Fleets in Far Eastern waters, would have had
to be urgently reinforced; and this might have had awkward consequences nearer home when the Anglo-French crisis flared up. But
in a war with France as the principal enemy it would be politically and
strategically possible to accept an initial setback in the Far East, for it
could be promptly reversed once the French Fleet had been put out of
action in European waters.[1]

Delcassé faced these facts when he admitted that France could not
hope to succeed at sea even if Russia fought by her side. But at no time
throughout the crisis did Russia even hint at the possibility of such
assistance. True, on 27 October Delcassé showed Monson a telegram
from St Petersburg in which Russia promised to associate herself 'avec
toutes les démarches' taken by France. Delcassé stated that four other
telegrams of a similar tenor had been received, and offered to show
them to Monson. On the strength of this Monson sent home a 'sensational telegram' stating his belief that France could rely on armed
Russian assistance. But Monson's fears were belied by reports from
other sources, and Sanderson pointed out that the word 'démarche'
normally implied diplomatic action only.[2] Monson also believed that
Delcassé's resistance had originally been stiffened by a series of
encouraging messages from St Petersburg, which had been disavowed
by Muraviev when on 15 October he arrived in Paris and discovered
the true dimensions of the crisis.[3] There had in fact been no such series
of messages; and Delcassé never seems to have relied to any extent on
Russian support. He procrastinated simply in the hope that Salisbury
would relent a little rather than carry the dispute to the point of war.

On 1 September Delcassé had communicated for Muraviev's
observations a recent despatch from London forecasting an imminent
crisis on the Upper Nile.[4] There was no reply from St Petersburg, and
on the 10th Delcassé sent a reminder. Muraviev then told the French
Chargé Toutain, on 12 September, that Britain would probably not
attempt to modify the status of Egypt proper ('la Basse-Egypte'), but
that she would undoubtedly strive to 'assure her predominance' in the
newly-conquered regions. He added the assurance that: 'dans cette
affaire, comme dans toutes les questions relatives à l'Egypte, le
Gouvernement impérial était résolu à marcher d'accord avec nous et à
conformer son attitude à celle du Gouvernement français.' Muraviev's
further remarks were however less encouraging. The Czar, he said,

[1] Marder, *loc. cit.*; cf. *supra*, Ch. XIV, p. 324. For Salisbury's confidence cf. G.P. XIV/2,
No. 3925, Hatzfeldt to Hohenlohe 22 Dec. 1898.
[2] FO 78/5051, Monson to Salisbury tel. No. 189, 27 Oct. (B.D. I, No. 218). FO 78/5052,
Monson to Salisbury No. 554, 28 Oct. (B.D. I, No. 221); minute by Sanderson, 29 Oct.
FO 78/5051, Milbanke (Vienna) to Salisbury tel. No. 47, 26 Oct.; FO 141/332, Fane
(Copenhagen) to Salisbury No. 90 (copy), 24 Oct.
[3] FO 27/3397, Monson to Salisbury No. 580, 7 Nov.
[4] D.D.F. XIV, No. 315, Delcassé to Montebello 1 Sept. 1898, enclosing Geoffray to
Delcassé 25 Aug. (*ibid.*, No. 305).

had suggested that a Turkish protest, supported by the Powers, might be useful; but Muraviev himself underlined the futility of this proposal when he expressed doubts whether Germany, 'actuellement en coquetteries avec l'Angleterre', would lend herself to such a course. Perhaps to avoid further importunities, Muraviev went off on holiday the next day.[1]

This telegram from Toutain was almost certainly the one which Delcassé showed to Monson on 27 October; the different wording reported by Monson is doubtless explained by his having been shown a paraphrase.[2] As for the other four telegrams of which Delcassé boasted to Monson, they have never come to light and it is very doubtful whether they ever existed. A memorandum by Félix Faure does indeed mention 'deux dépêches de Pétersbourg par lesquelles nous étions informés que la Russie nous suivrait jusqu'au bout dans les discussions avec l'Angleterre au sujet de la Haute-Egypte'. These two documents, like Delcassé's boasted five, it had been intended to include in the French Yellow Book, but they were on second thoughts omitted.[3] The first of these is presumably Toutain's telegram of 12 September. The second may have been an independent document, in which case it has disappeared; more probably, it was simply Toutain's extender. On 15 October, as a guide for Delcassé in his discussions with Muraviev, his Direction submitted to him a brief reminder of Toutain's September telegram.[4] Had there then been any other relevant messages from Russia they would surely not have been omitted. It seems safe to conclude that St Petersburg maintained an unbroken silence between 12 September and Muraviev's arrival in Paris on 15 October.

Muraviev's visit was not primarily concerned with the affairs of the Upper Nile. His mission, in company with the War Minister Kuropatkin and the Finance Minister Witte, was to negotiate for the raising of loans and the procurement of arms. But the Fashoda situation was of course discussed between Delcassé and Muraviev. Unfortunately the French documents are completely silent as to what passed,[5] and no relevant Russian documents have ever been published. The reports which do exist, probably or certainly based on what Muraviev revealed to other diplomatists, are not easy to assess, for Muraviev did not regard accuracy, or even consistency in inaccuracy, as a necessary part of his professional equipment. Count Münster, who probably got his information from Muraviev though he does not specifically say so, states very positively that Muraviev advised Delcassé to withdraw from Fashoda in return for the promise of a negotiation on Egypt and on

---

[1] Ibid., No. 342, Delcassé to Toutain 10 Sept.; No. 347, Toutain to Delcassé 12 Sept.
[2] Delcassé told Monson that it had originally been intended to include this tel. in the Livre Jaune; and there exists a file cover for the Livre Jaune bearing a minute which refers to the proposed insertion of Toutain's tel. of 12 Sept. (FO 78/5052, Monson to Salisbury No. 554, 28 Oct.; D.D.F. xiv, No. 429, editorial footnote).
[3] Faure, ubi supra, p. 38. D.D.F., loc. cit.
[4] Note du Département 15 Oct. 1898 (selected for publication in D.D.F. xiv, but omitted).
[5] D.D.F. xiv, Avant-Propos, p. ix.

African frontiers in which Russia would support France. If Muraviev really gave this advice, he must have completely failed to appreciate the real problem which confronted Delcassé. The story which Muraviev told Eulenburg, the German ambassador at Vienna, was very different, in emphasis at least: Delcassé had been anxious to treat the Upper Nile as a purely African question of sole concern to Britain and France, and had indeed strongly discouraged any Russian intervention! At this, said Muraviev, he had been 'most pleasantly surprised', for Egypt was 'dangerous ground' in that on this question Russia stood completely on the French side.[1] It looks very much as if Muraviev seized upon Delcassé's undoubted reluctance to touch the Egyptian question proper[2] as a proof that Fashoda was after all not 'relative to Egypt' and was therefore not covered by the assurance given to Toutain on 12 September.

However, the impression was widespread that Muraviev had strongly advised Delcassé to evacuate Fashoda, and had sugared this pill by a promise to open the Egyptian question in concert with France at some propitious moment. This was the impression that Münster gained; and Monson had it from a source which he does not name, but which he considered 'entirely trustworthy'. Moreover, on 31 October the new Russian ambassador Urosov told Monson that while France would probably yield over Fashoda, 'the underlying question'— presumably that of Egypt—was a much graver matter and might ultimately lead to a general war.[3] But the promise to re-open the Egyptian question, if it was made, was no less worthless than Muraviev's earlier assurances. Not many days after leaving Paris, Muraviev told Goluchowski that Egypt was unimportant to Russia, compared with her interests in the Far East. The British were naturally disturbed by Muraviev's reported promise; but when Sir Charles Scott taxed the Russian under-secretary with its 'glaring inconsistency' with the repeated assurances of St Petersburg's desire 'to avoid all complications with England', Lamsdorff replied that Muraviev could not possibly have held out 'any hope of Russian assistance in the event of a serious quarrel with England on the Egyptian question'. Delcassé, he said, must have misunderstood Muraviev's 'natural professions of sympathy'.[4] Muraviev had from first to last no intention whatever of involving Russia, even remotely, in either present or future French diplomatic defeats in the Nile valley.

Had the Russians been less totally unhelpful Delcassé might have held out a little longer. He would certainly have been no more ready to go to war, believing as he did that even with Russian help France

---

[1] G.P. xiv/2, No. 3893, Münster to A.A. 20 Oct. 1898; Nos. 3896, 3897, Eulenburg to A.A. and to Hohenlohe 24 Oct.

[2] *Supra*, p. 354; *infra*, Ch. xvi, p. 370.

[3] G.P. xiv/2, No. 3893. B.D. i, No. 215, Monson to Salisbury tel. No. 185, 25 Oct. FO 27/3397, same to same No. 572, 4 Nov.

[4] FO 78/5052, Rumbold to Salisbury tel. No. 50, 5 Nov., Scott to Salisbury No. 373, 17 Nov.

must lose. But a belief in Russian support might well have stiffened the determination of the French public to risk the hazards of war. Félix Faure, against Delcassé's strong opposition, insisted that the Russian telegrams (or telegram) should be omitted from the Yellow Book, because 'ces dépêches étaient de nature à surexciter le sentiment national de gens qui auraient tablé sur les promesses de la Russie pour faire des sottises'.[1] In the event, French opinion on Fashoda was divided almost as deeply, though not of course nearly so violently, as on the Dreyfus Affair itself. There was nothing in France remotely resembling the almost unanimous British determination to go to war rather than tolerate the continued presence of the French flag at Fashoda. In England only Morley and the *Manchester Guardian* sang out of tune. The working-class was no less bellicose than its betters; the Yeovil Workingmen's Liberal Association strongly approved the Government's stand, and the newspapers with the mass circulations were the most jingoistic of all. Only that narrowly sectarian body the Social Democratic Federation brought itself to denounce British as well as French imperialism. But in France the Socialists, already a force to be reckoned with, impartially denounced imperialism on both sides of the Channel; and the views of the less class-conscious working man may well be represented by the reported remark: 'Que ça nous fait Egypte? Anglais! c'est pas Prussiens.'[2] To most French workmen, fighting an even harder battle than their English counterparts for shorter hours and better pay, the quarrel with Britain over Egypt and the Upper Nile was utterly incomprehensible and irrelevant.[3] Even the suspicious and hostile Monson, who never wearied of predicting a French *coup de tête*, sometimes admitted that beneath all the noisy agitation the ordinary Frenchman had a profound desire for peace.[4]

The deep division of French opinion on Fashoda does not however coincide with any ready-made distinction between 'bourgeoisie' and, 'proletariat'. Middle-class views were themselves sharply divergent, if their expression in the press be any guide. In Paris most of the more solid journals—*Le Matin* (which was Delcassé's mouthpiece), *Le Temps*, the *Débats*—were usually moderate, and sometimes conciliatory. The Socialist *La Petite République* was also of course pacific. But the right-wing *Figaro* was combative; further to the right was the realm of doctrinaire anglophobia. Here were the papers that really kept the agitation going: *L'Eclair*, which sometimes expressed unofficially the views of the Army; the Orléanist *Soleil*, the chauvinistic *Gaulois*; and—

---

[1] Faure, *ubi supra*, p. 38.

[2] Arie, *ubi supra*, p. 355. Riker, *ubi supra*, p. 67. T. Barclay, *Thirty Years: Anglo-French Reminiscences* (London 1914), p. 161.

[3] At the beginning of Oct. 1898 the Paris building workers struck; on Oct. 15 they would have been followed by the railway workers but for the Government's action in occupying the railways by troops (*A.R.*, 1898, pp. [225-6]). Cf. Barclay, *loc. cit.*

[4] E.g. FO 78/5051, Monson to Salisbury No. 500, 7 Oct.; FO 78/5052, same to same No. 566, 30 Oct.

coming to the almost lunatic anti-Dreyfusard fringe—Déroulède's *La Patrie*, de Rochefort's *L'Intransigeant* and de Cassagnac's *L'Autorité*. But under the Third Republic Paris was no longer the bell-wether of French opinion; and in the all-important provinces there was little reflection of the bellicose fervour of some sections of the Paris press and population. Moreover, a large and important section of the provincial press was openly in favour of evacuation from mid-October onwards. This was not only true of petty-bourgeois organs like *Le Petit Marseillais*, *Le Petit Méridional*, *La Petite Gironde*. The newspapers which were bought by, and presumably reflected the views of, the solid businessmen of Lyon, of Marseille, of Toulouse, of Limoges, of the *Département du Nord*, also strongly supported evacuation and greeted Delcassé's decision with profound relief. Typical of these was *Le Lyon Républicain*, which on 19 October bluntly stated that 'l'hypothèse d'un conflit entre deux grandes puissances civilisées pour la possession des marécages malsains de Fachoda serait absurde'. The newspapers of the great seaports and the industrial towns, far from being the standard-bearers of an aggressive imperialism, were the strongest advocates of a peaceful solution even at the cost of wounded national self-esteem. The provincial bourgeoisie was disillusioned with colonial expansion, especially when it endangered peace and profits.[1]

Not the least worthy representative of this class was the President of the Republic himself. Félix Faure, the self-made industrialist from Le Havre, had in his day been one of the pioneers of colonialism. In 1881 he had entered Gambetta's Ministry as the first Under-Secretary of State for the Colonies. From 1883 to 1885 he had held the same office under Jules Ferry, who had revived the Under-Secretaryship, after its suppression by Gambetta's successor, largely in order to employ Félix Faure in it. In 1890 Faure was one of the founder-members of the *Comité de l'Afrique française*. Yet during the Fashoda crisis he threw every ounce of his influence on the side of conciliation, and by a possibly extra-constitutional assumption of responsibility stiffened Delcassé's backbone to carry on in the new Ministry and order the evacuation of Fashoda. His considered verdict on the whole affair would have been echoed by many a solid provincial bourgeois: 'Nous avons été comme des fous en Afrique, entraînés par ces gens irresponsables qu'on appelle les coloniaux.'[2]

The Dreyfus Affair has sometimes been regarded as a major factor in Delcassé's surrender;[3] but this cold civil war probably weakened his hand less than the division of opinion over Fashoda itself. Of course, the deepening crisis of the Affair made it more difficult to climb down. It may also have increased the Anglo-French tension by arousing fears in London of a French military coup d'état and thereby speeding up

---

[1] Arie, *ubi supra*, pp. 346-64. Cf. *infra*, Ch. XVI, pp. 374-6.
[2] Faure, *ubi supra*, p. 34.
[3] E.g. by Mlle Arie, *ubi supra*, p. 363. This seems a strange conclusion in view of her very clear demonstration of the profound division of opinion on the Fashoda issue itself.

the naval mobilisation.[1] But the measures which the British took immediately after 25 October could not in any case have been much longer delayed had Delcassé persisted in maintaining the French flag at Fashoda. As a motive for the French surrender Dreyfus counted for nothing beside the glaring naval inferiority of France, and for very little beside the determination of many Frenchmen not to fight for 'the pestilential swamps of Fashoda'.

Nor was it only ordinary Frenchmen who were unwilling to fight. The officials of the Quai d'Orsay, for all their 'extremely combative' attitude to England, had never seriously envisaged a war with the British even over Egypt, much less over the Upper Nile. In 1898 they were utterly taken aback by Salisbury's intransigence. J. Darcy, a well-informed publicist who must certainly have had official contacts, sadly remarked 'jamais on ne prévit qu'on pût être amené à quitter le terrain diplomatique'.[2] That this should have come as a surprise may itself seem strange, in the light of the Grey Declaration and of the Note, blunt to the point of brutality, which Salisbury addressed to Hanotaux on 10 December 1897. A despatch by Cogordan of November 1898 explains the psychology by which it was possible for otherwise intelligent and highly trained experts to ignore these unequivocal warnings:

> Les hommes intelligents n'avaient jamais pensé que nous irions jusqu'à faire la guerre pour le Nil, quand nous ne la faisons pas pour le Rhin; mais presque tous admettaient comme une vérité démontrée que jamais l'Angleterre n'ouvrirait les hostilités; que ses vaisseaux n'étaient destinés qu'à effrayer, que ses intérêts commerciaux l'empêcheraient toujours de s'exposer à voir ses communications avec le continent interrompues par l'état de guerre.[3]

Secure in its conviction that the British were a nation of pacific shop-keepers, the Pavillon de Flore went ahead with its projects almost as if Britain did not exist as a Power. The *bureaux* of the Quai d'Orsay, though by no means always kept officially informed, were doubtless pretty well aware, unofficially, of what was being hatched just over the Seine. But what did it matter? The British would never fight.

Hanotaux had discovered, in the course of the West African negotiations if not before, that the British might fight if pushed hard enough. But in July 1898 the *Direction Politique*, with a capacity for 'learning nothing and forgetting nothing' worthy of any restored Bourbon, warmed up for Delcassé the project of evacuation and partition which

---

[1] Cf. Robinson and Gallagher, *Africa and the Victorians*, pp. 374-5. But they seem to overlook the fact that the British precautions were initiated *before* the crisis of 25 Oct.

[2] Darcy, *France et Angleterre, Cent Années de Rivalité Coloniale*, p. 389. Cf. D.D.F. xiii, No. 154, Cogordan to Hanotaux 17 Mar. 1897: 'Ils [sc. the French at Fashoda] formeraient une barrière que l'Angleterre ne pourrait franchir qu'*au prix d'une guerre qui n'est guère à craindre*, ou de concessions qu'il nous appartiendrait d'apprécier.' (Emphasis supplied.)

[3] D.D.F. xiv, No. 531, Cogordan to Delcassé 21 Nov. 1898. Darcy also admits (*op. cit.*, pp. 444-5) that the directors of French policy had failed to take the British warnings seriously.

Hanotaux had rejected in February 1897.[1] Delcassé of course rejected it too, but he must have been shocked to find that the experts of the Quai d'Orsay were blind to facts which to him were already painfully clear. Already crippled by naval inferiority, by ignorance of the local position and by the profound division of public opinion, Delcassé had to devise a policy without expert assistance, for the thinking of the experts had never allowed for the situation which actually arose—and which many less intelligent men would have said was almost certain to arise. Delcassé had no real alternative but to yield; except as an irrational gesture of defiance, war with England was not a possible choice. But Delcassé, a newcomer to diplomacy, played his hopeless hand with a skill, tenacity and sang-froid which made his reputation and—a matter of some importance for the future—gained him the respect and admiration of his British adversaries.

[1] D.D.F. xiv, No. 258, *note du Département* 10 Feb. 1897/18 July 1898.

XVI

THE CONDOMINIUM AGREEMENT AND

THE ANGLO-FRENCH SETTLEMENT

NOVEMBER 1898–MARCH 1899

DELCASSÉ'S decision to withdraw Marchand from Fashoda at once relieved the tension between London and Paris; but it was far from bringing that tension to an end. Until the end of January 1899 it was widely believed in Europe that in spite of Delcassé's surrender England would go to war with France at a time, and on a pretext, of her own choosing. German diplomatists, with the exception of Hatzfeldt, were particularly convinced of this. The Kaiser firmly believed that war between England and France was inevitable, though this did not prevent him from trying to assist the inevitable.[1] At the beginning of November 1898 he had attempted to provoke the Czar into stiffening the French resistance; but his crude appeal to the vanity of Nicholas earned him a stinging rebuff: 'It is always awkward to interfere without being asked in others' business.'[2] The Kaiser thereupon tried to egg on the British by promises of benevolent neutrality and, if Russia intervened, of active support; and repeatedly urged London not to let slip such a magnificent and irrecoverable opportunity of forcibly settling accounts with France.[3] His disappointment at the settlement of March 1899 is reflected in the tasteless and spiteful comment that Salisbury had kept the peace with France 'just because the Queen wants to enjoy herself at Cimiez'.[4]

Still, the Kaiser had some grounds for his belief that the British had made up their minds to go to war. On more than one occasion during November and December 1898 British behaviour seemed to be gratuitously provocative to France. Chamberlain's speeches seemed to show that England was determined to pick a quarrel;[5] so, in French

---

[1] G.P. xiv/2, Nos. 3926, 3927, 3928, Münster to Hohenlohe 29 Dec. 1898, 6 and 10 Jan. 1899; Nos. 3923, 3925, Hatzfeldt to Hohenlohe 20 and 22 Dec., and minutes by the Emperor. FO 27/3455, Monson to Salisbury No. 67, 3 Feb. 1899 (B.D. 1, No. 243).

[2] *Ibid.*, No. 3900, the Kaiser to the Czar 28 Oct. 1898; No. 3905, the Czar to the Kaiser 3 Nov.; No. 3916, the Kaiser to the Czar 10 Nov. Goetz, *Briefe Wilhelms II an den Zaren*, p. 317, No. xviii, 9 Nov.

[3] L. Bittner, 'Neue Beiträge zur Haltung Kaiser Wilhelms II in der Faschodafrage', *Historische Zeitschrift*, clxii (1940), pp. 540-50. B.D. 1, No. 122, Lascelles to Balfour 23 Aug. 1898; No. 123, Rumbold to Salisbury 5 Dec.; No. 124, Lascelles to Salisbury 21 Dec.

[4] G.P. xiv/2, No. 3944, minute on Münster to Hohenlohe 24 Mar. 1899.

[5] Especially those at Manchester on 15 Nov. 1898 and at Wolverhampton on 18 Jan. 1899.

eyes, did the publication early in 1899 of the Madagascar Blue Book with its record of broken French promises.[1] A small but very painful pin-prick was the wounding suggestion that to obviate difficulties about the movements of Marchand's steamer *Faidherbe*, the vessel should be disposed of to the British 'at a fair valuation'.[2] No wonder Delcassé bitterly remarked 'ils me font avaler un crapaud par jour et ça ne finit pas et ne finira jamais'.[3] Then there was Monson's famous indiscretion of 6 December, provoked by Deloncle's proposal that French schools should be established at Khartoum and Fashoda in competition with the Gordon Memorial College. Monson denounced the French 'policy of pin-pricks', deplored the failure of the French to 'profit by the lesson of Fashoda [and] to appreciate the friendly consideration with which they had been treated', and threatened an abandonment of the British 'policy of forbearance' unless they mended their ways.[4] It seemed hardly possible that the notoriously punctilious and correct Monson, even after he had wined and dined with the British Chamber of Commerce in Paris, could have made so aggressive a statement unless he had been authorised to do so.[5]

Monson was indeed one of those who believed that it would have been to Britain's advantage had the Fashoda dispute 'been settled by the sword and not by negotiation'.[6] Other and more influential people, notably Chamberlain, held similar views; but once Delcassé had agreed to withdraw Marchand, Salisbury was always able to keep 'the preventive war school of thought' well in check.[7] Yet throughout November and December 1898 and most of January 1899, the British naval dispositions seemed to be strong evidence, almost proof, that such a stroke was being prepared. Not only was the regular Navy kept at maximum preparedness; apparently even more significant, the commissioning of the Reserve Fleet, begun on 24 October 1898, was not halted, much less countermanded. It seemed very probable that when the build-up had reached its maximum strength, London would present Paris with a string of unacceptable demands and go to war when these were rejected. On 9 December Delcassé frankly admitted his fears to Monson. A fortnight later Paul Cambon warned him from London that 'the slightest slip would be fatal for us'.[8] And at the beginning of January 1899 Delcassé thought it worth while to warn Monson through an intermediary that the destruction of the French Fleet would not be the end of a war; the French would fight on in the

---

[1] *France No. 1 (1899)* [C.-9091].
[2] This proposal was originated by Kitchener and pressed by him, through Cromer, against the advice of Monson. The French in fact used the *Faidherbe* on the first stage of their homeward journey through Ethiopia. It was ultimately abandoned at the limit of navigation of the Sobat.   [3] G.P. xiii, No. 3558, von Huhn to A.A. 5 Dec. 1898.
[4] The relevant part of Monson's speech is printed Barclay, *Thirty Years*, pp. 157-8.
[5] D.D.F. xiv, Nos. 563, 566, Paul Cambon to Delcassé 8 and 10 Dec. 1898.
[6] FO 78/5052, Monson to Salisbury No. 566, 30 Oct. 1898.
[7] Cf. Marder, *The Anatomy of British Sea Power*, p. 332.
[8] FO 27/3398, Monson to Salisbury No. 677, 9 Dec. 1898. D.D.F. xiv, No. 577, P. Cambon to Delcassé 22 Dec.

hope of a favourable change in the European situation. The scare was indeed now at its height. The Paris Bourse, which had been steady throughout the crisis of October 1898, was depressed and nervous in the first week of January 1899.[1]

Apprehension was increased by the very unconvincing explanations which Salisbury offered for this maintenance of full naval mobilisation. In his speech of 9 November he justified it by vague references to the generally unsettled international situation; in December he told an incredulous Hatzfeldt that the Admiralty was simply carrying out exercises which had been planned early in 1898.[2] No wonder the Kaiser pooh-poohed all Salisbury's disclaimers of hostile intent towards France.[3] The usual explanation is that the British were simply reacting to the naval precautions on the other side of the Channel, and that in this way a 'vicious circle of fear' was set up. It is certainly true that the Admiralty demanded the maximum security. On 7 December the Director of Naval Intelligence asserted that 'every day sees the French stronger at sea and better prepared for war', and as late as 18 February the First Sea Lord was still uneasy about the 'so-called defensive preparations' in France.[4]

Yet even the suspicious Monson reported, doubtless on expert advice, that the French preparations were indeed mainly defensive; nor did he believe that the French had any immediate intention of going to war.[5] By February 1899 even the Naval Intelligence Department concurred in this view; and if the First Sea Lord still considered it his duty to make security doubly secure,[6] this hardly amounts to a 'vicious circle of fear'. The British had in fact no reason for fear. Throughout the crisis their overwhelming naval superiority was taken for granted in London and fully recognised in Paris. Fear was an emotion of which neither the British Government, nor the British Navy, nor the British public, showed the slightest trace during the crisis with France. On the contrary, all three were confident to the point of vainglory. There could have been no objective danger whatever in quietly halting the commissioning of the Reserve Fleet once Delcassé had agreed to withdraw Marchand; nor, in the prevailing atmosphere of confidence, is it likely that either the Admiralty or public opinion would have raised insuperable objections had Salisbury wished to take this step.

Salisbury did not continue the naval build-up in order to frighten the French out of the Bahr al-Ghazal. Towards the end of January, just when the negotiations with Paul Cambon began in earnest, a gradual demobilisation began, and 'by the end of February [the

---

[1] FO 27/3455, Monson to Salisbury Nos. 6, 12, of 6 and 8 Jan. 1899.
[2] A.R., 1898, pp. [176-8]. G.P. xiv/2, No. 3925, Hatzfeldt to Hohenlohe 22 Dec. 1898.
[3] Cf. G.P. xiv/2, Nos. 3924-29, Dec. 1898-Jan. 1899, minutes by the Emperor.
[4] Marder, op. cit., pp. 329-35.
[5] FO 27/3455, Monson to Salisbury No. 67, 3 Feb. 1899. Cf. Marder, op. cit., pp. 328-9, citing a report of the British Consul at Cherbourg.
[6] Marder, op. cit., pp. 334-5.

scare] had passed away'.[1] There is however a very close, and surely significant, connection in time between the rise and decline of the British naval precautions and the conclusion in January 1899 of the Anglo-Egyptian Agreement establishing a condominium over the Sudan. This Agreement was the final development of the 'two flags' policy initiated by Salisbury in June 1898. On 4 September this policy had been communicated to the Egyptian Government with the intimation that it was:

> intended to emphasise the fact that Her Majesty's Government
> consider that they have a predominant voice in all matters
> connected with the Sudan, and that they expect that any advice
> which they may think fit to tender to the Egyptian Government
> in respect of Sudan affairs will be followed.

The pretence was still maintained that 'this decision will have no reference to the manner in which the occupied countries are to be administered in the future';[2] but, with an eye to the future, Salisbury forbade Rodd to publish the text of the Note lest this 'somewhat ambiguous' passage should 'give rise to embarrassing comment'.[3] Throughout the Fashoda Crisis the British maintained this prudent reserve,[4] but on 10 November, just a week after Delcassé's surrender, Cromer submitted to Salisbury a draft Anglo-Egyptian Agreement which already contained all the main features of the ultimate settlement.[5] The Agreement in its final form, which reduced the Khedive's authority in the Sudan to an even ghostlier shadow than Cromer's original draft,[6] was signed on 19 January 1899 and promulgated forthwith.

Cromer regarded the Condominium Agreement as a compromise between a direct British annexation of the Sudan, which was politically difficult and financially undesirable; and continuing to treat the Sudan as a part of the Ottoman Empire. The latter alternative would of course 'perpetuate all the international difficulties of which the British had complained during the last fifteen years in Egypt'.[7] But the Agreement did much more than merely remove international difficulties. The legislative and executive powers of the Governor-General, to 'be appointed by Khedivial Decree on the recommendation of Her Britannic Majesty's Government' were for all practical purposes unlimited. No Egyptian law, decree or regulation was to

[1] Marder, loc. cit. Cf. G.P. xiv/2, No. 3930, Hatzfeldt to Hohenlohe 26 Jan. 1899; No. 3931, Münster to A.A. 31 Jan.; P. Cambon, Correspondance 1870-1924, ii (Paris 1940), pp. 23-4, Cambon to Delcassé 1 Feb. 1899.
[2] FO 78/5050, Rodd to Salisbury No. 134, 4 Sept. 1898.
[3] FO 141/336, Salisbury to Rodd tel. No. 82, 22 Sept. 1898.
[4] The delay was deliberate. Cf. ibid., Cromer to Salisbury, Salisbury to Cromer, private unnumb. tels., 24 Oct. 1898.
[5] FO 78/4957, Cromer to Salisbury, separate and secret No. 1, 10 Nov. 1898 (printed, Mekki Abbas, The Sudan Question [London 1952], pp. 160-72). Cf. Shibeika, British Policy in the Sudan, pp. 410-18.
[6] Kitchener was responsible for the amendments: Cromer and Salisbury concurred (Shibeika, op. cit., pp. 418-9).
[7] Ibid., p. 411.

'apply to the Sudan or any part thereof, save in so far as the same shall be applied by Proclamation of the Governor-General'.[1] The British were to have a completely free hand in the whole of the Sudan, as well as in Wadi Halfa and Suakin coolly annexed from Egypt,[2] and not merely in the 'large tracts of useless territory' of a southern Sudanese 'sphere'. Egypt's only practical function in the Sudan turned out to be that of carrying the deficit on its budget. Before the Sudan budget was balanced in 1913 Egypt's payments on this head amounted to nearly a million and a half—the *fallāh*'s reward for the blood and sweat he had expended in the Sudan campaign.

Cromer admitted that the Agreement had created 'a status hitherto unknown to the law of Europe'.[3] But the right of either England or Egypt to conclude such an agreement was itself questionable. It was not easy to see how England, as a guarantor of the Ottoman Empire, could unilaterally create a special régime which practically excluded Ottoman influence from Ottoman territory. Egypt, for her part, appeared to be precluded from making the agreement by Firmans which debarred the Khedive from signing other than commercial treaties, and which expressly forbade him to alienate Egyptian territory. The undiluted application of the right of conquest thesis might however cover Britain, and cover this particular difficulty for Egypt; but this doctrine was itself not uncontroversial. There was also the more fundamental difficulty that Egypt, as an 'état mi-souverain', had in any case no capacity to make such a treaty with England.[4] In fact, the Condominium Agreement did not appeal to the right of conquest; its Preamble described the Sudan as 'certain provinces . . . which were in rebellion against the authority of His Highness the Khedive'. Cromer defended the legality of the Agreement on the grounds that the Khedive was merely making, without any diminution of his sovereignty, arrangements for the internal administration of his territory—a very unconvincing argument, of which no public use was ever made.[5] But the British never had to make a public defence of the Condominium Agreement, for it was never publicly challenged.

Yet in 1897 and 1898 opposition to the creation of a 'régime d'exception' in the Sudan, as a breach of Ottoman and Egyptian

[1] Art. V read: 'No Egyptian law, decree, ministerial arrêté, or other enactment hereafter to be made or promulgated shall apply to the Sudan or any part thereof . . .', save as proclaimed by the Governor-General. Although on the face of it this appears to exclude only *new* laws, etc., *no* Egyptian law was in fact ever applied under the Condominium except by Governor-General's proclamation.

[2] '. . . Whereas it is conceived that for many purposes Wadi Halfa and Suakin may be most effectively administered in conjunction with the reconquered provinces . . .' (Preamble). The territorial extent of the Sudan was also deliberately defined (Art. 1) so as to permit independent British acquisitions in the Equatorial regions. (The east bank of the Nile, south of Lat 5°N, was in fact administered as part of British East Africa until 1 Jan. 1914.)

[3] FO 78/4957, *loc. cit.*

[4] Cf. Cocheris, *Situation Internationale*, pp. 505-9, for an unsparing exposure of the Condominium Agreement's legal weaknesses.

[5] Cromer himself thought this argument 'weak', and preferred 'to take [his] stand boldly' on the right of conquest. But in view of the Preamble, this 'stand' seems even weaker.

rights, had been one of the major objectives of French policy on the Nile.[1] Here was a 'régime d'exception' with a vengeance. Not content with the humiliating ejection of France from Fashoda, England now faced her with the practical substitution of British for Egyptian authority throughout the Sudan. This had indeed become, since August 1898 at the very latest, the principal objective of Salisbury's policy, an end to which even the major crisis over Fashoda had been a means. The continued British naval mobilisation was a hint to Paris that France had better swallow the Condominium Agreement without fuss. Delcassé took the hint. Nisard, the *Directeur Politique*, did indeed toy with the notion of 'une constatation des violations de droit': 'Elle peut même être *concertée*, et servir de base à la négociation des compensations. En tout cas, le Directeur politique croit qu'il y a lieu de ne pas laisser se produire ce grand changement sans nous créer un titre auprès de l'Angleterre, grâce à notre tolérance.' Delcassé knew better. He answered this minute in one word—'Attendre';[2] and he waited for ever.

When Nisard suggested that the 'constatation' might be 'concerted', he was drawing attention to the fact that France was not the only Power whose rights and interests were violated by the Condominium Agreement. Its very doubtful legality was in itself, as Cogordan remarked, 'un défi lancé à l'Europe'.[3] Nor were the Powers involved merely in their capacity as guarantors of the Ottoman Empire. All the privileges which they enjoyed in Egypt—Control of the Public Debt, Capitulations, Mixed Courts, Consular Jurisdictions—were now swept away, at the stroke of a British pen, in the Sudanese provinces. So revolutionary was this change in the status of the Sudan that Cogordan doubted whether Salisbury would have ventured upon it without obtaining the consent of at least some of the Powers.[4] In fact Salisbury had consulted no other Power, and was 'strongly opposed' even to communicating officially the text of the Agreement to any of the Powers. 'What have they to do with it?' he exclaimed.[5] Of course Salisbury was well aware 'what they had to do with it', but he was determined that there should be no interference; and the naval mobilisation was a warning to the Powers in general, as well as to France, that any attempted intervention between Britain and Egypt would incur very serious risks.[6] If ever Salisbury's policy could pro-

[1] D.D.F. xiii, No. 360, Hanotaux to Cogordan 16 Nov. 1897; xiv, No. 11, Cogordan to Hanotaux 13 Jan. 1898; No. 176, Geoffray to Hanotaux 30 Apr.; No. 197, Cogordan to Hanotaux 22 May 1898.

[2] D.D.F. xv, No. 33, minutes on Cogordan to Delcassé 20 Jan. 1899.

[3] Cogordan to Delcassé 21 Jan. 1899 (*ibid.*, No. 29, footnote; cf. No. 33).

[4] 'Sans doute [l'Angleterre] a pris ses précautions pour ne pas se trouver exposée au sort des Russes . . . au lendemain du traité de San Stefano.' (Cogordan to Delcassé 20 Jan. 1899, D.D.F. xv, *ubi supra*. Cf. *ibid.*, No. 47, same to same 25 Jan.).

[5] FO 78/5025, Salisbury to Cromer tel. No. 13, 18 Jan. 1899.

[6] 'La mobilisation des forces anglaises doit être regardée comme un avertissement aux Puissances à ce sujet'—i.e. not to interfere with Britain's settlement in the Sudan (D.D.F. xiv, No. 507, *note d'un agent de renseignements* 10 Nov. 1898). Cf. Cromer, *Modern Egypt*, ii, p. 118: 'No one was prepared to bell the cat . . .'.

xiv The end of the trail: Marchand about to enter Obock, May 1899

xv Marchand acclaimed by a Parisian crowd after his return from Africa

perly be described as 'splendid isolation', it was in January 1899. The French were isolated too, but not splendidly. 'Que faire à nous tout seuls?' wrote Paul Cambon of the Condominium Agreement.[1] Once Salisbury had made quite sure that the French were indeed 'tout seuls' and therefore completely impotent, the naval 'precautions' could be, and were, relaxed.

At the end of October 1898 Monson had predicted that the most severe crisis would arise when the French realised that the British were demanding not only the evacuation of Fashoda but 'a much further abatement of claim' in the Bahr al-Ghazal.[2] But that was before the Condominium Agreement. Once the French had accepted this set-tlement without even putting on record their 'constatation des viola-tions de droit', the Anglo-French negotiation on the delimitation of 'spheres' amounted to no more than drawing an agreed line around territory over which France had already accepted the reality of British control. The negotiation was therefore, contrary to Monson's pre-diction, a very tame affair; and Salisbury and Delcassé tacitly co-operated to keep it so. Delcassé, under Paul Cambon's guidance, offered no serious resistance to the British determination, asserted by Salisbury on 11 January 1899, not 'to share with France political rights over any portion of the valley of the Nile'.[3] Salisbury, for his part, was careful not to push his successes to self-defeating lengths, and insisted to Cromer and Kitchener that the line to be drawn must be a reasonable one. He rejected out of hand their proposal for a frontier, strangely described by Kitchener as 'granting large concessions to France', which would have created a continuous band of British territory from Darfur to Lake Chad and thus have isolated the French Congo from the French possessions in West and North Africa.[4] When on 15 February Salisbury asked Cromer for a definition of the Darfur-Wadai boundary, he warned him to 'be moderate, for if your demands are excessive we may find it hard to defend our frontiers both on the spot and in Parliament'.[5]

It seemed at first as if agreement would be reached within a few days; the main difficulty appeared to be the avoidance of offence to the Turks, who had rights, and to the Italians, who had aspirations, in the hinterland of Libya adjacent to the north-western Sudan.[6] On 21 January Salisbury told Cambon that his colleagues approved the

[1] Cambon, *op. cit.*, ii, pp. 19-20, Cambon to Delcassé 21 Jan. 1899.
[2] FO 78/5052, Monson to Salisbury No. 566, 30 Oct. 1898.
[3] FO 27/3454, Salisbury to Monson No. 11, 11 Jan. 1899 (B.D. 1, No. 240). D.D.F. xv, Nos. 14, 15, Cambon to Delcassé 12 and 13 Jan. 1899. Cambon, *op. cit.* ii, pp. 15-16, Cambon to Jules Cambon, 12 Jan.; to d'Estournelles de Constant, 13 Jan.
[4] FO 141/333, Cromer to Salisbury No. 160, 9 Oct. 1898, enclosing Kitchener to Cromer 8 Oct. (B.D. 1, No. 207). Cf. FO 78/5025, Salisbury to Cromer tel. No. 29, 2 Feb. 1899; D.D.F. xv, No. 57, Cambon to Delcassé 2 Feb.
[5] FO 78/5025, Salisbury to Cromer tel. No. 37, 15 Feb. 1899. Cf. FO 78/5026, Cromer to Salisbury tel. No. 41, 3 Feb., for the suggestion, rejected by Salisbury, that Wadai should be preserved as a buffer-state.
[6] D.D.F. xv, No. 25, Cambon to Delcassé 18 Jan. 1899; Nos. 41, 42, same to same 23 Jan. Cambon, *op. cit.* ii, pp. 20-1, Cambon to Delcassé 23 Jan.

2A

ambassador's proposal, already unofficially blessed by Delcassé, for a frontier along the Nile watershed with merely commercial French access to the Nile. Salisbury even apologised to Cambon for the inconvenience caused by an inflammatory speech by Chamberlain on 18 January: ' "Toutes nos affaires s'arrangeraient bien mieux si M. Chamberlain parlait moins", a-t-il dit avec un soupir; "mais comment empêcher M. Chamberlain de parler?" '[1] But on 26 January a complication arose when Delcassé demanded, in strict and literal accordance with Salisbury's 'Nile-Valley' principle, a partition of Darfur along the line of the Nile-Shari watershed. On 2 February Salisbury insisted on retaining the whole of Darfur; he also raised the question of a possible British commercial outlet on the Ubangi as compensation for the French outlet on the Nile.[2]

Delcassé was prepared to sacrifice western Darfur; but he was prompted by the Colonial Ministry to demand as compensation that portion of the Bahr al-Ghazal lying to the west of the river Sueh and south of a line drawn from Wau on the Sueh to Hofrat en Nahas in southern Darfur.[3] The Pavillon de Flore, which had lain so low during the Fashoda crisis, had begun to raise its head again. Salisbury flatly refused to countenance this proposal, reiterating his objection to 'the floating of the French flag . . . in any part of the water basin of the Nile'. On 10 February Delcassé gave way without serious resistance. He was not prepared to jeopardise a general settlement for the sake of his Colonial colleague, whose proposal he had doubtless put forward in the first place more *pour acquit de conscience* than in any serious expectation of its being acceptable or even negotiable. At the same time he abandoned his claim to a commercial outlet on the Nile, in the face of Salisbury's hint that a similar British claim might be made on the Ubangi.[4]

Delcassé also proposed that the forthcoming Agreement should take the form of an Annex to that part of the 1898 West African Agreement which referred to the territories east and north of Lake Chad. 'Ma préoccupation est, vous le savez, d'éviter dans la convention toute rédaction qui semblerait reconnaître implicitement, en droit, la situation de l'Angleterre en Egypte.' This proposal was communicated to Salisbury on 15 February; he raised no objection, and it was in fact adopted.[5] Cambon now asked Salisbury for a trace of the proposed

[1] D.D.F. xv, Nos. 34, 39, 40, Cambon to Delcassé 21 Jan.; cf. No. 19, Delcassé to Cambon 14 Jan. Cambon, *op. cit.* ii, pp. 18-20: Cambon to Jules Cambon 21 Jan.; to Delcassé, 21 Jan. *Rev. Hist. Dip.* LXVIII (1954), pp. 189-201, 'Lettres de Paul Cambon', Cambon to Félix Faure, 21 Jan. FO 27/3461, Salisbury to Monson tels. No. 15 and 17, of 19 and 21 Jan.

[2] FO 78/5025, Salisbury to Cromer tel. No. 21, 26 Jan. D.D.F. xv, No. 57, Cambon to Delcassé 2 Feb.

[3] D.D.F. xv, No. 68, Delcassé to Cambon 7 Feb.; No. 70, Cambon to Delcassé 8 Feb. Cf. No. 57, footnote.

[4] *Ibid.*, No. 70; No. 76, Delcassé to Cambon 10 Feb. FO 27/3454, Salisbury to Monson No. 40a, 9 Feb.

[5] D.D.F. xv, No. 76; No. 81, Cambon to Delcassé 15 Feb. FO 27/3454, Salisbury to Monson No. 47, 15 Feb. (B.D. i, No. 244).

Darfur-Wadai frontier. This was communicated on 22 February, and detailed discussion began.[1] Early in March another difficulty arose. The British draft proposal of 2 March claimed as part of Darfur the district of Dar Sila, which had for long been disputed territory between Darfur and Wadai. Delcassé rejected this claim, with some indignation, as unsupported by the evidence of the map which the British had originally agreed to use. However, on 7 March he suggested that if the British wanted Dar Sila the French should retain the Zande sultanate of Tambura, with which Paris had a treaty going back to 1896 and which would be cut in two by a frontier running along the Nile watershed.[2] On 9 March Cambon submitted a draft in which the French claims to Dar Sila and to Tambura were presented as alternatives. Salisbury, anxious to retain a clear-cut natural frontier and to preserve the integrity of the Nile basin as an 'Anglo-Egyptian' sphere, waived his claim to Dar Sila. This was the only material concession made to the French in the entire negotiation.[3]

In the third week of March, after all the controversial issues had been settled, the negotiators ran into apparently insuperable difficulties when they attempted to define a frontier between Wadai and Darfur. It was not merely that this frontier was a purely theoretical concept and that in practice the boundary had fluctuated with the relative strength of the two Sultans concerned. Between Wadai and Darfur there existed four petty states—Dar Tama, Dar Sila, Dar Gimr and Dar Masalit—which both Sultans regarded as rightfully tributary to them. Between 15 and 19 March Salisbury cut the knot by suggesting that this frontier (between the eleventh and fifteenth parallels) should for the time being be left undefined, subject to its ultimately being drawn so as to fall entirely between the twenty-first and twenty-third meridians of east longitude.[4] The Agreement, officially disguised as an 'Additional Declaration' to the West African Convention of 14 June 1898, was signed on 21 March 1899.[5] The story of French enterprise in the basin of the Upper Nile had reached its melancholy conclusion.

Salisbury's insistence on the whole of the Bahr al-Ghazal was not prompted by any illusions about its value. In October 1898 he had minuted 'wretched stuff' on Gleichen's absurdly optimistic estimate

[1] D.D.F. xv, No. 81. FO 27/3454, Salisbury to Monson No. 57, 22 Feb. For the detailed discussions, see: D.D.F. xv, Nos. 84, 87, 88, 92, 96, 98; FO 27/3454, Salisbury's despatches No. 66, 28 Feb. and No. 95, 17 Mar. 1899.

[2] FO 97/561, British draft communicated to Cambon 2 Mar. 1899. D.D.F. xv, No. 102, Cambon to Delcassé 2 Mar., enclosing British draft; No. 106, Delcassé to Cambon 7 Mar.

[3] FO 97/561, draft communicated by Cambon 9 Mar. Cf. FO 27/3454, Salisbury to Monson No. 93, 15 Mar. (B.D. 1, No. 245); same to same No. 95, 17 Mar.

[4] D.D.F. xv, Nos. 111, 114, Cambon to Delcassé 15 and 18 Mar. FO 97/561, undated British draft, 15 (?) Mar.; 'Draft given privately by Lord Salisbury to M. Cambon, March 19th'.

[5] Hertslet III, No. 244. The final drafts and counter-drafts are at FO 97/561; cf. D.D.F. xv, Nos. 116, 117, 119, 120, 121, 122. The Agreement was ratified on 13 June 1899.

of its resources. One of the arguments with which in February 1899 he countered Delcassé's proposal for a partition was that such an arrangement would involve the setting-up of frontier-posts in a region where Britain did not wish to burden herself with the expense of an immediate occupation.[1] All the same, he was probably not personally unwilling to make at any rate a token concession here; but when the French were so half-hearted in demanding what British opinion and Salisbury's own colleagues were very reluctant to grant, he naturally took the line of least resistance. Nor did Delcassé set much intrinsic value on the Bahr al-Ghazal. He wanted some of it as a sop to French feeling; but he was not prepared to risk a new dispute with England by seriously trying to get it. For Paul Cambon, and indeed by now for the *Direction Politique*, the important point was to ensure the continuity of French Equatorial Africa and French North Africa by securing a title to Wadai, Bagirmi, Kanem and Borku, and to the oases of the Tibesti and Ennedi massifs.[2] Alphonse de Courcel, in his last despatch from London on 5 December 1898, had stated that:

> Notre principal intérêt, notre intérêt suprême dans cette partie de l'Afrique centrale et dans les prolongements du Soudan de l'est à l'ouest, consiste moins dans la création de débouchés peut-être problématiques vers le Nil, que dans la constitution d'un ordre de choses qui nous offre toute garantie contre l'ingérence d'influences étrangères sur les derrières de la Tunisie et de l'Algérie. Empêcher . . . que des rivaux dangereux puissent se glisser entre le lac Tchad et les territoires riverains de la Méditerranée centrale ou occidentale, pour prendre à revers nos établissements ou notre sphère d'influence légitime, tel me paraît devoir être le but de notre politique dans cette partie du monde. . . .[3]

Delcassé's actions, if not always his words,[4] during the Anglo-French negotiation of 1899 show that he fully shared the views of Cambon and Courcel. All the same, token compensation in the Bahr al-Ghazal would have been popular in France, and very useful for Delcassé's reputation. Delcassé might have fought on a little longer but for the fact that the internal situation in France—rather than any minatory hints from London—seemed imperatively to demand a speedy settlement. By January the French resentment at the surrender in November had indeed died down to a surprising degree. At the Chamber debate on 23 January Delcassé's speech was well received. The shock of Fashoda had dissipated many illusions; as Paul Cambon put it: 'Des choses utiles ont été dites et ont été entendues patiemment.

---

[1] FO 78/5051, minute on a report by Gleichen 20 Oct. 1898. D.D.F. xv, No. 70, Cambon to Delcassé 8 Feb. 1899.

[2] D.D.F. xv, Nos. 38, 40, Cambon to Delcassé 21 Jan. 1899; No. 98, *note du Département, Affaires du centre africain*, [ ] Feb. 1899.

[3] D.D.F. xiv, No. 558, Courcel to Delcassé 5 Dec. 1898.

[4] But sometimes his words too: cf. D.D.F. xv, Nos. 19, 43, despatches of 14 and 24 Jan. 1899.

Les énergumènes se sont tus; la raison seule a parlé.'[1] But this lull seemed most unlikely to last. On the domestic front the anti-Dreyfusard 'energumens' were anything but silent; the Affair was now at its paroxysm, and seemed to threaten the very survival of Republican institutions. The situation became critical with the sudden death, in embarrassing circumstances, of President Félix Faure on 16 February 1899; and the farcical collapse of Déroulède's attempted coup d'état on the 23rd was no more than a temporary alleviation.[2]

From Delcassé's point of view the most sinister feature of this situation was that the anti-Dreyfards were already beginning to build up Marchand not merely as a national, but as a nationalist, hero. From that it was not a long step to putting him forward as a saviour of society, a second and more satisfactory Boulanger; indeed, an attempt was later made to do this, though it did not get very far.[3] Meanwhile, there was plenty to be made of Marchand as the gallant soldier who had defied perfidious Albion, only to be basely betrayed by politicians sold to the Jews. The more extreme anti-Dreyfusards were already proclaiming that 'Dreyfus' and 'Fashoda' were the first and second stages in a vast Anglo-Jewish conspiracy for the total ruin of France. De Rochefort even founded a periodical—*L'Egypte*—the main object of which was to preach this gospel.[4] Marchand, a profoundly disappointed and embittered man, and even before Fashoda second to none in his detestation of *perfide Albion*,[5] was meanwhile on his way home. In November 1898 he had at first greeted Delcassé's orders to retire from Fashoda with violent and utterly insubordinate telegrams which he forced Lefèvre-Pontalis at Cairo to transmit through official channels by the threat to send them *en clair* from the nearest Post Office.[6] Had Marchand's return to a France in deep internal crisis coincided with another prolonged and severe dispute with England in the Nile valley, the consequences might well have been disastrous for the Republic. On 4 February 1899 the German ambassador had noted the extreme anxiety of the Republican leaders to avoid any additional causes of excitement.[7] As a good Republican, Delcassé did his bit.

*   *   *

[1] *Ibid.*, No. 46, Cambon to Delcassé 25 Jan. 1899. Cf. F O 27/3455, Monson to Salisbury No. 44, 25 Jan.
[2] Chapman, *The Dreyfus Case*, pp. 200, 237-8, 249-57. Chastenet, *La République Triomphante*, pp. 129-35, 160-3.
[3] Chapman, *op. cit.*, p. 265; Delebecque, *Vie du général Marchand*, pp. 181-5. Cf. C. Castellani, *Marchand l'Africain* (Paris, n.d. ?1901), pp. 316-51.
[4] For samples of *L'Egypte*, see FO 27/3455, Monson to Salisbury Nos. 66, 96 and 117, of 2, 18 and 27 Feb. 1899. Cf. Langer, *The Diplomacy of Imperialism*, pp. 566-7; Arie, 'L'Opinion publique . . .', *Rev. Hist. Cols.* 1954, pp. 352-6. The lunatic fringe of anti-Semitic anglophobia is well illustrated in Castellani, *op. cit.*, pp. 371-89.
[5] Marchand to Grandidier, 25 Nov. 1897, printed Ménier, *Rev. Hist. Cols.* 1958, pp. 103-5. In May 1899, at Obock, Marchand accepted a medal presented to him on behalf of the *Ligue des Patriotes* by Georges Thiébaud—whom Chapman describes (*op. cit.*, p. 255) as 'the journalist who practically invented Boulanger'. Cf. M C Afrique III 34d, Governor Jibuti to *Colonies* 13 May 1899.
[6] D.D.F. xiv, Nos. 484, 490, Marchand to Delcassé 4 and 5 Nov. 1898; No. 531, Cogordan to Delcassé 21 Nov. 1898.   [7] G.P. xiii, No. 3561, Münster to Hohenlohe 4 Feb. 1899.

In the not very long run Fashoda settled the question of Egypt as well as that of the Upper Nile, though not in the way that Marchand had hoped. Fashoda demonstrated *a fortiori* that Britain would fight rather than allow herself to be worried out of Egypt, and thereby destroyed an illusion which was widespread not only among the French public but in the *bureaux* and in the diplomatic corps. Had the Upper Nile been settled by a compromise—for instance, by an Anglo-French partition at the expense of a prior occupation by King Leopold—the illusion about Egypt itself would doubtless have survived to bedevil relations between London and Paris. No responsible French statesman had ever contemplated a war for the sake of Egypt, except perhaps as a member of a Continental League whose very existence would probably have made such a war unnecessary. To such a league Germany was indispensable, and experience had shown that Germany would co-operate only at the impossible price of a final renunciation of the Lost Provinces. Except perhaps during 1884-5, when the temporary entente with Germany had brought some useful gains, the policy of opposing Britain because of her occupation of Egypt had been dictated by wounded national pride rather than by any rational assessment either of French interests or of French diplomatic and military resources. Not surprisingly, it had turned out to be sterile and self-defeating. As early as March 1899 Paul Cambon had, by implication, written its epitaph: 'Si nous avions toujours cherché à réaliser le possible au lieu de nous perdre dans les rêves nous aurions évité à notre pays bien des déboires.'[1]

Still, a humiliation on the scale of Fashoda might well have been expected to freeze French opinion in this attitude of impotent but embittered protest. Instead, it convinced French opinion, other than the anti-Dreyfusard fanatics and traditionally anglophobe groups such as the nobility and the officer corps, that opposition to England in the Nile valley was pointless because success was demonstrably impossible. Even more surprisingly, this purely pragmatic reasoning soon began to make headway among the colonialists themselves. At about the turn of the century there seems to have been a change in the influences dominating the French colonialist movement. The military explorers—the Mizons, Monteils and Marchands—and the permanent officials—the Roumes, Bingers and Benoîts—all of whom were, on principle, combative towards England by the accepted tradition of their Service or their Office, seem to have lost ground to the commercial and industrial interests of whom Félix Faure, in his colonialist days, had been a not untypical representative.[2] For these men Egypt had long ceased to be a burning grievance. Indeed, they privately doubted whether any change could be an improvement on the exist-

[1] Cambon, *op. cit.*, II, p. 24, Cambon to his son 23 Mar. 1899.
[2] B. R. Leaman, 'The influence of Domestic Policy on Foreign Affairs in France, 1898-1905', *J. Mod. Hist.* XIV (1942), pp. 449-79. This article contains some useful hints and pointers; but further investigation of this subject is desirable.

ing situation, which admirably safeguarded their economic interests. Under their influence the colonialists jettisoned, with remarkable speed and completeness, the Egyptian grievance as a motive for policy.

From 1893 'business colonialism' had been organised in the *Union Coloniale Française*. This was indeed an organisation of firms rather than individuals; full membership was open only to Directors and 'fondés de pouvoirs'. It was a colonialist, but not originally an expansionist, body; its founders believed that 'l'empire actuel est déjà assez vaste et que la tâche à faire est, non plus de conquérir, mais de tirer parti de ce que nous avons déjà conquis'.[1] The *Union Coloniale* undertook serious, even scholarly, research into colonial affairs; it set itself to provide for its members, and for the interested public, reliable and practically useful information, not the propagandist rhetoric which too often filled the pages of the *Bulletin du Comité de l'Afrique française*. Its directing committees also seem to have taken their work much more seriously than those of the *Comité*. They met regularly and frequently, and there was no place here for a take-over by a venal adventurer like Harry Alis. The *Union Coloniale* began rich, and soon became richer. Its research and information services attracted many business subscriptions away from the *Comité*, though no doubt this process was helped by the almost open discredit into which Harry Alis fell towards the end of 1894. At all events, as the *Union Coloniale* grew in membership and resources, the income of the *Comité* declined catastrophically. Between 1891 and 1894 the *Comité*'s income rose from 187,600 francs to 346,800 francs; but in 1895 it plunged to 27,100 francs, and never again rose above the 60,000 mark.[2] By the end of the century the quiet but pervasive influence of the *Union Coloniale* was already overhauling that of the noisier *Comité de l'Afrique française*. Marchand himself, as an out-and-out expansionist, knew and feared this influence. In a letter written from Wau on 25 November 1897 he delivers a tremendous philippic against 'les coloniaux d'exploitation commerciale "rationnelle" ', who betray the true colonial destiny of France and use colonialism as an excuse for banquets, speeches and lectures.[3]

Eugène Etienne was by 1898 rapidly emerging from the ruck of colonialist politicians as the real statesman of the movement. As leader of the Parliamentary Colonial Group, he had worked in close liaison with the *Union Coloniale* from its foundation, and he was increasingly influenced by its technique and policies. When in 1901 he founded the *Comité de l'Asie française*, he modelled its policy on that of the *Union Coloniale* rather than of the *Comité de l'Afrique française*; he was duly rewarded by generous subscriptions from bankers and indus-

[1] H. Brunschwig, *Mythes et réalités de l'impérialisme colonial français* (Paris 1960), p. 149, citing Chailley-Bert in *La Quinzaine Coloniale*, 25 July 1901.
[2] Brunschwig, *op. cit.*, pp. 120-1, 124-32.
[3] Marchand to Grandidier 25 Nov. 1897, *Rev. Hist. Cols. ubi supra*. The monthly dinners and annual banquets of the *Union Coloniale* were important political and social occasions.

trialists. In 1904 he founded the *Comité du Maroc* on similar lines and was supported even more lavishly, especially by the bankers.[1] By 1904 the liaison between Etienne and the 'economic imperialists' was probably complete; but already by 1898 he seems to have begun to share the views of his capitalist friends on Egypt and the Nile valley. He had indeed never been a bigoted, nor even perhaps a very enthusiastic, 'Egyptianist'. When in office, he had given the Nile valley so low a priority that his policy amounted to complete inaction. Since 1892 he had made, at times of crisis, the gestures of defiance to Britain in the Nile valley which his position demanded of him; but he had never been directly involved in the planning of any of the Nile projects. Appropriately, Etienne undertook the task of defending the evacuation of Fashoda at a meeting sponsored by the *Union Coloniale*. He did so on 4 November 1898 in the words: 'il ne faudrait pas risquer les graves intérêts de l'avenir pour une question que nous pourrons reprendre plus tard'. But Etienne's 'reprendre' in November 1898 was like Delcassé's 'attendre' in January 1899—a postponement to the Greek Kalends. In April 1904 Etienne was to be one of the warmest supporters of the Anglo-French settlement both in the Chamber and in the colonialist press. In November 1897 Marchand had written: 'vous verrez que les coloniaux de "l'exploitation rationnelle" ne seront pas les derniers à crier "vive l'Entente" '. It was a sound appreciation and an accurate prediction.[2]

Even in the eighteen-nineties, however, there were one or two leading colonialists who were not merely free from doctrinaire anglophobia but open advocates of an Anglo-French entente. One of these was J.-L. de Lanessan, a former Governor of Indo-China; and it was a sign of the times when in November 1898 the journal *Questions Diplomatiques et Coloniales* opened its pages to him.[3] Another was the impenitent anglophile d'Estournelles de Constant, who had been one of the founders of the French administration in Tunisia and who played an important and conciliatory part in Chamber debates on colonial questions during 1899 and 1900.[4] More representative of the 'new colonialism', however, was an attitude of frank opportunism in foreign policy. The choice lay of course between England and Germany. By the end of the century the *Union Coloniale*, perhaps under the influence of the Algerian Etienne, had in one instance abandoned its policy of pure consolidation. It now regarded Morocco as the indispensable rounding-off of the French North African empire. But it was most unlikely that Britain would willingly permit France to acquire Morocco; a tactical alliance with Germany was therefore necessary.[5]

---

[1] Brunschwig, *op. cit.*, pp. 121-4.

[2] Arie, *Rev. Hist. Cols.* 1954, p. 357. *A.R.*, 1904, pp. [256, 265]. Marchand to Grandidier 25 Nov. 1897, *Rev. Hist. Cols.* 1958, *loc. cit.*

[3] J.-L. de Lanessan, 'L'évacuation de Fachoda; ses véritables causes', *Q.D.C.* v, Nov. 1898, pp. 321-9. Cf. *eundem*, 'Les relations de la France et de l'Angleterre', *ibid.*, vi, Mar. 1899, pp. 259-73.   [4] Brunschwig, *op. cit.*, pp. 116, 144-7.

[5] *Ibid.*, p. 149, quoting Chailley-Bert; Leaman, *ubi supra*, pp. 453-60.

This view was ably expounded in 1898 and 1899 by the publicist Robert de Caix, who was in 1904 to become secretary of Etienne's *Comité du Maroc*.[1] De Caix believed, and British behaviour between 1898 and 1901 gave him plausible grounds for the belief,[2] that Britain was not only opposed to all further French acquisitions but even coveted some of the existing French colonies. There was therefore no escape from collaboration with Germany, a fellow-sufferer from British rapacity who would surely welcome 'accords partiels' with France.[3] But de Caix explicitly refused to adduce the recent history of the Nile valley as a motive for this Franco-German entente. He was perfectly willing to recognise that 'Tell-el-Kebir et Omdourman ont été des étapes de l'histoire', if only Britain would not oppose the remaining colonial aspirations of France—above all in Morocco, 'qui vaudrait une guerre'. To de Caix Morocco was 'la dernière grande chance coloniale qui nous reste', a sentiment which was to be repeated almost *verbatim* by Etienne at the foundation of the *Comité du Maroc*. But once France had achieved her remaining colonial objectives with German help, de Caix looked forward to a substantial improvement in relations with England, quoting Gambetta's dictum that 'on n'a l'estime des Anglais qu'à la condition de s'en faire respecter'. Indeed, de Caix sometimes writes of the proposed Franco-German entente as if it were little more than a tactical move towards an ultimate reconciliation with England based on an equitable colonial settlement.[4]

No sensible person, least of all de Caix, believed that co-operation with Germany could reverse the verdict of Omdurman and Fashoda. The Nile valley, as de Caix insisted, simply had to be written off.[5] But if Britain ever brought herself to compromise on Morocco, the proposed alignment with Germany would evidently be pointless. Moreover, Delcassé was by now aware, even if de Caix was not, that no assistance from Germany, in Morocco or anywhere else, would be forthcoming until, in the words of the *Kölnische Zeitung*, 'the word Alsace-Lorraine shall have disappeared from the vocabulary of French statesmen and of the French press'.[6] Early in December 1898 Delcassé, under the shadow of the British naval threat, had proposed to Arthur von Huhn of this very newspaper a Franco-German alignment against British aggression overseas. He would make every concession to German colonial aspirations; he would even make a formal treaty

---

[1] Brunschwig, *op. cit.*, p. 123. Even before the Fashoda Crisis de Caix had been moving towards this position: cf. his 'Après la prise de Khartoum', *Bull. C.A.F.*, Sept. 1898, pp. 278-81. He developed his thesis in further articles: 'La Leçon de Fachoda', 'La France et l'Angleterre après Fachoda', *Bull. C.A.F.*, Nov., Dec. 1898; and in a book, *Fachoda: La France et l'Angleterre* (Paris 1899).

[2] E.g. the brusque opposition to the French attempt to secure a coaling-station at Muscat (cf. B.D. 1, Nos. 255-60).

[3] De Caix, *Fachoda, La France et l'Angleterre*, pp. 288-90, 305-14, 320-1.

[4] *Ibid.*, pp. 297, 315-20. Cf. Etienne in *Bull. C.A.F.*, Jan. 1904.

[5] De Caix, *op. cit.*, pp. 315, 318-9.

[6] *Kölnische Zeitung*, 15 Dec. 1898, cited Langer, *op. cit.*, p. 568.

and bring it before the Chambers. 'J'y irai demain, si vous voulez.'[1]
The Wilhelmstrasse was not impressed; in any case, its price was still
the same, and the French were evidently still unwilling to pay. Immediately after the French surrender at Fashoda, Münster had reported
that Britain was now more hated in France than Germany had ever
been, and that the idea of a Franco-German rapprochement was
making rapid headway. But by mid-December he had reached the
conclusion that this idea had no political importance, because the
French persisted in harbouring 'quite remarkably impractical ideas'
about Alsace-Lorraine.[2] Even Robert de Caix had never dared to
write the word 'Alsace-Lorraine'; he had taken refuge in such phrases
as 'considérer l'Allemagne comme toute autre puissance', or 'des
rapports normaux et pacifiques avec l'Allemagne'.[3] In his unofficial
discussions with von Huhn, Delcassé had shrouded this subject in
embarrassed generalities: French opinion might perhaps become
gradually reconciled to the *status quo*, in any case Russia would vouch
for the pacific behaviour of France in Europe.[4] By March 1899, when
the scare of a British preventive war had died away, such subterfuges
were no longer necessary. On 2 March *Le Temps* declared that France
had 'not yet reached the point of . . . passing off to the account of profit
and loss the sacrilegious mutilation which has taken from her the flesh
of her flesh and the purest of her blood'.[5]

Delcassé never seems in fact to have had much faith in German
support. His unofficial overture to Berlin in December 1898 was mainly
a tactical move intended to make the British think twice before launching a preventive war. On 9 December, just after his conversations with
von Huhn, Delcassé attempted to impress Monson with the bluff that
in case of war France could count upon German assistance; but almost
in the same breath he protested his fundamental goodwill towards
Britain and his earnest desire for her friendship.[6] Throughout the
Fashoda crisis Delcassé offered French friendship to Britain, admittedly
at the price of concessions in the Bahr al-Ghazal; and he even stated,
with emphasis, that he would prefer Britain to Russia as an ally.[7] No
doubt this was Delcassé's personal preference; but as a policy it can
hardly be taken seriously, for even the closest alliance with Britain
could not have compensated France for the loss of Russian military
support on land. But Delcassé was undoubtedly sincere in his desire
for a general settlement of disputes as the basis for a stable and cordial
friendship with England. Even Hanotaux had felt an urgent need for
more friendly relations when the Russian alliance threatened to bring

---

[1] G.P. xiii, No. 3558, von Huhn to A.A. 5 Dec. 1898.
[2] *Ibid.*, Nos. 3555, 3560, Münster to Hohenlohe 23 Nov. and 18 Dec. 1898; G.P.
xiv/2, Nos. 3911, 3926, same to same 9 Nov. and 29 Dec.
[3] De Caix, *op. cit.*, pp. 287-90, 295-6.
[4] G.P. xiii, No. 3558.
[5] Cited Langer, *op. cit.*, p. 569.
[6] FO 27/3398, Monson to Salisbury No. 677, 9 Dec. 1898 (B.D. i, No. 238).
[7] *Supra*, Ch. xv, p. 342.

French battleships into action side by side with those of Germany against Japan, and to drag France willy-nilly into the dangerous waters of the Bosphorus and the Dardanelles.[1] An Anglo-French rapprochement was indeed the only means by which France could demonstrate that Russia was not her only friend, and so insist that the profits of the alliance be more equitably shared.

Since the German seizure of Kiao-Chow, Russo-German relations had not indeed been so dangerously cordial, from the French point of view, as they had between 1895 and 1897. But political rivalry between Germany and Russia in the Far East was largely counter-balanced by the aristocratic distaste for the bourgeois Republic which was shared not only by Kaiser and Czar but by the entire German and Russian ruling class. Cheap sneers at French statesmen and French institutions were too often the staple of small-talk between German and Russian diplomatists. A very real class solidarity was expressed in the trivial form of denigrating Félix Faure—'ce foutu Président', as the Russian diplomat Osten-Sacken once called him[2]—and of derisively contrasting Faure's shortcomings with the brilliance and grandeur of the All-Highest and Our August Master. The French were made to understand that only a constant flow of gold to St Petersburg could compensate for their repulsive and contemptible political institutions and social structure. Like a smart cocotte, Russia extorted money by the threatened withdrawal of favours.[3] Nor was this an empty threat, even after Kiao-Chow; after all, in May 1897 Muraviev and Goluchowski had agreed to maintain and preserve the *status quo* in the Balkans and at the Straits.[4] Meanwhile the Russian financial demands were becoming more, not less, exorbitant. Early in 1897 the French Minister of Finance had become alarmed at the rate and volume of Russian borrowing, and Félix Faure fully shared his disquiet;[5] but by October 1898 Witte was in Paris asking for more. By 1898 Russian insolence in matters of detail had reached an intolerable level. The Russians were seeking to modernise their field artillery, and were likely to adopt the French 'soixante-quinze'. But in October 1898 Kuropatkin told the French military attaché that if the French gun were chosen, it would nevertheless be put out to Krupp's for manufacture unless French firms quoted a competitive price![6]

A rapprochement with some other Power was essential to France if she was ever to be anything more to Russia than a rather disreputable

---

[1] *Supra*, Ch. x, p. 222; Ch. xiv, pp. 314-5.

[2] Osten-Sacken used these words to the Kaiser himself: cf. the minute on G.P. xiv/2, No. 3927. William was never backward in reminding his cousin Nicholas that French Republicans were 'damned rascals', 'Revolutionists *de natura*', who in properly managed countries would be 'treated—rightly too—as people who must be shot or hung' (cf. Goetz, *op. cit.*, pp. 295-9. letters of 25 Sept. and 25 Oct. 1895).

[3] Cf. Taylor, *The Struggle for Mastery*, pp. 403-4; Chapman, *op. cit.*, pp. 112-3.

[4] Thereafter, a revival of the *Dreikaiserbund* was at least a possibility.

[5] D.D.F. xiii, No. 117, *note de la Direction Politique* 20 Feb. 1897; No. 266, Cochery (Finance) to Hanotaux 6 July; cf. No. 279, Montebello to Hanotaux 23 July 1897.

[6] D.D.F. xiv, No. 422, Moulin to Chanoine (War) 9 Oct. 1898.

client tolerated mainly as a source of money. This 'other Power' could only be Britain, for Germany ruled herself out by her attitude to Alsace-Lorraine. Thanks to Fashoda and to the changed outlook of the French colonialists, by the beginning of the twentieth century Egypt was rapidly ceasing to be a serious obstacle to Anglo-French friendship. The obstacle was now Morocco; and in June 1901 the Germans made it clear to Delcassé that their price for assistance to France here was exactly the same as it had been for assistance in the Nile valley before 1898.[1] In the spring of 1903 this obstacle began to disappear when Lansdowne admitted the possibility of French pre-ponderance in Morocco. By this time, too, a settlement with England had become for Delcassé a matter of great urgency, for it was already clear that Russia was heading straight for war with Britain's new ally Japan.[2]

The general conditions for an Anglo-French rapprochement were in 1903 more favourable than they had ever been since the days of Gladstone and Gambetta. The chastening experience of the South African War had deflated British jingoism. In France, the Dreyfusard Left had been firmly in the saddle since June 1902. Its leaders were in principle friendly to England; perhaps they tended to be even more friendly because doctrinaire anglophobia, abandoned by the colonial-ists, had by now become almost the monopoly of the anti-Dreyfusard Right. For all the hard bargaining that went into the Anglo-French settlement of 1904, agreement was never seriously in doubt. When in 1895 and 1896 Salisbury had attempted to 'disinterest' France in Egypt by the offer of Morocco, he had been met with a flat negative. In 1904 Delcassé was not only ready, but eager, to be 'disinterested' in this way; he had already written off Egypt, for all practical purposes, in 1899. The Anglo-French struggle for the Upper Nile had begun, both for England and France, as an obscure dispute with King Leopold over some of the most inaccessible and unattractive territory in Africa. It had developed into the most important, and indeed the critical, phase of the old dispute over Egypt. Its climax forced on France a humiliating collapse that awoke her from her dreams.[3] Thereafter France strove, as Paul Cambon had recommended, merely to 'réaliser le possible'—not only in Central Africa, not only in Egypt, but before long in the whole structure of her foreign policy.

[1] Taylor, *op. cit.*, p. 397.

[2] A useful summary of Anglo-French relations between 1900 and 1904 will be found in F. H. Hinsley, 'British Foreign Policy and Colonial Questions, 1895-1904', *C.H.B.E.* III, Ch. XIII, at pp. 530-7.

[3] 'Faut-il d'aussi dures leçons pour nous rendre raisonnables?'—Cambon to Delcassé 21 Jan. 1899 (D.D.F. xv, No. 40). Cf. Cambon to his son, 23 Mar. 1899 (Cambon, *op. cit.* II, p. 24).

XVII

DIPLOMACY, IMPERIALISM AND THE

UPPER NILE : POLICIES AND MOTIVES

OF the Powers involved in the struggle for the Upper Nile only Leopold II, in Africa a complete autocrat with no conflicting domestic interests to resolve, was able to pursue a policy of consistent territorial aggrandisement. From this he was deflected only by physical force, or by the direct threats of other Powers. He persisted in it even after 1899. In 1903, after rejecting as inadequate a proffered British cession in the western Bahr al-Ghazal, he attempted to occupy his leases under the 1894 Agreement. He met British refusals to recognise these leases by repudiating his recognition of the 'British sphere', and in October 1905 formally annexed the disputed territories to the Congo State. It was, once again, only under direct threat of force that in May 1906 he was constrained to abandon his claims and to accept as a consolation prize the Lado Enclave—a derisory memento of his dreams of Nilotic Empire.[1]

Leopold attempted to combine the role of a Great Power in Africa with that of a minor Power in Europe; and as African affairs began to loom larger in the relations of the Great Powers themselves, he was necessarily squeezed out. His ultimate failure should not however obscure the critical importance of the part which he played down to 1894. In 1886 it was his action in releasing Stanley, in Congolese interests, to lead the Emin Pasha Relief Expedition which far more than Mackinnon's rather woolly projects transformed this venture from an exercise in Egyptian withdrawal into an exercise in European expansion—albeit an unsuccessful one. Stanley's exploits put the Upper Nile on the map as a sphere of potential European competition. Leopold's drive for the Nile in 1890 and after kept it there, by challenging both France and Britain and by arousing fears, which the King carefully fostered, that the Congo State would align itself with either London or Paris. It was King Leopold's initiative, and the real or supposed French reactions to it, which forced London to come to terms with him in April 1894. The result was a confrontation of Britain and France as open rivals, and the transformation of the Upper Nile ques-

[1] For details see: Sanderson, 'Leopold II and the Nile Valley', *Proc. Sud. Hist. Assoc.*, 1955; R. O. Collins, 'Anglo-Congolese Negotiations, 1900-1906', *Zaïre*, xii, 5 and 6 (1958), pp. 479-512, 619-54.

tion from an obscure dispute with a minor Power to a major factor in both British and French policy.

King Leopold's role in the politics of the Nile basin between 1890 and 1894 was almost a repeat performance of the part he had played in the Congo basin some ten years earlier. On each occasion the King's restless encroachments prompted France to defend her interests, in 1882 by the ratification of de Brazza's treaty with Chief Makoko, in 1893 by the attempted launching of the Monteil Mission.[1] On each occasion the French action stirred up a previously dormant rivalry with Britain; and this rivalry, once awakened, led to far-reaching developments in the 'Partition of Africa'. Whatever the importance of other factors—and between 1882 and 1885 they were of course very important indeed—it was nevertheless King Leopold's initiative which had brought them into action. There would have very probably been a European partition of Africa even if Leopold had never existed. But the King's activities played a major part in determining the timing, and to some extent the development, of the partition that actually did take place between 1882 and 1899.

Leopold's motives for African aggrandisement are usually discussed in terms of his personal character: a hunger for power, and a skill in diplomatic and financial manœuvre, for which he could find no scope as the constitutional monarch of a small and permanently neutral country. This account is doubtless correct so far as it goes. But the King frequently claimed that by his African acquisitions he was safeguarding the economic future of Belgium; and he seems from a very early stage to have contemplated bequeathing his empire to the Belgian State. The political representatives of the Belgian people certainly looked this gift horse very much in the mouth; but the legend of Leopold's complete isolation from Belgian interests has been exaggerated. He was in fact able to obtain the collaboration of important sections of Belgian capital; of Albert Thys and the Sociétés de la rue Bréderode, and a little later of the Antwerp bankers' consortium led by Alexandre Browne de Tiège.[2] The dominant motive of these men was evidently financial gain; the same motive attracted much British and even French capital into the Congo State. As early as 1863 Leopold had written: 'Le Belge n'exploite pas le monde; c'est un goût à faire naître chez lui.'[3] In this task he succeeded. Once Belgium had at last taken over the Congo, its development and exploitation soon became a major Belgian interest.

Economic motives operated right down to the grass-roots of Con-

---

[1] The general argument is not affected by Stengers' contention ('L'Impérialisme colonial . . .', J.A.H. III, 3 (1962), pp. 471-2), that Leopold began to work for political domination only when French action began to threaten his earlier plans for purely economic control.
[2] Cf. Stengers, 'La première tentative de reprise', Bull. Soc. Roy. Belge Géog., 1949; eundem, 'Note sur l'histoire des finances congolaises', Bull. I.R.C.B., 1954. Cf. also B.C.B. II, Empain; III, Browne de Tiége; IV, Thys.
[3] Citation in Brunschwig, Mythes et Réalités, p. 32, Cf. Ascherson, The King Incorporated, pp. 239-40, for Leopold's role as 'the leader of the nation's industrial expansion'.

golese administration; the French noted with distaste the 'âpreté au gain matériel' of the King's agents on the upper Ubangi. Similar motives surely played their part in the King's thirst for territory on the Upper Nile and elsewhere; and since between 1890 and 1894 Leopold set the pace in the scramble for the Upper Nile, on this account alone economic motives cannot be excluded from the forces which promoted international competition for this region. To call 'economic imperialism' a 'mythological beast'[1] is doubtless a valid criticism of the unsatisfactory models which at present exist. But it would be both difficult and misleading to call by any other name those aspects of Leopoldian imperialism which attracted over thirty million francs in investments and which, in the thirty years between 1878 and 1908, brought in a profit of twenty-six million francs on a total outlay of just over forty.[2] King Leopold's economic imperialism seems to have been exceptional in its success rather than in its nature; and the continued expenditure of powder and shot on a 'mythological beast' seems extravagant when there is evidently a real animal available as a target.

Italian intervention in the politics of the Nilotic Sudan was as erratic as that of King Leopold was consistent. Here, too, policy was determined by personality; but in Italy economic calculations played no significant part in its formulation. Crispi sought to make Italy a truly great Power by a vision of imperial greatness and a burden of imperial responsibility which should wean her from the contemplation of her multiple internal divisions. He was not alone in this vision, nor in his attempt to realise it in Ethiopia and the eastern Sudan. What distinguished Crispi was his willingness, in pursuit of this objective, to hazard if not to sacrifice the indispensable friendship with England in the Mediterranean. This conflict of interests could not be reconciled. Crispi therefore attempted simply to conceal it. Again and again he was forced to deceive even his own supporters about the scope of his African operations and the state of his relations with England. On Crispi's fall, di Rudinì re-affirmed the friendship with England by a definitive renunciation of 'unimportant and even doubtful' claims in the Nile valley; he hoped to obtain in return positive British support for Italian aspirations in North Africa, where di Rudinì's imperial appetite seems to have been at least as keen as that of his predecessor. The return of Crispi in December 1893 led to renewed military and diplomatic probings in the eastern Sudan. But Rosebery and Cromer did not respond to offers of parallel action against the Mahdists; and di Rudinì's surrender in the Nile valley turned out to be irreversible. By 1895 increasing difficulties in Ethiopia had pushed Crispi's Nilotic aspirations into the background; and at Adowa they shared the common ruin of an imperialism based almost entirely on a romantically grandiose vision of Italy's place in the world.

[1] R. Robinson, reviewing Brunschwig, op. cit., at J.A.H. ii, 1 (1961), p. 158.
[2] J. Stengers, Combien le Congo a-t-il coûté à la Belgique?, Brussels 1957.

Prompted by a well-nigh mystical conception of national grandeur, Crispi invented interests for Italy in the Nile valley. From not entirely dissimilar motives, certain ultra-Orthodox and Slavophile groups invented interests for Russia in Ethiopia. It is, and doubtless always was, very far from clear just what these interests were; but they were evidently connected in some way with the profound spiritual affinity, discernible to the eye of faith, between Orthodox Russia and Monophysite Ethiopia.[1] These 'interests' had of course no economic basis and indeed no serious political basis; Ethiopia seems to have been no more than the political hobby of a few highly placed individuals. But this camarilla had the ear of the Czar, and its influence almost completely stifled the official policy of co-operation with France in Ethiopia. In the Nile valley itself Russia had of course no interests, except to keep the Egyptian Question in existence as a barrier between England and France. British expansion in the Sudan was indeed not unwelcome, as a distraction of England from regions of direct rivalry with Russia. Russian policy in the Nile valley, from Giers to Muraviev, never strayed far from these principles. Lobanov's sudden discovery, in March 1896, of a major Russian interest in Egypt and the Suez Canal, was a tactical move to forestall a possible *modus vivendi* between England and France, and if possible to free the hands of Russia by aligning Berlin with Paris in a quarrel with England over Egypt. When the Germans refused to act, Lobanov evaded collaboration with France, having already succeeded in his primary objective of fomenting an open dispute between France and England. In 1897 and 1898 Muraviev kept as aloof as possible from the Anglo-French conflicts in Africa; but having in September 1898 given a rather rash promise of support in matters 'relating to Egypt', he was forced to look for a loophole. He found one in Delcassé's thesis, developed for domestic reasons, that Fashoda was an 'African' and not an 'Egyptian' affair. But the excuse hardly mattered; Muraviev was in any case determined not to involve Russia in the inevitable defeat of France either by diplomacy or by armed force.

The Germans, having relinquished their direct interest in the Upper Nile in July 1890, did not thereafter take any serious initiative in its politics. Their Protocol with France in February 1894 was indeed intended to impress upon Rosebery, by a demonstration of Franco-German solidarity against Britain in Africa, how deeply Berlin resented his supposedly shifty policy in Europe and his very grudging co-operation overseas. But even when this determination had been strengthened by Rosebery's attempt to communicate with Rabīh Zubair, Berlin was careful not to drive Britain into outright enmity by supporting France in the Nile valley. The Franco-German Protocol of February 1894 did not re-open 'the road to the Nile' for the French;

[1] This idea had in fact been exploded in 1888 by the authoritative work of a certain Professor Bolotov (Jeśman, *The Russians in Ethiopia*, pp. 39-44).

it could not have done so, for that 'road' had never been effectively closed. It was meant to hurt Britain, and it did hurt Britain, not on the Nile but on the Niger. It was probably as a gesture of retaliation that Rosebery and Kimberley included the 'corridor clause' in the Anglo-Congolese Agreement. By mid-June 1894 the Kaiser, and German opinion generally, were imperatively demanding the cancellation of this clause; but Marschall had already, apparently without result, exhausted his resources of isolated pressure on London. He was therefore forced to seek the assistance of France, and to offer a cautiously limited collaboration in the Nile valley. Fortunately for Marschall, London capitulated before he had committed himself to any specific act of co-operation; twenty-four hours later Hanotaux submitted a detailed programme of action so far-reaching as to be quite unacceptable.

During the Transvaal crisis of January 1896 Marschall again suggested that France and Germany should co-operate against Britain in Africa; but as he was careful to exclude the Nile valley from the sphere of proposed action, his offer of collaboration was rejected without much ceremony. In the course of 1896 it became clear that the price of Germany's support on the Nile was the final renunciation of Alsace-Lorraine; and that the French must go the whole way to this renunciation before Germany would take a single step in the Nile valley. Meanwhile, collaboration with France in Africa was possible only on questions where there was a clear balance of tangible advantage to Germany. So unimaginative and penny-wise a policy was not likely to distract the French from 'the blue line of the Vosges'. But Marschall, Bülow and Holstein, differ as they might in personality and diplomatic technique, all shared a belief that it was unworthy of Germany's power and dignity to do favours which did not bring in an immediate cash return.[1] Berlin also completely miscalculated the strength of French feeling on Egypt as against its strength on Alsace-Lorraine. Whatever Frenchmen might say in moments of excitement, it was absurd to suppose that they would deliberately renounce the Lost Provinces for the merely psychological satisfaction of seeing the British ejected from Egypt. The Germans, not for the first or the last time, quite failed to realise the depth of resentment which their actions had aroused in others. They paid the penalty for this obtuseness when they permitted the Upper Nile question, and in effect that of Egypt too, to be settled without attempting more than a petty colonial squeeze, of which in the event they never drew the profits. It has indeed been suggested that by failing to support France at Fashoda, Germany threw away 'the last, and greatest opportunity by which [she] might have established a peaceful hegemony of Europe'.[2] Be this as it may,

[1] The Germans also over-rated their own indispensability. Bülow justified his much-vaunted 'Free Hand' by the argument that sooner or later either France, Britain or Russia would be forced to seek German friendship on Germany's terms.
[2] A. J. P. Taylor, 'Fashoda', in *From Napoleon to Stalin: Comments on European History* (London 1950), p. 96.

2B

Salisbury himself was always very uncomfortably aware of the potential German strength between March 1896 and March 1899, and was apt to interpret as 'blackmail' behaviour which was in fact no more than a rather crude display of self-assertion.

Except for a moment in June 1894, the Germans always kept their action, or inaction, on the Upper Nile subordinate to their general foreign policy. In France, at the other extreme, policy towards the Upper Nile often followed a completely autonomous course which was sometimes in direct opposition to the broader trends of French diplomacy. Indeed, by 1897 the Foreign and Colonial Ministries were pursuing two separate and irreconcilable policies. Something not dissimilar occurred in London during 1897-8, when Salisbury and Chamberlain differed radically on policy towards France in West Africa. But not even 'pushing Joe' ever dared to imitate the off-hand arrogance with which the Pavillon de Flore sometimes ignored the directives—indeed, almost the very existence—of the Minister for Foreign Affairs.

Between 1889 and 1892 Eugène Etienne had striven to introduce some order into the chaos of French activity and stagnation on the mainland of Africa. His scale of priorities, on which the upper Ubangi and the Upper Nile ranked very low, was maintained by his successor Jamais. But Jamais quite failed to control either the soldiers in West Africa, or the forces which Etienne himself had released. When Delcassé took over in January 1893, the under-secretary's control over expansionist activity was little more than a legal fiction. Mizon was levying private war in Adamawa, a region which London and Berlin regarded as their private bone of contention. In West Africa the *commandant supérieur* Archinard passed on Delcassé's instructions to his subordinate Combes—but with explicit orders not to obey them.[1] On the upper Ubangi the younger men were going as far as they dared in opposition to the 'politique de moindre effort' for so long enforced by Paris and by de Brazza. Even Liotard, normally the most loyal of subordinates, had caught the prevailing infection when he advanced on Bangasso in March 1893. In this situation Haussmann, the *Directeur Politique* at the *Colonies*, tended to regard his function as that of a brake on local excess of zeal. In 1893 he was not looking for new adventures, above all not on the Upper Nile, but rather to liquidate old ones, especially the potentially very dangerous Adamawa affair.

To these hazards Delcassé seems to have been quite indifferent. He did indeed recall Mizon, but evidently with the greatest reluctance. He did not get to grips with the *officiers soudanais* until in December 1893 heavy pressure from press and parliament forced him to appoint a civilian Governor-General, Albert Grodet, with the directive that 'the period of conquest and territorial expansion must be considered as

---

[1] E. Réquin, *Archinard et le Soudan* (Paris 1945), pp. 125-7. Cf. Monteil, *Souvenirs Vécus*, p. 35.

definitely over'.[1] Meanwhile, influenced by Victor Prompt's dangerous hydrological speculations and perhaps by the sudden enthusiasm
of d'Arenberg and Harry Alis, Delcassé launched a drive for the Nile.
Leopold had promoted this idea through his agent Harry Alis, hoping
to enforce a diplomatic settlement on the upper Ubangi as an indispensable preliminary to the French expedition; but to Leopold's dismay Delcassé proposed to challenge the Congolese by armed force as
well as to 're-open the Egyptian question' by a threat to the Nile
waters at Fashoda. Meanwhile, Delcassé kept even his own *Direction*
as far as possible in the dark. Develle, the Foreign Minister, was no
wiser, though he was on record as approving at any rate a mission
'towards' the Bahr al-Ghazal. However, Delcassé invoked the assistance of the President of the Republic himself to overcome Monteil's
reluctance to undertake the mission; and Sadi Carnot, usually regarded as a model of constitutional rectitude, associated himself
completely with a mere *sous-ministre*'s private and unauthorised project to challenge the British occupation of Egypt.[2]

The Monteil Mission of 1893 was not so much a policy as a conspiracy in the margin of policy. It was neatly frustrated when Leopold
II, a conspirator beside whom Delcassé was a beginner, inspired the
probably unwitting Monteil to insist on a previous agreement with the
Congo State as a *sine qua non* of his departure for Africa. Delcassé could
not dismiss out of hand the colonialist hero of the hour and a man who
still enjoyed the powerful support of Etienne. The Mission therefore
languished from August 1893, when Monteil delivered the ultimatum
embodying his 'conditions', until it was given its quietus by Casimir-
Périer early in 1894. Casimir-Périer's suppression of the mission was
certainly prompted by his desire to assert his own ministerial authority
against Presidential encroachment; he was moreover prepared, from
whatever motives, to go to almost any length to please King Leopold.
At the beginning of 1894 there were however good objective reasons
for putting a sharp curb on adventures in Africa. The British had
protested against Mizon's proceedings in language which, if used in
any but an African dispute, might have heralded an early ultimatum.[3]
In December 1893 there had been an accidental but bloody clash
between British and French troops in the hinterland of Sierra Leone.
In January 1894 a French column, sent to relieve a junior officer who
had advanced to Timbuktu in direct contravention of orders, was
ambushed and annihilated. *Le Matin* thundered: 'Les Romains, qui
furent le modèle des conquérants dans l'antiquité, châtiaient sans pitié
l'héroïsme indiscipliné.'[4]

The early months of 1894 were the high-water mark of 'héroïsme

[1] Gatelet, *Histoire de la conquête du Soudan français*, pp. 319-20. R. E. Robinson, *New C.M.H.* xi, p. 620, citing Delcassé to Grodet 4 Dec. 1893.
[2] Carnot's motives are still a matter for conjecture.
[3] D.D.F. x, No. 410, Dufferin to Develle 30 Oct. 1893.
[4] Gatelet, *op. cit.*, pp. 288, 290-9, *Le Matin*, 8 Feb. 1894.

indiscipliné'. Thereafter the *Colonies* (since April 1894 a full Ministry) seems to have exerted a more effective control over its agents overseas. The details of this process are unknown. Boulanger, despised for his lack of expert knowledge, initiated an internal re-organisation of his Ministry;[1] and this may have had some effect. The appointment of Grodet certainly went far to spike the guns of the *officiers soudanais*, in spite of—or perhaps because of—Grodet's quarrelsome, unscrupulous and generally unpleasing personality.[2] Haussmann's rather ineffective *immobilisme* began to be eclipsed by the influence of younger men, more in sympathy with a forward policy and perhaps for that very reason better able to control it. After his return to the Pavillon de Flore in June 1894, Delcassé no longer seems to have held his *Direction* at arm's length; he evidently worked closely with it in opposition to the proposed Phipps-Hanotaux settlement.

In the second half of 1894 the Colonial Ministry launched a series of successful missions—Decoeur, Toutée, Ballot—through the Dahomey gap towards the middle Niger. These successes, and the *esprit de suite* of the whole operation, showed a professional touch which had been lacking in the planning of the Monteil Mission; and they extorted the rueful admiration of a fellow-professional, Sir Percy Anderson: 'It is impossible not to be struck by the admirable way in which the numerous French expeditions are conducted by capable officers.'[3] In sharp contrast to these successes, the Liotard Mission to the Upper Nile, authorised by the French Cabinet in November 1894, made no progress worthy of the name. But compared with the West African expeditions, the 'Liotard Mission' was little more than a *façon de parler*. There was no independent mission under an experienced military explorer. Instead, the drive to the Nile was entrusted to a rather pedestrian administrator already over-burdened by routine tasks for which his resources were barely adequate. Delcassé's apparent satisfaction with this rather half-hearted arrangement invites speculation; it is at least possible that his policy towards the Upper Nile was no longer so headstrong as in 1893.

Delcassé's successor Chautemps was a clear-headed administrator, who took the first and decisive step towards remedying the 'situation anarchique' of conflicting and overlapping jurisdictions in French West Africa.[4] The setbacks to Delcassé's forward policy in the Ivory Coast and elsewhere had raised an outcry in the Chambers; Chautemps insured against a similar danger on the Upper Nile by simply neglecting to reinforce Liotard. This quiet reversal of Cabinet policy may not have been to the taste of his *Direction*; but no one else objected

[1] Monteil, *op. cit.*, p. 110. Cocheris, *Situation Internationale*, p. 431. Cf. Newbury, 'The Formation of the Government-General of French West Africa', *J.A.H.*, 1959, pp. 111-4.
[2] Gatelet, *op. cit.*, pp. 320-5. For Grodet's remarkable career, see Blanchard, 'Administrateurs d'Afrique Noire', *Rev. Hist. Cols.* 1953, pp. 411-20.
[3] FO 27/3232, minute by Anderson 18 Sept. 1895, on Dufferin to Salisbury No. 250, 14 Sept.
[4] Newbury, *ubi supra*, pp. 114-5.

—least of all Hanotaux, who had in November 1894 openly opposed the Liotard Mission. In September 1895, Marchand, presumably with support from the permanent officials, submitted his proposals to Chautemps. Administratively, the essence of Marchand's scheme was that the Upper Nile mission should be given an organisation and status similar to those of the successful West African expeditions. This was a technically sound proposal which Chautemps was prepared to consider; but he was not prepared to act until the political implications of Marchand's plan had been explicitly approved by the Quai d'Orsay. In September 1895 the relations of France with Russia, and of Russia with Germany, were moving Hanotaux actively to seek a rapprochement with England, rather than to initiate action which could, as he well knew, lead only to a violent quarrel. But he seems to have lacked the nerve to kill the project outright. Instead, he hedged and procrastinated. Meanwhile, so long as Chautemps was in office, the *Colonies* took no further action, and the Marchand Mission remained a paper project.

The mission was finally launched, after the fall of Chautemps and Hanotaux, by those who had doubtless supported it from the first—the permanent officials, notably Ernest Roume. Approval was obtained from Guieysse, the new and professionally inexperienced Colonial Minister, when he had been only a week in office. Berthelot, the new Foreign Minister, was if anything even less qualified for his position than Guieysse. Roume found an ally at the Quai d'Orsay, presumably Benoît, the high colonialist *Directeur des protectorats*. Pleading overwhelming urgency—a plea totally belied by their later action—these men rushed Berthelot into approving a project of which the full political implications had never been explained to him. This concealment was almost certainly deliberate; and the mission to the Upper Nile, in 1895 as in 1893, was promoted by methods which can only be described as conspiratorial.[1] But this time the conspiracy was not merely in the margin of policy; it was a conspiracy directly opposed to Berthelot's policy of amicable settlement with England, if possible even in Egypt.

In 1896 the able and aggressive Gustave Binger became *Directeur des affaires d'Afrique* at the Colonial Ministry. Given a tough-minded Minister who would underwrite their policies, the *bureaux* of the Pavillon de Flore could now disregard the directives of a mere non-political Foreign Minister like Hanotaux. The *Colonies* found their tough-minded Minister in André Lebon; and Hanotaux' efforts to assert his control over this formidable combination were pathetically futile. He apparently watered down Marchand's instructions by omitting all mention of the White Nile and of Fashoda, in the attempt

[1] Apropos of the Dreyfus affair, G. Chapman quotes from Nizan's *La Conspiration*: 'Little chances and little men manufacture great events' (Chapman, *The Dreyfus Case*, p. 360). The history of the Marchand Mission inspires similar reflections.

to convert the mission from 'a pistol-shot on the Nile' to a means of comparatively gentle pressure in the Bahr al-Ghazal. He certainly opposed the Colonial Ministry's foolhardy and irresponsible policy—supported, however, by his own *Direction*—of enlisting the military support of the Negus Menelik. But after he had been over-ruled in full Cabinet on Ethiopian policy in March 1897 he seems to have admitted defeat; and he took no traceable action when early in 1897 the Pavillon de Flore issued instructions quite incompatible not only with Hanotaux' own watered-down version but with the original objects of the Mission as approved by the Quai d'Orsay. While the *Colonies* did its best to set the Nile on fire, Hanotaux pursued an expectant and unprovocative policy in this sphere, presumably hoping that 'Marchand n'arriverait pas'—at least, not on the Nile itself.

The Marchand Mission was the last and most spectacular manifestation of the 'imperialism of prestige'[1] which came to dominate French colonial expansion in the eighteen-nineties. In this movement, economic motives played very little part; in the Marchand Mission itself, none at all. Marchand's own motives were those common to the *officiers soudanais* who conquered a sub-continent while Ministers protested and businessmen placed their investments elsewhere: a hunger for action and adventure, ennobled by the concept of 'la plus grande France', and in Marchand's particular case (which was certainly not unique) spiced by a hearty detestation for 'greedy and hypocritical' England.[2] Until 1893 the 'imperialism of prestige' had been restrained rather than encouraged, at least in its more extravagant forms, by the Office tradition at the *Colonies*; Haussmann was utterly opposed to its extension to the Nile valley. Moreover Etienne, from motives which can at least in part be justly described as economic,[3] saw French expansion in Africa largely as the creation of a 'Greater Algeria'. To this vision the Upper Nile was quite irrelevant. But from 1894 the control of policy fell increasingly into the hands of permanent officials who were, in Monson's words, 'extremely combative' towards England. To these men, always ready to assert the prestige of France by 'inventing and intensifying' difficulties with England,[4] the Nile project was very relevant indeed; for its fundamental object was to restore French prestige in the theatre where national pride had received its most grievous wound since 1871.

[1] Cf. Brunschwig, *op. cit.*, pp. 185-6. Stengers discusses this phenomenon at *J.A.H.*, 1962, pp. 472-86. He emphasises that there was, and not in France alone, a widespread belief that 'Ne pas agir, ne pas s'étendre, c'est se décerner à soi-même un brevet d'incapacité, prélude à la décadence politique' (p. 484).

[2] Cf. Marchand's published correspondence *passim*, and especially his letters to Grandidier (July 1896—June 1898), published *Rev. Hist. Cols.*, 1958.

[3] In his public speeches at least, Etienne repeatedly emphasised the economic advantages of colonial expansion (cf. Roberts, *History of French Colonial Policy*, pp. 17, 22, 44, 126, 347).

[4] Both the cited phrases are Monson's (FO 27/3455, Monson to Salisbury No. 48, 27 Jan. 1899).

Precisely because the British occupation of Egypt was so widely felt as an intolerable affront to national self-respect, the Nile project enjoyed support far outside the ranks of convinced colonialists once its connection with Egypt had been clearly established. In June 1894, at the close of the debate in which Etienne established this connection, the Chamber voted unanimously in favour of what at least appeared to be a policy of active reprisal against the Anglo-Congolese Agreement. In December 1896, when a Deputy queried the inflated upper Ubangi budget which, as almost everyone knew, concealed the credits for the Marchand Mission, even the Socialist Jean Jaurès demanded 'une vote nationale'; and obtained one, by an enormous majority.[1] It is hardly relevant to discuss the influence of the Parliamentary Colonial Group in this connection.[2] The Chamber needed no convincing; all that the Colonialists had to do was to make the keynote speeches and to provide any necessary detailed information.[3] In 1882 the French Chamber had shrunk from the largely imaginary hazards of joint intervention in Egypt. In 1885 it had destroyed Jules Ferry because he had become involved in petty hostilities, for the moment unsuccessful, with China. But in 1894 and 1896 the Chamber gave its overwhelming approval to a policy carrying risks beside which those of 1882 and 1885 were negligible. Behind this policy there was little rational calculation. It rested rather on a quite irrational conviction that a successful expedition to the Upper Nile *must* somehow lead to a favourable solution of the Egyptian question; and on the further assumption, less irrational but almost wilfully erroneous, that economic interests would always keep England from making the Nile a *casus belli*. These views were not confined to an ill-informed public and parliament. Astonishingly, they were shared by French diplomatists and by the professional experts not merely in the Colonial Ministry, but in the Foreign Ministry. Even had Hanotaux' position been stronger than it was, it is doubtful whether, after his return to office in 1896, he could have halted the Marchand Mission against the combined pressure of the permanent officials and of public opinion.

Beneath the surface of events, however, the 'imperialism of prestige' was losing ground to the economic imperialism of the *Union Coloniale Française*. The businessmen who formed this organisation relaxed their hostility to further expansion to the extent of regarding Morocco as an indispensable acquisition; but they never had the slightest sympathy for an imperialism of prestige in the Nile valley. They well knew that in Egypt Cromer safeguarded their investments better than any conceivable alternative régime was likely to do; better, indeed, than they

---

[1] *Journal Officiel*, Chambre, 8 Dec. 1896. Cf. Cocheris, *op. cit.*, pp. 490-2.

[2] Cf. however Leaman, 'The Influence of Domestic Policy . . .', *J. Mod. Hist.*, 1942, for some interesting reflections on this subject.

[3] The richest French collection of official papers relating to the Upper Nile was published not as a Yellow Book by the Quai d'Orsay, but by François Deloncle in his capacity as Deputy (*Journal Officiel*, Documents Parlementaires, Chambre 1894, Annexe No. 653).

were safeguarded by the *fonctionnaires* in some French possessions.[1] As for the Sudan, profits here were obviously a chimaera. In the shock and disillusion which followed Fashoda, the interests embodied in the *Union Coloniale* were able to use the influence which they had been quietly accumulating during the previous five years. If the Marchand Mission was the last grandiose fling of the old imperialism of prestige, its dénouement in 1898-9 was the first victory for an imperial policy based on more material calculations. It was at a meeting sponsored by the *Union Coloniale* that Eugène Etienne read the obituary of the imperialism of prestige; Marchand had known what he was about when he so bitterly denounced 'les coloniaux d'exploitation rationnelle'.[2]

French policy towards the Upper Nile was certainly the outcome of a conflict of interests; indeed of a multiple conflict which even included personal interests, not always of a reputable kind. But once the Upper Nile had been publicly linked to Egypt in 1894, French intervention was sustained by a wider enthusiasm which rose to a climax in 1897 and 1898, only to collapse thereafter with a surprising rapidity. In England, too, similar conflicts played their part in the determination of policy; but here too there was a wider enthusiasm for intervention and ultimately for acquisition. Until the end of 1894 this wider enthusiasm scarcely existed so far as the Sudan was concerned; but in 1898 and 1899 it reached a peak from which it did not decline until it had undergone the chastening experience of the South African War. By 1898 it had endowed with strongly acquisitive overtones a Sudan policy which had in the later eighteen-eighties been gradually and rather reluctantly initiated as a purely defensive strategy to protect the Nile waters and so to safeguard the British position in Egypt.

The precise point of origin of this early defensive strategy is very difficult to define. It is perhaps going beyond the positive evidence to assert that Salisbury's approval, in December 1886, of the Emin Pasha Relief Expedition marks even the germ of it. Yet Salisbury's evident reluctance to be pushed forward in East Africa between 1886 and 1889 has sometimes obscured the fact that he did repeatedly allow himself to be so pushed by Anderson and others. In December 1886 he must have known that the objectives of Mackinnon—and of Anderson— were not merely the final disengagement of Egypt from the southern Sudan which Baring wanted and was willing to pay for. But whatever the real motives of Salisbury, to other Powers the Relief Expedition looked like an essay in imperial expansion. Particularly in Germany, competitive interest in the Upper Nile was aroused; and although Bismarck gave no countenance to this, his new protectorate over the Tana-Juba region in October 1889 suggested that Germany might again be preparing to move forward in East Africa. Meanwhile, in

---

[1] Cf. the complaints of bureaucratic inefficiency and obstruction expressed at the 1894 banquet of the *Union Coloniale* (Brunschwig, *op. cit.*, p. 133).
[2] Marchand to Grandidier, 25 Nov. 1897 (*Rev. Hist. Cols.*, *ubi supra*).

Equatoria, the reaction of Emin's Sudanese soldiers to Stanley's intervention led to disturbances of which the upshot was anarchy and a vacuum of power. The status of the country was a standing invitation to imperial competitors; but its condition ruled out a possible penetration by the British East Africa Company, which was probably the solution towards which Salisbury was working by 1888. Before the end of 1889 Salisbury recognised that he would soon have to engage in a direct diplomatic defence of the Upper Nile; and the safeguarding of the Nile waters now became 'a separate and dominating factor' in his diplomacy.

Until the fall of Bismarck, however, Salisbury seems to have been confident that Germany would not sacrifice British goodwill by infringing the implicit veto on penetration into the Nile basin. The young Emperor's take-over in March 1890 implied both a danger and an opportunity: a danger that uncontrolled Anglo-German competition in Africa might threaten the Upper Nile and so disrupt the 'terms of amity' which were even more important to London than to Berlin; an opportunity of safeguarding the Upper Nile, and consolidating Anglo-German friendship, without making territorial concessions in Africa unacceptable to the 'Companies and missionaries'. In May and June 1890 Salisbury bargained with great skill and success, using Heligoland as a means of aligning the Emperor's naval enthusiasm against the demands of the German colonialists. Before the end of 1889 Italy had also appeared as a competitor, in the eastern Sudan; but her aspirations caused more anxiety to Baring than they did to Salisbury, who was better aware of her fundamental weakness as a Power and her dependence upon England in the Mediterranean. Especially after it became clear, in the course of 1890, that the supposed weakness of the Mahdist state had been greatly exaggerated, Salisbury was content to await the fall of Crispi; whereupon di Rudinì abandoned Italy's claims with a good grace in March 1891. But Salisbury's very skill in protecting the Nile waters without arousing resentment in Berlin and Rome led to French and Russian suspicions that he had secretly aligned himself with the Triple Alliance. The Anglo-German Agreement, which did at least represent a considered decision to maintain a loose link with Berlin, was particularly suspect; but these suspicions had no positive result, partly because Salisbury was able to make an immediate counter-gesture of conciliation to France in Africa. But the 1891 Agreement with Italy, to Salisbury no more than a slightly overdue piece of diplomatic tidying-up, initiated a series of events which led directly to Russian proposals for a closer entente with France.

Although Salisbury had in 1890 foreseen and evaded the diplomatic penalty which his skill incurred in 1891, he had been forced during the German negotiations to make a domestic concession which was later to have embarrassing diplomatic consequences. Germany's territorial sacrifices, substantial though they were, did not satisfy the British East Africa Company; and Salisbury's approval of the 'Mackinnon Treaty' was the Company's price for calling off its opposition to the Anglo-German settlement. It was a price which Salisbury's precarious parliamentary position compelled him to pay. But he took neither Mackinnon nor his treaty seriously; and once the Anglo-German Agreement had been safely concluded, he denounced the Mackinnon Treaty, by implication, both publicly in the Lords and privately to the Germans. Salisbury had taken Mackinnon's measure; but he had not taken that of Leopold, who occupied the Nile basin and insisted on the validity of his title. A problem was thus created which was solved only by the Anglo-Congolese Agreement; and this in its turn initiated the open Anglo-French dispute on the Upper Nile.

The Mackinnon Treaty shows how a private interest, usually regarded—and not least by Salisbury himself—as almost contemptibly unimportant, could in a particular domestic situation exert pressure which ultimately had far-reaching effects upon international diplomacy. The 'Mackinnon squeeze' seems however to be the only example of its kind in British policy towards the Upper Nile. Goldie did indeed dominate the West African side of the Phipps-Hanotaux negotiations through Anderson; but this was hardly by pressure, for pressure implies resistance. Confronted with Goldie's dynamic personality, Anderson's usual hardheadedness seems to have deserted him, and he accepted Goldie's most fantastic claims without a trace of doubt or misgiving.

Under the Gladstone administration from 1892 to 1894 the British struggle for the Upper Nile was only incidentally with King Leopold. The major struggle was between Rosebery and his colleagues. The Cabinet frustrated a positive decision on Uganda, and therefore a 'reasonable arrangement' with Leopold; and drove Rosebery to the almost futile expedient of ordering Portal to intervene on the Upper Nile, and to the very questionable expedient of attempting to influence the German-protected Rabīh Zubair. The latter episode initiated a series of provocations and counter-provocations between London and Berlin, of which the upshot was the withdrawal of the 'Corridor Clause' under heavy German pressure. Until Rosebery had presented Berlin with this handsome little diplomatic triumph, Hanotaux had been willing to talk about the possible 'suspension' of the leases to Leopold, a solution which might have been formulated so as tacitly to recognise the British sphere. Afterwards, of course, 'il fallait en finir tout de suite'.[1] Without the German complication, the Anglo-French dispute might just possibly have been settled before the 'prestige imperialists' at the Quai d'Orsay and the Pavillon de Flore had really played themselves in.

By 1894, however, there were 'prestige imperialists' in power on

---

[1] Cf. D.D.F. xi, Nos. 123 and 163.

both sides of the Channel. Rosebery's insistence on 'pegging out claims' implied more than the mere pre-empting of markets and raw materials. In March 1893 he told the Colonial Institute that it was 'part of our responsibility and heritage to take care that the world, so far as it can be moulded by us, shall receive an English-speaking complexion and not that of other nations'.[1] Rosebery's negotiations with France in 1894 were conducted in a very different spirit from those of Salisbury with Germany in 1890, when Salisbury seems to have refrained from demanding anything so positive as a 'sphere' until forced to do so by the formalistic exigencies of the Wilhelmstrasse. It was not merely that Rosebery rejected the self-denying arrangement; doubtless no Prime Minister in Rosebery's situation could have accepted this, for all its value as a practical safeguard for the Nile waters. The whole negotiation was dominated by a highly combative attitude towards France, in which Rosebery's affectation of contemptuous indifference to Hanotaux' proposals was reinforced by Anderson's aggressively acquisitive defence of supposed 'possessions' in West Africa. The British, in return for major demands both in West Africa and in the Nile valley, offered nothing except a grudging partition of Borgu; and Anderson looked upon Phipps' task as that of browbeating Hanotaux into accepting these very ungenerous terms. In the eighteen-seventies and eighteen-eighties the Foreign Office had often toyed with the idea of using Gambia as *matière d'échange*;[2] such a thought never crossed their minds in 1894. Hanotaux at one stage suggested that agreement might be easier if Britain would cede the small and barely inhabited Isles de Los, off French Guinea. Phipps replied: 'If I was to dare to mention such a thing I should expect, at best, to start for Brazil next week and pass my days there!'[3] Phipps had predicted with considerable accuracy the exile by which he expiated his failure to realise that the negotiation turned at least as much on 'possessions' as on the security of the Nile waters.

In the summer of 1894 popular 'imperialist' sentiment towards the Upper Nile seems to have rather lagged behind that of the African Department. When in July 1894 Lugard wrote in *Blackwood's* on 'The New African Crisis with France and Germany', his first task was to explain that there was indeed a crisis.[4] But if the analysis of d'Estournelles de Constant be any guide, by the end of 1894 such sentiment was not only very strong, but to be found in circles not previously regarded as 'imperialist'.[5] With the Grey Declaration of March 1895 it of course became clearly, even noisily, explicit. But there was no imperialist pressure for the Sudan advance of March 1896, perhaps not least

[1] Cited Langer, *Diplomacy of Imperialism*, pp. 77-8.
[2] Hargreaves, *Prelude to the Partition of West Africa*, pp. 145-252, *passim*.
[3] FO 27/3186, Phipps to Kimberley, private, 14 Sept. 1894.
[4] Anon. [F. D. Lugard], 'The New African Crisis with France and Germany', *Blackwood's Magazine*, CLVI, July 1894, pp. 145-58.
[5] D.D.F. XI, No. 303, d'Estournelles de Constant to Hanotaux, 3 Dec. 1894.

because the *northern* Sudan was still looked upon as a region where the profits of action would accrue, not to England, but to Egypt. If so, no wonder Chamberlain warned Salisbury that the Government would be deserted by its own supporters if British troops had to be sent to the rescue of the Egyptians. Nor was the advance an attempt to protect the Nile waters from French encroachment; in Salisbury's eyes an advance from the north was not a safeguard, but an almost certain sacrifice, of security on the Upper Nile. Salisbury's action was prompted by European motives: the need to make a gesture of solidarity with Italy, and to quiet German fears of an Anglo-French entente, as an insurance against the possible disintegration of the Triple Alliance and the emergence of new alignments less favourable to England.

Local factors soon began to extend the minimal advance which Salisbury had authorised as his gesture to the Triplice. Even as Hunter was making his military promenade from Sarras to Akasha, Cromer was insisting, on purely Egyptian grounds, that the advance must not stop short of Dongola. After the fall of Dongola, the development of the campaign—even the decision to send British reinforcements—was determined by the real or supposed strength of the Mahdists, not by fears about the security of the southern Sudan. Salisbury did indeed attempt to intervene directly on the Upper Nile. But the Macdonald Mission, ill-conceived, worse executed and in any case frustrated by the mutiny of the Sudanese in Uganda, had no effect whatever on the course of events.[1] Only in the summer of 1898 did it begin to appear probable that the advance from the north would after all play a critical part in the settlement of the south.

The British reaction to Marchand's presence at Fashoda disconcerted the French by its almost unanimous vehemence. British opinion still resented the humiliation of the Port Arthur climb-down, and there was a widespread feeling—just as d'Estournelles had predicted in 1894—that it was now or never to assert Britain's status as a Power. In March 1898 Francis Bertie had written: 'Unfortunately France, Russia and Germany have got it into their heads that we shall never stand up to one First Class Power, much less 2 or 3 . . .' In April he was echoed by the *Contemporary Review*: 'There is not a serious politician on the continent of Europe who believes that our present Government will risk a war, however great the provocation.'[2] France, too, had to be 'put in her place'. In 1897 Chamberlain had on at least one occasion reacted to French claims in West Africa by the marginal comment, 'Cheek!'.[3] At Fashoda the French were 'giving cheek' in

---

[1] Except to deepen the suspicions of Menelik, already aroused by Kitchener's advance into the Sudan.

[2] Bertie to Lascelles 16 Mar. 1898, cited Steiner, 'The Last Years of the Old Foreign Office', *H.J.*, 1963, p. 69. Anon., 'The Failure of our Foreign Policy', *The Contemporary Review*, April 1898, cited Langer, *op. cit.*, p. 488.

[3] FO 27/3373, minute by Chamberlain 11 Nov. 1897, on the Niger Commissioners' report of 10 Nov.

the most flagrant manner possible. Kitchener's reporting made their claim to occupation seem an impudent fraud; and on the strength of a bogus occupation, secretly launched, the French were challenging deeply held, if rarely expressed, convictions about the relative rank of Britain and France as Powers.[1] It was not for nothing that *Punch* depicted Marchand as a tattered organ-grinder disturbing the afternoon slumbers of a prosperous bourgeois John Bull.[2] Finally, in Churchill's words, 'the people of Great Britain . . . were confronted with the fact that a "friendly Power" had, unprovoked, endeavoured to rob them of the fruits of their victories'; had indeed launched 'covert and deceitful' operations 'designed solely for the mischievous and spiteful object of depriving them of the produce of their labours'.[3]

It may be that 'to the initiated few Fashoda was simply the climax to an old policy of imperial defence'.[4] But they must have been *very* few, for they did not even include all Salisbury's ministerial colleagues.[5] And even if Fashoda was 'the climax to an old policy of imperial defence', the climax to Salisbury's policy in the Sudan was not Fashoda but the Condominium Agreement, by which the British obtained 'the fruits of their victories'. Salisbury's 'right of conquest' had its point not primarily against the French on the Upper Nile, but against historic Egyptian and Ottoman rights. Indeed, by this doctrine Salisbury had not shaken off, but taken on, 'diplomatic hamper' in his dispute with the French; by conquest, Marchand's rights at Fashoda were as good as Kitchener's at Omdurman, as Salisbury tacitly admitted when he abandoned his original argument in his conversations with Courcel.[6] Nor can even 'the initiated few', unless they were adepts in self-deception, have regarded the Condominium as a necessary move in a merely defensive strategy. Certainly, control of the Nile waters tightened the British grip on Egypt herself, and would be a useful insurance against the day when it might be necessary to grant Egypt a form of independence.[7] But to this end the annexation of the 'British sphere' would have sufficed; even, at a pinch, the mere maintenance of British rule in Uganda and Unyoro.

In 1898 almost the whole of articulate British opinion did not so much demand as simply assume without question that Britain must

---

[1] G. Shepperson has recently written: 'In the re-interpretation of imperialism . . . the influence of nationalism probably cannot be stressed too much'—'Africa, the Victorians and Imperialism', *Rev. Belge Phil. Hist.* XL, 4 (1962), p. 1236. Brunschwig (*op. cit.*) and Stengers (*J.A.H., ubi supra*) both point with some emphasis to the 'chauvinistic' element in late nineteenth-century imperialism. It is noteworthy that as early as 1887 Salisbury himself equated the 'acquisitional' with the 'national' feeling (Salisbury to Drummond Wolff 23 Feb. 1887, cited Cecil, *Salisbury* IV, pp. 41-2).

[2] *Punch*, 22 Oct. 1898.

[3] Churchill, *The River War*, p. 319.

[4] Robinson and Gallagher, *Africa and the Victorians*, p. 378.

[5] Certainly not Chamberlain and Goschen; probably not Hicks Beach or Devonshire.

[6] *Supra*, Ch. XV, p. 345.

[7] Salisbury, for one, can hardly have forgotten Cromer's repeated warnings that 'whatever Power holds the Upper Nile Valley must, by the mere force of its geographical situation, dominate Egypt' (Baring to Salisbury 15 Dec. 1889). And cf. Churchill, *op. cit.*, p. 364: 'the command of the great river is an irresistible weapon' (sc., against Egypt).

have some tangible reward for her financial assistance and military exertions in the Sudan. The 'British sphere' would have been a negative reward; and the direction in which British appetite was looking is shown by the suggestion of both Cromer and Hicks Beach, towards the end of 1896, that Dongola should be retained as a 'pledge' for the repayment by Egypt of the British loan. In 1896 no action had been taken on these proposals;[1] but two years later this appetite had sharpened to a point where it could no longer be ignored. In October 1898 George Wyndham, speaking for the younger Tories, was proclaiming: 'We don't care whether the Nile is called English or Egyptian or what it is called, but we mean to have it. . . . The Khedive may be kept on for some years as a sort of Indian Maharajah.'[2] When in his speech of 9 November Salisbury referred to the rumour that 'we intend to declare a protectorate of Egypt', his audience responded by 'prolonged cheers'; and Salisbury was constrained, in an obviously improvised and slightly embarrassed passage, to defend the *status quo* in Egypt as reasonably satisfactory, 'looking at the matter all round, and considering the feelings of other people as well as ours'.[3] To the guests at a Lord Mayor's banquet, the Sudan Condominium was a necessary consolation prize for the failure to impose a protectorate on Egypt.

But the assumption that Britain must have her reward was not confined to Tory imperialists, nor to the City circles whose 'avidity' foreign diplomatists deplored.[4] English journalists had, naturally enough, written up the 1898 Sudan campaign as a glorious chapter in British military history;[5] by the end of the year the public saw it as an almost purely English enterprise, of which one of the objectives was to 'avenge' an Englishman—Gordon. Few knew and fewer cared that Egypt had made greater—relatively to her wealth and population, enormously greater—sacrifices of blood and treasure in the Sudan since 1896.[6] The facts were further obscured by the gigantic shadow cast by Kitchener in his new role as national hero; and a legend grew up which is still far from dead—that 'the British' reconquered the Sudan. But even those who were repelled by the military glories of

---

[1] *Supra*, Ch. xi, p. 266. It is of considerable interest to note that Hicks Beach put forward this proposal in the belief that it would be pleasing to the Commons. Another symptom, small but significant, is Kitchener's anxiety, after the fall of Dongola, 'to have a postage stamp different from the Egyptian ones . . .' (E. A. Stanton, 'The Sudan Camel Stamp', *S.N.R.* xviii, 1 [1935], p. 135).

[2] Blunt, *My Diaries*, pp. 299-300.

[3] *Annual Register*, 1898, pp. [176-7].

[4] Cf. D.D.F. xiv, No. 491, Courcel to Delcassé 5 Nov. 1898; G.P. xiv/2, No. 3909, Castell-Rüdenhausen to Hohenlohe 8 Nov. 1898.

[5] E.g. G. W. Steevens, the *Daily Mail* correspondent. Cf. this author's *With Kitchener to Khartoum* (London 1898).

[6] The total cost of the campaign from Mar. 1896 to Dec. 1898 was some £2,355,000. Of this England contributed just under £800,000. The Egyptians lost, in the same period, 235 all ranks killed in action; the British lost seventy. Deaths from wounds and from disease are difficult to compute accurately from the published material; but the Egyptian losses from the first cause were certainly heavier, and from the second cause very much heavier, than those of the British.

the Atbara and Omdurman, and who normally opposed territorial acquisition, did not oppose the Condominium Agreement. For the alternative was to restore Egyptian administration; and Exeter Hall had long ago convinced the public that Egyptian rule in the Sudan had been little better than 'a chapter in the history of crime'.[1] When in October 1898 the Rev. Drs Guinness and Goodrich denounced Marchand to the Congregational Union as an adventurer and a trespasser,[2] it was not *Egyptian* rights they were defending. Ecclesiastical and missionary interests would indeed have been scandalised had the Sudan been placed under a purely Muslim government. Missionary agitation was particularly strong, for a number of reasons, in 1898-9, and was being directed in particular against the 'threat' of Muslim expansion in Africa.[3] Nonconformists and humanitarian Radicals found themselves on the same side as out-and-out imperialists like Wyndham;[4] instead of attacking the Condominium Agreement, they attacked Kitchener's treatment of the wounded, and his desecration of the Mahdi's remains.[5] The one public figure to criticise the Condominium was the rationalist Radical Morley; and even he queried details rather than the principle.[6] The Sudan was annexed— for all practical purposes—'almost without a protest'.[7] The protest would have been raised, by almost every articulate section of opinion, had it *not* been annexed.

In January 1885 Gladstone had deprecated, as a very unwelcome innovation, the possible introduction into British politics of 'the demands now rife in some of the colonies for a system of annexations designed to forestall . . . other countries'.[8] By 1898 even the Liberal Party, having dropped both Harcourt and Morley as potential leaders, was presenting itself to the country as a party of imperialism— no doubt of a less aggressive and more prudent imperialism than that of their Tory rivals, but of imperialism none the less.[9] Views on colonial annexation which had been exceptional in 1885 were by now fully accepted by both great parties and presumably by the majority of the public which supported them. When a change of outlook takes place on this scale, the 'policy-makers' must adjust their policies to it;

[1] I owe this *mot* to R. L. Hill, 'The Period of Egyptian Occupation, 1820-1881', *S.N.R.* XL (1959), pp. 101-2. Cf. Cromer, *Modern Egypt*, II, p. 114: 'it was essential that . . . the Egyptians should not have conferred upon them a "bastard freedom" to repeat the misgovernment of the past'.
[2] *A.R.*, 1898, pp. [165-6].
[3] 1899 was the centenary year of the Church Missionary Society, which celebrated its second Jubilee in Nov. 1898. For this and other information concerning missionary activity I am indebted to my wife.
[4] Cf. Blunt's analysis of the Liberal press (*op. cit.*, p. 311).
[5] Even Blunt recognised the futility of a sustained protest against the political settlement, and devoted himself mainly to the humanitarian agitation against Kitchener (*ibid.*, pp. 313, 317, 319-25).
[6] Cf. the analysis of his Commons speech in *A.R.*, 1899, pp. [34-6].
[7] W. T. Stead, quoted in Robinson and Gallagher, *loc. cit.*, footnote.
[8] L.Q.V. 2, iii, pp. 593-4, Gladstone to the Queen 23 Jan. 1885.
[9] Cf. Asquith's speech at Birmingham on 16 Dec. 1898 (*A.R.*, 1898, pp. [194-6]); and that of Campbell-Bannerman at Hull on 21 Mar. 1899 (*A.R.*, 1899, p. [71]).

or they will be replaced by others who are willing to do so. In no society —and certainly not in late-Victorian England—do the policy-makers in fact take completely autonomous decisions. On the contrary, it is their task to translate into a workable policy the wishes and demands of 'those of the governed on whose support or acquiescence any government ultimately rests'.[1] In the autumn of 1898 Salisbury was especially ill-placed to resist the very strong and widespread demand in England for a political 'reward' in the Nile valley. In July 1898 *Punch* had published a cruel cartoon in which, above the title 'The Open Door', Chamberlain shows Salisbury an open door labelled 'Exit From Office'.[2] Three months later the talk was still of his senility and incapacity. There was more to this than mere journalistic rumour-mongering and club gossip; Salisbury's own colleagues were becoming 'alarmed lest some untoward event should occur'.[3] The choice before Salisbury was to 'retrieve himself politically'[4] by satisfying the public, or to make way for a 'strong man'—doubtless Chamberlain—who would have no truck with 'graceful concessions'.[5] To have denied to the British 'the fruits of their victories' in the Nile valley would have been no less politically suicidal than to have tolerated 'a French principality at Fashoda'.

Changes in the 'climate of opinion' such as that which took place in England between 1885 and 1898 are notoriously difficult to trace in detail. It is usually even more difficult—indeed, often frankly impossible—to trace in any convincing way the actual effect of such changes on the formulation of policy. It is easy enough to collect data; but a satisfactory technique for interpreting the data has, it seems, yet to be devised. Studies in 'public opinion' are therefore apt to seem intolerably conjectural and subjective, especially when compared with studies in 'pure' diplomatic history. Here the data, derived from the working papers of highly articulate experts, permit the accurate dissection of motives and often the formulation of impressively clear conclusions. 'Wovon man nicht sprechen kann, darüber muss man schweigen' is doubtless a good rule for historians as well as for philosophers. But mere inability to analyse the phenomena of 'public opinion' precisely and convincingly does not justify the conclusion that the phenomena themselves are necessarily of minor importance. Moreover, instances are not unknown where one can in fact demonstrate the broad effect of public opinion, though not of course the detailed processes by which this effect was achieved.

---

[1] W. G. Runciman, *Social Science and Political Theory* (Cambridge 1963), p. 81. Runciman's chapter on 'Elites and Oligarchies', from which these words are cited, is useful to anyone studying the activities of 'policy-makers'.

[2] *Punch*, 16 July 1898.

[3] Steiner, *ubi supra*, p. 59, citing Askwith, *Lord James of Hereford*, p. 256.

[4] Cf. 'Diplomaticus', 'Fashoda and Lord Salisbury's Vindication', *The Fortnightly Review*, New Series, LXIII, Dec. 1898, pp. 1002-14.

[5] In the number of 1 Oct. 1898, Mr Punch had enquired 'what "graceful concession" the Government will make to MARCHAND to induce him to evacuate Fashoda'.

Such a situation occurred during the 'Sudan crisis' of 1898-9. The upshot of this crisis was a settlement which went far beyond anything that was necessary for the defence of the Nile waters or indeed for defensive imperial strategy in general. True, Salisbury had originally put forward the two-flags policy, the basis of this settlement, as a defensive move in diplomatic tactics.[1] But a few days earlier he had warned the Khedive that it was doubtful whether the Sudan would be restored to him at all; more, he asserted a British 'right of conquest' *over Egypt itself*, based on the thesis that at the time of Tel-el-Kebir Ahmad 'Urābi had already acquired sovereign rights over Egypt at the expense of the Khedive Tawfīq.[2] These extreme claims suggest that Salisbury was already preparing the ground not only for a *de facto* annexation of the Sudan but also for the possible proclamation of a Protectorate over Egypt. Unless in the summer of 1898 Salisbury underwent a personal conversion to acquisitive imperialism—a possible but very unlikely hypothesis[3]—this behaviour is explicable only on the assumption that he already recognised the existence of a strong demand for a reward in the Nile valley, and was taking steps to meet that demand when the time came. The demand for a Protectorate over Egypt he ultimately rejected as too provocative to the Powers.[4] But having disappointed the public over Egypt, he simply could not afford to disappoint it again over the Sudan; especially as even those sections of opinion which did not positively demand acquisition would have rejected as intolerable the only alternative solution—the restoration of the Sudan to Egypt.

It may be doubted too whether the motives of diplomatists—even of strongly acquisitive diplomatists like Rosebery and Anderson—were the sole significant factor in the development of British policy towards the Upper Nile between June 1894 and April 1895. There is a sharp contrast between the indifference of the public to 'the new African crisis with France and Germany' in June 1894, and the widespread and vocal uneasiness which preceded the Grey Declaration. It now seems clear that this statement was an improvised response to press and Parliamentary agitation rather than a premeditated act of policy;[5] much as Rosebery may have desired to make some such declaration as a formal act of State, he had evidently been restrained from doing so by his inability to carry the Cabinet with him.[6] According to

---

[1] FO 78/5050, Salisbury to Cromer tel. No. 47, 3 June 1898.
[2] FO 141/336, Salisbury to Cromer tels. No. 41 and 43 of 15 and 25 May 1898. Cf. *supra*, Ch. xi, p. 267 footnote.
[3] Cf. his famous lament on the South African situation a year later: '. . . I see before us the necessity for considerable military effort—and all for people whom we despise, and for territory which will bring no profit and no power to England' (Salisbury to Lansdowne 30 Aug. 1899).
[4] Cf. Salisbury's speech of 9 Nov. 1898 (*supra*, p. 398).
[5] The evidence pointing in this direction, hitherto rather inconclusive, seems now to be clinched by the publication (James, *Rosebery*, p. 374) of Murray's letter to Bigge on 2 Apr. 1895.
[6] James, *op. cit.*, pp. 374-5.

2C

d'Estournelles de Constant a marked hardening of British opinion on the Upper Nile question, even in circles not usually regarded as 'imperialist', was already clearly visible by the beginning of December 1894.[1] If this analysis be reliable—and the penetration shown by d'Estournelles' despatch inspires confidence—the spectacular French successes on the Niger and the indiscreet utterances of de Brazza and Deloncle can have done no more than provoke the public expression of views which had developed between June and December 1894. To the agitation thus aroused the Grey Declaration was the response; had it not been for the movement of British opinion—still uninvestigated—in the second half of 1894, this declaration might well not have been made.

*   *   *

The waters of the White Nile linked the Sudan indissolubly to the security of Egypt, and therefore of the British position in Egypt. Even had the British succeeded in maintaining their predominance in Egypt without an indefinite occupation, they could not have remained indifferent to the fate of the Upper Nile; and once the continued occupation of Egypt had become a major British interest—as it did between 1887 and 1889—the protection of the Nile waters from European interference became an inescapable task of diplomatic strategy. As early as 1889 the Upper Nile question, both in the central Sudan and in the far South, was being drawn into the mainstream of Great-Power diplomacy. Between 1891 and 1894, however, it receded into a backwater; England and France, now the two major though undeclared rivals, transformed it in appearance into a petty affair of African frontiers by their inconclusive bickerings with the intruder Leopold. In 1894 the British attempt to install Leopold as a tenant led, instead, to his almost complete ejection from the Nile basin; England and France were now face to face, with their prestige as Great Powers heavily and publicly engaged. Meanwhile Egypt, and therefore the Upper Nile, had become and was becoming more important than ever in British strategic calculations. The development of the Franco-Russian alliance, and the recognition by London that it was impossible to seal the Straits against Russia, made the continued and unthreatened occupation of Egypt increasingly indispensable. By an accident of geography, events in the remote wildernesses of the Upper Nile might have an important, conceivably a decisive, effect on the balance of power in the Mediterranean. Not only did the Mediterranean imply the Suez route to India; it was the arena where British naval preponderance backed the paper of London's diplomacy in the Near East and even on the continent of Europe itself. These European implications of the Upper Nile dispute were further emphasised, at the formal level, by the policy of Hanotaux, which

[1] D.D.F. xi, No. 303.

through its insistence on Ottoman rights in the Sudan tended to assimilate the Upper Nile to the Eastern Question.

On the Upper Nile, if anywhere in Africa, imperial strategy had every opportunity of being the continuously predominant motive of British policy. Not only was the strategic motive enormously strong in itself; it had no serious material competitors. On the Upper Nile there were no settlers, no Chartered Companies already established on the spot, no Uitlanders, no gold, no young 'Dominions' to complicate imperial strategy with the brash chauvinism that the Australians and New Zealanders displayed in the Pacific. True, a few optimistic businessmen showed some interest between 1886 and 1890 and again in the excitement of 1898-9; but these were feeble flashes in the pan. Yet it was not until 1889 at the earliest that imperial strategy established a predominance; in the launching of the Emin Pasha Relief Expedition it had played, at most, only a subsidiary part. Nor was this predominance maintained unchallenged or unbroken; in the 'Mackinnon Treaty' episode of 1890, strategy had to accommodate itself to imperialist motives of a different kind. Between 1891 and 1894 strategic motives were indeed preponderant;[1] but in the Phipps-Hanotaux negotiations strategy took second place to considerations of national prestige and imperial 'possession'. By the beginning of 1895 similar considerations were being strongly emphasised by the 'public opinion' whose demands evoked the Grey Declaration; but once the excitement of March and April 1895 had died down, the strategists seem to have regained pretty complete control until the summer of 1898. In 1896 there was certainly no public enthusiasm for action in the northern Sudan; and if the project of offering Dongola to the Commons as a 'pledge' suggests the existence of acquisitive tendencies, the abandonment of this project testifies that these were still weak enough to be safely ignored. But by the summer of 1898 the demand for acquisition had become very much stronger; and the crude but convincing test of results permits the assertion that between June 1898 and March 1899 imperial strategy was no longer the decisive motive in British policy towards the Sudan.

---

[1] They were of course challenged, but hardly by rival imperialist motives; rather by Gladstonian traditions, of different kinds, both at the Treasury and within the Liberal Party.

BIBLIOGRAPHY

The material has been classified as follows:

I *Unpublished Documentary Sources*

    This class includes material printed for restricted circulation.

II *Published Documentary Sources*

    This class *excludes* works in which documentary material, however rich, has been incorporated in a connected narrative; these are classified under IV below. *Hansard* and its foreign analogues have been omitted. Blue books, etc., have been included selectively, on the basis of their practical usefulness in the writing of the book.

III *Bibliographies and Collected Biographies*

    Omits standard reference works of no special relevance to Africa—e.g. the *Dictionary of National Biography* and its foreign analogues. Some indication is given of the bibliographical value of selected works listed under IV.

IV *Narrative and Analytical Works*

    This is a selective list by alphabetical order of authors. No attempt has been made to distinguish between 'primary' and 'secondary' sources. Most of the earlier writing (down to say 1914) contains 'primary' material; many of the later works are in effect digests of unpublished sources.

    Particularly between 1894 and 1899, the Upper Nile question provoked much ephemeral writing of the 'current affairs' type. The bibliography includes only those items which contain useful factual information, or which seem to illustrate changes in the 'climate of opinion'.

I. UNPUBLISHED DOCUMENTARY SOURCES

I. BRITISH

(a) *Foreign Office Papers in the Public Record Office, London:*

FO 1 (Abyssinia), 1897-9
FO 2 (Africa), 1893-9
FO 10 (Belgium), 1893-5
FO 27 (France), 1894-9
FO 45 (Italy), 1890-1; 1894-6
FO 64 (Prussia/Germany), 1893-8
FO 78 (Turkey:Egypt), 1886-99
FO 83 (Miscellaneous), 1894
FO 84 (Slave Trade), 1886-92
FO 97 (Protocols of Treaties), 1899
FO 123 (Belgium: Legation Archives), 1890
FO 141 (Cairo: Agency Archives), 1886-7; 1890; 1896-8
FO 146 (France: Embassy Archives), 1898-9

FO 170 (Italy: Embassy Archives), 1890-1; 1896
FO 633/6 (Cromer Papers), 1883-99

N.B. Until 31 December 1892 almost all diplomatic correspondence on African affairs was filed, irrespective of the Power concerned, in the 'Slave Trade' class (FO 84). The 'Slave Trade' files were then closed, and African diplomatic correspondence filed (in a separate series) in the same class as other correspondence with the Power concerned.

The new class 'Africa' (FO 2) was at the same time created for the papers, mostly non-diplomatic, previously filed under 'Slave Trade: Miscellaneous'.

   (*b*) *Papers of the third Marquis of Salisbury deposited at Christ Church, Oxford:*

     Egypt 1890
     Egypt 1895-8
     Italy 1890-2
     France 1899
     Cabinet Memoranda, 1896-9
     Private Secretary and Memoranda, 1897-9

   (*c*) *War Office Papers:*

     Précis of Information obtained by the British Mission to Abyssinia (Confidential Print, 1897).

Sir T. Sanderson's complaint that Salisbury's diplomacy had left little record in the official papers is hardly borne out by the FO material available for the Upper Nile. It is true that some quite important documents seem to have escaped filing in the FO 78 series, and are to be found only in FO 141; but it is hard to point to any really serious gaps either in the purely Egyptian correspondence or in the negotiations with other Powers. Rosebery's diplomacy in Africa was very largely prompted by Sir P. Anderson; and Anderson's habit of thinking on paper has left a very complete record.

The main value of the Salisbury Papers is that they often state explicitly what can only be inferred from the official record. They are, however, particularly valuable for the origins of the Sudan campaign and of the Macdonald mission; and for the crisis which overtook the Sudan campaign between October and December 1897.

2. FRENCH

   (*a*) *Ministère des Affaires Etrangères:*

     Mémoires et Documents, Afrique:
       Tome 138 (Abyssinie 5): 1888-95
       Tome 139 (Congo et Gabon 14): 1892-5

   (*b*) *Ministère des Colonies:*

     (i) Correspondence:
       Gabon-Congo I, 37-45; VI, 13-14 (1890-5)
       Côte française des Somalis, 1016, 1027 (1894-8)

     (ii) Afrique III (Missions):
       III 14, 16, 17 (Mizon)
       III 18 (Maistre, Fourneau, Ponel)

III 19 (Monteil: Oubangui-Nil)
III 24 (Van der Kerkhoven [sic])
III 25 (Grimaux, Cazemajou)
III 26 (Missions to the Middle Niger)
III 34, 35, 36 (Marchand)

(c) *Archives Nationales:*

Papiers Monteil[1]

The two *Affaires Etrangères* volumes, with their wealth of local detail, usefully supplement the very full general documentation in the published *Documents Diplomatiques.*

The *Colonies* dossiers on the Marchand Mission are very disappointing, owing to the drastic weeding they have undergone. This enhances the importance of the *Côte Somalis* papers, which seem to have escaped this weeding, and which throw light on the development of policy towards the Upper Nile as well as towards Ethiopia. The *Gabon-Congo* series is indispensable for the policy of de Brazza, and of the *sous-secrétariat des Colonies*, down to 1894. Of the Afrique III dossiers, the most directly useful is III 19 (Monteil). It evidently has much material in common with the *Papiers Monteil.* Other Afrique III dossiers, notably III 18 (Maistre, etc.) and III 25 (Grimaux, Cazemajou), afford some very valuable sidelights on the policy of the *Colonies* and of the *Comité de l'Afrique française.*

3. SUDANESE (Archives of the Ministry of the Interior, Khartoum)

(a) *Egyptian Army Intelligence Reports:*

Intelligence Reports, Egypt, Nos. 1-59 (April 1892-May 1898)
Sudan Intelligence Reports, Nos. 60-86 (May 1898-September 1901)

(b) *Archives of the Mahdist State:*

Mahdia 1/5, 1/32, 1/33: Correspondence of the Khalifa with Mahdist commanders in Equatoria, 1893-5
Mahdia 1/34: Correspondence between the Khalifa and the Negus Menelik, 1895-8; between Fadl al-Mūla Bey and the Congolese, 1892-4; between 'Arabi Dafa'allāh and the Khalifa, 1897-8

(c) *Papers of the Intelligence Division, Egyptian Army:*

(i) Relating to the Fashoda Incident, September-December 1898:
Cairint 1/61/323: Kitchener's orders, despatches and correspondence with Marchand
Cairint 1/62/324: Correspondence, Cairo-Omdurman, Oct.-Dec. 1898
Cairint 3/15/243: Jackson's Intelligence Diaries; and his correspondence with Omdurman and with the French
Intel 5/4: Various correspondence and reports

(ii) Other relevant papers (all class 'Cairint'):
1/7/66: Wingate—Projected reconquest of Dongola Province, 6 May 1890

---

[1] I have not myself been able to use these, except at second-hand through Prof. J. Stengers' paper 'Aux Origines de Fachoda'. But it seemed desirable to include this important source.

1/45/263: Arrest of Karl Inger, October 1896

3/15/299: Wingate, appreciation, 30 Jan. 1893—Expansion of the French Congo

3/15/302: Wingate, appreciation, June 1893—Maistre's expedition to Bagirmi

3/214/11: Kitchener, memo. on Uganda, 16 Sept. 1892

3/218/1: Kitchener, 28 Jan. 1898—Policy towards the Abyssinians

The 'Intelligence Reports, Egypt' (continued, with consecutive numeration, as 'Sudan Intelligence Reports' from May 1898) are at first rather scrappy, but become much fuller from 1896 onwards. The reports for 1898 in particular are a very important source. Of the Mahdia series, 1/34 is indispensable for Sudanese-Ethiopian relations and very useful for Congolese activities in the southern Sudan.

The four files relating to the Fashoda incident give a complete, almost hour-by-hour, account of events at Fashoda and of Cromer's reactions to them. They contain the originals of almost all the letters addressed to British officers by Marchand and by his deputy Germain.

II. PUBLISHED DOCUMENTARY SOURCES

I. COLLECTIONS OF TREATIES

HERTSLET, E., *The Map of Africa by Treaty* (3rd Edn., revised R. W. Brant and H. L. Sherwood, London, 1909).

Trattati, Convenzioni, Accordi, Protocolli ed altri Documenti relativi all'Africa (Rome, Min. For. Affs., 1906).

A useful collection; includes some 'non-territorial' treaties omitted by Hertslet.

2. DIPLOMATIC CORRESPONDENCE: OFFICIAL PUBLISHED COLLECTIONS

British Documents on the Origins of the War, 1898-1914, ed. G. P. Gooch and H. W. V. Temperley (London, 1927f.).

Documents Diplomatiques Français (1871-1914), First Series (Paris, 1929f.).

I Documenti Diplomatici Italiani, Third Series (Rome, 1953-).

Die Grosse Politik der Europäischen Kabinette, ed. J. Lepsius, A. Mendelssohn-Bartholdy and F. Thimme (Berlin, 1922f.).

Of these by far the most satisfactory is D.D.F. From 1894 onwards its coverage of Upper Nile affairs is excellent, and very little of any real importance seems to have been omitted.

3. OTHER PUBLISHED DIPLOMATIC DOCUMENTS

(except Diplomatic Blue Books, listed under II 5 below)

CAMBON, PAUL: *Correspondance, 1870-1924*, Vol. II (Paris, 1940).

[CAMBON]: 'Lettres de Paul Cambon, Ambassadeur de France, au Président de la République Félix Faure (1895-1899)', *Revue d'Histoire Diplomatique*, LXVIII (1954), pp. 189-201.

[DE COURCEL]: 'France et Angleterre en 1895', *Revue Historique*, CCXII, 431 (1954), pp. 39-60.

Prints Courcel's private letters to Hanotaux.

[FAURE]: 'Fachoda (1898)', *Rev. Hist. Dip.*, LXIX (1955), pp. 29-39.
Prints a long and very important memorandum by Félix Faure on the crisis of 1898-9. Throws light on Hanotaux' policy—or lack of policy—between 1896 and 1898.

[HOLSTEIN]: *The Holstein Papers*, ed. N. Rich and M. H. Fisher. Vol. I, *Memoirs and Political Observations* (Cambridge, 1955); Vol. III, *Correspondence* (Cambridge, 1961).
Especially valuable for the light thrown on the German attitude to Rosebery and to Salisbury between 1893 and 1896.

[STAAL]: *Correspondance Diplomatique de M. de Staal, 1884-1900*, ed. A. F. Meyendorff, 2 vols. (Paris, 1929).
Staal was not always fully informed about Russian policy; nevertheless, his correspondence contains some important information.

TEMPERLEY, H. W. V., and PENSON, L. M.; *Foundations of British Foreign Policy from Pitt (1792) to Salisbury (1902)* (Cambridge, 1938).
Prints some important documents from the Vienna archives.

[WILHELM II]: *Briefe Wilhelms II an den Zaren*, ed. W. Goetz (Berlin, 1920).

4. NON-DIPLOMATIC CORRESPONDENCE

[KHALIFA 'ABDALLĀHI]: P. M. Holt, *A Calendar of the Correspondence of the Khalifa Abdullahi and Mahmoud Ahmed* (Khartoum, 1955—date misprinted '1950').

[ESHER, *Viscount* (R. B. Brett)]: *Journals and Letters of Reginald, Viscount Esher*, ed. M. V. Brett (3 vols., London, 1934, 1938).

MANGIN, C.-M.-E., 'Lettres de la Mission Marchand, 1895-1899', *Revue des Deux Mondes*, 15 Sept. 1931, pp. 241-83. Some sidelights on Franco-Ethiopian relations in the Nile Valley.

[MARCHAND]: M.-A. Ménier, 'Une lettre inédite de Marchand à Gentil', *Revue d'Histoire des Colonies*, XL (1954), pp. 431-40.

[MARCHAND]: M.-A. Ménier, 'Lettres du commandant Marchand à Guillaume Grandidier', *Rev. Hist. Cols.*, XLV (1958), pp. 61-108.
Affords not only factual material, but also a useful insight into Marchand's views and personality.

[QUEEN VICTORIA]: *The Letters of Queen Victoria*. Second series, Vol. III, ed. G. E. Buckle (London, 1928); Third series, ed. G. E. Buckle, Vols. I-III (London, 1930, 1931, 1932).
An indispensable source for British policy throughout the period.

5. BLUE BOOKS, ETC.

(a) British:

Abyssinia No. 1 (1888) [C.-5431]: Correspondence respecting Mr Portal's Mission to Abyssinia.

Africa No. 8 (1888) [C.-5601]: Correspondence respecting the Expedition for the Relief of Emin Pasha, 1886-7.

Egypt No. 1 (1889) [C.-5668]: Further Correspondence respecting Affairs in Suakin.

Africa No. 5 (1890) [C.-6043]: Despatch to Sir E. Malet, respecting the Affairs of East Africa.

Egypt No. 3 (1891) [C.-6321]: Report on the Administration . . . of Egypt.

Africa No. 2 (1892) [C.-6560]: Papers respecting the Proposed Railway from Mombasa to Lake Victoria Nyanza.

Africa No. 4 (1892) [C.-6555]: Papers relating to the Mombasa Railway Survey and Uganda.

Africa No. 8 (1892) [C.-6817]: Papers relating to Uganda.

Egypt No. 2 (1892) [C.-6561]: Correspondence respecting the re-occupation of Tokar by the Egyptian Government.

Egypt No. 3 (1892) [C.-6589]: Report on the Administration . . . of Egypt.

Africa No. 1 (1893) [C.-6847]: Further Papers relating to Uganda.

Africa No. 8 (1893) [C.-7109]: Further Papers relating to Uganda.

Egypt No. 3 (1893) [C.-6957]: Report on the . . . Administration of Egypt.

Egypt No. 1 (1894) [C.-7308]: Report on the . . . Administration of Egypt.

Africa No. 2 (1894) [C.-7303]: Reports relating to Uganda by Sir Gerald Portal.

Africa No. 4 (1894) [C.-7360]: Papers relating to [the Anglo-Congolese Agreement].

Africa No. 5 (1894) [C.-7390]: Further papers relating to [the Anglo-Congolese Agreement].

Africa No. 4 (1895) [C.-7646]: Correspondence respecting the retirement of the Imperial British East Africa Company.

Africa No. 7 (1895) [C.-7708]: Papers relating to Uganda.

Egypt No. 1 (1895) [C.-7644]: Report on the . . . Administration of Egypt.

Egypt No. 1 (1896) [C.-7978]: Report on the . . . Administration of Egypt.

Africa No. 10 (1898) [C.-9027]: Report . . . on the . . . Mutiny of the Soudanese troops in [Uganda].

Egypt No. 2 (1898) [C.-9054]: Correspondence with the French Government respecting the Valley of the Upper Nile.

Egypt No. 3 (1898) [C.-9055]: Further Correspondence respecting the Valley of the Upper Nile.

(*b*) French:

1894. *Documents Parlementaires, Chambre.* Séance du 28 mai 1894, Annexe No. 653 (Deloncle's collection).

1898. *Documents Diplomatiques:* Affaires du Haut-Nil et du Bahr-el-Ghazal, 1897-8.

1899. *Documents Diplomatiques:* Correspondance concernant la Déclaration Additionelle du 21 mars 1899.

III. BIBLIOGRAPHIES AND COLLECTED BIOGRAPHIES

I. BIBLIOGRAPHIES

R. L. Hill, *A Bibliography of the Anglo-Egyptian Sudan from the Earliest Times to 1937* (Oxford, 1939), is a very useful guide to the earlier publications on the various Sudan campaigns and 'missions'. Later publications in the same field are noted by Abdel Rahman el Nasri, *A Bibliography of the Sudan, 1938-1958* (London, 1962).

The Cambridge History of the British Empire, Vol. III (Cambridge, 1959), contains a very full bibliography by A. Taylor Milne. Material relevant to the Sudan and the Upper Nile is to be found particularly in the 'Special Bibliographies', Sections B and D.

Much of the Blue-Book literature is listed in H. W. V. Temperley and L. M. Penson, *A Century of Diplomatic Blue Books, 1814-1914* (Cambridge, 1938).

A number of works listed in Section IV below contain useful bibliographies. Of these by far the most valuable is that in W. L. Langer, *The Diplomacy of Imperialism*. The second edition (New York, 1951) lists, with judicious critical comments, almost all the work of major importance published down to 1949. The bibliography in J. Cocheris, *Situation Internationale de l'Egypte et du Soudan* (Paris, 1903), is still useful in spite of its early date of publication. That in M. P. Hornik, *Der Kampf der Grossmächte um den Oberlauf des Nil* (Vienna, n.d.), is worth consulting, though rather sketchy. Fairly up-to-date bibliographies of Leopold II and of Crispi are appended to the articles on these two figures, by J. Bruhat and G. Bourgin respectively, in *Les Politiques d'Expansion Impérialiste* (Paris, 1949). C. Jesman, *The Russians in Ethiopia* (London, 1958), has a bibliography of its rather obscure subject, but surprisingly few of the items are in Russian. For East Africa and Uganda during the period of competition, Margery Perham, *Lugard: The Years of Adventure* (London, 1956), has a useful bibliography of mainly British material; for the German side, there is a very valuable bibliography in F. F. Müller, *Deutschland-Zanzibar-Ostafrika* (Berlin, 1959). For West Africa see J. D. Hargreaves, *Prelude to the Partition of West Africa* (London, 1963); his bibliography is by no means confined to the pre-partition period. The bibliography in H. Brunschwig, *Mythes et Réalités de l'Impérialisme Colonial Français* (Paris, 1960), is a very valuable pioneer effort in its field.

2. COLLECTED BIOGRAPHIES

DELLICOUR, F., *et al.*, *Biographie Coloniale Belge (Belgische Koloniale Biografie)*, 5 vols. (Brussels, 1948f.—in progress).

HILL, R. L., *A Biographical Dictionary of the Anglo-Egyptian Sudan* (Oxford, 1951).

Neither of these is infallible, but both are quite indispensable.

IV. NARRATIVE AND ANALYTICAL WORKS

ANON., 'La Rencontre du commandant Marchand et du Sirdar', *Bulletin du Comité de l'Afrique Française*, Oct. 1898, pp. 332-7.

—— 'De l'Oubangui au Nil: Les Missions Liotard et Marchand', *Bull. C.A.F.*, Oct. 1898, pp. 325-32.

—— 'La Mission Marchand dans le Bahr el Ghazal', *Le Mouvement Géographique*, xv, 44 (Oct. 1898), cols. 535-8.

—— 'Dans le Bahr-el-Ghazal: l'Occupation de Dem Ziber', *Bull. C.A.F.*, Nov. 1898, p. 367.

—— 'La Mission Marchand', *Bull. C.A.F.*, Nov. 1898, pp. 363-7.

—— 'France, Russia and the Nile', *The Contemporary Review*, LXXIV (Dec. 1898), pp. 761-78.

—— XX, 'Le Dilemme de notre Politique Extérieure', *La Revue de Paris*, May 1899, pp. 224-32.

412   BIBLIOGRAPHY

ANON, 'Le commandant Henry sur le Haut-Nil', *M. Géog.*, xvii, 5 (Feb. 1900), cols. 61-3.
— 'Aus den Archiven des belgischen Kolonialministeriums: Theil III, Das Lado—und Bahr el Ghazal—Pachtgebiet des Kongostaates', *Deutsches Kolonialblatt*, xxvii (June 1916), pp. 135-61.
  Includes the only published documentary material on the Mackinnon Treaty, and on the Anglo-Congolese dispute in the Bahr al-Ghazal between 1903 and 1906.
— *History of 'The Times'*, Vol. iii (London, 1947).
  Some useful sidelights on Italian policy, 1894-96.
ABBAS, M., *The Sudan Question* (London, 1952).
ALBERTINI, L., *The Origins of the War of 1914* (English Edn., London, 1952).
ALLEN, B. M., *Gordon and the Sudan* (London, 1931).
ANCHIERI, E., *Storia della Politica Inglese nel Sudan, 1882-1938* (Milan, 1939).
ANSTEY, R. T., *Britain and the Congo in the Nineteenth Century* (Oxford, 1962).
ARIE, R., 'L'opinion publique en France et l'affaire de Fachoda', *Rev. Hist. Cols.*, xli (1954), pp. 329-67.
  A painstaking and very useful analysis.
ARTHUR, G. C. A., *The Life of Lord Kitchener*, 3 vols. (London 1920).
ASCHERSON, N., *The King Incorporated* (i.e. Leopold II) (London, 1963).
AUSTIN, H. H., *With Macdonald in Uganda* (London, 1903).

BARATIER, A.-E.-A., *Souvenirs de la Mission Marchand: I, Au Congo* (Paris, 1914); *II, Vers le Nil* (Paris, 1923); *III, Fachoda* (Paris, 1941).
  Vol. iii is useful for events at Fashoda; and for sidelights on the crisis at Paris at the end of October 1898.
BARCLAY, T., *Thirty Years: Anglo-French Reminiscences* (London, 1914).
BAUMONT, M., 'Carl Peters', in *Les Techniciens de la Colonisation*, ed. C.-A. Julien (Paris, 1947).
BAYER, T. A., *England und der Neue Kurs* (Tübingen, 1955).
BERG, T., 'Tillkomsten av Sir Edward Greys Tal i Underhuset den 28 Mars 1895', *Historisk Tidskrift* (Stockholm), 1956, I, pp. 56-64.
BILLOT, A., *La France et l'Italie 1881-1899* (Paris, 1905).
BITTNER, L., 'Neue Beiträge zur Haltung Kaiser Wilhelms II in der Faschodafrage', *Historische Zeitschrift*, clxii (1940), pp. 540-50.
BLANCHARD, M., 'Français et Belges sur l'Oubanghi (1890-1896)', *Rev. Hist. Cols.*, xxxvi (1950), pp. 1-36.
  Important. Cites lengthy extracts from some very interesting correspondence.
— 'Administrateurs d'Afrique Noire', *Rev. Hist. Cols.*, xxxix (1953), pp. 377-430.
  Based on personal dossiers; very useful.
BLUNT, W. S., *My Diaries* (London, 1919; reprint in one vol., 1932).
  To be used with caution; but cannot be neglected. Blunt was often very well informed.
BOBICHON, H., 'Le Haut-Oubangui', *La Revue Forézienne* (St. Etienne), 1902, pp. 391-404, 516-30, 604-16.

The only available synoptic account—albeit a mere sketch—of the French occupation of the Bahr al-Ghazal in 1898-9.

— 'Vers Fachoda: Le Gouverneur-Général Victor Liotard', *Revue des Questions Coloniales et Maritimes*, Nov.-Dec. 1935, pp. 97-102.

BOURDARIE, P., *Fachoda: La Mission Marchand* (Paris, 1899).

— 'La Mission du Prince Henri d'Orléans en Abyssinie', *Questions Diplomatiques et Coloniales*, 1 (Aug. 1897), pp. 68-71.

— 'Les Missions Liotard—Marchand—de Bonchamps et la Question du Nil', *Q.D.C.*, 111 (Feb. 1898), pp. 223-36.

BOURGIN, G., 'Francesco Crispi', in *Les Politiques d'expansion impérialiste*, ed. P. Renouvin (Paris, 1949).

BROGAN, D. W., *The Development of Modern France, 1870-1939* (London, 1940).

BRUHAT, J., 'Léopold II', in *Les Politiques d'expansion impérialiste.*

BRUNSCHWIG, H., *Mythes et Réalités de l'Impérialisme Colonial Français, 1871-1914* (Paris, 1960).
The first serious analytical work.

— 'Le Parti Colonial Français', *Revue Française d'Histoire d'Outremer* (continuation of *Rev. Hist. Cols.*), XLVI (1959), pp. 49-93.

DE CAIX, R., *Fachoda, la France et l'Angleterre* (Paris, 1899).
Important for the shift in French opinion on the Nile question after Fashoda.

— 'Après la prise de Khartoum', *Bull. C.A.F.*, Sept. 1898, pp. 278-81.

— Anon., 'La Leçon de Fachoda', *Bull. C.A.F.*, Nov. 1898, pp. 358-62.

— 'La France et l'Angleterre après Fachoda', *Bull. C.A.F.*, Dec. 1898, p. 391.

[CAMBON, H.] 'Un Diplomate', *Paul Cambon, Ambassadeur de France (1843-1924)* (Paris, 1937).

CARROLL, E. M., *French Public Opinion and Foreign Affairs 1870-1914* (New York, 1931).

CASTELLANI, C., *Marchand l'Africain* (Paris, n.d., ?1901).

CECIL, *Lady* G., *Life of Robert, Marquis of Salisbury*, Vol. IV (London, 1932).
Its value is hardly diminished by the passage of time. Study of unpublished material usually confirms the soundness of Lady Gwendolen's judgments.

CEULEMANS, P., *La Question Arabe et le Congo (1883-1892)* (Brussels, 1959).

CHAILLÉ-LONG, C., *My Life in Four Continents*, 2 vols. (London, 1912).

— 'England in Egypt and the Sudan', *The North American Review*, CLXVIII (May, 1899), pp. 570-80.

CHAPMAN, G., *The Dreyfus Case: A Reassessment* (London, 1955).
Useful for French domestic politics.

CHASTENET, J., *Histoire de la Troisième République: II, La République des Républicains* (Paris, 1954); *III, La République Triomphante* (Paris, 1955).

CHAUVEAU, J., 'Mizon à Yola', *Rev. Hist. Cols.*, XLI (1954), pp. 227-44.

DE CHAVANNES, C., *Le Congo Français* (Paris, 1937).

CHESNEL, E., *Plaies d'Egypte: Les Anglais dans la Vallée du Nil* (Paris, 1888).

CHURCHILL, W. S., *The River War* (London, 1899; 3rd edn., 1933).
— 'The Fashoda Incident', *The North American Review*, CLXVII, 1898, pp. 736-43.
COCHERIS, J., *Situation Internationale de l'Egypte et du Soudan (Juridique et Politique)* (Paris, 1903).
  Still of very great value. Cocheris was an indefatigable collector of facts and a shrewd observer. His biases (against England, against the Third Republic) are openly avowed and do not usually interfere with his presentation of factual material.
COLLINS, R. O., *The Southern Sudan, 1883-1898: A Struggle for Control* (New Haven, 1962).
  A useful factual chronicle, based mainly on Mahdist and Belgian material.
— 'Anglo-Congolese Negotiations, 1900-1906', *Zaïre*, XII, 5, 6 (1958), pp. 479-512, 619-54.
COLVILE, H. E., *The Land of the Nile Springs* (London, 1895).
CORNET, R.-J., 'A propos de deux dossiers: Le dossier diplomatique de l'Ubangi, et le dossier de Grelle Rogier sur l'Ubangi', *Bulletin de l'Institut Royal Colonial Belge*, XXIV, 3 (1953), pp. 876-904.
  Indispensable for the Franco-Congolese negotiations of 1892.
— 'Rapport sur les dossiers: "Création, administration et gouvernement de l'Association Internationale du Congo (A.I.C.) et de l'Etat Indépendant du Congo (E.I.C.)" ', *Bull. I.R.C.B.*, XXV, 2 (1954), pp. 556-95.
COUPLAND, R., *The Exploitation of East Africa, 1856-1890: The Slave Trade and the Scramble* (London, 1939).
CREWE, Marquess of (R. O. A. Crewe-Milnes), *Lord Rosebery*, 2 vols. (London, 1931).
  Deplorably sketchy on foreign affairs.
CROMER, Earl of (E. Baring), *Modern Egypt*, 2 vols. (London, 1908).
  For all Cromer's obvious anxiety to be discreet, some of his remarks are very suggestive when read against the background of archive material.
CROWE, S. E., *The Berlin West African Conference* (London, 1942).
CURATO, F., 'Il Rifiuto inglese di cedere Zeila nel 1894-96', *Gerarchia*, XVI (Nov. 1935), pp. 948-50.

DARCY, J., *France et Angleterre: Cent Années de Rivalité Coloniale* (Paris, 1903).
DEHÉRAIN, H., 'Le Soudan perdu et reconquis', in *Histoire de la Nation égyptienne*, ed. G. Hanotaux, Vol. VII (Paris, 1940).
— 'La Succession de l'Egypte dans la Province Equatoriale', *Revue des Deux Mondes*, May 1894, pp. 312-47.
— 'L'Occupation égyptienne du Haut-Nil', *Revue des Deux Mondes*, Nov. 1898, pp. 183-200.
DELEBECQUE, J., *Vie du Général Marchand* (Paris, 1936).
  Hardly adequate; but it contains much more factual material than other 'lives' of its subject. The author had access to Marchand's correspondence.
DELONCLE, J.-L., 'La Question de Fachoda: Avant et Après', *Revue Politique et Parlementaire*, XVIII (Nov. 1898), pp. 277-300.

DEMANCHE, G., 'Les Lettres de la Mission Marchand', *Revue Française*, XXIII (1898), pp. 79-88.

DEPAGE, H., 'Note au sujet de documents inédits relatifs à deux expèditions de H. M. Stanley en Afrique Centrale', *Bull. I.R.C.B.*, XXV, I (1954), pp. 129-52.

'DIPLOMATICUS' (pseud.), 'Fashoda and Lord Salisbury's Vindication', *Fortnightly Review*, New Series, Vol. LXIII (Dec. 1898), pp. 1002-14.

EDWARDS, F. A., 'The French on the Nile', *Fortnightly Review*, N.S. LXIII (Mar. 1898), pp. 362-77.

— 'The French on the *Niger*', *Fortnightly Review*, N.S. LXIII (Apr. 1898), pp. 576-91.

EMILY, J., *Mission Marchand, Journal de Route* (Paris, 1913).
    The best and most balanced French report of events at Fashoda.

— 'À Fashoda, le 19 septembre 1898', *Afrique Française*, March and April 1937, pp. 124-7, 192-4.

EYCK, E., *Bismarck and the German Empire* (English edn., London, 1950).

FERRY, R., 'L'Ethiopie et l'Expansion Européenne en Afrique Orientale', *Annales des Sciences Politiques*, XXV (1910), pp. 17-36, 199-224.

FLAMENT, F., *et al.*, *La Force Publique de sa Naissance à 1914* (Brussels, 1952).
    A rather jejune 'official history'; but useful as a factual chronicle.

FLINT, J. E., *Sir George Goldie and the Making of Nigeria* (London, 1960).

FOX-BOURNE, H. R., *Civilisation in Congoland: A Story of International Wrong-Doing* (London, 1903).
    Polemical in purpose, as its title indicates; but remarkably well-informed, especially about the structure and organisation of Leopold's companies in the Congo.

— 'The Uganda Protectorate and its relation to the Sudan', *Asiatic Quarterly Review*, 3rd Series Vol. VII (Apr. 1899), pp. 322-37.

GAGE, M. F., 'Sudd-Cutting', *Sudan Notes and Records* XXXI, I (June 1950), pp. 7-20.

GALLAGHER, J., and ROBINSON, R., 'The Imperialism of Free Trade', *Economic History Review*, 2nd Series, VI, I (1953), pp. 1-15.

GARDINER, A. G., *Life of Sir William Harcourt*, 2 Vols. (London, 1923).
    In spite of more recent publications, still indispensable for the policies of the Liberal ministries, 1892-5.

GARVIN, J. L., *The Life of Joseph Chamberlain*, Vols. II and III (London, 1933, 1934).

GATELET, A.-L.-C., *Histoire de la Conquête du Soudan Français* (Paris-Nancy, 1901).
    A useful factual chronicle.

DE LA GENARDIÈRE, G., 'Les Provinces Equatoriales de l'Ethiopie', *Q.D.C.*, IV (May 1898), pp. 12-19.

GIFFEN, M. B., *Fashoda: The Incident and its Diplomatic Setting* (Chicago, 1930).
    The earliest serious monograph.

GILLARD, D. R., 'Salisbury's African Policy and the Heligoland Offer of 1890', *English Historical Review*, LXXV, 297 (1960), pp. 631-53.

GILLET, L., *Gabriel Hanotaux* (Paris, 1933).
    Very flimsy.

GILMOUR, T. L., *The Ethiopian Railway and the Powers* (London, 1906).
    Prints some relevant correspondence.

GIRAUDEAU, C., 'Après Adowa—Avant Dongola', *Revue Politique et Littéraire*, Mar. 1896, pp. 362-4.
    A very perceptive assessment of the European motives for Salisbury's change of policy in the Sudan.

GLEICHEN, Count A. E. W., *With the Mission to Menelik* (London, 1898).

— (and others), *The Anglo-Egyptian Sudan* (London, 1905).

GRAY, [J.] R., *A History of the Southern Sudan, 1839-1889* (London, 1961).
    Important for the 'humanitarian' background of the Emin Pasha Relief Expedition, as well as for the internal history of the South.

GREENE, T. K., *Adamawa Past and Present* (London, 1958).
    Useful sidelights on French activities.

GRENVILLE, J. A. S., *Lord Salisbury and Foreign Policy* (London, 1964).

— 'Goluchowski, Salisbury and the Mediterranean Agreements, 1895-97', *The Slavonic Review*, XXXVI (1958), pp. 340-69.

GREY, Viscount (E. Grey), *Twenty-Five Years*, 2 vols. (London, 1925).

GUEBELS, L., 'Rapport sur le dossier J. Greindl', *Bull. I.R.C.B.*, XXIV, 2 (1953), pp. 583-619.
    Important for the Anglo-Congolese negotiations, 1892.

HANOTAUX, G., *Le Partage d'Afrique: Fachoda* (Paris, 1909).
    Hanotaux' apologia; mostly an exercise in 'double-talk'.

— 'Carnets' (selections, ed. G.-L. Jaray), *Revue des Deux Mondes*, April 1949, pp. 385-403, 573-88.
    Valuable, especially for the origins of the 'Liotard Mission'.

HARDY, G., *Histoire de la Colonisation Française* (2nd edn., Paris, 1947).

HARGREAVES, J. D., *Prelude to the Partition of West Africa* (London, 1963).

— '*Entente Manquée*: Anglo-French Relations 1895-1896', *Cambridge Historical Journal*, XI, 1 (1953), pp. 65-92.
    Important for the diplomatic background to the 'Dongola Expedition'.

— 'Towards a History of the Partition of Africa', *Journal of African History*, I, 1 (1960), pp. 97-109.

[HENRI D'ORLÉANS, Prince], 'La Question du Nil' (statement to Henri Pensa), *Revue Politique et Parlementaire*, XVI (May 1898), pp. 171-5.

HENRY, J., 'A la Conquête du Nil', *L'Expansion Belge*, 1933, No. 3, pp. 19-22.

HEYSE, T., 'Correspondance Léopold II—Janssen: Le Nil.—Réformes fiscales et Politique Economique.—Négotiations avec la France au sujet de la frontière nord.', *Bull. I.R.C.B.*, XXIV, 2 (1953), pp. 475-501.
    Contains the earliest revelation of the equivocal role of 'Harry Alis'.

HILL, R. L., *Egypt in the Sudan, 1820-1881* (London, 1959).

— 'The Suakin-Berber Railway, 1885', *S.N.R.*, XX, 1 (1937), pp. 107-24.

HILL, R. L., 'The Gordon Literature', *Durham University Journal*, XLVII, 3 (1955), pp. 97-103.

Includes a useful statistical table showing the volume of 'literary production' on Sudan Affairs, in England and elsewhere, during the 1880s and 1890s.

HINSLEY, F. H., 'International Rivalry in the Colonial Sphere, 1869-1885', *Cambridge History of the British Empire*, Vol. III (Cambridge, 1959), Ch. IV, pp. 95-126.

— 'International Rivalry, 1885-1895', *C.H.B.E.*, III, Ch. VIII, pp. 255-92.

— 'British Foreign Policy and Colonial Questions, 1895-1904', *C.H.B.E.*, III, Ch. XIII, pp. 490-537.

— 'Bismarck, Salisbury and the Mediterranean Agreements of 1887', *Historical Journal*, I, 1 (1958), pp. 76-81.

HOLLINGSWORTH, L. W., *Zanzibar under the Foreign Office, 1890-1913* (London, 1953).

HOLT, P. M., *The Mahdist State in the Sudan, 1881-1898* (Oxford, 1958).

Fundamental and indispensable.

— 'The Sudanese Mahdia and the Outside World, 1881-9', *Bulletin of the School of Oriental and African Studies* (London), XXI (1958), pp. 276-90.

HORNIK, M. P., *Der Kampf der Grossmächte um den Oberlauf des Nil* (Vienna, n.d., ?1939).

A premature attempt to solve the problem; the only unpublished material used is that from the Austrian archives. Perhaps for this reason, the book is much better on Italian policy than on that of other Powers.

— 'The Anglo-Belgian Agreement of 12 May 1894', *E.H.R.*, LVII, 226 (1942), pp. 227-43.

HOWELL, P. P., *et al.* ('The Jonglei Investigation Team'), 'A Short Account of the Equatorial Nile Project and its effects in the Sudan', *S.N.R.*, XXXIII, 1 (1952), pp. 3-41.

A very useful introduction to the hydrology of the White Nile.

HUGODOT, M., 'L'opinion publique anglaise et l'affaire de Fachoda', *Rev. Hist. Cols.*, XLIV (1956), pp. 113-37.

HURST, H. E., *The Nile* (London, 1952).

The standard work for the non-expert.

IIAMS, T. M., *Dreyfus, Diplomatists and the Dual Alliance: Gabriel Hanotaux at the Quai d'Orsay (1894-98)* (Geneva-Paris, 1962).

Adds little except a few sidelights upon Hanotaux' relations with his ministerial colleagues.

INGHAM, K., *The Making of Modern Uganda* (London, 1958).

JACKSON, H. W., 'Fashoda, 1898', *S.N.R.*, III, 1 (1920), pp. 1-9.

An unvarnished report by the 'Anglo-Egyptian' commandant at Fashoda.

JAMES, R. R., *Rosebery: A Biography of Archibald Philip, Fifth Earl of Rosebery* (London, 1963).

Important. Much unpublished material has been used. Goes far to solve the problem of the 'Grey Declaration'.

JENTGEN, P., *Les Frontières du Congo Belge* (Brussels, 1952).

JEPHSON, A. J. M., *Emin Pasha and the Rebellion at the Equator* (London, 1890).

> Valuable. Jephson was an intelligent and level-headed man, and had some inkling of what was really going on in Equatoria.

JEŚMAN, C., *The Russians in Ethiopia: A Study in Futility* (London, 1958).

> Inadequate as a scholarly account, but at times shrewd and perceptive.

DE JONGHE, E., 'Gordon Pacha au service de Léopold II', *Bull. I.R.C.B.*, VIII, 2 (1937), p. 133f.

JUDET, E., 'Autour de Fachoda', *Bulletin de la Société d'Histoire de la Troisième République*, No. 11 (1938), pp. 92-6.

> Tendentious; written with an eye to the current political situation.

KELLER, C., *Alfred Ilg* (Leipzig, 1918).

KELTIE, J. S., *The Partition of Africa* (2nd edn., London, 1895).

KENNEDY, A. L., *Salisbury, 1830-1903* (London, 1953).

— 'Fashoda', *Quarterly Review*, CCLXXXVI, 576 (April, 1948), pp. 145-61.

> Both of Kennedy's contributions are competent accounts, but neither adds very much.

DE KIEWIET, M. J., *History of the Imperial British East Africa Company, 1876-1895* (unpubl. Ph.D., thesis, London, 1955).

KOSSATZ, H., *Untersuchungen über den französischenglischen Weltgegensatz im Faschodajahr* (Breslau, 1934).

LABOURET, H., *Monteil* (Paris, 1937).

> Disappointing. Adds little to Monteil's own publication.

DE LANESSAN, J.-L., 'L'évacuation de Fashoda: Ses véritables causes', *Q.D.C.*, V (Nov., 1898), pp. 321-9.

— 'Les Relations de la France et de l'Angleterre', *Q.D.C.*, VI (Mar. 1899), pp. 259-73.

LANGER, W. L., *The Franco-Russian Alliance, 1890-1894* (Cambridge, Mass., 1929).

— *European Alliances and Alignments* (2nd edn., New York, 1950).

— *The Diplomacy of Imperialism* (2nd edn., New York, 1951).

> The chapters on the Upper Nile are an object-lesson in the art of shrewd yet cautious inference from fragmentary and often very biased material.

LEAMAN, B. R., 'The Influence of Domestic Policy on Foreign Affairs in France, 1898-1905', *Journal of Modern History*, XIV, 4 (1942), pp. 449-479.

> Embodies some suggestive analytical work on the French Colonialist movement.

LEBON, A., *La Politique de la France en Afrique, 1896-1898* (Paris, 1901).

> André Lebon's apologia. More factual—and more frank—than that of Hanotaux.

— 'La Mission Marchand et le Cabinet Méline', *Revue des Deux Mondes*, March 1900, pp. 274-96.

> This material was later worked up into the foregoing.

LEJEUNE-CHOQUET, A., *Histoire Militaire du Congo* (Brussels, 1906).

> Never at all satisfactory. Now quite superseded by the work of Flament (*q.v.*).

LEMOINE, R.-J., 'Finances et Colonisation: La concentration des entreprises dans la mise en valeur du Congo belge', *Annales d'Histoire Economique et Sociale*, No. 29 (Sept. 1934), pp. 433-49.
> Useful, but not nearly as exciting as it sounds.

LE ROUX, H., *Ménélik et Nous* (Paris, n.d., ?1902).

LEWIS, S. E., 'Anglo-German Diplomatic Relations 1898-1902', *Bulletin of the Institute of Historical Research*, IX (1931-32), pp. 123-7.

LOCKROY, E., *La Défense Navale* (Paris, 1900).
> Lockroy held the Marine portfolio in the Brisson Cabinet. A remarkably frank book.

LOTAR, L., *La Grande Chronique de l'Ubangi* (Brussels, 1936).
— *La Grande Chronique du Bomu* (Brussels, 1940).
— *La Grande Chronique de l'Uele* (Brussels, 1946).
> The last two are indispensable for Belgian operations on the Upper Nile.

— 'Redjaf', *Congo*, 1932, No. 1, pp. 54-76.

LOW, A., *The British and Uganda* (unpubl. D. Phil. thesis, Oxford, 1957).
— 'British Public Opinion and the Uganda Question, October-December 1892', *The Uganda Journal*, XVIII, 2 (1954), pp. 81-100.

LUGARD, F. D., *The Rise of our East African Empire*, 2 vols. (London, 1893).

[LUGARD] Anon., 'The New African Crisis with France and Germany', *Blackwood's Magazine*, July 1894, pp. 145-58.

LUGARD, F. D., 'England and France in the Nile Valley', *The National Review*, July 1895, pp. 609-22.

LUWEL, M., 'Catalogue des manuscrits exposés lors de la commémoration H. M. Stanley', *Bull. I.R.C.B.*, XXV, 5 (1954), pp. 1410-27.

LYALL, A. C., *The Life of the Marquis of Dufferin and Ava*, 2 vols. (London, 1905).

McDERMOTT, P. L., *British East Africa or IBEA* (London, 1893).

MACDONALD, J. R. L., *Soldiering and Surveying in East Africa, 1891-1894* (London, 1897).

MADDEN, A. F., 'Changing [Imperial] Attitudes and Widening Responsibilities, 1895-1914', *C.H.B.E.*, III, Ch. x, pp. 338-405.

MAGNUS, P., *Gladstone; a Biography* (London, 1954).
— *Kitchener: Portrait of an Imperialist* (London, 1958).
> Uses the Salisbury papers for the account of K's Sudan campaign.

MAISTRE, C., 'Le Président Carnot et le plan français d'action sur le Nil en 1893', *Afrique Française*, March 1932, pp. 156-7.
> An important testimony.

MANGIN, C.-M.-E., *Regards sur la France d'Afrique* (Paris, 1924).
— *Souvenirs d'Afrique* (Paris, 1936).

MANTOUX, P., 'The Début of M. Paul Cambon in England, 1899-1903', in *Studies in Anglo-French History*, ed. A. Coville and H. W. V. Temperley (Cambridge, 1935), pp. 143-58.

MARCHAND, J.-B., [Account of the Fashoda Encounter], *Le Figaro*, 26 Aug. 1904.
— Statements to *Le Matin*, 20 and 24 June 1905.
> The only account by Marchand of the origins of his mission.

— [Account of the Fashoda Encounter], *L'Illustration*, 27 Jan. 1934.

MARCUS, H. G., 'Ethio-British Negotiations concerning the Western Border with Sudan, 1896-1902', *J.A.H.*, IV, 1 (1963), pp. 81-94.

MARDER, A. J., *The Anatomy of British Sea Power: A History of British Naval Policy in the Pre-Dreadnought Era, 1880-1905* (New York, 1940).
Indispensable for all questions of naval policy and strategy.

MASOIN, F., *Histoire de l'Etat Indépendant du Congo*, 2 vols. (Namur, 1912, 1913).

MAURICE, F. B., and ARTHUR, G. C. A., *The Life of Lord Wolseley*, 2 vols. (London, 1924).

MAUROIS, A., *King Edward and his Times* (London, 1933).
Cites extracts from Delcassé's diary during the Fashoda crisis.

MAXSE, F. I., *Seymour Vandeleur* . . . (London, 1905).
V. reached Wadelai in January 1895.

MÉNIER, M.-A., 'La marche au Tchad de 1887 à 1891', *Bulletin d'Etudes Centrafricaines*, No. 5, 1953, pp. 5-18.

MICHEL, C., *Mission de Bonchamps: Vers Fachoda à la rencontre de la Mission Marchand* . . . (Paris, 1900).
Unvarnished first-hand account of the adventures of the French missions from Ethiopia. Very critical of Lagarde.

MILLER, T. B., 'The Egyptian Question and British Foreign Policy, 1892-1894', *J. Mod. Hist.*, XXXII, 1 (1960), pp. 1-15.

MOCKLER-FERRYMAN, A. F., *British Nigeria* (London, 1902).
Useful for the local Anglo-French crises in 1898.

— 'The Story of the Uganda Mutiny', *Macmillan's Magazine*, LXXVIII, 466 (Aug. 1898), pp. 308-20.

MONTEIL, P.-L., *Souvenirs Vécus: Quelques Feuillets de l'Histoire Coloniale* (Paris, 1924).
Full of errors, both inadvertent and deliberate, and to be used with great caution. But indispensable for the origins of the Monteil Mission.

MOREL, E. D., 'The Congo State and the Bahr-el-Ghazal', *The Nineteenth Century*, Aug. 1901, pp. 202-13.

MOUREY, C., 'De l'Atlantique au Nil', *Annales des Sciences Politiques*, XIV (1899), pp. 45-67.

MÜLLER, F. F., *Deutschland-Zanzibar-Ostafrika* (Berlin/D.D.R., 1959).
Müller's analysis of the internal structure of the German colonialist movement suggests that recent historians—particularly British historians—have tended to underestimate its strength and importance.

'NED NOLL' (pseud.), 'La Marche des Belges vers le Haut-Nil', *Q.D.C.*, 1 (Aug. 1897), pp. 71-8.

NETON, A., *Delcassé* (Paris, 1952).
Very disappointing. Consists mainly of summaries of D's public speeches, and in no way supersedes the work of Porter (*q.v.*).

NEWBURY, C. W., 'The Development of French Policy on the Lower and the Upper Niger, 1880-98', *J. Mod. Hist.*, XXXI, 1 (1959), pp. 16-26.
A little sketchy, but suggestive and useful.

— 'The Formation of the Government-General of French West Africa', *J.A.H.*, I, 1 (1960), pp. 111-28.

NEWBURY, C. W., 'Victorians, Republicans and the Partition of West Africa', *J.A.H.*, III, 3 (1962), pp. 493-501.

NEWTON, Lord (T. W. Legh), *Lord Lansdowne: a Biography* (London, 1929).

NUR, S. M., *The Memoirs of Yūsuf Mikhā'īl* (unpubl. Ph.D. thesis, London, 1962). Y. M. was Chief Clerk to the Khalifa's personal 'Black Flag' regiment.

OLIVER, R., *The Missionary Factor in East Africa* (London, 1952).

— 'Salisbury, Rhodes and Johnston', *Revue Belge de Philologie et d'Histoire*, XXXV, 3/4 (1957), pp. 729-30.

— and MATHEW, G. (Eds.) *History of East Africa*, Vol. I (London, 1963).

PALMER, A. W., 'Lord Salisbury's Approach to Russia, 1898', *Oxford Slavonic Papers*, 1955, pp. 102-14.

PAPADOPOULOS, G. S., 'Lord Salisbury and the projected Anglo-German Alliance in 1898', *Bull. I.H.R.*, XXVI (1953), pp. 214-18.

PENSA, H., 'La France au Bahr-el-Ghazal', *Q.D.C.*, v (Oct. 1898), pp. 165-71.

PENSON, L. M., *Foreign Affairs under the Third Marquess of Salisbury* (London, 1962).

— 'The Principles and Methods of Lord Salisbury's Foreign Policy', *C.H.J.*, v, 1 (1935), pp. 87-106.

— 'The New Course in British Foreign Policy, 1892-1902', *Transactions of the Royal Historical Society*, 4th series, XXV (1943), pp. 121-38.

PERHAM, M., *Lugard: The Years of Adventure, 1858-1898* (London, 1956). Indispensable for Rosebery's policy towards Uganda and the Upper Nile, 1892-4.

PETERS, C., *Die Deutsche Emin Pascha Expedition* (Munich, 1891).

— *Die Gründung von Deutsch-Ostafrika* (Berlin, 1906).

PORTAL, G. H., *My Mission to Abyssinia* (London, 1892).

— *The British Mission to Uganda in 1893* (London, 1894).

PORTER, C. W., *The Career of Théophile Delcassé* (Philadelphia, 1936). A competent attempt to work up the available published material. It has yet to be superseded.

PRIESTLEY, H. I., *France Overseas, a Study of Modern Imperialism* (New York, 1938).

PROMPT, V., 'Soudan Nilotique', *Bulletin de l'Institut Egyptien*, Series III, No. 4 (1893), pp. 71-116.

RANIERI, L., *Les Relations entre l'Etat Indépendant du Congo et l'Italie* (Brussels, I.R.C.B., 1959).

RENOUVIN, P., 'Les Origines de l'Expédition de Fachoda', *Rev. Hist.*, CC, 408 (1948), pp. 180-97. The first really coherent account, based on the French archives.

RÉQUIN, E., *Archinard et le Soudan* (Paris, 1946). Sidelights on the behaviour of the *officiers soudanais*.

RIKER, T. W., 'A Survey of British Policy in the Fashoda Crisis', *Political Science Quarterly*, XLIV, 1 (1929), pp. 54-78. Still useful for its analysis of the British press.

ROBERTS, S., *History of French Colonial Policy* (London, 1929; reprinted 1963).

ROBINSON, R. E., 'Imperial Problems in British Politics, 1880-1905', *C.H.B.E.*, III, Ch. V, pp. 127-80.

— and GALLAGHER, J., *Africa and the Victorians: The Official Mind of Imperialism* (London, 1961).
 Brilliant, if perhaps rather one-sided, interpretation of British policy. Somewhat sketchy on the policies of other Powers, especially on that of King Leopold.

— — 'The Partition of Africa', *The New Cambridge Modern History*, Vol. XI (Cambridge, 1962), Ch. XXII, pp. 593-640.

RODD, J. R., *Social and Diplomatic Memories*, 2 vols. (London, 1922, 1923).

ROEYKENS, A., *La Période Initiale de l'Oeuvre Africaine de Léopold II, 1875-1883* (Brussels, 1956).

ROULET, E., *La Mission Roulet* (Paris, 1933).
 Sidelights on the French occupation of the Bahr al-Ghazal.

RUBENSON, S., 'Some Aspects on [*sic*] the Survival of Ethiopian Independence in the period of the Scramble for Africa', *Historians in Tropical Africa* (Proceedings of the 1960 Leverhulme History Conference, Salisbury [S. Rhodesia], 1962), pp. 253-66.

SANDERSON, G. N., *Anglo-French Competition for the Control of the Upper Basin of the Nile, 1890-1898* (unpubl. Ph.D. thesis, London, 1959).

— ' "Emir Suleyman ibn Inger Abdullah" ', *S.N.R.*, XXXV, 1 (1954), pp. 22-74.
 A detailed study of Karl Inger and of his dealings with the French.

— 'Leopold II and the Nile Valley, 1880-1906', *Proceedings of the Sudan Historical Association*, I, VII (1955), pp. 1-68.

— 'The European Powers and the Sudan in the later Nineteenth Century', *S.N.R.*, XL (1959), pp. 79-100.

— 'Contributions from African Sources to the History of European Competition in the Upper Valley of the Nile', *J.A.H.*, III, 1 (1962), pp. 69-90.

— 'The Anglo-German Agreement of 1890 and the Upper Nile', *E.H.R.*, LXXVIII, 306 (1963), pp. 49-72.

— 'The Foreign Policy of the Negus Menelik, 1896-1898', *J.A.H.*, V, 1 (1964), pp. 87-97.

— 'England, Italy, the Nile Valley and the European Balance, 1890-91', *H.J.*, VII, 1 (1964), pp. 94-119.

— Article, 'Fāshōda', in *The Encyclopaedia of Islam*, Vol. II, Fasc. 35 (1964), p. 828.

SANDES, E. W. C., *The Royal Engineers in Egypt and the Sudan* (Chatham, 1937).
 Contains an eye-witness account of the Fashoda encounter.

SANTANDREA, S., 'The Belgians in Western Bahr el Ghazal', *S.N.R.*, XXXVI, 2 (1955), pp. 188-91.

— 'Sanusi, Ruler of Dar Banda and Dar Kuti, in the History of the Bahr el Ghazal', *S.N.R.*, XXXVIII (1957), pp. 151-5.

SCHWEITZER, G., *Emin Pascha: Eine Darstellung seines Lebens und Wirkens* (Berlin, 1898).
 Cf. R. W. Felkin's *Introduction* to the English Edn. (London, 1898).

SELLASSIÉ, G. (trans. T. Sellassié, ed. M. de Coppet), *Chronique du Règne de Ménélik II, Roi des Rois d'Ethiopie*, 2 vols. (Paris, 1930, 1931).
The official *res gestae*; the author was Minister of the Pen to Menelik. Very discreet about European activities.

SHEPPERSON, G., 'Africa, the Victorians and Imperialism', *Rev. Belge Phil. Hist.*, XL, 4 (1962), pp. 1228-38.

SHIBEIKA, M. T., *British Policy in the Sudan, 1882-1902* (London, 1952).
A very detailed account of policy as revealed by the F.O. archives.

SIEBERT, F., 'Adua, eine Wende italienischer und europäischer Politik', *Historische Zeitschrift*, CLXXXI, 3 (1956), pp. 533-79.

SIMAR, T., 'Léopold II et l'Erythrée', *Congo*, 1924, No. 2, pp. 319-26.
— 'Léopold II et le Soudan', *Congo*, 1924, No. 2, pp. 506-28.
Contains the report of a conversation in November 1898, between Marchand and the Belgian Consul at Cairo.

SLADE, R., *King Leopold's Congo* (London, 1962).

SMETS, G., 'Rapport sur le dossier: "Abyssinie 1894-1903" ', *Bulletin de l'Académie Royale des Sciences Coloniales*, New Series, I, 2 (1955), pp. 139-52.

SMITH-DORRIEN, H., *Memories of Forty-Eight Years' Service* (London, 1925).
The author was O.C. Troops to Kitchener's Fashoda force.

STANLEY, H. M., *The Congo and the Founding of its Free State*, 2 vols. (London, 1885).
— *In Darkest Africa*, 2 vols. (London, 1891).
— (ed. D. Stanley), *The Autobiography of Sir Henry Morton Stanley, G.C.B.* (London, 1909).

STANTON, E. A., 'The Sudan Camel Stamp', *S.N.R.*, XVIII, 1 (1935), pp. 135-7.

STEINER, Z. F., 'The Last Years of the Old Foreign Office', *H.J.*, VI, 1 (1963), pp. 59-90.

STENGERS, J., 'La Première Tentative de Reprise du Congo par la Belgique', *Bulletin de la Société Royale Belge de Géographie*, LXIII (1949), pp. 43-122.
Indispensable for the understanding of Leopold's manœuvres, both political and financial, in 1894-5.
— 'Rapport sur les dossiers relatifs aux territoires cédés à bail', *Bull. I.R.C.B.*, XXIV, 2 (1953), pp. 576-82.
— 'Rapport sur le dossier "Correspondance Léopold II—Strauch" ', *Bull. I.R.C.B.*, XXIV, 4 (1953), pp. 1193-1209.
— 'Note sur l'histoire des finances congolaises: le "trésor" ou "fonds spécial" du Roi-Souverain', *Bull. I.R.C.B.*, XXV, 1 (1954), pp. 153-95.
Very important. Cf. the author's 'réponse aux interventions', *ibid.*, pp. 250-2.
— 'Aux Origines de Fachoda: L'Expédition Monteil', *Rev. Belge Phil. Hist.*, XXXVI (1958), pp. 436-50; XXXVIII (1960), pp. 366-404, 1040-65.
Fundamental. Embodies very important new material, notably from the *Papiers Monteil* and the *Papiers Janssen*.
— 'L'Impérialisme Colonial de la fin du XIXe Siècle: Mythe ou Réalité', *J.A.H.*, III, 3 (1962), pp. 469-91.
A searching critique of the Robinson-Gallagher thesis.

STENMANS, A., *La Reprise du Congo par la Belgique* (Brussels, 1949).
STUHLMANN, F., *Die Tagebücher von Emin Pascha*, Vol. IV (Brunswick-Berlin-Hamburg, 1927).

TAYLOR, A. J. P., *Germany's First Bid for Colonies, 1884-1885. A Move in Bismarck's European Policy* (London, 1938).
— 'Fashoda', in *From Napoleon to Stalin; Comments on European History* (London, 1950).
— *The Struggle for Mastery in Europe, 1848-1918* (Oxford, 1954).
— 'Prelude to Fashoda: The Question of the Upper Nile, 1894-5', *E.H.R.*, LXV, 254 (1950), pp. 52-80.
    The first informed analysis of the Anglo-Congolese Agreement and the Phipps-Hanotaux negotiations.
— 'Les premières années de l'alliance russe', *Rev. Hist.*, CCIV, 415 (1950), pp. 62-76.
TERRIER, A., 'La Marche vers le Nord-Est et la Question du Haut-Nil', in *Histoire des Colonies Françaises et de l'expansion de la France dans le Monde*, ed. G. Hanotaux and A. Martineau, Vol. IV (Paris, 1931).
THEOBALD, A. B., *The Mahdiya* (London, 1951).
THORNTON, A. P., 'Rivalries in the Mediterranean, the Middle East and Egypt' [1870-1898], *New C.M.H.*, XI, Ch. XXI, pp. 567-92.
THRUSTON, A. B., *African Incidents* (London, 1900).
    Describes the British expedition to Wadelai in June 1894.
THURIAUX-HENNEBERT, A., 'L'expédition du Commissaire de District Léon Roget au Nord de l'Uele', *Bulletin de l'Académie Royale des Sciences d'Outremer*, New Series, VII, 4 (1962), pp. 559-79.
TREVELYAN, G. M., *Lord Grey of Falloden* (London, 1937).
TREVES, P., *Il Dramma di Fascioda: Francia e Inghilterra sull'Alto Nilo* (Milan, 1937).
    The author was granted an interview by Marchand.
TUNSTALL, W. C. B., 'Imperial Defence, 1870-1897', *C.H.B.E.*, III, Ch. VII, pp. 230-54.

VANDELEUR, S., *Campaigning on the Upper Nile and Niger* (London, 1898).
    Describes the British expedition to Wadelai in January 1895.
VERGNIOL, C., 'Fachoda: Les Origines de la Mission Marchand', *La Revue de France*, Aug. and Sept. 1936, pp. 416-34, 630-45, 112-28.
    The evidence is sometimes treated rather uncritically; but these articles contain information still not available elsewhere.
[DAL VERME, L.] L.d.V., 'L'Italia nel Libro di Lord Cromer', *Nuova Antologia*, Series 5, Vol. CXXXVII (Oct. 1908), pp. 353-83.
    Useful for the Anglo-Italian negotiations of Oct. 1890, where dal Verme's account is evidently based on his notes or diaries.
VIGNERAS, S., *Une Mission Française en Abyssinie* (Paris, 1897).
VILLOT, R., *Eugène Etienne* (Oran, 1951).
VUILLOT, P., 'La France dans le Haut-Nil', *Q.D.C.*, II (Oct. 1897), pp. 337-40.
— 'La France et l'Angleterre sur le Niger', *Q.D.C.*, III (April 1898), pp. 404-30.

WAUTERS, A.-J., *L'Etat Indépendant du Congo* (Brussels, 1899).
— *Histoire Politique du Congo Belge* (Brussels, 1911).
— 'Autour de l'Abyssinie', *M. Géog.*, XIV, 41, 42, 43 (Oct. 1897), cols. 481-4, 493-5, 517-20.
— 'Les Territoires pris à bail du Haut-Nil', *M. Géog.*, XX, 15, 16, 17 (April, 1903), cols. 175-82, 187-91, 199-202.
— 'Le Conflit entre l'Etat du Congo et la Grande Bretagne dans le Bahr-el-Ghazal', *M. Géog.*, XXIII, 6 (Feb. 1906), cols. 61-4.
— 'Souvenirs de Fachoda et de l'Expédition Dhanis', *M. Géog.*, XXVII, 20, 21, 22 (May, 1910), cols, 247-54, 259-63, 271-6.
    Still useful if treated with caution.
WESTLAKE, J., 'England and France in West Africa', *The Contemporary Review*, LXXIII (April, 1898), pp. 581-92.
WINGATE, F. R., *Mahdiism and the Egyptian Sudan* (London, 1891).
    Digest of an I.O.'s appreciations. Still of value for the factual material it contains.
WINGATE, R., *Wingate of the Sudan* (London, 1955).
    A few sidelights on the Fashoda Incident from F. R. Wingate's correspondence. Otherwise very disappointing.
WOOLF, L., *Empire and Commerce in Africa* (London, n.d., ?1919).
    Woolf's answers are doubtless now outdated; but the questions he poses are still very much alive.
WORK, E., *Ethiopia: A Pawn in European Diplomacy* (New Concord, Ohio, 1935).
WYLDE, A. B., *Modern Abyssinia* (London, 1901).

ZAGHI, C., *Crispi e Menelich* (Turin, 1956).
    An elaborately annotated edition of the journal of Count A. Salimbeni.
— 'La Conquista di Cassala', *Nuova Antologia*, Oct. 1934, pp. 601-12.
    This and the following papers by Zaghi print (or digest) much unpublished Italian material. They form by far the best guide to the Italian side of the Anglo-Italian negotiations of 1890-1.
— 'La Missione Antonelli in Etiopia e il fallimento della politica scioana', *Rassegna di Politica Internazionale*, III (1936), pp. 473-85.
— 'La Conferenza di Napoli tra l'Italia e l'Inghilterra e la questione di Cassala', *ibid.*, pp. 661-9.
— 'I Protocolli italo-britannici del 1891 e la guerra contro i Dervisci', *ibid.*, IV (1937), pp. 936-47.
— 'L'Italia e l'Etiopia nel 1891 in alcuni dispacci inediti . . .', *Storia e Politica Internazionale*, 1939, No. 2, pp. 507-31.
— 'Il Problema di Cassala e l'Italia. Le Trattative italo-britanniche del 1890 alla luce del carteggio dal Verme—Crispi', *ibid.*, 1940, No. 2, pp. 412-65.
ZETLAND, *Marquess of* (L. J. L. Dundas), *Lord Cromer* (London, 1932).
    The standard 'life' of Cromer. Useful, but is far from exhausting its subject.

INDEX

2E

——————S——————

———T———

MAPS

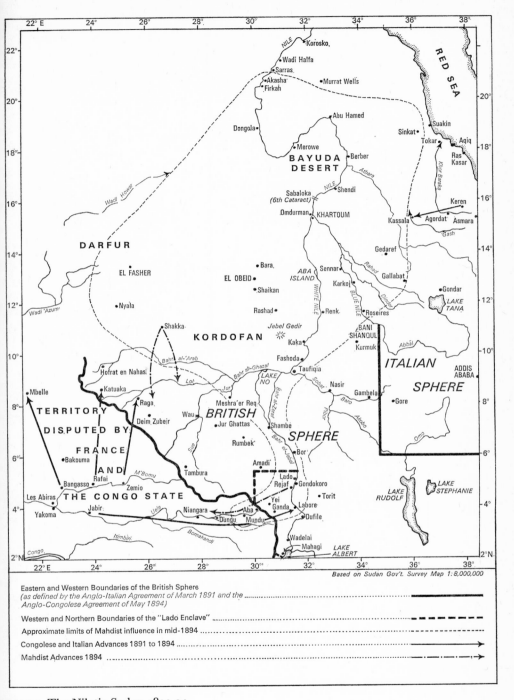

MAP I. The Nilotic Sudan 1893-94

Eastern and Western Boundaries of the British Sphere
*(as defined by the Anglo-Italian Agreement of March 1891 and the .... ▬▬▬▬▬
Anglo-Congolese Agreement of May 1894)*

Western and Northern Boundaries of the "Lado Enclave" .... ▬ ▬ ▬ ▬ ▬

Approximate limits of Mahdist influence in mid-1894 .... ▪▪▪▪▪▪▪▪

Congolese and Italian Advances 1891 to 1894 .... ➝

Mahdist Advances 1894 .... ▪—▪—▪➝

Based on Sudan Gov't. Survey Map 1:8,000,000

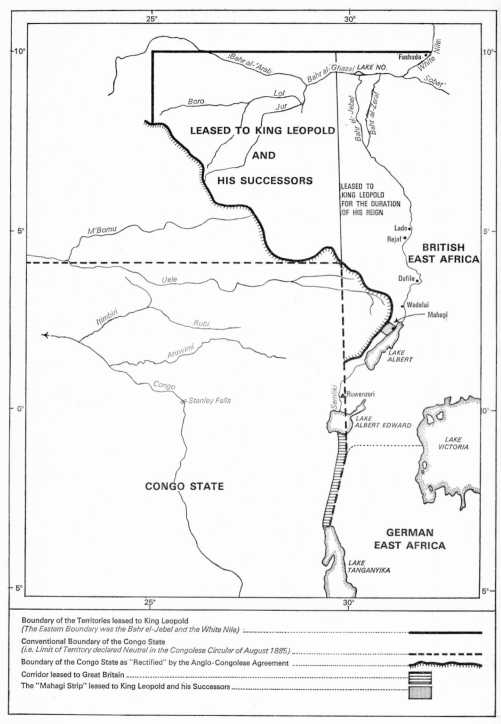

LEASED TO KING LEOPOLD

AND

HIS SUCCESSORS

LEASED TO
KING LEOPOLD
FOR THE DURATION
OF HIS REIGN

BRITISH
EAST AFRICA

CONGO STATE

GERMAN
EAST AFRICA

LAKE
ALBERT

LAKE
ALBERT EDWARD

LAKE
VICTORIA

LAKE
TANGANYIKA

Fashoda

Bahr al-'Arab

Bahr al-Ghazal LAKE NO.

White Nile

Sobat

Boro   Lol

Jur

Bahr el-Jebel

Bahr al-Zeraf

M'Bomu

Uele

Itimbiri

Rubi

Aruwimi

Congo

Stanley Falls

Lado
Rejaf

Dufile

Wadelai

Mahagi

Semliki

Ruwenzori

Boundary of the Territories leased to King Leopold *(The Eastern Boundary was the Bahr el-Jebel and the White Nile)*	
Conventional Boundary of the Congo State *(i.e. Limit of Territory declared Neutral in the Congolese Circular of August 1885)*	
Boundary of the Congo State as "Rectified" by the Anglo-Congolese Agreement	
Corridor leased to Great Britain	
The "Mahagi Strip" leased to King Leopold and his Successors	

MAP II. Sketch to illustrate the Anglo-Congolese Agreement of 12th May 1894. (after the map appended to *Africa No. 4* [1894])